# SAGE Premium Video

## BOOST COMPREHENSION. BOLSTER ANALYSIS.

- SAGE Premium Video **EXCLUSIVELY CURATED FOR THIS TEXT**
- **BRIDGES BOOK CONTENT** with application & critical thinking
- Includes short, auto-graded quizzes that **DIRECTLY FEED TO YOUR LMS GRADEBOOK**
- Premium content is **ADA COMPLIANT WITH TRANSCRIPTS**
- Comprehensive media guide to help you **QUICKLY SELECT MEANINGFUL VIDEO** tied to your course objectives

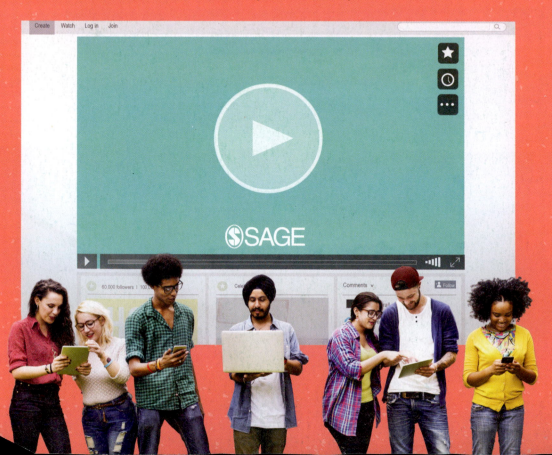

# SAGE Publishing:
# Our Story

Founded in 1965 by 24-year-old entrepreneur Sara Miller McCune, SAGE continues its legacy of making research accessible and fostering **CREATIVITY** and **INNOVATION**. We believe in creating fresh, cutting-edge content to help you prepare your students to thrive in the modern communications world and be **TOMORROW'S LEADING COMMUNICATORS**.

- By partnering with **TOP COMMUNICATIONS AUTHORS** with just the right balance of research, teaching, and industry experience, we bring you the most current and applied content.

- As a **STUDENT-FRIENDLY PUBLISHER**, we keep our prices affordable and provide multiple formats of our textbooks so your students can choose the option that works best for them.

- Being permanently **INDEPENDENT** means we are fiercely committed to publishing the highest-quality resources for you and your students.

# The Interpersonal Communication Playbook

*For Beckham Myles, the youngest but most naturally gifted communicator in our family. Your smile and love of life make our hearts young again.*

Sara Miller McCune founded SAGE Publishing in 1965 to support the dissemination of usable knowledge and educate a global community. SAGE publishes more than 1000 journals and over 800 new books each year, spanning a wide range of subject areas. Our growing selection of library products includes archives, data, case studies and video. SAGE remains majority owned by our founder and after her lifetime will become owned by a charitable trust that secures the company's continued independence.

Los Angeles | London | New Delhi | Singapore | Washington DC | Melbourne

# The Interpersonal Communication Playbook

**Teri Kwal Gamble**

*College of New Rochelle*

**Michael W. Gamble**

*New York Institute of Technology*

Los Angeles | London | New Delhi
Singapore | Washington DC | Melbourne

FOR INFORMATION:

SAGE Publications, Inc.
2455 Teller Road
Thousand Oaks, California 91320
E-mail: order@sagepub.com

SAGE Publications Ltd.
1 Oliver's Yard
55 City Road
London EC1Y 1SP
United Kingdom

SAGE Publications India Pvt. Ltd.
B 1/I 1 Mohan Cooperative Industrial Area
Mathura Road, New Delhi 110 044
India

SAGE Publications Asia-Pacific Pte. Ltd.
18 Cross Street #10-10/11/12
China Square Central
Singapore 048423

Printed in Canada

ISBN: 978-1-5443-3277-2

Acquisitions Editor:   Lily Norton
Content Development Editor:   Jennifer Jovin
Editorial Assistant:   Sarah Wilson
Production Editor:   Bennie Clark Allen
Copy Editor:   Lana Todorovic-Arndt
Typesetter:   C&M Digitals (P) Ltd.
Proofreader:   Sue Schon
Indexer:   Michael Ferreira
Cover Designer:   Scott Van Atta
Marketing Manager:   Staci Wittek

This book is printed on acid-free paper.

18 19 20 21 22 10 9 8 7 6 5 4 3 2 1

# Brief Contents

# Detailed Contents

## Chapter 2: Self-Concept, Identity, and Communication Presence   34

**Chapter 7: Conversations: Social Glue 186**

## Chapter 11: Conflict in Relationships   294

## Chapter 14: Relationships in Context: Family, Work, and Health-Related Settings   394

# Preface

There's nothing as useful as a *playbook* when it comes to building interpersonal communication skills. Interpersonal communication plays a pivotal role in all our lives. We wrote *The Interpersonal Communication Playbook* to help ensure that students have the knowledge needed to make the personal and professional relationships we share, whether face-to-face or online, successful.

A number of factors affect our ability to be interpersonally effective—an understanding of culture and gender and the norms and rules we internalize; an appreciation for how media and technology are omnipresent, streaming incessantly into our relationships; and a recognition of the roles that self-understanding and empathy play in life—often best exemplified by literary and pop-culture examples. To this end, we have woven each of these threads throughout the book and also into the boxes that enhance the content we cover.

It was especially important to us that readers have the opportunity to participate actively as they make their way through the text and the course. We provide abundant opportunities to offer personal observations, analyze personal experiences, and assess personal growth across interpersonal contexts. *The Interpersonal Communication Playbook*, by design, has an applied focus—identifying the student as the text's central player and the text as the tool the student uses to figure out and practice how to use interpersonal knowledge and apply interpersonal skills to enrich life.

The text has a natural progression, moving from the building blocks of interpersonal communication, to a consideration of interpersonal communication messages, to an exploration of the dynamics of interpersonal variables in action, to an examination of specific interpersonal contexts and the range of relationships we share as interpersonal communicators. Every chapter features sections on culture, gender, and media and technology—weaving the text's content into these three repeating motifs.

Chapters in *The Interpersonal Communication Playbook* also contain a number of integral features to reinforce each chapter's content and help hone the student's interpersonal skill development. Every chapter features clear learning outcomes; an end-of-chapter summary connecting content covered to the learning outcomes; an upfront student assessment of what they know; and an integrated array of *Try This*, *Reflect on This*, and *Analyze This* boxes that are designed, in turn, to promote active learning and skill building, help students clarify and apply theory, and enable students to demonstrate the ability to think both critically and empathically. There also are case studies to promote student consideration of how to do interpersonal communication better. Additionally, at the end of every chapter are *Check Your Understanding* questions keyed to specific text pages that focus student attention on the concepts and practical applications students are expected to master. Highlighted in-chapter key terms and a glossary at the text's end direct students to the field's key terminology.

## DIGITAL RESOURCES

*The Interpersonal Communication Playbook* offers comprehensive ancillary resources for instructors and students to support teaching and learning in the classroom and beyond.

## INSTRUCTOR TEACHING SITE: WWW.SAGEPUB.COM/GAMBLEICP

A password-protected instructor teaching site provides one integrated source for all instructor materials, including the following key components for each chapter:

- **Test bank**, available in Word format and to PCs and Macs through Diploma software, offers a set of test questions and answers for each chapter. Multiple-choice, true/false, and short-answer/essay questions for every chapter will aid instructors in assessing students' progress and understanding. The software allows for test creation and customization. The test bank is also available in Microsoft Word format.
- **PowerPoint® presentations** designed to assist with lecture and review, highlighting essential content, features, and artwork from the book.
- **Sample syllabi** for semester and quarter classes provide the instructor with suggested models for creating a course syllabus.
- Carefully selected **Web resources** and **audio and video links** feature relevant content for use in independent and classroom-based exploration of key topics.
- **SAGE Journal Articles:** A "Learning From SAGE Journal Articles" feature provides access to recent, relevant full-text articles from SAGE's leading research journals. Each article supports and expands on the concepts presented in the chapter. This feature also provides discussion questions to focus and guide student interpretation.

## STUDENT STUDY SITE: WWW.SAGEPUB.COM/GAMBLEICP

An open access student study site provides a variety of additional resources to build students' understanding of the book content and extend their learning beyond the classroom. Students have access to the following features for each chapter:

- **Self-quizzes** with multiple-choice and true/false questions for every chapter allow students to assess their progress in learning course material independently.
- **eFlashcards** reinforce student understanding and learning of key terms and concepts that are outlined in the book.
- **Study questions:** Chapter-specific questions help launch discussion by prompting students to engage with the material and by reinforcing important content.
- **Web resources** direct students to relevant online sites for further research on important chapter topics.
- **Video and audio links** feature meaningful content for use in independent or classroom-based exploration of key concepts and skills.
- **SAGE journal articles:** A "Learning From SAGE Journal Articles" feature provides access to recent, relevant full-text articles from SAGE's leading research journals. Each article supports and expands on the concepts presented in the chapter. This feature also provides discussion questions to focus and guide student interpretation.

We believe *The Interpersonal Communication Playbook*, together with the ancillaries described above, will motivate students to internalize the knowledge and develop the skills they need to develop meaningful and healthy interpersonal relationships across contexts, in both physical and digital arenas. We hope you agree!

# Acknowledgments

We owe a debt of gratitude to the unsurpassed SAGE team for being the best communicators in publishing! To Matthew Byrnie for making us feel at home in the SAGE family, to Terri Accomazzo for having a vision and making it come alive, to Sarah Calabi for helping to make our work better, to Scott Van Atta for the book's fresh design, to both project editor Bennie Clark Allen and copy editor Lana Todorovic-Arndt for not only keeping us informed and on track, but also for their close reading and attention to detail. We also owe a special thanks to our content development editor, Jennifer Jovin. To our executive publisher, Monica Eckman, we'd like to say, "Kudos!" You stepped into this project without missing a beat. Your enthusiasm and commitment are inspiring.

We also want to thank the instructors and students who are our motivation. It is because of you, and for you, that we wrote *The Interpersonal Communication Playbook*. What happens in your Interpersonal Communication classroom can transform the world.

# About the Authors

**Teri Kwal Gamble**, a full professor of communication at the College of New Rochelle in New Rochelle, NY (PhD New York University; MA and BA, Lehman College CUNY), and **Michael W. Gamble**, a full professor of communication at the New York Institute of Technology in New York City (PhD, New York University; BA and MFA, University of Oklahoma) are long-time partners in life and work. Professional writers of education and training materials, the Gambles are the coauthors of numerous text and trade books. Their most recent publications were the second edition of *The Public Speaking Playbook* (2018) and *The Communication Playbook* (2019). Among some of the other books the Gambles have written are *Nonverbal Messages Tell More: A Practical Guide to Nonverbal Communication* (2017), *The Gender Communication Connection* (2nd ed., 2014), and *Leading With Communication* (2013).

Prior to Michael's career as a college professor, he served as an officer and taught leadership skills for the U.S. Army Infantry School. Together, Teri and Mike founded Interact Training Systems, a communication consulting firm. They love living and working together!

iStock.com/monkeybusinessimages

**1**

# Interpersonal Communication

## Why It Matters

## Learning Objectives

### AFTER COMPLETING THIS CHAPTER, YOU SHOULD BE ABLE TO

1. Define and explain the importance of *communication presence*

2. Define *interpersonal communication*, distinguishing it from other types of communication

3. Use a communication model to identify the essential elements and transactional nature of interpersonal communication

4. Explain the functions interpersonal communication serves

5. Describe the characteristics, core principles, and axioms of interpersonal communication

6. Explain how gender and culture affect interpersonal communication

7. Provide examples of how digital media influence interpersonal contacts

8. Develop a plan to improve interpersonal communication

> I truly believe that life is a contact sport. You never know just who you'll meet and what role they might play in your career or your life.
>
> —Ken Kragen

. . . . . . . . . . . . . . . . . . . . . . . . . . . . . . . . . . . . . . . . . . . . . . . . . . . . . . . . . . . . . . .

Let's talk about interpersonal communication. Do you ever stop what you're doing to think about it? Have you, for example, ever wondered how others assess your interpersonal presence? For instance, after being with you, might they describe you as attentive or distracted, authentic or fake, empathic or distant? And how should you react to their description? Might you take steps to change in response to assessments that are less than positive?

What about your own assessment of your communication behavior and choices? How, for example, do you decide if it would be better to interact with another person face-to-face or via text? What if you had to choose between texting or calling? What if your options were to post on someone's Facebook wall or to Instagram? What do your answers suggest about your interpersonal availability and preferences? What's your go-to means of communicating—the one you usually find most comfortable and appealing? Are you best at communicating with others who are physically present or communicating via social media? And why does any of this matter? ■

# COMMUNICATION PRESENCE

Ours is a complex world. With so many communication options at hand, the choices we make reflect our approach to managing our identity or ==communication presence==—the unique composite of characteristics we present in both the physical and online worlds. How others respond to us in each of these domains reveals our effectiveness at navigating between communication spaces. How others assess our communication presence—how positive or negative they are toward the characteristics they attribute to us—shapes the relationships we will share with them.

Becoming better at connecting and establishing meaningful interpersonal relationships with others, whether face-to-face or digitally, is something we all can benefit from. Are you on board?

## TRY THIS

### A First Look at Digital Branding

Based solely on the name of your wi-fi network, what impressions might others form of you?

In an effort to influence others' reactions, wi-fi network names have morphed from boring series of digits to personalized monikers much like vanity license plates.

Choose a wi-fi name that you believe will reveal to others something they may not know about you. For example, one ballet dance instructor branded her wi-fi network "PointToMe."[1] How do you want to brand yours? What would you want your branding to communicate about you?

## HOW DO YOU DECIDE WHETHER TO SPEAK WITH A PERSON FACE-TO-FACE OR TEXT?

Are you among the two-thirds of people more likely to use your smartphone to connect with others?[2] If you're like many young adults, your smartphone serves as your prime personal connector. You likely use it to check Facebook, text, tweet, or post on Instagram—but less often to make a phone call. For some people, actually talking to another person creates discomfort. Such individuals find technology freeing, because they don't have to be in the physical presence of others. They feel able to say what they want without fear of being interrupted or even having to listen to another's response.

We have an abundance of communication choices.(See Figure 1.1) With so many available options, making the right choice is not always easy, and our choice may not necessarily be the one favored by those with whom we interact. Our goal is to help you explore your communication choices and the potential benefits and drawbacks they present for becoming as effective as you can be at communicating interpersonally.

# WHAT DO YOU KNOW?

Before continuing your reading of this chapter, which of the following five statements do you believe to be true, and which do you believe to be false?

1.  Communication is normally intentional.                                          T          F
2.  Interpersonal communication is always between two people.                        T          F
3.  If you already consider yourself a good communicator, then how you
    engage others does not need to change.                                          T          F
4.  Interpersonal communication affects your health.                                T          F
5.  Machines are altering the nature of interpersonal communication.                T          F

Read the chapter to discover if your answers are right or if you've made any erroneous assumptions.

## FIGURE 1.1
Texting Is Most Common Daily Communication Method for Teens

**Percentage of teens who contact their friends daily by different methods, by age**

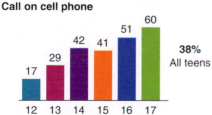

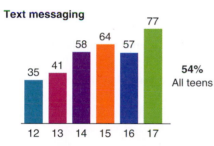

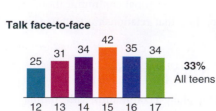

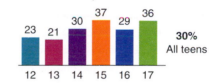

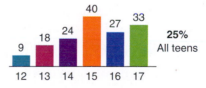

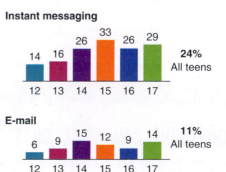

Source: Based on information from the Pew Internet & American Life Project.

How would others describe your communication presence?

# WHAT IS INTERPERSONAL COMMUNICATION?

**Communication** is our link to humanity. In its broadest sense, it is a process involving the deliberate or accidental transfer of meaning. One person does or says something, while others observe what was done or said and attribute meaning to it. Whenever you observe or give meaning to behavior, communication is taking place.

## INTERPERSONAL COMMUNICATION IS ABOUT RELATIONSHIPS

There are many kinds of communication. We distinguish them based on the number of people involved, the interaction's formality, and the opportunity to give and receive feedback. For example, since **intrapersonal communication** occurs when you think or talk to yourself, it requires only a single communicator—you! In contrast, **interpersonal communication** occurs when you interact with another person, forming a **dyad**, or pair. Both individuals in a dyad share the responsibility for determining the nature of a relationship by creating meaning from the interaction, whether it is in person or mediated by technology.

## INTERPERSONAL COMMUNICATION TAKES TWO

The fact that interpersonal communication takes two people means that it is indivisible. Without the second person, interpersonal communication is impossible. Thus, the parties to interpersonal communication are a duo: a couple, a pair, or perhaps adversaries. From an interpersonal perspective, even groups of three or more individuals are viewed as composites of dyads, effectively serving as the foundations for separate pairings and potential coalitions. Without a dyad, a relationship does not exist, and without a relationship, there is no interpersonal communication.[3] This means that if one person withdraws from the relationship, then that relationship terminates—unless or until the connection between them is reestablished.

## INTERPERSONAL COMMUNICATION ESTABLISHES CONNECTION

We measure the quality of an interpersonal relationship along a continuum, with "intimate communication" at one end and "impersonal communication" at the opposite end. The more personally we interact with another person, the more "interpersonal" our relationship becomes. When we engage in interpersonal communication, our goal is to treat one another as genuine people, not as objects, and to respond to each other as unique individuals with whom we create a distinct relational culture, not as people merely playing roles.[4]

The more personal a relationship becomes, the more interdependent the members become, sharing thoughts and feelings with each other. Our lives become interconnected, especially when contrasted with how we relate to people with whom we are uninvolved and to whom we don't reveal much about ourselves. We develop personal relationships because of the intrinsic rewards we derive from them; we find them emotionally, intellectually, and perhaps even spiritually fulfilling. In contrast, we have impersonal relationships usually because of the extrinsic rewards they offer, such as maintaining professional working relationships with others to help us reach our goals. Which kinds of relationships do you have more of—those that are impersonal, or those that are personal in nature?

## INTERPERSONAL COMMUNICATION IS A LIFELONG PROJECT

The effectiveness of interpersonal relationships depends on the extent to which we practice and exhibit interpersonal skills. While we may be born communicators, we are not born with effective interpersonal skills—those we need to learn. Nor are effective skills static; the same techniques may not work for all people in all situations. The culture of each person, his or her gender, the environment, and the individual's goals will determine how that person approaches and processes interpersonal communication.

Just as every person represents a unique combination of physical, psychological, education, gender, and cultural characteristics that distinguish us from one another, each new relationship teaches us a little bit more about the nature of people and interpersonal communication. Each new relationship increases our comfort at interacting not only with those who share our characteristics, but also with those whose attitudes, life experiences, and perspectives differ from ours.

## TRY THIS

### Strangers at the Door?

When you were a young child, your parents and/or caregivers probably cautioned you not to speak to strangers. However, travel opportunities and social networks such as Facebook make interacting with strangers much more commonplace, even ordinary. Answer the following questions:

1. In which arena are you more willing to interact with a stranger: online, at the mall, or when taking public transportation? Explain.

2. How does the anonymity or privacy of online relationships increase or decrease your level of personal comfort?

3. In your opinion, which is more likely to result in a lasting interpersonal relationship—a friendship that begins online, or a relationship that begins with the parties face-to-face? Explain your answer.

As we grow and learn, we should continually revise and update our personal theories of what works during interpersonal contacts, or our assumptions will compel us to repeat interpersonal scenarios or scripts that are doomed to fail. The effective interpersonal communicator does not take others or the means of communicating for granted. Instead, he or she attempts to continually enhance communication presence.

Our sense of personal identity results from and influences our interpersonal relationships. When we do it well, interpersonal communication helps us work through problems, and enhances our feelings of self-worth. When we do it poorly, however, personal growth and achieving our unique potential may be frustrated.

Whether an interpersonal relationship is productive or not depends on how satisfying it is and how much attention we pay to its health. Having good interpersonal skills can mean the difference between happiness and unhappiness or success and failure in multiple life contexts—home, job, school, health care settings, and society—as well as across cultures and generations. Enhanced understanding of the factors in play when two people communicate, whether in a personal or a professional relationship, increases the chance of developing **interpersonal competence**—the ability to communicate effectively.[5]

As you read the rest of this chapter, consider the following questions about yourself:

- How effective am I at communicating with people from diverse cultures?
- Am I equally effective interacting with men and women and with individuals whose sexual orientations differ from my own?
- How easy is it for me to develop relationships with people my own age and those of different ages?
- To what extent am I able to maintain self-control when I interact with others? Under what conditions do I lose control?
- How and to what extent do I use technology in my interpersonal relationships? In what ways is technology changing my interpersonal communication?

# MODELS OF INTERPERSONAL COMMUNICATION

Whether we are able to share meaning during person-to-person encounters depends on how well we handle the essential elements active in the process. For example, depending on the situation, patting someone on the back may be perceived as friendly and supportive or as a form of sexual harassment. There are seven key elements that influence interpretation of this act (see Table 1.1). Let's discuss each one.

## TABLE 1.1  THE ESSENTIAL ELEMENTS OF INTERPERSONAL COMMUNICATION

| | |
|---|---|
| **People** | The senders and receivers of communication messages |
| **Messages** | The content of communication |
| **Channels** | The media through which messages travel |
| **Noise** | Interference with the ability to send or receive messages |
| **Feedback** | Information received in exchange for messages |
| **Context** | The environmental, situational, or cultural setting in which communication takes place |
| **Effect** | The result of a communication episode |

In the poem *Anonymous*, 21st century poet Samuel Manashe suggests that when in the company of another person, too often we pretend to be someone we are not, keeping our actual identity secret and hoping to remain unknown or anonymous.

**Anonymous**

*Truth to tell,*

*Seldom told*

*Under oath,*

*We live lies*

*And grow old*

*Self-disguised—*

*Who are you*

*I talk to?*

1. How might remaining anonymous be enabling to someone?

2. What could compel you to disguise yourself when interacting with another person online or offline?

3. How would you handle the pain, frustration, and anger caused by feeling the need to suppress your cultural identity or hide your feelings to maintain a relationship?

Source: "Anonymous," from New and Selected Poems of Samuel Menashe copyright © 2005 by Literary Classics of the United States, Inc. All rights reserved. Reprinted by permission.

## PEOPLE

Recall that interpersonal communication between any two people ranges from "impersonal" at one end of an imaginary continuum to "intimate" at the other end.

When you respond impersonally to another person, you communicate based on limited knowledge of the categories into which to place that person—that is, the social groups or the culture to which you believe the person belongs—rather than on your personal experience interacting with that individual.

In contrast, when you respond to someone personally, you respond to an individual, drawing on your knowledge of their personality to guide your interactions. In other words, your past experience with the individual allows you to differentiate that person from the groups to which that individual belongs. You now take this unique person and their needs into account.

As a relationship develops and you get to know someone better, not only can you describe the person's behavior, but you also can more accurately predict their behavior in a particular situation. When you know someone really well, you also are able to explain the reasons for their actions. For instance, when you share an impersonal relationship with someone at work, you likely can describe the individual's behavior—maybe how they procrastinate in completing assignments. When you see a supervisor giving that person a project to work on, you may be able to predict that the project will not be completed on time. Were you to share an even more personal relationship with your coworker, however, you also might be able to explain the reasons behind the procrastination, such as concerns about a child's illness or feelings of inadequacy.

Each party in an interpersonal relationship participates in the functions of sending and receiving messages. Each serves simultaneously as sender and receiver, both parties giving out and taking in messages. For example, in the following exchange, both Jana and Karl give and receive messages:

**Jana:** I'm so tired. I wish we didn't have to go to the Joneses' party.

**Karl:** You always feel tired whenever we have plans to go to a party for someone I work with.

**Jana:** Why do you have to attack me when I say how I feel?

**Karl:** What's the matter with you? I'm not attacking you. I'm only commenting on what I observe and experience directly.

**Jana:** Give me a break. Don't I have a right to be tired?

**Karl:** Sure you do. Just tell me one thing. Why do you never feel tired when we're going to a party hosted by your friends?

Interpersonal communication is transactional in nature. It is a process in which transmission and reception occur simultaneously, and source and receiver continually influence one another. What we think of each other and what we believe the other to know affect the messages we send.[6] Each party in a dyad simultaneously performs the roles of sender and receiver, also known as **role duality**. How the individuals perform the roles, or how good they are at sending and receiving, depends on what they bring to the relationship, including their feelings about themselves, their knowledge about communication, and their attitudes, values, and goals. All these elements influence how well a sender encodes his or her thoughts, feelings, emotions, and attitudes by putting them into a form another can relate to, and how the receiver decodes the thoughts, feelings, emotions, and attitudes of the sender.

## TRY THIS

### Rating Relationships

Think about some of the relationships you have had over your lifetime.

1. Identify an extremely satisfying interpersonal relationship and an extremely frustrating one.

2. Identify the specific aspects of each relationship that made it satisfying or frustrating for you.

3. After summarizing the characteristics and qualities that differentiate your most satisfying relationship from your most frustrating one, propose steps you might have taken to increase your satisfaction with the relationship you found frustrating.

## MESSAGES

We negotiate the meaning we derive from interpersonal communication by sending and receiving verbal and nonverbal **messages**. Whom we speak to, what we choose to speak about, what we do as we interact, the words we use, the sound of our voices, our posture, our facial expressions, our touch, and even our smell constitute the message or the content of our communication. Everything we do has potential message value for the person with whom we are interacting or for someone observing the interaction.

Messages can be conveyed through any one of our five senses. Some messages—such as a kiss or the words "I love you"—are more personal than others. Some of our messages we send purposefully, while others, such as nervous tics, we emit unconsciously or accidentally. Everything we do when interacting with another person has potential message value as long as the other person is observant and gives meaning to our behavior.

## CHANNELS

A message travels via a <mark>channel</mark>, a medium that connects sender and receiver, much as a bridge

We use each of our five senses to convey messages.

connects two locations. We may use multiple channels at the same time to communicate a single message. In fact, under most circumstances, interpersonal communication is a multi-channeled interaction using visual, auditory, tactile, olfactory, and situational means to convey both verbal and nonverbal messages. Consider a first date: You make sure you look and smell nice; you choose a quiet setting to ensure you can hear each other; and you generally put your best face forward in both verbal and nonverbal ways in order to say, "I like you and I hope you like me too."

Capable communicators are adept channel switchers. They know how to use sound, sight, touch, taste, smell, and the environment, as well as words and nonverbal signs, to get messages across. However, if you find yourself consistently tuning in on just one channel, you might miss the most salient parts of a message. For instance, if you speak to people only by text, you might miss the underlying tone of concern when your best friend asks, "Is everything okay? I haven't seen you in a while." While we may prefer to send or receive messages through a particular channel, we should pay attention to and use all of the available channels.

Being adept at channel switching means that if one channel is closed or damaged, we can open another to compensate. For instance, rather than assuming that a blind person will be able to recognize us by our voice, we also should name ourselves. Since the blind person is unable to see the visual cues we use to shade the meaning of a verbal message, we also may need to take special care to ensure that the meanings we want conveyed are contained in the words we choose and the expressiveness of our voice.

## NOISE

In communication studies, <mark>noise</mark> includes anything that interferes with or impedes our ability to send or receive a message. Noise distracts communicators by focusing their attention on something extraneous to the communication act. As the level of noise increases, it becomes increasingly unlikely that we will be successful at negotiating or sharing meaning. Effective communicators find ways to ensure their messages get through accurately despite any noise.

Noise emanates from both internal and external sources. Among the external sources of noise are the sight, sound, smell, and feel of the environment. A drab room, an overly warm space, a loud siren, an offensive odor, and too many conversations occurring at the same time are all examples of environmental noise.

Among the internal sources of noise are personal thoughts and feelings. Racism, sexism, ageism, feelings of inadequacy, hunger, excessive shyness or extroversion, and deficient or excessive knowledge can all interfere with the ability to send and receive messages effectively. Most of us find it easier to cope with external noise than with internal noise because closing a window, for example, is usually a lot easier than opening a mind or changing a personality. Have you created or been influenced by noise in any of your relationships today? Which kind(s) of noise typically causes you the greatest problems? (See Table 1.2.)

## TABLE 1.2  TYPES OF NOISE

| Semantic noise | Noise due to the failure to understand the intended meaning of one or more words or the context in which the words are being used (people speaking different languages, using jargon and "technicalese") |
|---|---|
| Physiological noise | Noise due to personal illness, discomfort, or a physical problem including speech, visual, auditory, or memory impairment (difficulty articulating, hearing or sight loss, fatigue, disease) |
| Psychological noise | Noise due to anxiety, confusion, bias, past experience, or emotional arousal that interferes with communication (sender or receiver prejudice, closed-mindedness, rage) |
| Intellectual noise | Noise due to information overload or underload (over- or under-preparedness) |
| Environmental noise | Noise due to the sound, smell, sight, and feel of the environment or physical communication space that distracts attention from what is being said or done (cars honking, garbage rotting, people talking at once, cellular or computer interference) |

## FEEDBACK

**Feedback** is information we receive in response to messages we have sent. Both verbal and non-verbal, it lets us know how another person is responding to us. Feedback offers clues as to how we are coming across, whether we were heard through the noise, and how the receiver interpreted our communicative efforts. Feedback reveals whether or not our message was interpreted as we hoped and, if not, which portions of the message need to be resent.

Feedback can be positive or negative. **Positive feedback** enhances behavior in progress. It serves a reinforcing function, causing us to continue our behavior. In contrast, **negative feedback** stops behavior in progress. It serves a corrective function, prompting us to discontinue one or more behaviors because of their apparent ineffectiveness. In this way, negative feedback helps eliminate behavior that others judge inappropriate.

Because we constantly communicate with ourselves (even as we communicate interpersonally), feedback can emanate from both internal and external sources. **Internal feedback** is the feedback you give yourself as you assess your own performance during an interpersonal transaction. **External feedback** is feedback you receive from the other person. Competent communicators are sensitive to both feedback types, since both serve important functions.

Feedback often focuses on a person or a message. We can, for example, comment on a person's appearance or message effectiveness. In addition, we can be totally honest about feedback, offering **low-monitored feedback**, or we can carefully craft a response designed to serve a particular purpose, offering **high-monitored feedback**. Whether our feedback is spontaneous or guarded depends on how much we trust the other person and how much power that person has over our future.

We also can offer immediate or delayed feedback. For example, we can nod our head every time the other person says something we agree with. Or we can withhold our reaction until after she or he has finished speaking. When we interview for a job, we are rarely told immediately after the interview whether we will be given the position. Instead, we receive delayed feedback; sometimes days, weeks, or even months pass before we know whether or not the interview was successful.

**Feedforward** is a variant of feedback. However, instead of being sent after a message is delivered, it is sent prior to a message's delivery as a means of revealing something about the message to follow. Feedforward introduces messages by opening the communication channel and previewing the message, much as this book's preface does.

## CONTEXT

The environmental and situational or cultural **context** in which the communication occurs (its setting) can also affect its outcome. The physical setting includes an interaction's specific location, that is, its appearance and condition. A candlelit exchange may have a different feel and outcome from one held in a busy, brightly lit office. The social setting derives from the status relationships and roles assumed by each party. Some relationships seem friendlier and are less formal than others. The psychological setting includes the interaction's emotional dimensions. It influences how people feel about and respond to each other. The temporal setting includes not only the time of day an interaction takes place but also the history, if any, that the parties share. Any previous communication experience that you and another person have had will influence the way you treat each other in the present. The cultural context is composed of the beliefs, values, and rules of communication that affect your behavior. If you and the other person are from different cultures, the rules you each follow may confuse the other or lead to missing chances for effective and meaningful exchanges. Sometimes the context is so obvious or intrusive that it exerts great control over our interaction by restricting or dominating how we relate to one another; other times it seems so natural that we virtually ignore it.

## EFFECT

As we interact, we each experience an **effect**—meaning that we are influenced in some way by the interaction. One person may feel the effects more than the other person. One person may react more quickly than the other. The effects may be immediately observable or initially not observable at all.

How does your current physical setting affect you?

An effect can be emotional, physical, cognitive, or any combination of the three. As a result of interacting with another, we can experience feelings of elation or depression (emotional); we fight and argue or walk away (physical); or we can develop new ways of thinking about events or become confused (cognitive).

## VISUALIZING COMMUNICATION

To be sure, the thinking about interpersonal communication has evolved over the years. The earliest model—a linear or unidirectional model—depicted communication as going in one direction only. Questions such as "Did you get my message?" statements such as "I gave you that idea," and acts such as leaving someone a note with instructions suggest this one-way perspective.

Gradually, a more realistic two-way model—known as an **interaction model**—came to be preferred. The interaction model visualized interpersonal communication as a back-and-forth process, much like a game of tennis; it also acknowledges the presence and effects of both feedback and context. However, though more accurate than the one-way model, the interaction model fails to capture the complexity of interpersonal communication, including the reality that interpersonal communication does not involve a straightforward back-and-forth action and reaction as might occur when you send a text and a friend responds.

In reality, however, communication exchanges involve source and receiver responding to one another simultaneously rather than sequentially. A new and even more realistic **transactional model**, as shown in Figure 1.2, emerged to capture this reality. The transactional model's strength is that it depicts sending and receiving as simultaneous rather than distinctly separate acts. In so doing, it helps us visualize the vital complexity of interpersonal interaction. (See Table 1.3 for a summary of the various models' strengths and weaknesses.)

## FIGURE 1.2
Transactional Model of Interpersonal Communication

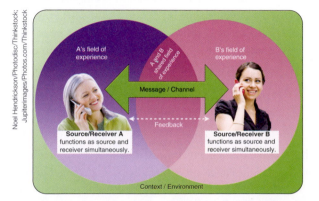

## TABLE 1.3 ADVANTAGES AND LIMITATIONS OF COMMUNICATION MODELS

| MODEL | COMMUNICATION EXAMPLES | ADVANTAGES | LIMITATIONS |
|---|---|---|---|
| Linear | Television and radio<br><br>E-mail and texts<br><br>Packaged presentations that do not allow for modifications | Simple and direct | Not useful for most face-to-face encounters |
| Interaction | Instant messaging<br><br>Class presentations where content is adjusted based on feedback | Wider applicability | Still discounts receiver's active role in creating meaning |
| Transactional | Any encounter in which meaning is co-created | Most realistic depiction of interpersonal communication | Does not apply to texting, tweeting, and posting |

## TRY THIS

# Making Model Sense

Use the transactional model of interpersonal communication in Figure 1.2 to analyze the following dyadic scenario. Identify how each of the essentials of interpersonal communication included in the model—people, messages, channels, noise, feedback, context, and effect—makes its presence felt during the interaction.

**Simona:** (approaching a restaurant table): Hi, Kevin. I thought I recognized the back of your head. How ya doing? Long time no see.

**Kevin:** (turning, somewhat startled): I recognized your perfume—I used to love it when—(abrupt break). It's been a while, hasn't it? When was the last time we got together? Is it a year?

**Simona:** (smiling): Longer than that. I haven't heard from or seen you since your divorce from Jan.

**Kevin:** Haven't seen me since the divorce. That makes it almost 2 years and 24 days, then.

**Simona:** Time sure goes fast when you're having fun, doesn't it? Well, you look great. Life's been good to you, huh?

**Kevin:** Yeah, I just got back from 6 months troubleshooting in Singapore. I got a promotion, and I'm finally making the kind of money I deserve.

**Simona:** Good for you! Emilio and I still see Jan, you know.

*(Continued)*

(Continued)

**Kevin:** Do you? How's she doing? I haven't spoken to her in 2 years, either.

**Simona:** You haven't spoken to your ex since the divorce? Actually, I'm meeting her for lunch today.

**Kevin:** Didn't seem to be anything left to say to her. *(Does a double take)* Did you say you're meeting Jan here? I was just leaving. I've got to get back to the office. I've got a key client coming. It was sure nice running into you.

**Simona:** Sure thing. I'll tell Jan you say hi.

**Kevin:** No. Don't even tell her you saw me. It would just open up her old wounds.

**Simona:** Why would it do that? She's great, has a great job, and she's seeing one of Emilio's friends. Besides, I'm sure she'd like to know you're doing so well.

**Kevin:** So, she picked up the pieces, did she? I didn't think it would happen that fast. She was so broken up, so devastated by my leaving.

**Simona:** Life goes on.

**Kevin:** Guess it does. Well, gotta go. Be good.

**Simona:** *(Under her breath, as he walks away):* What a conceited jerk!

| Messages | Simona's message:<br>Kevin's message: |
|---|---|
| Channels | |
| Noise | |
| Feedback | Simona's feedback:<br>Kevin's feedback: |
| Context | |
| Effect | The effect on Kevin:<br>The effect on Simona: |

# HOW DOES INTERPERSONAL COMMUNICATION ENHANCE LIFE?

Communicating interpersonally helps us discover who we are. It fulfills our need for human contact and personal relationships, and it can contribute to our changing our attitudes and behavior. In these ways, interpersonal communication serves psychological, social, information, and influence functions.

## IT FULFILLS PSYCHOLOGICAL FUNCTIONS

First and foremost, just as we need water, food, and shelter, we need people. When we are cut off from human contact, our health suffers. In fact, being in at least one good relationship appears to be a prerequisite of physical and psychological well-being.[7] For example, some maximum-security prisoners are locked alone in their cells for up to 23 hours each day. The feelings of isolation the inmates experience result in their becoming restless, angry, violent, and potentially suicidal. When restrictions are loosened, however, and inmates allowed out of their cells for hours each day, able to play sports and mingle and dine with others, their behavior and emotional health improve.[8]

Interpersonal communication also enhances self–other understanding. Through our interactions with others, we learn how different individuals affect us. In fact, we depend on interpersonal communication to develop our self-awareness, hone our communication presence, and maintain our sense of self. To quote communication theorist Thomas Hora: "To understand oneself, one needs to be understood by another. To be understood by another, one needs to understand the other."[9]

Because interpersonal communication is a fluid process that depends on constantly changing components, it offers lots of opportunities for self–other discovery. Different contexts help us figure out who likes or dislikes us and why, when and why to trust or distrust someone, what behaviors elicit the strongest reactions, under what conditions we have the power to influence another person, and whether we have the ability to resolve relational conflict.

## IT FULFILLS SOCIAL FUNCTIONS

Through interpersonal communication, we are able to begin and sustain relationships. Our interpersonal contacts meet our social needs to varying degrees. Although we vary greatly in the extent to which we experience these needs, according to psychologist William Schutz, our relationships reflect the following in particular:

- Our need for *affection*—to express or receive fondness

- Our need for *inclusion*—to be included or include others as full partners

- Our need for *control*—to direct or exert influence over the self and others so that we feel we are able to deal with and manage our lives and environment.[10]

When we are in a relationship with someone whose needs complement or balance our own, each of us is able to have our needs met. When our needs are not complementary, however, we are more apt to experience relationship struggles or conflict. Do your experiences confirm this? (We explore the work of William Schutz in more depth in Chapter 12.)

Good interpersonal communication also allows us a glimpse into another person's reality. For example, developing an interpersonal relationship with someone whose culture differs from our

Have you ever felt isolated when in a crowd?

own broadens our point of view. Our interpersonal styles may differ, but we adapt to the sound, form, and content of their messages and pay attention to how members of different cultures feel about displaying affection, exerting control, defining roles, and meeting goals. While it may be easier to identify with and associate with those who are like us, coming from different cultures does not preclude our learning to share similar meanings.

Interpersonal communication similarly fulfills our need to *be friended* and to *friend* others. It helps alleviate feelings of isolation, fulfilling our desire to feel needed, loved, wanted, and capable. Because of this, interpersonal communication may increase our personal satisfaction, helping us feel more positive about ourselves.

## IT FULFILLS INFORMATION FUNCTIONS

During interpersonal contacts, as we share information, we reduce the amount of uncertainty in our lives. By taking in information, we meet the need to acquire knowledge.

Information is not the same thing as communication. Just as more communication is not necessarily better communication, more information is not necessarily better information. Sometimes no information and no communication may be the best course. We can, after all, talk a problem or issue to death. Thus, just as there is a time to talk, there is a time to stop talking and listen.

## IT FULFILLS INFLUENCE FUNCTIONS

We use interpersonal communication to influence others—sometimes subtly and sometimes overtly. As we exercise influence, our need to gain agreement is met. Interpersonal communicators are both the users of and targets of persuasion.

As we observed earlier in this chapter, interpersonal communication is often goal directed, methodically planning how to get what we want. We seek contact with and advice from others whom we believe can help us. This is not to say that human beings are naturally manipulative or deceptive, as neither of these practices supports the interdependent and transactional nature of interpersonal communication.[11] Communication is not something we do to others or have done to us. It is a mutually reinforcing activity we engage in together. We are both affected by what each of us does and says.

## TRY THIS

### Functions in Action

Consider three conversations: one you recently had with a significant other, one between you and a friend, and one between you and an acquaintance or co-worker you usually don't see outside of work. Explain which interpersonal communication function(s) each interaction fulfilled: psychological, social, information, and/or influence. Be specific in describing and assessing how each interaction illustrates the function(s) you identify.

| | CONVERSATION WITH SIGNIFICANT OTHER | CONVERSATION WITH A FRIEND | CONVERSATION WITH A COWORKER |
|---|---|---|---|
| Psychological | | | |
| Social | | | |
| Information | | | |
| Influence | | | |

# UNDERSTANDING INTERPERSONAL CONTACT

Every interpersonal communication contact has certain essential elements and serves one or more functions. Every interpersonal communication contact also features the following:

- *Key characteristics:* descriptions of the communication that are common across different situations or contexts
- *Core communication principles:* identifiable behavioral patterns and motivations
- *Axioms:* the fundamental rules by which communication may be analyzed or explained

## FIVE CHARACTERISTICS OF INTERPERSONAL COMMUNICATION

Let's first explore the noteworthy characteristics of interpersonal communication (see Table 1.4).

### TABLE 1.4 CHARACTERISTICS OF INTERPERSONAL COMMUNICATION

| COMMUNICATION IS . . . | IN OTHER WORDS . . . |
|---|---|
| A dynamic process | It is ongoing, continuous, and in a constant state of flux. |
| Unrepeatable and irreversible | It is unique. |
| Learned | We find out over time what works for us and what does not work if we remain conscious of the communication. |
| Characterized by wholeness and nonsummativity | It operates as a complete entity, much like a team functions. |

### Interpersonal Communication Is a Dynamic Process

By dynamic process we mean that interpersonal communication is ongoing and in a constant state of flux. All the components continually interact with and affect each other. What one person says or does influences what the other person says or does. Every interpersonal encounter is a point of arrival from a previous encounter and a point of departure for a future encounter.

### Interpersonal Communication Is Unrepeatable

Every interpersonal contact is unique. It has never happened in just that way before, and it will never happen in just that way again. Why? Because every contact changes us in some way and, as a result, can never be exactly repeated or replicated. Try as we might, we can never recapture exactly the same feelings, thoughts, or relationship that existed at a specific point in time. We are no longer exactly the same person we were before we made contact.

### Interpersonal Communication Is Irreversible

In addition to being unrepeatable, interpersonal communication is irreversible. Once we have said or done something to another, whether in person or online, we cannot erase its impact. After exhibiting behavior, we cannot simply say, "Forget that!" and substitute a better or more appropriate behavior in its place (though we sometimes try). We cannot unhear words, unsee sights, or undo acts. They are irretrievable. Presenting a new stimulus does not change the previous stimulus. It merely becomes part of a behavioral sequence.

### Interpersonal Communication Is Learned

Over time, we learn what works for us in an interpersonal relationship and what does not. We can hinder our communication with another person if we remain unconscious of how we affect him or her, and vice versa. Part of the art of interpersonal communication involves recognizing how our words and actions affect others, how their words and actions affect us, and then, based on our observations, making the necessary adjustments.

Once sent, it is virtually impossible to take back an e-mail message.

### Interpersonal Communication Is Characterized by Wholeness and Nonsummativity

When we say that the interpersonal relationship is characterized by "wholeness," we mean that we consider more than the individuals who are in the relationship; we look at the unique ways in which the people involved influence each other. When we say that interpersonal communication is characterized by "nonsummativity," we are saying that the whole is more than the sum of its parts; interpersonal communication is about more than just its participants per se. We cannot understand a couple by looking at each of the partners individually. The nature of the relationship must be examined. The "us" must be explored. The relationship takes on a quality that we cannot understand merely by possessing information about its parts.[12]

## INTERPERSONAL PATTERNS

Interpersonal communication involves understanding patterns of behavior, predicting what others will do and say, and providing reasons for their actions, as well as our own.[13] Thus, understanding an individual's patterns of behavior, not just a single behavior, provides the basis for understanding the person's interpersonal communication. In other words, a single isolated behavior is not what we need to focus on; rather, we must take into account entire behavioral sequences.

Interpersonal communication involves not only interpreting but also predicting and accounting for another person's behavior. If we are able to distinguish individuals from a general group, then we recognize their uniqueness and are able to know and understand them. For example, were we to date a number of different people yet not distinguish one date from another, we would not be very effective interpersonal communicators. To the extent that we can predict the behavior of a specific romantic interest, and account for that behavior—what we term **reasoned sense making**—we can understand that individual more than we might understand others.

We also reason retrospectively. **Retrospective sense making** means making sense of our own behavior once it has occurred. We interpret our own actions in light of the goals we have or have not attained. We look back on interactions and continually redefine our relationships, which is our way of making sense of them. As our interactions with another person progress, the events of our relationship increase in number, and as a result, the relationship and how we feel about it changes.

## FIVE COMMUNICATION AXIOMS

A classic study by Paul Watzlawick, Janet Beavin, and Don Jackson identified five axioms, or universally accepted principles, of communication that enable us to understand interpersonal interactions more fully.[14] (See Table 1.5.)

### TABLE 1.5   AXIOMS OF COMMUNICATION

| |
|---|
| 1. You cannot not communicate. |
| 2. Interactions have content and relationship dimensions. |
| 3. Interactions are defined by how they are punctuated. |
| 4. Messages are verbal symbols and nonverbal cues. |
| 5. Exchanges are symmetrical or complementary. |

From a study by Paul Watzlawick, Janet Beavin, and Don Jackson.

### Axiom 1: You Cannot Not Communicate

Behavior has no opposite. We cannot voluntarily stop behaving. Even if we consciously decide not to respond, even if we do our utmost not to move a muscle or utter a sound, our stillness and silence are responses and have message value and influence others.

### Axiom 2: Every Interaction Has a Content and Relationship Dimension

The content dimension of a message involves the literal meaning of the words used, while the relationship dimension involves how the message was said, indicating how it is to be interpreted. The relationship dimension reveals what one party to the interaction thinks of the other. For example, a husband says to his spouse, "Get over here right now." The content level is the husband's words. But the message can be delivered in a number of ways: as an order, a plea, a flirtation, or an expression of sexual desire, for example. Each manner of delivery suggests a different kind of relationship. It is through such variations that we offer clues to another person regarding how we see ourselves in relation to that person.

## Axiom 3: Every Interaction Is Defined by How It Is Punctuated

Though we often feel as if we can label the beginning and the end of an interaction, in actuality, communication has no definitive starting or finishing line. It is difficult to determine exactly what is stimulus and what is response. Consider this example:

*A woman is usually late getting home from work. When she does get home, she often finds her partner asleep. Both are angry. The woman might observe that she works so much because all her partner does is sleep. The partner might say that all he does is sleep because she's never home.*

Neither of them interprets the other's behavior as a response to their own. For the woman, her partner's behavior is the stimulus, and hers is the response; he causes her behavior. For the partner, it's just the opposite. Whereas he sees the sequence as going from working to sleeping, she sees it as going from sleeping to working. Which is it, really?

We all segment experience somewhat differently because we each see it differently. We call the dividing of communication into segments *punctuation*. The way a communication is punctuated usually benefits the person doing the punctuating. Punctuation also reveals how an individual interprets a situation and offers insight into the nature of an interpersonal conflict in particular and the interpersonal relationship in general.

## Axiom 4: Messages Consist of Verbal Symbols and Nonverbal Cues

During face-to-face or online interactions, we emit two kinds of messages: discrete, verbal symbols (i.e., words) and continuous, nonverbal cues. According to Watzlawick, Beavin, and Jackson, the content of a message is more apt to be carried via the verbal system, whereas the relationship level of the message is typically carried via the nonverbal system. Although we can usually control what we say or write, it is much more difficult to control the nonverbal cues we emit. Thus, we may not speak angry words, but our face may betray our rage. As a result, it is easy to lie with words but hard to produce behavior that supports the lie. Nonverbal behavior often gives us away.

## Axiom 5: Interactions Are Either Symmetrical or Complementary

Watzlawick, Beavin, and Jackson categorize relationships as either symmetrical or complementary. In a **symmetrical relationship**, the parties mirror each other's behavior. If one person is solicitous, the other is as well. If one person whines, the other does also. In contrast, in a **complementary relationship**, the parties engage in opposite behaviors. If one person is docile, the other is assertive. If one leads, the other follows.

Neither symmetrical nor complementary relationships are trouble-free. In a symmetrical relationship, the parties run the risk of experiencing "symmetrical escalation." Believing they are "equal," both people might assert, for example, the right to exert control. Once this starts, each may feel compelled to engage in battle to demonstrate his or her equality. And so, a status struggle begins. The main danger facing those in a symmetrical relationship is a runaway sense of competitiveness.

In contrast, those who share complementary relationships may face a problem called "rigid complementarity." This problem surfaces when one party begins to feel that control is automatically his or hers. An overly protective mother who cannot accept that her child is grown, an employer unable to share leadership, and a teacher who cannot learn from others—all illustrate the rigidness that can develop in people who become locked into self-perpetuating, unchanging, unhealthy patterns of behavior. Switches in power are natural; we need to be prepared for them.

Taken together with the characteristics and principles of communication, the five axioms of communication provide additional knowledge as we seek to enhance our understanding and increase the effectiveness of our interpersonal contacts. Now let's widen our focus.

# DIVERSITY AND CULTURAL CONSIDERATIONS

Because U.S. society is multicultural, and because cultural values help shape our acceptance of and preference for specific communication styles, we should understand the role culture plays in our interpersonal contacts. Even though the United States is the most demographically diverse country in the world, how regularly do you take cultural differences into account in your person-to-person interactions?

## DIVERSITY AND COMMUNICATION STYLE

Developing **cultural awareness**, the ability to understand the role that cultural prescriptions play in shaping communication, is an asset. Intercultural ignorance too frequently slows our ability to create meaningful interpersonal relationships with people who are culturally different from us.

Whenever cultural variability influences the nature and outcomes of interpersonal communication, culture is having an effect. Learning about other cultures, including their systems of knowledge, belief, values, customs, and artifacts, facilitates person-to-person interaction. Every culture can be subdivided into co-cultures consisting of members of the same general culture who differ in some ethnic or sociological way from the dominant culture. In the United States, African Americans, Hispanic Americans, Japanese Americans, Korean Americans, the physically challenged, gay people, and the elderly are examples of co-cultural groups. To engage in effective interpersonal communication with members of these and other groups, it is important to enhance your knowledge of the norms and rules that characterize their interactions. Remember, the lessons taught to you by your culture are not necessarily the lessons others have been taught by theirs.

Among culture's lessons are how to say hello and goodbye, when to speak and when to remain silent, how to behave when angry, how much eye contact to make when interacting, and how much

iStock.com/deshabara

Becoming culturally aware increases communication competence.

gesturing and touching is appropriate. If culture guides behavior, we must make the effort to understand someone's culture if we are to understand the person.[15]

When interacting with someone whose cultural background differs from yours, considering the following questions can improve your communication:

- How do this person's feelings about socialization differ from mine?
- How does his or her concept of self differ from mine?
- To what extent do our attitudes, values, and thinking processes differ?
- To what degree is he or she more or less competitive than me?
- In what ways does his or her use of nonverbal cues differ from mine?

## ORIENTATION AND CULTURAL CONTEXT

While an array of variables allows us to distinguish one culture from another, the two we focus on here are individual and collective orientation and high-context and low-context communication.[16]

### Individual and Collective Orientation

Cultures that are more individualistic in nature, such as those of the United States, Canada, Great Britain, and Germany, stress individual goals. In contrast, cultures more collectivistic in nature, such as those represented by many Muslim, African, Asian, and Latin American countries, stress group goals.[17] In an individualist culture, you are responsible for yourself and maybe your immediate family; in a collectivist culture, you are responsible for the entire group. Likewise, whereas individualist cultures promote competition, collectivist ones stress cooperation.

### High-Context and Low-Context Communication

Cultures are also distinguished from each other by their use of high- or low-context communication. High-context cultures are tradition bound; cultural traditions guide members' interactions, causing them to appear to outsiders as overly polite and indirect in relationships. Members of low-context cultures, in contrast, usually exhibit a more direct communication style, one that is verbally explicit. Members of Western cultures tend to use low-context communication, whereas members of Asian and other Eastern cultures typically use high-context communication.[18] Because they also place a premium on face-saving behavior, members of high-context cultures are much less confrontational. Preferring to preserve harmony, they avoid arguing for fear the other person might lose face. For similar reasons, members of high-context cultures are also reluctant to say "no" directly to another person. Thus, members of low-context cultures may have difficulty deciding when and if the "yes" of a member of a high-context culture really means yes.

## THE IMPACT OF GENDER

Culture also shapes **gender**, and gender shapes communication.[19] Socially accepted variations in the definitions and views of masculinity and femininity, gender differences, are taught to us as we grow up. As historian Elizabeth Fox-Genovese writes, "To be an 'I' at all means to be gendered."[20]

## GENDER AND COMMUNICATION STYLE

Gender is a social creation that imposes a sense of social order by reflecting the societal characteristics associated with the biological categories of male and female. Subtly or overtly, we are pressured to conform to social norms, encouraged to learn accepted interaction scripts, and usually develop preferences for using different communication styles. Though attitudes have evolved, in U.S. society, many still expect women to be more nurturing, sensitive to others' needs, and more emotional than men. Similarly, they expect men to be more independent, assertive, and emotionally restrained than women. Some families even persist in dividing responsibilities along gendered lines, assigning more physically demanding outdoor chores to males, while expecting females to clean the home's interior, cook, and care for other family members, including younger siblings and aging parents. Some hospitals still wrap baby girls in pink blankets and baby boys in blue blankets. Girls and boys similarly are provided with different kinds of toys—perhaps dolls for girls and action figures for boys. Schools have been criticized for encouraging students to pursue different curricula depending on their gender. So, from the delivery room to the home, to the school, and on to romantic relationships and career paths, we see gender shaping lifestyle. However, as we become more conscious of arbitrarily created gendered meanings, we are able to broaden our understanding of what is appropriate behavior and what we accept as "normal."

While we all express gender through behavior that we believe is normal, what we define as normal changes with time. By identifying how arbitrarily created gendered constructions, or conventions, affect interpersonal communication and our relationships, we take a step toward understanding what we hope for when it comes to our interpersonal lives. Do you see your options as unlimited? What tasks do you feel free to perform? What limits, if any, do you believe should be placed on the role gender plays in our social, professional, and family relationships? While all societies promote gender ideologies that specify appropriate behaviors for males and females, what should you do if you believe a gendered construction is privileging, disadvantaging, empowering, or paralyzing you or a partner?

# THE IMPACT OF MEDIA AND TECHNOLOGY

"The medium is the message." "The medium is the massage." We can trace both of these sayings to the musings of the late media critic and communication theorist Marshall McLuhan. According to McLuhan, the channels of communication affect both the sending and the receiving of messages. The same words convey different messages depending on whether they are sent using face-to-face interaction, print, a cell phone, a video, or a podcast. The medium changes things, altering the message by massaging its contents.

It is now over half a century since McLuhan predicted that the introduction of new technologies would transform our world into a mobile global village.[21] Technology makes it increasingly possible for us to watch and listen to, introduce ourselves to, and have continuing contact with individuals across the country and around the world without ever leaving our homes. Technology also is altering our sense of self, our social norms, our views of reality, our images of success and failure, our happiness, our interpersonal options, and the communication rules we adhere to. All these changes impact our communication presence.

Years ago, Apple's Steve Jobs observed that computers really were personal and should be renamed "inter-personal computers."[22] Today we use computers, tablets, and smartphones to log on to Facebook, LinkedIn, Twitter, or an endless litany of other sites, to connect with others. In the year 2000, the average person spent 2.7 hours a week online. In 2010, that number jumped to 18 hours a week.[23] In 2017, teens spent up to 9 hours a day on various social platforms.[24] On average, in 2017, Americans spent 12 hours, 7 minutes a day consuming media, including radio and television.[25] However, when we form a relationship online, we are likely to idealize and create heightened expectations for it, expectations that might not be realized should we actually meet. In fact, online partners feel greater intimacy with and attraction for one another than when they actually meet one another face-to-face.[26] Have any of your online relationships developed into flourishing offline ones? To what do you attribute their success or failure?

## TRY THIS

### What's Okay With You?

What guidelines do you think people ought to follow when using electronically enhanced communication? For example, have you ever engaged in any of the behaviors identified in the chart below yourself? Would you become annoyed, insulted, or feel at risk if another person engaged in any of the identified behaviors? Use the chart to record your answers.

| THE BEHAVIOR | EXHIBITED THE BEHAVIOR MYSELF | MY REACTION TO ANOTHER EXHIBITING THE BEHAVIOR |
|---|---|---|
| Texting while walking in the street | | |
| Texting another person while dining out with a friend | | |
| Answering a cell during a movie | | |
| Talking loudly on your cell on public transportation | | |
| Texting back in response to a missed call | | |
| Talking on a cell with one friend when out with someone who is talking on a cell to another friend | | |
| Not liking an Instagram post right away | | |
| Tweeting about one friend to another | | |
| Accessing Facebook while watching TV with a significant other | | |

1. What rules, if any, would you advise we adhere to when using digitally enhanced communication?

2. What makes certain uses of digitally enhanced communication either acceptable or unacceptable in your eyes?

3. How would you react if a rule important to you were violated?

In addition to broadening the network of people we communicate with, technology makes it possible for those who experience communication apprehension when face-to-face with another person to connect without such fear. We can interact remotely or in person, be anonymous, someone else, or ourselves. If the choice were yours alone, would you opt to increase or decrease the number of your virtual interactions compared to those you experience face-to-face? Why?

As well as spending more time in the digital dimension, we also devote more time to viewing and talking about reality TV and other programs. As a result, our mediated experiences are influencing our real-life experiences and relationships. Mediated reality is often sexier or more violent than real life. Despite this, we sometimes try to apply what we learn from them to our own lives, only to end up disappointed. Our love affairs are rarely as poignant or as passionate as those in the media. Our friends are rarely as attractive, giving, or fun to be with as those we see depicted. Physicians and lawyers are rarely as successful treating or representing us as their fictional counterparts are. Somehow, real life falls short of the lives we encounter either online or via television and film.

Years back, parents used to cajole, "Turn off the TV." Their plea has now changed to something like "Turn off the device and come watch television." Or are your parents as plugged into Facebook and other apps as you are? Do you or they take the smartphone to bed as you once did a stuffed animal? The claims we make about Internet addiction, while much like the claims people used to make about television being a plug-in drug, are being taken seriously by consumers and creators alike. Might you be addicted to your device? Facebook, Instagram, and Twitter are hypnotically compelling for many of us, in part because they deliver unscheduled "variable rewards"—much like slot machines do. Messages, alerts, notifications, photos, and "likes" are sent to us randomly, making it virtually impossible for us not to react to them. They induce large numbers of us to become compulsive site checkers looking for a dopamine boost—almost as if we were seeking a fix.

Quite simply, a machine is altering our consciousness and the nature of our interpersonal interactions.[27] We need to think about that. In coming chapters, we will look at the extent to which our devices are personalizing or depersonalizing our contacts, improving or harming communication with friends and family members, and fostering or impeding the development of what we call a community. When immersed in the digital domain, for example, do you gravitate toward cliques of people who share your interests, or do you seek to widen and diversify your interpersonal circle?

How are phones affecting relationships?

# ON THE WAY TO GAINING COMMUNICATION COMPETENCE

Even though interpersonal communication is an inevitable part of life, few, if any, of us are as effective or as successful at it as we could be. Therefore, we invite you to treat this class as your interpersonal communication laboratory. Use the information you gain and the skills you practice as guides when you interact with others. There is no such thing as being too good at interpersonal communication. Whatever your capabilities are right now, to help yourself become better at communicating interpersonally, promise yourself you will do the following.

## ADD TO YOUR STOREHOUSE OF KNOWLEDGE ABOUT INTERPERSONAL COMMUNICATION

Your chance of influencing your interpersonal encounters depends, at least to some extent, on your knowledge of how interpersonal relationships work. While our relationships vary significantly, with some being plagued by problems and others proceeding smoothly, one of our objectives in this book is to share with you a number of techniques you can use to enhance the quality of your relationships and the satisfaction you derive from them.

## RECOGNIZE THE EFFECTS OF YOUR RELATIONSHIPS

Every relationship affects you in some way. Some influence your understanding of others; some alter the quality of your life. Some add to your confidence; others diminish your belief in yourself. While healthy relationships enrich your life, unhealthy ones too often rob you of energy, leaving you demoralized or apathetic. Another goal of this course is to help you understand the forces at work during person-to-person contacts and the complex ways in which interpersonal communication changes you. If you understand the challenges you face, identify alternative modes of responding, and learn how to think about your relationships, then you will be better prepared to deal effectively with them.

## ANALYZE YOUR OPTIONS

The interpersonal communication choices you make have impacts on you and your partner. Rather than responding automatically, take time to think about your options. What happens in a relationship usually is not beyond your control. In most situations, you have freedom to respond in any number of ways. Every contact you engage in offers opportunities to improve it if you remain flexible and open. Another of our goals is to help you learn to take advantage of this.

## INTERACT ETHICALLY, RESPECT DIVERSITY, AND THINK CRITICALLY

Effective interpersonal communicators act ethically in their relationships, demonstrate their respect for diversity, and think critically about the interactions they share. Ethical communicators demonstrate the ability to adhere to standards of right and wrong. They follow appropriate interaction rules, treat other people as they would like to be treated, and never knowingly harm someone else in an effort to achieve personal goals.

Interpersonal communicators who respect diversity understand culture's role in person-to-person interactions, tolerate difference and dissent, willingly interact with people from a variety of backgrounds, demonstrate a decreased use of stereotypes to guide behavior, process experience from the viewpoints of others, avoid imposing their cultural values on other people, and refrain from holding discriminatory attitudes.

Individuals who think critically about their relationships know that communication is complex, and they don't know all there is to know. They are open-minded; reflect on others' ideas rather than respond impulsively; open themselves to new ideas and new ways of perceiving; challenge themselves to reexamine their beliefs, values, and behaviors; and concern themselves with unstated assumptions in addition to overt discourse. They think things out, analyzing and evaluating outcomes, seeking to understand and remember what worked or didn't, and creating opportunities for their own personal growth together with the personal growth of others.

# REFLECT ON THIS

## *The Cell Effect*

Over a decade ago, researcher Noelle Chesley wanted to find out if the time people spent on cellphones enhanced or detracted from their overall feelings of happiness. To answer the question, Chesley surveyed more than 1,200 adults and concluded that a correlation existed: The more time individuals spent on cellphones, the less happy and less satisfied they became with their family relationships. Chesley attributed this, at least in part, to the work lives of people spilling over into their personal lives and causing stress at home.

### Consider these questions:

1. Do your experiences today confirm Chesley's findings? Does time spent on your phone stress the relationships you share with people important to you, or does it help bring you closer?

2. Do you think Chesley would have found the same results if she had studied the time we spend on tablets or computers? Explain your answer.

3. What recommendations can you offer for alleviating such relationship stressors? For example, would you expect others to abide by rules specifying when to rely on smart phones or other digital tools?

Source: Noelle Chesley, "Blurring Boundaries? Linking Technology Use, Spillover, Individual Distress, and Family Satisfaction." *Journal of Marriage and Family*, 67, 2005, p. 1237–1238.

How omnipresent is technology in your life? Could you live without it? Would you want to?

## PRACTICE AND APPLY SKILLS TO IMPROVE INTERPERSONAL PRESENCE

This text shares skills you can practice to enhance your interpersonal presence. Commit to practicing them. How you present yourself, perceive others, use words and nonverbal cues, listen, progress in a relationship, overcome relational obstacles, demonstrate trust and trustworthiness, and handle your emotions all affect your effectiveness when interacting with friends, family members, coworkers, health providers, and others. The extent to which you practice and apply the skills we discuss will determine whether you add to your interpersonal behavioral repertoire, demonstrating your interpersonal versatility and resourcefulness.

## CONNECT THE CASE

### The Case of Sylvia and Khalil

"After he left my dorm, he texted me, 'I'm sorry, it's over.' That's all he said," Sylvia told her roommate Justine. "How could he end things just like that? Why didn't he talk to me when we were together? I thought everything was fine with us."

Sylvia and Khalil had been together for several months. They had met on campus at the beginning of the semester and had been seeing each other regularly. Sylvia had even invited Khalil to spend Thanksgiving with her at her parents'. They had returned to campus after the holiday, and then this happened. "What did I do to cause this?" Sylvia asked Justine. "Do you think he met someone else?"

Sylvia was despondent. Questions raced through her mind. She tried to access Khalil's Facebook page, but he had already defriended her, deleted her pictures, and changed his relationship status to single. She decided to text him back, asking, "What happened? What did I do?" Then she turned off her cell, afraid of what he would text back to her.

Khalil was sitting in his off-campus apartment staring blankly at his iPad. He had just defriended Sylvia and changed his Facebook status. He didn't feel good about it, but he told himself he had no choice. Now she was texting him. He didn't want to read it. "How can I tell her the truth?" he wondered. Sure, they had had some great times together—but that was until he went home with her for Thanksgiving dinner. Soon after entering Sylvia's parents' home, Khalil had begun to feel uncomfortable. Her folks were nice enough, but he sensed a certain amount of distance on their part.

By the time they had finished dinner, Khalil was certain that because he was Egyptian, Sylvia's parents had reservations about him. They hadn't done or said anything directly to him; he just had a feeling. Maybe he should have raised his concerns with Sylvia. But he told himself that ending things this way was easier. Was he right? Khalil just didn't know. He turned off his cell.[28]

## Demonstrate your understanding by answering these questions:

1. What do you think about the way Sylvia and Khalil handled their situation?

2. What does the behavior of each suggest about his or her communication weaknesses and strengths?

3. Would you have used texting and Facebook in the same way as Sylvia and/or Khalil? Explain your answer.

4. Given the current status of their relationship, what advice would you give each of them?

# REVIEW THIS

## CHAPTER SUMMARY

1. **Define and explain the importance of *communication presence*.** ☐

Communication presence is the unique composite of characteristics we present when interacting both digitally and in the real world. Communication presence affects interpersonal effectiveness and relationship development.

2. **Define interpersonal communication, distinguishing it from other types of communication.** ☐

Interpersonal communication occurs between two people, forming a dyad. Interpersonal communicators make personal contact, build a connection, and establish a relationship. The process of interpersonal communication is ongoing and ever changing, and it occurs whenever we interact with another person, sharing responsibility for creating meaning (what we extract from the interaction) and managing our relationship (determining its nature).

3. **Use a communication model to identify the essential elements and transactional nature of the interpersonal communication process.** ☐

Every interpersonal interaction is transactional in nature, meaning it involves two people who simultaneously function as sender and receiver; it contains messages (the content of communication), channels (the medium or media carrying the message), noise (anything interfering with the reception of a message), feedback (information returned to a message source in response to a message sent), context (the physical, psychological, temporal, and cultural setting for communication), and effect(s) (the emotional, physical, and/or cognitive influence of the communication).

4. **Explain the functions that interpersonal communication serves.** ☐

Interpersonal communication fulfills psychological functions by enhancing self–other understanding; social functions by meeting our needs for affection, inclusion, and control; information functions by promoting the sharing of knowledge and reduction of uncertainty; and influence functions by enabling us to use strategic communication to achieve goals.

5. **Describe the characteristics, core principles, and axioms of interpersonal communication.** ☐

Among interpersonal communication's characteristics are that it is a dynamic process, unrepeatable and irreversible, learned, and noted for its wholeness and nonsummativity. Among the principles underlying interpersonal communication are the importance of using behavioral patterns and both reasoned and retrospective sense making to predict and interpret behavior. The following five axioms add to our understanding of interpersonal relationships: (1) You cannot *not* communicate; (2) every interaction has content and relationship dimensions; (3) every interaction is defined by how it is punctuated; (4) messages consist of verbal symbols and nonverbal cues; and (5) interactions are either symmetrical or complementary.

**6. Describe how gender and culture affect interpersonal communication.** □

Gender and cultural prescriptions shape interpersonal communication. Because of their potential to enhance or complicate interpersonal relations, we can demonstrate sensitivity and avoid misunderstandings by increasing our awareness of the culture and gender preferences of others and recognizing the importance of respecting and adjusting to differences.

**7. Provide examples of how digital media are reshaping interpersonal contacts.** □

Digital media have broadened our options for communicating interpersonally. They are altering our sense of self, social norms, and views of reality. We send an increasing number of texts, using our cell phones more than ever before. Whether such options are personalizing or depersonalizing interaction is still open to debate.

**8. Develop a plan to improve your interpersonal communication.** □

Adding to your storehouse of knowledge about interpersonal communication, critically analyzing how your relationships affect you as well as the behavioral options open to you, committing to interacting ethically, respecting diversity, and thinking critically about person-to-person interactions, together with developing and practicing skills, will make you a more effective interpersonal partner.

## CHECK YOUR UNDERSTANDING

1. Can you explain the different kinds of communication you use in a day and how they help meet your needs? (See pages 1–2 and 12–14; and *Try This*, page 16.)

2. Can you give examples of what makes communication interpersonal? (See pages 2–5.)

3. Can you name and define the elements and axioms at work during interpersonal communication by using them to analyze some of your recent communication exchanges? (See pages 20–22.)

4. Can you summarize how communicating online as opposed to face-to-face alters the nature of interpersonal communication? (See pages 25–27; and *Try This*, page 5 and page 24.)

5. Can you write a paragraph describing the steps you will take to enhance your interpersonal skills? (See pages 27–29.)

## KEY TERMS

Channel 9

Communication 4

Communication presence 2

Complementary relationship 20

Get the tools you need to sharpen your study skills. **SAGE edge** offers a robust online environment featuring an impressive array of free tools and resources. Access practice quizzes, eFlashcards, video, and multimedia at **edge.sagepub.com/gambleicp**.

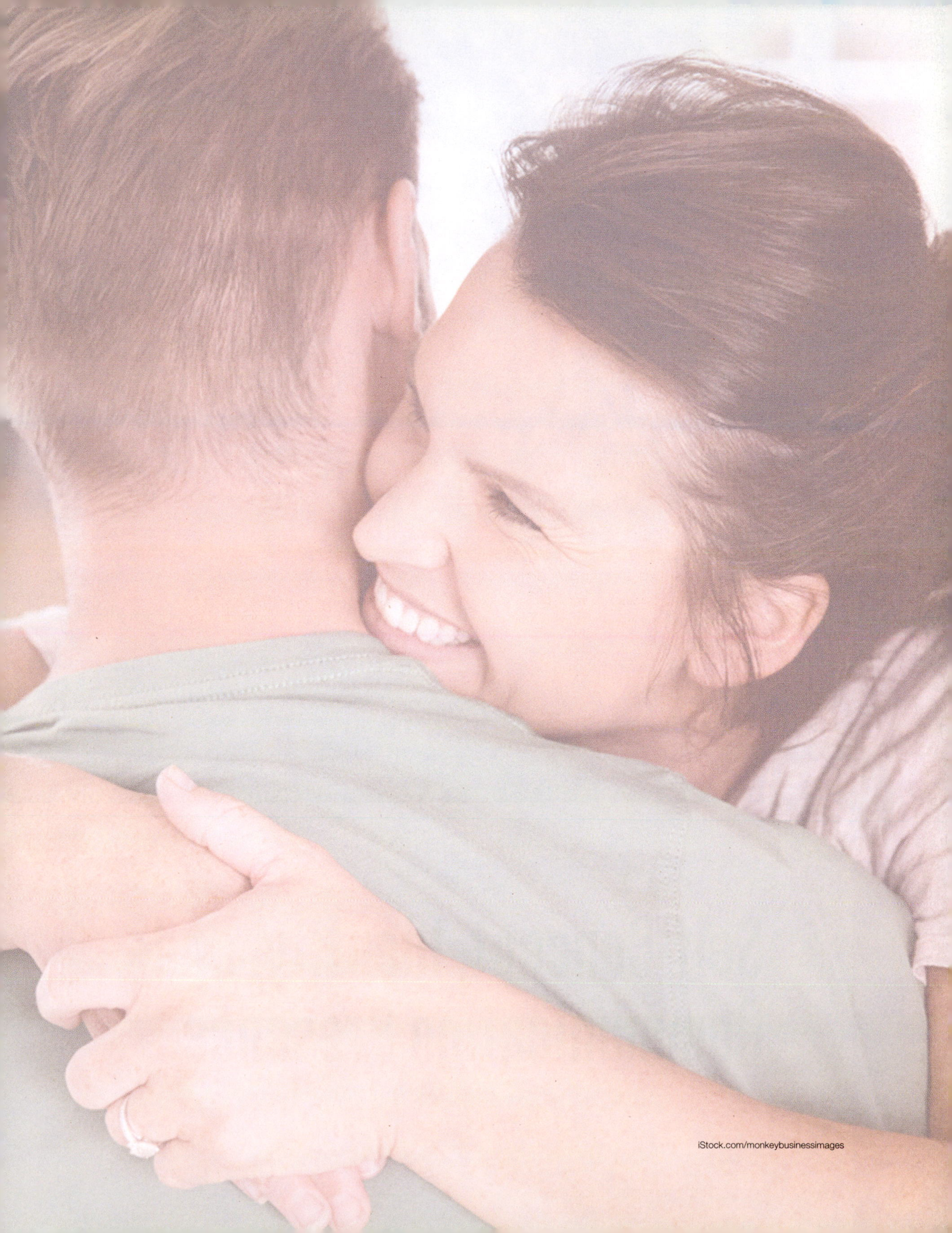

iStock.com/monkeybusinessimages

**2**

# Self-Concept, Identity, and Communication Presence

## CHAPTER 2

## Learning Objectives

**AFTER COMPLETING THIS CHAPTER, YOU SHOULD BE ABLE TO**

> Know thyself.
>
> —Socrates

1. Define self-concept, distinguishing it from the self, and noting its effect on your communication presence and relationships

2. Define self-esteem, distinguishing high self-esteem from low self-esteem and discussing the effects of each on performance

3. Explain reflected appraisal theory, social comparison theory, and confirmation, rejection, and disconfirmation, using them to discuss the role you and others play in shaping the self-concept

4. Define self-fulfilling prophecy and distinguish between a positive and negative Pygmalion

5. Explain the importance of periodically reexamining and revising your self-concept

6. Explain the influence that cultural diversity and gender have on the self

7. Describe how media and technology affect self-conceptions

8. Identify how you can change and strengthen your self-concept

. . . . . . . . . . . . . . . . . . . . . . . . . . . . . . . . . . . . . . . . . . . . . . . . . . . .

What role do social networks play in our lives? Do they encourage us to put our best "face" in front of others? Do they cause us repeatedly to fall in and out of love with ourselves as we compare ourselves to others? If set today, would the Greek myth find Narcissus in love with his Instagram or Facebook feed rather than with his reflection?[1] Might we also find him counting his followers or friends as we do?

The feature film *The Social Network* introduces us to a fictional portrayal of the real Mark Zuckerberg, the entrepreneur who created Facebook. As one writer observed, Zuckerberg created *Face*book, not Footbook or Elbowbook.[2] Zuckerberg was acting on the belief that it is human for people to want to know what is going on in each other's lives. And we have proven him right. You likely are among the 68 percent of Americans who use Facebook.[3] We are not just Facebook's users, however. We are also Facebook's products. We log on, post selfies that display ourselves as attractively or enticingly as possible, and update our lives for others to share by the minute if we're obsessed, by the hour if we're driven, and by the day if we're typical users.

What motivates participation on Facebook and other social networks? A deep interest in each other and a desire to be noticed. We feel the need to tell about a new shirt, car, promotion, hairstyle, significant other, or status change. Facebook capitalizes on our longing for connection and attention—to be virtually alive. Zuckerberg understands that we want others to know about us. He understands that showing our face helps us validate our identity—and our concept of self.[4] The question is, Do Facebook and other social media platforms have positive or negative influences on our concept of self as we engage in self-promotion? What do you think? ■

## WHAT DO YOU KNOW?

Before continuing your reading of this chapter, which of the following five statements do you believe to be true, and which do you believe to be false?

1.  People with high self-esteem are less likely to be bullies.                                    T          F

2.  Your perceived self is the one others see.                                                      T          F

3.  Engaging in face-work improves your looks.                                                      T          F

4.  Positive expectations have no impact on performance.                                            T          F

5.  Childhood experiences influence our ideas about gender.                                         T          F

Read the chapter to discover if you're right or if you've made any erroneous assumptions.

ANSWERS: 1. F; 2. F; 3. F; 4. F; 5. T

iStock.com/iridi

How we see ourselves and how we imagine others see us affects our communication presence and relationships.

Do you know yourself? Consider these questions: Who are you? What do you think of yourself? Do you consider your relationship with yourself to be a good one? When you evaluate yourself, do you characteristically give yourself a thumbs-up or a thumbs-down?

This chapter offers you the opportunity to develop **self-awareness** as you reflect on and monitor your physical and digital presence. It encourages you to explore the nature of the self and identity; to analyze how culture, gender, media, and technology influence self-concept; and to examine how the intrapersonal level of communication (the individual level, the communicating you do with yourself) affects the choices you make, your behavior, judgments of your interpersonal presence, and your relationships.

The poet–philosopher Alan Watts noted, "Trying to define yourself is like trying to bite your own teeth."[5] Exactly how confident are you that you really know yourself? And how willing are you to try to get to know yourself better?

Who you think you are and how you think about yourself in relationship to others influences every one of your interpersonal contacts. What you think of yourself is your baseline, your starting point for communication.

# SELF-CONCEPT: YOUR ANSWER TO WHO YOU ARE

Where does self-concept come from? While we are not born with a self-concept, over time we certainly develop one. The day a child first says "me," the day there is recognition of the self as separate from one's surroundings, life begins to change as a child strives to fit into the world as they see it. In short order, our concept of self—that relatively stable set of perceptions each of us attributes to ourselves—becomes our most important possession.

Beginning in childhood, the **self-concept** is a composite of everything we think and feel about ourselves. It is the perceived self—our self-identity—and it has two key components: self-image and self-esteem (see Table 2.1). **Self-image** is the mental picture you have of yourself— it sums up the kind of person you *think* you are. It is a composite of the roles you claim and the attitudes and beliefs you use to describe who and what you are to others, and your understanding of how others see you. **Self-esteem** is your self-evaluation—your estimation of your self-worth. In many ways, it is an indication of how much you like and value yourself, including your feelings, positive and negative, about your abilities, character, and feelings.

With this as background, it becomes apparent that self-concept affects communication presence and behavior, including what we think possible. As a result, it is important to use every opportunity to think carefully about self-concept.

## TABLE 2.1  LOOKING AT YOURSELF

| Self-concept | Everything you think and know about yourself |
|---|---|
| Self-image | Your mental picture of you |
| Self-esteem | Your estimation of your self-worth |

How you complete the sentences in the "Who Are You?" "Try This" box on page 38, and the categories into which your answers can be grouped, offers clues to your self-concept, including your self-image and self-esteem. For example, you might conceive of yourself in reference to your gender, religion or spirituality, race, nationality, physical attributes, roles, attitudes and emotions, mental abilities, or talents. The words you use to express your self-perceptions reveal what you think you are like. In many ways, your answers represent a construct that you have built to make sense of who you are. Remember, however, that the self-concept is not necessarily the same as the self.

## Who Are You?

Begin the exploration of your self-concept by answering the following question: Who am I? How many answers can you give? Complete the sentence "I am _____" with a minimum of 10 different ways you view yourself.

As we hope you now realize, there are lots of ways to complete the sentences. For example, did you give information about personal traits, such as, "I am spiritual," "I am attractive," or "I am friendly"? Did you describe your social identity, such as "I am a Christian" or "I am Chinese"?

Taken together, your answers describe the elements or specific beliefs that constitute your self-concept. Look back at your answers. What do they reveal regarding how you define yourself? What roles do you see yourself playing? How do you describe yourself socially? As you completed the sentences, how did social comparisons, whether online or face-to-face, influence what you wrote? In what ways, if any, did past successes and failures as well as other people's judgments play a part in determining your responses?

## ANALYZE THIS: THE CLOWN

As you read the following poem by Teri Gamble, consider these questions: What do you think is the significance of the clown's omnipresent rainbow smile? Like the poem's subject, do you ever "play" to people around you? Like the clown, do you ever wonder who you really are?

*The rubber man in the spotlight*

> *Propels himself*
>
> *Beyond the reach*
>
> *Of reality.*
>
> *Midway between today and tomorrow*
>
> *He pauses*
>
> *Suspended in his reverie by the crowd.*

*The rubber man in the spotlight*

> *Warmed by laughter*
>
> *Finds a face*
>
> *To play to.*
>
> *Dancing upon an ever-turning spindle*
>
> *He plays to another*
>
> *And another, and another.*

*The rubber man in the spotlight*

> *Sweeps up the dreams*
>
> *That remind him*
>
> *Of yesterday.*
>
> *Then tumbling out of the ring*
>
> *His face frozen in a rainbow smile*
>
> *He wonders who he is.*

## HOW ARE THE SELF AND SELF-CONCEPT RELATED?

The self and the self-concept differ from each other in a number of ways. First, the self is very fluid and in a state of constant change, whereas the self-concept is more highly structured and difficult to change (see Figure 2.1). Second, a portion of the self-concept may not actually be included in the self; this area represents the part of ourselves that we invent. Third, there is much more to the self than is included within the self-concept; this area represents our untapped potential. For example, you may think of yourself as friendly and outgoing, while others see you as snobbish and reserved. You may have the potential to become a leader, but because of your inability to convince others that you would like to work with them, you might not have the opportunity to demonstrate this talent.

To put it another way, the self-concept is a "map" that we create to chart the "territory" that is the self.[6] Our map or mental picture is, at least in part, a result of our interpretations of the messages others send us. As such, it may be accurate or inaccurate, positive or negative. The self-concept is depicted in Figure 2.1 as a rigid, geometric design to indicate that we like to make sense to ourselves. Experiencing uncertainty about the self is not a comfortable state for us, and so we work to develop consistency in the way we perceive ourselves.

## HOW ACCURATE IS YOUR SELF-CONCEPT?

Although change is a constant in life, the thirst for constancy can lead us to cling to outdated self-notions even in the face of evidence that renders them obsolete. Instead of revising our self-concepts to conform to new information, we are likely instead to do our best to acquire information that confirms what we already believe is true. Our reluctance to let go of set ideas allows outmoded notions about the self to persist.

It is understandable that we might resist changing an inaccurate self-concept when the new information available to us is negative, because our self-concept could become more negative. For example, this could happen when we are no longer considered to be as bright or hardworking as we once were. It is harder to comprehend why we similarly resist changing when the information is positive and would enhance our self-concept, such as when we are no longer perceived to be gawky or unfriendly. By rejecting such information, we deny ourselves a chance for growth and self-renewal.

Defending an unrealistic negative or positive self-concept keeps us from redefining ourselves. Our cognitive conservatism keeps us from seeing the real need for change and allows us to continue deluding ourselves. Refuting new information that could lead us to change limits us and obscures our view of how others see us. Conducting a reality check is necessary to validate or invalidate who we think we are. Have you conducted one recently?

**FIGURE 2.1**
The Self and the Self-Concept

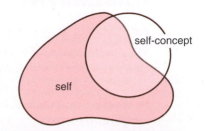

self-concept

self

REUTERS/Mario Anzuoni (UNITED STATES ENTERTAINMENT)

Do you see yourself as others see you?

# SELF-ESTEEM: ASSESSING SELF-WORTH

When we feel good about our achievements, we tend to value and feel good about ourselves. Self-esteem, our positive or negative evaluation of our self-concept, is important because it can either nurture and feed success or make succeeding more difficult. We build self-esteem when we exhibit determination to overcome obstacles, acquire specific skills or achievements, or are given increased responsibilities. Feeling good about the self and what we are capable of contributes to our performing well.

We carry our self-esteem with us from one interpersonal experience to another. What is more, we relay our level of self-esteem to others by how we interact with them.

## HIGH VERSUS LOW SELF-ESTEEM

People with high self-esteem differ from those with low self-esteem in communication style. They tend to display different eye contact, posture, and expression. Think about your friendly and romantic relationships. What role does your opinion of your self-worth play in them?

Individuals with high self-esteem often think better of others, expect others to like them, evaluate their own performance favorably, perform well in front of others, work hard for those who demand it, feel comfortable interacting with superiors, and defend themselves against others' negative appraisals.

Photodisc/Photodisc/Thinkstock

Belief in yourself shapes what is possible for you.

In contrast, individuals with low self-esteem often disapprove of others, expect others not to like them, evaluate themselves unfavorably, perform poorly in the presence of others, feel threatened by their superiors, and find it hard to defend themselves against those who view them critically, equating criticism with rejection.[7]

When we perceive ourselves as failures, we are more likely to present ourselves and behave in ways that cause us to fail. When we perceive ourselves as successes, we are more apt to act confidently and in ways that bring about success. Every success we have helps build our self-esteem.

## SELF-ESTEEM AND PERSONAL PERFORMANCE

When self-esteem is not connected to personal performance, it can be self-defeating. Feeling good about yourself when you have no reason to—that is, when you have not added to your achievements or competencies—can lead to your developing a favorable self-appraisal that will not be matched by others' views of you. Thus, when we talk about the importance of developing self-esteem, we are not talking about simple cheerleading. Rather, we are talking about opening yourself to opportunities that will help you develop your skills and abilities to their fullest potential.[8]

And here's a note of caution: Research reveals that individuals with high self-esteem may pose more of a threat to others than people with low self-esteem.[9] In fact, research indicates that over-emphasizing the importance of self-esteem in those who possess an unrealistically inflated self-appraisal can precipitate a culture of bullying. These findings have led some to argue for balance in the amount of praise given, to prevent inflated perceptions of self-importance in already self-centered individuals.[10] Researchers advise that instead of fostering self-esteem, we should be fostering resilience, because resilience helps people recover from personal disappointments and defeats.[11] By learning to cope with personal setbacks, we may help optimize our behavior.

# OTHERS HELP SHAPE OUR SELF-CONCEPT

While your experiences help to shape your self-concept, your self-concept, in turn, helps to shape your future experiences. How you see yourself in relation to others guides your behavior. Probably, you behave differently depending on the people you are with. You may be outgoing when with one friend but be intimidated by another. You may feel like a star in art class but inferior in chemistry, or vice versa. At any given moment, the nature of your self is affected by the nature of the situation in which you find yourself. And your interactions shape your view of yourself. Consequently, your language, attitudes, and appearance are apt to change as you move from one set of conditions to another. In a way, you become different selves as you adapt to perceived changes (see Table 2.2).

## TABLE 2.2   THEORIES REVEAL HOW OTHERS HELP SHAPE US

| Reflected appraisal theory | We build a self-concept that reflects how we think others see us. |
| Social comparison theory | We assess how we measure up against others. |

## WE REFLECT OTHERS' APPRAISALS

More than a century ago, psychologist William James put it this way: "A man has as many social selves as there are individuals who recognize him and carry an image of him in their mind."[12] In similar fashion, in his reflected appraisal theory, psychologist Charles Cooley described the mirror-like image we derive from our contacts with others and then project into our future experiences. In other words, we build a self-concept that reflects how we think others see us.[13] According to Cooley, the self we present is in large part based on the way others categorize us, the roles they expect us to play, and the behaviors or traits they expect us to exhibit. Cooley believed that by reflecting back to us who we are and how we come across, other people function as our mirrors. In fact, he coined the term "looking glass self" to represent the self that comes to us from others. For example, if others see you as a capable and outgoing leader, you may reflect their appraisals by viewing yourself in those ways. Of course, the roles we play and how we play them affect both how and with whom we communicate. They all influence the content, objectives, and frequency of our communication contacts.[14]

## TRY THIS

## Feelings About Age and Physical Ability

Feelings about aging may affect notions of self-worth. Society sends powerful messages about the capability and worth of people depending on their ages and physical abilities.

### Consider these questions:

1. How do you think your view of yourself would change if you were 30 to 40 years older? How do you imagine you would you feel about your appearance? How do you suppose you would feel about your potential to find a good job? How would you feel reporting to someone younger than yourself in your workplace?

2. How would your view of yourself change if instead of being able-bodied you suddenly had to use a wheelchair or vice versa?

3. What steps could you take to foster resilience in yourself when you are faced with forces that challenge your self-conceptions?

Of course, not all messages others send us about how they see us carry the same weight. Those sent by our significant others and by individuals whose opinions we respect and trust normally exert more influence on us than do the opinions of strangers and mere acquaintances.

## WE COMPARE OURSELVES WITH OTHERS

According to social comparison theory, we compare ourselves to others to develop a feel for how our talents, abilities, and qualities measure up to theirs.[15] In other words, to learn more about ourselves, we use others as measuring sticks, evaluating ourselves against them. As we compare ourselves to others, we form judgments of our skills, personal characteristics, and so on. We can, for example, decide whether we are similar or different, better or worse, stronger or weaker, or more or less creative than those with whom we compare ourselves. Often, as we assess our similarities and differences, we also make decisions regarding the groups we fit into. Generally, we are most comfortable interacting with others we perceive to be like us.[16]

Our self-esteem suffers if we continually feel we fall short when gauging ourselves in relation to others. When this happens, however, it could be because we have chosen to compare ourselves to an inappropriate reference group. For example, if we compare our looks with those of a supermodel, our musical ability with those of the winner of *The Voice,* or our athletic prowess with that of an Olympian, we probably are making an unfair comparison and, as a result, will develop an unrealistic assessment of our appearance, talent, or ability. If we compare ourselves with members of a more appropriate reference group, we might be able to inflate rather than deflate our sense of self.

Our accuracy in assessing our self-concept and self-esteem depends on how successful we are at processing experience and receiving feedback. If we pay more attention to our successes than to our failures and to positive reactions than to negative ones, we could end up overinflating our sense of self. On the other hand, if we pay more attention to our failures and give more credence to negative reactions, then our sense of self could deflate. In neither instance would our sense of self conform to reality.

People with normally high self-esteem tend to be happier[17] and less affected by peer pressure than those who have low self-esteem.[18] Individuals with healthy self-esteem are not self-absorbed. Rather than filling themselves with "unwarranted self-regard," they have a realistic sense of their abilities.[19] In touch with both their strengths and their weaknesses, they display **grit**—a combination of passion and perseverance for a singularly important goal, together with resilience and a tolerance for feeling frustrated.[20] Ultimately expecting a positive outcome, they persist in spite of failure. They are both confident and resilient, traits necessary for success.[21] To build resiliency and increase your chances of adjusting positively to change or disappointments try the following:

- Limit negative self-talk. In lieu of telling yourself that "I'm a loser," think, "I did something foolish, but I can fix it."

- To regain composure after a disappointment, place yourself figuratively or physically in another setting for a few moments.

- To improve your mood and productivity, relax your posture, put a smile on your face, and engage others with a warm tone of voice.

- Seek a friend to spend time with, even if it's just to take a walk. Having a friendly relationship increases satisfaction and energy.[22]

Researchers assert that high self-esteem is an effect of good performance, rather than its cause. According to J. D. Hawkins, President of the National Self-Esteem Association, "Self-esteem is more than just feeling good about yourself. It's about being socially and individually responsible."[23]

## TRY THIS

## Me, You, and Popular and Social Media

1. Consider how celebrities online and offline affect your picture of yourself. For example, how is your self-evaluation influenced by exposure to the lifestyles and standards of living experienced by pop-culture icons such as the Kardashians?

*(Continued)*

(Continued)

2.  When texting or messaging friends, many of us now use a personal emoji, often a caricature of ourselves. Typically, while the emoji we create may resemble us, and we may even make it lightly mocking, many of us make it more physically pleasing—as if it represents our "better self."

3.  If you haven't done so, download the Bitmoji app and create one to represent you. Explain the ways in which this selected public image represents an extension of yourself and what you hope it communicates to others.[24] Also explain what it suggests about your online level of honesty.

4.  Consider how you feel after spending time on social media. Do you ever find yourself suffering from FOMO (fear of missing out) after discovering your friends at an event without you? In general, do you feel better about yourself or worse about yourself once you log off? Be specific. To what do you attribute these feelings?

## WE HAVE PERCEIVED, IDEAL, POSSIBLE, AND EXPECTED SELVES

Each of us possesses a perceived self, an ideal or possible self, and an expected self. Sometimes, these views of the self can conflict with one another.

The **perceived self** is a reflection of your self-concept. It is the person you believe yourself to be when you are honest with yourself. Usually, there are some aspects of the perceived self that you wish to keep secret from others. For example, you might hesitate to let others know that you do not think you are good-looking or intelligent, that you are fixated on becoming wealthy, or that you are more concerned for your own welfare than theirs. To accomplish this, you engage in **impression management**; you exercise control over your behavior in an effort to elicit the desired reaction.[25] The **possible self** is the self you might become one day—the one you think about becoming. You may, for instance, want to be a passionately loved self, an accomplished self, or a rich self. The **expected self** is the one others assume you will exhibit. It is based on behaviors they have seen you display in the past or stereotypes they hold. Your **ideal self** is an idealized version of you—the person you wish to be and admire in your role models. For example, you may want to be likable, and so you try to be a likable person. If your ideal self is very different from you, then you might feel dissatisfied with your life.

### Goffman's Dramaturgical Approach

Through his concept known as the dramaturgical approach to human interaction, Erving Goffman explains the role that the skillful enacting of impression management plays in person-to-person interaction.[26] If we consider social interaction a performance and the setting in which interaction occurs the stage, then the actors (the people interacting) play their parts to manage the impressions of others sharing the stage with them, so that they, the actors, may achieve their personal objectives. The more skillful the actors, the more effectively they convince others that they are knowledgeable and trustworthy and that they possess a charisma that makes them attractive to others.

We can use several dramatic elements to make the best impression in any given scene. First, we can employ *framing*, specifically defining a scene or situation in a way that helps others interpret its meaning in the way we desire. Picture this: On a first date, you go on stage when you arrive to meet your date at a restaurant. You are seated and employ *framing* when you decide how to look and what to do while waiting for your date to arrive. You also use *scripting*, when you go through standard small talk upon your date's arrival. As you chat, you are convincing your date to play their role too. Of course, you use *engaging dialogue*—storytelling together with colorful and descriptive language and effective use of nonverbal cues—to guide your date's responses. Together, these elements underlie your *performance*.

When performing, we can also choose from among a number of techniques to encourage others to see us as we wish to be seen. For example, we may use *exemplification*, in which we serve as an example or act as a role model for others; *promotion*, in which we elucidate our personal skills and accomplishments and/or a particular vision; *face-work*, in which we take steps to protect our image by reducing the negative aspects of ourselves visible to others; or *ingratiation*, in which we employ techniques of agreement to make others believe us to be more attractive and likable and less threatening, harmful, or pernicious.

Describe a performance, face-to-face or online, that you or another person you know has enacted in an effort to come off as authentic. Were you or the other person successful? Were you or the other person authentic? How do you know?

## TRY THIS

## The "Authentic" Self

How do you define authenticity? What does the word mean to you? Can a person who decides to act authentically still be authentic? Do you know anyone who engages in "calculated authenticity," consciously managing others' impressions of him or her? Such a person effectively turns human interaction into a staged performance. Is this what we do on Facebook or Instagram—brand ourselves in such a way that others find us authentic?

Track your Facebook or Instagram activity for a week. What messages do you think your posts send to others regarding your self-image and its authenticity? Might there be a benefit to opening yourself up to other possibilities of who you are and who you might grow into in the future?

Source: See Stephanie Rosenbloom, "Authentic? Get Real," *New York Times*, September 11, 2011, pp. ST1, ST2, and Michael Puett and Christine Gross-Loh, "The College of Chinese Wisdom," *The Wall Street Journal*, Saturday/Sunday, April 2–3, 2016, pp. C1, C2.

## REACTIONS TO YOU: CONFIRMING, REJECTING, AND DISCONFIRMING RESPONSES

As we interact with others, how we feel about ourselves changes. Some people we interact with provide **confirmation** of our opinion of ourselves, communicating with us in ways consistent with our own appraisal of ourselves. How they treat us during our interactions with them reflects the way we think we are. For example, if you believe yourself to be intelligent, confirmers might reflect this by asking you to tutor them.

Others with whom we interact signal **rejection** of our self-appraisals by treating us in ways inconsistent with our sense of self—whether that is good or bad. For example, if you believe yourself to be hardworking, but rejecters treat you as if you are lazy, over time, their treatment of you might cause you to revise your picture of yourself.

Still others provide **disconfirmation** of our self-appraisals by sending us messages that tell us that, as far as they are concerned, we are not even important enough for them to think about; in their eyes, we do not exist—we are irrelevant. Someone who disconfirms you ignores you and goes about her business as if you were not present. By treating other human beings like nonentities, consistent disconfirmers may eventually rob others of their sense of self, without which it becomes virtually impossible for them to relate to the world effectively.[27]

Thus, those around us help shape our self-concepts in both positive and negative ways. Virtually every interpersonal contact we share sends a message regarding our importance, our capabilities, and how others view both our potential and our inadequacies.[28] (See Table 2.3.)

### TABLE 2.3  THE SELF IN RELATIONSHIPS

| Confirming response | Supports self-appraisal |
|---|---|
| Rejecting response | Negates self-appraisal |
| Disconfirming response | Robs the individual of a sense of self |

# THE SELF-FULFILLING PROPHECY

Do you tend to be pessimistic or optimistic? Optimists believe eventually they will succeed, and so they persevere; pessimists, expecting failure, tend to give up when confronted with challenges. Consequently, pessimists fail more frequently than do optimists. Optimists are resilient; they have feelings of **self-efficacy**, a positive belief in their abilities and competence.[29] Unfortunately, the pessimist's outlook and lack of resilience may lead to failure even as success is within reach. In many ways, both pessimists and optimists live out self-fulfilling prophecies.

## IT'S A CYCLE

A **self-fulfilling prophecy** occurs when we verbalize a prediction or internalize an expectation that comes true simply because we act as if it already were. For example, have you ever been invited to a function you did not want to attend because you expected to be bored? Were you? If you were, to what extent is it possible that your prediction of boredom increased the likelihood of its occurrence?

There are five basic steps in the self-fulfilling prophecy cycle (see Figure 2.2).[30] First, we form expectations of ourselves, others, or events—for example, "Monica won't like me." Second, we communicate the expectation by exhibiting various cues—"so I'll keep my distance from Monica." Third, others respond to the cues we send by adjusting their behavior to match our messages—Monica tells herself, "Ed is stuck up. I don't even want to talk to him." Fourth, as a result our initial expectation comes true—"I was right; Monica does not like me." Fifth, our interpretation of the actions of others strengthens our original belief—"Every time I see Monica, I am reminded that she does not like me."

## FIGURE 2.2
The Self-Fulfilling Prophecy Story

1. We develop expectations of people or events.
2. We express those expectations verbally and/or nonverbally.
3. Others adjust their behavior to match our verbal and/or nonverbal messages.
4. Our expectation becomes reality.
5. The confirmation of our expectation strengthens our original belief.

A self-fulfilling prophecy can be either self-imposed or other-imposed. When your own expectations influence your behavior, the prophecy is self-imposed. When the expectations of others help direct your actions, the prophecy is other-imposed. Either way, we exhibit behavior that we or another person expects.

## THE PYGMALION EFFECT

Among the most widely reported examples of the self-fulfilling prophecy is that used by psychologists Robert Rosenthal and Lenore Jacobson in their classic study *Pygmalion in the Classroom,* named for George Bernard Shaw's play *Pygmalion.* In the play, later adapted into the musical and film *My Fair Lady,* Henry Higgins transforms Cockney flower girl Eliza Doolittle into a duchess by believing that he can help her learn to speak and act like one.

Rosenthal and his associates informed a number of teachers that certain of their students were expected to "bloom"—that is, perform exceptionally well—during the following academic year. The teachers were unaware that the student names had actually been selected randomly, and there

How often do you compare yourself to others?

was no basis for predicting who would succeed. Despite this, the students who were singled out to bloom did so, improving their IQs and performing at higher levels than would otherwise have been expected.[31] Apparently each teacher had functioned as a **positive Pygmalion**, causing the students to live up to the labels placed on them.

The teachers gave the "about to bloom" students extra positive verbal and nonverbal reinforcement, waited patiently for the students to respond if they hesitated, and did not give them negative feedback when they offered incorrect answers. Thus, the teachers' behavior influenced the students' perceptions of their own abilities. The "about to blooms" responded to the teachers' prophecies by fulfilling them. Like Eliza Doolittle, the students acted like the people others perceived them to be.

The Pygmalion effect, as this form of the self-fulfilling prophecy has come to be known, influences performance in a variety of settings, from work-related to educational to social, and it does so in both positive and negative ways. When others have high expectations for a person, their opinions tend to result in enhanced performance, but when a **negative Pygmalion** has low expectations for others, the result is typically diminished performance. Consequently, managers' expectations can help or hinder worker production, and teachers' expectations can boost or deflate student grades. We live up to—and down to—expectations.

# REVISING YOUR SELF-CONCEPT: REEXAMINING IMPRESSIONS AND CONCEPTIONS

How others treat us and how we treat ourselves influence the person we think we are. Thus, if we wish to change our self-concept, we need to update the way we think about ourselves and assess the accuracy of our self-concept. Figuratively speaking, we need to turn on a light inside ourselves so we become more self-aware, recognize the kinds of messages others send us, and be cognizant of messages we typically ignore, discount, or purposefully misinterpret.

## CAN YOU REINVENT YOURSELF?

While we tend to hold on to our existing self-concept—even when it is proved false—this does not mean that we cannot change it. We just have to work to overcome our natural resistance. To combat the tendency to cling to an erroneous self-concept, we need to develop the willingness and skills to reevaluate or reinvent ourselves. That way, we will be better able to shed outdated conceptions.

To start this process, we need to understand how we manage to maintain a self-image that others may regard as unrealistic. Perhaps because we are overly concerned with how we come across to others, we put all our energy into presenting ourselves in as favorable a light as possible. When we focus on ourselves, however, we are less likely to notice others' reactions to us, and we may miss feedback revealing how they really see us. Sometimes, however, others are reticent to provide accurate feedback for fear of hurting our feelings. Other times, we base our assessment of ourselves on obsolete information, clinging to memories rather than face current realities.

We can also be our own worst critics and view ourselves more harshly than others. For example, we might convince ourselves that we are fat despite others insisting we are a perfect weight. Why do we do this? We might be acting on information that was true at one time but is no longer. Or we might receive distorted feedback from an overly critical friend that warps our view of ourselves. Or we might criticize ourselves simply because we believe that society prefers we own up to our inadequacies, while downplaying our strengths.

When you visualize yourself, do you see a person who can achieve anything or a person with limitations who is likely to fail? To change your self-concept, assess your strengths and shortcomings honestly, freeing yourself to reshape your self-image and grow.

# DIVERSITY AND CULTURE IN RELATIONSHIPS: HOW IMPORTANT IS THE "I"?

Individuals in most, if not all, cultures have a notion about the self, although the specific notions held vary across cultures, affecting person-to-person interactions in subtle to dramatic ways.[32]

## THE SELF IN INDIVIDUALISTIC AND COLLECTIVISTIC CULTURES

In North American and Western European cultures, the word *self* reigns supreme, reflecting the importance individuals place on realizing their personal goals. Members of such individualistic cultures, in which individual identity is paramount, value uniqueness and personal identity; they tend to believe in themselves, seek to do their own thing, and shun conformity. In contrast, in the collectivistic cultures of Asia, Africa, and Central and South America, group goals are given a higher priority.[33] Japanese parents, for example, typically refrain from lavishing praise on their children, believing that children who are overpraised are likely to end up being self-centered and not focused enough on the group's needs.

For the members of collectivistic cultures, the self is not the center of the universe. For them, the group—not the individual—is the primary social unit. Where individualistic cultures link success with personal achievement, collectivistic cultures link it to group cohesion and loyalty. Members of collectivistic cultures gain a sense of identity through their group memberships, not by promoting themselves, as members of Western cultures are apt to do.[34] Thus, while some of us have been raised to call attention to ourselves and develop ourselves at the group's expense, others of us have been reared to avoid such behavior by nurturing the *interdependent self* instead.[35]

# REFLECT ON THIS

## *Changes*

Digital Vision./Digital Vision/Thinkstock

In his book *Uh-Oh,* philosopher and author Robert Fulghum presents his observations concerning when and how our self-conceptions change:

> Ask a kindergarten class, "How many of you can draw?" and all hands shoot up. Yes, of course we can draw—all of us. What can you draw? Anything! How about a dog eating a fire truck in a jungle? Sure! How big you want it?

Do you like to act in plays? Yes! Do you play musical instruments? Yes! Do you write poetry? Yes! Can you read and write and count? Yes! We're learning that stuff now.

Their answer is Yes! Over and over again, Yes! The children are confident in spirit, infinite in resources, and eager to learn. Everything is still possible.

Try those same questions on a college audience. A small percentage of the students will raise their hands when asked if they draw or dance or sing or paint or act or play an instrument. Not infrequently, those who do raise their hands will want to qualify their response with their limitations: "I only play piano, I only draw horses, I only dance to rock and roll, I only sing in the shower."

When asked about the limitations, college students answer that they do not have talent, are not majoring in the subject, or have not done any of these things in years, or worse, that they are embarrassed for others to see them sing or dance or act.

What went wrong between kindergarten and college?

What happened to YES! Of course, I can?

### Consider these questions:

1. To what extent, if any, do your experiences support Fulghum's observations?

2. What factors do you believe cause us to change our answers to Fulghum's questions as we mature?

3. Based on Fulghum's insights, what advice would you give today's kindergarten and college students?

Source: Robert Fulghum, *Uh-Oh,* New York: Villard Books, 1991, pp. 228–229.

People who are primarily individualistic in their thinking and behaving have an **idiocentric orientation**. Those who are primarily collectivistic in the way they think and behave have an **allocentric orientation**.[36] To which group do you belong?

Do you think American culture is becoming more individualistic or more communal?

Our unique personal experiences and shared group membership influence how we define our-selves. Together with culture, these factors play integral parts in forming our self-concept. Still, care should always be taken against rigidly categorizing people from any given culture, whether indi-vidualistic or collectivistic in orientation. Keep in mind that variations occur within countries. For example, in the United States, people from the South exhibit higher levels of collectivism than do people living in the West.[37] In addition, after people from the Western and Eastern worlds interact with each other, their cultural orientations moderate.

## THE SELF IN HIGH- AND LOW-CONTEXT CULTURES

People from different cultures also exhibit different communication style preferences. Individuals belonging to **high-context cultures** tend to be very polite and indirect when interacting with oth-ers, while people from **low-context cultures** typically exhibit a more direct communication style.[38] When meeting someone for the first time, a person from a low-context culture is likely to ask direct questions in an effort to gather background information and get to know the person; their priority is the discovery and expression of individual uniqueness.

People from high-context cultures, however, hesitate to ask direct questions, preferring to rely on nonverbal, contextual information. They value silence and reticence, believing that people of few words are thoughtful, trustworthy, and respectable. As a result, they also are likely to find unsolicited self-disclosures inappropriate. And because they would view such behavior as a sign of disrespect or disloyalty, they are less likely than people from low-context cultures to criticize one another publicly. When their words hurt another person, they believe they hurt themselves as well.

## THE SELF IN HIGH- AND LOW-POWER-DISTANCE CULTURES

Attitudes toward the self also differ along the dimension of **power distance**, or the extent to which individuals are willing to accept power differentials. People from high-power-distance cultures, such as Saudi Arabia and India, perceive power as a fact of life. In these cultures, people in low-power positions are apt to defer automatically to people in authority. In contrast, people from low-power-distance cultures, such as the United States and Sweden, are more likely to emphasize and value their independence even when superiors are present.[39] A general feeling of equality prevails in such cultures (see Table 2.4).

## TRY THIS

### Are You an "I" or Part of a "We"?

Evaluate how much the statements in categories A and B below reflect how you think and act in regard to yourself and others. Rate each statement on a scale of 1 to 5, with 1 being *not at all important* and 5 being *very important*.

*Category A*

1. I want to demonstrate my personal worth. _____

2. I want to be me. _____

3. I want others to consider me an asset. _____

4. I want to achieve my personal goals. _____

Total _____

*Category B*

1. If I hurt you, I hurt myself. _____

2. I want harmonious relationships. _____

3. I put the welfare of others before my own welfare. _____

4. I act in accordance with tradition. _____

Total _____

Compare your totals. The higher your Category A total, the greater your idiocentric tendencies. The higher your Category B total, the greater your allocentric tendencies.

## TABLE 2.4  CULTURE AND INFLUENCES ON THE SELF

| People with individualistic orientations | Conceive of the individual as the basic social unit<br>Make individual goals a priority<br>Link success and individual achievement |
|---|---|
| People with collectivistic orientations | Conceive of the family/group as the basic social unit<br>Make interdependence/group goals a priority<br>Link success and group achievement |

| People from high-context cultures | Exhibit an indirect communication style<br>Make face-saving a consideration |
|---|---|
| People from low-context cultures | Exhibit a direct communication style<br>Seldom think of face-saving |
| People from high-power-distance cultures | Defer to superiors |
| People from low-power-distance cultures | Value independence |

## LONELINESS AND SELF-DISCONTENT ACROSS CULTURES

Even though their cultures may differ, young people throughout the world are likely to share common perceptions regarding the self. Most hope to develop and sustain social relationships, especially with their peers, and most are optimistic regarding their abilities to assume responsibilities for themselves in the future. Despite the optimism of a majority of young people, between 25 and 30 percent of them also describe themselves as lonely, overwhelmed by life's problems, and frequently sad,[40] though the percentage varies widely from country to country. Among Japanese teens, 55 percent reported frequently feeling sad, and 39 percent reported feeling lonely.[41] Britain also has a loneliness problem, with some 9 million Brits reporting in a 2017 report that they often or always feel lonely. Now the country has appointed a minister for loneliness.[42]

Those who find themselves with fewer people to talk with or share thoughts and experiences with more frequently report feeling lonely. Loneliness does not discriminate; it affects all whose opportunities for person-to-person contact are diminished, perhaps because of a fear of being rejected or the belief that they don't fit in. Many people who are lonely wish they had a larger network of people to contact, yet, even when they do, for one reason or another they avoid reaching out, which can cause their feelings of social isolation to spiral out of control. To combat the tendency some of us have to isolate ourselves when feeling lonely, try the following:

- Accept. When isolated, connection becomes difficult. Accept opportunities for connection even if you don't want to go out.

- Plan. Scatter potential opportunities to connect socially across your calendar. If you need to, plan something and invite one or more others to join you.

- Join. Think of things you love to do and find others who share your passion. If you love reading, join a book club. If you love running, try road-runners.

- Think positively. Feelings of loneliness or isolation can lead to our misinterpreting others' words and actions. Give others the benefit of the doubt. They may not be rejecting you. They may just be having a bad day.[43]

In 1991, clinical psychologists Darlene Powell Hopson and Derek Hopson reported that African Americans expressed discontent with the self, finding that as early as the age of 3, black children expressed the desire to be white, even expressing a preference to play with white dolls.[44] Do you experience such feelings today? Another study did not find that African Americans had negative attitudes toward the self because of skin tone.[45] Might greater diversity in dolls have helped in changing the self-discontent of children? In 2016, the Mattell Corporation further diversified the 57-year-old

Barbie doll by adding new body types with diverse ethnicities to the doll options. Film and television saw an uptick in nonwhite characters and creators, exemplified by the 2018 film *Black Panther*.

If you're white, seeing people who look like you in toys and media offerings isn't unusual. Historically, those who aren't white have had to search for pro-social cultural representations resembling them. Being able to relate to such representations is necessary, not only to feel seen and valued, but to challenge institutional bias.[46]

To what extent, if any, do you think that being in another marginalized group, such as the elderly or physically or mentally challenged, contributes to feelings of isolation and negative attitudes toward the self?

## TRY THIS

## Young and Old

1. Interview a male relative and a female relative, both of whom are older. Ask them these questions:

   a. Who are you? What roles do you perform? What adjectives describe you?

   b. How has the way you see yourself today changed from how you saw yourself when you were a child, a young adult, and middle-aged?

   c. How do you believe the ways your family and friends see you have changed through the years?

   d. Is there an era of your life you would want to repeat? Why?

2. The following quotations reveal the self-perceptions of two older people. These quotations are not meant to characterize all older people; rather, illustrate two individuals' perspective on how aging affects self-perception:

   > The young want everything to move fast. They let their impatience show in their eyes. When you are hard of hearing it is worse. People get impatient when you try to join in. They yell in your face. Finally, they just give up on you and act like you are not there because it is too much trouble to try and keep you in the flow of things.[47]

   > You ask me if I enjoy remembering things from the past. Well I do. . . . [I]t is as if there are reels of movies in my head, all starting at different eras. I can go back and start one up any time. Different people, dressed differently, living in rooms and houses without electricity. And all starring a different me, of course . . . the past—what I did and accomplished and endured and loved—are all part of who I am.[48]

   Compare and contrast the answers your interviewees provided to the questions listed above with the perceptions of these two people.

## GENDER AND SELF-CONCEPT

If you awoke one day to discover that you had changed into a member of the opposite sex, how would that affect you? In what ways, if any, would this alteration change your plans for the day? The week? The month? The year? What impact would it have on the rest of your life?

As we noted in Chapter 1, *sex* refers to the biological characteristics that define men and women. *Gender,* in contrast, refers to the socially constructed roles and behaviors that the members of a given society believe appropriate for men and women. Thus, gender is a variable that influences how others treat us and how we treat them because of our sex. Our gender becomes integrated into our self-concept, providing us with a **gender identity**, that is, an inner sense of being male or female. The experiences we have during our formative years influence our views of masculinity and femininity, affecting our identities in later years. As we internalize the attributes of maleness and femaleness, what we have come to believe about our gender affects the way we conceive of our self. Transgender activist Chaz Bono has been quoted as saying, "I believe gender is between your ears, not between your legs."

Men and women are likely to see and describe themselves differently. Men generally characterize themselves as possessing initiative, control, and ambition. In contrast, women see themselves as sensitive, concerned for others, and considerate. While appearance plays a major role in the self-image of women, until recently, it was not considered integral to the self-image of a man.[49] Young women are still teased about both their looks and their weight more often than are young men, but the macho male, muscular and fit, is making a comeback, placing pressure on men to "bulk up" or be thought of as unmanly.[50]

Unfortunately, in our society, social and cultural expectations cause women to be vulnerable to damage to their self-concepts, in part because of the many conflicting and confused messages they receive.[51] Our society expects those who are feminine to be nurturing, unassertive, sensitive, caring, deferential, and emotional. As a result of such expectations, society rewards young women for a pleasing appearance, revealing their feelings, being forgiving, and being nice or helpful to others. In contrast, our society expects men to be strong, ambitious, in control of their emotions, and successful; unlike women, men are rewarded for displaying these qualities and achieving results.[52]

Of significance is the finding that our society values male characteristics more highly than female characteristics. Thus, men typically feel better about themselves than do women. The upshot is that many women try to attain success by attempting to be it all and do it all. The comedian Carol Leifer perhaps put it best in her act when she said, "I just had a baby an hour ago and I'm back at work already. While I was delivering, I took a course in tax-shelter options." Of course, the "me too." movement has provided women with role models and a movement within which to combat unhealthy gender stereotypes particularly when it comes to sexual harassment.

# SEEING THE SELF THROUGH THE MEDIA AND TECHNOLOGY LOOKING GLASS

Entertainment programs, films, music, platforms, and applications help us forge our identities, sense of self, and who we want to be. They teach us how to dress, look, interact, and consume. We learn who has power and who does not, who has followers and who does not. The websites and media we frequent also influence our sense of ethnicity and race, gender, and class.

# REFLECT ON THIS

## Beauty Standards and Dying to Be Thin

In "The Girl Who Could Never Be Thin Enough: One Family's Tragedy," we learn about Stacy Asbury, a teenager suffering from anorexia nervosa who sadly succumbed to the disorder. Her father, Tom, was left heartbroken at his inability to help his daughter overcome its ravages. Approximately 100,000 people, both female and male, but predominantly female, have this disorder. Because of a desire to be thin and the distorted images they have of their own bodies, 3 to 5 percent of sufferers starve and exercise themselves to death, as Stacy did.

### Consider these questions:

1. In your opinion, is it appropriate for any industry to send the message that beauty and thinness are requisites for success?

2. What role do the cosmetic and diet industries play in feeding a person's longing to attain a self that mirrors the ideal presented in media?

3. In what ways, if any, are the messages the media send women any different from the messages they send men regarding athleticism and the ideal muscular build?

4. Should we blame the media and technology for individuals' feelings of inferiority or inadequacy?

5. What, if anything, can we do to counter the effects of media messages and campaigns featuring male and female ideals? For example, why do you think Facebook removed "feeling fat" from its list of status update emoticons?[53] What effect, if any, has "fat talk" had on you or others?

Source: Gene Wojciechowski, "The Girl Who Could Never Be Thin Enough: One Family's Tragedy," special to *Los Angeles Times,* December 27, 1993. See also Naomi Wolf, *The Beauty Myth,* New York: Morrow, 1991.

## THE IMPACT OF THE MEDIA

Media depictions help us assess the general public's preferred patterns of behavior and appearance. They help shape our opinions about how our bodies should look, how men and women should interact, and the meaning of success. The way we interpret their offerings reinforces or negates our own sense of self by influencing our sense of who we are as compared to who we should aspire to be.

Often, we are not conscious of the extent of the media's influence, of how much they are "**make-believe media**"—that is, they make us believe.[54] Our concepts of what we should be like or, for that matter, what our relationships should be like, or even more specifically what African Americans, Latino Americans, Asian Americans, and men and women are supposed to be like, are conveyed to us via the media, so much so that some critics complain that the media preempt real life, offering us fabricated views of the world in its place.

Among the media's messages are that violence against women is commonplace; that men are hard, tough, and independent; and that minorities and women are less visible than men. Women, for example, have been underrepresented in film (especially aging women), which features fewer female than male protagonists and female characters who were younger than the male characters. Women also have been less likely than men to be portrayed as leaders and more likely to be identified by their marital status.[55] Other media messages are that African American males are either athletes or unlawful, that Asian males are awkward, and that Muslim men are terrorists. Such messages often distort how we see ourselves and influence our perception of what is normal and desirable behavior. In addition, media models adversely affect our evaluations of ourselves as attractive, successful, or smart. And all too often, the thirst the media develop in us to attain some ideal turns into painful and enduring feelings of inadequacy when we are unable to acquire what we covet.[56]

## THE IMPACT OF TECHNOLOGY

We derive our sense of self not only from communicating face-to-face, but also from communicating online. By using technology, we participate in the creation of new worlds and new ways of finding out about ourselves. Interacting digitally, we can be ourselves or, at times, someone else—that is, we can exist as personas.

For some of us, the lives we live are more virtual than real. Some of us regularly inhabit virtual worlds, participating in simulations and assuming different personas. We may have a number of e-mail and Twitter accounts and various screen names as we use the digital domain to experiment with multiple identities—while concealing our real identities from both friends and strangers with whom we interact online.[57] We might, for example, pose as a member of the opposite sex, conceal our age or ethnicity, hide physical characteristics, or otherwise pretend to be someone we are not. In other words, online we can be genderless, raceless, rankless, and appearanceless.[58]

We also can create parallel identities that facilitate the exploration of murkier aspects of the self, something very different from being an employee part of the day, a student another part of the day, and a family member at home. As psychologist Sherry Turkle notes, "The obese can be slender, the beautiful plain, the 'nerdy' sophisticated" due to the construction of an identity that is not part of their authentic selves. Turkle asserts that instead of developing internally, as a result of our being overly influenced by the opinions of others, the self is being externally manufactured. She contends that when we tweet and communicate via Facebook or Instagram, we are playing to the crowd—presenting a self that is based on what others respond to positively.[59]

How do manufactured images affect your sense of self?

Research shows that we try to present ourselves in as positive a light as possible online—especially, as we noted as the outset of this chapter, when using a social networking site such as Facebook. In effect, we psychologically boost our ego, enhancing our self-esteem.[60] Some researchers, however, believe that Facebook has a dark side, in that it feeds users' narcissistic tendencies by providing opportunities for self-promotion, access to shallow relationships and detached communication, and numerous self-solicitations for support.[61] Other researchers disagree, contending that frequency of Facebook use is not associated with narcissism—a trait they assert applies only to those Facebook users who gather unrealistically inflated numbers of friends—but rather with greater openness and lower concern regarding privacy.[62] For avid online game players, spending too much time online can result in depression and anxiety, because failing in game playing becomes as real as failing in real life.[63]

Researchers continue to weigh in on how life in the digital domain influences thoughts about identity. A 2017 survey of 1500 young people aged 14–24 suggests that social media platforms affect their sense of self including their body image—but in different ways. YouTube was found to have the most positive impact. In contrast, Facebook, Snapchat, Twitter, and Instagram demonstrated negative effects—with Instagram being the most negative particularly because of its ability to cause young women to compare themselves with curated, Photoshopped, unrealistic versions of reality.[64] Among the most prevalent negative effects of social media was their tendency to contribute to feelings of anxiety and depression, leading to a lack of sleep, unhappiness with one's appearance, increased bullying, FOMO, or not being present at social events that others frequented. Together, these contributed to decreased feelings of adequacy.[65]

Does your communication presence change when you go online? Does frequenting social media tend to make you more or less social? More or less inhibited? Do you act more or less authentic? Do you assume multiple identities, negotiate identities, or stay true to yourself? What have you learned about yourself by interacting with others online?

## ANALYZE THIS: MEDIA

In Sidney Lumet's classic award-winning 1976 film *Network,* written by Paddy Chayefsky, the main character, a television news anchorman, speaks these words to his audience:

> Television is not the truth. We lie like hell. . . . We deal in illusions, man. None of it is true. But you people sit there day after day, night after night. . . . We're all you know. You're beginning to think that the tube is reality and your own lives are unreal. You do what the tube tells you to do. You dress like the tube, you eat like the tube, you raise your children like the tube. In God's name, you people are the real thing; we're the illusion.

1. What does the preceding quotation suggest about our relationship with media? Substitute the words *the internet* for *the tube*. Does the quotation still ring true? Why or why not?

2. Compare and contrast the image you have of each of the following with the image portrayed in the media. Which image do you prefer and why?

   A nurse

   A lawyer

   The police

   A corporate executive

   The wealthy

   Arabs

   Teenagers

   Older people

3. Divide your life into three approximately equal segments. For example, if you are currently 21 years old, divide your life into the following segments: ages 1 to 7, 8 to 14, and 15 to 21. From each life segment, select a television program or film, song, book, and app or social networking site that you believe exerted a significant influence on your self-perception and interaction with others. For each of your selections, explain its significance and what it reveals about you.

4. If you could trade places with any media/YouTube/Instagram personality or character, who would it be and why?

Source: Quote from *Network*, written by Paddy Chayefsky, MGM and United Artists, 1976

# GAINING COMMUNICATION COMPETENCE: WAYS TO STRENGTHEN YOUR SELF-CONCEPT AND COMMUNICATION PRESENCE

We all carry a visualized "selfie" of the person we think we are wherever we go. Our selfie is a collage of merged images: what we think we were like in the past, what we wish we had been like, what we think we are like right now, and what we expect to be like in the future. It is a composite of how we see ourselves, how we wish we saw ourselves, and how we imagine others see us. Use the following suggestions to improve your mental picture-taking ability and to develop a clearer sense of self.

## UPDATE YOUR SELFIES

Although changing your mental image of yourself is not easy, it is possible. To do it, remind yourself that a selfie captures but a moment in time linked to a particular environment and communication context. Photos are frozen in time. We are not. Thus, while our memories are important and help us construct our sense of who we are, we need to keep the mental picture we carry with us current. By doing this, we will be better able to discount images that no longer accurately represent us, and thereby avoid focusing on regrets—"the lost lives, lost selves a person could have lived or been if s/he had done a few things differently."[66]

## CONDUCT AN IMAGE REVIEW

Watch yourself in action. Review your images, periodically taking time to reassess the roles you perform, the statements you use to describe yourself, and the extent to which you approve of your own values and behavior. Are you satisfied as you scroll through them? Do you have realistic goals? It takes courage and open-mindedness to do this.

## EXPLORE OTHERS' IMPRESSIONS OF YOU

The people we interact with regularly often see the strengths or weakness we tend to overlook or underplay. While we need not become what others think we are, if we are willing to explore others' perceptions of us, we at least open ourselves to the possibility of change. If we are receptive to how others see us, we may be able to make adjustments and become more effective in other person-to-person contacts.

## PICTURE INFINITE POSSIBILITIES

The self is flexible and changeable. In a constant transitional state, it has the capacity to adapt to changing circumstances and conditions. By asking yourself, "Who am I now?" instead of "Who am I always?" you will be able to take picture after picture of a changing you, someone who opens him- or herself to the possibilities that today and tomorrow offer. As a Xerox executive said in a speech aptly titled "Butterflies, Not Pigeonholes":

> In a knowledge-driven economy, self-confidence means a willingness to champion new ideas and the resilience to roll with the punches when ideas turn out to be better in the abstract than in reality. Plus, self-confidence provides the persistence to try again from another angle. Self-confidence enables an individual to withstand the criticism of colleagues, to live with the fact that not everyone will like everyone else.

> And it gives one the ability to listen to others, to work as part of a team, to be willing to let others share the load . . . and the spotlight, confident that one's contribution to the success of the whole will be recognized.

> In short, self-confidence enables people to feel comfortable outside the pigeonholes, to contribute in an ever-changing environment. Without it, the most gifted individual can toil in the shadows, their gifts never fully realized.[67]

Isn't it better to picture yourself as a butterfly, free, than stuck in a pigeonhole?

# The Case of Aisha's Term Paper

"I'll never be able to pass this course," Aisha moaned to herself as she sat at Starbucks staring at her laptop with her text opened beside her. "I've been trying to write this paper all weekend, and I'm still on the first page." She sighed deeply and then rose to get another cup of coffee.

As Aisha sipped her coffee, she began to thumb through the Sunday paper. She stopped to read an article about the Efficacy Institute, a school that provides students with instruction on self-concept. The article noted that studies on "efficacy" suggest that any person can succeed if he or she is motivated and works hard. Efficacy programs help students believe in themselves by repeatedly delivering messages such as "Work hard!" "Think you can!" "Believe in yourself!"

Aisha began to think about her own situation. She had dropped out of college years earlier and had only recently reenrolled. Now she found herself stuck in the same old trap—she didn't think she could do the work. Aisha wondered—should she also enroll at the Efficacy Institute? Aisha remembered how bad she had felt after dropping out of college, and now she was experiencing those same feelings of failure—all because of this paper. Then she had a brainstorm. She typed the following lines on her laptop and posted them on her Facebook wall:

### Recipe for Success in College

1. Believe in your abilities to succeed.

2. Work hard on all assignments.

3. You can do it!

She stared at the words. Then she started writing. Her head was filled with so many new ideas that her fingers could barely keep up. Could all these ideas have come from the simple lines she had just posted?

Aisha didn't dwell on the question. She was working too hard and writing too fast to ponder that possibility.

### What Do You Think?

1. Do you believe that improving a college student's self-esteem will enable him or her to earn better grades? Why or why not?

2. Are there recipes for success you believe a student should follow to succeed in college? What about in the world of work? In life? If so, describe them, comparing and contrasting your various success recipes.

3. Does *self-talk*—that is, what you tell yourself—influence your chances of succeeding? Explain.

# REVIEW THIS

## CHAPTER SUMMARY

1. **Define self-concept, distinguishing it from the self and noting its effect on your communication presence and relationships.** ☐

Self-concept, the baseline for communication, is that relatively stable set of perceptions we attribute to ourselves. Composed of everything we think and feel about the self, it guides our communicative behavior. By watching ourselves in action, we see the effect that our communication presence has on others.

2. **Define self-esteem, distinguishing high self-esteem from low self-esteem and discussing the effects of each on performance.** ☐

Self-esteem is our positive or negative evaluation of our self-concept. We carry it from one interaction to another. Self-esteem that is high nurtures success, while low self-esteem makes its attainment more difficult. When self-esteem is not connected to personal performance, however, it can be self-defeating.

3. **Explain reflected appraisal theory, social comparison theory, and confirmation, rejection, and disconfirmation, using them to discuss the role you and others play in shaping the self-concept.** ☐

According to reflected appraisal theory, our self-concept reflects how we believe others see us. According to social comparison theory, we compare ourselves to others to develop a feel for how we measure up to them. *Confirmation* supports our self-appraisal, *rejection* negates our self-appraisal, and *disconfirmation* reveals a total disregard for us as a person, suggesting that for the other person, we do not exist, robbing us of a sense of self.

4. **Define self-fulfilling prophecy and distinguish between positive and negative Pygmalions.** ☐

A self-fulfilling prophecy is a prediction that increases the likelihood that an anticipated outcome will occur. A positive Pygmalion has positive expectations and fosters positive change in us, while a negative Pygmalion has low or no expectations and fosters diminished performance in us.

5. **Explain the importance of periodically reexamining and revising your self-concept.** ☐

We need to develop the willingness and skills to reevaluate or reinvent ourselves. Only by doing this are we able to shed outdated conceptions.

6. **Explain the influence that cultural diversity and gender have on self-concept.** ☐

Cultural differences influence our self-notions. Whether we are from an individualistic or collectivistic culture, display an idiocentric or an allocentric orientation, or ascribe to masculine or feminine gender prescriptions is derived from the lessons taught us by society and culture.

7. **Describe how media and technology affect self-concept.** ☐

Media and technology provide us with information about preferred patterns of behavior and appearance, sometimes causing us to develop unrealistic expectations for ourselves and at times either adversely or positively affecting our feelings of adequacy.

**8. Identify how you can change and strengthen your self-concept.** ☐

To strengthen our feelings of self-worth, we need to reassess the nature of our self-concept periodically, visit and revisit others' perceptions of us, and keep ourselves open to the possibility of change.

·························································

## CHECK YOUR UNDERSTANDING

1. Can you identify the components of self-concept and then use them to describe yourself? (See pages 36–37.)

2. Can you describe how the social comparisons you make with others influence your thoughts about yourself? How does reflected appraisal theory play out in your own life? (See pages 40–42.)

3. Can you name individuals who have served as positive and negative Pygmalions in your life, making you feel better or worse about yourself? (See pages 44–46.)

4. Can you explain how living in an individualistic or collectivistic culture affects a person's self-concept? What about living in a social media-obsessed culture? (See pages 47–51.)

5. Can you identify steps you can take to strengthen your self-concept? (See pages 55–56.)

## KEY TERMS

Allocentric orientation  50

Collectivistic cultures  49

Confirmation  46

Disconfirmation  46

Expected self  44

Gender identity  55

Grit  43

High-context cultures  51

Ideal self  44

Idiocentric orientation  50

Impression management  44

Individualistic cultures  49

Low-context cultures  51

Make-believe media  57

Negative Pygmalion  48

Perceived self  44

Positive Pygmalion  48

Possible self  44

Power distance  51

Reflected appraisal theory  41

Rejection  46

Self-awareness  36

Self-concept  37

Self-efficacy  46

Self-esteem  37

Self-fulfilling prophecy  46

Self-image  37

Social comparison theory  42

Get the tools you need to sharpen your study skills. **SAGE edge** offers a robust online environment featuring an impressive array of free tools and resources. Access practice quizzes, eFlashcards, video, and multimedia at **edge.sagepub.com/gambleicp**.

3

# Perception and Social Experience

## Learning Objectives

**AFTER COMPLETING THIS CHAPTER, YOU SHOULD BE ABLE TO**

1. Explain the nature of perception and its relationship to reality

2. Describe the perception process in action

3. Explain how schemata, perceptual sets, unconscious bias, ethnocentrism, and stereotypes influence perception

4. Distinguish among the following perceptual barriers: fact-inference confusions, allness, indiscrimination, frozen evaluations, snap judgments, and blindering

5. Discuss how culture and gender influence perceptions of social experience

6. Discuss how media and technology influence perceptions of social experience

7. Identify strategies you can use to enhance your perceptual abilities

> We don't see things as they are.
> We see them as we are.
>
> —Anais Nin

How accurate are the quick perceptions we form of each other? And how good are the decisions we make based on these instant perceptions? Consider speed dating, for example. In speed dating, we rely on "thin slicing"—basing our impression of another person solely on an abbreviated behavioral glimpse.[1] During a speed-dating event, we may interact round-robin style with as many as 12 possible partners, with each individual "date" lasting on average from 3 to 8 minutes. While some believe we should be able to make judgments about how close we want to become with a potential dating partner during such a short time—even as short as 30 seconds—others are not so sure.[2]

Interestingly, researchers report that thin slicing produces judgments that are pretty accurate.[3] Within 30 seconds, speed-dating participants find themselves either attracted to someone or not. Speed daters acknowledge a lack of attraction or negative physical qualities as potential partner turnoffs, with women reporting three times as many negative judgments as do men. Reported turn-ons are physical attractiveness and positive behavior and demeanor, including positive perceptions of a potential date's communication and presentation skills.[4] Participants also are likely to report more attraction for those they perceive themselves to share attributes with, whether or not their perceived similarities are accurate.[5] And men report that similarity influences their attraction to a potential partner more than do women.[6]

While we are good at forming rapid, relatively accurate perceptions of others when deciding whom to date (consider the popularity of the online dating site Tinder), are we as capable of forming quick and accurate perceptions when it comes to making other decisions, including whether a person is racially biased? What do you think? ■

## WHAT DO YOU KNOW?

Before continuing your reading of this chapter, which of the following five statements do you believe to be true, and which do you believe to be false?

| | | | |
|---|---|---|---|
| **1.** | Differences in perception are rare. | T | F |
| **2.** | We can process unlimited amounts of data each second. | T | F |
| **3.** | We have a tendency to fill in perceptual gaps. | T | F |
| **4.** | Dividing people into in- and out-groups improves perceptual accuracy. | T | F |
| **5.** | "The sun will rise tomorrow" technically is not a statement of fact. | T | F |

Read the chapter to discover if you're right or if you've made any erroneous assumptions.

ANSWERS: 1. F; 2. F; 3. T; 4. F; 5. T

To advance the understanding of perception and its impact on us, Paul Allen, cofounder of the Microsoft Corporation, donated US$300 million to a project devoted to mapping the brain's circuitry of perception and analyzing the billions of cells and synapses at work in vision, memory, and awareness.[7] Because the brain has been described as the "gatekeeper to our interactions with the world," scientists hope the decoding of these processes advances understanding of perception in action.[8]

## OUR PERCEPTION DEFINES OUR REALITY

Should we believe our eyes? To answer this question, researchers study the relationships among perception, reality, and performance. For example, psychologists have learned that when baseball and tennis athletes are playing well, they report the ball looks larger than when they are playing poorly. Golfers playing well likewise report that the cup looks bigger than when they are playing poorly.[9] Perceive the ball, hole, or hoop to be larger, and you may be on your way to improving your athletic prowess—even if what you perceive is not really there.[10]

Today it's so easy to alter visual images that it's become normal to be skeptical regarding which are real and representative of reality.[11] The yellow line that appears across the football field on your TV screen is added digitally. The ads you see behind home plate when watching baseball on TV are computer-generated effects. Dead celebrities appear in new commercials and reprise their roles in movies. Much of the time we are unable to tell if a photo has been digitally doctored or altered, and if we can tell, we typically are unable to say definitively what's changed.[12] Were they used in court, fake photos could pose real problems. More troubling, eyewitness testimony given during trials is wrong about one-third of the time.[13] Our eyes are deceivable.

Can we believe the eyes of an eyewitness?

## DO WE PERCEIVE THE SAME SOCIAL REALITY?

Our lack of agreement about what we see is particularly apparent when we consider art. For example, take the work of performance artist Marina Abramovic. Would you call a person sitting still in a room "art"? The fact that answers to this question vary illustrates a key aspect of perception—different people do not always view the same situations in the same ways. For the same reason,

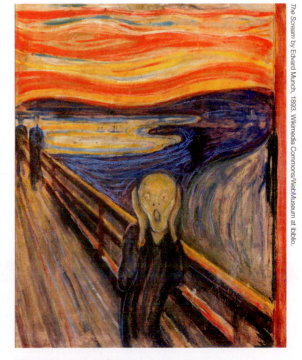

people do not agree on the meaning of Edvard Munch's painting *The Scream*, pictured here. Our perception is a consequence of who we are, where we are, and what we choose to see.

Culture, race, age, gender, geographic location, and life experiences combine to create perceptual gulfs between us and those whose culture, race, age, gender, geographic location, and life experiences differ from ours. Confronted with issues such as race relationships, gender equity, an economic crisis, and the political divide, many of us see different realities. It is not uncommon for our perceptions of events and people to conflict. In fact, differences in how we see, hear, taste, smell, or feel specific stimuli—that is, differences in how we perceive—occur all the time. Is it because we cannot perceive what is really there? Is it because we perceive what we want to perceive? Is it because we never experience the exact same reality as anyone else?[14]

As we learn more about the perception process, we prepare ourselves to handle the interpersonal problems that perceptual variations and

What does *The Scream* mean to you?

disagreements present. By exploring why we experience the same stimuli differently, we may better understand why we think and act differently as well. Only by getting behind the eye of the "I" can we come to understand why "where we stand depends on where we sit."[15]

### Standpoint Theory

Our experiences as members of particular groups shape how we perceive situations, people, and ourselves, at least in part, because of our standpoint. According to **standpoint theory**, people in positions of power have an overriding interest in preserving their place in the social hierarchy. Therefore, they develop views of social life that are likely to be more distorted than those of people who stand to gain little, if anything, from their positions in the social hierarchy.[16] For example, a recent survey of 1,302 adults found that 82 percent of women believe sexism currently is a problem. Men, in contrast, significantly underestimate the sexism felt by women.[17] It is easier for the powerless to feel inequities than for the empowered. People who occupy less powerful or marginalized positions develop keener insights into how society works, if only because they need to develop these understandings to survive.[18]

By becoming aware of diverse perspectives and interacting with people whose standpoints differ significantly from our own, we can develop better-balanced perception.[19]

# THE PERCEPTION PROCESS IN ACTION

**Perception** is the process we use to make sense of experience. Through perception, we give meaning to the world, making it our own:

- We actively select or choose to focus on relatively few stimuli.
- We organize or give order to the stimuli.
- We interpret sensory data or explain what we have selected and organized.
- We remember what we have observed.
- We respond.

We use our perceptual powers to decide what people are like and to give their behavior meaning. While waiting to order in a restaurant, for example, we may observe two people having lunch, size them up as businesspeople, and decide that they are meeting to close an important deal. When engaging in interpersonal perception, we also ask questions about others regarding their relationship to us, draw conclusions about their personalities, and make judgments about their intentions.

According to **uncertainty reduction theory**, we monitor the social environment to learn more about each other and reduce our uncertainty regarding another person's intentions.[20] We seek such information because if we lack it, we could fail in our efforts to predict behavior and its consequences. Thus, upon meeting someone, we will choose certain cues to attend to. We might note, for example, that the person is female, older than we are, speaks with a foreign accent, is well groomed, and seems approachable. Our next step would be to organize the information we have gathered so that we are able to store it and/or use it. This is followed by an effort to evaluate and interpret the meaning of our perceptions, which are placed in our memory for retrieval whenever we need or choose to respond.

## SELECTION

Although our senses can process approximately 5 million bits of data every second, our brains can handle only about 500 bits per second.[21] Because of our inability to perceive everything, we are compelled to be selective about stimuli.[22] As a result, we focus on certain cues and ignore others. Figure 3.1 illustrates the process of perception in action.

As you read this chapter, stop and look around you. What do you see? What captures your attention? Is it the hum of the refrigerator, the feel of your chair, the color of the walls, or voices coming from another location? Consciously turn your attention to something different. What did you fail to notice initially that now makes an impression on you?

### FIGURE 3.1
The Perception Process

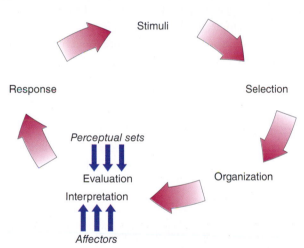

Since we can attend to only a limited number of stimuli, we choose which people, situations, or events to perceive. When we interact with others, some of us focus on appearance, others on the strength of a handshake, and still others on the sound of the voice or the look in the person's eyes. We direct our attention to certain qualities and not others. Multiple factors influence what we pay attention to, what enters our awareness and what exists unobserved and unnoticed.

Usually we focus on a stimulus that is more intense than others or that reflects our motives or interest more than others. For example, we pay attention to a loud noise that disrupts our concentration. Likewise, we overhear a conversation near us in a diner if the two people are speaking about a topic that concerns us. Our interests influence our perceptions, as do our motives. When, for example, we are concerned with our financial situation, we notice more information about how to save money. When we are hungry, we become more aware of food establishments, or we notice the aroma of what someone else is eating. When we are late for an appointment, we might run right past a close friend without even realizing it.

According to psychologist Herbert Simon, "A wealth of information creates a poverty of attention."[23] When we direct our attention to some stimuli, while choosing to ignore others, we demonstrate **selective perception**. What are the specific cues you focus on when first meeting someone? What do you look for? What do you listen for? Three components of the perceptual process provide answers to these questions:

- **Selective exposure** is our preference for people and messages that confirm our existing beliefs, values, or attitudes, such as paying attention to messages delivered by a candidate we are supporting.

- **Selective attention** is the means by which we focus on certain cues but ignore others, such as not noticing the look of disgust on the face of someone we like.

- **Selective retention** is the practice by which we recall things that reinforce our thinking and forget things we find objectionable, such as recalling positive qualities of people we like and negative qualities of people we dislike.[24]

In using any of these, we may bias the perceptual process of selection and end up with distorted views of people or events. For example, think about a relationship you once shared but ended. Once you made the "end-it" decision, did you start to notice more about the person that you disliked? This is known as the **horn effect**, which occurs when our perception tends toward the flaws of a person or thing. Compare this phenomenon to what happens when you decide to take a personal relationship to a more serious level. Once you have made this kind of decision, instead of perceiving what is negative about the other person, you are more likely to perceive additional things that you like. The reverse of the horn effect is known as the **halo effect**.

Selective perception helps us create a somewhat limited but more coherent and personally meaningful picture of the world—a picture that conforms to our beliefs, expectations, and convictions.[25]

## ORGANIZATION

Just as we use a number of strategies to select what impressions we notice, we do the same to facilitate our meaningful organization of these impressions. One strategy is to categorize a stimulus according to the **figure-ground principle**. What we choose to focus on becomes the figure, and the rest of what we experience is the ground. We are able to alternate the figure and ground of what we perceive. In a classroom, for example, if you focus on what a fellow student is doing during your professor's lecture, the student becomes the figure, while the professor recedes into the background. When you focus your attention on the professor, she is the figure, and the rest of the classroom is the ground.

A second organizing strategy is **closure**. Every time we fill in a missing perceptual piece, we employ closure. Look at the stimuli pictured in Figure 3.2. What do you see? Most see a dog and a circle. Because we seek to close gaps, we mentally fill in the incomplete figures. We want to perceive a completed world, as it were, so we supply elements that are not really part of the stimuli or messages we process. For example, the assumptions we make about others' motivations help us make sense of our own relationships. We might conclude that a friend invited us to a party only because she needed our help in passing a course. Whether the sense we make is right or wrong, justified or unjustified, it fills in certain gaps. Just as what you choose to notice is up to you, you can choose how to organize what you perceive.

**FIGURE 3.2**
Illustrations of the Closure Principle

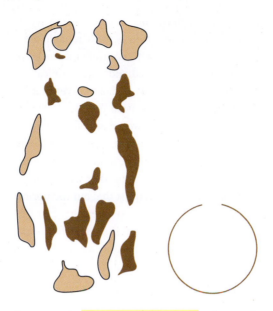

A third organizational strategy is <mark>perceptual constancy</mark>—the tendency we have to maintain the same perception of stimuli over time. As a consequence of perceptual constancy, we often see people not as they are, but as we have been conditioned to see them. The constancy principle helps explain why we find it difficult to alter a perception once we form it. A large number of our perceptions are learned and then reinforced over time.

Perceptual constancy is facilitated by our use of <mark>schemata</mark>, which are the mental templates or patterns of thought we carry with us. A <mark>script</mark> is a type of schemata, through which we enact the general ideas we have about people and situations and how things should play out during routine activities. We develop schemata and scripts based on both real and vicarious experiences. By reverting to schemata, we are able to classify people into manageable categories, according to their appearance, psychological traits, group memberships, and so on. Sometimes schemata, as we will discover later in this chapter, also contribute to stereotyping, which can lead us to see what is not there while ignoring what is.

## EVALUATION AND INTERPRETATION

As we evaluate and interpret experience, the meaning we see in it is influenced by individual affectors—factors that color our responses—including culture, roles, biases, present emotional state, past experiences, and physical limitation or capabilities. If you are looking for a fight, you may perceive an insult. If you are hungry, you may smell food. If you are looking for a date, you are more likely to interpret a statement as a flirtation. The horn and halo effects come into play as affectors shape our perceptions.[26]

Among other variables influencing the interpretation/evaluation process are the degree of involvement we have or expect to have with a person, the knowledge we have relative to the person's intentions, our feelings about ourselves in relation to the other person, and the assumptions we make about human behavior in general and this person's behavior in particular.

# MEMORY

Memory is a composite of what we read, piece together, experience, and/or want to be true.[27] How we interpret and evaluate a stimulus determines whether or not what we experience enters our memory and can later be retrieved. The question is, how reliable are our recollections? Can we count on our perceptual abilities to supply us with accurate memories of experience?

Consider this: When Americans were surveyed and asked to recall their memories of what they observed early on September 11, 2001, 76 percent of those surveyed in New York and 73 percent of those surveyed nationwide recalled watching television broadcasts of the two planes that struck the twin towers of the World Trade Center.[28] These, however, were false memories. In fact, there is no video of the first plane hitting the tower. What people experienced was a "flashbulb memory"—memories that feel as sharp as though they just happened, but are almost always wrong.[29] Memories can be unreliable and often are a mingling of what did happen together with information acquired days or even years after the actual event. Despite this, we often insist that our memories are totally correct.

We do not simply reproduce what we store in our memory. Instead of objectively recalling an experience, we try to reconstruct a memory at the time of withdrawal. However, as we engage in retrospection or backward reasoning, inaccuracies may creep in. While trying to remember, we infer past occurrences based on who we are and what we now believe and know. We tend to recall information consistent with our schemata and discount or forget information that is not. On the other hand, if information dramatically contradicts any of our schemata, compelling us to think about it, this can lead us to revise the schemata we use.

Nostalgia, a special kind of memory, can be defined as a bitter-sweet longing for memories of experiences that we cannot recapture. Experiencing nostalgia inspires us to live fuller lives by reminding us of experiences and people that mattered to us in the past. Nostalgic feelings contribute to our wanting to build and nurture our present social lives.[30]

# RESPONSE

Perception is a mixture of external stimulation and a person's internal state. We actively participate by controlling our responses to stimuli. We are both the cause of perception and its controlling force. The result is how we make sense of the world and relate to others.

The terrorist attack of 9/11 is the most memorable TV event of the past 50 years. But do we remember it as it happened?

**Attribution theory** helps us understand our response to social experience. It also speaks to the fact that we like to be able to explain why others behave as they do.[31] We assign meaning to the others' behavior by ascribing motives and causes for their actions. When we attribute behavior to something in the disposition of the people involved, we assume it to have an internal cause—that is, we believe it is caused by their characteristics. When we attribute it to something about the situation or environment, we identify an external cause—that is, we believe the behavior to be caused by something outside of them.

Let's say, for example, that your date arrives to pick you up early, and you want to figure out why. An internal attribution might be that he was eager to see you or that he did not want you to have to wait for him. Each of these reasons points to an internal characteristic of your date as the cause of the behavior. External attributions might be that the traffic was much lighter than it usually is or that he was able to leave work early. Each of these point to something in the external environment as causing the behavior.

## ANALYZE THIS: THE DECEPTIVENESS OF APPEARANCE

Can Stock Photo Inc./wacker

In "Childhood," by Frances Cornford, a child's initial perception of old age matures:

> I used to think that grown-up people chose
>
> To have stiff backs and wrinkles round their nose,
>
> And veins like small fat snakes on either hand,
>
> On purpose to be grand.
>
> Till through the banisters I watched one day

> My grand-aunt Etty's friend who was going away.
>
> And how her onyx beads had come unstrung.
>
> I saw her grope to find them as they rolled;
>
> And then I knew that she was helplessly old,
>
> As I was helplessly young.

How do you account for the change in the child's perception? Why is it possible to perceive a person, situation, or event one way at one point in time and differently at another? What happened that led the child to discover that what she or he saw at one point in time did not tell the entire story?

Identify challenges that stand in the way of your accurately evaluating people, situations, or events. What steps can you take personally to ensure that what you see in a person, situation, or event is not limited to what you are looking for?

Source: Frances Cornford, "Childhood," in *Frances Cornford: Selected Poems,* ed. Jane Dowson. London: Enitharmon Press, 1996. Reprinted by permission.

We use four principles as guides when attributing behavior to a particular cause: consensus, consistency, distinctiveness, and controllability. With *consensus,* we consider commonalities of behavior. For instance, we might ask a question such as "Do the friends of my friend also speak with different accents when they are at home as opposed to when they are at work?" If the answer is no, we are more apt to decide that the exhibited behavior has an external cause—perhaps a concern with their employer's impression of them.

When focusing on *consistency* to make an attribution, we look at repeated behavior. For example, if our friend is chronically late, then there is high behavioral consistency, and we are more apt to attribute the behavior to internal causes.

When focusing on *distinctiveness,* we ask if the person displays similar behavior in different situations. If the answer is yes, we are likely to conclude the behavior has an internal cause.

Finally, when focusing on *controllability,* we seek to determine if the person's behavior was under his or her control. For example, if someone is flying in to see you and is delayed because of a mechanical problem with the airplane, the delay was not under his or her control.

### Attribution Errors

A common error in making attributions is that of assuming that the primary motivation for behavior is in the person, not in the person's situation, a tendency known as the **fundamental attribution error**. When, for example, a friend disappoints us by failing to arrive on time for a party, we make a fundamental attribution error if we conclude that the friend is inconsiderate, rather than believe that external factors interfered with his or her ability to attend. The fundamental attribution error causes us to overemphasize internal factors or personality traits, and to de-emphasize or discount the role played by the situation or factors external to the person.[32]

Things change dramatically, however, when we provide reasons for our own behavior. In offering reasons for why we behave as we do, we overemphasize external factors and downplay internal ones. This tendency, known as the **self-serving bias**, functions as a barrier to accurate perception, while simultaneously helping to raise our own self-esteem. We take credit for the positive and attribute the negative to factors beyond our control.

Another perceptual barrier is over-attribution—the attributing of everything an individual does to a single or a few specific characteristics. For example, we may ascribe a person's alcohol use, preference for certain kinds of friends, and lack of interest in close relationships to the fact that she or he was sexually abused when young.

When it comes to human beings, accounting for behavior can be complex. To understand our own behavior and that of others, we need to do our best to make accurate, reasoned attributions rather than excuse or blame ourselves or other people based on habitual attribution biases.

# FRAMEWORKS OF PERCEPTION

The mental templates and life experiences we bring to any situation strongly affect how we process experience and relate to others. Our schemata, when combined with our preconceived ideas (or sets), along with unconscious bias, ethnocentrism, and stereotyping, define our perceptions and reveal our perceptual vulnerabilities. What is more, we often enact our perceptions without any conscious awareness.[33]

## SCHEMATA

Four perceptual schemata, or cognitive frameworks, help us decide what others are like and whether we would like to get to know them better:

1. *Physical constructs* enable us to classify people according to their physical characteristics, including age, weight, and height.

2. *Interaction constructs* point us toward their social behavior cues; for example, are they friendly, arrogant, aloof?

3. *Role constructs* focus on their social position; for example, are they professors, students, administrators?

4. *Psychological constructs* lead us to classify people according to such things as their generosity, insecurity, shyness, and sense of humor.

Which of these schemata are you conscious of using when you first meet someone?

## REFLECT ON THIS

### Attribution Theory

Reverend Jesse Jackson speaks at the UN for the International Day for the Elimination of Racial Discrimination. March 21, 2012. United States Mission Geneva.

*Licensed with CC BY 2.0, https:// creativecommons.org/licenses/by/2.0/deed.en.*

Research has confirmed our tendency to attribute another's behavior to internal variables while underestimating the impact of situational or environmental variables. Can you show how this works?

1. Use attribution theory and the fundamental attribution error to provide a rationale for the following lines from a speech by the Reverend Jesse Jackson:

   *Most poor people are not lazy. They catch the early bus. They raise other people's children. They clean the streets. No, no, they're not lazy.*

2. Using your understanding of the nature of perception, explain this statement:

*We find causes where we look for them.*

Then, draw an example from personal experience to illustrate the statement's meaning.

Source: See, for example, Jessica Li Yexin, Katherine A. Johnson, Adam B. Cohen, Melissa J. Williams, Eric D. Knowles, and Chen Zhansheng, "Fundamental(ist) Attribution Error: Protestants Are Dispositionally Focused," *Journal of Personality and Social Psychology,* 102, 2012, pp. 281–290; and Didier Truchot, Gwladys Maure, and Sonia Patte, "Do Attributions Change over Time When the Actor's Behavior Is Hedonically Relevant to the Perceiver?" *Journal of Social Psychology,* 143, 2003, pp. 202–208.

## PERCEPTUAL SETS AND SELECTIVITIES

The lessons that our family, friends, and culture teach us condition us to perceive stimuli in set ways, effectively helping us to construct our social reality. These organizational constructions are known as **perceptual sets**. They are established gradually over time and help us decide which stimuli we should attend to. For example, if we are raised in a family that values education, we are likely to perceive learning-related activities more positively than we would if we had been raised in a family that dismisses education as unimportant. Likewise, if we grow up in a home where a particular religious or ethnic group is consistently demeaned, we would be more likely to believe in that group's inferiority.[34] Because past lessons and experiences are part of us at every new encounter, our past influences our interpretations and evaluations of the present.

Education and culture also influence perception, helping us make sense of our environment by selecting stimuli significant to us. For example, American culture supports the open expression of opinion, whereas in Japanese culture, talk may be considered a sign of shallowness.[35] Therefore, an American may perceive long silences to be embarrassing and uncomfortable, but a Japanese person accepts periods of silence as perfectly normal. Culture helps to condition us to communicate in distinctive ways. As you will see later in this chapter, it also influences our communication preferences and styles.

Like education and culture, our motivation or internal state also causes us to exhibit perceptual preferences. For instance, hungry people are more apt to see food when shown a series of ambiguous pictures than are individuals who are full. Similarly, our financial position can influence our perceptions of matters such as the U.S. welfare system and clothing fads.

## TRY THIS

### Lessons Learned

1. To better understand the concept of perceptual sets, quickly read the statements that appear in the following triangles.

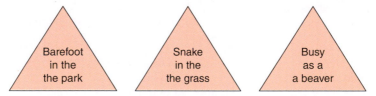

Barefoot
in the
the park

Snake
in the
the grass

Busy
as a
a beaver

2. After you have read them, examine each more carefully. Did you notice the second *the* or *a* in the statements the first time? Because we are conditioned to see words in groups or clusters and not to read individual words, we actually can fail to see what's before our eyes. What lessons about social perception can you draw from this experience?

3. How do preconceptions or prejudgments (perceptual sets) affect your ability to relate to others? For example, how might your judging a person to be hostile affect your assessment of behavior the person displays that others might see as ambiguous?

## UNCONSCIOUS BIAS, ETHNOCENTRISM, AND STEREOTYPES

**Unconscious bias** is a bias we are unaware that we harbor. Unknowingly, we take mental shortcuts derived from social norms and stereotypes. **Ethnocentrism** is the tendency to perceive right and wrong according to the categories and values of one's own culture. When we are ethnocentric, we formulate categorizations that are familiar and comfortable to our "in-group" and apply categorizations that are unfamiliar and awkward to an "out-group." Unconscious biases together with more overt feelings of ethnocentrism can lead us to rely on stereotypes that reduce our communication effectiveness.

**Stereotypes** are widely held but oversimplified preconceived generalizations applied to all members of a group regardless of individual variations.[36] Once generalizations become rigid stereotypes, they contribute to our losing touch with the real world. Such stereotypes share two key characteristics: (1) They lead us to categorize others on the basis of easily recognized, but not necessarily significant, qualities (for example, a person's ethnicity), and (2) they lead us to ascribe an array of qualities to most or all members of a group (for example, assuming that all people of Asian descent are soft-spoken). When our generalizations harden, we are likely to disregard any differences in individuals that set them apart from the stereotyped group.

Stereotyping and **racial profiling**, a specific kind of stereotyping, have the potential to plague both interracial and intercultural communication. When we stereotype instead of responding to the communication or cues of individuals, we create expectations, assume those expectations are valid, and behave as if they have already occurred. We judge people on the basis of what we believe regarding the group in which we have placed them. We emphasize similarities and overlook differences. Stereotyping leads us to oversimplify, generalize, and grossly exaggerate our observations.

Sometimes we find ourselves in situations requiring a decision based on little information other than appearance. Unfortunately, in addition to making clothing-trait associations, we also are prone to making "feature-trait associations," relying on physical appearance to make judgments regarding the categories people belong to and the traits they possess. While we may believe we are responding to a specific person, what we are really acting on is a stereotype. For example, certain physical features—dark skin, coarse hair, full lips, and a wide nose—signal to some people that a person is African American. This is a stereotype that produces a stereotypic judgment. And the more "Afrocentric" an individual's features, the more he or she is ascribed traits stereotypical of African Americans.[37] Colorism researchers report that more prejudice and discrimination are directed against dark-skinned African Americans than against light-skinned African Americans; the latter are more likely to have better jobs and to attain higher levels of education than those with darker skin.[38]

Researchers note that although we may see more African American lawyers and doctors in prime-time television offerings, those characters tend to be lighter skinned. Unconscious bias, ethnocentrism, stereotyping, and lack of diversity are connected.

Lazy perceivers rely on stereotyping as their key perceptual process. Because it discourages careful observation and encourages pigeonholing and categorization, some have observed that stereotyping brings on a malady called "hardening of the categories," in which we insist on fitting everyone into a niche. When we do this, we fail to recognize that every person is unique in some way and in fact constitutes his or her own category.

The marriage of African American Meghan Markle to Prince Harry shattered stereotypes.

Karwai Tang/WireImage/Getty Images

Together, schemata, sets, unconscious bias, ethnocentrism, and stereotypes play major parts in structuring our social perceptions. By recognizing their roles and understanding their potential effects, we can prepare ourselves to question whether we are processing experience accurately and are thinking critically and reflectively about our judgments.

# MORE BARRIERS TO ACCURATE PERCEPTION

In addition to barriers already discussed, a number of other barriers can interfere with our developing accurate perception by causing us to behave unreflectively—that is, acting only on the basis of our personal interests, making erroneous assumptions, and so forth. Perhaps the best way to eliminate such barriers is to learn to recognize them in our behavior.

## REFLECT ON THIS

### Stereotypes at Work

1. Jerry Bembry, a sports journalist and senior writer at ESPN, described the following incident that happened a long time ago:

   At a basketball media day at the Naval Academy, a ranking Navy official was greeting the news media. Each journalist received a gracious hello, but when the Navy man got to me, I was asked a question.

   "So," the official said, extending his hand. "Where did you play ball at to get this job?"

   His assumption: Because I'm an athletic-looking African-American male, my education must have come in combination with an athletic scholarship. It's a question I'm often asked, although I've never played collegiate sports.

   No matter how many times such instances happen to me, it's unsettling.

   In your opinion, could something similar happen now?

2. Facebook's Chief Operating Officer, Sheryl Sandberg, wrote:

   Studies show that job applicants with "black-sounding names" are less likely to get call-backs than those with "white-sounding names"—and applicants called Jennifer are likely to be offered a lower salary than applicants called John. And organizations which consider themselves highly meritocratic can actually show more bias.

   Where else in professional or social settings have you encountered bias making itself visible? What steps do you suggest we take to increase awareness of it?

   Source: Jerry Bembry, "The Pain That Whites Don't See," *The Record*, January 23, 1994, p. E3; Jessica Guynn, "Facebook Develops Unconscious Bias Training," *USA Today*, July 30, 2015, p. 3B.

## AGE AND PERSON PERCEPTION

Throughout the life span, we continually change age-group memberships. How old we are at any point in time influences our perceptions of others.[39] When perceiving an elderly person, younger people may engage in **category-based processing**. In contrast, if the perceiver is also older and views the target individual as similar, in age, he or she would probably rely on **person-based processing**, rather than on stereotypic category-based processing. Person-based processing reduces the influence of group attitudes on our perceptual judgments. Because we are likely to be more familiar with people in our own age group, we are motivated to use person-based processing when forming impressions of members of that group.[40]

## TRY THIS

### Age Wise

Imagine yourself in the following situation. You work on campus in one of the chemistry labs from 6:00 p.m. until midnight. It is late in your shift, and you're alone. You're a bit more nervous than usual because there's been an increase in campus crime and students have been warned to travel in pairs. You're relieved when midnight comes, and you can close the lab and go home. As you are about to lock the door to the lab, you hear someone yell, "Wait! Don't lock the door!" A person runs down the hall toward you and pleads with you to be let in so that work can be completed on an experiment. The person isn't carrying any student ID but tells you that it was left in a car. You don't recognize the individual.

Do you trust what you are being told? Do you let the person in? How would you respond if the person were your age? What if the person was significantly older than you? Would your answer differ if it was a man or a woman at the door? What if the individual was Asian? Latino? Muslim? Dressed shabbily? Wearing designer clothes? Explain your answers.

Young people have the highest level of anxiety about aging.[41] As a result, younger people tend to place older adults into a number of different stereotypes and are likely to perceive them more negatively than they view young and middle-aged adults. Older people, in contrast, have more positive attitudes about their own aging process and perceive other older adults as exhibiting more instrumentality and autonomy. While this may be due to an in-group favoritism effect, the same effect may explain why younger people rate characteristics of people their own age more favorably than do older people.

Gender also affects attitudes toward age. Young women who attribute any negative attitudes toward older people to their own fear of aging tend to stereotype older people less than do other women. In contrast, young men who acknowledge their own fears about aging tend to stereotype older people more than do other men. This may be attributed to the fact that men and women have different mental representations for aging.[42]

## FACT-INFERENCE CONFUSIONS

A fact is something we know is true on the basis of observation. Unlike opinions or inferences, facts are not disputable. An inference is a conclusion we draw, whether or not it is supported by facts. If you assume your neighbor is having an affair based solely on the fact that an unfamiliar car comes to her house every few days for an hour or so, you are making an inference.

When we mistake what we infer for something we have observed, we experience **fact-inference confusion**. Inferences have varying degrees of probability of being correct; their validity depends on the facts that underlie them. For instance, "The sun will rise tomorrow" is not technically a statement of fact; it is an inference with a very high probability of being correct. In contrast, if you see a friend talking and laughing with another person, and you conclude that the two of them are hooking up, that would be an inference with average to low probability of being correct.

Inferences can have serious consequences for our relationships. They can cause us to jump to erroneous conclusions, create embarrassing moments, and result in our responding inappropriately to others. Thus, we need to take time to evaluate whether we are relying on facts or on inferences when we perceive and interpret another's behavior. The question is not whether we make inferences but whether we are *aware* of the inferences we make. If we are aware that we are inferring and not observing, and we can accurately assess the probability that our inferences are correct, we take a giant step forward in improving our perceptions.

## TRY THIS

# Can You Tell the Difference?

To test your understanding of facts and inferences, read the following brief story and the statements that follow it. If you think a statement is true, circle T; if you think it is false, circle F. For an inference that might be either true or false, circle the question mark. (Answers appear below at the bottom of this box.)

You arrive at school one day and see that a number of police cars and an ambulance are parked at the front gate of the campus. Also parked there is a car with "Dr. Smythe" on the license plate.

| | | | | |
|---|---|---|---|---|
| 1. | Police cars are parked at the front gate of the campus. | T | F | ? |
| 2. | Someone at the college has been shot. | T | F | ? |
| 3. | The police summoned the ambulance. | T | F | ? |
| 4. | The car with "Dr. Smythe" on its license plate is not parked at the front gate. | T | F | ? |
| 5. | The man who owns the car is Dr. Smythe. | T | F | ? |

Fiction and drama frequently revolve around fact-inference confusion. Think of a TV show, film, or novel plot that is held together by fact-inference confusion. Analyze what occurs in the story and describe what the involved characters could have done or said to avoid it.

Answers: 1. T; 2. ?; 3. ?; 4. F; 5. ?

There are other problems with facts. Sometimes indisputable facts are not accepted. In 2016, the *Oxford Dictionary* declared the word *post-truth* its word of the year. Relentlessly repeating false claims somehow helps them stick. Because some people are increasingly willing to dispute facts—labeling them as fake news—fact-checking has grown into its own industry with the goal of identifying lies or errors.[43]

## ALLNESS

**Allness**, or thinking that we can know all there is to know about a person, place, or situation, is an attitude that some people carry with them from one relationship to another. These people exhibit very little tolerance for ambiguity, which causes an unwillingness to withhold judgment.

Thinking we know it all limits our ability to perceive accurately. When we insist that our viewpoint alone is correct, we in effect are saying that any differing perceptions are incorrect. We would be wiser to open ourselves to alternative ways of perceiving. To correct a tendency toward allness, we could add an implied "et cetera" to each of our perceptions, acknowledging that there is more to be known than what we see.

## INDISCRIMINATION

When we fail to discriminate *among* individuals, we may end up discriminating *against* an individual. When this occurs, we exhibit **indiscrimination**.[44] In other words, the more we are discriminating and look for differences in all individuals, the less likely it is that we will be prejudiced against the members of any one group or treat people belonging to these groups unfairly.

Accurate perception depends on our being able to identify differences, not just recognize similarities. Too frequently, however, just the opposite happens, increasing our tendency to stereotype. If you remind yourself that no two people are absolutely alike, that every person is unique, your ability to perceive each as an individual will improve.

## FROZEN EVALUATIONS

When we assume that situations and people stay the way they are, always, we make **frozen evaluations**. "Once a thief," we reason, "always a thief." Such statements fail to acknowledge that people can change. If our perception does not permit us to be flexible, but freezes our judgment instead, then we fail in perceiving the constant change that characterizes all of us.

To avoid making such fallacious perceptions, we should attach a date to every perception we acknowledge. Doing so will also help prevent us from clinging to our first impressions. Maintaining an open mind should be a goal if we are to develop more valid assessments of experience. For example, consider the following initial impression and subsequent reevaluation of perception:

> For years I had seen octopuses as terrible, evil creatures that were intent on grabbing swimmers with their tentacles and dragging them under water to be crushed and drowned. Now I perceive them as being gentle, inoffensive, intelligent creatures, who enjoy playful contacts with swimmers.
>
> Probably I have changed my perceptions of octopuses because of changes in the filters of past experience and mind-set. My early experiences were reading horror

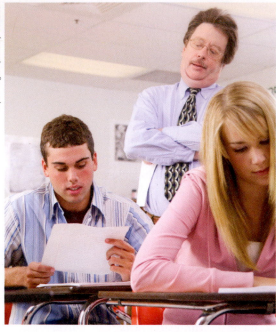

stories and seeing horror movies. . . . I wanted to believe the horrible stories were true because that enhanced my enjoyment. Later experiences were seeing undersea documentaries by Cousteau. . . . My mind-set now is that I respect what scientists tell me. . . . I saw a movie of one of Cousteau's divers doing a little battle dance with an octopus. . . . I saw the octopus and the diver embrace affectionately.[45]

Can you think of an experience in your life that led you to form an initial impression that you subsequently changed? How challenging is it for you to reevaluate a first impression?

Has an instructor ever made a snap judgment about you?

## SNAP JUDGMENTS

In the rush to give meaning to our perceptions, we can end up making snap judgments, or instant decisions. Instead of delaying our responses, we jump to conclusions, which are often incorrect or dangerous. For example, if we see a friend talking with a police officer, we may rush to judgment and conclude that the officer was giving him a ticket. Accurate perception usually takes time. Better perceivers do not rush to respond; rather, they try to synthesize as many data as possible, explore alternative evaluations of the situation, and thus increase their chances of understanding what is really going on.

## BLINDERING

What we tell ourselves about what we perceive can also limit our ability to perceive accurately. In effect, the act of **blindering**—that is, forcing ourselves to see people and situations only in certain ways, as though we are wearing blinders—keeps us from seeing who or what is really before our eyes.

Accurate perception depends on the ability to see what is there without being limited by imaginary restrictions or boundaries. When, for example, scientists stopped searching for the cause of malaria in the air (the word *malaria* comes from the Italian for "bad air") and looked for other causes, they soon traced the origin of the disease to the *Anopheles* mosquito and were then able to find a cure. The following exercise can help you understand the concept of blindering: Draw four straight lines to connect all of the dots below, without lifting your pencil or pen from the page or retracing a line.

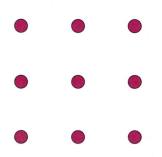

Most people have difficulty completing this exercise because they add a restriction that is not actually there—they assume the figure is a square. (See the solution at the end of this chapter.)

## JUDGING OTHERS MORE HARSHLY THAN OURSELVES

Point your finger at a person near you. The gesture feels natural, doesn't it? Now point that same finger at yourself. That doesn't feel quite so natural, does it?

Related to the self-serving bias discussed earlier in this chapter, when perceptual disagreements arise, we tend to assume that the problem in perceiving lies with the other person, rather than with ourselves. We are quite comfortable evaluating our perceptual capabilities more charitably than we judge those of others.

When asked to compare their ability to communicate with that of their peers, parents, professors, significant others, or siblings, most people report communicating at least as well as if not better than others. Thus, whenever communication goes awry, that finger points outward—directly at another—rather than inward to the self. We shift responsibility for communication problems and perceptual distortions away from ourselves and place it with others with whom we have relationships.

# DIVERSITY AND CULTURE: INTERPRETING THROUGH DIFFERENT *I*'S

Many persist in seeing the world not necessarily as it is but as they have been conditioned to perceive it. Culture and past experience create in us a quest for perceptual constancy—it is easier for us to keep seeing things as we have in the past than it is to revise our perceptions.

The more similar two people's life experiences, the more similarly they tend to perceive things. The more dissimilar our life experiences, the wider the gap between us with respect to how we see and make sense of things. Cultural habits or selectivities ensure that not everyone makes sense out of experience in the same way.

The members of every culture develop particular cultural perspectives or ways of looking at the world. As we have noted, most Americans perceive it to be important to express their uniqueness and independence, whereas in Asian cultures, the group and not the individual is paramount. These contrasting orientations have implications for interpersonal communication. American children are taught to separate from their parents and develop self-reliance, but cultures that value interdependence nurture cooperation, helpfulness, and loyalty instead. Thus, people from these cultures tend to have more close-knit relationships and expect more from others.

We also see these differences play out in the processing of information. The Japanese, for example, develop a wider-angle view of experience than do Americans. They do not see themselves as being at the center of the universe. When students at the University of Michigan and Kyoto University were shown animation of an underwater scene with a "focal fish" and other fish swimming among an array of undersea objects, the Japanese students made more references to the background elements, while the Americans focused on the "focal fish." Americans believe that each person has a separate identity that needs to be reinforced. They value the ethic of competition. This orientation can cause difficulty for Americans when they need to interact with people from other cultures who do not share this value and may perceive it as threatening.

Culture teaches us a worldview, influencing assessments of reality. Whether we are judging beauty, evaluating the meaning of success, or reacting to someone's age, culture plays a role. In the United States, for example, we have a culture that values youth. People in Muslim, Asian, Latin American, Native American, and African cultures do not share this perception. Individuals from different cultures are simply trained to observe the same cues differently; we interpret what we perceive through a cultural lens. Some years ago, researchers used an apparatus resembling binoculars to compare the perceptual preferences of Native Americans and Mexicans. Each subject in the study was shown ten pairs of photographs; one photo in each pair was of an element of Native American culture and one was of Mexican culture. After viewing the paired images through the device, the subjects reported their observations. Results revealed that both the Native American and the Mexican subjects were more likely to report having seen scenes from their own culture.[46]

Race also influences perception. When it comes to views on how much progress we have made since the days of the civil rights movement, a racial divide persists. For example, when asked who will be hired, whites perceive a level playing field, whereas African Americans believe that discrimination persists. In 2015, a majority (69 percent) of African Americans, compared with 31 percent of white Americans, believed the United States needed to enact new civil right laws to reduce discrimination.[47] How might such disparate perceptions affect relationships between white people and black people in the United States?

Because we have not all experienced the same life lessons, even within cultures, we may not attribute the same meanings to the same sets of conditions or behavioral cues. If we are to relate effectively to one another, we need to take steps to eliminate cultural nearsightedness.

## GENDER AND PERCEPTION

Would you see things differently if you were a different gender? Gender, like culture, influences how we make sense of our experiences. Men and women are conditioned to perceive different realities, encouraged to perform in different ways, and prefer to use different communication styles. In addition to influencing how men and women perceive one another, beliefs about gender-appropriate behavior influence how we relate to each other.

From early childhood, boys and girls are rewarded for gender conforming behaviors. For example, boys are commended for displaying strength and independence, whereas girls are praised for expressing their feelings and being kind to others. We even categorize them differently—men as rational and women as emotional.[48]

As a result of interacting with parents, teachers, peers, and others, we internalize the lessons of what others label as appropriate gendered behavior. Such lessons instruct us in how society would like us to behave, framing our perceptions. These constructs, however, can limit our perceptions and may lead to the judging of men and women based on gender expectations rather than on observed cues.

Additionally, we continually monitor ourselves and others. We sort stimuli, selecting

CBS Photo Archive/CBS/Getty Images

Do personal gender beliefs affect reactions to persons exhibiting gender non-conforming behavior?

some and rejecting others. The information we store in our internal database helps us build our view of reality and gives our lives a sense of stability. For example, if we develop the perspective that men are persistently more dominant than women, then we use that belief to categorize both genders and predict their actions. However, when our expectations cause us to misperceive others and their intentions, undesirable consequences can result. All too frequently, rigid categorizing creates communication problems and precipitates interpersonal fiascoes.

We do not have to accept the **gender prescriptions** our culture provides. We can reject those that limit our development, and in doing so, we can elicit changes in the behavior of others toward us. When we refuse to support a gender-based definition, we in effect participate in redefinition. For example, when one woman encourages another to be more autonomous, she may help that woman to expand her definition of behaviors appropriate for women. As women change their behavior and roles, men may perceive both women and themselves differently and may change as well. In the process, we recast the meanings of masculinity and femininity.

# THE MEDIA, TECHNOLOGY, AND PERCEPTION

The media and technology also influence perceptions of social experience. For better or worse, they have the ability to radically change our views of reality. By being mindful of where our perceptions come from—aware of how both media and technology affect our processing of the self, each other, and events—we can better understand and improve our perceptual accuracy.

## THE MEDIA AND PERCEPTION

Because the mass media tend to depict us in ways that reinforce cultural views of race, culture, and gender, the more time we spend with media, the more accepting we tend to become of social stereotypes, and the more likely we are to help perpetuate the unrealistic and limiting perceptions presented to us.

How do stereotypes in media influence our expectations and relationships? First, they help us identify and generalize about what we consider to be appropriate behavior. They offer us categories into which people fit, and they provide us with an array of models in action so that when similar situations arise we think we know how to deal with them. Second, they provide us with perceptual shortcuts; they cause us to forget that we communicate with individuals, not stereotypes, and they contribute to our becoming lazy perceivers—too accepting of the inaccurate or false images presented to us. We need to acknowledge our role. An exploration of the web traffic of 148 news organizations demonstrates that publications across the political spectrum report on the same news daily, but we gloss over what we prefer not to see. Quite simply, we prefer information consistent with the beliefs and views we hold and go out of our way to avoid information that's inconsistent.[49]

What are some of the specific lessons we learn from the media that help shape our perceptions? One lesson, which we glean from the significant underrepresentation of women and older people in leading roles in the media, is that men matter more than women (and younger males matter most). Even in news programming, stories about men outnumber stories about women.

A second media lesson involves our internalization of stereotypic portrayals of gender. Whereas media offerings present men as active, independent, powerful, and sexually virile, they portray women as the objects of males' sexual desires, incompetent, manipulative, and passive. The media focus on women's looks and their relationships with family members and others, while men are typically portrayed taking care of business.

A third lesson concerns the extent to which the media lead us to perceive minority groups inappropriately. Minorities have an even smaller media presence than women, for the most part being cast in supporting roles and often depicted as lazy, unlawful, dumb, or, in the case of Muslims, as terrorists. Even positive portrayals are based in stereotypes: The media tend to pigeonhole the Asian character as "the smart one" or the African American as "the athletic one." There has been some recent improvement on this front, for instance with the success of Marvel's film recent *Black Panther*, which features an almost entirely black cast, and the rising prominence of directors and creators of color, such as Ryan Coogler, Ava DuVernay, Taika Waititi, and Jordan Peele.

The media also influence our perception by molding our conceptions of the real world and people in ways that are inconsistent with facts. Heavy television viewers are more likely than those who view little TV to be fearful and to exaggerate the amount of violence in the world.[50] Heavy viewers perceive the world to be meaner and a more dangerous place.[51] Research demonstrates that by distorting our perception of risk, the media induce in us a sense of fear that is out of proportion with any actual danger.[52] Such perceptions affect real-life judgments of what is safe, whom we should fear, and whom we are safe with. What steps can you take to counteract the false sense of reality brought to you by media?

Media lessons often cause us to misperceive reality. As they perpetuate what is unreal and untrue (even on so-called reality shows), they encourage us to reach for what is impossible. Because we use the media as reference points for what is normal, we are more likely to perceive ourselves, our relationships, and our lives as inferior by comparison. The media present the human body in perfect form, thus causing us to develop negative images of ourselves in comparison. The media's unreal images perpetuate unrealistic perceptions of what our lives should be like and cause us to internalize and anticipate unreasonable outcomes from relationships.

## TECHNOLOGY AND PERCEPTION

Like media in general, technology has the potential to alter self- and self–other perceptions.[53] Some, for example, see digital social connections pulling us closer into new kinds of communities. Others see them as pulling us apart by separating us from more local, personal interactions. Some contend that the ease with which we can link with others who share our interests and goals only helps to confirm our way of thinking creating communities of sameness. What do you think? Online, are we reproducing real social interactions or creating something altogether different? Might we be sacrificing serendipity for a false sense of companionship?

When digitally engaged, we make judgments of others—just as we do when others are physically present. Often these judgments involve other people's cultures or gender. According to the **social identity model of de-individuation effects** (known as SIDE), we have different identities that make themselves visible in different situations.[54] When we interact online, the lack of nonverbal cues, especially those related to appearance and sound, cause us to hold on more tightly to what we know about the other person's group affiliations.[55] This could compel us to become more judgmental, to make over-attributions (that is, single out one or two characteristics of a person), or to exaggerate the importance of the minimal information we have. We practice closure, often filling in the gaps by using stereotypes. If we assume that people share social categories with us, making them like us, we tend to find them more likable than if we believe they are different.

Technology affects us in other ways, too. Playing violent games online may increase aggressive behavior by causing heavy players to perceive annoying provocations as more hostile.[56] The games also are apt to expand the repertoire of aggressive behaviors of users and emotionally desensitize players to aggression and violence.[57] The potential effects of online gaming are not all negative, however. Playing action games has been found to enhance an individual's ability to pay attention to objects and changes in the environment. Experienced gamers are 30 to 50 percent better than non-gamers at perceiving everything happening around them. It appears that gaming not only precipitates better spatial skills but also improves attention skills and facilitates the accurate understanding of a visual landscape.[58]

Virtual reality may have transformative effects on our perception of what's real.

What about virtual reality technology? It may well have transformative effects on perception—widening experience by its use of immersive stories that help enlarge human empathy, simulations that improve observational skills, imagined experiences that can help those affected recover from trauma, as well as opportunities for connection. On the other hand, it could also be used to spread propaganda and be employed to simulate torture that actually feels real.[59]

Because of the vastness of the virtual landscape, interacting online may be affecting our perceptual focus by making it difficult for us to concentrate on any one thing for a sustained period of time. We frequently divide our focus, viewing multiple screens simultaneously, as we watch TV, Web surf for information related to what we are watching, or exchange messages with others about what we are viewing.[60] Typically, we hurry from one stimulus to another, sneaking peeks at people and sites, but not paying close attention to any.[61] Continued decreases in attention is one reason theorists give to account for the migration of younger users from Facebook to Snapchat. When interviewed, younger users complain that interacting on Facebook consumes too much time, while Snapchat is less demanding and allows their minds to move more quickly.[62]

The Internet also affects how we remember. We pay more attention to and are more likely to remember information if we think we will not be able to find it later. For many, the Internet is becoming a primary system for information storage. We have found a new means of outsourcing memory.[63]

# GAINING COMMUNICATION COMPETENCE: ENHANCING YOUR PERCEPTUAL SKILLS

Your ability to relate to others is affected by how capable a perceiver you are. Understanding your role in perception, including how and why you perceive people and events as you do, is essential if you are to experience new and healthy relationships, minimize misunderstandings, and broaden your horizons. Take the following steps to improve your perceptual abilities.

## RECOGNIZE THE PART YOU PLAY

Because we are all unique, we each experience a reality that is somewhat different from that experienced by others. Until we acknowledge our part in perceiving and making sense of reality, we are apt to experience numerous relational and communication problems. Just because others may not see the world the way we do does not mean their views are wrong. Variations in physiological, psychological, and cultural factors lead us to adopt different perspectives and attribute different meanings to experience. Perception is not something that happens to us. It is something we do.

You may like a person who seems similar to you and dislike someone who seems different. Your friend's jokes may strike you as funny when you are in a good mood and tasteless when you are preoccupied with a personal problem. By taking stock of yourself, including your emotional state and biases, you accept responsibility for what you bring to the perception process.

## BE A MORE PATIENT PERCEIVER

Because we tend to live at an accelerated pace in U.S. society, we expect things to happen quickly. Patient perceivers, however, do not jump to conclusions, cling to first impressions, or believe they know it all. Instead, they open their minds to possibilities, look beyond the obvious, and genuinely attempt to check the accuracy of their interpretations.

## TRY THIS

### Facebook in Focus

Peruse the walls of the Facebook pages of various friends. Then answer these questions:

1. To what extent does each wall contain clues that help others form an initial impression of each person?

2. If you know the person well, how does his or her wall reinforce or contradict your face-to-face perception?

Patient perceivers question their perceptual acuity. Ask yourself if there is any chance you could be wrong. By acknowledging that you might have made an error in judgment or misevaluated observed behavior, you motivate yourself to seek further information. If you make the effort either to verify your judgment or to prove yourself wrong, you increase your chances of forming more accurate impressions of others and of situations in which you find yourself.

## BECOME A PERCEPTION CHECKER

To avoid treating interpretations as if they were indisputable facts, develop the skill of perception checking: Observe the behavior of another, describe and interpret what his or her behavior means to you, and put your interpretation into words in the effort to determine if your perception is correct.

For example, imagine your friend Leila walks into the classroom and flings her books down on the desk next to yours. As she takes her seat, you notice that her eyes are narrowed, and her face is in a scowl. You might be inclined to ask, "Why are you angry at me?" But a perception checker would quietly say to her, "Leila, I get the feeling that you're angry about something. Am I right? Can I do anything to help?"

By making an initial statement followed by questions that assume nothing you aim to explore Leila's thoughts and feelings, not to prove that your interpretation of what you have observed is right. Leila might not even be angry. If you ask, she might state, "I'm not angry. I'm upset with myself for not getting the paper done on time." By seeking verification of the impression you received from Leila's nonverbal behavior and giving her the opportunity to share her thoughts and feelings, you take some of the guesswork out of perception.

Keep in mind that perception checking works best with people from low-context cultures. Typically, it involves straight talk and direct statements of observation. People from high-context cultures might become embarrassed if they are asked so directly about their feelings and the meanings of their actions.

## WIDEN YOUR FOCUS

Keep the big picture in mind as perceptual clues surface. Avoid jumping to a conclusion based on a single piece of evidence. By cautiously assessing what is happening, you refrain from over-attributing meaning to any single behavior or circumstance. We tend to pay extra attention to what we see or hear first (known as the primacy effect) or last (the recency effect), but you should search for more evidence so that you do not draw inaccurate conclusions based on the partial picture to which you have access.

## SEE THROUGH THE EYES OF ANOTHER

Try to exhibit empathy—that is, experience the world through the eyes of another person by recreating that person's perspective. This means you need to socially decenter, or take the focus off yourself, and place it on another by considering that person's thoughts and feelings first.[64] Doing this allows you insight into the other person's state of mind and lets you see things from his or her perspective.

When you empathize, you also engage in perspective taking—you develop a personal sense of what the person is going through. You imagine what it would be like to be in the person's position. Through *emotional contagion*, you experience the same feelings as the person has. Can you imagine, for example, how your significant other feels when you forget his or her birthday? While it is easier to feel empathy for those with whom we identify, it is equally important to be able to put yourself into the shoes of a person with whom you may have little in common. The third ingredient in empathizing is *genuine concern* for the other person's well-being. Do you find it easy to empathize with others? Some researchers fear that the ability to empathize is on the decline due to social media's encouragement of self-promotion as opposed to other-understanding.[65] On the other hand, others believe that by engaging in virtual reality simulations and having the opportunity to inhabit the body of someone completely different from ourselves, we can develop new attitudes and understandings. Which position is closer to your own?

## BUILD PERCEPTUAL BRIDGES, NOT WALLS

Although perceptual disagreements can drive us apart, if we exhibit a willingness to experience the world from another person's perspective, we can enhance communication. Rather than argue over whose point of view or behavior is right, it is more productive to understand the factors that create differences in our interpretations and then work to adapt to and bridge those differences.

## CONNECT THE CASE

### The Case of Dax's Trial

Dax had not been happy when he received the notice to report to the courthouse for jury duty. He was even less happy when he found that he had no valid reason to be excused from the obligation.

When he reported to the courthouse, things went just fine. He was not called during the morning session, so he was able to finish reading a novel. Then it all began.

Dax was called for the jury selection phase of a murder trial. Before he knew it, he was on the jury, and the trial had started.

Two days into the trial, Dax began to wonder about the entire process. Twelve different witnesses had been called to testify about what had happened on the street corner where the murder had occurred. All twelve described different versions of the event.

Was this possible? How could so many people not agree on what had happened? Dax wished he could have a chance to question the witnesses himself. Was each of them certain of his or her perception? To what degree did the relationship each did or did not share with the defendant or the victim influence the reports? How could the jury decide?

#### Answer these questions:

1. Do you think several people observing one event will perceive it the same way? Why or why not?

2. What is there about the perception process that enables us to observe different realities?

3. How do you explain the differences in the testimony Dax heard at the trial? Do you think any or all of the 12 witnesses who testified lied?

# REVIEW THIS

## CHAPTER SUMMARY

1. **Explain the nature of perception and its relationship to reality.** ☐

We do not all perceive reality similarly. Standpoint theory suggests that people in positions of power have an overriding interest in preserving their place in the social hierarchy. Thus, our view of reality is a consequence of the person we are, where we are, and what we choose to see. Perception is the personally based process we use to make sense of experience. When we perceive, we select, organize, and interpret sensory data in an effort to make sense of and give meaning to our world.

2. **Describe the perception process in action.** ☐

Perception is a multi-stage process involving selection, organization, interpretation, remembering, and responding. We rely on a number of strategies to facilitate perceiving. The figure-ground principle addresses our tendency to focus on a particular person or item, while the surrounding context becomes background. Closure is the process we use to fill in missing perceptual pieces or gaps. Perceptual constancy is our tendency to maintain the way we see the world.

3. **Explain how schemata, perceptual sets, unconscious bias, ethnocentrism, and stereotypes influence perception.** ☐

Schemata are cognitive frameworks, the mental templates or knowledge structures we carry with us. Perceptual sets are organizational constructions that influence our readiness to perceive in predetermined ways; each set or selectivity helps us decide what stimulus to focus on and how to construct our social reality. Unconscious bias is a prejudice we possess of which we are unaware. Ethnocentrism is the tendency to perceive right or wrong according to the values of one's own culture. A stereotype is a rigid perception that is applied to an individual because of their membership in a particular group, regardless of individual variations.

4. **Distinguish among the following perceptual barriers: fact-inference confusions, allness, indiscrimination, frozen evaluations, snap judgments, and blindering.** ☐

Each of these makes it difficult for us to perceive people and events accurately. Fact-inference confusions cause us to confuse observations and assumptions. Allness leads us to think we know it all. Indiscrimination causes us to emphasize similarities and neglect differences. When we make frozen evaluations, we ignore change. Snap judgments lead us to jump to conclusions. Blindering causes us to add restrictions where none actually exist.

5. **Discuss how culture and gender influence perceptions of social experience.** ☐

Culture teaches us acceptable ways of looking at our world, as well as acceptable ways of behaving. Gender conditions men and women to perceive different realities, exhibit different behaviors, and use different communication styles.

· · · · · · · · · · · · · · · · · · · · · · · · · · · ·

**6. Discuss how media and technology influence perceptions of social experience.** ☐

The media influence our self-perception, as well as our perception of each other and our social experiences. Because the media tend to reinforce cultural views of gender and ethnicity, they contribute to our becoming more accepting of social stereotypes. Technology is altering the way we perceive social connection, changing our view of what is real, and enhancing our perceptual acuity.

· · · · · · · · · · · · · · · · · · · · · · · · · · · ·

**7. Identify strategies you can use to enhance your perceptual abilities.** ☐

To improve your chances of developing more accurate perceptions, you need to recognize the part you play in perception, develop patience, become a perception checker, see through others' eyes, work to bridge perceptual differences, and carefully consider how technological innovations are affecting your perceptions.

· · · · · · · · · · · · · · · · · · · · · · · · · · · ·

## CHECK YOUR UNDERSTANDING

1. Can you provide evidence of your own personal basis of perception? For example, what aspects of your environment are you attending to right now? (See pages 62–63.)

2. Can you offer examples showing how stereotypes have affected your judgments? What do you see as the ethical implications of stereotyping? (See pages 69–72.)

3. Can you describe instances when one or more barriers to perception impeded your response to another person or situation? (See pages 72–78.)

4. Can you offer examples of how attitudes toward masculinity and femininity influence perception? How about media portrayals of race and ethnicity? (See pages 79–83.)

5. Can you describe steps you can take to develop your perceptual ability? In your opinion, is developing accurate perception a moral issue? (See pages 83–85.)

## KEY TERMS

Allness  81

Attribution theory  72

Blindering  82

Category-based processing  79

Closure  70

Empathy  89

Ethnocentrism  76

Fact-inference confusion  80

Figure-ground principle  70

Frozen evaluation  81

Fundamental attribution error  74

Gender prescriptions  85

## Solution to Blindering Exercise on Page 82

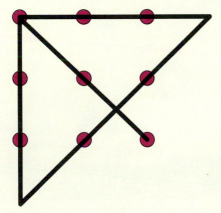

Get the tools you need to sharpen your study skills. **SAGE edge** offers a robust online environment featuring an impressive array of free tools and resources. Access practice quizzes, eFlashcards, video, and multimedia at **edge.sagepub.com/gambleicp**.

# 4

# Listening and Life Contexts

## Learning Objectives

### AFTER COMPLETING THIS CHAPTER, YOU SHOULD BE ABLE TO

1. Define and distinguish between hearing and listening, and between effective and ineffective listening

2. Identify and explain the six stages of listening identified in the HURIER model

3. Define and distinguish among four styles and four types of listening contexts

4. Explain the importance of ethical listening and identify behaviors to avoid in order to listen effectively

5. Define the different kinds of feedback, explaining their dependence on listening

6. Explain how gender and culture influence listening

7. Analyze how media and technology affect listening

8. Identify strategies to improve listening effectiveness

There is a difference between listening and waiting for your turn to speak.

—Simon Sinek

Students are known to engage in a number of different activities at the same time—even during class. Be honest. How often do you multitask, dividing your attention, while trying to listen to and absorb what your instructor or peer is sharing? Perhaps you use a laptop or smartphone to browse the Web, secretly text a friend, or monitor Facebook—all while listening to a lecture. But is it possible for you to listen effectively while distracted by competing interests?

Studies suggest that if you multitask during class, you may not be listening and absorbing as much as you think.[1] While heavy multitaskers are the people most overconfident about their multitasking abilities, the research reveals that students who multitask during class do not perform as well as those who focus on the lesson.[2] What is more, multitaskers often are completely unaware of what they have missed. Multitasking inhibits a person's acquisition of a deep understanding of the information being presented.[3] ■

# LISTENING IN YOUR LIFE

Consider this statement: "In our talking-head, Twitter-finger culture, learning to listen, engage, and observe are valuable skills, whether you are a journalist, employer, or friend."[4] Many of us, however, are quick to speak and hit "send," but slower to listen, engage, and observe.

We experience different listening contexts and engage different listening levels daily. On an intrapersonal level, we always are listening to the voice within ourselves. On an interpersonal level, we need to listen to another's voice. We also need to listen in public arenas, where a multitude of voices are competing for our attention.

But just because we should be listening doesn't mean we are listening. Have you encountered individuals whom you decided that you "just couldn't talk or listen to"? Perhaps you thought "We have nothing in common and nothing to say to each other"?[5] Selecting the few we are willing to engage with functions as a symptom of our unwillingness to listen. There is not an individual on earth with whom we have absolutely nothing in common. We need to be willing to listen to and learn from one another—even those with whom we disagree and whose opinions we may find offensive. The purpose of listening is

iStock.com/Steve Debenport

We spend more of our time listening than we do speaking.

to understand. By listening effectively, we can transcend differences, that is, if we're patient, skilled, and disciplined listeners.[6]

Most of us spend more of our communication time listening than doing anything else—even speaking. Studies have found that the average college student spends more than 50 percent of the available communicative time in an average day listening, and the average employee spends more than 60 percent of an average workday listening.[7] That we spend a great deal of each day listening is undeniable—whether we do it well, however, is another issue.[8] The use of digital media complicates things further by helping to distract us. In fact, many of us have grown so accustomed to receiving quick bursts of information, including tweets, that we expect all messages to be delivered succinctly and in small bits of time.[9] Many find it increasingly taxing to listen to more detailed and complex information.[10]

Research reveals that while the average person hears a great deal throughout the day, he or she processes just half of what is said, understands about a quarter of the message, and retains even less of the content. Too frequently, we take listening for granted, and that is not good news for us. It is also not good news for the people we're supposed to be listening to, and it does not bode well for our relationships. When it comes to making relationships work, listening is just as important as other communicative behaviors.

## DIFFERENCES BETWEEN HEARING AND LISTENING

Effective listeners do not listen only with their ears—they also rely on their minds. To listen well, you need to think effectively. Hearing is the first step in a two-part process.

**Hearing** is an involuntary, physiological process. Just as we do not need to think to breathe, neither do we need to think to hear. As long as our eardrums are functional, when sound waves hit them, the subsequent vibrations cause the tiny bones of the middle ear to vibrate. Once these vibrations reach our auditory nerves, they are transformed into electrical impulses and automatically processed by our brains, and we hear. What we do with these impulses once we receive them takes us into the complex arena of listening.

**Listening** is a voluntary, psychological process. It is "the process of receiving, attending to, and assigning meaning to aural and visual stimuli."[11] As we assign meaning to a spoken message, a number of components come into play, including understanding, remembering, interpreting, and responding. If we don't listen well, we likely won't understand what we hear, and we may pass misinformation onto others. Far too often, instead of listening actively to others, we only *hear* them. Our minds are asleep rather than alert, and we passively receive, rather than actively process, what they are saying. When we listen, however, we not only hear the message, but also make sense of it—or at least we try to.

## DIFFERENCES BETWEEN EFFECTIVE AND INEFFECTIVE LISTENERS

Think of the worst listener you know. What does this person do that suggests to you he or she does not really listen to you? What words would you use to describe this person as a listener? Typically, words such as *distracted, inattentive, closed-minded, daydreamer, bored, impatient, nonresponsive,* and *rude* might come to mind. Now think of the best listener you know, and select adjectives to describe his or her behavior. Do they include *concerned, open-minded, intelligent, attentive, interested,* and *respectful*? Which words on your lists would you use to describe your own listening behavior? Which words do you imagine others would choose to describe you when you interact with them?

# ANALYZE THIS: UNDERSTANDING "UNDERSTANDING"

What is the listener's intention? In this excerpt from *The Seven Habits of Highly Effective People*, Stephen R. Covey describes a specific behavior that hurts a relationship. Identify the behavior and then cite your own examples to illustrate how either you or another person you know has been guilty of acting as Covey describes.

> "Seek first to understand" involves a very deep shift in paradigm. We typically seek first to be understood. Most people do not listen with the intent to understand; they listen with the intent to reply. They're either speaking or preparing to speak. They're filtering everything through their own paradigms, reading their autobiography into other people's lives.
>
> "Oh, I know exactly how you feel!"
>
> "I went through the very same thing. Let me tell you about my experience."
>
> They're constantly projecting their own home movie onto other people's behavior. They prescribe their own glasses for everyone with whom they interact.

If they have a problem with someone—a son, a daughter, a spouse, an employee—their attitude is, "That person just doesn't understand."

A father once told me, "I can't understand my kid. He just won't listen to me at all."

"Let me restate what you just said," I replied. "You don't understand your son because he won't listen to you?"

"That's what I said," he impatiently replied.

"I thought that to understand another person, you needed to listen to him," I suggested.

"Oh!" he said. There was a long pause. "Oh!" he said again, as the light began to dawn. "Oh yeah! But I do understand him. I know what he's going through. I went through the same thing myself. I guess what I don't understand is why he won't listen to me."

This man didn't have the vaguest idea of what was really going on inside his boy's head. He looked into his own head and thought he saw the world, including his boy.

Source: Stephen R. Covey, *The Seven Habits of Highly Effective People,* New York: Simon & Schuster, 1989, pp. 239–240.

Are you the best listener you could be? We lose when we listen ineffectively, and we stand to gain much when we listen effectively. But what exactly is it that we lose or gain? To find out, consider the following questions yourself.

- What consequences have you suffered when you have displayed a lack of respect for someone you were conversing with?

- What problems have you encountered after losing your temper with someone else?

- What challenges have you faced when you have failed to understand what another person was telling you?

- How has jumping to an incorrect conclusion caused problems for you?

- What happened when you missed a key conversational segment because you were distracted?

- How did the person you were conversing with respond upon realizing that you were not really listening?

When we fail to listen to each other, our relationships usually experience problems. In contrast, effective listening helps to enhance our relationships by doing the following:

Being distracted or daydreaming impedes listening.

- *Decreasing stress*. Stress levels are reduced as ideas and feelings are communicated clearly and understood as intended.

- *Increasing knowledge*. We learn more about each other when we listen effectively. Each of us learns more about what the other responds to and how the other reacts to our ideas.

- *Building trust*. We all need someone to listen to us. We appreciate those who listen much more than those who fail to give us their complete attention. In fact, careful listening can be a reciprocal act: We pay closer attention to those who do the same for us, and we tend to avoid those who do not.

- *Improving analysis and decision making*. Careful listening can provide you with information and insights that enable you to exercise better judgment. You are more likely to spot faulty reasoning and identify invalid arguments or gross appeals to prejudice when you listen critically. In the process, you protect yourself against others who may act irresponsibly. Careless listeners are more likely to end up accepting the unacceptable.

- *Increasing confidence*. When another person perceives you to be giving him or her your rapt attention and believes that you are open, alert, and actively involved, that person will be more comfortable interacting with you and more likely to share his or her feelings. By listening effectively, you also increase your own confidence and understanding. As you increase your comprehension of another's ideas and feelings, you gain confidence in your ability to respond appropriately.

## STAGES OF LISTENING

The **HURIER model** of listening, developed by listening expert Judi Brownell, suggests that listening is a system of interrelated components that includes both mental processes and observable behaviors. The model focuses on six aspects, or stages, of listening: hearing, understanding, remembering, interpreting, evaluating, and responding (see Figure 4.1).[12]

### FIGURE 4.1
Listening Stages

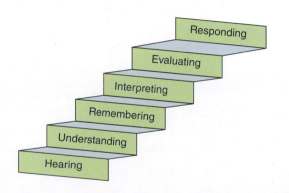

# How's Your LQ (Listening Quotient)?

First, take the following quiz to gauge your listening effectiveness:

1. Do you ever find yourself labeling either the person you are conversing with or his or her subject as uninteresting?　　Yes　　No

2. Do you ever find yourself becoming overstimulated by what someone says to you?　　Yes　　No

3. Do you ever jump ahead of the person speaking to you?　　Yes　　No

4. Do you ever pretend to pay attention?　　Yes　　No

5. Do you ever "turn off" when a message gets complicated?　　Yes　　No

6. Do you ever daydream when you are in a conversation with another person?　　Yes　　No

7. Do you ever try to process every single word someone says to you?　　Yes　　No

8. Do you ever let a person's manner of delivery or mannerisms or gestures interfere with your reception of his or her words?　　Yes　　No

9. Do you ever let the environment or personal factors distract you?　　Yes　　No

10. Are there some individuals you refuse to listen to?　　Yes　　No

Every yes response indicates a behavior that can function as an impediment to listening and, as such, merits your attention.

Next, answer the four questions below.

1. On a scale of 0 to 100, I give myself a rating of _____ as a listener.

   0　25　50　75　100

2. I would use the following three words to describe myself as a listener:

   _____　_____　_____

3. Others would give me a rating of _____ as a listener.

   0　25　50　75　100

4. Others would use the following three words to describe me as a listener:

   _____　_____　_____

Finally, ask two people with whom you interact regularly to answer these two questions:

5.   On a scale of 0 to 100, how would you rate me as a listener?

6.   What three words would you use to describe me as a listener?

How does your self-rating compare to the ratings others gave to you?

## STAGE 1: HEARING

We exist in a world filled with aural stimuli. Background noises permeate our listening environment, with incessant beeps, ringtones, text-message dings, and alarms intermingling with the sounds of nature.[13] Sounds surround us, competing to be noticed, but we choose to pay attention only to the ones that interest us. Eugene Raudsepp of Princeton Creative Research tells the story of a zoologist who was walking with a friend down a busy street filled with the sounds of honking car horns and screeching tires. Turning to his friend, the zoologist says, "Listen to that cricket!" The friend, with astonishment, replies, "You hear a cricket in the middle of all this noise?" The zoologist takes out a coin and flips it in the air. As the coin falls to the sidewalk, a dozen heads turn in response to its "clink." The zoologist responds, "We hear what we listen for."[14]

**Attending** involves our willingness to focus on and organize particular stimuli. We attend to a sound by concentrating on it, even if just for a moment. Unless the sound holds our attention, we will soon refocus our attention elsewhere. Consequently, it is not enough to capture another's attention; attention needs to be maintained.[15] This requires developing sensitivity to the interests of those with whom we make contact.

## STAGE 2: UNDERSTANDING

During the understanding stage, we absorb the meaning of a person's statement or sound. In a sense, we work to decode what is being said using our own reservoir of information, and we refrain from judging the message until we are certain we comprehend it. In an effort to ensure understanding, we might reply to the speaker with questions aimed at clarifying the message's content. Rephrasing or paraphrasing what we have heard also helps us comprehend the message.

## STAGE 3: REMEMBERING

During the remembering stage, our brain assigns meaning to the spoken words. Once that is accomplished, we may or may not commit the information to our memory for further use. Here again, we make choices, as we decide what has value and is worth remembering and what we can discard. If we have intense feelings for the person we are with, or if the message is reinforced, we increase our chances of remembering. We remember personal and public events of significance. For example, you likely remember the birthdays of people close to you, as well as where you were when you learned of a loved one's death or a public tragedy.

Two key kinds of memory concern us: short-term memory and long-term memory. We store most of what we hear, if only briefly, in the limited space of our brain's short-term memory bank. Unless we continually use and apply what we store in short-term memory, we will forget it before we can transfer it into our long-term memory bank for use at a later date. Our long-term memory plays an important role in listening by connecting new experiences to previous images and information.

## STAGE 4: INTERPRETING

When we interpret a message, we attempt to make sense of it. To interpret effectively, we consider the message from the sender's perspective. Doing this keeps us from imposing our meaning onto another's ideas.

For example, suppose your friend says, "I've had enough!" By listening to his tone of voice and observing his facial expressions, you can decide whether your friend is talking about the meal he is eating with you or he is upset by the conversation you are having with him. Each represents a very different interpretation of his words. The meaning you settle on will determine how you respond.

## STAGE 5: EVALUATING

When we evaluate a statement, we weigh its worth and critically analyze what we were told. We decide if the message has relevance for us. As with all the stages of listening, we have choices to make. Separating facts from inferences, weighing evidence, and identifying prejudices and faulty arguments are part of the evaluation process. When we fail to evaluate a message effectively, we risk agreeing with ideas or supporting actions that violate our values or have been slanted to earn our support.

For example, if you ask your congressional representative if she supports increasing taxes on those who earn more than one million dollars annually, and she says, "Don't worry about me. I'm okay on that!" she is counting on you to believe she agrees with whatever stance you support. Unless you follow up with additional questions, however, you do not have adequate information to determine where she actually stands on the issue.

## STAGE 6: RESPONDING

When we respond to someone, we react and provide feedback. We communicate our thoughts and feelings about the received message. We let the person know whether we think the message was communicated successfully or is flawed. In effect, we become the sender's radar. We will address responding in more depth later in this chapter, in our discussion of feedback.

# WAYS OF LISTENING

When interacting with others, we likely use one of four listening styles: people oriented, action oriented, content oriented, or time oriented.[16] We likely also find ourselves engaged in one of four types of listening: appreciative, comprehensive, critical or deliberative, or empathetic. (See Tables 4.1 and 4.2.) While most of us prefer a particular style and type, we probably all use each of the four styles and four types of listening on occasion.

## STYLES OF LISTENING

Users of each of the following listening styles display different attitudes and beliefs about listening. Which one of the following styles is your personal favorite?

## People-Oriented Listening

A focus on the emotions and interests of others is characteristic of the people-oriented style. When you take your time and work to understand what others think and feel, you improve your chances of getting to know them well. Thus, the people-oriented style fosters relating to others in more meaningful ways.

## Action-Oriented Listening

If you value clarity and preciseness above all else, you are apt to use the action-oriented style often. Action-oriented listeners don't like to feel frustrated by others' indirect messages. They want the people they speak with to be direct and straightforward.

## Content-Oriented Listening

Those who enjoy being intellectually challenged and having to work ideas through practice the content-oriented style. Comfortable listening to messages that are ambiguous and spark debate, content-oriented listeners commonly relate what they are listening to with their own views.

## Time-Oriented Listening

Time-oriented listeners expect the speaker to get to the point. They like others to impart messages quickly, allowing the listeners to work through them efficiently.

### TABLE 4.1 STYLES OF LISTENING

| STYLE | FOCUS |
|---|---|
| People oriented | Emotions and interests |
| Action oriented | Clarity, precision, and assumptions |
| Content oriented | Facts, details, and ambiguities |
| Time oriented | Efficiency and succinctness |

# REFLECT ON THIS

## When Is Listening Not First and Foremost?

Listening may well be the most important skill in our communication arsenal because it is necessary for relationship building. However, while the research demonstrates listening's value, there are also times when the act of listening itself may pose a danger to the listener and others.

*(Continued)*

(Continued)

According to the research, the act of listening while behind the wheel of a car can distract from the primary responsibility of driving, endangering the driver, passengers, those in other vehicles, and pedestrians. Texting and cell phone use—even when conducted with hands-free devices—cause drivers to lose focus and contribute to decreased driving accuracy. The risk faced by drivers who access their phones while driving is four times the risk undistracted drivers face—and similar to the risk associated with driving while intoxicated. It appears that simply attempting to comprehend a spoken or texted message competes with the driver's need to focus on driving. Thus, driving and listening both require your full attention and should not be placed in competition with each other.

Sources: F. E. Gray, "Specific Oral Communication Skills Desired in New Accountancy Graduates," *Business Communication Quarterly,* 73:1, 2010, pp. 40–67.

See Marissa A. Harrison, "College Students' Prevalence and Perception of Text Messaging While Driving," *Accident Analysis and Prevention,* 43, 2011, pp. 1516–1520; Amy N. Shys, "The Most Primary of Care—Talking about Driving and Distraction," *New England Journal of Medicine,* 362, 2010, pp. 2145–2147; and M. S. Just, T. A. Keller, and J. A. Cynkar, "A Decrease in Brain Activation Associated with Driving When Listening to Someone Speak," *Brain Research,* 1205, 2008, pp. 70–80.

## TYPES OF LISTENING

We listen for different reasons and with different goals in mind.

### Appreciative Listening

Sometimes we listen for pleasure—we go to a concert, view a film, or go to a comedy club, actively seeking out an **appreciative listening** activity. Such activities help us unwind or escape.

Empathetic listening builds strong relationships.

### Comprehensive Listening

When you listen to gain knowledge, you engage in **comprehensive listening**. When you ask for directions, listen to a friend's description of her new job, or pay close attention to lectures in class, you're listening to derive information. Because your primary purpose is to learn, you listen with an open mind and suspend judgment.

### Critical/Deliberative Listening

Have you ever questioned the truth of a message, its usefulness, or the reliability of the person delivering it?

Frequently, we must analyze information, assess its worth, validity, and soundness, and ultimately, decide whether to accept it. We perform these functions when we engage in **critical or deliberative listening**.

## Empathetic Listening

When another person reaches out to us for support, he or she needs us to engage in **empathetic listening**. This type of listening is important to master if you wish to build strong interpersonal relationships. When you help someone else work a problem through by offering her or him your ear, you are listening empathetically.

### TABLE 4.2  LISTENING IS GOAL RELATED

| TYPE | EXAMPLE | GOAL |
|---|---|---|
| **Appreciative** | Listening to music | Be entertained |
| **Comprehensive** | Listening to a lecture | Acquire information |
| **Critical/deliberative** | Listening to a political debate | Make an evaluation |
| **Empathetic** | Listening to a friend talk about a breakup | Therapeutic—to be a sounding board |

Empathetic listening facilitates problem solving; it lends a different, clearer perspective to any given situation; and it helps individuals regain emotional balance. When you listen empathetically, you understand the dilemma another is facing from their viewpoint, not yours. You do your best to interpret the situation as if you were the other person.

Those who score high in emotional intelligence are generally better at de-centering themselves while listening. That is, an empathetic person places the focus on another to understand that person as he or she desires to be understood. In this way, empathetic listening is a relationship enhancer.[17]

When empathizing, you activate three skills: empathetic responsiveness, perspective taking, and sympathetic responsiveness.[18]

When we exhibit **empathetic responsiveness**, we experience an emotional response that corresponds to the emotions the other person is experiencing. For example, when Samira tells Tong that she has to leave school because her family needs her at home, Tong's empathetic responsiveness will allow her to understand and feel the same regret and sadness that Samira feels.

When we employ **perspective taking**, we place ourselves in the shoes of the other person. For example, not only does Samira feel regret and sadness about leaving school, but she feels guilty for not wanting to help her family at home. If Tong is able to recognize this and perhaps offers Samira a clearer perspective on it, she is practicing this particular type of empathetic skill.

Finally, if Tong feels concern and compassion for Samira because of the situation Samira faces, then Tong also will have succeeded in demonstrating **sympathetic responsiveness**. Sympathetic responsiveness is different from empathy because, while the receiver *feels for* the other person, without perspective taking and empathetic responsiveness, she does not *feel with* the other person. For example, when you sympathize with and console a friend whose dog has died, even though you are afraid of dogs and you cannot imagine what she is feeling, you are being sympathetically responsive.

What can you do to increase your empathetic abilities? If you're very individualistic, or I-oriented, empathizing may not typically be easy for you. You may be so used to being the center of attention that you may find it challenging to look at the world from anyone else's point of view. Yet, if you want to improve your effectiveness at developing meaningful interpersonal relationships, empathizing is a skill you ought to master. Here are six steps you can take to improve your empathy quotient:

1. Make a concerted effort to become other-oriented, paying careful attention to what others are saying and feeling. If, for example, your partner comes home depressed after a hard day at work, try to imagine how you would feel if you were in his or her situation.

2. Take in the whole scene. Focus not just on words, but also on the nonverbal cues that are part of the other person's message. Tune in to how the person moves, sits, looks, and sounds.

3. Work to understand the other person's emotions by asking questions and then paraphrasing how you think he or she feels by saying something like, "I guess you are feeling . . . ?" Your goal is to obtain more details, clarify the nature of the situation, or get at the root cause of what the other person is feeling.

4. While processing the other person's information, repeatedly ask yourself why you believe the other person is experiencing what he or she is, and try to identify what it is that makes you think and feel that this is so. Is it what the person says to you, his or her facial expressions, or something else? By focusing on the person's emotions and the cues you are using to draw your conclusions, you also increase your attentiveness and become better at sensing the other person's emotional state.

5. Again, use the skill of perception checking, discussed above and in the preceding chapter, to facilitate your understanding of what the other person is experiencing. Acknowledge what you think the person has said, and then inquire whether your interpretation is correct.

6. Once you fully understand the other person's feelings, you may still need to provide her or him with emotional comfort and support. Help the other person feel better and/or show that you care about what happens to him or her. When you comfort and support someone, you provide affirmation, acknowledging the person's right to feel as he or she does. You also offer reassurance, consolation, and assistance and, if appropriate, try to cheer the person up or divert his or her attention. And remember that you can comfort someone using both verbal and nonverbal cues.

If you fail at empathizing, usually it is for one of the following reasons:

- You deny the other person the right to his or her feelings, suggesting that what he or she is feeling is either wrong or inappropriate. You might say something like "You shouldn't be so upset," or "Don't let that get you down." By uttering such a statement, you "de-legitimize" his or her emotions.

- You minimize the importance of the situation by saying something like, "It's no big deal." Such statements reveal that you really don't understand what the other person is going through.

- You pass judgment on the other person by saying something such as "Well, you asked for it." Such comments do little more than make the other person defensive.

- You feel the urge to defend yourself and say something self-centered like "Don't blame me," which does nothing to help the other person.

- You place the focus on tomorrow rather than on today. Empathizing occurs in the present, not in the future. Avoid statements like "You won't even remember this next year." While that may be true, it is not what he or she wants or needs to hear from you right now.

The closer you feel to another person, and the more familiar you are with his or her situation, the easier it should be for you to demonstrate empathetic responsiveness. You'll likely have to work harder to exhibit genuine empathetic responsiveness toward someone you've known only briefly. By using phrases such as "I'm listening," "I hear you," and "I get it," you can demonstrate your respect, understanding, and acceptance of another person, even someone you don't know very well.[19]

# LISTENING ETHICS

At one time or another, we have all committed an unethical listening act—preferring not to engage. Instead we pursue our private thoughts, reminisce, or worry about something personal rather than concentrate on what the other person was saying. Unethical listeners believe their own thoughts are worthier of attention than others'. Thus, in the competition for thinking space, their thoughts win and others lose. Not listening to another can have serious consequences. For example, imagine what could happen if a physician is more concerned with her own thoughts than with listening to a patient describe his symptoms. Regardless of the role or position of the listener, listening not only fulfills a personal obligation, but also confirms a societal bond.

To become a more effective listener, you need to recognize the internal and external factors that lead to deficient listening (see Table 4.3), and then do your part to eliminate them. Ethical listeners don't engage in **non-listening**—that is, they don't answer any of the following questions with a yes.

## DO YOU TUNE OUT?

A listener who doesn't care about the person with whom he or she is conversing tunes out. When someone tries to start a conversation, share ideas, or influence them, unethical listeners don't pay attention. They're preoccupied—too busy thinking about their own problems or something else. As a result, they fail to focus fully or actively on the messages that others send.

# ANALYZE THIS: ACTIVE AND INACTIVE LISTENING

iStock.com/RuslanDashinsky

Active listening has a lot in common with perception checking, since it involves feeding back to the speaker your understanding of what the speaker has communicated to you, both in content and in feeling. By providing feedback, we enable the other person to clarify his or her thoughts and emotions and correct misperceptions.

Consider the following exchange:

**Maya:** I'm screwed! Dr. Rodriguez wants me to redo this entire paper. I spent so much time researching it, but it's still not good enough for him. He's giving me 2 days to improve it, or I'll get a C. How am I going to get this done? Does he have any idea how busy my life is?

**Davilla's response:** Lucky you. At least you got 2 days. I just got the C.

**Dave's response:** Two days isn't so bad. You can do it. All you need to do is focus.

**Doreen's response:** Ugh, you worked so hard on that paper! You're totally stressed out, aren't you?

Which of the three friends do you think demonstrated active listening?

Davilla focused on herself. Dave attempted to diminish Maya's problem. Only Doreen attempted to promote a meaningful exchange. Doreen paraphrased Maya's message to make sure she got it right and reflected her feelings, recognizing their legitimacy.

Source: See B. R. Burleson, "Explaining Recipient Responses to Supportive Messages: Development and Tests of a Dual-Process Theory," in S. W. Smith and S. R. Wilson, eds., *New Directions in Interpersonal Communication Research,* Thousand Oaks, CA: Sage, 2010, pp. 159–179; and D. Johnson, "Helpful Listening and Responding," in K. M. Galvin and P. Cooper, eds., *Making Connections: Readings in Relational Communication,* Los Angeles: Roxbury, 1996, pp. 91–97.

## DO YOU ENGAGE IN FAKE LISTENING?

Listeners who don't care about those they interact with often engage in pseudo-listening. They look at you, smile or frown appropriately, nod their heads, and even utter sounds such as "hmmm," or "uh-huh." All their external cues tell you they're listening, but in fact, they let no meaning get through.

## DO YOU IGNORE SPECIFIC INDIVIDUALS?

Before even giving another person a chance, a deficient listener may decide that the person looks uninteresting or sounds dull, or that there is no future for a relationship with him or her. Ineffective listeners' tendency to prejudge limits their potential for developing meaningful relationships.

## TABLE 4.3  BEHAVIORS OF POOR LISTENERS

| BEHAVIOR | CONSEQUENCES |
|---|---|
| Tuning out | Listener's loss of focus and preoccupations make understanding less likely. |
| Faking attention | Listener's pseudo-listening behavior deceives the speaker. |
| Losing contact opportunities | Listener's misjudging has potential effects on both message relevance and relationship. |
| Losing control | Listener's emotions and lack of patience lead to ambushes, message distortions, and defensiveness. |
| Laziness | Listener's lack of effort and refusal to work at listening make comprehension unlikely. |
| Selfishness | Listener's focus is on the self rather than on the other person. |
| Being distracted by external factors | Listener's oversensitivity to setting or context interferes with listening. |
| Wasting time | Listener's failure to use the speech–thought differential to advantage compromises listening effectiveness. |
| Apprehensiveness | Listener's fear of the new leads to defensiveness. |
| Burnout | Listener's inability to cope with information overload closes down the mind. |

## DO YOU LOSE EMOTIONAL CONTROL?

Sometimes we let disagreements with another get in the way of our listening carefully. Some of the words others speak function as **red-flag words**—words that interfere with our ability to listen because they trigger in us an emotional deafness that causes our listening efficiency to drop to zero as we take an emotional side trip. Among the words and phrases that might contribute to emotional deafness in some of us are *Nazi*, *you should*, *entitlement*, and *what's wrong with you*? Are you aware of any specific words or phrases that cause you to erupt emotionally, disrupting your ability to continue interacting meaningfully and calmly?

## DO YOU AVOID CHALLENGING CONTENT?

Listening is voluntary, and, unfortunately, some of us refuse to volunteer to listen to people whose ideas or manners of expression challenge us. Believing that we will not understand the other person, we don't even give ourselves a chance to exercise our minds.

When was the last time you dismissed another person because you told yourself, "I won't understand what she has to say anyway"? To what extent are you willing to stretch your mind to accommodate the challenge of new ideas instead of merely focusing on those people or ideas that validate your preconceived notions?

## ARE YOU EGOCENTRIC?

When was the last time you tuned out someone because you felt his or her ideas were irrelevant to you? People who are egocentric do this regularly. Seeing themselves as the center of the universe and seeking only self-satisfaction, they are so wrapped up in themselves that they fail either to realize or to value their interconnectedness with others. Ironically, egocentric listeners still expect those they converse with to listen to them.

## DO YOU WASTE POTENTIAL LISTENING TIME?

We typically speak at a rate of 150 to 200 words per minute. However, we can comprehend 400 to 600 words per minute.[20] The difference between the two is known as the **speech–thought differential**. Ineffective listeners waste this extra time by daydreaming instead of focusing on, summarizing, and asking themselves questions about the substance and meaning of the other person's remarks. They would rather drift off than attend closely to what the other person is telling them.

## ARE YOU OVERLY APPREHENSIVE?

Have you ever been so fearful of new situations, people, or information that you became overly anxious? Apprehensive listeners are fearful of psychologically adjusting themselves to messages that others send to them.[21] Anxiety can cause us to become overly defensive, which, in turn, inhibits effective listening.

## ARE YOU SUFFERING SYMPTOMS OF LISTENING BURNOUT?

Sometimes, people who once were effective listeners become ineffective because they are burned out. When exposed to too much information at one time, our minds simply close. For example, if you were a psychologist and had to listen daily to clients' disclosures, you might experience listening burnout and seek to spend your free time not listening so attentively.

Certainly, we cannot listen at full capacity all the time. However, we need to become aware of how often and why we fail to listen and determine what we can do to become better at listening. Being an effective listener has implications for how well we perform our jobs and whether we live up to our relational responsibilities.

## HURDLING LISTENING ROADBLOCKS

Listening consumes energy. When you listen actively, your body temperature rises, your palms become moist, and your adrenaline flow increases. Your body actually prepares itself to listen. You are the catalyst in this operation—you set in motion the listening process. Taking to heart the following principles will make your listening efforts more productive:

- Listening requires your full attention. You can't half listen—the half you miss could be critical.

- Evaluation follows reception. Withhold your evaluation until you are certain you have understood the other person's message. Anger and hostility can impede understanding, as can rapture and hero worship. A heightened emotional state impedes your ability to comprehend.

- The other person's appearance or delivery is not an excuse for not listening. Overlook a speaker's monotone or lack of eye contact. Concentrate on the message. A polished speaking manner can be equally harmful if you let it blind you to an absence of substance.

- Likewise, judging another person based on your own existing negative or positive prejudice impedes listening. You either become busy arguing against the other person or are too quickly impressed to accurately process the message being sent.

- How you listen affects how others feel about you. The more adept you are at exhibiting empathetic and supportive behaviors, the more others will want to interact with you.

- If you seek opportunities to practice skillful listening, you will become a better listener.

# RESPONDING WITH FEEDBACK

Listening is a collaborative process. Both parties to a conversation have the power to complicate or facilitate listening. Listening is a dialogic, or give-and-take, process in which speakers help listeners participate in and coordinate what is a joint activity.[22] In return, receivers provide feedback, which is an integral part of the listening process.

## DEFINING FEEDBACK

When we listen actively, we provide the other person with feedback. Recall from Chapter 1 that the term *feedback* implies that we are returning to another person our reactions to their verbal and nonverbal messages. Whenever you consciously or unconsciously emit a message that another perceives to be a response to something he or she said or did, your message serves as feedback.

During interpersonal communication, we're not always totally honest when we provide feedback. At times, when bored with a conversation, you may nevertheless put on your "I'm interested" expression and nod approvingly. Unfortunately, we can mislead others by providing dishonest feedback.

The feedback you offer another person affects how he or she interprets your relationship. Tiffany Cooper Gueye, CEO of Building Educated Leaders for Life, has noted that the most important thing she can provide to the people she works with is "direct, honest, clear feedback."[23] Many believe the need for such feedback exists in all relationships. Do you?

When given effectively, feedback has positive consequences.

## FEEDBACK OPTIONS

Like communication, feedback is a continuous process. We constantly send feedback, whether or not we intend to. Another person can interpret everything we do or don't do—a raised eyebrow, folded arms, every word we speak or fail to speak—as feedback. Sometimes our feedback is purposeful, because we hope to evoke a specific response. For instance, your partner tells a joke, and you laugh heartily because you want him or her to know you enjoyed it and would like him or her to feel comfortable telling you more. On the other hand, sometimes the feedback we send is unintentional and elicits unexpected reactions. Without our consciously realizing it, our words and behavior may provoke responses in another person that we never intended. When facing such an occurrence, we may say something like "That's not what I meant!" Other times, a person simply ignores the feedback we sent. Have you ever tried to convey your romantic interest to another person without receiving a response? Sometimes another person is not ready, willing, or able to process our honest reaction.

The kind of feedback we offer and its content are dependent on the kind of relationship we share. Our partner is likely to give us feedback regarding our relationship strengths; our teachers probably will not. Well-given feedback has positive consequences for our relationships; poorly given feedback does not. Whether your feedback is likely to elicit positive or negative reactions from another person depends on three questions:

1. Do you offer feedback at the right time?
2. Are you clear and specific about the feedback you give?
3. Is your feedback appropriate, tactful, and conducive to sustaining the relationship?

## Feedback May Be Immediate or Delayed

Much of the feedback we send during interpersonal communication occurs virtually simultaneously with our reception of a message. This is generally most effective because our reaction can lose its impact on the other person if we wait too long. Sometimes, however, we may consciously withhold responding. For example, it can be wiser to cool down before offering a response to a message that angers you. Feedback sent in anger can damage a relationship.

## Feedback May Be Person or Message Focused

We can center feedback on either the person or the message. Feedback such as "You're just about the most compassionate person I know" focuses on the person, while a statement such as "While I understand your position, I believe the reasons you offer are flawed" focuses on the message.

## Feedback May Be Low or High Monitored

Feedback that's sincere and spontaneous is low-monitored feedback. It occurs constantly through the interpersonal communication process. As we exchange messages, we reveal our responses without consciously monitoring or censoring them. In contrast, feedback that we offer to serve a specific purpose is high-monitored feedback. We are more guarded and think about whether our feedback will serve a desired purpose before sending it. For example, if your instructor were to ask you what you think of the course, you would probably monitor your feedback before responding.

## Feedback May Be Evaluative or Non-Evaluative

When we provide **evaluative feedback**, we provide positive or negative assessments to another; we let him or her know what we think of his or her ideas, abilities, looks, and so on. By its very nature, evaluative feedback is judgmental; it either confirms or refutes the communication of another.

Positive evaluative feedback serves a reinforcing function. For example, if you get positive feedback in response to you flirting with someone, you'll tend to continue flirting. Negative evaluative feedback serves a corrective function—it helps reduce undesirable behavior. When we perceive feedback as negative, we're apt to change or modify our behavior accordingly. For example, if you tell an off-color joke and then receive feedback indicating that another person found it offensive, you probably won't tell another. Negative evaluative feedback alerts us to discontinue behavior in progress.

Unlike evaluative feedback, which tends to be judgmental, **non-evaluative feedback** does not direct the action of another. Instead, we use it when we want to find out more about another person's feelings. When providing non-evaluative feedback, we refrain from revealing our own personal opinions or judgments. We simply question, describe what we observe, or demonstrate our interest in listening to the person.

Because non-evaluative feedback is nondirective in style, a receiver may perceive our support as reinforcing his or her behavior and thus assign it a positive tone. In reality, however, non-evaluative feedback goes beyond positive feedback, because it does more than merely reinforce behavior; it enables others, without our direction, to explore their own thoughts and feelings and arrive at their own solutions. Non-evaluative feedback tends to fall into one of four categories: probing, understanding, supporting, and "I" messages.

**Probing.** When we solicit additional information from another person in an effort to draw him or her out, as well as to demonstrate our willingness to listen, we are **probing**. For example, suppose a friend who's concerned about a job-related conflict tells you, "I'm really over the edge. My boss keeps pushing and pushing me. I'm going to snap." If you are probing, you might inquire, "What's she doing that is so annoying?" or "Why do you think this is happening?" By responding in this way, you give the other person the opportunity to think through the problem, while also offering him or her the chance for emotional release. On the other hand, responses such as "Oh, they're all like that," could cause your friend to become defensive, preventing him or her from thinking through and discussing the troublesome situation with you.

**Understanding.** When we offer understanding, we try to comprehend what the other person is telling us, and we check our interpretations by paraphrasing (restating in our own words) what we have heard. By paraphrasing, we show that we care enough about the other person and the problem he or she is facing to be certain we understand the message's meaning. If a friend says, "I don't think I'm good enough to get the job," you could paraphrase by responding, "You mean you think you lack the skills to get promoted?"

If we use understanding early in a relationship, we communicate our willingness to listen and the person's importance to us. Understanding responses encourage a relationship's development in part by demonstrating our sensitivity to and concern for the other person, and also by allowing the other person more time to describe and detail his or her feelings and perceptions to us.

**Supporting.** When we respond by supporting, we indicate that we share the other person's perception of a problem as important. Suppose your friend comes to you with a problem she believes is so serious that she has become agitated, and she says that you couldn't possibly understand her predicament. In offering **supportive feedback** you would do your best to calm her down by assuring her that you understand the problem, that her world is not ending, and that you are there to help her work through it.

When you offer supportive feedback, you acknowledge another person's problem as important.

By offering supportive feedback, we accomplish a number of things: First, we do what we can to reduce the intensity of the other person's feelings. Second, we let him or her know we consider the problem real. Instead of offering comments such as "Why are you worrying about that?" we say things like "I can tell you're upset. Let's sit down and discuss it. I'm sure you can find a way to work it out." A friend who is distraught because he or she has just been fired or has just broken up with a lover does not need to be told, "There's no reason to be so upset," or "I warned you about this." When we provide supportive feedback, we acknowledge the importance of the other person's predicament, but we do not attempt to solve it; we simply listen, show the person we care, and in so doing, help him or her to discover a solution.

**"I" messages.** By delivering non-evaluative feedback in the form of "I" messages, we refrain from passing judgment on the other's actions; however, we do reveal our feelings about the situation.

When we say things like, "You're a pain in the neck!" or "You're wasting my time!" we place blame for something on someone else. When we experience relationship problems, we sometimes resort to name-calling and place blame on others as a means of coping with the situation. Such feedback, however, builds barriers between us, which then become increasingly difficult to remove.

To avoid building these barriers, we can replace "you" messages with "I" messages. Instead of saying, "You're really getting on my nerves"—which could be interpreted by the recipient as "I'm not liked"—explain how you feel. For instance, if you clarify the situation by saying something like "I've just walked in the door and you're asking about our plans for tonight, which stresses me out. I need some time to unwind before talking about tonight," your friend's internal reaction is apt to be along the lines of "Okay, she's had a really tough day," which is much less likely to evoke a defensive or self-serving reaction.

## TRY THIS

### It's the "I."

When phrased appropriately, "I" messages contain three parts: (1) a description of the other person's behavior, (2) a description of how you feel about the behavior, and (3) an explanation of how the other person's behavior affects you—its consequences. "You" messages begin with the word *you* and often express blame.

> Imagine you and a colleague have been assigned the joint task of completing a complex project. You find your partner difficult to work with because he or she will not spend the time you think necessary to complete the task.
>
> Respond to this situation by first using a "you" message and then by using a three-part "I" message. Describe how you think the "you" message and the "I" message might each influence your relationship.

# DIVERSITY AND CULTURE IN LISTENING

Listening plays a vital role in the development of our social relationships. Just as culture and gender play a part in our perception of the self and others, so it plays a part in listening.

## CULTURE'S INFLUENCE ON LISTENING

**Dialogic listening**, the give-and-take process that occurs between people as they respond to one another, is an important focus during interpersonal communication.[24] However, how we engage in dialogic listening differs from culture to culture. For example, in the United States, we practice a people-oriented listening style that focuses on the feelings and concerns of the individuals interacting and the social aspects of their interaction. In contrast, those from Eastern cultures tend to practice speculative, metaphoric thinking.[25] Members of Western cultures tend to be less open and tentative in their listening behaviors than do members of Eastern cultures. Reflecting this, the Chinese emphasize the receiving process over the sending process, a demonstration of their concern for interpretation and anticipation.[26]

Cultural attitudes about when it is appropriate to talk and when one should remain silent also play roles. People from Eastern cultures view **silence** as signaling respectability and trust; they believe that words can corrupt an experience[27] and that people should listen more than talk.[28] Thus, when interacting with people from Eastern cultures, Westerners need to listen with more than their ears and understand that what is important may be implied rather than spoken directly. Additionally, because people from China and Japan have been raised to be comfortable with silence, they simply do not talk as much as Americans do.[29]

The ancient Arab proverb "A man's tongue is his sword" suggests that when they speak, Arab people may use language as a means of offense, to chastise or punish others, and to boast about their abilities. They may make assertions regarding others' faults and failures, contributing to impressions among people from non-Arab cultures who are listening that they could be aggressive or threatening.[30] A contrasting Arab proverb, "When you have spoken the word, it reigns over you. When it is unspoken you reign over it," suggests an alternative explanation for how people of Arab cultures approach listening. It confirms their hesitation to be negative and their desire to maintain peace. Those who are unaware of this may easily misinterpret the intentions of individuals from Arab cultures.

As we speak with and listen to members of different cultures, we need to remind ourselves that the meanings we give to words vary based on our experiences and backgrounds. Because culture influences how we use language, it also influences how we listen to and interpret language.

## TRY THIS

## Culture, Communication Style, and Feedback

In the United States and Europe, individuals prefer direct communication, expecting feedback to be honest and reflective of the feelings of the person giving it. In contrast, members of Asian cultures prefer communicating in a less specific and more indirect way, perhaps because of the value they place on politeness and the maintenance of a positive image. Consequently, members of Asian cultures may expect feedback also to be more indirect, confirming their belief that bluntness could injure the self-esteem of the person to whom feedback is directed.

1. Would you adapt how you offer feedback when interacting with someone from a culture different from yours? Why or why not?

2. In what ways, if any, might using your typical way of offering feedback pose problems for you when you are responding to someone of a different culture? Explain.

3. Pair up with a classmate and discuss a controversial topic of your choice, such as universal health care, capital punishment, or immigration policy. Before you respond to what the other person says, count to 4. How does this short silence affect your comfort level and the tone of your discussion? Be specific.

Sources: See John C. Condon, *With Respect to the Japanese,* Yarmouth, ME: Intercultural Press, 1984, pp. 43–44.

See William B. Gudykunst, *Bridging Differences: Effective Intergroup Communication,* 3rd ed., Thousand Oaks, CA: Sage, 1998, pp. 173–174.

## GENDER'S INFLUENCE ON LISTENING

To what extent, if any, do the listening behaviors of the men and women you know differ? Sociolinguist Deborah Tannen reports that women and men exhibit different listening styles and that they listen for different reasons. To what extent, if any, do your experiences confirm this? According to Tannen, women listen to confirm both the relationship and the person with whom they share a relationship.[31] When a woman processes information, her real goal is to zoom in on an emotional level. This is another reason women excel at empathizing and at identifying another person's communication mood; they are ready, willing, and able to allow others to open themselves up and reveal what is important to them.

In contrast, research reveals that men are more at home with comprehensive listening, hearing a message's facts or informational dimension, and less comfortable handling its emotional content.[32] Men have been conditioned to desire power and control.[33] As a result, they are more likely to listen for solutions so they can give advice rather than empathize. They also are apt to turn off their listening when they come across a problem they cannot solve right away.[34]

Empathetic listening, as we learned earlier, is essential for the development and maintenance of a meaningful relationship, so men may need to work to develop and demonstrate empathetic listening skills. They can help others perceive them to have such skills by using more vocal cues when listening, interjecting responsive sounds such as "uh-huh" and "hmmm" into their reactions. Such cues help others feel listened to.[35]

In interactions between men and women, men tend to spend more time in the speaking role and women in the listening role. If women want to disengage themselves from the role of listener or responder, they probably need to take action, rather than wait for men to stop speaking. When women exercise their right to enter the conversation, they also relieve men from feeling they have to give a solo conversational performance. Both men and women can expand their behavioral repertoires when it comes to listening.

Not only do men and women listen differently, but they also are listened to differently. For example, when men and women speakers use an equal number of tag questions (". . . right?") or qualifiers ("I think . . ."), listeners still perceive the women to use these speech forms more often.[36] Listeners perceive the speech of men as stronger, more active, and more aggressive than women's speech, which they perceive as more polite, pleasing, and sweet.[37] And when women and men speak similarly, women's speech is evaluated more negatively—being perceived as aggressive rather than strong, for example. Perhaps if listening were perceived not as a source of power differences between men and women, but as a means of relationship building, our ability to process the speech of men and women equitably would improve.

# MEDIA AND TECHNOLOGICAL INFLUENCES ON LISTENING

Media and technological innovations are playing roles in affecting how we listen, especially in light of our short attention spans and urge to multitask.

## MEDIA INFLUENCES

Critics have long contended that watching too much television shortens the attention spans of viewers. They argue that because we are offered information and entertainment in shorter and shorter segments, partly because programmers fear that if segments were made longer we would lose focus and tune out, our ability to give sustained attention to anything is undermined. Fast-paced editing and rapidly changing images delivering quick bursts of content are the rule.

Consider the advertisements for various brand-name prescription drugs that we see and hear repeatedly on television, such as one for the antidepressant Cymbalta. Ask yourself whether the ad has been created to make it less likely you will listen to the words spoken? The ad features a dad, thin, young, and handsome, twirling his young daughter around their living room, while a newborn baby sleeps nearby. After witnessing the sense of well-being that permeates this scene, viewers suffering from depression are encouraged to ask their doctors to prescribe Cymbalta for them—even though they are also presented with a warning regarding the drug's potentially harmful side effects, as mandated by the U.S. Food and Drug Administration. The ad was successful; a significant increase in sales was attributed to it.[38]

The advertiser understood the science of attention—that the typical viewer pays attention for only the first 6.5 seconds of a TV ad.[39] The warning about side effects comes later in the ad. Using emotional appeals, the ad quickly captures viewer attention up front—we learn depression hurts, but Cymbalta can help. The detailing of the side effects comes at the point in the ad where we are least likely to pay attention, because we have been led already to imagine the ending. We hear the tone of the voice-over but pay little attention to the words. The warning about potential liver damage is delivered in softened consonants and end sounds, almost a murmur, as the ad's visual imagery changes from tragic to happy—and we know a happy ending is upon us, whereas when the product is introduced and the punch line is delivered at the ad's end, the voice-over diction is slower, and the words more carefully enunciated. The makers of this commercial clearly understood how viewers listen (or fail to listen) and then respond to such advertising.

The media have other problematic influences on listening aside from diverting attention. Too frequently on opinion shows, whether on radio or TV, speakers talk over each other, competing for airtime and acting like spoiled children who will not wait their turns to speak. Meaningful discussion has become a rarity on the airwaves and on cable television.

## TECHNOLOGY'S INFLUENCES

Given the ubiquity of cell phones, we exercise our ears and mouths regularly. Still, the question is whether we spend more of our listening time being entertained than we do talking to or listening to each other. How frequently, for example, do you respond passively to another person because you're preoccupied listening to music or a podcast? Some believe that our connections to digital media through smartphones and tablets and laptop computers cause us to focus on the visual rather than the aural—to emphasize the eye over the ear. How are we adapting to technological listening?

### Visual listening

With the explosion of texting and around-the-clock Web access, we "listen" more visually, rather than aurally. Texting and e-mailing provide messages devoid of a person's voice or body language.

### Social outcomes

Technology continues to alter social outcomes of listening. Research suggests that speaking on cell-phones increase feelings of social support and connection.[40] And according to **social presence theory**, most who engage with social media

Howard Lipin/TNS/Newscom

Do the benefits of a digital assistant outweigh privacy concerns?

convince themselves that others are listening to them when they post. Many even feel as if they are face-to-face—rather than in a digital environment. This perception is known as *telepresence*, and it leads to our thinking of ourselves as actually talking and listening even though that is not the case.[41] In this new listening environment, we demonstrate listening through liking, sharing, retweeting, and other supportive responses. We engage when we want to. It can be part of our daily routine or serve as "background listening," much as radio and television have.[42] More often, however, the volume of messages can become overwhelming, precipitating stress and feelings of disconnection in users.

## Divided attention

Additionally, our affinity for technology makes it likely that we will multitask when listening. For example, how often do you find yourself texting, tweeting, or checking e-mail while talking with another person? In such a circumstance, technology interferes with our relationship by making it difficult for us to listen to each other. Unfortunately, because of multitasking, we frequently find ourselves not focusing exclusively on any single interaction. Consequently, we often fail to give a person we are with our full attention.

## Secretly listeners

How do you feel upon discovering that another person has eavesdropped on you? You would probably feel violated because you did not intend your words to be heard by this individual. Despite this, we have shown ourselves willing to trade privacy for convenience in the form of digital assistants like Siri or Alexa. These assistants sometimes eavesdrop on us, retaining our conversation history.[43]

## TRY THIS

## The Ethics of Illusionary Listening

Is it possible for people to face an operating television without really watching it? Likewise, can a person ignore a radio that is turned on? Is it possible for people to speak to each other without listening?

1. How often, would you guess, do individuals with whom you regularly converse "turn off" their listening skills even while they are still in front of you?

2. Do you prefer having an "illusionary listener" to having no listener, much as television and radio stations are content to have "illusionary viewers or receivers" (people whose TVs or radios are on but who do not watch or listen) as long as they are counted in their program ratings?

3. Do you consider your Facebook friends to be real or illusionary listeners? Explain.

# GAINING COMMUNICATION SKILLS: BECOMING A BETTER LISTENER

In this chapter, we have explored the role of listening in relationships. You should now recognize that you can never be too good a listener. No matter how effective you believe your listening skills currently are, doing the following can help you become a better listener.

## CATCH YOURSELF EXHIBITING A BAD HABIT

Recognition of a fault precedes correction of it. If you monitor your listening behavior, you can catch yourself before you display an undesirable trait. That is the first step toward positive change.

## SUBSTITUTE A GOOD HABIT FOR A BAD ONE

Think about the new listening habits you would like to have. For example, if you tend to daydream when someone is speaking to you, encourage yourself to display greater attentiveness and concentration. Visualize yourself listening effectively when conversing. Imagine the positive impact your new behavior will have on your relationships.

## LISTEN WITH YOUR WHOLE BODY

Take steps to ensure that your physical mannerisms do not distract or confuse the person you are interacting with. Instead of leaning back with your arms crossed, fidgeting, playing with your hair or jewelry, gazing repeatedly at your watch, or otherwise signaling that you are uninterested in what the other person is saying, make a commitment to convey a more positive listening demeanor. Assume an attentive posture, make good eye contact, and display appropriate facial expressions. In other words, get physically ready to listen. If you look more like an effective listener, you will be apt to behave like one.

## CONSISTENTLY USE YOUR EARS, NOT JUST YOUR MOUTH

When you converse with another, shift naturally and frequently from a speaking to a listening mode. Rather than monopolizing the speaking role or spending your time planning what you will say next, make a sincere effort when not speaking to focus on the other person's message when he or she is talking. Avoid completing another's statements because you "know for sure" what he or she is going to say. Conversing with another compels us to develop not just a speaking presence, but also a listening attitude.

## SEE THE OTHER SIDE

One of the greatest detriments to listening is an unwillingness to look at a situation from another's point of view. If you begin a conversation by telling yourself you are willing to see and feel from the other person's perspective, you increase your chances for more meaningful interaction. You may not end up agreeing with what you have heard, but you will be more likely to understand where the thoughts and feelings are coming from.

## LISTEN NON-ASSUMPTIVELY

Every message a person delivers to another person exists in at least four different forms:

1. The message as it exists in the mind of the person speaking to you (his or her thoughts)

2. The message as it is spoken (encoded by the person)

3. The message as the listener interprets it (decoded by you)

4. The message as the listener ultimately remembers it (influenced by personal selectivity or rejection biases)

When passed from person to person, messages become distorted. We usually try to simplify the message we hear, losing nuance as we decode it, or we may not want to admit that we did not understand what someone told us; instead, we may try to make sense of what we heard by making certain assumptions. This usually results in our adding to, subtracting from, or otherwise altering the message. Try to listen without filling in the gaps. Ask questions to clarify anything you don't understand.

## PARTICIPATE ACTIVELY

Listening is an active and responsive process, not a passive behavior. Ask questions. Paraphrase what the other person has said, and ask for confirmation of your understanding. In this way, you can determine whether you are processing the other person's words and feelings correctly.

## CONNECT THE CASE

### The Case of Non-Listening Flora

"I didn't mean to do it," Flora told Fred, her boss. "I just misheard you."

Tuesday had begun as a fairly typical day in Flora's busy life. She had attended her morning classes, eaten a late lunch with several friends, and then left campus for a nearby factory outlet store where she was employed as an assistant manager on the evening shift to help pay her way through college.

As she arrived, Flora's boss said, "Be sure and mark the silk designer blouses down to $19.99." It seemed a little low, but who was she to question Fred's

*(Continued)*

(Continued)

instructions? She told Joe, one of the stock workers, to adjust the price immediately.

About an hour later, Adel, a salesclerk, told Flora that the blouses were moving off the shelf. Flora instructed Joe to bring out another case. Before her shift's end, eager shoppers had purchased the entire contents of five more cases of the silk designer blouses.

As Flora prepared to close the store, she gazed at the now-depleted blouse display and saw the problem: the blouses had been marked down to $9.99 erroneously.

Just then, Fred called Flora to see how things were going. She explained, "I told Joe to mark the blouses down to $19.99 like you said, but he mistakenly marked them down to $9.99. He just didn't listen. Should I reprimand him or fire him?"

"Fire him?" came the reply. "I told you to mark the blouses up to $99.99. We've now lost $90 for every blouse we sold tonight! You and Joe are two of the worst listeners ever!"

Flora felt terribly. She wondered, "How could I have made such a costly mistake?"

### Consider these questions:

1. Why do you imagine Flora made the initial listening error?

2. What steps can Flora take to ensure that she listens to others correctly and others listen to her correctly?

3. If you were in Flora's shoes, do you think you would have made the mistake she did, or are you a more proficient listener than she?

# REVIEW THIS

## CHAPTER SUMMARY

**1. Define and distinguish between hearing and listening and effective and ineffective listening.** □

Hearing is an involuntary physiological process; listening is a voluntary psychological process we use to understand and retain aural messages. While listening effectively can improve our relationships and understanding of information, ineffective listening may create relational and other problems.

**2. Identify and explain the six stages of listening identified in the HURIER model.** □

The six stages in the HURIER model are hearing (the physical act of perceiving sound), understanding (comprehending meaning), remembering (the storing and retrieving of information as needed), interpreting (the assigning of meaning based on the other's perspective), evaluating (assessing the truth and accuracy of a message), and responding (demonstrating to another that you are listening by providing feedback).

**3. Define and distinguish among the four styles and four types of listening.** □

The four styles of listening are people oriented (listening to discover commonalities), action oriented (listening to process errorless, concise messages), content oriented (listening to be intellectually stimulated), and time oriented (listening to receive quick and to-the-point communications). The four types of listening are appreciative (listening for enjoyment), comprehensive (listening to gain knowledge), critical (listening to analyze, assess, and decide to accept or reject a message), and empathetic (listening to think and feel as another does by functioning as a sounding board or in a therapeutic role).

**4. Explain the importance of ethical listening and identify behaviors to avoid to listen effectively.** □

Unethical listeners tune out, fake attention, lose opportunities for meaningful contact, become overly emotional, look for the easy way out, act in an egocentric manner, are overly sensitive to context, waste time, are overly apprehensive, and/or exhibit symptoms of listening burnout. Ethical listeners are active participants in the listening process, asking questions, paraphrasing, and controlling their emotions and biases in the effort to ensure understanding.

**5. Define the different kinds of feedback.** □

Feedback is a reaction fed back to the source of a message. It can be positive or negative, immediate or delayed, person or message focused, low- or high-monitored, and evaluative or non-evaluative. Probing, understanding, supporting, and "I" messages are among the non-evaluative forms of feedback.

**6. Explain how culture and gender influence listening.** □

Culture affects attitudes toward talk and silence. Gender affects listening style as well as our reasons for listening.

**7. Analyze the impacts of media and technology on listening.** ☐

Media and technology are changing how we listen to one another, including whether we multitask or pay full attention to another person when listening.

**8. Identify strategies to improve listening effectiveness.** ☐

Effective listeners catch themselves when not listening, make listening a habit, use their whole body to listen, listen more than they speak, see the other side, listen non-assumptively, and participate actively.

## CHECK YOUR UNDERSTANDING

1. Can you distinguish between hearing and listening? What listening style do you believe you exhibit most frequently? Why do you think this is so? (See pages 93–95 and pages 98–100.)

2. Can you explain how the kind of listening in which someone is engaging influences his or her behavior? What kind of listening do you prefer to engage in? (See pages 101–103.)

3. Can you apply the HURIER model to a personal listening experience? (See pages 95–98.)

4. Can you provide a dialogue (real or hypothetical) that demonstrates one or more listening challenges and the effects of faulty listening? (See pages 103–107.)

5. Can you distinguish between the different kinds of feedback, identifying what makes each valuable? (See pages 107–111.)

## KEY TERMS

Appreciative listening  104

Attending  101

Comprehensive listening  104

Critical or deliberative listening  105

Dialogic listening  115

Empathetic listening  105

Empathetic responsiveness  105

Evaluative feedback  112

Hearing  97

HURIER model  99

"I" messages  114

Listening  97

Non-evaluative feedback  113

Non-listening  107

Perspective taking  105

Probing  113

Red-flag word  109

Silence  115

Social presence theory  118

Speech–thought differential  110

Supportive feedback  113

Sympathetic responsiveness  105

Get the tools you need to sharpen your study skills. **SAGE edge** offers a robust online environment featuring an impressive array of free tools and resources. Access practice quizzes, eFlashcards, video, and multimedia at **edge.sagepub.com/gambleicp**.

5

# Communicating With Words

## Learning Objectives

1. Define language, explaining its uses and distinguishing among semantic, syntactic, and pragmatic codes

2. Explain the triangle of meaning

3. Identify ways to remove semantic barriers

4. Discuss the effects of word walls, euphemisms, emotive language, polarizing words, politically correct language, bypassing, and intensional orientation

5. Explain how language affects relationships

6. Identify how language helps reinforce attitudes toward culture, gender, and age

7. Discuss the interface between language and media and technology

8. Take steps to use language more effectively

> Words can be like X-rays if you use them properly—they'll go through anything.
>
> —Aldous Huxley

Historically, language and culture go hand in hand. Back in 1972, in response to broadcast censors, the late comedian George Carlin delivered a monologue that remains popular today on the seven words that never could be said on TV. The words were *sh-t*, *piss*, *cu-t*, *f—k*, *c—ksucker*, *mother—cker*, and *tits*. Out of thousands and thousands of words, these were the ones that at that time were considered terribly inappropriate. Sensitivities change, however, and you've probably heard at least a few of these words on basic cable.

The word-ban issue is global. In 2018, the Polish legislature passed a law outlawing the phrase *Polish death camps*, making it a crime, punishable by fine and/or prison, to accuse the Polish nation of complicity in the Holocaust.[1] And in Quebec, provincial legislators passed a resolution advising shopkeepers to take the word *hi* out of their customer greeting and use only the word *bonjour* instead.[2]

What messages do the preceding examples send? The words we embrace and dismiss provide clues to our values and communication practices and goals. Words have power. They are tools and can be used for good as well as for nefarious purposes. So much of what happens in our lives depends on words and how we use them. What does your choice of words say about you? ■

## CHAPTER 5

# WHAT DO YOU KNOW?

Before continuing your reading of this chapter, which of the following five statements do you believe to be true, and which do you believe to be false?

| | | | |
|---|---|---|---|
| **1.** | Meaning exists in words. | T | F |
| **2.** | The personal meaning that we have for a word is permanent. | T | F |
| **3.** | You can substitute a politer word for one that is less polite to make yourself crystal clear. | T | F |
| **4.** | Advertisers realize that words do not easily fool us. | T | F |
| **5.** | Spotlighting highlights a person's appearance. | T | F |

Read the chapter to discover if you're right or if you've made any erroneous assumptions.

ANSWERS: 1. F; 2. F; 3. F; 4. F; 5. F

Being unable to use words helps us understand their importance.

Comstock Images/Comstock/Thinkstock

Depending on our choices, words can clarify or confuse, making meaning apparent or obscure. Interpersonal effectiveness and word mastery are related. How we use words has an impact on our sense of self and on the nature and development of our relationships. After all, language is the tool we use to form, maintain, and end relationships. It makes it feasible for us to cooperate, plan, and share. Without language, we would be far less effective communicators, more isolated, and significantly less social. So, let's talk about language. Let's talk about using words to communicate.

# DEFINING LANGUAGE

**Language** is a code or system of arbitrary symbols that permits a group of people to communicate and share meaning. Without the ability to use words to create verbal messages, we would find interacting with one another far more difficult and certainly more frustrating. If unable to use words to express ourselves, how would we talk about our relationships, career goals, or dreams? Yet, as we do with so many other important things, we take our ability to use words for granted. Often it is only when we are prevented or restrained from communicating with words that we value their utility and importance.

We use language to negotiate meaning, and meaning is at the heart of communication. Because words are symbols, in and of themselves, they have no meaning. They are letter combinations or spoken sounds that arbitrarily were selected at some point to stand for the things about which we speak. If enough people agreed, we could create new symbols—new words—to use in place of the ones we currently use. The word *water* is not drinkable. The word *snow* is not colder than the word *coffee,* any more than the word *coffee* is hotter than the word *pepper.*

Meanings for words do not reside in their symbols—their letters or their sounds—but rather in the minds of their users. Thus, words are not reality; they merely *represent* reality. Meaning exists in us, not in words. You have your meaning, and other people have their meanings. To the degree that we can negotiate our meanings so that they overlap, we are able to relate to and understand each other.

## THE MEANING OF WORDS

How did the words we use to communicate develop their meanings? To explain how words came to have meaning, we will examine a trio of language codes (rules specifying language use): the semantic code, the syntactic code, and the pragmatic code (see Table 5.1).

### TABLE 5.1  THE LANGUAGE CODE TRIO

| SEMANTIC CODE | SYNTACTIC CODE | PRAGMATIC CODE |
|---|---|---|
| Denotative and connotative meaning | Conventions and rules (grammar) | Appropriateness based on context |
| Variability through time and place | Ignoring rules makes language incomprehensible | Dependent on cooperation and coordination |

### The Semantic Code

According to the semantic code, we agree to use the same symbols to communicate. By agreeing on a set of semantic rules, we make it possible to understand each other. The semantic code, which we explore in more depth as we proceed through this chapter, establishes that words have both a dictionary definition and more subjective, personal meaning, that they vary through time and place, and only represent or symbolize reality. Were we to use symbols in unpredictable ways, perhaps arguing over whether an apple is something to eat or wear on your foot, we would be unable to communicate with each other meaningfully.

### The Syntactic Code

The syntactic code establishes the conventions guiding word use. When proper syntax is lacking—that is, when we ignore grammatical rules—we may render our words incomprehensible, even nonsensical. When a person fails to follow widely accepted linguistic or syntactic rules, our impressions of that person may be negatively affected. Until popularized by the music industry, for example, the syntax of the hip-hop community was neither widely accepted nor understood by people outside the culture, who

Do you understand the grammatical conventions of hip-hop?

initially maligned it, before eventually emulating it. Understanding and respecting another person's mode of expression, regardless of whether we share the grammatical conventions, is important.

### The Pragmatic Code

Communicating with words works best when all parties understand and use the same rules. To be pragmatic, we coordinate our efforts and cooperate with each other to agree on an appropriate code. When, for example, is it appropriate to tell a joke, and what kind of joke may be told? Are there jokes that you might consider tasteless or denigrating to others? Kathy Griffin, for example, was much maligned for sharing a satirical image of herself holding President Trump's severed head. How do you know how another will interpret your humor? Answering these questions brings the **pragmatic code** into play. This code requires us to consider the context of an interaction, the interdependent nature of our relationship, and the goal of our exchange.

When we begin by holding dissimilar perspectives, our interpretations of meaning are also likely to diverge. For example, have you ever observed how the same words can take on different meanings depending on a person's perspective? Imagine you work for a software company that is about to lay off 50 employees. Your boss walks by and says, "You look like you've been through the wringer. Why don't you take the rest of the week off?" If you feel secure in your position, you would likely understand that your boss is appreciative of how hard you have been working and is rewarding you with a well-deserved rest. If, on the other hand, you fear you are about to be laid off, you might view the boss's comments as the beginning of the end of your employment. If you were in this situation, what pragmatic rules would you use to guide your interpretation of the messages? What is the chance you would jump to the wrong conclusion?

## THE TRIANGLE OF MEANING

In their classic work *The Meaning of Meaning,* C. K. Ogden and I. A. Richards use the **triangle of meaning** to illustrate the relationships among words, things, and thoughts (see Figure 5.1).[3]

#### FIGURE 5.1
The Triangle of Meaning

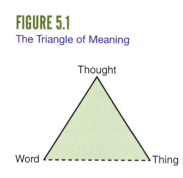

Their model uses a broken line to connect the word and the thing to which the word refers. The broken line underscores that an arbitrary relationship exists between a symbol and its referent. It reminds us that the word is not the thing, and that there is no direct connection between these two points on the triangle. In contrast, the solid lines between words and thoughts and things and thoughts reflect the personal meanings we attach to words and things. When you say the word *wealth,* for example, it does not necessarily mean the same thing to you that it does to another person. Each of us has different associations that we likely attach to the word based on our stored mental images and personal experiences. No one else will react to a stimulus—whether a word or a thing—exactly as you do, because no one else has had your exact experiences.

Meanings exist in thoughts, not in words or things. For you and another person to understand each other, you must both attribute the same meaning to the words being used. When your language is ambiguous or contains what we call **word masks**, misunderstandings may result. When words wear masks, we are apt to misunderstand them.

# REMOVE SEMANTIC BARRIERS

When we use language to impede understanding, we figuratively build a **word wall**. In Lewis Carroll's *Through the Looking Glass,* Humpty Dumpty explains to Alice how easy it is to build one:

> "I don't know what you mean by 'glory,'" Alice said.
>
> Humpty Dumpty smiled contemptuously. "Of course you don't—till I tell you. I meant, "There's a nice knock-down argument for you!"
>
> "But 'glory' doesn't mean 'a nice knock-down argument,'" Alice objected.
>
> "When *I* use a word," Humpty Dumpty said in a rather scornful tone, "it means just what I choose it to mean—neither more nor less."

Word walls impede understanding. Have you ever built one?

iStock.com/Andrew_Howe

In the real world, we cannot make words mean whatever we want them to. If we don't consider how another person may interpret our words, we're apt to have problems communicating. Although there are a number of semantic barriers that complicate the sharing of meaning, we can overcome them by identifying them, recognizing when they are present, and taking steps to facilitate—not mask—meaning transference.

## DIFFERENTIATE DENOTATIVE AND CONNOTATIVE MEANING

Words have both denotative and connotative meanings. Can you distinguish one from the other?

### Denotative Meaning

A word's **denotative meaning** is its standard dictionary definition. It is the general or objective meaning that members of a particular language community attribute to the word. The more denotations a word has, the greater the possibility for confusion when the word is used. A *run* in baseball is different from a *run* in a stocking, which is different from a 10K *run*. When another person does not understand the denotative meanings of our words, we have a potential semantic barrier.

## Connotative Meaning

**Connotative meaning**, in contrast, is much more subjective, personal, and contextual by nature. Unlike denotative meaning, it is influenced by an individual's personal experience with a word and its referent. Thus, if the person you are speaking with does not share the connotative meaning you have for a word, it becomes even more likely that a semantic barrier will form. A word can have as many connotations as there are people using it; in effect, connotative meanings are limitless. To understand just how limitless, complete the Try This: Measuring Meaning activity that follows.

## TRY THIS

## Measuring Meaning

Below is a scale designed to measure how you feel about particular words, similar to the one developed by psychologists Charles Osgood, George Suci, and Percy Tannenbaum to measure the meaning of words.

1. Use the scale below to score each of the following words: *college, feminism, immigrants,* and *celebrity*. Think about whether each of these words gives you feelings of happiness or sadness, hot or cold, strength or weakness. Using a different color for each of the four words, circle the number on the scale that best represents your rating.

| | | | | | | | | |
|---|---|---|---|---|---|---|---|---|
| Good | 1 | 2 | 3 | 4 | 5 | 6 | 7 | Bad |
| Happy | 1 | 2 | 3 | 4 | 5 | 6 | 7 | Sad |
| Strong | 1 | 2 | 3 | 4 | 5 | 6 | 7 | Weak |
| Honest | 1 | 2 | 3 | 4 | 5 | 6 | 7 | Dishonest |
| Hot | 1 | 2 | 3 | 4 | 5 | 6 | 7 | Cold |
| Active | 1 | 2 | 3 | 4 | 5 | 6 | 7 | Passive |
| Valuable | 1 | 2 | 3 | 4 | 5 | 6 | 7 | Worthless |
| Sweet | 1 | 2 | 3 | 4 | 5 | 6 | 7 | Bitter |
| Fast | 1 | 2 | 3 | 4 | 5 | 6 | 7 | Slow |

2. Compare your scores with those of your peers. How do your feelings for each word compare? To what extent, if any, does the sex or age of the respondent appear to affect ratings?

Source: See Charles E. Osgood, George J. Suci, and Percy H. Tannenbaum, *The Measurement of Meaning*, Urbana: University of Illinois Press, 1957.

## RECOGNIZE HOW TIME AND PLACE MAY CHANGE MEANING

The meanings that words trigger in people's minds may change with time. Just because we used a word one way at a particular time does not mean that individuals born into a different generation or era will use it in the same way or even be able to understand our message. Our language system is open to expansion and alteration. Words may lose old meanings and evolve new ones, sometimes as often as every year. Consequently, especially if you are interacting with someone older or younger than yourself, it is important to find out whether you attach the same meaning to a word. The word *queer* has transitioned from meaning *odd* to an umbrella term for LGBT (lesbian, gay, bisexual, transgender) people to a slur and now denotes a refusal of traditional sexual identity categories. Words lose their luster for a variety of reasons. For example, at Princeton University, the term for the leaders of residential colleges was changed from *master* to *head*, at least in part because of the former term's associations with slavery.[4]

The meanings of words also may change by geographic region. Thus, a soft drink is known as a *soda* in some parts of the country, a *Coke* elsewhere, and *pop* in other regions. Because of such regional differences, to determine meaning, you have to consider where you are. Unless you are sensitive to how regional differences affect words, you could find yourself facing a communication gap.

# CONSIDER THE EFFECTS OF YOUR WORDS

Words matter. We can choose words that are candid and explicit or vague and misleading. Similarly, our words can announce or conceal our true feelings. To influence people's feelings, we may revert to using euphemisms and linguistic ambiguity, emotive language, polarizing and hateful language, or language that is politically correct, depending on our message objectives.

## EUPHEMISMS AND LINGUISTIC AMBIGUITY

Sometimes we substitute less direct or inoffensive language for language we think may be too blunt or potentially offensive. Such substitutions, called **euphemisms**, mask meaning by "softening the blow" of a message. However, because we substitute a pleasant term for a less pleasant one, they also may obscure or fog meaning and alter our receiver's response.[5] As a case in point, few companies *fire* people today—instead, employees are "let go" or "given a pink slip." While people in most cultures value politeness, there are cultural variations in how important politeness and honesty are. People from Asian cultures, for example, value politeness in interpersonal relations more than do people in the United States. Eager to spare the feelings of those with whom they are interacting, Asians frequently use euphemisms to soften their words' impact.[6]

While euphemisms help spare feelings, they also may obscure or mislead those we speak with by camouflaging the truth. According to American linguist William Lutz, euphemisms wage "linguistic fraud and deception."[7] Politicians also use euphemisms to soften the impacts of government policies. A tax increase becomes "increased revenue," and a war becomes a "freedom operation."

The euphemism isn't the only way to reduce the sting of words. Linguistic ambiguity fulfills a similar function. Purposefully saying something that can be taken in at least two ways can help avoid a confrontation. It also can defuse tense situations, as when a U.S. spy plane collided with a Chinese EP-3E fighter that had been tailing it. The Chinese wanted the United States to issue a *formal* apology, something the U.S. government did not want to do. The solution was found in linguistic ambiguity—via the writing of a nuanced note in which the United States expressed "sincere regret" over the incident and offered two "very sorrys," expressions satisfactory to both the United States and China.

## RECOGNIZE EMOTIVE LANGUAGE

In contrast to euphemisms, which we use to mask or conceal our real meaning, we use ==emotive language== to announce our attitude toward a particular subject of discussion. If, for example, you approve of a friend's cutting back on expenses, you might call her *thrifty*; if you disapprove, you might call her *cheap*. While the behavior or object being described is the same, the term used to describe it expresses the user's opinion of the behavior. Notice, for example, how your reactions change as the words change in the following word trios describing the same things:

| | | |
|---|---|---|
| War | Defensive response | Massacre |
| Third World | Undeveloped | Backward |
| Undocumented immigrant | Undocumented workers | Illegal immigrant |

In many ways, the word you select to describe a person or an action becomes more a matter of personal feeling than one of objective fact. Hence, *inheritance tax* and *death tax* may represent the same thing, but not the same feelings toward that thing. Now, using the following statements, demonstrate how you can share your feelings about the subject of each description merely by altering the italicized word:

She's *messy.*

He's *principled.*

I'm *reserved.*

## ACKNOWLEDGE THE POWER OF POLARIZING AND HATEFUL LANGUAGE

The English language can lead us to think in extremes, even though the world is much more gray than black or white. When we describe experience in *either/or* terms, we may use ==polarizing language==. How many of these expressions sound familiar to you? "Either you're for us or against us." "She's either a patriot, or she's a traitor." Either/or thinking conditions us to categorize experience and people according to polar opposites.

Our language makes it easy for us to use polarizing thinking and talk. Just see how easy it is to fill in the opposites for each of the following words:

Bold   _____

Brave   _____

Tall   _____

Then try filling in two or more words between each pair of opposites. That is more difficult, isn't it? It is harder to find words that express all possibilities, not just the extremes. Because polarizing leaves out the middle ground, it does not reflect reality and causes us to perceive gulfs where none really exist.

Language is polarizing in another way when it's used for hateful purposes. Words can be used to dehumanize, attack, and intimidate a target. Hate speech degrades another either because of their national origin, race, sex or sexual orientation, religion, disability, or political views. Calling people profanities, intimidating them, or advocating for violence against specific groups are examples of hate speech.[8]

Do you try to avoid using polarizing language?

## BALANCE POLITICALLY CORRECT LANGUAGE

The term *political correctness* means different things to different people—in fact, it may have different connotations for each of us. For some, being politically correct means using words that convey respect for and sensitivity to the needs and interests of different groups. For others, political correctness means feeling pressured by society to avoid some words for fear of being perceived as offensive. Still others view political correctness as a form of censorship and a very real danger to free speech. Which of these three views comes closest to your own?

## TRY THIS

### Is It Politically Correct or Incorrect?

1. In your opinion, should an individual pay a price for being politically incorrect and making statements that some judge to have negative moral and social consequences?

2. To what extent, if any, do you believe that the political correctness movement interferes with our rights under the First Amendment, which was designed to protect unpopular speech from government restriction?

3. How do you believe we can balance the right to say what we want—no matter how provocative or controversial—with watching what we say so that we do not offend others or considering how our remarks might play in another context?

4. How do you differentiate and where do you personally draw the line between politically incorrect speech and unpopular speech?

In addition to disparaging a person's sex, sexual orientation, age, ethnicity, or race, politically incorrect language also may demean a person's social class or physical or mental abilities. When, for example, one person calls another white trash or a retard, the user's words announce his or her attitude toward the other person while excluding the speaker from the same group, thereby establishing or enhancing their sense of superiority.

Using sexist or non-gender-neutral language is a form of political incorrectness. In early 2018, Prime Minister Justin Trudeau of Canada objected when a reporter used the word *mankind*, noting that *personkind* would be more appropriate. Similarly, in the effort to be more gender-inclusive, some colleges have been rethinking the use of Mr., Ms., and Mrs. in written communications, advising that a student's full name be used instead. Others object, noting that doing this could be culturally insensitive because in some parts of the word using a person's first name is unacceptable.[9] What do you think? How would you prefer others to address you?

Using ageist language such as *geezer* indicates little regard or respect for older people. Using language that is ethnically or racially biased indicates disdain for individuals of particular ethnic or racial heritage and also reveals the stereotypical images the user holds of the members of groups different from their own. Because they demean and disparage others, words like these promote distance rather than interpersonal approachability.

Language can have repercussions depending on the words and symbols used and who uses them. For example, while one African American may casually refer to another African American as a nigger and not have that reference taken pejoratively, it is highly unlikely that a white person's use of the word would be construed in the same way. Members of a group may reclaim and redefine words that were once used to stigmatize or degrade them. It has become increasingly common for women to refer to themselves as *girls*, for instance.

The language we use conveys our feelings and attitudes toward an object of discussion, reflecting our point of view. In effect, we use language to express and shape attitudes.

## BEWARE OF BYPASSING

**Bypassing** occurs when individuals think they understand each other but actually miss each other's meaning because one or both are using **equivocal language**, words that can have more than one interpretation. Instead of making contact with an agreed-upon meaning, their words simply pass by one another, leaving both parties confused.

Two types of bypassing concern us.[10] The first occurs when people are unaware that they are talking about the same thing or fail to see that they agree with each other because they are using different words or phrasing. For example, a pair argue vehemently over proposed changes in the health care system. One insists that the health care system needs to be "revamped," while the other says that's foolish, since only "small changes" are needed. Neither realizes that what one means by revamped is what the other means by small changes. Too often, we argue because we're unaware that we basically agree. We simply are using different words.

The second and more prevalent type of bypassing occurs when our words suggest we and another are in agreement when in fact we substantially disagree. While this form of bypassing is often harmless and may even provoke laughter, it can have more serious consequences. Consider that in Britain *knock you up* means "come and see you." What would happen if a young British man visiting the United States were to tell his American friend that he will knock her up before he returns home?

Again, not all bypassing is funny. During World War II, it was thought that the Japanese had decided to ignore the Potsdam Declaration calling on them to surrender, when the Japanese announced that they would be adhering to a policy of *mokusatsu*. It was only after the atomic bomb was dropped on Hiroshima that interpreters realized that *mokusatsu* could also have been translated as "make no comment at the moment" rather than "reject" or "ignore," as it had been translated initially.[11]

A first step in limiting the damage that bypassing may do to our relationships is to develop an awareness that it exists. If it's possible for others to misunderstand us, they probably will. With this in mind, make the effort to become "person minded" and take the time to make sure that your meaning has been understood. The alternative is being "word-minded," which usually results in the protest "I never thought you'd think I meant . . ." Recognize the responses your words can precipitate. If you anticipate these responses, then you will be doing your part to prevent mismatched meanings from interfering with effective communication.

## REFLECT ON THIS

### Which Do You Prefer?

Digital Vision./Digital Vision/Thinkstock

When members of various groups were asked what words they prefer that others use to describe them, the majorities of respondents expressed the following preferences: *older people* is preferred to *elderly* or *senior citizen*, *gay* and *lesbian* are preferred for men and women who have affectional orientations toward members of their own sex; *Black* or *African American* is preferred to *black* (*Black* and *African American* place the emphasis on cultural heritage, while *black* focuses on a color), *Latinx* is preferred to *Latino/a*, *Inuit* is preferred to *Eskimo*, *Muslim* is preferred to *Moslem*, *Asian* is preferred to *Oriental*, and *Native American* is preferred to *Indian*.

The reasons for these preferences vary. For example, the word *Muslim* is preferred to *Moslem* because in Arabic the word *Moslem* actually means "one who is evil and unjust," while the word *Muslim* means "one who submits to God." See if you can discover the rationales for the various groups' preferences for some terms over others.

Sources: See Paul Ortiz, *An African American and Latinx History of the United States*. Boston: Beacon Press, 2018.

See Yii-Ann Christine Chen, "Why Do People Say Muslim Now Instead of Moslem?" History News Network, July 8, 2002, http://hnn.us/articles/524.html.

## DON'T BE MISLED BY LABELS

How label-conscious are you? To what extent do you respond to labels themselves, rather than to what the labels represent?

At times, the words we use as labels help obscure reality. When we respond to a label rather than to what the label actually represents, we display what's known as **intensional orientation**. Intensionally oriented individuals are easily fooled by words and labels, and as a result, they fail to inspect what the labels represent. For example, perfume and cologne manufacturers and advertisers take advantage of our intensional tendencies by giving their products names such as Intimate and Obsession. They count on us to buy the products based on our desires—to become intimate with another or to be the object of another's obsession. In contrast, when we inspect whatever a label refers to instead of letting the label blind us, we exhibit what's known as **extensional orientation**. Extensionally oriented individuals refuse to be conned by words. When we confuse labels with reality, or words with things, we can make major misinterpretations.

# LANGUAGE AND RELATIONSHIPS: COMMUNICATION STYLE, WORDS, AND FEELINGS

Language plays an integral part in expressing social identity.[12] Our preferred speaking style tends to reflect our values and helps emphasize similarities and differences between us. For example, Japanese and Americans are likely to display contrasting communication styles. The qualities valued by the Japanese—reserve, formality, and silence—are discouraged by Americans, who generally prefer self-assertion, informality, and talkativeness. For Americans, a key function of speech is to prevent silence.[13] Unlike Americans, who typically use a direct conversational style, the Japanese tend to practice conversational indirectness. From the Japanese perspective, communication failures are the result of receiver deficiencies, not message deficiencies, even when the message contains imprecise and ambiguous words. Because of such culture-based differences, when Japanese and American people interact, there is a potential for tension and bad feeling.[14]

## ANALYZE THIS: HURTFUL WORDS

Consider the old nursery rhyme, "Sticks and stones may break my bones, but words will never harm me." In your opinion, can words do another person harm? Have you ever been harmed by another's words? Is there any difference between words that are harmful, those that are insensitive, and those that are hateful? Defend your position.

For Americans, social conversation helps establish and maintain friendships. Americans use talk to bring themselves and others together. As communication researcher Steve Duck observes, we talk our relationships into being.[15] Although the use of language serves an information function—it lets us get things done—it also helps us express our feelings about things and each other. In other words, the words we use to describe subjects or people also displays our attitudes toward them. We can, for example, call a person *homeless, displaced,* or a *bum.* Our words announce our attitudes. The words *mangy animal, adorable puppy, goofy pup,* and *vicious beast* may all refer to the same dog. Our description of the dog demonstrates our tendency "to snarl" (register disapproval) or "purr" (register approval). In actuality, when we use **snarl words** and **purr words**, we describe our preferences. We snarl and purr about people all the time, don't we?

Using social conversation, we talk our relationships into being.

In addition to facilitating the expression of feelings, language can be used to exclude or include others in a conversation. Groups of people who share a profession or a culture different from our own, for example, often engage in "in-group" discussions during which others may feel quite left out. In contrast, people who use more inclusive language enable everyone present to feel more of a connection to the conversation; they explain terms that may be confusing, translate foreign terms, and use analogies that make it possible for all involved to understand the content more readily.

We also use language to influence perceptions of power. For example, compare the following statements:

Um, could I talk to you for a second? I probably shouldn't mention this, and I'm not really sure it's your fault, but I'm kinda upset about the fact that you didn't meet with me at the restaurant like you were supposed to. Can you meet me tomorrow maybe? If you're free?

I'd like to talk to you. I waited for you at the restaurant and I'm upset that you didn't call when you realized you wouldn't be able to meet me as we planned. While I'm willing to set another date, you need to be more considerate of my time. Just let me know if you can't make the appointment. Okay?

The speaker in the second example sounds stronger, more in control, and more self-confident than the speaker in the first example, who comes across as weak, powerless, and certainly non-authoritative.

However, we must be careful not to confuse powerful speech with rude or profane speech. They are quite different. Imagine if the speaker had stated:

What's wrong with you? You kept me waiting at the restaurant without so much as a phone call. If you know what's good for you, you'll never do that again!

Effective wordsmiths state their feelings clearly without being rude or using profanities that could be offensive and damaging to a relationship.

We also enact the principles of **communication accommodation theory** during interactions with others.[16] This theory explains that we adjust our language patterns to reflect how we feel about another person. For example, when we feel positively about another person and want to show our interest in and desire to affiliate with him or her, we may adapt our speech style to match theirs. When done effectively, the result is **communication convergence**. By matching our vocabulary, speaking rate, and use of pauses to those of the other person, we build our relationship. For example, if you work in an environment where polite language is the norm, mirroring the congenial patterns of your boss and coworkers may enhance the feelings of connection between you and the group.[17]

The accommodation principle also works in reverse. When the goal is to stress our differences, we may revert to the strategy of **communication divergence**—that is, purposefully adopting a style of speaking that contrasts with the style of the person from whom we desire to distance ourselves. How have you used the strategies of communication convergence and divergence in your relationships?

# LANGUAGE CONVEYS AND REINFORCES ATTITUDES TOWARD CULTURE, GENDER, AND AGE

Language conveys social attitudes regarding culture, gender, and age. Let us explore how cultural and social contexts modify our use of words.

## CULTURESPEAK

Words help us share meaning. The more diverse our experiences, however, the more difficult it becomes to achieve mutual understanding.

### The Sapir–Whorf Hypothesis

One of the key, but disputed, theories concerning how language reflects culture is the **Sapir–Whorf hypothesis**, developed by the linguist Edward Sapir and his student Benjamin Lee Whorf, which states that language reveals social reality. According to Sapir,

> The real world is to a large extent unconsciously built upon the language habits of the group. No two languages are ever sufficiently similar to be considered as representing the same reality. The worlds in which different societies live are distinct worlds, not merely the same world with different labels attached.[18]

Some view the Sapir–Whorf hypothesis as an expression of **linguistic determinism**, which means that language shapes thinking. Others view it as an expression of **linguistic relativity**, which means that languages contain unique embedded elements such as a language's grammar. According to Sapir and Whorf, words are not neutral vehicles conveying meaning, but rather tools structuring our perception of reality and participating in the construction of our social world. As a result, not everyone speaks or thinks in the same way. For example, some languages have separate words for "blue" and "green," while others have one that means "sort of bluish, but kind of greenish too." Individuals whose language clearly distinguished between blue and green could better recall objects they saw a few days earlier that were either blue or green than were those whose language made no such differentiation.[19]

## TABLE 5.2  SAPIR–WHORF HYPOTHESIS

| ARE YOU A RELATIVIST, A DETERMINIST, OR A NONBELIEVER? | |
| --- | --- |
| **Relativist** | Language influences thought and feeling. |
| **Determinist** | Language conditions us to process experience. |
| **Nonbeliever** | Language does not influence thought. |

According to linguistic relativists, language influences both human thought and meaning. It mediates between the symbols and the ideas they represent.[20] In fact, Whorf states,

> We cut up and organize the spread and flow of events as we do largely because, through our mother tongue, we are parties to an agreement to do so, not because nature itself is segmented in exactly that way for all to see.[21]

From this perspective, language defines, rather than reports, experience. It influences how we think and how we perceive the world.

Those who are extreme advocates of the Sapir–Whorf hypothesis believe that we are "at the mercy of the particular language which has become the medium of expression" for our society.[22] Believing that language determines reality, they contend that language conditions users to process experience in a certain way. For example, the Hopi language has no concept of time as an objective entity. This, according to adherents of extreme Whorfianism, affects the Hopi conceptualization of the world. They claim that the way the Hopi rely on preparation, announcing events well in advance, shows a concept of continuous time, in contrast to the segmented time of Western societies.

Those who disagree with the premise of the Sapir–Whorf hypothesis contend that language does not influence thought. They point out that, although languages may differ in grammar and syntax, it is still feasible to translate meaning from one language to another. Furthermore, as Noam Chomsky observed, there are universals, deep grammatical structures that are common to all languages.[23]

Despite having its critics, the Sapir–Whorf hypothesis has influenced the way we conceive of language.[24] Even those who support the hypothesis only moderately believe that language does influence us by functioning as a barometer of cultural behavior and offering ways of perceiving and interpreting reality. We may study a culture by examining the words that the members of the culture use. In effect, the languages that groups of people use mirror their experiences. For example, if your talk abounds with words such as *text, tweet,* and *download,* receivers are able to learn something about what is important to you and what your culture is like.

## Reasoning Patterns and Expression Preferences

Language also reflects reasoning patterns and expression preferences. For example, people in Western cultures rely on inductive and deductive reasoning to make and understand an argument. Those in the Arab world rely on the expression of personal emotions. Because of these differences, Westerners may have difficulty locating the main idea in an Arab's message, and vice versa.[25] Arab speech is filled with repetitions that highlight an idea's importance. Its stress patterns often confuse

Western listeners, causing them to interpret messages as either aggressive or disinterested when they are intended as neither.[26] Likewise, whereas members of Asian cultures are apt to use language sparingly and carefully, preferring to keep their feelings to themselves in an effort to preserve social harmony, members of Spanish and Latin American cultures eagerly engage in conversation and are typically open and willing to share their feelings with others.[27] Thus, our culture influences how we use language.

According to researchers in the field of cultural neuroscience, culture shapes brain activity in addition to language use. They assert that the region of the brain called the medial prefrontal cortex represents the self. For example, when Americans think of the word *me*—their personal identity and traits—the medial prefrontal cortex is activated. For Chinese subjects, however, the same brain region is activated when subjects think of the word for *me* as well as the word for *mother*. Therefore, the research indicates that neural circuitry differs between those raised in cultures that conceive of the self as a part of a larger whole, such as the Chinese, and those raised in cultures that hold the self as autonomous and unique, such as Americans.[28]

### Language and Co-Cultures

We also need to understand how language functions within co-cultures. **Co-cultures** are groups of people living within a society but outside its mainstream or **dominant culture**. The language within a given co-culture will differ in some ways from that of the dominant culture, because it reflects a different reality, including differences in lifestyle, values, and behavior. The special vocabulary that a co-culture evolves, its **argot**, enables the members of the co-culture to develop both an identity and a sense of community. In time, some words developed within co-cultures begin to be used by the dominant culture. When this happens, members of the co-cultures often stop using them. Thus, argots undergo constant change.

Language is a part of identity. In fact, changing how you talk can influence how you think. Thus, sometimes in studying a new language you also open your mind to new ways of looking at the world.[29] The same is true of studying how members of different cultures use language.

## GENDERSPEAK

Language is a prime means of communicating cultural views of gender. Once we internalize the transmitted social prescriptions, we then enact them during our relationships. Language is not neutral, and it can both express and reinforce gender stereotypes and perceptions of power.

### TRY THIS

## Language–Gender Links

In your opinion, should we eliminate the use of gender-named hurricanes? Explain your answer. What might we name hurricanes instead of male and female names?

Consider the pairs of Hurricane names below. Which do you think would have higher wind speeds and why?

Alexandra/Alexander

Christina/Christopher

Gender stereotypes might be lurking anywhere. Research reveals that hurricanes with female names cause more deaths. Why? Because subjects judge hurricanes with male names as potentially more dangerous. As a result, they are more likely to heed warnings and evacuate when advised to do so.

Source: Robert M. Sapolsky, "Language Shapes Thoughts and Storm Preparations," *The Wall Street Journal,* April 25–26, 2015, p. C2.

## Language Can Diminish and Stereotype Women and Men

Language helps shape what we see as "normal," "appropriate," or an exception to the rule.[30] It can, for example, symbolize a devalued perception of women by presenting the experiences of men as the norm and those of women as departures from that standard. Consequently, although male generic language was once thought to be inclusive of both women and men, research has revealed that many of us interpreted male generics as including men but excluding women.[31] While they have faded from common usage, male generic terms such as *mankind, businessman,* and *congressman* caused our culture to perceive men as more prominent and numerous than women. To combat such perceptions, many organizations and individuals have adopted policies of avoiding the use of male generics and other sexist and non-gender-neutral language.

Similarly, it used to be common to refer to women as *girls,* while refraining from calling men *boys,* leading many to perceive women as childlike. In like fashion, the highlighting of a person's sex, referred to as **spotlighting**, also reinforced gender norms. Although we rarely hear combinations such as *male lawyer* or *female teacher, woman firefighter* and *male nurse* remain widely used. Eliminating spotlighting should make it easier to revise gender perceptions.

Language also distinguishes between men and women when our words define them differently. We tend to define men by their independence, activities, status, and accomplishments. We more often define women by their appearance and relationships. Defining a person by physical qualities or appearance diminishes that person's achievements. Definitional biases reinforce the idea of women as decorative accessories whose claim to fame is how they look and the idea of men as capable and qualified individuals whose claim to fame is how they perform.

On the other hand, some have asserted that words also are used to emasculate men by promoting a cartoonish idea of them. They point to the new words invented to describe men's fashion as examples: *manties* for male undergarments and *manbag* or *murse* for a men's version of the purse or pocketbook.[32] How do you feel about these terms?

## Language Can Convey Gendered Feelings About Power

In general, men and women use language to accomplish different goals.[33] Typically, men use it to achieve something or assert themselves, whereas women use it to create and sustain relationships. Men use language to attract and keep an audience, whereas women use it to indicate they're paying attention. Men use language to compete; women, to collaborate. For women, talk is at the very core of a relationship, not a means to achieve conversational dominance.[34]

Because women are more likely than men to exhibit an affiliative, or socially based and mutual, orientation, they are less likely to use words to assert status. Unlike most men, who express ideas firmly and then wait to see if someone challenges them, many women prefer to use language to foster connection, gain support, and display understanding. Women are more likely to interpret challenges to their ideas as personal attacks. Since women are socialized to weigh others' opinions, they also are apt to ask others for their ideas before rendering decisions. Whereas men interpret questions as information requests, women characteristically use questions to keep conversations going. Should a man provide the requested information, the woman typically asks another question, which usually succeeds in frustrating the man. Why is this? When neither understands the other's behavior, the likely result is frustration.[35]

The sensitivity women display to others' reactions probably explains their unobtrusive and smoothing style. In comparison with men, women have a lower threshold for identifying behavior as offensive. This also accounts for why women's speech is often labeled as deferential, as well as why women are prone to offering ritual apologies—saying "I'm sorry" on numerous occasions every day.[36]

Differences in male and female orientations result in differences in the structure of utterances. Tentative phrases such as *I guess* and *I wonder if* characterize the speech patterns of women but not those of men. Unlike men, women frequently turn their statements into questions. Thus, a woman might ask, "Don't you believe it would be more effective to put this paragraph in the introduction rather than in the conclusion?" In contrast, a man would deliver a more definitive statement: "It would be more effective to put this paragraph in the introduction rather than in the conclusion."[37]

According to linguist Robin Lakoff, unlike most men, women don't lay claim to their utterances.[38] Additionally, women's tendency to add "tag questions" to their comments contributes to their being perceived as more tentative. While a woman may say, "Mel is right, isn't she?" men usually make such statements minus the "isn't she" question tags. Women also reinforce their reputation for tentativeness by prefacing utterances with phrases such as "This probably isn't important, but . . ." Some researchers contend that such habits further weaken the impact of the messages women send, while others suggest that the tentativeness noted in women's speech is not a sign of powerlessness, but rather reveals their desire to keep conversation open and inclusive.[39]

Linguist Deborah Tannen has coined the term **genderlect** to describe the different languages that men and women use.[40] According to Tannen, the genderlect that women hear and speak is one of connection and intimacy, of seeking to preserve relationships. Men, in contrast, speak and hear a language of status and independence. Tannen contends that women use "rapport talk" (using conversation as a means of emotional validation and connection), while men use "report talk" (getting to the heart of the matter—here's what happened and why).[41]

Age can account for variations in language use.

## AGE AND LANGUAGE VARIATION

Just as gender and culture help account for language use variations, so does age. People who grew up in different generations may experience more difficulty understanding each other than people who grew up in the same generation. Significant age differences may make individuals more prone to misunderstanding one another or to misperceiving what others are telling them.[42]

Research also reveals that young people tend to adjust their language when interacting with older people, but sometimes, they over-accommodate. Reacting on the basis of their stereotype of older people, younger people may consciously alter their word choices, making them simpler and more concrete, believing erroneously that older people have a diminished capacity for conversation. Those who are younger also are likely to think they ought to speak more slowly and in a more nurturing tone when conversing with an older person. Because younger people have the tendency to speak to the elderly as if they are incompetent, the older person may soon *feel* incompetent, which contributes to both individuals, young and old, feeling unfulfilled by their interactions.[43]

Of course, individual accommodations are sometimes necessary, but even if an older person has a hearing loss, this does not reflect diminished mental ability. To avoid interacting with an older person in a way he or she could find demeaning, young people should treat people of any age group as individuals rather than as members of a social category.

# REFLECT ON THIS

## The Muted Group

Jupiterimages/Comstock/Thinkstock

According to muted group theory, the group that is dominant in a social hierarchy uses language to shape societal perceptions. As a consequence, those who have less power can find themselves repressed by language. For all practical purposes, their voices are muted.

Those who control language use also are able to control thought and behavior. For example, by calling a law that includes significant limits on individual freedoms the Patriot Act, Congress succeeded in silencing those who questioned the act's contents by implying that non-supporters were unpatriotic.

1. In what ways, if any, have authorities who have more power than you used language to attempt to mute your voice, and to what extent have you done the same to people whom you perceive to have less power than you?

2. How should we react when someone in power defines a situation as a means of silencing any opposition?

Sources: See, for example, Cheris Kramarae, "Classified Information: Race, Class, and (Always) Gender," in Julia T. Wood, ed., *Gendered Relationships,* Mountain View, CA: Mayfield, 1996, pp. 20–38; and Cheris Kramarae, *Women and Men Speaking: Frameworks for Analysis,* Rowley, MA: Newbury House, 1981.

See, for example, Ann Burnett, Jody L. Mattern, Liliana L. Herakova, David H. Kahl, Clay Tobola, and Susan E. Bornsen, "Communicating/Muting Date Rape: A Co-cultural Theoretical Analysis of Communication Factors Related to Rape Culture on a College Campus," *Journal of Applied Communication Research,* 37, 2009, pp. 465–485; and Cheris Kramarae, "Muted Group Theory and Communication: Asking Dangerous Questions," *Women and Language,* 28:2, 2005, pp. 55–61.

# LANGUAGE, MEDIA, AND TECHNOLOGY

As we have seen, how we use language reveals both our attitudes toward and our assessments of the subjects of our discussions and each other. This practice also is reflected in countless media examples.

## TRY THIS

### How Would You Reengineer a Media Image?

Describe a media representation that you find potentially degrading to you or the members of a specific group.

1. In your opinion, should we be holding the media more accountable for their representations of people of color and various other groups, such as gays, the elderly, and the physically challenged? Explain.

2. If the representations the media offer us were reengineered in an effort to deliberately eradicate stereotypical portrayals, how do you imagine that would affect our daily interactions?

## EXPERIENCING MEDIA

Reflecting societal judgments of what is important for each sex, media coverage of female politicians and athletes often contains references to their physical appearance, whereas stories about their male counterparts are more likely to stress their accomplishments rather than their hair, dress, weight, or physical appeal.[44] We also see societal judgments affecting story placement, with stories about women appearing more often in the lifestyle pages rather the front pages of newspapers.[45] And although strides have been made, even when women have careers as physicians or lawyers, they are apt to be portrayed in stereotypical ways in the media and defined by their marital and familial status. Unfortunately, such practices can increase sexism.

## EXPERIENCING TECHNOLOGY

Are we in danger of becoming a wordless society? Sometimes people choose to communicate using only GIFs—video loops often lasting only a few seconds. GIFs are emotion heavy and fact light; we don't need to think about the cute image of a cat dancing. Sending sentences composed of GIFs constitutes a new visual language, one we can use to communicate our feelings (but not necessarily our thoughts).[46]

More typically, when interacting online, we use both words and pictures to encode our on-screen identities. The particular words and pictures we use, as well the actual or fabricated stories we share about who we are communicates our digital identity, shaping our online presence. Together, personae interact with each other, forging a collective culture.[47] We tend to separate ourselves from others online based on our needs and interests, affiliating ourselves with those belonging to communities reflective of our mutual concerns.

Because young people are addressing issues of race, class, and gender online, they likely reveal their personal struggles, just as they would offline—only not necessarily to their parents.[48] As in face-to-face conversation, the use of inflammatory, insulting, imprecise, or discriminatory language can lead to problems online. What we write, text, or tweet in haste or in anger may reach a wider audience and have more influence than imagined, causing potentially serious consequences. For example, when a teacher posted on her Facebook page that she was "a warden for future criminals," the school board of her district scheduled a hearing to consider whether to revoke her tenure.[49] When online, we are apt to share our thoughts without displaying concern for others' feelings and more likely to comment *about* one another than to talk *with* one another. Gossip, sexist and homophobic remarks, trash talk, and hate speech are all too common in the digital domain—posted for all to read, no longer merely whispered by one person to another. Particularly virulent hate speech messages have been directed at immigrants and women. During the "Gamergate" controversy, for instance, game developer Zoe Quinn was inundated with hateful and intimidating postings made via Twitter and social networking sites including threats to rape and murder her.[50]

Some people display more enthusiasm when communicating online than they do in face-to-face interactions. Do you?

Americans send more than a trillion text messages every year.[51] Some believe that the prevalence of texting is causing us to speak in shorter sentences and has the potential to wipe out spoken conversation.[52] Others believe that our use of text-speak is leading us to speak in acronyms, a form of private language.[53] Still others contend that texting is destroying our ability to use grammar correctly, while others counter that this is not the case, noting that written language is merely becoming more flexible.[54] There has been interest in the new grammar springing up around texting that helps add nuance to the text messages we send. Even the presence or absence of a simple period communicates a subtext of whether a conversation via text is over, or open for additional comments.[55]

How do your online interactions differ from those occurring face-to-face? Some report that they display more enthusiasm during online interactions. Online speech can have a breathless, yet emphatic feel to it—as if users are jumping up and down to capture their receivers' attention.[56]

Women's use of highly expressive language online projects their desire for connection. While men post about sports games and politics, women use social media more like a public diary, revealing personal bits of their lives, such as relating a funny thing a boyfriend just did or posting questions about their appearance.[57]

# GAINING COMMUNICATION COMPETENCE: MAKING YOUR WORDS WORK

Taking language for granted is dangerous. With this in mind, what can you do to master meaning and improve your relationships? Answering the following questions will help you learn to make your words work.

## ARE MY WORDS CLEAR?

Far too often we understand the words we are using, but others do not. If we choose words with the individual we are interacting with in mind, that person will be more apt to respond as we had hoped. Ask yourself the following questions when considering your words' clarity:

- Are the words I am using reflective of the education level of the person with whom I am interacting?
- Is this person familiar with any technical language (jargon) or argot I might use with members of my particular co-culture?

## ARE MY WORDS APPROPRIATE?

Our word choice should change as the situation we are in changes and as the individual with whom we are interacting changes. For example, we might use slang when speaking with friends, but probably not with a professor. Ask yourself the following questions when assessing the appropriateness of your word choice:

- Will my receiver find my words offensive?
- Am I using the right words in the right place at the right time?

## DO I USE CONCRETE WORDS?

Our words are concrete when they enable us to describe a feeling, an event, or a circumstance unambiguously. When we eliminate vague and confusing words from our conversation and substitute more exact ones, we are able to shape the meaning we transmit to others more effectively. Ask yourself the following questions when evaluating the concreteness of your expression:

- Do my words enable my receiver to formulate a clear picture of my thoughts?
- Do my words communicate my intended feelings?

## DO MY WORDS SPEAK TO THE OTHER PERSON AND REFLECT THE CONTEXT?

Many people use words differently than you do. When this occurs, remind yourself that their experiences may have led them to develop different points of view or different ways of thinking. When you are sensitive to the person and the context, you increase your chances of "talking the same language."

Keep in mind that the meaning of a word can change from one time period to another and from one culture to another. In the 1970s, when the Ford Motor Company tried to sell its car the Pinto in Brazil, it failed miserably—at least in part because in Brazilian slang the word *pinto* means "tiny male genitals."[58] We all use words, just not necessarily in the same ways.

## DO I SHARE "TO ME" MEANING?

Words can confuse or clarify, conceal or reveal meaning. When you take time to share your perception of the "to me" nature of language, you let another person know that you are aware that he or she may not be processing experience the same way you are. That person then also becomes more willing to share his or her "to me" perceptions with you.

You share "to me" meanings by eliminating the accusatory "you" from your vocabulary. By using the word *I* in place of *you,* you describe your own feelings and thoughts instead of berating others for theirs. For example, instead of telling a friend, "You are selfish. You didn't think about how I would feel when you asked Karen to go shopping with you but not me," you say, "I feel like I didn't matter when you asked Karen to go shopping with you but not me."

By sharing your "to me" meanings, you practice dual perspective talking. Once you acknowledge that everyone has a "to me" meaning and their own feelings and thoughts, you take responsibility for yourself. We do not need to give up our "to me" perspective to respect and understand the perspectives of others. Using "I" or "to me" language decreases the defensiveness of others, opens the door to dialogue, and empowers the self.

## DO I RESPECT UNIQUENESS?

No two people, events, or things are exactly alike. Whenever we make a blanket judgment about others, such as "Lawyers are liars," we are thinking in generalities and ignoring differences. Because expecting a behavior can help to precipitate the behavior, we must consciously avoid forming fixed mental pictures of anyone or any group. When we form a fixed mental picture, we fail to notice the unique characteristics that distinguish one person or group from another.

What can you do to ensure you look beyond the category? Indexing generalizations can prevent you from using language to conceal important distinctions between people. When we index generalizations, we acknowledge individual differences within a group. For example, all professors are not alike: Professor Orion is different from Professor Berger, who is different from Professor Sanchez, and so on. An action as simple as this can help you avoid the problems that stereotyping encourages.

## DO I LOOK FOR GROWTH?

People and situations change. We are constantly in the process of becoming. Experiences change us. Just as people are not fixed in time, neither are we or our ideas.

Take the opportunity to allow your words to reflect this growth. Demonstrating such flexibility will facilitate more effective interpersonal communication and relationships. Keep in mind that when you make general or static evaluations of others and situations, you deny the reality of change. Static evaluations limit interpersonal effectiveness by preventing you from acknowledging the changes in people and situations.

Check yourself periodically to see if you are holding on to any static evaluations about people or situations that are no longer valid. Dating your observations will remind you that nearly everything—even the meanings of words and our interpretations and reactions to them—changes with time.

## CONNECT THE CASE

## The Case of the Wounding Words

Like many college students, Aiden gave little thought to how his words affected others. He was shocked to discover that his shouting a few words and then tweeting about it could actually precipitate demonstrations on and off campus. What words had Aiden shouted and tweeted?

One day, when he was disturbed by a group of African American students who in his opinion were socializing much too loudly beneath his window, Aiden had yelled, "Shut up, you water buffalo!" He then tweeted about how annoyed he was. Though Aiden later explained that he had previously attended a yeshiva where the Hebrew term for "water buffalo" was slang for "foolish person," he was threatened with prosecution for racial harassment. Eventually, persecuted by the press, the students who had been outside Aiden's window dropped their charge against him, and the case died down.

### Answer the following questions:

1. Are some words so racist or sexist that no one should use them? Explain your stance with reasons.

2. To what extent, and in what ways if any, can the words one person uses to describe another person change our views of both the person using the words and the person the words describe?

3. If you were a friend of Aiden, what advice would you offer?

4. Are you in favor of political correctness? If so, why, and if not, why not?

Note: This case is based on the 1993 racial harassment case of Eden Jacobowitz. See Scott Lanman, "Jacobowitz Settles 'Water Buffalo' Lawsuit," *Daily Pennsylvanian,* September 8, 1997, http://www .thedp.com/index.php/article/1997/09/jacobowitz_settles_water_buffalo_lawsuit.

# REVIEW THIS

## CHAPTER SUMMARY

**1. Define language, explaining its uses and distinguishing among semantic, syntactic, and pragmatic codes.** □

Language is a system of symbols used by a group of people to communicate. We use language to facilitate social contact, the sharing of perceptions, and the negotiation of meaning. The semantic code consists of our agreed-upon uses of symbols or words. The syntactic code consists of the rules that guide our use of words. The pragmatic code involves the coordination and cooperation necessary to derive meaning.

**2. Explain the triangle of meaning.** □

Ogden and Richards's triangle of meaning illustrates the relationships that exist among words, things, and thoughts. The model specifies that there is no direct connection between a symbol and its referent, underscoring the fact that the word is not the thing, and that meaning exists in thoughts, not in words or things.

**3. Identify ways to remove semantic barriers.** □

Semantic barriers complicate the sharing of meaning. We need to identify them, recognize when they are present, and take steps to facilitate—not mask— meaning transference. Understanding the difference between denotative and connotative meaning, as well as how time and place affect meaning facilitates this.

**4. Discuss the effects of word walls, euphemisms, emotive language, polarizing words, politically correct language, bypassing, and intensional orientation.** □

When we build a word wall, we use words in a way that impedes understanding and the sharing of meaning. A euphemism masks a communicator's meaning by substituting polite or inoffensive language for blunt, direct language. Emotive language editorializes our feelings. Polarizing language describes the world in extremes. Language that is politically correct is sensitive to the listener's interpretation. Bypassing occurs when we think we understand each other but miss each other's meaning. When we respond to a label rather than to what the label represents, we display intensional as opposed to extensional orientation.

**5. Explain how language affects relationships.** □

The language we use reflects our values, helping to emphasize the similarities and differences between us, including the nature of our conversations, how we express feelings, and whether our use of words enhances or detracts from our power.

**6. Identify how language conveys and reinforce attitudes toward culture, gender, and age.** □

Language exerts a powerful influence on our social identity and perceptions of one another. The language we use to describe one another can cause stereotypes to persist or can foster their eradication.

· · · · · · · · · · · · · · · · · · · · · · · · · · ·

7. **Discuss the interface between language and media and technology.** ☐

The types of words used to describe people in print, broadcast, and cable media and on the Internet reflect societal judgments of worth and importance.

· · · · · · · · · · · · · · · · · · · · · · · · · · ·

8. **Take steps to use language more effectively.** ☐

To use language more effectively, we need to ensure that our words are clear, appropriate, and as concrete as possible. We also need to work our way carefully and sensitively through the world of words, be committed to sharing meaning, respect the uniqueness of every individual, and seek opportunities for growth.

· · · · · · · · · · · · · · · · · · · · · · · · · · ·

## CHECK YOUR UNDERSTANDING

1. Can you provide an example that demonstrates how the triangle of meaning works? (See page 126.)

2. Can you provide an example of how time and place influence word choice? Whom do you believe should be held accountable when problems in understanding occur because of time and place differences? (See page 127.)

3. Can you give an example of a time when the use of euphemisms affected one of your relationships? In what ways does masking meaning complicate things?

What about the use of polarizing language or displaying an intensional versus extensional orientation? (See pages 129–131.)

4. Can you create a scenario illustrating how gender and/or culture affect your use of language? Can you create another showing how media and/or technology affect your use of language? (See pages 136–141; and pages 142–144.)

5. Can you put into action a plan to improve your command of words? (See pages 144–146.)

## KEY TERMS

Get the tools you need to sharpen your study skills. **SAGE edge** offers a robust online environment featuring an impressive array of free tools and resources. Access practice quizzes, eFlashcards, video, and multimedia at **edge.sagepub.com/gambleicp**.

6

# Nonverbal Communication

## Learning Objectives

### AFTER COMPLETING THIS CHAPTER, YOU SHOULD BE ABLE TO

1. Define nonverbal communication, explain its metacommunicative nature, and discuss its functions and characteristics

2. Define and distinguish among the following kinds of nonverbal messages: kinesics, paralanguage, proxemics, haptics, artifactual communication and appearance, olfactics, color, and chronemics

3. Discuss culture's influence on nonverbal behavior

4. Compare and contrast the nonverbal communication styles of men and women

5. Describe how the media and technology influence use of nonverbal messages

6. Identify steps you can take to improve your nonverbal effectiveness

> Beware of people whose bellies do not move when they laugh.
>
> —Chinese Proverb

. . . . . . . . . . . . . . . . . . . . . . . . . . . . . . . . . . . . . . . . . . . . . . . . . . . . . . . . . . . . . . . . .

In the digital domain, video and audio communication rule. Sound and images are fast becoming our universal language, influencing our understanding of each other and the world.[1] The film industry has a long history of relying on visual communication. In 2012, The Academy Award winner for Best Picture was *The Artist*, a mostly silent black-and-white film. Most of the communication occurring in the movie was nonverbal. The film's starring actress, Bérénice Bejo, commented, "We give ourselves so much pressure with words. I like it very much that our intention is not conveyed solely through dialogue but by the body, the walk, the attitude, the precision of each gesture."[2]

The actors did not need to use spoken words to make their characters' messages clear. By observing how the actors moved, by paying attention to their facial expressions, by looking at how they sat and adjusted their heads, we understood them and connected with them emotionally. We do this in our daily lives too.

Consider, for example, what these descriptive phrases have in common:

*The twinkle in his eye. The edge in her voice. The knowing look of their smiles. The confidence in her walk. Your dress. How closely you stand to another.*

Each of the phrases highlights a clue to a person's attitudes, feelings, and personality. Despite the presence of such cues, too often we remain unaware of the messages our bodies, our voices, or the space around us send to others. ■

## WHAT DO YOU KNOW?

Before continuing your reading of this chapter, which of the following five statements do you believe to be true, and which do you believe to be false?

1. You are a message.                                                              T       F
2. Words used, not nonverbal cues, are more likely to reveal the telling of a lie.   T       F
3. Suspicious people are better at spotting deception.                              T       F
4. Your hands reveal more about your feelings than does your face.                  T       F
5. Some women purposefully make their teeth crooked.                                T       F

Read the chapter to discover if you're right or if you've made any erroneous assumptions.

ANSWERS: 1. T; 2. F; 3. T; 4. F; 5. T

In this chapter, we transition from focusing on *what* we say to *how* we say it, for another's words on their own rarely lead to our wanting to begin, continue, or end a relationship. By taking time to better appreciate that nonverbal messages tell more, we take another step forward in expanding our ability to understand person-to-person interaction.[3]

# DEFINING NONVERBAL COMMUNICATION

Interpersonal effectiveness depends on more than words. It depends on the use and understanding of nonverbal messages. We become the message, with our nonverbal cues announcing our state of mind, expectations, and sense of self. Our entire being chatters incessantly, revealing what we really feel and think.

Nonverbal communication is expressed through nonlinguistic means. It is the actions or attributes of humans, including their appearance, use of objects, sound, time, smell, and space, that have socially shared significance and stimulate meaning in others.

## THE NATURE OF METACOMMUNICATION

We send nonverbal messages deliberately or accidentally with the meaning attributed to them dependent on others' interpretations. Such messages fulfill metacommunicative functions, meaning they communicate about communication, clarifying both the meaning of our words and the nature of our relationship. In fact, researchers conclude that nonverbal cues carry approximately two-thirds of a message's communicative value. Even when used independently of words, as long as an observer derives meaning from them, nonverbal messages speak volumes. Of course, the amount of information they convey varies according to their clarity, and how receptive and perceptive the receiver is. Based on interpretations of our nonverbal cues, others may decide if they like us, trust us, will or won't listen to our ideas, or want to sustain a relationship. The ability to understand and respond to nonverbal messages helps unlock meaning's door.

## THE FUNCTIONS AND CHARACTERISTICS OF NONVERBAL COMMUNICATION

With the wink of an eye, a certain facial expression, voice tone, bodily movement, use of space, or touch, we can change the meaning of our words. As our ability to use and interpret nonverbal behavior and contextual cues improves, so will our understanding of interpersonal relationships. Let's see how this works. What do you make of these examples?

- The woman who says, "I love you," to her spouse while hugging him and smothering him with kisses.

- The child whose eyes are downcast and shoulders are rounded as she says, "I'm sorry for breaking the vase."

- The supervisor who, when asked a question by an employee, leans forward with a hand cupped behind one ear.

Each message contains nonverbal cues revealing a person's feelings. These cues are integral to communication, because as the preceding situations illustrate, they may (1) contradict words, (2) emphasize or underscore words, (3) regulate words' flow, (4) complement words, or (5) substitute for or take the place of spoken words (See Table 6.1). Whereas words are best at relaying

## TABLE 6.1  FUNCTIONS OF NONVERBAL COMMUNICATION

| FUNCTION | EXAMPLE |
|---|---|
| Contradicting | Your face is contorted into a grimace. Your eyes are narrowed and eyebrows furrowed. Yet, you are yelling, "I am not upset!" Your nonverbal cues negate your words, creating a mixed message. |
| Emphasizing | You wave your finger accusingly and raise your voice to demonstrate your anger as you say, "It is your fault, not mine." Your behavior reinforces your words. |
| Regulating | After explaining your opinion, you raise and then lower your intonation as you say, "And that's why I feel the way I do." This, together with your silence, signals you are finished speaking and another person may comment. Your behavior establishes turn-taking and influences the flow of verbal interaction. |
| Complementing | Your head is bowed and your body posture is slouched as your boss tells you how unhappy she is with your job performance. Your nonverbal cues reinforce your regret and help convey your attitude toward your boss. |
| Substituting | You run into a friend who asks, "So, how do you like your new job?" You just roll your eyes, using nonverbal cues in place of words. |

We rely on nonverbal cues to emphasize spoken words.

We use nonverbal cues to signal our attraction for another person.

thoughts or ideas, nonverbal cues are best at conveying information about relational matters such as liking, respect, and social control. To be sure, the meaning of neither verbal nor nonverbal messages should be interpreted without carefully considering the other.

## All Nonverbal Behavior Has Message Value

While we can stop speaking, it is impossible for us to stop behaving. Behavior, whether intentional or unintentional, is ongoing. As long as someone is aware of your presence and is there to decode your nonverbal communication, it is impossible for you not to communicate. Even if you turn your back on the observer, you are communicating. With this in mind, if someone were to enter the space in which you are now reading, what messages might they derive from your nonverbal demeanor? Are you seated at a desk or reclining on a bed? What does your face suggest regarding your level of interest and degree of understanding?

## Nonverbal Communication Is Ambiguous

What we communicate may be ambiguous and subject to misinterpretation. One nonverbal cue can trigger a variety of meanings. For example, wearing jeans can be symbolic of a relaxed mode of dress or construed as a statement of support for the gay community, as when LGBT organizations surprise blue jean wearers by posting signs that say, "Wear jeans if you advocate gay rights."

All nonverbal behavior should be interpreted within a specific context. There could be any number of reasons why a person looks at a watch, coughs, or rubs his or her eyes.

## Nonverbal Communication Is Predominantly Relational

Many find it easier to communicate emotions and feelings nonverbally. We convey liking, attraction, anger, and respect for authority nonverbally. In fact, our primary means of revealing our inner states is through nonverbal communication. For example, we usually look to the face to assess emotional state. We look to the mouth to evaluate contempt. We look to the eyes to evaluate dominance and competence. We base our judgments of confidence and relationship closeness on our reading of gestures and posture, and we listen to the voice to help us evaluate both assertiveness and self-confidence.

## Nonverbal Communication Can Be Unintentional

Sometimes we're unaware of the nonverbal cues we send, leading us inadvertently to reveal information we'd rather conceal. Without intending it, our nonverbal messages let others know how we feel about ourselves and about them. As we take control of our nonverbal messages, their informational value may decrease. In effect, a conscious intention to manage the impression we convey means that we will try to communicate messages that are in our own best interest.

## Nonverbal Behavior May Reveal Deception

When a person says one thing but means another, the person's behavior contradicts his or her words. Under most circumstances, when there's a discrepancy between verbal and nonverbal messages, researchers advise that you

Transportation Security Administration agents are trained to pick up signs of deception.

believe the nonverbal cues, which are more difficult to fake.[4] Clues to this deception, known as leakage, can be detected in changes in facial or vocal expression, gestures, or slips of the tongue.[5] In fact, once strong emotions are aroused, these changes may occur automatically, with our words, body, and voice betraying us by thwarting our attempts to conceal them.

According to David Buller and Judee Burgoon's research on deception, we make poor lie detectors. Many liars, it seems, strategically monitor and control their deceptive displays giving us only a 60 percent chance of being able to identify when someone is lying to us.[6] In fact, our ability to spot the deception depends on how suspicious we are.

Psychologist Paul Ekman, however, believes that with training, it is possible for us to become more skilled at detecting dissemblers. Ekman and his co-researcher, Wallace Friesen, identify 43 muscular movements that we are capable of making with our face. They also identify more than 3,000 facial expressions that have meaning, compiling them into the **Facial Action Coding System**, a taxonomy of facial expressions used to interpret emotions and detect deception. Ekman and Friesen have worked for the Central Intelligence Agency, the Federal Bureau of Investigation, and more recently Homeland Security to create experimental scenarios for studying deception intended to help their agents correctly identify untruths.[7] Paul Ekman's work was the subject of the television program *Lie to Me* that first aired in 2009 and for which he served as a consultant.

Theatrical and media performances demonstrate how possible it is for skilled communicators to control nonverbal cues, thereby persuading audience members to suspend their disbelief and accept the façade. Yet most of us don't spend weeks, days, or hours rehearsing for our daily encounters. Nevertheless, when interacting with another, sometimes we may wish to misrepresent our real feelings or intentions, perhaps by masking a facial expression so that we do not insult or embarrass the other person. In general, we are more successful at such deceptions if the other person trusts us. The more a person plans and rehearses a deceptive message, the more confident the person is, and the less guilty the person feels about the deception itself, the less likely it is that others will suspect or uncover the lie.

If we are watchful, however, we can improve our ability to detect deception. Unskilled liars leak clues.[8] It may be a change in facial expression, a shift in posture, or other leaked nonverbal cue that gives them away (See Table 6.2).

**TABLE 6.2 NONVERBAL CLUES TO DECEPTION**

| WHEN TELLING A LIE, YOU ARE MORE APT TO | YOUR LIE IS MORE APT TO BE DISCOVERED IF YOU |
|---|---|
| Smile falsely, using fewer facial muscles than usual | Intentionally want to conceal your emotions |
| Blink more frequently | Feel intensely about concealing the information |
| Have dilated pupils | Feel guilty |
| Rub your hands or arms together | Are unfulfilled by lying |
| Scratch the side of your nose | Are unprepared and unrehearsed |
| Cover your mouth | |
| Shift body posture frequently | |
| Articulate words more carefully | |
| Speak more slowly | |
| Say less than you otherwise would | |
| Exhibit speech that contains more errors and/or hesitation than is typical for you | |
| Raise your pitch | |
| Deliver a mixed message | |

Sources: Adapted from R. G. Riggio and H. S. Freeman, "Individual Differences and Cues to Deception," *Journal of Personality and Social Psychology,* 45, 1983, pp. 899–915; and Paul Ekman and Mark G. Frank, "Lies That Fail," in Michael Lewis and Carolyn Saarni, eds., *Lying and Deception in Everyday Life*, New York: Guilford Press, 1993, pp. 184–200.

## TRY THIS

## It's Not Just What You Say . . .

Can you detect a lie? Behavioral slipups sometimes betray us. For example, if a person is trying to communicate an aura of confidence, but his or her foot shakes uncontrollably, others may determine that the person is actually anxious or uptight.

1. Think of a time a friend or coworker's behavior contradicted what she said. What specific behavior(s) exhibited by the person leaked his or her true feelings?

2. Think of the last time you interacted with someone you thought was telling you the truth but whom you now know was lying to you. What was it about this person's behavior that initially caused you to believe that he was being truthful? Now, looking back, how many of the following nonverbal clues to deception do you recall the person exhibiting during your interaction?

   • Pausing

   • Hesitations

- Rapid speaking rate
- Self-adaptors, such as touching the face and body
- Object-adaptors, such as touching to playing with objects
- Deficient eye contact
- Averted gazes
- Excessive blinking
- Pupil dilation
- Masked Smiles

3. When have you attempted to use nonverbal messages to conceal your actual intentions or feelings? Were you successful? If you were, what do you attribute your success to? If not, why not?

# READING NONVERBAL MESSAGES

To improve our ability to read another person, we explore eight nonverbal message categories: (1) kinesics, (2) paralinguistics, (3) proxemics, (4) haptics, (5) olfactics, (6) artifacts and appearance, (7) color, and (8) chronemics (see Table 6.3). Although for purposes of examination we will discuss each category separately, these behaviors don't occur in isolation. Instead, they interact with each other, whether reinforcing or diminishing the impact of the perceived cues.

## TABLE 6.3  TYPES OF NONVERBAL CUES

| MESSAGES ARE SENT BY | |
| --- | --- |
| Kinesics | Facial expressions, gestures, eye movement, posture, rate of walk |
| Paralinguistics | How words are spoken, variations in the voice |
| Proxemics | How space and distance are used |
| Haptics | Different types of touching |
| Clothing and artifacts | Appearance, style |
| Color | Variations in clothing and environmental colors |
| Chronemics | Using time to communicate |

## KINESICS

Kinesics is the study of human body motion. It includes such variables as facial expression, eye movement, gestures, posture, and walking speed. Valuable communicator information is contained in the look on your face, whether you stare or avert your gaze, whether your shoulders are straight or drooped, whether your lips are curved in a smile or signal contempt with a sneer, and whether your gait suggests eagerness or anxiety.

## Face and Eye Talk

Picture yourself in the following scenario: Your significant other has had an operation. You are meeting with the doctor to discuss the prognosis. You search the doctor's face, looking for clues. Almost immediately, the face of the doctor could cause you to cry, put you at ease, or frighten you.

**The Face.** The face is the main channel we use to decipher another's feelings.[9] Faces talk. It is wise to depend on facial cues to facilitate person-to-person interaction.

What do faces reveal? Faces tell us many things, including

- Whether parties to an interaction find it pleasant or unpleasant
- How interested an individual is in sustaining or terminating contact
- The degree of involvement of the parties
- Whether responses during contact are spontaneous or controlled
- The extent to which messages are understood and shared

The face is also the prime communicator of emotion. Our ability to read the emotions depicted in facial expressions determines whether we will be able to respond appropriately to others' feelings.

In general, being able to read another's face increases with familiarity, an understanding of the communication context, and an awareness of behavioral norms. Not everyone is good at it. Deficiency in interpreting facial cues of teachers and classmates, for example, may even be a factor in unpopularity and poor grades. Psychologist Stephen Nowicki notes, "Because they are unaware of the messages they are sending, or misinterpreting how other children are feeling, unpopular children may not even realize that they are initiating many of the negative reactions they receive from their peers."[10]

Since they are the most visible and reliable means we have, we also use facial features to identify others and distinguish one person from another.[11] Just as security analysts use faces to identify potential terrorists, crime victims describe suspects' faces for police artists to draw, parents of missing children describe their children's faces to authorities, and relatives, friends, and acquaintances describe your facial features to others. Facial recognition software appears to have a glitch, however. Good at identifying Caucasian faces, it is error prone when identifying the faces of darker-skinned subjects. In part, this is attributed to a lack of diversity in the Artificial Intelligence community.[12]

Facial appearance influences judgments of your physical attractiveness, approachability,[13] and dominance,[14] which in turn influences how your messages, both verbal and nonverbal, are received. We speak of a baby face, a face as cold as ice, a face as strong as a bulldog's, and so on. What words would you use to describe your face, a friend's face, or the face of your significant other?

**The Eyes.** *Shifty eyes. Goo-goo eyes. The evil eye. Eye to eye.* Eye behaviors are a key part of interpersonal communication, as we use our eyes to establish, maintain, and terminate contact. As with all nonverbal cues, the messages we send with our eyes may be interpreted in a variety of ways, but in general they serve three central functions:

1. Eyes reveal the extent of interest and emotional involvement.

2. Eyes influence judgments of persuasiveness and perceptions of dominance or submissiveness.

3. Eyes regulate person-to-person interaction.

The pupils of our eyes are a reliable emotion indicator. When interested in what another is saying, our blinking rate decreases and our pupils dilate; when we're uninterested, our pupils contract.[15] Similarly, our pupils dilate when we experience a positive emotion and contract when we experience a negative one. They rarely, if ever, lie, because regulating pupil size is a nonverbal cue beyond our conscious control.

In order for others to find us persuasive, we need to not blink excessively, maintain a steady gaze, and not exhibit eye flutter. In some cultures, including Arab, Latin American, and southern European cultures, individuals judge those who look them in the eye as more honest and credible than those who don't. In American culture, when others avoid meeting our eyes or avert their gaze, we're likely to assume they have something to hide, they lack confidence, or are unknowledgeable on some matter.[16]

Visual dominance correlates with increased eye contact. Humans may "stare down" each other to establish dominance. Look away first, and you may well find that you have become the less powerful player in an interaction.

Eye contact also indicates whether a communication channel is open. It is much easier to avoid interacting if we have not made eye contact, because once we do, interaction virtually becomes an obligation.[17] When we like one another or want to express our affection, we also increase our eye contact.

The eyes can enhance the establishment of behavior synchrony or behavioral mirroring with another in an effort to establish or advance our relationship. We establish behavioral synchrony by using nonverbal cues that are in sync with the other person's.

## The Ethics of Face-Work

"Put on a happy face!" instructs a once popular song. Have you ever followed such advice when not feeling happy inside? Could others tell you were not really happy?

When we use our facial expressions to communicate genuine feelings, we exhibit **representational facial expressions**.[18] Conversely, when we consciously control our face to communicate a message meant only for public consumption, we are giving a performance and displaying **presentational facial expressions**. It is when we consciously control our facial expressions that we likely are engaging in interpersonal deception.

# ANALYZE THIS:
# FACECRIME AND THE FAKE FACE

In his classic novel *Nineteen Eighty-Four*, author George Orwell alludes to the practice of masking facial expressions so as not to reveal what you are really thinking to those in authority. The citizens of Orwell's dystopia make great efforts not to look nervous or give others a reason to think they have something to hide. Anyone who fails at this may be arrested for "facecrime."

While we may try to conceal our real feelings, it is not typically because we fear the state's retribution, but instead because we fear that others may not approve of them or may be hurt by them.

1. Can you remember a time when you (or someone near you) were called out for committing a facecrime (faking a facial expression)? What might have led you or the other person to commit the act? What was the outcome?

2. Should the concept of facecrime exist? Explain your position.

Source: George Orwell, *Nineteen Eighty-Four* (1949), New York: New American Library, 1983.

What techniques do we use to "put on a face"? First, we may qualify our facial expression—that is, we add another expression that modifies the impact of the original expression. Second, we may modulate our facial expression to reflect feelings that are somewhat more or less intense than what we actually feel. Third, we may falsify directly. This requires that we simulate an unfelt emotion, show no emotion when we actually feel some, or mask a felt emotion by displaying one that we do not really feel.[19] Which of these techniques have you caught yourself using?

Face-faking usually leaves an array of clues for astute observers. For example, our "face-work" may lack spontaneity or be out of sync with our words or actions, or we may exhibit involuntary cues, in which an expression appears on our face for only a fraction of a second. What begins as a smile becomes ever so briefly a grimace and then is reengineered back into a smile. We call these fleeting emotional changes, lasting a fraction of a second, microfacial or micromomentary expressions. Such expressions reveal our emotional states and typically occur when we attempt to disguise or conceal those states. Thus, a twitch of the mouth or the eyebrow can suggest that the emotion being communicated is not the emotion actually being felt.

## TRY THIS

## Ethics and Impression Creation

The TV program *Bull* focuses on the world of trial consultants. Hired usually by defense attorneys, these consultants work with defendants and witnesses to ensure that the nonverbal behaviors they exhibit create as favorable an impression as possible on the jury. Similarly, career, college, and political consultants work with individuals to help present each person in as favorable a light as possible in situations such as interviewing for a job or campaigning for public office.

1. Imagine you have been hired as a consultant to help in building a more successful image for you. What changes would you suggest regarding your nonverbal behavior?

2. In your opinion, is it ethical to employ consultants to work with individuals on their nonverbal displays just to ensure they make a positive impression on others? In other words, should consultants be helping people to appear more credible, confident, and likable than they actually are? Explain your position.

## Gestures and Posture

We move and stand in distinctive ways—so distinctive that often others can identify us by our characteristic walk or posture. The movements and alignment of our body communicate. Although some of our body's messages facilitate effective person-to-person interaction, others—whether sent consciously or unconsciously—impede it.

**Cue Categories.** Paul Ekman and Wallace Friesen identify five categories of nonverbal behavior that we can use to describe bodily cues: emblems, illustrators, regulators, affect displays, and adaptors.[20] We explore each in turn in the following.

**Emblems** are movements of the body that are consciously sent and easily translated into speech, such as a wave that means "come here." We often use emblems when noise or distance makes it hard for others to understand us through our words alone.

**Illustrators** support or reinforce spoken words and are used consciously and deliberately. For example, when you want to stress the shortness of a member of a basketball team compared to the average height of his teammates, you use your hands to emphasize the difference.

**Regulators** are cues we use intentionally to influence turn taking—who speaks, when, and for how long. For example, gazing at someone talking to you and nodding your head usually encourages the person to continue speaking, while leaning forward in your seat, tensing your posture, and breaking eye contact traditionally signals that you would like a turn. If we ignore another's use of regulators, the other person may accuse us of rudeness. Your use or misuse of regulators reveals much about your social skills.[21]

**Affect displays** are body movements reflecting emotional states of being. While our face, as we have noted, is the prime indicator of the emotion we're experiencing, it is our body that reveals the emotion's intensity.[22] For example, you might describe another person's body as slumping and defeated or proud and victorious. Those of us who characteristically show a lack of affect make it especially difficult for others to relate to us meaningfully.

**Adaptors** involuntarily reveal information about our psychological state while simultaneously meeting our own physical or emotional needs. Adaptors include movements such as nose scratches, hand over lips, chin stroking, and hair twirling. Individuals interacting with or observing us interpret these as signs of nervousness, tension, or lack of self-assurance.

### Decoding the Body's Messages

Others may judge us to be more or less likable, assertive, or powerful based on observations of our physical behavior. Watching a person's body can help us answer the following questions:

*Do individuals like or dislike one another?* When we like each other, we tend to exhibit open postures and more direct body orientation, and we stand more closely together than when we don't. Our bodies are also relatively relaxed, and our gestures are uninhibited and natural. Such cues tend to stimulate interaction. In contrast, if we don't like each other, we exhibit incongruent and indirect body orientations.

*Is a person being assertive or nonassertive?* Typically, a nonassertive person adopts a rigid posture, exhibits an array of nervous gestures, avoids sustained eye contact, and hunches his or her shoulders in a protective or closed stance. In contrast, the assertive counterpart exhibits comfortable eye contact and employs illustrators in place of confidence-deflating adaptors that announce vulnerability.

*Is an individual powerful or powerless?* If you have an erect but relaxed posture, gesture dynamically, feel free to stare at others, and interject your own thoughts even if it means interrupting another person, others are likely to perceive you as powerful. On the other hand, visible bodily tension, a downward gaze, and closed posture will contribute to perceptions of you as powerless.

Our bodies talk constantly about how we feel about ourselves and others. Even when we try to "stonewall" another in an effort to cut off our communication, our body continues talking.

## PARALINGUISTICS

Messages sent via voice are known as **paralanguage**. Often, it's not what we say but how we say it that determines our interaction's outcome, with vocal cues helping us determine the "actual" meaning of words spoken. Such cues are especially important when deciding whether someone is being sarcastic. The words "Yeah, right" convey different meanings depending on whether they're spoken sincerely or sarcastically.

The tone of your voice can help communicate what you mean to convey, or it can reveal thoughts you mean to conceal. It can reinforce or negate your words. The sound of your voice reveals your emotional state, attitudes, personality, status, and turn-taking, needs. How you speak influences how others interpret your intentions, as well as how credible, intelligent, or attractive they judge you to be.[23] With this in mind, respond to the following questions:

- Does my voice enhance or detract from the impression I make?

- Does my voice support or contradict my intended meaning?

- If I were interacting with me, would I want to listen to the sound of my voice?

Among the elements of paralanguage are pitch, volume, rate, articulation, pronunciation, hesitations, and silence. Each plays a part in the impressions others form of you.

Digital Vision./Digital Vision/Thinkstock

The sound of your voice affects how others respond to your words.

## Pitch

Pitch is the highness or lowness of your voice. We associate higher pitches with female voices and lower pitches with male voices. We also develop and act on vocal stereotypes. We associate low-pitched voices with strength, sexiness, and maturity, and high-pitched voices with helplessness, tension, and nervousness. Although we each have a modal or habitual pitch—one that we use most often when we speak—we also vary our pitch to reflect our mood and interest. For example, we often lower our pitch when sad and raise it when excited. A lively animated pitch encourages interaction, whereas a monotone discourages it.

Others rely on your pitch to decide whether you're making a statement or asking a question or whether you're expressing concern or conviction. Your pitch expresses your emotional state; it can communicate anger or annoyance, patience or tolerance.

## Volume

The loudness of your voice also affects perceptions of intended meaning. While some whisper their way through encounters, others blast through them. An individual who is typically loud may alienate others and often is viewed as overbearing or aggressive. In contrast, soft-spokenness may be interpreted as timidity. Your volume can cause others to turn you off in an effort to turn you down or to lose interest in your words simply because they cannot comfortably hear them.

**Regulating Volume to Promote Meaningful Interaction.** Volume should reflect a message's nature, the size and acoustics of a space, proximity to another person, and any competing noise or conversations. Typically, we increase volume to stress particular words and ideas and to reflect the intensity of our emotions. A sudden decrease in volume can add suspense or sustain another's attention. Volume that is varied is most effective.

## Rate

Most of us speak at a rate of 150 words per minute. When we speed up, exceeding 275 words per minute, it's difficult for others to comprehend what we're saying. If we speak too slowly, others may perceive us as tentative or lacking in confidence or intelligence. An overly deliberate speaking pace contributes to boredom, lack of attentiveness, and unresponsiveness in others. Rate also affects others' judgment of our intensity and mood. As your rate increases, so do assessments of your level of emotional intensity.[24] When talking about more serious subjects, we often slow down. On the other hand, our speaking rate usually accelerates as we shift to talking about lighter topics.

## Articulation and Pronunciation

Message intelligibility as well as perceptions of credibility are affected by articulation (the way you pronounce individual sounds) and pronunciation (whether the words themselves are said correctly). Ideally, even during person-to-person contact, the sounds of your speech are sharp and distinct. When you fail to utter a final sound (a final *t* or *d*, for example), fail to produce the sounds of words properly, or voice a sound in an unclear, imprecise way (*come wimme* versus *come with me*), perceptions of your credibility drop, and those listening to you may find it more difficult to make sense of what you are saying.

### Hesitations and Silence

Knowing when to pause is a critical skill. When nervous or tense, we may exhibit a tendency to fill all pauses, often by inserting meaningless sounds or phrases such as *uh*, *you know*, or *okay* in the effort to fill voids. These nonfluencies, or hesitation phenomena, disrupt the natural flow of speech and adversely affect how others perceive your competence and confidence.

In addition to slowing the rate of speech and emphasizing key ideas, brief periods of silence give us a chance to gather our thoughts. This is not to suggest that a pause's message is always positive. Sustained pauses—significantly extended periods of silence—can constitute the "silent treatment," a means by which we ignore a person, communicating the message, "As far as I am concerned, you do not exist." We also tend to become silent during moments of extreme anxiety or annoyance.

## PROXEMICS

Generally, we use physical proximity and distance to signal whether we desire to communicate. The closer we stand, the greater the chances are that we like one another. Proximity or lack of it also indicates how dominant or submissive we are in a relationship. The more dominant we feel, the more likely we are to move closer to another.

Perceptions of friendliness or unfriendliness and extroversion or introversion, as well as our privacy and social contact needs, are also reflected in our spatial relationships. As we study how we use space and distance to communicate, keep in mind that a gap may exist between the messages we intend to send using space and distance and the messages that others actually receive and interpret.

The father of proxemics research, Edward T. Hall, coined the term **proxemics** to indicate that "proximity" influences human interaction. The word itself refers to how we use the personal space around us as we interact with others as well as how we structure the space around us in our homes, offices, and communities.[25]

### Spatial Relationships

Hall identified four distances that distinguish the kinds of interactions we have and the relationships we share during them (it should be noted that Hall's research involved only white Americans):

| | |
|---|---|
| Intimate distance | Contact to 18 inches |
| Personal distance | 18 inches to 4 feet |
| Social-consultative distance | 4 to 12 feet |
| Public distance | 12 feet to the limit of sight |

**Intimate distance** ranges from skin contact to 18 inches from another person. At this distance, physical touching is normal. While we usually share such closeness with those we trust and with whom we share an emotional bond, this is also the distance used for physical combat and sexual harassment. At times, in crowded spaces such as elevators or buses, we have to put up with intimate distance between ourselves and strangers.

**Personal distance** ranges from 18 inches to 4 feet. While we can still shake the hand of another at this distance, we are most likely to converse informally. We use this distance at social events or when talking between classes. If we unilaterally close the gap between personal and intimate distance, we may make the person we are interacting with feel uncomfortable. On the other hand, if we widen the distance between us, we may make him or her feel rejected.

**Social distance** extends from 4 feet to 12 feet. At this distance, we're less apt to talk about personal matters and thus more likely to conduct business or discuss issues that are neither private nor personal. Many of our discussions during meals, conferences, or meetings are held within social distance range. Often, we use objects such as desks or tables to maintain appropriate distance in these settings.

**Public distance**, 12 feet and beyond, is the distance we use to remove ourselves physically from interaction, to communicate with strangers, or to address large groups. Public distance is much less likely than smaller distances to involve interpersonal communication.

The amount of distance we maintain between us reveals the nature of our relationship.

People from different cultures maintain the same four categories, but not necessarily the same distances. For example, Latin Americans use the smallest conversational space, European Americans use more space than Latin Americans do, and African Americans use even more impersonal space than European Americans do.[26] Cultural and family backgrounds also influence our use of space and personal body boundaries. In the United States, land tends to be plentiful, and family size averages three or four; in countries where land is scarcer and families are larger, people live in tighter spaces, spaces that by our standards might be small or confining.

What happens when we violate distance norms? **Expectancy violation theory** researchers tell us that the outcomes of such violations can be positive. For example, if we perceive the approaching person closing the distance between us as attractive, our evaluation of him or her may become more favorable, especially if the distance violation is accompanied by other behaviors, such as compliments.[27] More frequently, however, we may feel uncomfortable or violated when another person invades our personal space.

Understanding proxemics affords us opportunities to improve our relationships. By becoming aware of how space communicates, we attune ourselves to the nature of acceptable and unacceptable proxemic behavior. Although some studies reveal that "spatial invasions" may, under some conditions, achieve positive outcomes, we ought to remember that spatial violations have also led to lawsuits and violence.

## Places and Their Spaces

Three kinds of environmental space concern us: fixed-feature space, semi-fixed-feature space, and informal space (see Table 6.4).[28] Each affects communication in different ways.

**Fixed-feature space** involves the permanent characteristics of an environment—walls, doors, built-in cabinets, roads—that functionalize it and determine how we will use it. For example, window placement often identifies the front of a classroom, swimming pools provide opportunities for increased interaction, and aisles in shopping malls and stores route customers in an effort to promote sales.

## TABLE 6.4  IT'S ABOUT SPACE

| TYPE OF SPACE | REPRESENTED BY | EXAMPLE |
|---|---|---|
| Fixed-feature space | Permanent characteristics of the environment | Walls, Doors |
| Semi-fixed-feature space | Movable objects | Plants, Furniture |
| Informal or non-fixed-feature space | Our space | Personal bubble |

**Semi-fixed-feature space** uses movable objects such as furniture, plants, temporary walls, and paintings to identify boundaries and either promote or inhibit interaction. For instance, desks can reduce contact, while chairs facing each other can increase it. Some rooms say, "Use me" and actually bring people together, while others say, "Look at me," and keep people out.

**Informal space or non-fixed-feature space** is the space we carry around with us. It is invisible, highly mobile, and enlarged or contracted at will as we try to keep individuals at a distance or bring them closer. The amount of personal space we claim, the size of our personal bubble, changes as we move from interaction to interaction, relationship to relationship.

## Territoriality

Each of us lays claim to, or identifies as our own, spatial areas that we seek to protect or defend from intrusion. This is **territoriality**. We devise various means to accomplish this, some more formal than others: nameplates, fences, or assigned chairs. While it may not be logical to claim certain spaces, it is typical. Think of how often you have stopped someone from taking a specific seat, saying, "Don't sit there—that's Dad's seat."

In professional settings, territory claimed tends to reflect status. Senior executives typically are accorded more favorable office spaces than are managers. The former also employ more markers, such as outer offices with assistants, to keep others out. While higher-status individuals can enter the spaces of lower-status people unannounced, the opposite is rarely true.

## HAPTICS

Touch, or **haptics**, is usually involved in our closest relationships, those that happen within intimate space. While always part of sexual communication, touch also plays a role in helping us develop closer relationships and is a key ingredient in the establishment and maintenance of many of our personal relationships.

Touching signals the desire for closeness and conveys degrees of emotion and meaning that other forms of communication can't match.

The amount of touching we find acceptable tends to be culturally conditioned. Although some cultures promote only limited touching, others promote more frequent touch. Members belonging to a given culture generally conform to its established norms. When others violate these norms, we may experience discomfort. In the United States, for instance, it is more acceptable for women to touch each other than it is for men to touch each other.[29] Touch also correlates positively with openness, comfort with relationships, and the ability to express feelings.[30]

We use touch to communicate attitude or affect, to encourage affiliation, and to exert control or power.[31] In some ways, beginning early in our lives, touch serves a therapeutic function. To demonstrate our concern for others, we often touch them. Infants wither emotionally and physically when not touched. Although touch is our most effective means of demonstrating affection or support, and it is important for the maintenance of both physiological and psychological health, as we get older, we often are touched less.

Touch also helps us exert status or power in relationships. People of higher status usually initiate touch. Thus, it is more likely you will see the CEO pat a worker on the shoulder than vice versa.[32] The person who initiates touch is also the one who usually controls the interaction. Sometimes, however, rather than communicating liking or concern, touch signals dislike, dominance, aggression, or abuse; shoves, pokes, and slaps fall into this category.

The amount of consensual touching two people engage in indicates how much they like each other. Touch is part of relationship development and is used as a guide to gauge the amount of intimacy desired. We touch those we like and try not to be touched by those we dislike.

What we wear and how we look helps others form impressions of us. What do the artifacts you wear suggest to others about you?

Touch also marks greetings and leave-takings. Even a handshake can be coolly polite or friendly and warm.

## ARTIFACTS AND APPEARANCE

What clothing or jewelry do you like to wear? How does it affect you? What do your appearance, hairstyle, and mode of dress and personal adornments suggest to others about you?[33]

What we wear and how we look affect first impressions and may even lead to our being accepted or rejected. In addition, the clothing and jewelry we wear can cause others to form judgments regarding our success, character, power, and competence. Typically, we respond more positively to those we perceive to be well dressed than to those whose attire we find questionable or unacceptable. In the past, Americans were more apt to respond to requests from well-dressed individuals, including those in uniform, than they were to listen to or emulate individuals whose dress suggested lower status or a lack of authority,[34] but things may be changing. During the past few presidential campaigns, for instance, candidates have dressed more casually in the effort to come off as accessible, "empathetic, regular Joes."[35]

Many believe we live in a looks-based culture. Unfortunately, they may be right. It appears that tall men, slender people, and attractive women are awarded a premium.[36] For example, when it comes to height, taller people seem to win elections and jobs. Men actually make almost $800 a year more for every extra inch of height. When it comes to weight, obese or overweight individuals are treated more unkindly, and heavier people earn less than slim or average-weight people. In like fashion, people others judge to be unattractive receive lower salaries than do people judged attractive. Attractiveness also appears to be a factor for people facing prison, with less attractive people receiving longer sentences than their more attractive peers.[37]

What we wear affects our cognitive processes, which is reflected in the findings of a new scientific field called "embodied cognition." According to a study on the subject conducted by Hajo Adam and Adam D. Galinsky, if you wear a white coat you believe belongs to a physician, your ability to pay attention improves significantly. If, however, you think the same white coat belongs to a painter, no such improvement occurs. Quite simply, the clothing we have on not only influences how others see us but, by transforming our psychological state, also affects how we think about ourselves.[38]

## OLFACTICS

Who smells good to you? How good do you smell to others? Through the years, the desire to use and appeal to the sense of smell, or **olfactics**, has spawned numerous industries offering products such as perfumes and colognes, mouthwashes and deodorants, household disinfectants, scented candles, and aromatherapy oils. Many of us go out of our way to avoid smells we find objectionable such as body or spoiled food odors. Americans often seek to hide or enhance their natural bodily odors, preferring to use smell as an attractor by adding pleasant smells in the effort to trigger emotional reactions, sexual arousal, romance, or friendship. Women prefer men who smell similar to them.[39] Gay men respond to smell much as women do, and in ways that are distinct from those of heterosexual men.[40]

Smell and the recall of good and bad memories go hand in hand. When something bad happens, for example, our sense of smell sharpens, as if going on high alert to warn us of impending danger.[41] Of course, we also have good memories related to the presence of pleasing smells, such as freshly baked cookies and flowers blooming.

## COLOR

Color talks both to and about us. The colors we wear and surround ourselves with affect us physically and emotionally. For example, when a person is exposed to pure red for extended periods, the nervous system is excited, and blood pressure, respiration rate, and heart rate rise. In contrast, when the person is similarly exposed to dark blue, a calming effect occurs, and blood pressure, respiration, and heart rate fall.[42] Color may help compel us to move more quickly or slowly, help us relax, or cause us to become agitated. People who regularly wear red tend to be more active, outgoing, and impatient than those who avoid the color.

Fast-food chains, product marketers, department stores, and law enforcement agencies use our predictable reactions to various colors as behavioral conditioners. Because the color green encourages oral interaction, it is common practice for investigators to question suspects in green rooms, or in rooms where the lighting is green. Of course, green also prompts ecological associations. The following table indicates how marketers use color to target consumers.[43] In which group would you place yourself?

Colors do not evoke the same meanings in all cultures. For example, whereas in the United States and Europe brides routinely wear white, in Asian countries, white is the color of mourning and so not considered suitable for weddings. In India, if a bride wears white, at least a touch of another color is usually added. In Ghana, blue signifies joy; in Iran, it has negative connotations. What meanings do different colors have for you?

### TRY THIS

## Color Matters

First, look only at the color palette in the first column of the following chart. Rank the colors shown, from the color you prefer (your favorite) to the color you like least.

Once you have completed your ranking, consider the accompanying color preference descriptions. To what extent, if any, do you think they accurately describe you?

*(Continued)*

(Continued)

| COLOR | MEANING/ PERSONALITY | COMMUNICATES |
|---|---|---|
| Gray | Neutrality | Noninvolvement, concealment, or lack of commitment |
| Blue | Calmness | Contentment, being at peace |
| Green | Growth | Persistence, high self-esteem, constancy |
| Red | Energy | Intensity, conquest, fullness of living |
| Yellow | Happiness | Lack of inhibition, a desire for change |
| Violet | Enchantment | Longing for wish fulfillment, a desire to charm others |
| Brown | Security | Need for physical ease and contentment, for release from discomfort |
| Black | Nothingness | Surrender, renunciation |

*Source:* Based on Max Luscher, *The Luscher Color Test*, translated and edited by Ian Scott, New York: Random House, 1969.

## CHRONEMICS

The study of how we use time to communicate is called **chronemics**. Some of us are preoccupied with saving time; others waste it. Some approach life with a sense of urgency; others prefer a more leisurely pace. Some of us are early birds, functioning best in the morning; others perform best at night.

### FIGURE 6.1
How Often Are You Late for Work?

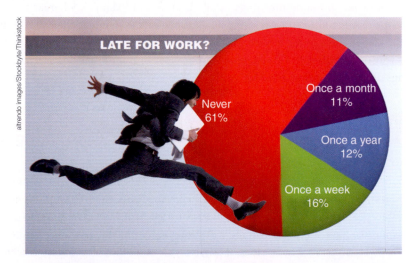

Source: Based on information from a CareerBuilder survey of 7,780 workers.

Misunderstandings, miscalculations, and disagreements involving time can create communication and relationship problems. What does it mean to be "on time"? To be "on time" for a job interview may be different from what it means to be "on time" for a cocktail party. The latter usually allows more flexibility. Many of us can't stop watching the clock, structuring time in an effort to ensure we accomplish needed tasks. As a result of focusing on time rushing by, we become anxious.[44]

How long we are willing to wait to meet with someone or for something to occur is a reflection of our status and the value we place on what we are waiting for. Status affords us greater power to control both our own and others' time. The more status a person has, the longer others with less status will wait to see him or her.[45] High status people also perceive themselves to have more control of time because they believe they have more time available to them.[46]

Our culture influences how we use and think about time. In some cultures, people live for today, but in others, they are waiting for tomorrow. Thus, even the meaning of the phrase *a long time* is influenced by how a culture's members conceive of time.

# CULTURE AND NONVERBAL BEHAVIOR

Culture modifies use of nonverbal cues. For example, individuals belonging to contact cultures, such as Saudi Arabia, France, and Italy, relish the intimacy of contact. When interacting, they tend to display their warmth, closeness, and availability to one another, tend to be comfortable standing close to each other, seek maximum sensory experience, and touch each other frequently. In contrast, members of noncontact or lower-contact cultures, such as Scandinavia, Germany, England, Japan, and the United States, place more value on privacy and are more likely to discourage the behaviors exhibited by higher-contact culture members.[47]

Individuals growing up in different cultures may display emotion or express intimacy in different ways. For example, members of Mediterranean cultures tend to display uninhibited, exaggerated highly emotional reactions, expressing grief or happiness with open facial displays, magnified gestures, and vocal cues supportive of their feelings. In contrast, neither the Chinese nor the Japanese readily reveal their feelings in public, preferring to maintain more self-control; for these reasons, they often remain expressionless.[48]

Even when members of different cultures use the same nonverbal cues, they may not mean the same thing. In the United States, for instance, a nod symbolizes agreement or consent, while in Japan, it means only that a message was received.

Misunderstandings become more likely when we fail to understand that people around the world and from different co-cultures use nonverbal cues that adhere to cultural rules that are different from ours. For example, individuals from Latino cultures tend to avoid making direct eye contact with another person as a sign of respect or attentiveness, a cue that people from the dominant U.S. culture may misinterpret as a sign of inattentiveness or disrespect.[49] While African Americans are apt to use more continuous eye contact than European Americans when speaking, they tend to use less when listening.[50] They also prefer authority figures to avert their gaze.[51] African Americans tend to be comfortable with public displays of fervent emotion, however, while the mainstream culture may regard such displays as inappropriate.[52]

Culture influences other kinds of nonverbal cues as well. For example, while a timepiece may be a great gift to give someone in the United States, in China clocks are associated with death and funerals, so a gift of a clock may be interpreted as a sinister act.[53] And while Americans are prone to spending money to straighten less-than-perfect teeth to improve their smiles, in Japan, a new fashion has women paying to have their teeth purposefully made crooked—a look called *yaeba*. This practice is meant to make the women more girl-like and approachable, sexualizing them in the process.[54]

For us to interact effectively with individuals from different cultures, we need to make the effort to identify and understand how culture shapes nonverbal communication. Acknowledging that one communication style is not intrinsically better than any other can help foster more successful multicultural exchanges.

# GENDER AND NONVERBAL BEHAVIOR

Our nonverbal interaction style likely contributes to our gendered identity, because the preferred styles of men and women tend to reflect a number of gendered patterns. Researcher Judith Hall suggests that "'male' and 'female' are roles, each with its set of prescribed behaviors."[55] As a result, men and women commonly use nonverbal communication in ways that reflect societal expectations. For example, men are expected to exhibit assertive behaviors that demonstrate their power and authority; women, in contrast, are expected to exhibit more reactive and responsive behavior. Thus, it should not surprise us that men talk more and interrupt women more frequently than vice versa.[56]

Men are also more apt to be dominant during interactions. To measure visual dominance, we compare the percentage of time spent looking while speaking with the percentage of time spent looking while listening. Men spend more time looking while speaking and less time looking when listening. Thus, the visual dominance ratio of men is higher than that of women, again reflecting the ability of nonverbal cues to reinforce perceptions of social power.[57]

Men and women also differ in their use of space and touch. Men tend to use space and touch to assert their dominance over women. As a result, men are much more likely to touch women than women are to touch men. Men usually also claim more personal space than do women, and when they walk with women, they are more likely to take a position in front of the women than behind them. In general, when it comes to same-sex touch, it is considered more appropriate for women to touch other women than for men to touch other men. Men, it appears, have more of a concern with being perceived as homosexual than women do.[58]

One of the nonverbal behaviors that women display more than men is smiling. Accustomed to using a smile as an interactional tool, women even smile when under stress.[59] In contrast, men, who are customarily taught to display less emotion than women, are likely to suppress their facial expressions, thereby conveying their sense of reserve and self-control. Women also commonly display their feelings more overtly than do men. In general, women are more expressive and exhibit higher levels of involvement during person-to-person interaction. Women also use nonverbal signals to draw others into conversation to a greater extent, perhaps smiling at them or opening their hands in the direction of others to solicit comments. While women characteristically demonstrate an interest in affiliation, men generally are more interested in establishing the strength of their ideas than in sharing the floor.[60] On the other hand, women tend to be better interpreters of nonverbal messages. Gender differences in behaviors such as smiling don't necessarily cross over to co-cultures, however. Unlike their Caucasian counterparts, African American women do not tend to smile more than African American men.

When it comes to use of artifacts, use of color, and clothing, men and women are likely to reflect the stereotyped characteristics attributed to the sexes. For instance, women use artifacts such as jewelry, cosmetics, and hair adornments that help reinforce the image of a woman as a decorative object. Similarly, men's clothing tends to be less colorful and more functional than women's clothing. Men's clothing is more likely to promote utility, activity, and ease of movement, and it does not call the same kind of attention to the body as does women's clothing. Consequently, women are perceived as more sexual.[61]

Despite these habitual proclivities, in recent years, some men have taken to wearing heels, and some women have taken to wearing classic male oxfords. In fact, in France, the wearing of high-heeled shoes, by men as well as women, used to be perceived as a sign of nobility. Today, they help men bring a look to dance floor clubs. While it appears to be acceptable for women to wear shoe styles that were previously reserved for men, how long do you think it will be before contem-

Hemera Technologies/AbleStock.com/Thinkstock

How would you describe what this man is wearing over his shoulder? Would you change the terminology were a woman wearing it?

porary society finds it acceptable for men to wear stilettos?[62] Interestingly, men are also wearing "wristwear" (not called bracelets) and carrying "holdalls" (not purses).[63]

Remember, according to standpoint theory (discussed in Chapter 3), it was women's subordinate societal status that compelled them to become better message decoders so that they could accurately predict the behavior of the more dominant or powerful men.[64] On the other hand, as Carol Gilligan notes, since women are more concerned than men with relationship maintenance, it follows that they are likely to develop an enhanced sensitivity to nonverbal cues that facilitate and sustain relationship development.[65]

## NONVERBAL CUES AND FLIRTING: EXPRESSING INTEREST OR DISINTEREST

Flirting is a means of self-promotion as well as a vehicle to express interest in another. How do men and women signal interest in potential partners? Men do so by preening and stretching (actions that makes them seem larger). They also are likely to stiffen their stance and flex

Jupiterimages/Polka Dot/Thinkstock

Flirting is a means of self-promotion as well as a means of expressing our interest in another.

their muscles. Men may also talk in a low voice and are likely to stand or sit with their hands on their belt. Women, in contrast, display nonverbal actions designed to make them appear smaller. They may play with or flick their hair, tilt their heads, exposing their necks, and even display their inner wrists. They also are apt to glance, gaze, primp, preen, pout, lip lick, smile, giggle, laugh, and nod in agreement. Both men and women flash or raise their eyebrows slightly to indicate their interest, make eye contact (even from across the room) or exhibit sideway glances, and play with accessories such as earrings, necklaces, or neckties. They also tend to lean in closer, exhibit open body language, gaze at the other's lips or jaw, laugh, and lightly touch the other's arm or knee.[66]

Gender influences men's and women's use of nonverbal cues as they define their expectations for each other, express their feelings about and toward one another, and convey their interest in pursuing or not pursuing an interpersonal relationship. By sensitizing yourself to the differences associated with gender, you can reduce misunderstandings and increase your personal communication effectiveness.

# MEDIA, TECHNOLOGY, AND NONVERBAL MESSAGES

All too often, the media and technology help to legitimatize stereotypical nonverbal displays. They depict a plethora of open sexual appeals, portrayals of women obsessed with men, and male–female interactions in which men are physically dominant and women subordinate. They also include numerous repetitions of the message that "thin is in."

## ADVERTISING AND PROGRAMMING

In her video series *Killing Us Softly*, Jean Kilbourne explores how media representations help convey gender norms for dominance and subordination. Kilbourne argues that advertising, the primary storyteller in our culture, takes agency away from women. According to Kilbourne, by exploiting the social anxieties women have and espousing the American value that transformation is possible, advertisers encourage women to be excessively thin. Kilbourne also warns that the images advertisers use undermine how women see themselves, while at the same time participating in the normalization of violence directed at them by men. Kilbourne further observes that advertising's objectification and sexualization of men is also on the rise.[67]

With repeated exposure to such media messages, men and women come to believe and ultimately emulate what they see and hear. Thus, women are primed to devote considerable energy to improving their appearance, preserving their youthfulness, and nurturing others, while men learn to display toughness. In the media, nonverbal behaviors portray women as vulnerable and men in control.[68]

Even mediated vocal cues suggest that it is the male and not the female who is the authority. In up to 90 percent of all advertisements, male voices are used in voice-overs—even when the product being sold is aimed at women. Interestingly, however, when we consider the digital domain, we find that computer voices are mostly female, as exemplified by the iPhone's virtual assistant Siri. The reason: Research reveals that people find women's voices more pleasing. This is also the rationale for the use of female voices in most navigation systems—except those sold in Germany, where German men refuse to take directions from a woman.[69]

## TECHNOLOGY

The continued growth of the use of virtual reality simulations is cause for some concern. While facilitating our feeling as if we are really interacting in different, but make-believe, environments and even giving us the opportunity to change our gender, such simulations also are being used to enforce violent gender scenarios resulting in women being threatened and killed. Even when erotic rather than violent, computer games all too often reinforce the notion that men have physical control over women.

Although we experience the most social presence when face-to-face, online we have emoticons, emoji, and gifs to replace physical gestures and facial expressions, substitute for nonverbal cues, and help us convey action, emotion, and emphasis in our online interactions. Emoticons and emoji are relational icons that add personalization and emotional expressiveness to online dialogue. They are a way to approximate the warmth and intimacy of face-to-face interactions. They also help us establish our online personas. Gifs are becoming a mainstay of digital expression. Nothing has changed written expression like the three preceding substitutes for physical cues.[70] Yet, their meanings can be ambiguous.[71] Consider this statement: "You are unreal!" Which emoji(s) would you use to express this sentiment? Did your peers choose the same ones?

Online punctuation also makes its mark (or not). Exclamation points can express emotional state! Ellipses can signal that the thought is ruminating, you are about to respond, or to register the sender's confusion. . . . Even the period has power.[72] Based on receiver reports, the presence of a period in one word texts makes them less sincere or even snarky.[73]

When online, it is common to seek out those who share our needs and interests. On the other hand, it's also easy to present multiple aspects of ourselves and multiple identities. Some of us adopt more than one screen name, or pose as members of the opposite sex or another race. We use emoji either to conceal who we really are as we perform the role of someone else or to reveal one or more aspects of ourselves that we have kept hidden. We manufacture or present an alternative identity to get the reaction we want from others and/or to test others' reactions to those parts of ourselves we have kept submerged.

Humans and computers now converse with most of the digital assistants, including Alexa, Siri, and Cortina having female voices.[74] Might this be because we give them orders, they have pleasing sounding voices, and we have been conditioned to expect women to serve in administrative positions?

## TRY THIS

### Can You Read the Cues?

In 1959, anthropologist Edward T. Hall coined the expression "the silent language" to describe nonverbal communication. Hall's writings on nonverbal communication attracted significant attention, both scholarly and popular. Hall argued that when we fail to decode the manners, gestures, and subtle protocols that accompany words, we leave ourselves vulnerable to miscommunications.

Today it is estimated that high school students alone devote in excess of 9 hours a week to social networking. Add texting, blogging, and tweeting on top of that. The prevalence of texting and other forms of messaging leaves a dearth of opportunities to learn to read posture, facial expressions, intonation, and eye movements—all the expressive behaviors of nonverbal communication that are so essential for mutual understanding.

1.  In your opinion, are we in danger of losing the "silent fluency" that comes from experiencing face-to-face communication, a needed key in reading another's behavior? Explain your answer.

2.  How do you suggest we ensure that such skills are acquired?

3.  To what extent do you believe that using FaceTime and Skype, enablers of online face-to-face interaction, solve some of these issues? How does reading someone's face when you are virtually face-to-face with him or her compare with reading faces when you are really face-to-face?

Source: Mark Bauerlein, "Why Gen-Y Johnny Can't Read Nonverbal Cues," *Wall Street Journal*, September 28, 2009, p. W11.

# GAINING COMMUNICATION COMPETENCE: USING SKILLS TO ENHANCE RELATIONAL UNDERSTANDING

By using nonverbal cues appropriately, you can create a more favorable impression and aid in the development of your relationships. To enhance our abilities to develop effective interpersonal relationships, we need to be fully aware of the nonverbal messages we send and receive.

## FOCUS ON RELATIONAL LANGUAGE

Nonverbal communication is a "relationship language." It expresses how we feel about one another. Even though it may be a challenge to interpret how people really feel, because they may not want us to know, the key is to observe them as they interact with you. For example, when in your company, do other people lean toward you or pull away? Do they face you directly or face away from you? Do their facial expressions suggest they're happy you're around, interested in pursuing a relationship, fearful to approach you, or angry with you? Is their posture relaxed, indicating they feel comfortable, or uptight, indicating that they feel threatened? What does their use of touch, space, clothing, color, and time suggest about your relationship?

## WHEN UNCERTAIN ABOUT A NONVERBAL CUE'S MEANING, ASK!

What a particular nonverbal cue signifies in one culture may not transfer to another culture. Even if you and those with whom you interact come from the same culture, it is important to remember that nonverbal cues can have multiple meanings. It's a good idea to check your perception, perhaps by paraphrasing, to determine if your interpretation is correct. By asking for verbal clarification of your observations, you increase the chances for mutual understanding.

## REALIZE INCONSISTENT MESSAGES HAVE COMMUNICATIVE VALUE

When words and facial expressions, gestures, postures, or vocal cues contradict each other, rely more on the nonverbal information you are receiving than on the words. Even though the words may be precisely what we want or expect to hear, we must also heed unintended mixed messages to help us decide, for example, whether the other person is incompetent, nervous, or a liar.

## MATCH THE DEGREE OF CLOSENESS
## YOU SEEK WITH YOUR NONVERBAL BEHAVIOR

Nonverbal behavior should be compatible with the kind of relationship sought. Touch, for example, typically varies in duration, location, and strength, depending on our relationship with another person. Similarly, intimacy and distance also correlate with relationship type. Thus, your proximity to the other person and the amount of touching you use should be compatible with the kind of relationship you seek. Should you find yourself in close proximity with someone with whom you're not emotionally close, you can use nonverbal cues to compensate for your discomfort. For example, you may decrease eye contact, helping to psychologically increase the distance between you. Similarly, if you are separated from someone with whom you feel emotionally close, you can use nonverbal cues to close the distance gap, perhaps increasing eye contact or smiling.

## MONITOR YOUR OWN NONVERBAL BEHAVIOR

Monitoring your own nonverbal behavior is a critical component of interpersonal goal attainment. By engaging in self-reflection, you become better able to judge if your nonverbal cues project the message you hope to send. For example, how well do you use facial expressions and body movements to foster relationships you want to pursue and terminate relationships you want to end?

When you want to change the tenor of a relationship from one that is close to one that is more restrained, or vice versa, what nonverbal cues do you characteristically put into play? How do they affect your partner?[75] Keep in mind, the more you hone your nonverbal abilities, the more likely it is that others will perceive you as socially adjusted and that you will be able to exert social influence and have satisfying relationships.[76]

## CONNECT THE CASE

# The Case of Surprised Sam

Sam entered the conference room. He couldn't put his finger on what was up, but things just didn't feel right to him as he observed the people already present in the room. At the head of the impressive mahogany table sat the company president. Senior vice presidents sat to the president's right and left, and several managers—including Sam's immediate supervisor—lined the table's sides.

There was one seat open. As Sam approached, he couldn't help but feel uneasy. Sure, the people at the table were drinking coffee, smiling, checking their smartphones, and chatting among themselves, but as Sam took his seat, not one person looked up or said a word to him.

Sam asked himself why he was feeling uncomfortable. Was it because no one had greeted him, except maybe his immediate supervisor, who Sam thought had nodded her head at him? Whatever it was, Sam felt like an outsider.

Then the president looked up—and made eye contact directly with Sam. Everyone else looked Sam's way too. The president called the meeting to order, explaining that there was a single agenda item: Sam.

Sam's heart sank. How could he have missed it? Was this going to be the end of his career? Here they were, he told himself, about to fire him, and he had had no clue that any problem existed before now.

At that moment, the president reached under the table and brought out a bottle of Champagne. Sam, he announced, was being promoted to senior vice president in charge of his entire division. Slowly, a smile appeared on Sam's face, and Sam rose to shake hands with all assembled, including his soon-to-be former supervisor.

### Answer these questions:

1. Have there been times when you have felt just as uncomfortable as Sam did on entering a room but could not identify what caused you to feel that way?

2. What steps can we take to ensure that we pick up and do not misread nonverbal cues?

# REVIEW THIS

## CHAPTER SUMMARY

1. **Define nonverbal communication, explain its metacommunicative nature, and discuss its functions and characteristics.** □

Nonverbal communication consists of the actions or attributes of human beings, together with the use of objects, sounds, time, and space that have socially shared significance and stimulate meaning in others. Because nonverbal communication helps clarify the nature and meaning of verbal messages, it also fulfills metacommunicative functions. Nonverbal cues can add to, negate, accent, regulate, or replace verbal messages. Nonverbal behavior also has message value, is ambiguous, is predominantly relational in nature, and provides clues to deception.

2. **Define and distinguish among the following kinds of nonverbal messages: kinesics, paralanguage, proxemics, haptics, artifactual communication and appearance, olfactics, color, and chronemics.** □

Kinesics is the study of body motion, including expressions, gestures, eye movement, posture, and rate of walk. Paralinguistics includes a consideration of vocal cues, such as how words are spoken and the impact of vocal variations. Proxemics is the use of space and distance. Haptics includes different kinds of touch. Artifactual communication and appearance involve the significance of clothing, personal adornments, beauty, height, and weight for our feelings and others' reactions to us. Olfactics is the study of the sense of smell. Color has effects on us both psychologically and physically. Chronemics explores the communicative value of time.

3. **Discuss culture's influence on nonverbal behavior.** □

Contact cultures value the intimacy of contact by promoting interaction and displays of warmth, closeness, and availability. Noncontact cultures value privacy and the maintenance of distance. Misunderstandings become more likely when we fail to understand that people around the world and from different co-cultures use nonverbal cues that adhere to cultural rules that are different from ours.

4. **Compare and contrast the nonverbal communication styles of men and women.** □

Most men and women use nonverbal communication in ways that reflect societal expectations of their respective genders. Thus, men exhibit assertive behaviors and women are more responsive and reactive.

5. **Describe how the media and technology influence use of nonverbal messages.** □

Media and technology frequently participate in the legitimization of stereotypes. When interacting online, some individuals use emoticons to try to replace the nonverbal cues that would be present in face-to-face interaction.

**6. Identify steps you can take to improve your nonverbal effectiveness.** ☐

By paying attention to nonverbal cues, cultural differences, and inconsistent messages; matching nonverbal behavior to relationships; and monitoring our nonverbal behavior, we improve the likelihood of communicating effectively.

· · · · · · · · · · · · · · · · · · · · · · · · · · · · · ·

## CHECK YOUR UNDERSTANDING

1. Can you offer an example of metacommunication in action? How might you use it to better understand the nature of a relationship? (See pages 152–154.)

2. Can you create a scenario illustrating the role nonverbal cues play in creating a false impression? Why is it easier to lie with words than with nonverbal cues? (See pages 155–158.)

3. Can you explain the kinds of messages conveyed by personal appearance? What about those that voice and use of space and distance communicate? (See pages 172–174.)

4. Can you offer two examples of nonverbal messages in action, one demonstrating how gender or culture influences the use and interpretation of nonverbal cues, and the other demonstrating the role that media and technology play in nonverbal messaging? (See pages 175–182.)

5. What can you do to enhance your ability to send and receive nonverbal messages? (See pages 182–184.)

## KEY TERMS

Adaptors  165

Affect displays  165

Chronemics  174

Emblems  165

Expectancy violation theory  169

Facial Action Coding System  159

Fixed-feature space  169

Haptics  170

Illustrators  165

Informal space or non-fixed-feature space  170

Intimate distance  168

Kinesics  161

Metacommunicative functions  156

Nonverbal communication  156

Olfactics  173

Paralanguage  166

Personal distance  168

Presentational facial expressions  163

Proxemics  168

Public distance  169

Regulators  165

Representational facial expressions  163

Semi-fixed-feature space  170

Social distance  169

Territoriality  170

Get the tools you need to sharpen your study skills. **SAGE edge** offers a robust online environment featuring an impressive array of free tools and resources. Access practice quizzes, eFlashcards, video, and multimedia at **edge.sagepub.com/gambleicp**.

**7**

# Conversations
## Social Glue

## CHAPTER 7

## Learning Objectives

**AFTER COMPLETING THIS CHAPTER, YOU SHOULD BE ABLE TO**

1. Define small talk, enumerating the skills that good conversationalists share

2. Explain conversation's importance and nature

3. Explain conversational management

4. Discuss how to navigate a difficult conversation and repair conversational damage

5. Describe how cultural differences influence feelings and perceptions of the value of conversation

6. Describe how gender differences influence the nature of conversation

7. Discuss how media and technology are helping to reinforce or change both the substance and the nature of conversation

8. Identify specific steps you can take to improve your conversational skills

> A conversation is a dialogue, not a monologue.
>
> — Truman Capote

· · · · · · · · · · · · · · · · · · · · · · · · · · · · · · · · · · · · · · · · · · · · · · · · · · ·

Fans of popular TV shows like to connect with one another, engaging in conversation and analysis both during and after viewing a program. They relish deconstructing their favorite episodes—often using Facebook posts, tweets, and opportunities provided by call-in after-shows to chat and weigh in. Prior to social media's widespread use, highly rated television programs were the topics of "watercooler conversations" on mornings after a program aired. Today, it's easier for viewers to converse even as they watch. Each new online chat venue functions as a substitute for those conversations that in the past would have been held around the proverbial office watercooler.[1]

Posting comments about what we watch on Twitter, Facebook, and other social platforms has become increasing prevalent. Some 70 percent of viewers discuss programs via social media, and 83 percent discuss it by the next day.[2] And the tweeting doesn't just occur during commercial breaks. It happens whenever there is an OMG moment in a show. Fans thrive on sharing reactions as viewing morphs into a social experience.

While many of us chat online about television shows or other subjects simply because we enjoy it—treating our discussions as add-ons to the conversing we do face-to-face—others, perhaps because of social anxiety, prefer connecting digitally to talking face-to-face.[3] Consider this: While some of us are comfortable entering a room filled with people whom we don't know, easily conversing with strangers, others of us muddle along, unable to make a connection.[4] Have you ever found yourself tongue-tied at a party, or afraid you would say something stupid? According to a *Wall Street Journal* article, this is a pretty common occurrence. Many of us find speaking up in the presence of others difficult, especially if we think our social status is in question.[5] ■

## WHAT DO YOU KNOW?

Before continuing your reading of this chapter, which of the following five statements do you believe to be true, and which do you believe to be false?

| | | | |
|---|---|---|---|
| 1. | Rules guide conversation. | T | F |
| 2. | A skilled conversationalist can control a conversation's direction. | T | F |
| 3. | Conversations are essentially the same everywhere in the world. | T | F |
| 4. | Once you have said something wrong in a conversation, you can never repair the damage. | T | F |
| 5. | Texting is taking the place of face-to-face conversations. | T | F |

Read the chapter to discover if you're right or if you've made any erroneous assumptions.

ANSWERS: 1. T; 2. T; 3. F; 4. T; 5. T

## SMALL TALK: SOCIAL LUBRICANT

While making small talk or engaging in spontaneous conversation is not a challenge for some, it presents real concerns for others. Yet it is through conversation that we lay the foundation for interpersonal relationships.[6] Because most people enjoy being in the company of a good communicator, one of the most important skills you can master is that of carrying on a conversation. After all, being able to connect with others is important for personal well-being.[7] Besides being a social lubricant, conversation helps build empathy and collaboration. When you're a good conversationalist, you're adept at approaching others, starting a conversation, listening, changing a topic to one of interest or importance to the other person, and also graceful at ending the interaction. Above all else, a good conversationalist also has a curious mindset.

## PRELIMINARY POINTERS

To be successful at striking up a conversation, follow these preliminary pointers: (1) Begin by identifying common ground. If at a party, you might ask: "How do you know the host?" (2) Commiserate. You can initiate talk by sharing a frustration: "This line is endless. How long are you willing to wait?" (3) Find out more. Rather than flit from subject to subject, dig deeper in the effort to sustain talk. (4) Say you don't know. Make it your business to learn something new from another person. (5) Be curious. Ask interesting questions. If someone says the room is stifling, for example, ask, "What's the hottest you've ever been?" (6) Exit gently. Instead of abruptly ending a conversation, first send a hint that you'll soon need to go.

# WHAT IS CONVERSATION? WHY IS IT IMPORTANT?

==Conversation== is a relatively informal social interaction in which the parties involved exchange the roles of sender and receiver, collaboratively and spontaneously.[8] It facilitates contact and the establishing of interpersonal relationships. As such, it plays a critical role in our lives.

## WHAT IS CONVERSATION DEPRIVATION?

Some years ago, in an effort to prevent prison inmates from sharing information about how to commit different crimes, prison reformers reduced the amount of conversation inmates were able to have with each other. The result? "The prisoners spent much of their time tapping out coded messages on walls and pipes, devising means of passing information to one another, and working out other clever ways of communicating."[9] Even when the inmates were denied opportunities to be face-to-face, they found other ways to converse.

Devising secret means of conversing is by no means new. Retired Navy captain Gerald Coffee, one of hundreds of American pilots shot down during the Vietnam War and held as a prisoner of war in a facility known as the "Hanoi Hilton," offers a moving example that illustrates the lengths humans will go to in order to compensate for face-to-face ==conversation deprivation==. In his book *Beyond Survival*, Coffee describes an ingenious method he and his fellow prisoners relied on to communicate within the prison walls. The prisoner who previously had occupied the small cell that was now Coffee's had scratched into the wall a system of taps that represented the letters of the alphabet. Once they learned the system, the prisoners were able to sustain contact with one another by covertly tapping messages.[10] Because of the system, the prisoners were able to compensate for a lack of aural communication and thereby maintain their sense of connection to others.

Which shows do you text your friends about?

## WHAT ARE THE RULES AND NORMS OF CONVERSATION?

While conversation is a mainstay of human interaction, if unchecked, the extremely extroverted may fill any conversational opening, rushing to speak, rather than thinking reflectively before speaking, as introverts, who may find nonstop socializing stressful, tend to do.[11] Thus, being comfortable in the spotlight is not the sole requisite for being an effective conversationalist. Another important element is a desire to share real-life experiences—to be fully present.[12]

What happens when we are fully present in a conversation? How do we act? According to relationship expert and researcher Steven Duck's **serial construction of meaning model**, before we engage in conversation with another person, we may share things in common with that person, expressed as *commonality*. As we converse about something that we share in common, we establish *mutuality* and seek to determine if we evaluate the shared experience similarly. Once we establish the *equivalence of our evaluation*, we then process what Duck calls *shared meaning*. In other words, it is through conversation that we create a shared world.[13] We seek to converse with people who resemble us and share our attitudes.[14]

## TRY THIS

### Do You Like to Talk?

Assess how you feel about striking up a conversation with another person. Using a scale of 1 to 5, where 1 represents an extremely negative response and 5 represents an extremely positive response, answer each question below as honestly as possible.

1. How much do you enjoy yourself in situations that compel you to mingle and strike up conversations with people you don't know well or at all?

2. How much do you enjoy engaging in small talk?

3. Do you look forward to spending a lot of time talking with others?

4. How comfortable are you around people who don't talk a lot?

5. How at ease are you sharing personal information with others when face-to-face?

What do your answers suggest regarding whether or not you are conversationally apprehensive?

During a conversation, there's no set time limit for each party to speak or listen. The participants determine the time frame themselves. However, describing conversational exchanges as spontaneous does not mean that conversations are random or without rules. In fact, **conversational rules** and norms reveal the behaviors we prefer and those we would like to prohibit in various social situations.[15] For instance, if someone says, "Hello," how do you respond? Typically, with a "Hi," or a "Hello, how are you?" Rules and adherence to norms guide much of our person-to-person behavior. Reflect for a moment on the rules you use to guide you: What do you say when disagreeing with a parent? What about an employer? We tend to rely on learned social and conversational rules to guide us as we interact. We may not be able to state the rules explicitly, but we've been subconsciously conditioned to follow them.

As we explore conversation, we also need to apply what we've learned about verbal and nonverbal messages directly to our daily interactions and our efforts at relationship building. After all, Duck notes, "If you were to sit and list the things that you do with friends, one of the top items on the list would surely have to be 'talking.'"[16] By exploring the dynamics of conversational exchange, we enhance our ability to engage in everyday talk wherever our conversations occur—whether on the playing field, at work, at home, during a date, or at a social gathering. While many of our conversations occur spontaneously and are casual interactions with others that involve no preplanned agenda, others are more pragmatic and involve a specific goal on the part of at least one of the conversational parties. Which of these kinds of conversations do you engage in more?

## TRY THIS

### The Elevator

What rules do most people follow regarding conversing with others in elevators?

1. While in an elevator, break a rule you usually follow and observe how the other person reacts. For example, does he or she respond in kind, refrain from responding, or exhibit some other noteworthy behavior?

2. Why do you imagine such elevator rules exist?

## CONVERSATION GAMES AND GAME PLAYERS

Some theorists suggest that conversation is a kind of game and that we can therefore apply game rules to our conversational interactions.[17] Adopting this approach, Robert Nofsinger, a communication researcher who studies conversation, notes, "The idea is to apply what we know about ordinary, everyday games (chess, checkers, tic-tac-toe, card games, competitive sports, and so on) to the conduct of conversation."[18] When we use this analogy, we find people making moves, taking turns, and aiming to achieve some goal. We also find them using specific tactics, employing strategies, and devising game plans.

According to Nofsinger, a conversation's moves consist of talk itself. When we talk, however, we do not simply *say* something, but we also *do* something. Our talk, for example, may direct others, signal our acceptance or rejection of another, or insult another. How we act and respond or subsequently conduct our conversations depends on our understanding of conversational events.

While the rules of board games and sports games are codified and written down so that they may be enforced easily—and violators can be corrected or penalized—we don't usually find the rules of everyday conversation in print. There are topics we may consider taboo when we interact with some people but that we consider acceptable when we converse with others. We simply are able to change the rules to guide our conversations from day to day and from minute to minute.

## CONVERSATIONAL STRUCTURE

Most conversations adhere to a general five-stage **conversational structure**: the greeting, topic priming, the heart of the conversation, preliminary processing, and the closing (see Table 7.1). Let us explore each.

### TABLE 7.1  THE STAGES OF A CONVERSATION

| STAGE | FUNCTIONS |
|---|---|
| Greeting | Ask a question.<br><br>Tell something about yourself.<br><br>Deliver a compliment.<br><br>Make a cute/flippant statement.<br><br>Say something innocuous.<br><br>Issue a direct invitation. |
| Topic priming | Preview the nature of and reason for the conversation.<br><br>Ask one or more open-ended questions. |
| Heart of the conversation | Introduce and then discuss the conversation's focus or goal. |
| Preliminary processing | Reflect back on the conversation in an effort to evaluate conversational progress. |
| Closing | Let the other person know the conversation is ending.<br><br>Express appreciation.<br><br>Summarize topics discussed. |

## TRY THIS

# Conversational Analysis

Watch a brief segment of a film or TV show focusing on interpersonal relationships in which two characters converse. For example, you might use an excerpt from *Modern Family*, *The Simpsons*, or a soap opera. Then analyze the conversation as follows:

1. Describe the nature, purpose, and results of the conversation.

2. Describe how the communicators regulate their interaction, including who appears to be in control of interaction ebb and flow. Be sure to note how turn taking is managed, who asks questions, who interrupts, and who shifts topics.

The Interpersonal Communication Playbook

3. Discuss the degree to which the characters conversing appear to be involved in the conversation. Identify the cues you have relied on to distinguish involved from uninvolved characters.

4. Evaluate the conversational adaptability (flexibility), responsiveness (the extent to which they appear to know what to say, understand their role, and feel part of the interaction), perceptiveness (the extent to which they demonstrate an awareness of how the other perceives them and responds to them), and attentiveness (the extent to which they listen carefully to the other party or are preoccupied with personal thoughts) of each party.

5. Evaluate whether any party to the conversation displays conversational narcissism—that is, exhibits cues suggesting that a participant is overly self-concerned—and how the presence or absence of this quality affects the outcome of the interaction.

6. Identify which conversational participant exhibits more empathy—that is, which is best able to show his or her conversational partner that emotions are shared and the situation is understood.

7. Evaluate whether the goals of the conversation are achieved and at what, if any, cost.

## The Greeting

The interpersonal greeting is our routine way of initiating conversation with someone, and we usually adjust it based on our perception of our relationship with a specific person, our mood, and how we imagine the other person will respond. We cannot, however, script our opening lines in advance to guarantee success. "Didn't I meet you in Dallas?" and "Do you have an aspirin?" and "Bet I can make you laugh" have all been tried, and they have worked in some instances but not others.

Conversational analyst Thomas E. Murray identifies three different categories of conversational openers:

1. Questions ("How are you?")
2. Advertisements ("My name is . . .")
3. Compliments ("I like your suit.")[19]

Researcher Chris Kleinke also identifies three types of openers:

1. Cute/flippant ("Is that really your hair?")
2. Innocuous ("What do you think of the band?")
3. Direct ("Since we're both eating alone, would you like to join me?")[20]

Note that each of Kleinke's approaches relies on a question. While men and women both use

Greetings are conversational openers.

indirect opening lines that are cute/flippant or innocuous, women particularly tend to dislike the use of cute and flippant openers by men.

Whatever type of greeting we employ, we use it to let others know that we are accessible and would like to talk. Normally the person we greet will return our greeting in a similar way. When this does not happen—when the other person responds coolly or with caution to our greeting or conversational overture—we assume that the other person does not want to establish contact, that he or she is shy or fears establishing contact, and that we will have to work harder and be more creative if we hope for a more sustained conversation.

## Topic Priming

We prime a conversation by keeping the communication channels between us open and by previewing for the other person what the topic or focus of our conversation will be. For example, we might say, "I need your input. What do you think of X?" or "I have some bad news to share with you." Priming prepares the person we are conversing with for what is to follow.

If we are unable to find a topic to discuss with another person, our conversation ends after the greeting. In general, we usually end up talking about one of three kinds of topics: ourselves, the other person, or a particular situation. Sometimes we test a particular topic by pairing a statement with a question: "I liked what you said today at lunch. What do you think businesses should be doing to avoid having to downsize their operations?" By asking ==open-ended questions==, which allow the respondent free rein in answering, rather than ==closed-ended questions==, which force the respondent to choose a specific response, we are better able to involve and interest another person in conversing with us.

Gregory Stock, author of *The Book of Questions,* notes that far too frequently we exchange small talk without becoming involved in deeper conversation. To combat this, he suggests that we ask questions that are more "dangerous," ones that we may have never been willing to ask before and that might provoke more interesting reactions in others. The following are examples of such questions, as suggested by Stock:

- Would you accept $1,000,000 to leave the country and never set foot in it again?
- What would constitute a "perfect" evening for you?[21]

Jack Hollingsworth/Photodisc/Thinkstock

At the heart of every conversation is its focus or goal.

We err in conversation when we either cut short the priming stage or extend it beyond what is considered appropriate. If we get stuck in this stage, our conversational partner may wonder if we really have anything to discuss. On the other hand, if we omit this stage and head straight for our goal, the other person may judge us to be rude, insensitive, or interpersonally deficient.

## The Heart of the Conversation

At the heart of a conversation, we find its focus or goal. Perhaps we want to share new information with another person. Or perhaps we want to persuade him or her to act or think in a specific way. Maybe we want to offer the person our help—perhaps just a friendly ear. Whatever our specific goal, in this part of our conversation, we get to the heart of the matter—why we opened the conversation in the first place and why we did our best to prepare the other person for what was to come next.

How good we are at getting to and explaining the heart of our conversation is directly related to conversational maintenance skills, which will be discussed a little later in this chapter. The substance of the conversation involves conversational partners exchanging speaker and listener roles.

## Preliminary Processing

The preliminary processing stage is the inverse of topic priming. Here, instead of preparing the other person for what is to come, we process what has just occurred. We consider the effects that our conversation has had on each of us and, based on our assessment of the other person's response, we may decide to adjust or alter our message and strengthen or modify our content. During this stage, we may also assess how much we have learned about the other in an effort to determine the extent to which we have been able to reduce our uncertainty about him or her.

As we review our conversation's progress, we may realize that while we feel that we have accomplished our conversational purpose, our partner may not agree. Thus, we may need to take a step back instead of proceeding to the closing.

## The Closing

The closing is the reverse of the greeting. How we take our leave often lets the other person know whether we intend to meet with him or her again. "It was good to catch up about you and Joe, but I've got to go now" or "I really enjoyed hearing about your trip. When can I see you again?"—each kind of closing sends a message that is very different from a mere good-bye.

Renowned communication scholar Mark Knapp and his colleagues note that a good closing to a successful conversation serves three functions:

1. It lets the other party know that the conversation is nearing an end and thus signals the impending inaccessibility of one party.

2. It is supportive in tone and contains expressions of appreciation for the conversation and the desire to renew contact.

3. It summarizes the main topics discussed.[22]

Closings based on these three rules leave both parties feeling good about the possibilities for continued contact.

Sometimes we merge conversational stages—the processing and closing stages may be combined, for example—or we may mutually agree to skip a stage because the time we have together is short. Thus, not all conversations contain all five steps in the model. However, if you listen and observe carefully, you should be able to identify at least some, if not all, of these stages during many of your conversations. You will probably realize that the conversations you find most fulfilling and least frustrating are those that develop sequentially according to the five-stage model.

# CONVERSATION MANAGEMENT

When a conversation flows smoothly and naturally, the roles of speaker and listener are performed simultaneously by both parties, with each party engaging in conversational turn taking—the alternating of speaking and listening, cooperating, and engaging in dialogue to fulfill the conversation's purpose.[23]

How does one get a turn to speak during a conversation? Is this something that we can determine ahead of time? Do perceptions of wealth or status play a role? What behaviors promote conversational dialogue? Consider this: When we say "mm-hmm" "huh," or "uh," we are using words as traffic signals. These non-content insertions guide our conversations, cueing us when to speak and letting us know when someone is done speaking.[24]

## TURN TAKING: MAINTAINING AND YIELDING THE FLOOR

We regulate our conversations by using and responding to turn-maintaining and turn-yielding signals. Turn-maintaining signals include both paralinguistic and kinesic cues. For example, we may vocalize pauses (*ummm, uhhh*) to indicate we have not yet completed a thought, inhale a breath to suggest we have more to say, exhibit a gesture that suggests we are not yet finished, or avoid making direct eye contact with the other party until we are fully ready to surrender our speaking turn.

Turn-yielding signals let our conversational partner know that we are prepared to let him or her speak. For example, we may make direct eye contact, ask a question requiring a response, nod in the other person's direction, drop our pitch, or remain silent. When someone interrupts or overlaps what we consider to be our turn, we may become upset or agitated, fight to maintain our turn, or reluctantly yield it prematurely.

Turn-taking control does not rest in the hands of one person. An individual who is listening may also exert regulatory control over conversational turn taking by emitting turn-requesting signals or turn-denying signals that let the person speaking know whether the listener would like to switch roles. To signal interest in having a speaking turn, the listener might use a vocalized filler such as *umm* or *ah,* merely open his or her mouth as if to interject a thought, lean forward and look directly at the speaker, or gesture for attention with his or her hand. Similarly, the listener may signal a reluctance to take over the speaking role by avoiding eye contact with the speaker, shaking his or head to indicate that he or she has nothing to add, engaging in some activity that is incompatible with a speaking role (such as taking copious notes), closing his or her eyes, coughing, or exhibiting a gesture that encourages the speaker not to yield the floor but to continue speaking instead. The use or absence of these signals also contributes to the continuing or ending of talk.

## THE COOPERATION PRINCIPLE

For both parties to be satisfied with a conversation, they need to cooperate. According to the cooperation principle, conversations are most satisfying when the comments of the conversational partners are consistent with the conversation's purpose. Based on this premise, researchers offer the following conversational maxims: quality, quantity, relevancy, and manner.[25]

### The Quality Maxim

According to the **quality maxim**, people engaged in conversation should not offer a comment if they know it to be false. Offering an opinion when you have no knowledge of the topic or are only speculating is inappropriate. Violating this maxim leads to distrust.

### The Quantity Maxim

The **quantity maxim** tells us to provide as much information as is needed to communicate the meaning of our message and continue the conversation. This means neither party talks too much or too little. Each should avoid single-word responses but say what is needed to deliver the message while allowing the other person to continue the conversation. Monopolizing the conversation and failing to give another his or her chance to speak undermines cooperation.

### The Relevancy Maxim

The **relevancy maxim** asks that we not go off on tangents or purposefully switch subjects when the other party still wants to discuss our initial topic. Interjecting irrelevant comments illustrates uncooperativeness. Effective conversationalists work to sustain conversational coherence by relating their comments to previous remarks.[26] They prefer to ask relevant questions that others enjoy answering.

### The Manner Maxim

According to the **manner maxim**, diction should be appropriate to the receiver and the interaction's context; that means using terms the other party understands and providing background information to avoid confusion. Conversation is informal, but that does not mean it should be disorganized. Adherence to this maxim requires organizing thoughts to facilitate sharing meaning.

These four maxims apply to conversations occurring between people living in the United States. People from other cultures may adhere to other maxims, such as the *maxim of face-saving*, which would require the parties to a conversation to avoid contradicting, embarrassing, or correcting one another. The *maxim of politeness* might require that people avoid self-praise or taking credit for an accomplishment.[27] While people from Asian cultures as well as the British tend to adhere closely to these two maxims, people from all cultures value face-saving and politeness.[28]

## TRY THIS

# Whose Turn Is It, Anyway?

Keep a log of all the significant conversations you are involved in for one day. Every time you converse with another person, note the following:

1. The person you conversed with

2. How the conversation was initiated and terminated

3. The topic of conversation

4. The cues you used to determine when it was your turn to talk

5. Your ratings of the extent to which the conversation satisfied both you and the other person, where 1 represents completely dissatisfied and 5 represents completely satisfied

6. Your reasons for each rating

## THE DIALOGUE PRINCIPLE

When conversing, we often display either a preference for monologue, in which we speak while the other person listens, or dialogue, in which we both speak and listen. Unlike dialogue, monologue involves little, if any, conversational ebb and flow and expresses minimal concern for the thoughts and feelings of the other person. The monologist is self-centered and exhibits an obsession with achieving personal conversational goals and objectives. Approximately 40 percent of our everyday talk is devoted to letting others know our thoughts and feelings.[29]

Why do we find it so enjoyable to talk about ourselves? Harvard University neuroscientists have suggested that self-disclosure becomes its own reward, triggering the same sensations in the brain as food and money.[30] What is more, we would rather talk about ourselves even when we are promised an incentive of food or money for speculating about other people.[31] What we love is for other people to listen to us.

# ANALYZE THIS: RELATIONSHIP TURNS

A RAISIN IN THE SUN, Claudia McNeil, Sidney Poitier, 1961 / Everett Collection

Read the following excerpt from Lorraine Hansberry's play *A Raisin in the Sun,* paying special attention to the nature of turn taking and the state of conversational cooperation exhibited:

**Mama:** *(Still quietly)* Walter, what is the matter with you?

**Walter:** Matter with? Ain't nothing the matter with *me*!

**Mama:** Yes, there is. Something eating you up like a crazy man. Something more than me not giving you this money. The past few years I been watching it happen to you. You get all nervous acting and kind of wild in the eyes—*(Walter jumps up impatiently at her words)* I said sit there now, I'm talking to you!

**Walter:** Mama—I don't need no nagging at me today.

**Mama:** Seem like you getting to a place where you always tied up in some kind of knot about something. But if anybody ask you 'bout it you just yell at 'em and bust out the house and go out and drink somewheres. Walter Lee, people can't live with that. Ruth's a good, patient girl in her way—but you getting to be too much. Boy, don't make the mistake of driving that girl away from you.

**Walter:** Why—what she do for me?

**Mama:** She loves you.

**Walter:** Mama—I'm going out. I want to go off somewhere and be by myself for a while.

**Mama:** I'm sorry 'bout your liquor store, son. It just wasn't the thing for us to do. That's what I want to tell you about—

**Walter:** I got to go out, Mama—

*(He rises.)*

**Mama:** It's dangerous, son.

| Walter: | What's dangerous? |
| Mama: | When a man goes outside his home to look for peace. |

- What do the turn taking and yielding behaviors of Mama and Walter tell us about their relationship?

- Do they adhere to the cooperation principle?

Effective communication is dialogic and requires that communicators exhibit concern for each other and their relationship. Dialogic conversational parties display respect for each other, invite each other to participate actively in the conversation, display an accepting manner, request clarification of the other person's perspective, and show empathy by adopting an "other-oriented" perspective that helps the other person feel understood.

# HAVING DIFFICULT CONVERSATIONS AND REPAIRING CONVERSATIONAL DAMAGE

Sometimes in a conversation, we need to tackle difficult subjects and serious matters. Rather than being composed of small-talk, these conversations are more like "hard-talk" or what conversational specialists call "consequential unscripted interactions."[32] Perhaps you need to discuss health issues, finances, give corrective feedback, or hold someone accountable for problematic behavior. When facing such an interaction, it's important to commit to having an honest conversation so that you can air what's troubling you. This is often easier said than done, however.[33] Techniques that work include these:

- Set a clear goal (know your purpose for having the conversation and the outcome you seek).

- Identify your assumptions about the other person's motives (recognize that they may not really be the other's intentions).

- Review the backstory (acknowledge what has contributed to your current emotional state).

- Be willing to engage confidently and assertively: Clearly express how you feel (see Chapters 2, 8, and 11) while relying on non-threatening, non-accusatory "I-messaging" (see Chapter 4).

Every now and then we commit or are on the receiving end of a conversational blunder—a faux pas—during which something we or our partner find objectionable is said. When this occurs, a prime means of repairing the damage done by the blunder is to offer an excuse designed to lessen the potential negative consequences of the remark. For instance, after insulting a friend, we might offer an excuse such as "I don't know why I said that. Can you forgive me? I'm just stressed because of what's happening at work."

To avoid committing such blunders, we need to remind ourselves that, as we converse, it is important to engage in dual perspective talking. This requires us to make a concerted effort to take the other person's feelings into account, as well as our own, as we interact.

Insensitivity is not the only cause of conversational blunders. Sometimes **prejudiced talk**, including racist, sexist, or ageist comments, also damages conversations.[34] Because it emphasizes differences rather than similarities, such talk functions to separate, distance, and enhance feelings of power for the user of the questionable language. Because most of us try to present ourselves as unprejudiced when we converse with others, we are apt to preface prejudiced talk with a disclaimer in which we claim not to be prejudiced. As noted earlier, however, once we speak words aloud, we cannot easily take them back. The damage is done, and the people in the relationship will feel its effects.

# CULTURAL DIFFERENCES AND CONVERSATION

Culture and conversational norms are related. Culture influences beliefs about the nature and value of conversation. For example, conversation is more important to European Americans than it is to native-born Chinese or Chinese Americans. For that reason, European Americans are much more likely to initiate and engage in conversations with others than are Chinese Americans. Whereas European Americans view talk as a tool to gain social control, the Chinese view the absence of talk as a control strategy.[35] From their collectivist perspective, talk is not necessary for relationship development, whereas from the individualist perspective held by European Americans, it is.

The difference between high-context cultures such as those of Asia and Africa and low-context cultures such as those of the United States and most Western European countries is also reflected in the words members choose in conversation. During their conversations, members of low-context cultures are more likely to utter words such as *absolutely, positively,* and *most definitely,* while members of high-context cultures are more likely to use fewer categorical words while employing more provisional language, such as *maybe, possibly,* and *probably.*[36] These practices are reflective of contrasting worldviews—the Western worldview being linear and the non-Western worldview being relational and therefore focused on avoiding the use of more extreme wordings.[37] Do your experiences confirm this observation?

The Japanese share the collectivist perception; in general, they tend to trust those who are silent more than those who talk a lot. The Japanese value discretion; they believe that talking can be dangerous to a relationship because it may precipitate social disapproval and the embarrassment of others.[38]

In contrast, people from Arab cultures tend to engage others in conversation much more directly and to use an abundance of over-assertions or exaggerations when conversing.[39] Often, for example, a simple no is construed by other Arabs to mean yes, and thus, Arabs must rely on verbal exaggeration to make a point.[40]

Puerto Rico, a collectivist, high-context culture, shares a number of characteristics with Asian cultures. Like Asians, Puerto Ricans typically do their best to reduce the risk of any conversational confrontation, preferring to be more imprecise and indirect when it comes to clarifying a message's meaning. What is *not* said in a conversation with someone from Puerto Rico may be more significant than what is said.[41]

Feelings about turn-taking also vary among cultures. Because they value succinctness, for example, people from Asian cultures tend to take short turns when conversing and try to distribute turns evenly.[42] In contrast, North Americans tend to take longer turns, which they distribute unevenly, with the participant who initiated a topic characteristically attempting to monopolize conversation. By understanding such differences, we increase our chances of facilitating effective conversations with people from diverse cultures.

# GENDER DIFFERENCES AND CONVERSATION

Conversation is a collaborative effort.

Men and women view and define conversation differently. A number of the differences are attributable to the value men place on instrumental behavior and their preference for engaging in organized activities or interacting in groups and the value women place on talk and their preference for engaging in one-on-one, person-to-person communication.[43] Underscoring this basic difference, linguist Deborah Tannen notes that for men, conversations "are negotiations in which people try to achieve and maintain the upper hand if they can, and protect themselves from others' attempts to put them down and push them around," whereas for women, conversations "are negotiations for closeness in which people try to seek and give confirmation and support, and to reach consensus. They [women] try to protect themselves from others' attempt to push them away."[44] As a result, women and men often misunderstand each other's intentions. Women wonder why men are not interested in discussing a situation's details, and men wonder why women want to waste their time talking about trivial matters.

Conversation is a collaborative effort. Everything that happens during conversation is the doing of the participants, including interrupting. For interruption to succeed, one speaker begins speaking before being yielded the floor, and another speaker must stop speaking as a result. Men and women differ in the amount of interrupting they do during their conversations with each other. Interrupting violates the turn-taking system, and it allows the interrupted to exercise his or her conversational power and assume greater conversational control.

## REFLECT ON THIS

*Interruptitis*

Who do you think interrupts more—men or women?

In this excerpt from her book *Gender and Discourse,* researcher and sociolinguist Deborah Tannen focuses on a gender-based conversational perception:

*(Continued)*

Creatas Images/Creatas/Thinkstock

**(Continued)**

A joke has it that a woman sues her husband for divorce. When the judge asks her why she wants a divorce, she explains that her husband has not spoken to her in two years. The judge then asks the husband, "Why haven't you spoken to your wife in two years?" He replies, "I didn't want to interrupt her."

This joke reflects the commonly held stereotype that women talk too much and interrupt men. On the other hand, one of the most widely cited findings to emerge from research on gender and language is that men interrupt women far more than women interrupt men. This finding is deeply satisfying insofar as it refutes the misogynistic stereotype and seems to account for the difficulty getting their voices heard that many women report having in interactions with men. At the same time, it reflects and bolsters common assumptions about the world: the belief that an interruption is a hostile act, with the interrupter an aggressor and the interrupted an innocent victim. Furthermore, it is founded on the premise that interruption is a means of social control, an exercise of power and dominance.

To what extent do your experiences support or contradict the observations of Tannen and others? Explain your answers using specific examples.

Sources: See V. Chand, "Linguistic Anthropology," *Current Anthropology,* 46, 2005, pp. 261–362.

Deborah Tannen, *Gender and Discourse,* New York: Oxford University Press, 1994, pp. 54–55.

However, in other situations, interruptions can be construed not as power plays, but as a sign of conversational or social comfort, where one party feels free to interrupt the other and the interrupted party does not feel infringed on and does not resent the interruption.[45] When this occurs, it actually greases a conversation's wheels, encouraging and reinforcing the speaker.[46]

## ANALYZE THIS: DON'T FINISH MY THOUGHTS

Read the following selection from Henrik Ibsen's classic play *A Doll's House,* in which Torvald Helmer and his wife, Nora, whom he has always treated as though she were a child, are engaged in a conversation:

**Nora:** (*Looking at her watch.*) It's not so late yet. Sit down, Torvald; you and I have much to say to each other. (*She sits at one side of the table.*)

**Helmer:** Nora—what does this mean? Your cold, set face—

**Nora:** Sit down. It will take some time. I have much to talk over with you. *(Helmer sits at the other side of the table.)*

**Helmer:** You alarm me, Nora. I don't understand you.

**Nora:** No, that is just it. You don't understand me; and I have never understood you—till to-night. No, don't interrupt. Only listen to what I say.—We must come to a final settlement, Torvald.

**Helmer:** How do you mean?

**Nora:** *(After a short silence.)* Does not one thing strike you as we sit here?

**Helmer:** What should strike me?

**Nora:** We have been married eight years. Does it not strike you that this is the first time we two, you and I, man and wife, have talked together seriously?

**Helmer:** Seriously! What do you call seriously?

**Nora:** During eight whole years, and more—ever since the day we first met—we have never exchanged one serious word about serious things.

**Helmer:** Was I always to trouble you with the cares you could not help me to bear?

**Nora:** I am not talking of cares. I say that we have never yet set ourselves seriously to get to the bottom of anything.

**Helmer:** Why, my dearest Nora, what have you to do with serious things?

**Nora:** There we have it! You have never understood me—

1. What can you tell about Nora and Torvald's relationship from this brief conversation?

2. Have you ever initiated a conversation similar to this one that signaled a turning point in a close relationship?

3. If so, did the person you were addressing attempt to interrupt you? Did you attempt to interrupt him or her? How did each of you respond?

Source: Henrik Ibsen, *A Doll's House* (1879), translated by William Archer, in *Six Plays by Henrik Ibsen,* New York: Barnes & Noble Classics, 2003, pp. 311–312.

# MEDIA AND TECHNOLOGY TALK

Media and technology continue to change the tone and nature of our conversations.

## MEDIA TALK

Conversation on radio and television talk shows has coarsened over the years. Too frequently participants demonstrate their incivility. On news programs featuring "talking heads," for example, hosts and guests commonly use insults, speech that degrades, and pronouncements that encourage defensiveness or hostile reactions. They verbally attack and chronically interrupt one another, exhibit little patience for alternative points of view, belittle each other, and raise their voices so that they literally yell at each other. While the media offers a few examples of genuine, well-mannered, and well-informed conversation, they provide a multitude of negative models of conversation for listeners and viewers to emulate.[47]

## TRY THIS

### Squawk Talk

Think about the ways that films and videos have influenced your conversational habits. To what extent, if any, do you think we use such offerings to learn how to talk to each other and what to talk about?

1. Cite an example of conversation initiation, topic focusing, and termination used in a film or television show that you have copied or used in conversation with another person. Compare and contrast the results you achieved with the media results.

2. Listen to or view a talk show. Count the number of times the show's host or guests attack, embarrass, and/or insult each other; raise their voices; interrupt each other; or otherwise display anger, frustration, or impatience with one another.

3. In your opinion, does poor conversational behavior make "good" entertainment? If yes, why? If no, how do you account for the popularity of shows featuring such behavior?

## TECHNOLOGY TALK

As we observed in the introduction to this chapter, technology increases connection. The question is, whether we are sacrificing meaningful conversation for mere connection—a concern expressed by author, psychologist, and MIT professor Sherry Turkle. Turkle observes that we have become too comfortable being "alone together."[48] Technology frees us to be with each other and elsewhere simultaneously. We want to pay attention to what interests us, but not necessarily the person whom we're with. Even as we connect, Turkle notes, we hide. She quotes the words of a wistful 16-year-old: "Someday, someday, but certainly not now, I'd like to learn how to have a conversation."[49]

### Technology and Conversation

Far too many of us are not comfortable conversing when face-to-face. We wear headsets connected to smartphones and computers, keeping even people who are near us at a distance. According to Turkle, no matter how valuable Twitter and Facebook are, connecting with others through them does not substitute for conversation—the means of communicating that calls on us to see things from another's perspective.[50] Unfortunately, even when conversing face-to-face, we sometimes fail to achieve that goal.

Studies reveal that the mere presence of a visible cell phone signals that our conversation could be interrupted causing us to keep our discussion more superficial. The visibility of the cell phone affects not only the depth of a conversation, but how connected to each other the parties to the conversation feel.[51]

## Influences of Digital Connectivity

Advances in technology also are contributing to some of us finding it difficult to imagine person-to-person contact apart from digital connections. An outcome of the obsession with digital devices is that while fewer of us engage in face-to-face conversation with those whom we don't know well,[52] legions of people walk down the street or sit in cafés communicating with others not physically present. We can converse with virtually anyone, and when we do so digitally, we are more apt to be blunt, sometimes even cruel, than we are in face-to-face encounters.

For some, conversing face-to-face or on cell phones is passé—texting is preferred, even when the person we are texting is seated next to us. Too many of us think nothing of interrupting a face-to-face conversation to respond to someone not present, but who has just texted or tweeted us. For some reason, we tend to give people reaching out via digital technology priority by allowing them to interrupt our face-to-face conversations. Some observers even assert that face-to-face conversation may be in jeopardy, that we may be jettisoning aural communication.[53] Texting may be fine, but it's what texting is doing to conversation that's troublesome. Turkle notes that in a conversation involving five or six people, only three are likely to be paying attention at any given time. Conversation may be proceeding, but when you look at who's engaged, you see only three heads that are up.[54]

When communicating face-to-face, we typically are aware of who we are conversing with. When we tweet or post online, however, we may be doing so without full knowledge of our audience because the person we intend our posts for can send them on to others without our permission or knowledge.

## Multi-Tasking Multiplies

In addition, technology makes multi-tasking while online commonplace. We often find ourselves participating in any number of digitally based conversations simultaneously. While we sometimes do the same when engaged face-to-face, usually those with whom we are interacting are aware of our side conversations. This is not necessarily so when we go online. When online, we can conduct an array of conversations with different people, each of whom might believe we are interacting solely with them when that's far from the truth. While our attention is divided, we somehow manage to keep numerous conversational threads going. What is more, Twitter gives us a means of listening in on millions of conversations daily.[55]

How is all this media multitasking affecting us? It may be hurting some of us—especially teenagers—socially and emotionally. In fact, face-to-face time correlates with higher levels of social confidence.[56] It may well be that watching others' faces lets us better interpret their emotions, which makes us feel more comfortable socially and more emotionally engaged. Looking at people, not just devices, also builds empathy.[57]

## Blogging and Podcasting

Blogging and podcasting provide two other means we use to compose and share our thoughts with others. People once recorded their secret wishes, regrets, and social problems in personal diaries or journals. Today, we use blogs and podcasts to record our problems, vent, relieve stress, and permit others to respond. For the most part, reader responses to personal revelations tend to be supportive, helping us put things in perspective.[58] As with all forms of conversation, however, we can also use a blog or podcast to spread rumors and gossip.[59] Unlike face-to-face conversations, which are for the most part spontaneous, blog entries and podcasts can be revised before they are posted for others to read and respond to.

### Ending the Connection

Whereas face-to-face conversations have clear beginnings and endings, a conversation begun in cyberspace may terminate without our full awareness. In other words, our conversational partner can disengage without notifying us. How do you feel when, in the midst of an online chat, you discover that you literally are talking to yourself? Would you prefer that your partner clue you in to his or her departure, perhaps by typing "gotta go"? What if a partner you had been talking to face-to-face simply walked away without so much as a word? Are the two situations comparable? While the latter is unexpected, sadly, more and more people are accepting abrupt technological disconnections as normal. Do you?

# GAINING COMMUNICATION COMPETENCE: IMPROVING YOUR CONVERSATION SKILLS

Developing the skills noted in the following can facilitate your ability to participate in and manage conversations more effectively.

## DEVELOP META-CONVERSATIONAL ABILITIES

Just as metacommunication is communication about communication, meta-conversation is conversation about conversation. Be willing to talk with your conversational partner about *how* you talk to one another. Share your insights about intentions, perceived contradictions or inconsistencies, and impressions of each other's thoughts and feelings. It is important to commit to developing a greater understanding of the factors involved in effective conversation.

## BE AWARE OF HOW CULTURE AND GENDER DIFFERENCES AFFECT CONVERSATION

What works in China may not work in the United States or in Muslim countries. To facilitate interaction with people whose cultural background or gender differs from your own, you need to open yourself to the differences that exist, maintain a flexible outlook, and engage in conversation to increase your understanding of one another. This means that you need to be unconditionally accepting of differences; you should not make others feel that they have to conform to your preferences for you to interact with them.

## STRIVE TO IMPROVE YOUR CONVERSATION INITIATION, MANAGEMENT, AND TERMINATION ABILITIES

Every communicator shares responsibility for beginning, managing, and terminating conversations. This means we are each responsible for performing speaking and listening functions, and we are each responsible for ensuring that we take advantage of conversational opportunities.

To that end, you need to monitor your own behavior in addition to monitoring the behavior of the person you are conversing with. Demonstrate your concern for others in addition to your concern for yourself. Practice active listening, be sensitive to expressions that signal turn-taking preferences, find ways to communicate your level of personal involvement and interest in appropriate ways, and attain conversational closure in a manner that is confirming and non-offensive, leaving the door open for possible future encounters.

Do you let cellphones interrupt face-to-face conversations?

## STRIKE A BALANCE BETWEEN FACE-TO-FACE AND DIGITAL CONVERSATIONS

Conversing with others using digital means is not a substitute for face-to-face interaction. If face-to-face conversations continue to be de-emphasized in favor of texting and tweeting, we may also lose our ability to make eye-contact and learn how to empathize. Texting during social gatherings hurts conversation.

## CONNECT THE CASE

### The Case of the Company Party

It would be one of those company parties—the kind where you don't really know anyone, so you stand around and feel awkward and totally unconnected. Even though he wasn't the chit-chatty type, Alberto knew he was expected to attend. He told himself that it meant he would have to spend time interacting with people he really didn't want to spend any extra time with. He had no interest in them, just as they probably had no interest in him.

Alberto thought about trying to get out of going to the party. He considered using the old "car trouble" excuse, but he dismissed that idea quickly because it seemed too obvious. He had gone so far as to mention to a coworker that he wasn't feeling well, but he knew that his not showing up at the party would only create more problems for him. So a little while after testing out the "sickness" excuse, he had said he felt better.

*(Continued)*

(Continued)

From the moment Alberto arrived at the party, he felt out of place, just as he thought he would. Not one person approached him, and he didn't approach anyone either. He longed to find a quiet little corner, sit down, and do his best to look introspective. He considered interacting with the catering staff so that he wouldn't stand out as unapproachable. He took out his cell and pretended to text.

Suddenly, seemingly out of nowhere, a person Alberto had never spoken to before stood before him. Alberto was dumbstruck. He could think of nothing to say. He opened his mouth, hoping some interesting words would come out, but his nerves got the better of him. Alberto was a wreck. He excused himself, uttering something about having just received an emergency text, and hurried to leave the room, as an even sicker feeling consumed him. Looking at the framed picture on the wall of the hallway, Alberto realized that the person he had just turned his back on was the company's president.

### Consider these questions:

1.  If you were Alberto's friend, what advice would you give him about how to survive and thrive at a company party or similar function?

2.  Have you ever been in a situation similar to the one Alberto found himself in? How did you handle it? How would you handle it now?

# REVIEW THIS

## CHAPTER SUMMARY

**1. Define small talk and enumerate the skills that good conversationalists share.** ☐

Small talk is spontaneous conversation; it facilitates our making contact with others. Above all else, a good conversationalist has a curious mindset.

**2. Explain conversation's importance and nature.** ☐

Conversation facilitates contact and the establishing of interpersonal relationships. It is a relatively informal social interaction in which the parties involved exchange the roles of sender and listener, or receiver, collaboratively and spontaneously. Conversational rules reveal the behaviors we prefer and would like to prohibit in various social situations. Most conversations proceed in the following five stages: greeting, topic priming, heart of the conversation, preliminary processing, and closing.

**3. Explain conversational management.** ☐

We regulate our conversations by using and responding to turn-maintaining and turn-yielding signals. The parties cooperate, adhering to the maxims of quality, quantity, relevancy, and manner, and following the dialogue principle.

**4. Discuss how to navigate a difficult conversation and repair conversational damage.** ☐

Rather than being composed of small-talk, difficult conversations are more like a "hard-talk" or what conversational specialists call "consequential unscripted interactions." Conversational damage is caused by a conversational blunder during which something we or our partner find objectionable is said. When this occurs, a prime means of repairing the damage done by the blunder is to offer a disclaimer designed to lessen the potential negative consequences of the remark.

**5. Describe how cultural differences influence feelings and perceptions of the nature and value of conversation.** ☐

Cultural differences influence our attitudes about the nature and value of conversation. For example, while the members of some cultures view talk as a means of gaining social control, others use silence for this purpose.

**6. Describe how gender differences influence the nature of conversation.** ☐

Whereas for men conversations are negotiations for achievement, for women, they are negotiations for closeness.

**7. Discuss how the media and technology are helping to reinforce or change both the substance and the nature of conversation.** ☐

Media talk shows are providing models of incivility, leading to the coarsening of conversations. New technologies are widening the kinds of conversations we are having, freeing us to conduct multiple conversations simultaneously, some of which are face-to-face and some of which take place in cyberspace.

8. **Identify specific steps you can take to improve your conversational skills.** ☐

By working to increase your understanding of conversations and taking the time to develop your conversational skills, you can enrich your potential for developing meaningful relationships.

## CHECK YOUR UNDERSTANDING

1. Can you offer an example that displays the role small talk plays in relationship building? (See page 190.)

2. Can you create a scenario to illustrate the difference between an effective and an ineffective conversationalist? (See pages 190–191.)

3. Can you deconstruct a recorded conversation by identifying its parts? (See pages 192–196.)

4. Can you describe specific ways in which gender, culture, media, and technology affect your conversational exchanges? (See pages 200–206.)

5. Can you devise a plan to enhance your conversational skills? (See page 206.)

## KEY TERMS

Get the tools you need to sharpen your study skills. **SAGE edge** offers a robust online environment featuring an impressive array of free tools and resources. Access practice quizzes, eFlashcards, video, and multimedia at **edge.sagepub.com/gambleicp**.

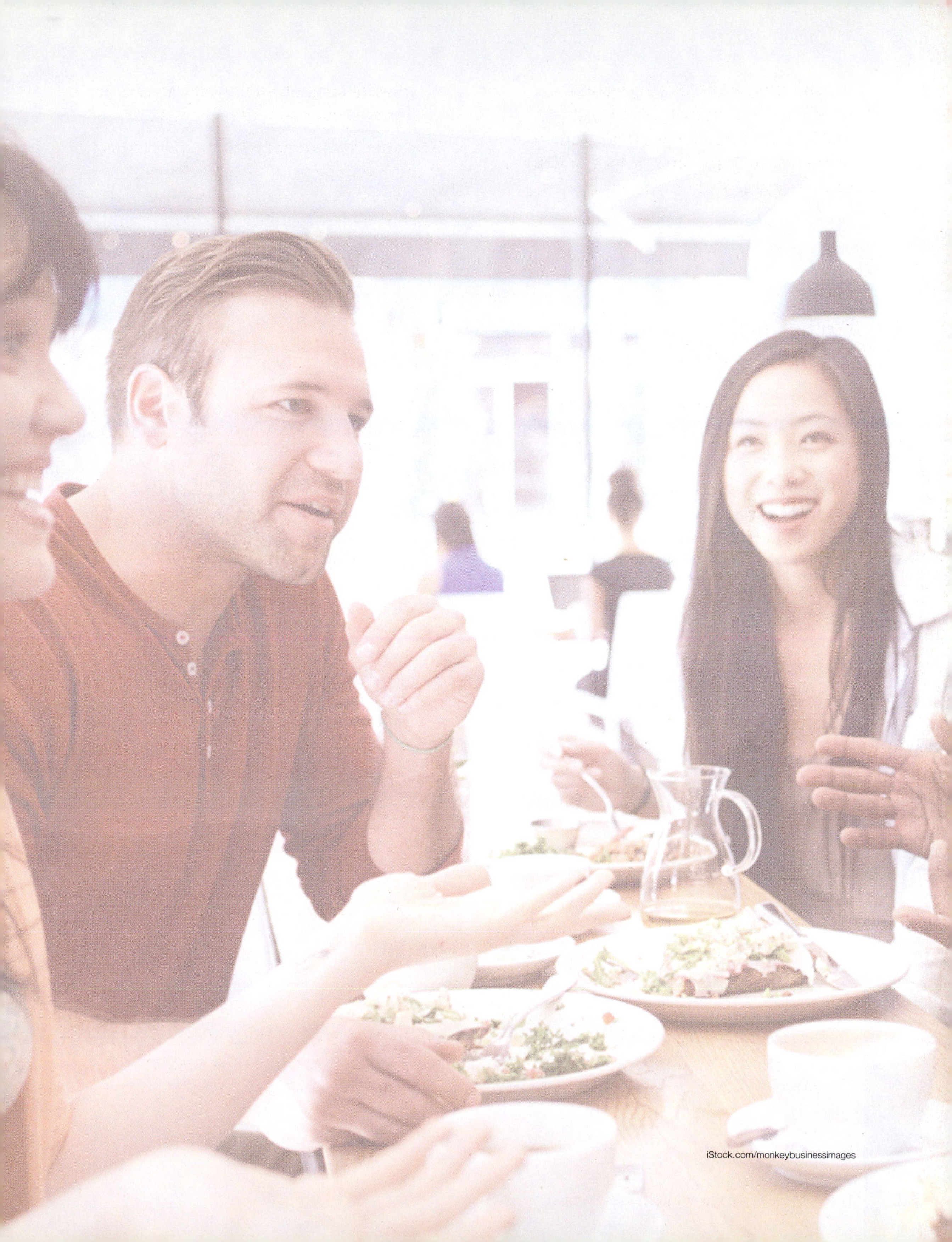
iStock.com/monkeybusinessimages

iStock.com/PeopleImages

# 8

# Emotions

## Learning Objectives

**AFTER COMPLETING THIS CHAPTER, YOU SHOULD BE ABLE TO**

1. Explain what emotions are, identifying the connection between emotional awareness and resilience

2. Discuss the relationship between emotional management, emotional intelligence, and emotional ineptitude

3. Describe the look and feel of emotions

4. Identify factors influencing how emotions affect relationships

5. Describe culture's effects on the expression of emotion

6. Describe gender's effects on the expression of emotion

7. Discuss how the media and technology serve as both models and channels for the emotions we exhibit

8. Apply guidelines for sharing emotions more effectively

**Emotions are contagious.**

—Carl Jung

Surprise—your friend's hair is now PINK! Sadness—your grandparent's cancer is incurable. Anger—your BFF has been secretly going out with your significant other. Fear—you hear a series of gunshots right outside your classroom. Emotions are powerful forces that help to mark the high and low points of our lives. Leaving home, falling in love, having a baby, grieving, experiencing an act of violence—all these arouse our emotions. Our emotional responses reveal what we care about and what we think is of consequence.

Because our emotions may move us in ways we fail to anticipate, sometimes they get the better of us.[1] They can affect our judgments and ability to make rational decisions.[2] This can happen, for example, if we over-identify with another person's pain or joy, or become paralyzed by fear.[3] Once overwhelmed with emotion, we may find it challenging to control our reactions. And when we handle them poorly, emotions can have frightening effects. Daniel Goleman notes numerous examples of this happening in his often-cited book *Emotional Intelligence*.[4] When a student goes on a violent rampage after being suspended from school, a motorist experiences road rage after being cut off, or a Neighborhood Watch member responds to a perceived threat by "standing his ground" and shooting a weaponless teenager, we are witness to the terrible effects of out-of-control, badly managed emotions.

In this chapter, we explore what we need to understand about our emotions to be able to lead an emotionally rich and complex life. We also identify steps to take to prevent emotions from causing relational damage, including how to recognize your feelings and better understand your emotions so that when you respond, you do so assertively rather than aggressively and don't end up hurting yourself or others. By shaping our emotional habits, we act to harness positive emotions and prevent either out-of-control or festering emotions from destroying our relationships—overtly or insidiously. ■

## WHAT DO YOU KNOW?

Before continuing your reading of this chapter, which of the following five statements do you believe to be true, and which do you believe to be false?

| | | | |
|---|---|---|---|
| 1. | Feeling depressed affects your breathing. | T | F |
| 2. | Anger is the briefest of all emotions. | T | F |
| 3. | We feel closer to those people we laugh with. | T | F |
| 4. | The use of Botox contributes to emotional expressiveness. | T | F |
| 5. | On Twitter, good news travels faster than bad news. | T | F |

Read the chapter to discover if you're right or if you've made any erroneous assumptions.

ANSWERS: 1. T; 2. F; 3. T; 4. F; 5. F

iStock.com/silverkblack

Our feelings influence our emotional response.

## WHAT ARE EMOTIONS?

Emotions are the feelings we experience in reaction to our surroundings and other people. Emotions are our responses to the differences we perceive between the self and the environment.[5] For example, if we sense a personal gain from a relationship, we likely feel confident. On the other hand, if we feel threatened by the relationship, we are apt to feel anxious.

Our emotions are accompanied by physiological changes within our bodies and physical changes in our appearance. Some emotions, such as anger, increase respiration and heart rate and may cause us to become tense and flushed. Other emotions have the opposite effects. For example, depression slows respiration and may cause us to be visibly pale.

As noted in our discussion of perception in Chapter 3, not everyone responds to the same stimulus in the same way or with the same intensity. Each of us experiences unique physical and psychological sensations as our emotions affect us in complicated ways. By focusing on both response differences and similarities, we can learn about our unique emotional style and how we react to and try to cope with our feelings.[6] As one theorist observes,

> The joyful person is more apt to see the world through "rose colored glasses," the distressed or sad individual is more apt to construe the remarks of others as critical, and the fearful person is inclined to have *tunnel vision*, that is, to see only the frightening object.[7]

Emotions color our outlooks and relationships.

Developmental psychologist Howard Gardner believes that at the very core of intrapersonal and interpersonal intelligence are the ability to gain "access to one's own feelings and the ability to discriminate among them and draw upon them to guide behavior," together with our "capacities to discern and respond appropriately to the moods, temperaments, motivations, and desires of other people."[8] By developing a broader awareness of and sensitivity to feelings, we also cultivate greater **resilience**, the ability to cope with and recover and bounce back quickly from disappointments, setbacks, and upsets.[9] With greater resilience, we are better able to shake off feelings that otherwise might debilitate and/or de-energize us.

# MANAGING EMOTIONS

Can we learn to manage our emotions? In the Disney Pixar animated film *Inside Out*, viewers were introduced to personifications of five basic emotions that lived within the main character's mind: joy, sadness, fear, disgust, and anger. Riley (the film's main character) had to relocate with her family to an unfamiliar town. As a result, she went on an emotional roller coaster ride as her emotions did their best to guide her on her journey, sometimes working in harmony and other times being contentious. As Riley sought to cope, ultimately, she was able to manage her emotions, adjust, and live an emotionally complex life. As she came to understand her emotions, Riley grew in emotional intelligence.

## DEVELOPING EMOTIONAL INTELLIGENCE

**Emotional intelligence** helps us maintain emotional balance. It also helps us keep our relationships healthy. Having emotional intelligence motivates us to persist in the face of frustration, to control impulses and delay gratification, and to regulate our moods so we keep distress from swamping our ability to think, to empathize, and to hope.[10] In contrast, **emotional ineptitude**, or the inability to control an emotional response, is the root cause of many relationship problems. Once we have an emotional outburst, we may regret it, but the relational damage is done.

Emotional intelligence is a form of ==social intelligence==—the ability to understand and relate to people.[11] According to Gardner, both intrapersonal and interpersonal intelligence are integral components of social intelligence. With intrapersonal intelligence, we are able to recognize our emotions and manage them, finding ways to handle such feelings as fear, anxiety, anger, and sadness. Developing emotional self-control frees us to channel our emotions in the service of a goal. By knowing ourselves, we are more likely to recognize similar emotions in others, a skill that strengthens interpersonal intelligence. However, monitoring our own emotions is but a first step in developing self–other understanding.

When emotionally intelligent, we monitor both our own and others' emotions, discriminating among them and using what we discern to guide our thinking and actions when in another's presence.[12] For example, does arguing with a friend ruin the rest of your day? If a dinner engagement is canceled, do you feel depressed for hours? How quickly do you recover from disappointments? Once we develop an awareness of how others affect us, we are no longer at the mercy of the emotions we feel when in their company.

As we discussed in Chapter 4, empathy, the ability to tune in to what others are feeling and to feel with them, is an important interaction skill. Those who are ==emotionally tone-deaf== usually don't have as many fulfilling relationships as do the emotionally attuned. In fact, to become interpersonally effective, we need to develop our ability not only to understand our own emotions, but to empathize with others as they experience an array of emotions as well.[13] By employing appropriate emotions in response and displaying emotional self-control and a willingness to delay self-gratification, we facilitate self–other understanding.

# EMOTIONS HAVE A LOOK AND FEEL

Years ago, there was a hit song titled "The Look of Love." Have you ever stopped to consider what love actually looks like? When we are in love, our facial expressions and body language often reveal our emotions to others. (See Chapter 6.) In fact, while cultures may have different rules that guide emotional displays, the physical expressions associated with particular emotions appear to be virtually universal. For that reason, even without understanding another's language, we are often able to identify the emotion the person is expressing—we can tell whether he or she is angry, feels threatened, or feels at ease and is having a good time.

We read emotions partly by mirroring facial expressions. Notably, research suggests that Botox dulls the user's ability to understand others' emotions. Because the drug paralyzes users' facial muscles, they cannot make a number of the facial movements normally active in facial expression mimicking. Thus, Botox not only impedes a user's ability to express emotions, but it may also impede the ability to empathize with others.[14]

We register the experience of an emotion not just in our minds, but in our bodies as well.[15] Happiness, for example, makes us feel warm all over, while fear can make us feel cold and tightens our chest. Emotions also register on our face. According to nonverbal communication expert Paul Ekman, particular facial patterns reflect each emotion.[16]

## SURPRISE

Surprise is the briefest of all emotions, flitting quickly across our faces. We express surprise by lifting our eyebrows, creating horizontal wrinkles across the forehead, slightly raising our upper eyelids, and usually opening the mouth in an oval shape. The lifting of the eyebrows also allows us to take in a larger visual area and enables more light to strike the retina. Surprise may transform into happiness if the stimulus that caused it leads to something favorable or into anger or fright if the event that created it initially leads to a perceived threat or outrage.

## ANGER

Anger garners a lot of attention because of the damage it can do if poorly handled. We feel anger when someone interferes with our ability to attain a goal, restraining us, physically or psychologically. Disregard for our feelings or disdain for us also may produce in us feelings of anger and hostility. Of interest is that when women display angry feelings they are labeled as "out of control" and judged more harshly than men.[17] Thus, they often suppress their anger—even smiling when furious.[18]

When experiencing anger or hostility, we usually lower our eyebrows and draw them together to create a scowl or a frown. We often stare at the object or person that elicited these feelings and tightly compress our lips or draw them back in a square-like shape to reveal our clenched teeth. Our face may redden, and the veins in our neck and head may become more visible. As anger surges through us, blood flows to our hands, making it easier for us to strike out; our heart rate increases, and adrenalin prepares us for possible action.[19]

Because contemporary American society discourages overt expressions of anger, we might conclude that expressing anger is dangerous or unhealthy. If communicated properly, however, it is neither. In fact, while it may be unhealthy to express a lot of anger often, it is better to express some anger than to avoid expressing anger at all. Research has found that the moderate expression of anger, compared with little or no expression, cuts the risk of heart attack and stroke in half.[20] People who fail to express their anger at all have been found to be more likely to exhibit passive-aggressive behavior or a negative and hostile personality. It is important to learn constructive ways to express angry feelings, using assertiveness rather than aggressiveness. Also of value is learning how to redirect angry feelings and calm down.

An effective response to anger is to figure out what triggered it so that we can express our angry feelings assertively by clarifying for the person(s) involved what our needs are and how they can be met without harming anyone else. This requires that we calm down, perhaps by doing some deep breathing or visualizing appropriate imagery, before responding so that we can control not just our outward behavior, but also our internal responses. Expressing angry feelings in assertive ways—ways that are respectful of our own needs and feelings as well as those of others—rather than in aggressive or suppressive ways is the healthiest means of dealing with anger.

Lashing out unthinkingly takes a toll on a relationship.

Approaching anger by using cognitive restructuring, problem solving, and humor has been shown to be useful. *Cognitive restructuring* involves changing the way we think. If, for example, we commonly react by swearing when we become angry because we exaggerate the seriousness of the situation, we need to change that dramatic response by reminding ourselves that this is not the end of the world. While we may feel frustrated, anger will not help. Instead, we need to adopt a more balanced perspective that lets us identify the problem and focus on handling it. This involves mapping out a plan and monitoring progress toward it. Adding a dose of humor also can help to defuse anger that is in danger of escalating out of control. This is not to suggest that we laugh away the problem by making light of the situation or becoming overly sarcastic. Rather, humor is useful for helping us to avoid taking ourselves or the situation too seriously.[21]

## HAPPINESS

Like anger, happiness has received particular attention in recent years as researchers have explored its impact and tried to gauge the happiness of people living in different countries.[22] Happiness is the feeling that pulls our lips back and curves them gently upward in a smile. Our cheeks rise, and the corners of our lips create wrinkles that run from the nose and eyes and out beyond our lips and cheeks.

Social laughter, a nonverbal expression of happiness, contributes to interpersonal bonding and feelings of closeness and is a source of health and well-being.[23] The physical act of laughing triggers an increase in endorphins, brain chemicals that contribute to our feeling good. In recent years, researchers in an array of fields have sought to unravel the secrets of happiness.[24] Pleasure, purpose, and pride appear to be three key variables in the happiness equation that determines life satisfaction.[25]

Joy and laughter precipitate feelings of well-being. How much you smile and laugh is an indication of how happy you feel. Happy people are likely to be more creative and productive. They also tend to have strong bonds with friends and family members.

Interestingly, the frequency of positive experiences in life is more important than their intensity. In fact, happiness researcher Daniel Gilbert asserts that happiness is the sum of hundreds of small things.[26] Nurturing social connections is one of them.

Can you predict what will make you happy and how long the feeling of happiness will last? Most of us are not terribly accurate at predicting this. In fact, few experiences—whether good or bad—affect us for longer than a few months. Yet, resilience and the ability to produce "synthetic happiness," or the happiness we create even when not getting what we want, make it possible for us to make the best of every experience.[27] It seems that we are able to look for and find things that can make our lives happier. Suggestions for increasing happiness include the following: Write a thank you note to a friend. Snap a photo. Do one thing at a time. Get some sun. Remind yourself of what you're grateful for. Think about doing a favor for someone. Engage in mini-meditation. Experience an event—make memories.[28]

## SADNESS

When we experience the opposite of happiness, sadness, we often exhibit a loss of facial muscle tone. We arch the inner corners of our eyebrows upward and draw them together. We may also raise our lower eyelids and draw down the corners of the mouth, and our lips may tremble. Accompanying sadness are a drop in our energy and a slowing of the body's metabolism.

## FEAR

When we experience fear, we raise our eyebrows slightly as we draw them together. We open our eyes wider than usual, and our lower eyelids tense. We stretch our lips back tightly, and the center of the forehead wrinkles. Our body tells us that something is wrong.

## DISGUST

Think of what your face looks like when you take a bite of a lemon. While this is not exactly the face of disgust, it comes close. Unquestionably, feelings of disgust do more than upset your stomach. Finding something disgusting alters your behavior, affecting virtually all aspects of your interpersonal relations, from romance to how close you get to others whom you choose to sit near.[29]

**FIGURE 8.1**
Wheel of Emotions

Primary emotions are inside the wheel.
Mixed emotions are outside the wheel.

Source: Based on Robert Plutchik, "Emotions: A General Psychoevolutionary Theory," in Klaus R. Scherer and Paul Ekman, eds., *Approachable to Emotion*, Hillsdale, NJ: Lawrence Erlbaum, 1984, p. 197–218.

Relationships don't experience emotions; we do.

## PRIMARY AND MIXED EMOTIONS

Sometimes putting on the facial expression associated with an emotion can actually precipitate the feelings that the expression represents. In other words, facial expressions are not merely the visible signs of emotions: In some instances, they may in fact be the *cause* of emotions.[30] As the mind can influence the body, the body can also influence the mind.

Psychiatrist Robert Plutchik asserts that there are eight primary emotions: surprise, anger, fear, sadness, disgust, acceptance, anticipation, and joy. According to Plutchik, these eight emotions can combine, like paint on a canvas, to form mixed emotions: remorse, a mixture of disgust and sadness, love, awe, submission, disappointment, contempt, optimism, and aggressiveness (see Figure 8.1).[31] Does your experience support or contradict the hierarchy of primary and secondary emotions that Plutchik describes? With a greater understanding of the amalgams of emotions we experience—mixtures involving emotions that sometimes conflict with one another—we can describe our feelings more accurately, develop a keener awareness of how they affect us, and process and respond to them appropriately.

## EMOTION CONTAGION

It is also possible for us to catch a mood much as we catch a cold. We call this **emotion contagion**. People expose us to their moods in much the same way they pass their germs on. The better able we are to tune in to the moods of others—the more empathetic we are—the better our chances of catching the mood of the person with whom we are communicating. Highly empathetic people tend to develop emotional support and unconsciously mirror or imitate the moods and emotions of others.[32] People who are weak at both sending and receiving moods tend to have more relationship problems than do those who are more emotionally expressive and receptive.

# EXPERIENCING EMOTIONS IN RELATIONSHIPS

Although relationships affect our emotions, relationships don't experience emotions—*we do*. When we feel good or experience what we perceive to be a positive emotion when interacting with another person, we tend to attribute that feeling to the other person and to the kind of relationship we share.[33] But when we feel a particular emotion, such as depression or rage, persistently, we are exhibiting an emotion trait. An **emotion trait** exists when we experience a specific emotion during person-to-person interactions regardless of whom we are interacting with.[34]

During any interpersonal encounter, we have various thoughts or feelings about the person with whom we are interacting and the situation itself. These thoughts elicit an **emotion state**, an emotional process of limited duration lasting from seconds to hours and varying from mild to intense.[35] This contrasts with the emotion trait, which persists for a long time. Examples of emotion states are the temporary sadness and happiness that come from hearing certain kinds of news.

Women report being in negative moods or emotion states about twice as often as do men and, as conflicting as it may seem, also report being in positive moods about twice as often as do men.[36] One reason cited for the disparity between women's and men's reports is that women's moods simply tend to be more intense than men's.[37]

We generally seek to interact with those who share our mood. As a result, our moods tend to perpetuate themselves. Further, our moods influence our perceptions of the future. After viewing a comedy, for example, we are likely to evaluate our relationships and careers more positively that we do after viewing a tragedy. Thus, a good or bad mood can create in us an optimistic or pessimistic frame of mind and, in turn, influence how positively or negatively we view others and our future.

## TRY THIS

## Emotional Checkup

1.  Which of the emotions on the following list do you recall experiencing during the past month? List them on a separate sheet of paper. (If necessary, add other emotions not listed here.)

| | | |
|---|---|---|
| Accepted | Contemptuous | Happy |
| Angry | Curious | Hostile |
| Anticipatory | Depressed | Hurt |
| Anxious | Desperate | Impatient |
| Apathetic | Disappointed | Insecure |
| Apprehensive | Disgusted | Jealous |
| Ashamed | Eager | Joyful |
| Bewildered | Ecstatic | Loving |
| Bored | Embarrassed | Optimistic |
| Calm | Envious | Outraged |
| Concerned | Excited | Paranoid |
| Confident | Fearful | Pessimistic |
| Confused | Guilty | Proud |

*(Continued)*

(Continued)

| | | |
|---|---|---|
| Rejected | Surprised | Vengeful |
| Relieved | Stressful | Vicious |
| Remorseful | Sympathetic | Violent |
| Sad | Tense | Worried |
| Shy | Useful | |
| Supported | Useless | |

2. Go back through your list and place a checkmark next to each of the emotions you experience most frequently.

3. Think about the specific people you tend to be with when you experience your most frequent emotions. Write their names next to the appropriate emotions.

4. Review the emotions and the names you have written. What relationship variables can you point to as being the cause or precipitating factor for each emotion?

5. Finally, complete these sentences:

I am anxious when I interact with _____.

I am confident when I interact with _____.

I am frustrated when I interact with _____.

I am embarrassed when I interact with _____.

I am happy when I interact with _____.

I am stressed when I interact with _____.

## EMOTIONS IN HEALTHY AND UNHEALTHY RELATIONSHIPS

Emotions can facilitate as well as impede the development of healthy relationships.

When we perceive that our interactions support our well-being, we usually experience positive or **facilitative emotions**, and we act in ways that permit our emotions to help our relational goals. When we perceive that others impede our well-being, we usually experience negative or **debilitative emotions**, and the actions accompanying these feelings typically get in the way of our developing a healthy relationship or realizing our relational goals.[38]

Although we all experience an array of emotions in our relationships, those most closely associated with relationship facilitation or goal attainment are compassion, happiness, hope, love, pride, and relief. Those most closely associated with debilitation, or that lead to our failing to attain our relational goals, are extreme anxiety, disgust, envy, terror, guilt, jealousy, paranoia, rage, sadness, and shame.

Both facilitative and debilitative emotions run the gamut of different types of feelings, but they differ from each other in two key ways—intensity and duration. We tend to feel debilitative emotions more intensely and for longer periods than facilitative emotions. Because of this, debilitative emotions interfere with our ability to engage in productive interactions. For example, although some anger can propel us to act, anger that is out of control—rage—typically reduces our ability to behave rationally and, therefore, usually impedes our ability to make things better. Thus, how we experience and express our emotions can be facilitating or debilitating and can significantly affect our relationships with others.

## MANAGING EMOTIONS

**Coping** involves the management of our emotions. We use two key coping strategies. First, we may try to remove the problem. This is often difficult—if not impossible—to accomplish when it involves another human being. For example, when we are angry with someone, it is not always practical or desirable for us simply to remove the person from our surroundings. The second, more feasible and usually more effective, means of coping involves changing the way we interpret a situation and our emotional response to it. In the following subsections, we look at ways of coping with emotions.

### How Does Making Sense of Another's Behavior Facilitate Coping?

How you interpret events often holds the key to handling your emotions. Consider the following two situations:

Imagine you are walking by a friend's house. Suddenly your friend opens the door, throws a rock at you, and starts shouting obscenities at you.

Imagine that you are walking by a psychiatric hospital in which your friend is a patient. Suddenly your friend opens the door, throws a rock at you, and starts shouting obscenities at you.[39]

You would probably think about and react to these two situations differently. Whereas in the first situation you might feel angry and upset, most likely in the second you would feel saddened and distraught. Your interpretations cause you to experience different feelings.

What you tell yourself about the nature of an experience determines whether you feel outrage or sympathy, compassion or disdain. We interpret the actions of others based on our feelings and the reasons we use to explain their behavior. Recall from Chapter 3 that attribution theory describes how we explain the causes of social behavior. Whether a specific behavior is due to a person's personality or to the situation the person finds himself or herself in affects our evaluation of that person. In other words, what we determine to be the reasons for someone else's behavior—rightly or wrongly—directly influences our perception of and feelings toward that person.[40]

## TRY THIS

### Do You Have Resilience?

With yourself in mind, indicate whether you think each of the following statements is true or false. Do not overthink your responses—answer with your first reactions.

1. A minor disagreement with a close friend or significant other typically leaves me feeling down for hours or longer.

*(Continued)*

(Continued)

2. If another driver uses the shoulder instead of waiting in line to merge, I typically shake it off quickly rather than fume about it.

3. Grief caused by the loss of a loved one has made it impossible for me to function for months.

4. If I am reprimanded for a mistake, I interpret it as a learning experience and continue.

5. If I go to a restaurant for dinner and the food and service are way below par, it ruins my night.

6. If I'm stuck in traffic because of an accident down the road, I vent my frustration by flooring it once I pass the scene.

7. If an appliance breaks in my home, I don't let it bother me. I just call someone to repair it.

8. If I'm turned down when I ask out someone I'm attracted to, I am down for days.

9. If I'm up for a promotion but it goes to someone I think doesn't deserve it as much as I do, I get over it quickly.

10. If I'm at a party and get tongue-tied while conversing with an interesting guest, I replay the scene over and over again afterward, rehashing what I should have said.

## Scoring the Test

1. For statements 1, 3, 5, 6, 8, and 10: give yourself 1 point for each you labeled as true and 0 points for each you labeled as false.

2. For statements 2, 4, 7, and 9: give yourself 1 point for each you labeled false and 0 for each labeled true.

## Interpreting Your Results

If your total score is higher than 7, you are slow to recover. If you scored below 3, you are very resilient.

Source: Based on a test by Richard J. Davidson with Sharon Begley titled "How Resilient Are You?" which appeared in "Tired of Feeling Bad? The New Science of Feelings Can Help," *Newsweek*, February 27–March 5, 2012, pp. 47–51.

## How Does Describing or Displaying Your Feelings Facilitate Coping?

How do you tell others what you are feeling? How do you explain your anger without becoming angry? How do you explain your disappointment without withdrawing into a shell? **Describing feelings** and **displaying feelings** are not the same thing. When we describe our feelings, we are not judging the other person. In contrast, an overt display of feelings—such as shouting, "That was the most stupid thing you've ever done!"—conveys an evaluation. By making the effort to describe your feelings, rather than enact them, you increase your chances of keeping lines of communication open and improving your relationship.

## ANALYZE THIS: SHOULD YOU TELL?

What do these lines from a William Blake poem reveal about the power of our emotions?

*I was angry with my friend:*
*I told my wrath, my wrath did end.*
*I was angry with my foe.*
*I told it not, my wrath did grow.*

1. Do you agree with Blake? Is the expression of anger always beneficial?

2. In your own experiences with anger, have you found that verbally expressing it helps you purge yourself of anger, or does it cause you to feel even angrier? Explain.

Source: William Blake, "A Poison Tree." 1794.

When we describe our feelings, we are also communicating how we would like the other person to treat us as well as the effect that person's behavior is having on us. By sharing such information, we give that individual the opportunity to decide whether her or his behavior toward us is appropriate or is having the intended effect. For example, if you politely tell a friend that you get exasperated when she doesn't stop talking long enough to listen to you, maybe next time you interact she will seek a response from you instead of merely delivering a monologue. When we share feelings, we make the other person more aware of how his or her actions affect us.

Although we find it easier to share positive emotions than negative ones, and we are reluctant to send messages that could hurt or embarrass another, it is important that we let someone know when we are angry with or disappointed in him or her. Because emotion is one of the most consequential outcomes of interaction, it is necessary that we let others know what causes us to feel as we do.[41] When our relationship partners understand how we feel, they are in a better position to make appropriate interpersonal choices regarding how best to interact with us.

## How Does Understanding Your Emotional Attachment Style Facilitate Coping?

Some of us easily express our emotions, whereas others prefer to be more reserved. Researcher Amir Levine differentiates three styles of attachment: avoidant, anxious, and giving.[42] People with an avoidant attachment style tend to feel overwhelmed if bombarded with too much emotion. Too much physical and emotional closeness is likely to irritate them, making it difficult for them to be emotionally supportive. Avoidant people also are apt to devalue their relationship partners by joking about their habits or appearance. In contrast, people who display an anxious attachment style typically are uncomfortable communicating feelings, yet they are constantly looking for cues

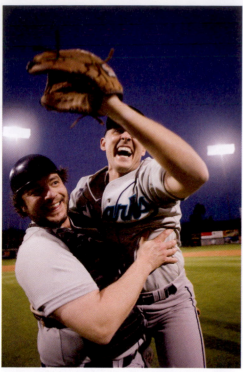

Sharing positive emotions is easier than is sharing negative ones.

of rejection in their partners. They want their partners to notice when they are upset or acting out and take corrective action without their having to give voice to their feelings. Emotional givers, on the other hand, tend to be secure in showing affection. They enjoy being on both the sending and receiving ends of displays of love and are comfortable showing intimacy.[43]

What style of emotional expresser do you think you are? Identifying your style and recognizing the style another person displays can help prepare you to handle emotional challenges and cope with disappointments.

# CULTURE AND THE EXPRESSION OF EMOTION

As we have discussed, there are basic emotions that we all experience regardless of where we live. No matter what our cultural background, at one time or another, we all feel anger, disgust, fear, happiness, and sadness. As members of a multicultural society and citizens of a shrinking world, we must understand how our own cultural filters influence how we assess the behavior and the propriety of emotions displayed by people from cultural groups other than our own. What generates those feelings in us and how expressively we display them are affected, in part, by the rules and norms of our culture.

For instance, the Japanese generally refrain from expressing negative emotions in public.[44] This is because members of collectivistic cultures, such as Japan, China, and India, place great value on preserving harmony and consequently discourage the expression of any negative feelings that could create disharmony among the group's members. In contrast, members of highly individualistic cultures, such as the United States and Canada, are comfortable "telling it like it is"—revealing their feelings to others.[45] In such cultures, keeping feelings secret so that others are unable to tell when you are hurt, happy, or sad is, for the most part, regarded as both inappropriate and an ineffective way to manage feelings. Similarly, traditional Mexican culture encourages the open display and discussion of emotion; in fact, Mexican Americans who maintain their connection to traditional Mexican culture are even more likely than other Americans to express negative emotions openly.[46] It appears that people from warmer places tend to be more emotionally expressive than people living in cooler climates.[47]

When individuals from collectivistic and individualistic cultures interact with one another, the former might easily perceive the latter as too frank. Similarly, those from individualistic cultures may perceive members of collectivistic cultures as not completely forthcoming, in part due to the importance collectivistic cultures place on helping all parties in an interaction save face.[48] **Face-saving**, or the preservation of dignity, is so important that should people from individualistic cultures violate this norm when interacting with members of collectivistic cultures, the relationship they share can suffer.

When we are sensitive to another's cultural beliefs regarding emotional expression, we equip ourselves with the skills we require to modify how we express our own emotions.

## TRY THIS

### Are You a Face-Saver?

Consider this example of a negotiation between two businesspeople, one Japanese and one American. After you read it, identify what you believe the problem was.

> Phil Downing . . . was involved in setting up a branch of his company that was merging with an existing Japanese counterpart. He seemed to get along very well with the executive colleagues assigned to work with him, one of whom had recently been elected chairman of the board when his grandfather retired. Over several weeks of discussion, Phil and the chairman of the Japanese branch had generally laid out some working policies and agreed on strategies that would bring new directions needed for development. Several days later . . . the young chairman's grandfather happened to drop in and he began to comment on how the company had been formed and had been built up by the traditional practices, talking about some of the policies the young executives had recently discarded. Phil expected the new chairman to explain some of the innovative and developmental policies they had both agreed upon. However, the young man said nothing; instead, he just nodded and agreed with his grandfather. Phil was bewildered and frustrated, . . . and he started to protest. The atmosphere in the room became immediately tense. . . . A week later the Japanese company withdrew from the negotiations.

Phil failed to understand that the fact that the Japanese company's chairman had saved face for his grandfather by agreeing with him did not negate the agreements the chairman had earlier negotiated with Phil. Phil's overt protest and disagreement with the grandfather caused the grandfather to lose face, and the young chairman was now unwilling to do business with him. What would you have done in Phil's place?

*Source:* Richard W. Brislin, Kenneth Cushner, Craig Cherrie, and Mahealani Yong, *Intercultural Interactions: A Practical Guide,* Beverly Hills, CA: Sage, 1986, pp. 155–156.

# GENDER AND THE EXPRESSION OF EMOTION

There are numerous differences between women and men in the handling of feelings. Because some men are taught to be more emotionally reserved than women, many tend to be less expressive. As a result, some researchers say that men's friendships lack the emotional depth that characterizes

Men and women are likely to express feelings and closeness differently.

women's friendships.[49] However, others counter that men lack neither feelings nor emotional depth; rather, they prefer to express their feelings and develop closeness with others through *doing* rather than through talking, through activities rather than through self-disclosure.[50]

Men and women vary in both expressiveness and sensitivity to others' emotions. Women are more likely than men to reveal a wide range of feelings, precipitating the stereotypes of women as overly expressive and of men as inexpressive. For example, women are known to cry more than men. Most would expect them to feel better after a good cry, but this is not necessarily the case. In one study, the mood of women on a crying day was found to be worse than on one during which they did not cry. Surprisingly, the negative mood characteristic of crying days persisted for the two subsequent days as well. The researchers found, in addition, that the less dark the woman's mood, the more likely crying was to help. What also helped was crying in the presence of another person. Crying in front of a group, as compared to a single individual, however, made things worse.[51]

Men may try to hide feeling frightened, sad, lonely, or embarrassed. On the other hand, they tend to unabashedly reveal their strengths. As a result, observers are less accurate in discerning men's emotions than they are women's.[52] Women are also better than men at noticing the nonverbal clues that others provide regarding their emotions[53] and tend to outperform men at decoding the emotions of others.[54]

## TRY THIS

## Sharing Feelings

Think of a specific male and a specific female friend, sibling, or parent. Using a scale of 1 to 10, where 1 represents little if any comfort and 10 represents complete comfort, indicate how comfortable you are sharing the following feelings with each:

|  | MALE | FEMALE |
|---|---|---|
| A problem you have with him or her |  |  |
| A problem you have with someone else |  |  |

|  | MALE | FEMALE |
|---|---|---|
| Anger directed toward him or her | | |
| Anger directed toward someone else | | |
| A recent disappointment directed at him or her | | |
| A recent disappointment directed at someone else | | |
| Fears about him or her | | |
| Fears about someone else | | |
| What he or she does that makes you feel insecure | | |
| What someone else does that makes you feel insecure | | |
| What he or she does that causes you stress | | |
| What someone else does that causes you stress | | |
| What he or she does that makes you happy | | |
| What someone else does that makes you happy | | |

1. With which of the two people you have chosen are you most comfortable sharing your emotions? To what extent, if any, does gender appear to be a factor?

2. Which emotions are easiest for you to share with a female? With a male? Which are the hardest to share with a female? With a male? How do you account for the differences or similarities?

3. What general conclusions can you draw regarding individuals sharing emotions with person(s) of the same or opposite gender?

It appears to be more acceptable for men to express anger than it is for women. An angry woman tends to make people uneasy. Women are expected to restrain their anger. For this reason, women sometimes mask their anger as sadness, which receivers for some reason find more palatable.[55]

Most women prefer intimate talk, whereas most men prefer instrumental demonstrations of commitment.[56] By recognizing and understanding this stylistic difference, we can take a giant step forward in being able to relate effectively to each other. This difference may also explain why, when under stress, both men and women report wanting to be with a woman friend, and why both men and women are in general more comfortable revealing feelings to women than to men.[57] These differences are played out in online communication as well, with women more likely than men to use emoticons and emoji as emotional clarifiers.[58]

# MEDIA AND TECHNOLOGY: MODELING AND CHANNELING FEELINGS

The media and digital technology provide both the models and the channels we use daily to form attitudes about the most effective ways to handle and display our feelings. What we view in the media and the technologies we prefer affect both our willingness to communicate our emotions and the means we employ to express them.

## MEDIA MODELS

The images that we see on television, in advertising, and in movies—**media models**—have the potential to affect our emotions. Heavy television viewers (those who watch more than 4 hours a day) have different attitudes and hold different beliefs than do light viewers (those who watch fewer than 2 hours daily). For example, heavy viewers hold an exaggerated view of the prevalence of violence in society and believe that older people are fewer in number and less healthy today than in years past. In general, heavy television viewers perceive the world to be a meaner and more sinister place than do light viewers, believing that, if given the chance, people will take advantage of you because they are looking out only for themselves. The opinions that heavy viewers hold reflect the fictional world that television brings to them, not the world in which they actually live.[59] The fearfulness they experience, however, is all too real.

What we see in the media influences what we believe and how we evaluate experience, affecting how we feel and express our feelings. For example, heavy television viewers are less likely to presume innocence on the part of those accused of crimes and tend to take more of a hard line when serving on juries than do light viewers. This helps them handle the anger they feel about the perceived prevalence of societal violence. They also develop more fear of crime than do light viewers and have less sympathy or empathy for rape victims. For heavy viewers, television serves as a vital source of information for constructing their image of the world.[60]

## TRY THIS

### Modeling

First, identify a media offering that you believe convinced you that a certain way of behaving was legitimate or appropriate. For example, have any television programs or films affected your way of dressing or manner of speaking?

1. Explain how what you viewed influenced how you felt and expressed your feelings and as a result affected your response to a real-life situation.

2. To what degree, if at all, did the emotional rewards obtained by the mediated characters also accrue to you?

3. If given the opportunity, would you act the same or differently today? Explain.

Now answer the following questions regarding the media models provided by extremely angry talk-show hosts, guests, and music artists:

4. In your opinion, what effect, if any, do such models have on you and other members of the viewing and listening public? Do you think they help educate us? Do you think they harm us?

5. What do you believe we stand to gain and/or lose from listening to hosts and other celebrities who make their living demonstrating an inability to handle their emotions, becoming aggressive, lashing out, and giving in to verbal impulses that trample on others?

Media models also have the potential to influence our behavior. We simply are more likely to do what we have seen. After viewing a dramatized suicide, we may come to feel that suicide may be a reasonable way to deal with the problems life presents; after watching a televised fight, we may conclude that physical violence is an acceptable way to deal with disappointment.

## TECHNOLOGICAL CHANNELS

We are in control of both channels of mass and personalized communication. We now can call up television programs and movies on demand and

CBS/Photofest

The amount of television we watch influences our emotions and our perceptions of the world.

view them whenever we want to on our tablets or smartphones. What is more, we are now able to create our own interactive media experiences.

### We Actively Participate

We are no longer merely watchers; we are active participants. We may experience media versions of real worlds, or we can enter a virtual world. For a long time, we have vicariously experienced other worlds by watching television programs and movies and playing computer games, but virtual reality does something these media do not: It endows us with **telepresence**—it takes our body with us into another world, giving us the sense of physically being in a different place or time, allowing us to participate more fully in sensory experiences that elicit feelings and emotions we otherwise might never have experienced. Just as the National Aeronautics and Space Administration and the military use virtual reality environments for space travel and war, we can use virtual reality environments to train for future communication encounters unlike any we have had to date. How would you describe your use of virtual reality?

### Sharing Emotions Digitally

Social networking sites such as Twitter have given researchers new media to investigate. For example, they have found that social networks composed of company workers and family members

## FIGURE 8.2
Emoticons

| | |
|---|---|
| :-1) | smiley with a mustache |
| :D | big smile |
| ;- | wink |
| :* | kiss |
| :**: | returning kiss |
| :-J | tongue in cheek or joking |
| () | hug |
| :-( | sad |
| :'( | crying |

facilitate the sharing of emotion and that Twitter messages containing negative emotions are retweeted more frequently than other messages, leading them to conclude that bad news travels faster than good news.[61] Researchers who explored the Twitter messages posted by more than two million people in 84 countries discovered that the emotional tones of these messages exhibited similar patterns, not only through the day but also through the week and alternating seasons. After analyzing the posts and their accompanying emoticons, the researchers concluded that our moods reflect a shared underlying biological rhythm that transcends culture. We tend to be happiest on weekends, and we usually awaken in a good mood that deteriorates as the day progresses and then drifts upward again after dinner.[62] Still, some researchers caution that tweets may reveal what the tweeter thinks the follower wants to hear rather than the tweeter's actual feelings.[63] Do your experiences confirm these findings?

Of course, emoticons and emoji are available to help us express our emotions in cyberspace when we aren't using a webcam, Facetime, or Skype and are unable to see or hear the nonverbal cues of the person we are interacting with (see Figure 8.2). Emoji are a bit more elaborate in their communication of emotion, and so let users convey more feeling in their messages. Long popular in Asia, emoji may suffer in translation because of a failure to understand cultural differences. For example, in Japan, the emoji of a smiling coil of human waste expresses dissatisfaction. This may not resonate with people in the United States. Other emoji may be more easily understood by Americans, such as one titled "Titanic" that depicts both a ship's anchor and a broken heart.[64] For clarity's sake, we sometimes also include statements describing our feelings.

The disinhibition effect, a characteristic of interaction online, can contribute to online emotional outbursts and tirades. **Flaming**, or the loss of emotional self-control while sending a message online, can precipitate **flame wars**, the exchange of out-of-control online messages. Sometimes we express our anger online by CAPITALIZING ALL OUR WORDS. Other times, our loss of control is signaled by our use of obscene or inappropriate language. And yet other times, we are just plain nasty and resort to using derogatory words, hurling vile insults and threats, and bullying.[65]

Finally, how we use technology and what we use it for reveals our feelings about it as a conduit for interpersonal communication. When your smartphone or computer in unavailable, for example, are you relieved by the fact you are no longer connected, or do you panic because you may be unreachable and unable to reach anyone else for the time being? Does forgetting your phone completely stress you out? Technology can arouse us, involve us, affect our relationships with others, or leave us cold. For example, one researcher examined the brain activity of subjects viewing both religious images and consumer images involving brands such as Apple. The brain activity was strikingly similar for both stimuli. Another experiment demonstrated a "synesthesia" (cross-sensory effect), with subjects having activation in both the audio and visual cortices of their brains when they were exposed separately to audio or video of a ringing and vibrating iPhone. What is more, subjects' brains responded to their phones' sounds just as they did to the presence of a loved one. For some, technology appears to be a love affair.[66]

For others, what they see on Facebook, Instagram, and other social networking apps provokes feelings of jealousy—especially among women.[67] Active online surveillance of friends and significant others can leave us emotionally drained.

# GAINING COMMUNICATION COMPETENCE: COMMUNICATING EMOTION SKILLFULLY

A number of factors facilitate our accurate communication of our feelings. To enhance your abilities to develop effective interpersonal relationships, keep the following in mind.

## RECOGNIZE THAT THOUGHTS CAUSE FEELINGS

The rational-emotional approach to emotion management posits that in order to turn off debilitative feelings and replace them with feelings that are facilitative, we first need to learn how to change unproductive thinking.[68] According to rational emotive behavior therapy founder and cognitive behavioral psychologist Albert Ellis, the negative *beliefs* we hold about events and people, and not the actual events or people, cause us mental anguish and lead to mental and even physical discomfort. How we react emotionally to a person or event elicits different feelings in us and different consequences in our behavior. The key to understanding our feelings is to review our self-talk—our continuous internal monologue about what is occurring,

Do you panic when your smartphone fails or your laptop crashes?

the thought process that takes place before an emotion is expressed—and analyze whether the thoughts we have debilitate or facilitate our interactions and relationships.[69]

By taking responsibility for our own emotions and actions and by monitoring our emotional reactions to specific people or situations, we can get in touch with our feelings. Once we realize how we feel, we can look for factors that trigger debilitative reactions in us. We need to identify the irrational beliefs we hold, explain why they are a product of irrational thinking, and choose a more rational and realistic way of thinking for the next time we are faced with the same person or situation. Why should we allow our feelings to debilitate us when we can use them as facilitators instead? According to Ellis, we create our own moods and emotional states with the words we use during self-talk.[70] We can reframe events by using different words to describe what has occurred. A person who persistently places a pessimistic frame around events will debilitate himself or herself, whereas a person who places an optimistic frame around events helps to facilitate instead.

## CHOOSE THE RIGHT WORDS

Many of us have a hard time letting others know exactly what we are feeling: We say we feel "good," "okay," or "bad." By relying on words that are not as specific as they could be or that do not adequately describe our emotions, we make it more difficult for others to understand us. If we can figure out what triggers a particular emotion, we can be more specific when we talk about it. We can also try to find words to describe what we feel happening to us: For example, we might say, "I feel like a robot, robbed of my personal identity." And we can describe what we would like to do in response to our feelings: "I feel like sticking my head in the sand." It is important that we work hard to describe our feelings and their intensity.

## SHOW THAT YOU ACCEPT RESPONSIBILITY FOR YOUR FEELINGS

It is important to acknowledge that you own your feelings. To do this, you need to identify yourself as the feelings' source. This means that you need to start your comments with "I," not "you." Instead of saying, for example, "You're always embarrassing me," you need to say, "I get embarrassed when . . ." Remember, no one can make you feel an emotion that you refuse to feel.

## SHARE FEELINGS FULLY

Often what we feel is an amalgam of emotions rather than one single emotion. For example, we may feel anger, confusion, embarrassment, and sadness at the same time. To call such feelings simply anger would be misleading and not candid. To refuse to discuss what we are feeling at all could be even worse. Once the feelings have surfaced, they will continue to exist, and they will not go away even when we try to ignore them. You ought to be able to share all feelings fully in the interest of openness.

## DECIDE WHEN, WHERE, AND TO WHOM TO REVEAL FEELINGS

When you are angry is usually not the best time to let others know just how angry you are. Often it is wiser to wait a bit, collect your thoughts, and consider the best way to express your feelings to whoever you believe triggered your anger.

Deciphering our emotions and deciding how to deal with them can be a lengthy process. Be sure before you start a discussion of your feelings that you will have the time needed for a fair consideration of them.

## DESCRIBE THE RESPONSE YOU SEEK

It is helpful if the person you are speaking to understands how you want him or her to respond to your expression of feelings. For example, you might end your statement by noting, "I need you to help me unwind after a busy day." By revealing how we feel, how we see things, and how we would like things to change, we take steps toward achieving a greater state of relational health and set the stage for continued relational growth.

# The Case of Late Jean

John was furious. Jean had promised she would be home for dinner on time for once. But once again, she was more than an hour late.

John had rushed home from work just so that they would be able to spend some time together, but here he was spending it alone. Obviously, he told himself, Jean does not consider our relationship as important as I do. Clearly, he reasoned, she always puts her work before me.

John felt disappointed. His emotions mixed together: annoyance fused with resentment, exasperation turned into outrage. His once adoring and caring spouse for some reason preferred work to being in his company. She was becoming more like a boarder, he told himself, not a wife. Feeling dejected and almost desperate, he picked up his cell to text her.

Just as he was about to press "send," the front door opened. It was Jean—and she was carrying a bottle of his favorite wine. "Sorry honey," she said. "I meant to be here an hour ago, but one thing led to another, and time got away from me."

After considering this case from the perspective of both John and Jean, answer the following questions:

1. If you were John, what would be the next words out of your mouth? Why?

2. Does Jean's bringing home John's favorite wine solve the problem? Does it to some extent help to alleviate the problem, or is it an attempt to camouflage the issue?

# REVIEW THIS

**1. Explain what emotions are, identifying the connection between emotional awareness and resilience.** ☐

Emotions are the feelings we experience in reaction to our surroundings and others. As we develop awareness of our feelings, we also cultivate greater resilience, or the ability to cope with and recover quickly from disappointments.

**2. Explain the relationship between emotional management, emotional intelligence, and emotional ineptitude.** ☐

By learning to understand and handle our emotions—that is, by making a commitment to become emotionally intelligent—we increase our potential for sharing meaningful, effective relationships. On the other hand, when we display emotional ineptitude, or an inability to discuss or cope with our emotions, we contribute to continued relationship difficulties.

**3. Describe the look and feel of emotions.** ☐

We use our faces and bodies to reveal a panoply of emotions, and these displays may be mirrored by others. Some people are better than others at both communicating and reading emotions.

**4. Explain factors influencing how emotions affect relationships.** ☐

An emotion state is an emotional process of limited duration that varies in both duration and intensity. An emotion trait is an emotion state that persists beyond a period that is considered appropriate.

Emotions are reactions that influence our appraisals of interpersonal situations. The emotions we feel are accompanied by physiological changes in our bodies and physical changes in our appearance. By becoming more aware of our emotional responses and the emotional responses of others, we become better at managing them. We gain awareness of the extent to which our emotions help color our relationships.

**5. Describe culture's effect on the expression of emotion.** ☐

Among the emotions that members of all cultures experience are anger, disgust, fear, happiness, and sadness. However, individual emotional expressiveness and contributing factors may vary across cultures.

**6. Describe gender's effect on the expression of emotion.** ☐

Men tend to be less emotionally expressive than women, while women tend to be more attuned to others' emotions.

**7. Discuss how the media and technology serve as both models and channels for the emotions we exhibit.** ☐

Media models affect our internalization and display of emotion. Technological channels allow us to personalize and control our interactive experiences, as well as monitor our emotional responses.

8. **Identify steps you can take to share emotions more effectively.** ☐

The following factors facilitate the accurate communication of feelings: recognizing that our thoughts cause feelings, choosing the right words to describe our feelings, showing that we accept responsibility for our feelings, being able to share feelings fully, knowing when and where to reveal feelings, and describing the response we seek.

## CHECK YOUR UNDERSTANDING

1. Can you offer examples to illustrate the difference between an emotionally intelligent and an emotionally inept response? (See pages 212–213.)

2. Can you describe what it feels like to be happy, sad, or angry and use your description to explain the processes of cognitive restructuring and emotion contagion? (See pages 213–217.)

3. Can you compare and contrast an emotion trait with an emotion state and assess the extent to which each has influenced your interaction in a relationship? (See page 217.)

4. Can you create a scenario illustrating how gender and culture affect the handling of emotion and another depicting the roles that media and technology play in affecting the internalization and display of emotion? (See pages 222–227.)

5. Can you compile a list of recommended strategies for improving the sharing of emotions? (See pages 227–229.)

## KEY TERMS

Coping 223

Debilitative emotion 222

Describing feelings 224

Displaying feelings 224

Emotion contagion 220

Emotion state 221

Emotion trait 221

Emotional ineptitude 215

Emotional intelligence 215

Emotionally tone-deaf 216

Emotions 214

Face-saving 226

Facilitative emotion 222

Flame war 232

Flaming 232

Media models 230

Resilience 215

Social intelligence 216

Telepresence 231

Get the tools you need to sharpen your study skills. **SAGE edge** offers a robust online environment featuring an impressive array of free tools and resources. Access practice quizzes, eFlashcards, video, and multimedia at **edge.sagepub.com/gambleicp**.

AP Photo/Jorge Silva

# 9

# Trust and Deception

## Learning Objectives

**AFTER COMPLETING THIS CHAPTER, YOU SHOULD BE ABLE TO**

1. Define trust and explain the bases for it

2. Discuss the nature of forgiveness and its impact on relationship rebuilding

3. Explain cost-benefit theory, including its relationship to trust

4. Explore relational situations, identifying factors contributing to the development of cooperative/supportive and competitive/defensive interpersonal climates

5. Describe how lying affects interpersonal relationships

6. Discuss how gender and culture influence the development of trust

7. Describe how media portrayals and technology can foster or impede the development of relationships based on trust

8. Identify and use behaviors that promote the development of trusting relationships

> The best way to discover if you can trust somebody is to trust them.
>
> —Ernest Hemingway

• • • • • • • • • • • • • • • • • • • • • • • • • • • • • • • • • • • • • • • • • • • • • • •

While we expect our significant other to tell us the truth, 92 percent of us admit to lying to a romantic partner.[1] Sadly, our romantic partner is the person to whom we are mostly likely to tell our biggest lies. One or both partners in a romantic relationship attempt to deceive the other all too often, each believing that it is possible to keep the other from discovering the deceit. Such beliefs often turn out to be wrong. ■

# WHAT DO YOU KNOW?

Before continuing your reading of this chapter, which of the following five statements do you believe to be true, and which do you believe to be false?

| | | | |
|---|---|---|---|
| 1. | When you trust your partner, your relationship is safe. | T | F |
| 2. | Trust violations hurt the body. | T | F |
| 3. | Being unforgiving can cause you to become depressed. | T | F |
| 4. | Most students lie to their parents. | T | F |
| 5. | Liars use more indirect language than do truth tellers. | T | F |

Read the chapter to discover if you're right or if you've made any erroneous assumptions.

ANSWERS: 1. F; 2. T; 3. T; 4. T; 5. T

Deception breeds mistrust and nothing erodes a relationship like mistrust. Americans are deeply cynical when it comes to assessments of the trustworthiness of politicians, public officials, and business leaders because reports of their dishonesty and corruption are all too frequently reported. Even physicians have admitted to lying to patients about the state of their health and recovery prospects. Some also admitted to failures to disclose conflicts of interest when prescribing drugs.[2] Of course, our trustworthiness concerns are not limited to the political, public, business, or health care spheres. We all are familiar with stories about friendships ending or couples splitting up due to the discovery of deception. We condemn lies, but we regularly tell them.

So, how do we decide who to trust?[3] Why do we trust some people, but not others? And what causes us to lose trust in a person?

# WHAT IS TRUST?

Trust is a willingness to rely or depend on another person. Sometimes our trust is merited, and we are rewarded for it. Other times, however, it is misplaced, resulting in our feeling disappointment or becoming disillusioned with a relationship partner.

## WHY WE PLACE TRUST IN OTHERS

We place our trust in others for various reasons. We may rely on others because we expect them to perform basic services for us, such as drive us to work. Sometimes we expect them to give us direction, such as helping us pick out what to wear for an interview. Still other times we expect others to meet our emotional needs—commiserate with us when we're sad. The degree to which another person fulfills our expectations determines whether we will depend on or trust that particular person again. As the maxim says, *Fool me once, shame on you. Fool me twice, shame on me.*

Although we freely use the word *trust*, not everyone is able to express clearly what the word personally means to them. Try expressing what it means to you. Then consider the following excerpt from Antoine de Saint-Exupéry's *The Little Prince,* in which the fox tries to explain to the little prince what trust means to him by telling the prince, who is seeking friends, that he will permit the prince to "tame" him:

"What does that mean—'to tame'?"

"It is an act too often neglected," said the fox. "It means to establish ties."

"'To establish ties'?"

"Just that," said the fox. "To me, you are still nothing more than a little boy who is just like a hundred thousand other little boys. And I have no need of you. And you, on your part, have no need of me. To you, I am nothing more than a fox like a hundred thousand other foxes. But if you tame me [if we establish ties], then we shall need each other. To me, you will be unique in all the world. To you, I shall be unique in all the world.[4]

Essential for relationship satisfaction, trust develops over time. Once you trust another person, your willingness to make yourself vulnerable by engaging in personal disclosures increases, primarily because you have confidence in the person's dependability and believe you can reliably predict how the person will behave.

## THE BASES OF TRUST

How does establishing personal ties serve as a basis for building trust? The amount of trust we place in another, in large measure, is based on our perception of that person's character. In other words, when we judge someone to be of good character, we are likely to have faith in their integrity, motives, consistency of behavior, and discretion.

When we trust another because of their integrity, we think the person possesses a basic honesty. When we trust another's motives, we don't think that they would exhibit malevolent behavior toward us. When we trust someone on the basis of their consistency, we feel that we know the person well enough to predict their actions. Finally, when we trust another on the basis of their discretion, we conclude that the person will not violate our confidence or disclose information about us to anyone who could harm us.

When you place your trust in another, you display your willingness to rely on that person.

## THE COMPONENTS OF TRUST

Trust is an amalgam of two basic components: **trusting behavior** (confidence in another person's behavior) and **trustworthy behavior** (behavior exhibited by the other person that confirms our confidence). The two behaviors are reciprocal: Trusting precipitates trustworthiness, and vice versa. Your faith in another person therefore will either grow or weaken over time.

### Trusting Behavior

When we are confident in another person's behavior, (1) we are aware that their behavior can have either harmful or beneficial results (your friend can choose either to embarrass you in front of others or to do her best to make you look good); (2) we are aware that whether the outcome is positive or negative depends on the other person's actions (whether you end up being embarrassed or looking good is in your friend's control); and (3) we think the other person will behave in ways that produce beneficial results (you are confident that your friend will try to make you look good). In other words, you think that your friend's behavior has "positive" predictability.

### Trustworthy Behavior

When we behave in a way that earns another's trust, we are exhibiting trustworthy behavior. We (1) become aware of another person's motivational preferences (you realize that your coworker wants to impress his boss); (2) recognize that the other person has confidence in us and is relying on us to help them accomplish this (you understand that your coworker is counting on you to help him look good to the boss); and (3) respond by exhibiting the expected behavior (you make it a point to tell the boss how much you enjoy working with your coworker).

## TRY THIS

### Can I Depend on You? Can You Depend on Me?

1.  Identify three people whom you trusted or depended on recently. Reflect on your relationship with each and fill in the chart below. Consider whether your trust in the person was justified and explain why or why not.

| NAME | BEHAVIOR YOU EXPECTED THE PERSON TO EXHIBIT | EXTENT TO WHICH YOUR EXPECTATIONS WERE FULFILLED |
|---|---|---|
|  |  |  |
|  |  |  |
|  |  |  |

2.  Identify three people who recently trusted or depended on you. Reflect on your relationship with each and fill in the chart below. For each, explain why you think this person should or should not have trusted you.

| NAME | BEHAVIOR THE OTHER PERSON EXPECTED YOU TO EXHIBIT | EXTENT TO WHICH YOU BELIEVE YOU FULFILLED THE EXPECTATION |
|---|---|---|
|  |  |  |
|  |  |  |
|  |  |  |

3.  Examine both of your charts. What does your analysis of each reveal about your trust choices?

## FAILED TRUST

If any ingredient for trusting or trustworthy behavior is missing, trust does not exist. While developing trust takes time, unfortunately, it's relatively easy to destroy. When individuals depend on each other, each party in the relationship is taking a risk. The element of risk means that either party to the relationship can be personally harmed as a result of the other's behavior. When you place your faith in another, you recognize that it is possible for this person to use your belief in them against you. Should this occur, it usually shatters your trust.

To be sure, we cannot trust everyone.[5] You would be wise to avoid depending on anyone who repeatedly behaves in a way that brings you pain or causes you to feel rejected or betrayed. When you say, "I don't trust Ralph," for example, you probably mean that when you trusted Ralph in the past, he disappointed you. In effect, you no longer feel able to predict how Ralph will act in a given situation. In contrast, it makes sense for you to continue relying on those people whose behavior you believe you can predict with relatively consistent accuracy.

According to psychologist Abraham Maslow, people who believe in themselves and others tend to make "growth" choices. Maslow describes such individuals as self-actualizers who are close to fulfilling their unique potential as human beings.[6] The trusting behavior of self-actualizers permits them to experience the world fully and vividly, for they have the ability to be open and honest with others and themselves. Because trust can lead us to reveal important information about ourselves, it also can help improve our self-awareness and understanding. Thus, trust, openness, and self-actualization go hand in hand.

As you have probably learned from experience, there are numerous reasons we continue or end our relationships. If we feel we can no longer trust another person, we cease the reciprocation of disclosures, thereby bringing on the relationship's failure. Trust is a kind of interpersonal glue. When present, the parties to the relationship psychologically stick together.

# FORGIVENESS: REBUILDING A RELATIONSHIP AFTER TRUST WAS BETRAYED

What happens when someone close to you commits an interpersonal transgression against you, hurting you? Are you likely to respond by holding a grudge and being resentful or by forgiving the other person? The choice is yours.

Researchers describe forgiveness as the sense of peace and understanding that we experience when we stop blaming another person for a perceived wrong and instead interpret the transgression less personally.[7] Forgiveness is not condoning unkindness. Rather, it is a manifestation of the personal control we have over our lives, just as deciding whether or not to take offense in the first place also is a choice.[8]

## THE FORGIVENESS PROCESS

For us to be able to repair and rebuild a relationship jeopardized by a betrayal, we need to find a way to forgive that person so that we're able to let go of negative feelings.[9] The act of forgiving involves a multistage problem-solving process similar to the one associated with grief. Initially a person feels anger and hurt but then finds a way to excuse the specific offense, putting forth more personal and situational understanding of the offender and of themselves.[10] The forgiveness process may be broken down into four stages:

1. Experiencing self-justified anger
2. Recognizing that anger does not feel good and desiring to repair the damage to the relationship

3. Realizing that forgiveness has beneficial effects and choosing to let go of our anger fairly quickly

4. Making the proactive choice to rarely, if ever, get angry

## ANALYZE THIS: MISPLACED TRUST

Ferdaus Shamim/Contributor/WireImages/ Getty Images

Edward Albee's play *Who's Afraid of Virginia Woolf?* explores the negative outcomes of misplaced trust. During the course of an evening spent at the home of George and Martha, guests Nick and Honey and their hosts engage in some rather heavy "social" drinking. While the wives are elsewhere, George discloses some personal information about his youth to Nick. Nick reciprocates by telling George that he was forced to marry Honey because she believed— falsely—that she was pregnant. As the evening progresses, George feels that Nick has humiliated him, so retaliates by revealing to Honey and Martha the story that Nick had confided in him. Honey, quickly sickened, rushes from the room. The scene ends with Nick vowing to get revenge for George's behavior.

1. Cite an incident in which you witnessed or participated in an interaction in which someone who was trusted acted in an untrustworthy manner. What did you and others learn from this?

2. Describe a relationship you share that is based on trust. Identify the trusting and trustworthy behaviors exhibited by you and your relationship partner and the relationship factors that you believe facilitated the development of a climate of trust.

3. Describe a second relationship that you mistakenly believed to be based on trust. Identify the trusting and trustworthy behaviors that were missing, and describe the negative consequences resulting from this. Account for factors in your relationship that inhibited the development of a climate of trust.

The four stages are not necessarily experienced in the same way. There are some people in our lives for whom we have such love that we stabilize at Stage 4. And there are others who have hurt us so badly that we might spend years at Stage 1. The choice, again, is ours.[11]

## ARE YOU FORGIVING? AND WHAT IF YOU'RE NOT?

Willingness to forgive may be influenced by gender. For example, when Stanford University psychologists solicited volunteers to participate in a study on forgiveness, they found it easy to attract female participants but had difficulty attracting men. To determine why men were hesitant to participate, one of the researchers, Dr. Carl Thoresen, randomly asked a group of men about it. The consensus among the men was that the word *forgiveness* is too soft and acquiescing, suggesting that the forgiving person is a doormat. The men advised the researchers to use the harsher, more masculine-sounding word *grudge* in place of the word *forgiveness* in their solicitations. Once the researchers started distributing flyers reading "Got a grudge?" male participants surfaced.[12]

People unable to forgive a violation of trust put themselves in danger of experiencing not just emotional difficulties and interpersonal problems, but also impaired cardiovascular, neurological, and immune systems. The more we experience anger or hurt, the more our bodies secrete "stress chemicals" that over time take a toll on our well-being.[13] People who are unwilling to forgive experience more depression and are likely to have less fulfilling relationships than those who are more forgiving. In contrast, giving up grudges improves both emotional and physical well-being. By accepting not only others' flaws, but also our own, we increase our chances of deriving satisfaction from our relationships. Learning to forgive yourself is as important as learning to forgive others.

# COST-BENEFIT THEORY: THE PRICE WE ARE WILLING TO PAY FOR A RELATIONSHIP

Our relationships thrive or falter as a consequence of the energy we expend on them. They succeed or fail based on what we are willing to do with and for one another. For example, if we have worked to hold up our side of a relationship, we may expect a high level of trust, commitment, respect, and even love in return. When such expectations are met, we find the relationship satisfying. However, when they go unfulfilled, we find the relationship lacking.

According to **cost-benefit theory**, also known as social exchange theory, we work to sustain those relationships that give us the greatest total benefit.[14] Perceived relationship rewards include increased self-esteem, an enhanced sense of security, and better coping skills. Perceived relationship costs are the price we pay, or the personal energy that we must expend, to receive any of the rewards. Typical costs include the time we need to invest to make a relationship work, psychological and physical stress, and damage to our self-image. We can represent the relational equation as follows:

*Perceived Relationship Rewards – Perceived Relationship Costs = Perceived Relationship Benefits.*

If the rewards are greater than the costs, we experience a net gain. If the reverse is true, the relationship represents a net loss.

To see how this equation works, imagine you want to develop a closer relationship with someone you have been dating for a few weeks. To acquire a benefit of intimacy in that relationship, you have to be willing to trust that person enough to reveal personal information to them. Or what if you are seeking social acceptance? You might have to adopt certain beliefs, attitudes, and values. In each case, to obtain a benefit, you have to pay a price.

Cost-benefit theory tells us that we will work to continue a relationship only as long as the benefits we perceive ourselves to be receiving outweigh our emotional expenditures. As we compare a relationship's profits and costs, we also establish a **comparison level for alternatives** with which to weigh the profits and costs of one relationship against those we might derive from another. If we believe we can easily find another person to give us whatever a current partner is not providing, we are more apt to extricate ourselves from an unsatisfactory relationship and enter a new and potentially more rewarding one. In contrast, if we believe such a person *cannot* easily be found, we are more likely to stay in the relationship even though it carries with it great costs and the potential for significant loss.[15]

# EXPLORING RELATIONAL SITUATIONS

A relationship will thrive or wither depending on its situation or climate. Whether we perceive a relationship as cooperative or competitive, supportive or defensive, makes a difference in the establishing of trust.

## COOPERATIVE AND COMPETITIVE RELATIONSHIPS

How we define a relational situation determines if trust develops. If we view our relationship as primarily competitive, then we are more apt to try to protect ourselves when communicating with one another. If, on the other hand, we view our relationship as primarily cooperative, we avoid a dog-eat-dog situation, and sharing, interdependent efforts, and trust become more likely. Defining an interpersonal relationship as competitive precipitates defensive and threatening behavior on the part of the communicators, whereas defining it as cooperative precipitates supportive, nonthreatening behaviors and the exchange of more honest and forthright messages.

The goals the parties bring to a relationship affects the level of trust possible. If we perceive our goals to be congruent, then it is easier to create a cooperative atmosphere. But if we perceive our goals to be at odds, then we are more apt to display competitive mindsets.

Thinkstock Images/Comstock/Thinkstock

Whether a relationship is perceived as cooperative or competitive, supportive or defensive, affects its nature.

## TRY THIS

## Cooperative or Competitive?

Identify two people with whom you interact regularly. For each person, summarize three recent shared encounters and how each one made you feel. Characterize each interaction as being predominantly competitive or cooperative in nature.

Reflect on how you act in situations you define as competitive in contrast to those you define as cooperative?

Looking back, were there times when it would have been more productive for you to cooperate rather than compete or vice versa?

To what extent, if any, do you think the sex or the ethnicity of the other person influences your perception of a relationship's nature? Explain.

In order for cooperation to take place, certain requirements need to be met. We need to agree that we each have an equal right to satisfy our needs. Additionally, we have to ensure that conditions allow each of us to get what we want at least some of the time. For this to occur, we need to discourage the use of power plays that rely on techniques such as threatening, yelling, and demanding. Additionally, neither of us should attempt to manipulate the other by holding back information or dissembling. When two people are interacting cooperatively, one party does not aim to "win" or to "outsmart" the other. Cooperative relationships don't depend on one person gaining an edge over the other and don't promote defensiveness or lying.

## SUPPORTIVE AND DEFENSIVE RELATIONSHIPS

When entering into a new relationship, one of the first challenges we face is that of developing the ability and willingness to trust. For trust to develop, we will need to feel valued,[16] which occurs when messages a person sends make us feel recognized, let us know that our ideas and feelings are important, and project interest in our thoughts and feelings. When valuing goes uncommunicated, usually we take steps to protect ourselves from future hurt. The result may be a **defensive climate** because a party to the relationship now perceives or anticipates a threat. The threat need not be physical. Typically, it takes the form of a comment or behavior by one person that the other person perceives as a direct attack on the image they've been working to project.

When insecure in a relationship, we're more likely to experience a negative feeling and respond by exhibiting a defensive reaction. For example, you might respond to a threat to your image by counterattacking and becoming verbally aggressive toward the other person: "Who made you king?" With such a response, you take the focus off yourself and shift the blame to the other person.

We might also defend ourselves by distorting what the other person says in such a way that we're able to preserve our sense of self. We rationalize the attack by creating an explanation that's untrue but self-protective. Or we try to compensate for the criticism by emphasizing one or more strengths that we contend are more important than the weakness pointed out to us. Or we could choose simply to avoid an attack by steering clear of people we believe pose a threat to our image. None of these attempts at image preservation are particularly healthy responses.

To minimize or eliminate the arousal of defensiveness in our relationships, we need to understand what causes us to become defensive in the first place and substitute supportive behaviors.

When Stanley Kowalski confronts Blanche BuBois in Tennessee William's *A Streetcar Named Desire*, Blanche exhibits a series of defensive behaviors in an effort to preserve her false image and sense of self.

United Archives GmbH/0000015_AOK/Alamy Stock Photo

In a classic article, Jack R. Gibb identifies six such defense-causing behaviors and six contrasting behaviors that, when exhibited, help create a ==supportive climate==. These behaviors are listed in Table 9.1 and are discussed in the following sections.[17]

## Evaluation Versus Description

A relationship may run into trouble if one party makes ==evaluative statements==. If, as a result of our manner of speaking, tone, or words, we seem to be judging the other person, they are likely to be wary of our intentions. For example, once we label another's actions using overly critical descriptors such as *stupid* or *ridiculous*, we impede the development or continuance of a positive communication climate.

In contrast to evaluative statements, ==descriptive statements== recount a person's particular observable actions without labeling them good or bad, right or wrong. When we use descriptive language, we do not admonish another to change his or her behavior but simply report or question what we saw, heard, or felt. (See Table 9.1.)

Describing what concerns you instead of going on the attack is usually more productive than is being judgmental. Consider the difference between the evaluative statement, "You don't know what you're talking about!" which is judgmental in tone and phrased in a way that can easily provoke defensiveness, and the evaluative sentence, "I would like to understand how you came to that conclusion," which focuses on the speaker's thoughts and feelings.

### TABLE 9.1 CATEGORIES OF BEHAVIOR CHARACTERISTIC OF DEFENSIVE AND SUPPORTIVE CLIMATES

| DEFENSIVE CLIMATE | SUPPORTIVE CLIMATE |
|---|---|
| Evaluation<br>*Judgmental statements impede communication* | Description<br>*Neutral statements promote communication* |
| Control orientation<br>*Promotes resistance* | Problem orientation<br>*Promotes cooperation* |
| Strategy<br>*Presence of a hidden agenda* | Spontaneity<br>*Deception-free* |
| Neutrality<br>*Communicates indifference* | Empathy<br>*Communicates concern* |
| Superiority<br>*Encourages jealousy or resentment* | Equality<br>*Encourages trust* |
| Certainty<br>*Encourages perceptions of inflexibility* | Provisionalism<br>*Encourages perceptions of flexibility* |

## Control Versus Problem Orientation

Communication perceived as an effort to exert control also provokes defensiveness. In other words, if your intent is to control another person—to get someone to do something or to change his or her beliefs—you are apt to encounter resistance. How much resistance you meet depends, in part, on the openness with which you approach the other person and the degree to which your behavior causes the other to question or doubt your motives. If we conclude that someone is trying to control us, we tend also to conclude that the other believes that we're incapable of making decisions. A problem orientation, on the other hand, promotes the opposite response. When we communicate that we have not already formulated a solution and are not going to attempt to force an opinion on the other person, that person feels freer to cooperate with us to solve the problem.

How two people argue affects their relationship.

Consider the difference between asking another person how to spend shared vacation funds and issuing a declaration such as "Well, I like Barbados more than Aruba, and since my bonus is paying for the vacation, I'll decide where to go." In such an instance, the problem-oriented individual would say, "It appears that we have different vacation destinations in mind. Let's see if we can find somewhere we can enjoy ourselves together." This kind of approach keeps the relationship intact rather than provoking disharmony.

## Strategy Versus Spontaneity

Our defensiveness is likely to rise if we feel another person is trying to put something past us. No one enjoys being conned or made the victim of a hidden agenda. We become suspicious of strategies we discover have been concealed or are underhanded. We resent it when someone makes a decision for us and then tries to make us feel that we made the decision. Once we feel manipulated, we tend to become defensive and self-protective. In contrast, honest, spontaneous, deception-free behavior, helps to reduce defensiveness. Under such conditions, we exhibit less doubt regarding the other's motivations, and trust is more likely to develop.

With this in mind, consider a situation in which a person says, "Would you help me out if I told you it was really important?" and also fails to reveal what "helping out" means. We might feel that something is being kept from us, and we might begin to feel that we are being set up. It is better to be open and honest. For example, saying "I could really use your help to prepare for this exam" is a natural, straightforward way of asking for another's assistance.

## Neutrality Versus Empathy

Another behavior that can increase defensiveness is neutrality. For the most part, we like and need to feel that others see us as worthwhile, value our presence, like us, and are willing to take the time to establish a meaningful relationship with us. If the person with whom we're interacting communicates neutrality or indifference, instead of warmth and concern, we may conclude that the individual has no interest in us or that they perceive us as a nonperson. Comments such as "The boss doesn't even know me by name" indicate that someone is bothered by another's perceived indifference. In contrast, empathy erases feelings of indifference by implying care and regard for others. When you accept another's feelings, you send a message of concern and respect.

## Superiority Versus Equality

The development of either defensiveness or trust in interpersonal relationships is also influenced by behaviors showing superiority or equality. Our defensiveness is aroused if the person with whom we're communicating looks down their nose at us or expresses feelings of superiority about social position, power, wealth, intellectual aptitude, appearance, or other such characteristics.

When someone says something like "You should shop where I shop," they convey an attitude of superiority; we're apt to react by competing with them, becoming jealous, or ignoring the message altogether. If similar information had been communicated to us in a way that didn't cause us to feel inadequate, we would probably be less likely to get our guard up. The more secure we feel, the easier we find it to treat others as equals.

## Certainty Versus Provisionalism

When someone expresses absolute or total certainty about a disputed issue, we may become defensive. We are suspicious of individuals who think they have all the answers and who view themselves as our "guides" through life rather than fellow travelers.

Communicating an attitude of provisionalism, or open-mindedness, makes it possible for others to perceive us as flexible and open. We neither feel nor convey the need to be right and do not defend our ideas to the bitter end. Saying something such as "Only a nerd would think this assignment is fun" closes the door to continued discussion because the speaker appears unwilling to consider other positions. Alternatively, prefacing remarks with something such as "The way I look at the assignment . . ." encourages further discussion.

Various nonverbal cues support the development of either a defensive or a supportive interpersonal climate; these are summarized in Table 9.2. As you review the cues, consider the extent to which a defensive or supportive climate characterizes each of your relevant social or job-related relationships.

**TABLE 9.2   NONVERBAL SYMBOLS THAT CAN CONTRIBUTE TO THE DEVELOPMENT OF A SUPPORTIVE OR DEFENSIVE CLIMATE**

| BEHAVIOR PRODUCING DEFENSIVENESS | BEHAVIOR PRODUCING SUPPORTIVENESS |
| --- | --- |
| Evaluation | Description |
| *Maintaining extended eye contact* | *Maintaining comfortable eye contact* |
| *Pointing at the other person* | *Leaning forward* |
| *Placing your hands on your hips* | |
| *Shaking your head* | |
| *Shaking your index finger* | |
| Control | Problem orientation |
| *Sitting in the focal (central) position* | *Maintaining comfortable personal distance* |
| *Placing your hands on your hips* | *Crossing your legs in the direction of the other person* |
| *Shaking your head* | |
| *Maintaining extended eye contact* | *Leaning forward* |
| *Invading the personal space of the other person* | *Maintaining comfortable eye contact* |

| BEHAVIOR PRODUCING DEFENSIVENESS | BEHAVIOR PRODUCING SUPPORTIVENESS |
|---|---|
| Strategy<br><br>*Maintaining extended eye contact*<br><br>*Shaking your head*<br><br>*Using forced gestures* | Spontaneity<br><br>*Leaning forward*<br><br>*Crossing your legs in the direction of the other person*<br><br>*Maintaining comfortable eye contact*<br><br>*Using animated natural gestures* |
| Neutrality<br><br>*Crossing your legs away from the other person*<br><br>*Using a monotone voice*<br><br>*Staring elsewhere*<br><br>*Leaning back*<br><br>*Maintaining a large body distance (4½–5 feet)* | Empathy<br><br>*Maintaining close personal distance (20–36 inches)*<br><br>*Maintaining comfortable eye contact*<br><br>*Crossing your legs in the direction of the other person*<br><br>*Nodding your head*<br><br>*Leaning toward the other person* |
| Superiority<br><br>*Maintaining extended eye contact*<br><br>*Placing your hands on your hips*<br><br>*Situating yourself at a higher elevation*<br><br>*Invading the other person's personal space* | Equality<br><br>*Maintaining comfortable eye contact*<br><br>*Leaning forward*<br><br>*Situating yourself at the same elevation*<br><br>*Maintaining a comfortable distance* |
| Certainty<br><br>*Maintaining extended eye contact*<br><br>*Crossing your arms*<br><br>*Placing your hands on your hips*<br><br>*Using a dogmatic voice* | Provisionalism<br><br>*Maintaining comfortable eye contact*<br><br>*Nodding your head*<br><br>*Tilting your head to one side* |

# LYING AND RELATIONSHIP ETHICS

An old Moroccan proverb says: "Why are you lying to me who is your friend?" What does the word **lie** mean to you? To whom have you recently lied? Who has recently lied to you? What kinds of situations do you feel justify lying? How do you react when you catch someone in a lie? How do you react when caught in a lie? How does lying or being lied to affect a relationship?

To examine your practices when it comes to lying, complete the sentences that follow:

- A lie is _____.
- I would lie to _____.
- I would lie if _____.
- In the past week, I lied _____ times.
- In the past week, I was caught lying _____ times.

It is difficult to know for sure how pervasive lying is in U.S. culture because the nature of lying is to deceive others without their noticing. Still, when surveyed, more than eight in ten students confessed to having lied to a parent about something important, despite the fact that 92 percent of the students in the same survey said they believe their parents want them to behave ethically.[18]

## TRY THIS

## Cornered

First, think of several interpersonal encounters during which you believe the other person succeeded in challenging the image you were trying to project. For example, how would you feel if a friend told you that you always put yourself first? If the criticism was justified, you would more than likely feel defensive. Create a list of people who have put you on the defensive. Identify aspects of yourself that these individuals caused you to defend and the means you used to protect yourself from their perceived attacks. Use the chart below to record your observations.

| INDIVIDUALS WHO HAVE MADE ME FEEL DEFENSIVE | WHAT THE PERSON FOUND FAULT WITH IN ME | WHAT I DID TO PROTECT MYSELF |
|---|---|---|
| | | |
| | | |
| | | |

Next, think of several interpersonal encounters during which you sent one or more messages to someone that led him or her to feel a threat to their image. How did each person respond to your criticism? What consequences did your behavior have for each relationship? Use the chart below to record your observations.

| INDIVIDUALS WHOSE IMAGE I THREATENED | WHAT I DID TO PRECIPITATE THE THREAT | HOW THE PERSON RESPONDED | RELATIONSHIP CONSEQUENCES |
|---|---|---|---|
| | | | |
| | | | |
| | | | |

Finally, consider both situations from the perspective of each party. What advice would you give the person whose image was threatened regarding how to handle feelings of defensiveness? What would you say to the person doing the threatening regarding how to reduce the level of threat projected?

## WHY DO WE LIE?

Deliberately lying by distorting the truth is committing an overt lie. Concealing sensitive information is committing a covert lie. Both practices are all too common in person-to-person interaction.[19] Whenever we hope to convey a false impression or convince another to believe something that we ourselves don't believe, we're lying. Whether we want to admit it or not, our goal is to intentionally deceive another person into accepting what we know to be untrue. Our verbal and nonverbal communicative intent is to mislead, either by providing false information or by purposefully failing to provide the relevant informa-

Can the truth be as harmful as a lie?

tion the person needs to make a decision or come to an understanding.[20] When we lie, we try to manipulate someone into making choices they would not otherwise make. By manipulating the truth, we manipulate each other.

Rarely do we tell only one lie. Liars work hard to cover their tracks. As your experience probably reveals, to sustain a lie, we frequently have to tell another, and another, and another. Thus, whenever we lie, we usually are left with a significant amount of mending. We spend a lot of time and energy concentrating on what lies we told and to whom and our reasons for lying to them.

Some think that lying, for any reason, is morally and ethically wrong. Others hold that the motive for lying matters: Is harm intended? Still others believe it is a lie's outcome that merits consideration. What do you believe?

## REFLECT ON THIS

### *Building Company Trust*

Here are five principles that corporate leaders (and others, for that matter) can adopt to encourage others to trust them:

1.  *Demonstrate shared interests.* Before we trust another, we need to learn whether our interests are aligned.

2.  *Demonstrate concern for others.* We trust those we believe care about our welfare and, when push comes to shove, will do the right thing for us even if doing so will put them personally at risk.

3.  *Deliver on promises.* We trust those who deliver on the commitments they make.

*(Continued)*

4.  *Demonstrate consistency and honesty.* We respect those who admit their mistakes and take steps to ensure that they do not happen again.

5.  *Communicate clearly and often.* Clear and transparent communication engenders confidence; miscommunication frequently leads to distrust.

If you were the leader of a company that had lost the public's trust, what means would you use to build and sustain trust?

Sources: Jason Sturman, "Are You Inspiring Trust in the Workplace?" January 30, 2018, https://www.peoplehr .com/blog/index.php/2018/01/10/are-you-inspiring-trust-in-the-workplace/; Steven M. R. Covey, and Douglas R. Conant, "The Connection Between Employee Trust and Financial Performance," *Harvard Business Review*, July 18, 2016, https://hbr.org/2016/07/the-connection-between-employee-trust-and-financial-performance; Susan Adams, "Trust in CEOs Plummets, but Still Beats Trust in Government," *Forbes* online, January 23, 2012, http:// www.forbes.com/sites/susanadams/2012/01/23/trust-in-ceos-plummets-but-still-beats-trust-in-government.

At times, we fail to realize that under some circumstances, a truth that hurts someone can be as harmful as a lie. Now and again, we succeed in taking away false beliefs from those who need them to survive. Wittingly or unwittingly, when we do this, we can do as much damage as callous liars. For example, if someone believes she is attractive to others, but you find her unappealing and a bore, would you say so? Some people need their illusions.[21] If you analyze your life, it may become clear that some of your relationships rely on the silent agreement made between parties that certain illusions will be sustained and certain memories will be suppressed. This, too, is a form of trust.

## WHITE LIES: MOTIVATION MATTERS

A white lie is a minor falsehood that is not meant to harm or injure anyone. Individuals use white lies to provide moral support or cheer, or to maintain the "humanness" of the social relationship itself, as when you tell your roommate you like her haircut even if you don't.

## LYING TO OURSELVES: DEFENSIVE STRATEGIES

We don't lie only to others. We also lie to ourselves, employing a number of defensive strategies to protect ourselves from having to face truths. For example, according to his biographer, Steve Jobs believed, up until the very end, that he would beat his cancer.[22] It seems we need illusions to feel good about ourselves and to maintain a sense of continuity in our lives.[23] People who lie to themselves commonly employ three defense mechanisms: displacement, repression, and rationalization.

### Displacement

When we release our anger or frustration by transferring our negative feelings to people or objects we perceive to be more accessible and less dangerous than whoever or whatever precipitated the feelings in the first place, we practice **displacement**. For example, you yell at a younger brother or sister when you really want to yell at your boss.

### Repression

We use the self-protective strategy of **repression** when situations are too painful or unpleasant for us to face. We "forget" the stimulus that has disturbed us by denying its existence. For example, if someone was subjected to verbal abuse as a child, he or she might "solve" any problems that such abuse might engender by pretending it never happened. Although the facade erected would say "nothing is wrong," feelings of anger and aggression would be building and might surface and affect the individual's present-day relationships.

### Rationalization

When we use **rationalization**, we give ourselves a logical or reasonable explanation for our unrealistic pictures, thoughts, or feelings. For instance, a person who interviews for a position but is not hired might convince himself or herself that he or she didn't really want the job.

Thus, beneath deception and lying are strong feelings and the desire to protect our emotional well-being. Our lies may be self-serving, or they may be motivated by our desire to demonstrate caring and support for others.[24]

## RELATIONSHIP COUNTERFEITERS

What motivates us to create a **counterfeit relationship**—one based on deception that will invariably lead to interpersonal failure? What causes us to lie? While there are many reasons for lying, two appear most prevalent: to gain a reward or to avoid a punishment. Specifically, lying is motivated by our desire to protect our self-esteem, continue to meet our basic needs, initiate or preserve desired affiliations, and attain personal satisfaction.[25] Achieving these goals is rewarding. Having them taken away can be punishing. We most frequently lie to protect ourselves, less often to protect someone with whom we have a relationship, only occasionally to benefit a third party (see Table 9.3). Lies help us negotiate situations that have exposed us or another person to levels of vulnerability exceeding our comfort zone.

## THE EFFECTS OF LYING

If discovered, lying can destroy the very basis of a relationship. Imagine a relationship, no matter how effective in other respects, in which you could never believe his or her words or gestures. Imagine feeling that you have been taken advantage of, treated as a pushover, or duped. Such a relationship would be difficult to sustain simply because you would probably suspect the other's motives, resent how they treated you, and feel disappointed—in your partner for lying and in yourself for believing the lies. You would reinterpret and reevaluate your past, present, and future with this person in light of the lies and be wary of ever fully trusting them again.

Although "bending the truth" to keep peace in a relationship is a common practice, it may also reveal that the relationship is in trouble and not

A relationship based on deception is likely to fail.

**TABLE 9.3 WHO LIES?**

| WHERE DO YOU FIT INTO THE FOLLOWING STATISTICAL DATA ON LYING? |
| --- |
| Approximately 80% of all job seekers' résumés are misleading. |
| 100% of dating couples surveyed reported lying to each other in about one-third of their conversations. |
| 20%–30% of middle managers surveyed admitted to writing fraudulent internal reports. |
| 95% of participating college students surveyed were willing to tell at least one lie to a potential employer to win a job, and 41% had already done so. |
| We are lied to about 200 times each day. |
| Most people lie to others once or twice a day and deceive about 30 people per week. |
| The average rate of lying is 7 times per hour if you count all the times people lie to themselves. |
| We lie in 30% to 38% of all our interactions. |
| College students lie in 50% of conversations with their mothers. |

Sources: Data in this table are derived from information contained in the 2000 U.S. Census and on the websites of the U.S. Census Bureau (http://www.census.gov) and the U.S. Bureau of Labor Statistics (http://www.bls.gov).

likely to last. By sucking trust out of a relationship, lies destroy it. If you discover a partner's lies, you are much less likely to take the risk of displaying the vulnerability required for trust to grow between you in the future. In fact, an inability to trust one's partner is the reason most commonly given for a relationship's deterioration, and it is after such a discovery that the lied-to partner typically ends things.

# REFLECT ON THIS

## Richard S. Lazarus and the Case for White Lies

A little more than three decades ago, disagreeing with prevailing notions of the importance of facing the truth, psychologist Richard S. Lazarus asserted that illusion and deception have important roles to play in mental health.

Lazarus observed that many people believe facing the truth, however painful, is necessary to live successfully and that to have "authentic" relationships, we have to be absolutely honest with one another and ourselves. Lazarus disagreed, noting that many poets, playwrights, and novelists base their work on the opposite notion—that we need our illusions. Lazarus embraced the view that illusion and self-deception have positive value, if only because they are part of the fabric of our lives. He pointed out that we hold countless unexamined and idiosyncratic beliefs about ourselves that give life meaning and substance and that we pass down unchallenged to succeeding generations even though they have no basis in reality.

What do you think of Lazarus's position? What illusions do you believe are key in the life of someone close to you?

SOURCE: Richard S. Lazarus, "Positive Denial: The Case for Not Facing Reality," *Psychology Today,* November 1979, p. 47.

## THE EFFECTS OF GOSSIP

How do you feel about gossip? Have you ever begun a conversation with a friend with these words: "Wait until you hear this!" If you have, then more than likely you have spread gossip. Telling a friend a juicy story or sharing a rumor lets the other person know that you trust him or her enough to share your confidence. While many believe that gossip is negative, much of it is benign small talk, sprinkled with statements such as "Did you know Kaleisha got a really great grade on her presentation?" and "Can you believe that Paula and Sean are engaged? I never thought they'd get back together after she left him for Raul." This kind of gossip is basically harmless because no secrets are being revealed. Although many believe erroneously that women gossip more than men, the opposite is actually true: Men gossip at least as much as women. Men, however, give gossip another label, calling it "shop talk."[26]

Do you gossip?

While many people today consider gossip wrong, until the 1800s, gossip was seen as denoting friendship. Now, more than two centuries later, a number of psychologists once again contend it is a natural activity and critical to human survival. In fact, if you review your conversations during the past 24 hours, you may discover that a large number of them consisted of gossip. Gossip can be a powerful socializing force.[27]

In their book *Gossip: The Latest Scoop,* Jack Levin and Arnold Arluke note that gossip functions like social grooming, setting the boundaries of social behavior and letting us know when we have crossed a line. As such, it may hold one key to our understanding the social environment, help us develop and maintain relationships, cement social ties, and bond with other members of our social group.[28] In *Grooming, Gossip, and the Evolution of Language,* Robin Dunbar provides support for these notions, contending that verbal communication evolved from a need to gossip, which reduces stress and enhances feelings of social cohesion.[29] Dunbar asserts that humans gossip because, unlike other primates, we do not groom each other; instead, we use speech to maintain contact. For Dunbar, *gossip* is a synonym for *social communication.* Humans learned to talk so we could talk about each other.

### The Dark Side of Gossip

There is, however, a darker side to gossip. Gossip's potential to be harmful can be seen in cyberbullying—the sustained use of digital technology to share mean-spirited messages designed to threaten, embarrass, harass, or torment—which challenges the resilience of its targets. Cyberbullies, who often remain anonymous, post false rumors, start offensive websites, post information designed to encourage others to laugh at their targets, and otherwise harass their targets relentlessly.[30]

Thus, while gossip can have a prosocial side, it also can be unethical, malicious, and vicious. It is particularly egregious when the information being shared is inaccurate and directed at those not present or equipped to defend themselves. Sometimes the gossiper is particularly subtle and deceptive, pretending to be sympathetic to the subject of the gossip, while actually trying to do harm. When used in this way, gossip can do untold damage.

# CULTURE AND GENDER

Both culture and gender play a part in determining how much trust we are willing to place in others. Have you considered the extent to which your culture and gender identification have led you either to trust or suspect others' intentions toward you?

## CULTURE AND TRUST

Our expectations and predictions regarding how members of various cultural groups will communicate with us may facilitate or impede the development of trust when we actually interact with members of these groups. Some of us are less apt to trust a person whom we perceive to be different from us than someone we think similar. For example, consider that people from Western cultures expect friends to maintain approximately an arm's-length distance when conversing. When people enter our private space, we feel uncomfortable and violated and are unlikely to enter a trusting relationship with them. In contrast, many members of Arab cultures expect friends to stand so close they can smell each other's breath. In fact, some people in Arab cultures believe that not to allow a friend to smell one's breath is insulting and may lead to decreased trust and intimacy.[31]

Remember that ethnocentrism—the perception that one's culture is superior to all others—also limits development of trusting relationships among people identifying with different cultural groups. It causes members of one group to conclude that members of other groups have inferior values and that they should maintain a social distance from them. Ethnocentric feelings make it difficult to dispel preconceptions, impede the personalization of communication, make satisfying conversations of self-disclosure difficult, limit acceptance of "outsiders," and hinder development of trusting relationships among people of difference.[32]

The more ethnocentric someone is, the more anxious he or she is about interacting with members of other cultures. When we are fearful, we are less likely to expect such interactions to have positive outcomes and less willing to trust. For relationships between people from diverse cultures to thrive, the individuals involved at least "need to act *as if* a sense of trust were justified, and set their doubts aside."[33]

People from different cultures also differ in emotional expressiveness. In the United States, for example, people operate from the premise that expressing feelings is positive and, as a result, are particularly emotionally expressive, but members of other cultures may be much more likely to mask their emotions and behave in ways that belie their actual feelings. It is difficult to trust others if we attribute their lack of expressiveness to a desire to deceive, rather than to cultural difference.

## TRY THIS

## How Prepared Are You to Trust?

Use the following series of statements to gauge the degree to which you are prepared to trust people you perceive to be significantly different from yourself. Label each statement either true or false. Be honest.

1. I usually trust most people whom I perceive to be like me more than I do those who are different. _____

2. I am more apt to cooperate with someone I perceive to be like me than with someone who is different. _____

3. I fear interacting with people from other cultures. _____

4. I believe people from other cultures create problems. _____

5. I use my values as a standard against which I judge the values of others. _____

If your answer to the majority of these questions is *true,* you likely need to work on trusting others who are different from you.

## GENDER AND TRUST

All of us want close friends whom we can trust. Women generally like to share feelings and men typically enjoy sharing activities, but both kinds of interaction can engender trust.[34] Unless there is reason to doubt trust in a relationship, men assume trust and rarely discuss it, whereas women are likely to talk about a relationship's dynamics more overtly.

For men and women to trust each other, they need to recognize each other's concerns and interpret each other's behavior appropriately. We enhance trust by supporting each other, and making ourselves emotionally reliable and mutually attentive. Women are more likely than men to sense when a partner is in trouble and provide an empathetic response. Men, upon sensing something is wrong, tend to respond by attempting to change the subject. While from a female perspective such a response may be interpreted as a lack of caring or understanding, when viewed from a male perspective, it is construed as appropriate.[35]

Because of our mismatched perceptions of communication, gender may also influence the kinds of lies we tell. Whereas men tend to tell self-centered lies, the lies of women tend to focus on others' feelings. Women generally put a positive spin on events or falsely derogate themselves to make another feel more confident; men are apt to pretend to be more bothered than they actually are to manipulate others into acting the way they want.[36]

Sometimes women pretend not to detect a lie so they do not have to put a relationship in jeopardy. Because of this practice, some believe that women are more self-deceptive than men. Men tend to be more apt to confront deception or, at the very least, to let on that they are aware another person is trying to deceive them.[37]

# MEDIA, TECHNOLOGY, AND LESSONS IN TRUST

The messages delivered to us via media and technology influence whom we are willing to trust. Because we are exposed to them daily, media and technology leave an imprint on our relationships, often without our being aware of it.

## THE MEDIA AND TRUST

Of the many influences on how we view different groups in society, the media are among the most powerful. Integrated into our daily lives, media messages are repeated to us incessantly. They communicate images of the sexes, older people, businesspeople, medical professionals, ethnic groups, and so forth, and a significant percentage of the messages encoded in the media help sustain stereotypical or unrealistic perceptions regarding who is trustworthy.[38]

For too long the media were prone to categorizing women as either good or bad. "Good" women typically were portrayed as deferential and focused on home and family, while "bad" women were depicted as hard, cold, aggressive, ambitious, embittered, and not to be trusted.[39] In addition, media portrayals of women may undermine the ability of women to trust each other.[40] For example, in advertising, films, and television, women and girls often are presented as hyper-sexualized and as being in competition with each other—often for men. Such depictions may cause women to become suspicious of one another, contributing to an inability to trust each other and leading others to stereotype women as "catty." Now, some advertisers are starting to avoid hyper-sexualized and unrealistic images of women in their advertising. Although primarily in response to the "me too." and Time's Up movements, it also is an effort to earn the trust of millennial and i-gen women.[41]

Similarly, the media have all too frequently handled minority groups by either stereotyping or neglecting them.[42] Either depiction affects our judgments of their trustworthiness. For instance, until recently, the portrayal of Native Americans in the U.S. media was consistently inaccurate, depicting them as bloodthirsty, marauding, untrustworthy savages.[43] Likewise, the media still often portray minorities and people from less developed countries in extremes: African Americans have been portrayed as incapable, shiftless, or inferior; Hispanics as illegal aliens; and Italians as mobsters. The media also portray overweight people as lazy, older people as childlike and helpless, and the disabled as problems. By unfairly labeling or stigmatizing individuals, media portrayals may negate the human value of honesty, perpetuate misinformation, lead to human degradation, and adversely influence person-to-person understanding and a willingness to trust.

## TECHNOLOGY AND TRUST

With the ever-increasing popularity of social networking, we are spending increasingly more time online. We communicate with our fingertips, sharing our deepest secrets—virtually at warp speed. Technology helps speed up romance by compelling people to communicate verbally at the same time that it helps de-emphasize distracting visual signals such as frowns, smirks, and rolling eyes, which can inhibit in-person contact.

### Disinhibition

While we tend to detect lies or deception only at the rate of chance in our face-to-face relationships, when communicating in the digital domain, we show even less inhibition in trusting. When online, not only do we display higher rates of trust, but we also more readily share our personal information. We do this even though it is harder for us to tell if we are being deceived. At least in part, this is attributed to the online disinhibition effect.[44] Social networking sites and other online venues find people revealing secrets and sharing vulnerabilities much sooner than they would in more traditionally formed relationships. Online communication, however, may lack the security or inherent privacy

There is danger in sharing our deepest secrets and vulnerabilities online.

that the now hardly used sealed letter once promised. In fact, we might compare our social networking pages more to postcards: We shouldn't be surprised when something we write is read by people other than the one for whom it was intended. Consequently, while technological innovations have made us more accessible to each other, they also have made us more accessible to everyone.

On the other hand, for some, computer-mediated communication encourages the sharing of personal information that they might have found too difficult to communicate were they actually required to do so face-to-face. Somehow, using technology to communicate helps reduce our inhibitions and frees us to reveal information we would otherwise hesitate to share.

This leads us to pose three questions that each of us should ask ourselves before we entrust others with our more intimate disclosures on social networking sites:

1. If we would not discuss something on the richest channel available to us—face-to-face communication—should we be revealing the information at all?

2. How much of the real meaning of our disclosures is being lost in the electronic translation of personal information?

3. To what extent should we trust social networking sites to ensure our privacy at the same time they reduce our inhibitions and link us more closely to each other?

Whereas we may have been taught to assume that members of the community in which we live are trustworthy, online communities are a different story. We know many of the people we interact with online only by their screen names, making it more difficult for us to establish genuine trusting relationships with them. When we interact with people who surrender their fictional identities so that we can verify who they really are, the establishment of trust becomes easier.

## Detecting Deception Online

Since so much interaction has moved online, it would be a benefit if we were able to spot online deception. According to information technology and deception specialist Jeffrey Hancock, "Most people believe that given the opportunity, everything else equal, people will lie more online than they would face-to-face."[45] Lies told online are motivated by the same human needs as are any other lies, but their quantity may be greater.

Can you trust your eyes when it comes to online photos? A program called FakeApp lets users create fake videos in which an individual's face is superimposed on another person's body. While Snapchat already offers face-morphing technology, newer tools are more realistic and powerful, and leave behind few clues to the digital manipulation involved. It's not hard to imagine the potentially dangerous outcomes of such apps, leaving us to question the ethics and potential abuses of merging representation and reality deceptively.[46] Perhaps the next app created will help us detect and debunk these images.

Research on deception in online dating reveals that approximately 80 percent of people embellish their profiles with "small" fibs, such as a man representing himself as 6 feet tall when he is really 3 inches shorter. In such cases, those who tell the fibs find that the potential cost of being caught is outweighed by the self-presentation benefit of having others find them more appealing because they are thought to be taller than they really are. Lying in an online dating profile is a means to create interpersonal attraction. The requirement to post photos of themselves online, however, does make people less likely to lie—at least until now.[47]

With dating services so popular, how can you spot a lie when searching online for a potential date? Online prospects who are being less than honest are less likely to refer to themselves as "I"; use indirect adjectives, such as "not boring" rather than "exciting"; and keep their descriptions brief. Using these criteria, researchers were able to identify liars about 65 percent of the time.[48]

## More Digital Dangers

Some couples share their passwords to e-mail and social networking accounts, which facilitates opportunities to read each other's private e-mails and texts. This may be seen as a means of proving their trust in one another, but it can cause a lot of damage.[49] One danger is the potential for each person to reveal the other's secrets should the relationship turn dark or end.

Another danger involves the willing sharing of intimate photos. The amount of sexting is increasing—with one in four young people surveyed having received sexts. The problem is that one in seven have sent sexts they have received to others—often without the subject's consent. Revenge porn, a digital betrayal of trust in which intimate photos intended only for the recipient are shared widely, often results in the subject featured in the sext being harassed, cyberbullied, or blackmailed.[50]

Digital social networks are also dangerously effective at spreading rumors and misinformation. The pace of delivery makes it very difficult to stop the flow of lies. Merely seeing the same lie repeatedly stated makes it more credible in the eyes of the viewer.

# GAINING COMMUNICATION COMPETENCE: DEVELOPING SKILLS NEEDED TO NURTURE TRUSTING RELATIONSHIPS

As our examination of trust reveals, being trustworthy means working to build real relationships, not working to get to know others just so you can take advantage of their vulnerabilities. When you use your knowledge to harm a partner, you destroy your partner's trust in you. Fear, distrust, and other defensive feelings are common roadblocks to an individual's ability to function and self-actualize, as well as barriers to the development and maintenance of a good relationship. The key to building trust in a relationship is to behave in a trustworthy manner.

## BE WILLING TO DISCLOSE YOURSELF TO ANOTHER PERSON

Like self-disclosure, trust is a reciprocal process. Trusting behavior on your part can often lead to trusting behavior in another. Thus, self-disclosing to another can help the other come to know you, understand you, and realize that he or she must also take a risk if a relationship based on mutual trust is to develop.

## LET THE OTHER PERSON KNOW YOU ACCEPT THEM

When you reduce threats to the ego of another individual, you increase the level of trust between you and create a trusting or **supportive environment**. If the other person feels accepted by you and feels that you perceive him or her as a significant human being who is worthy of your time and attention, then he or she will be less likely to experience anxiety about being placed in a vulnerable position. Such feelings of acceptance will also deter others from attempting to defend themselves by lying or concealing the truth. They simply will have no reason to do so. Thus, support and acceptance encourage trust and honesty.

## DEVELOP A COOPERATIVE/SUPPORTIVE RATHER THAN A COMPETITIVE/DEFENSIVE ORIENTATION

Working to "win" in a relationship can destroy it. If your primary aim is to increase your personal gain, even though that means sacrificing the well-being of a partner, the degree of trust your partner is willing to put in you will diminish rapidly. You will be perceived as a manipulator. In contrast, healthy relationships depend on the problem-solving abilities of the individuals involved.

## TRUST ONLY WHEN IT'S WARRANTED

Taking inappropriate risks can cause as many problems as being unwilling to take a risk. In other words, always trusting people who do not merit your trust is as dysfunctional as never trusting anyone. People who consistently trust exploitative people find themselves taken advantage of and will not build relationships based on trust. Instead, you must be willing to question the other person's motives and behavior openly. The other person may learn to respect you for feeling strong or capable enough to call out the duplicity. Remember, trust is sustained only if both parties to a relationship behave in trustworthy ways.

# The Case of the Trusting Agent

Fifty houses! Angela was devastated. She had shown the Williams family 50 houses over the summer—and now this!

At the end of the spring term, Angela had completed a real estate sales course. A summer job selling houses had seemed like a great idea. She liked people, the hours were flexible, and the potential for earning high commissions as a sales agent with a company in her hometown was great. Of course, the downside was that there would be no pay if she failed to make a sale, but Angela figured that was too remote a possibility for her to take seriously.

Selling was not an easy job. There were houses to preview, owners to call, and buyers to show houses to 7 days a week. After working days and evenings for 6 weeks with no success, Angela finally found "live" buyers—Rita and Tom Williams—who desperately wanted to buy a $600,000 home in an upscale neighborhood. The fee she would earn from selling them a house would pay most of her school expenses for the next year.

Angela worked tirelessly, taking Rita to houses in the morning and showing Tom the same houses in the evening. She got to know their 3-year-old son, Evan, better than she knew her own nieces and nephews. Evan was a nice kid; it wasn't his fault that he often got carsick and threw up in her backseat . . .

Rita and Tom had finally narrowed it down to two homes. Angela was sure she could close the deal before September, when she would return to college. Showing them 50 houses had been exhausting, but now that she could see the light at the end of the real estate tunnel, she decided it had been fun.

Then Rita called. She and Tom had also been looking at houses with another real estate agent. In fact, they had already made an offer on a house that had been accepted several days ago; they would be closing on it soon. They had continued to look at houses with Angela just to convince themselves that the one they had made the offer on was the best they could find. Now they were convinced that they had made the right choice. Unfortunately, nothing Angela showed them had compared to the one they had decided to bid on. Rita thanked Angela for all her help.

Angela dropped the phone. How could Rita and Tom do this to her? Because of the time she had spent with them, Angela had worked the entire summer without earning a cent.

"Whom can I trust?" she cried to her sales manager. Just then, the door opened and a couple walked in. They wanted to look at homes. The sales manager introduced them to Angela.

### Consider these questions:

1. Should Angela trust the new couple and show them houses?

2. What could Angela do, if anything, to ensure that the trust she might place in these new buyers would not be misplaced?

# REVIEW THIS

**1. Define trust and explain the bases for it.** ☐

Trust is the belief that you can depend on another person to act in your best interest. It consists of two basic components: trusting behavior and trustworthy behavior. The amount of faith we have in one another is based in large measure on our perceptions of each other's character. Among character-based sources of trust are trust in the other's integrity, consistency of behavior, and discretion.

**2. Discuss the nature of forgiveness and its impact on relationship rebuilding.** ☐

Forgiveness is the sense of peace and understanding we experience once we stop blaming another person for a perceived wrong and instead interpret the transgression less personally. To repair and rebuild a relationship jeopardized by a betrayal, the betrayed person finds a way to forgive the transgressor by letting go of negative feelings.

**3. Explain cost-benefit theory, including its relationship to trust.** ☐

According to cost-benefit theory, we work to sustain relationships that enable us to maximize the profit side of our relational balance sheets. As long as the benefits we receive from our relationships outweigh our emotional expenditures, we will work to sustain them.

**4. Explore relational situations, identifying factors contributing to the development of cooperative/supportive and competitive/defensive interpersonal climates.** ☐

Whether a relationship is defined as cooperative or competitive plays a part in determining whether the individuals involved develop trust. An interpersonal relationship that is competitive precipitates defensive and threatening behavior in interactions, whereas a cooperative relationship tends to precipitate more supportive and honest communication.

**5. Describe how lying affects interpersonal relationships.** ☐

Deception, or the effort to manipulate truth, affects the nature and outcomes of a relationship. Although some people differentiate between white lies and bigger lies, all lies help us negotiate situations that expose us to levels of vulnerability exceeding our comfort zones.

**6. Discuss how gender and culture influence the development of trust.** ☐

Both culture and gender influence whom we trust. Ethnocentrism can decrease our trust in those whom we find different, and men and women differ when it comes to their trust assumptions and reasons for lying.

**7. Describe how media portrayals and technology can foster or impede the development of relationships based on trust.** ☐

Stereotyped portrayals in media affect our views of different groups in society, fostering unrealistic perceptions of who is and is not trustworthy. Technology and social networks facilitate the sharing and disclosure of

266   The Interpersonal Communication Playbook

personal information, leading us to trust people who may not deserve to be trusted.

8. **Identify and use behaviors that promote the development of trusting relationships.** ☐

For trust to develop, you need to be willing to disclose yourself to another person, let the other person know you accept and support him or her, develop a cooperative orientation, and believe that trusting behavior will be reciprocated and is, therefore, appropriate.

## CHECK YOUR UNDERSTANDING

1. Can you provide examples that highlight the nature of both trusting and supportive relationships? (See pages 236–239 and 243–248.)

2. Can you create a scenario illustrating how lying and/or a willingness or unwillingness to forgive may affect a relationship? (See pages 239–240.)

3. Can you develop a story to explain the value of cost-benefit theory? (See page 241.)

4. Can you create a list of ways in which your culture, your gender, or your preference for particular media offerings and social networks could influence your feelings about trust? (See pages 255–259.)

5. Can you identify behaviors you can adopt to foster more trusting relationships? (See page 260.)

## KEY TERMS

Comparison level for alternatives  245

Competitive relationship  246

Cooperative relationship  246

Cost-benefit theory  245

Counterfeit relationship  255

Defensive climate  247

Descriptive statements  248

Displacement  254

Evaluative statements  248

Lie  251

Rationalization  255

Repression  255

Supportive climate  248

Supportive environment  263

Trust  240

Trusting behavior  241

Trustworthy behavior  241

Get the tools you need to sharpen your study skills. **SAGE edge** offers a robust online environment featuring an impressive array of free tools and resources. Access practice quizzes, eFlashcards, video, and multimedia at **edge.sagepub.com/gambleicp**.

iStock.com/SvetaZi

# Power and Influence

## Learning Objectives

1. Define power, comparing and contrasting the following types of power: reward, coercive, expert, legitimate, referent, and persuasive

2. Define and distinguish among attitudes, beliefs, and values as persuasive forces, discussing strategies to help elicit compliance and restore relational balance

3. Discuss how culture, gender, and media and technology influence both the perception and exercise of power

4. Identify guidelines for balancing relational power

> Influence is the new power—if you have influence, you can create a brand.
>
> —Michelle Phan

Can you imagine anyone having the power to get you to do something that you absolutely have no intention of doing? For instance, might an authority figure who instructed you to inflict pain on someone succeed?

Power has a dark side. A half century ago, the psychologist Stanley Milgram conducted a series of studies on power and obedience. Over and over again, Milgram demonstrated that a large number of his well-intentioned subjects delivered what they thought were increasingly painful electric shocks to another person in what the subjects believed was an experiment about learning. Unbeknownst to the subjects, however, the "learner" was actually an actor who was only pretending to receive the painful shocks.[1]

The study showed that human beings have the capacity to act destructively without being coerced. They merely comply with the instructions of those in authority. They cede their personal power to those they believe to be in control.

Milgram's subjects had a choice, though, and so do we. We all have some power that we use in our daily interactions with others. By better understanding the relationship between power and influence, we can more capably respond to perceived power imbalances in our interpersonal relationships. ■

# WHAT DO YOU KNOW?

Before continuing your reading of this chapter, which of the following five statements do you believe to be true, and which do you believe to be false?

1. Giving perks reflects a need to influence behavior.           T     F

2. Asking someone to do something for you that he or she can easily do works about half the time.           T     F

3. We feel obligated to return a favor.           T     F

4. If someone pays you $100 to speak in support of a person or an issue that you do not support, you are more likely to come to support the person or issue than if the person pays you only $10 for your efforts.           T     F

5. If you always do as you are told, you likely are a member of a culture with a low-power-distance preference.           T     F

Read the chapter to discover if you're right or if you've made any erroneous assumptions.

ANSWERS: 1. T; 2. F; 3. T; 4. F; 5. F

# THE CONTROL FACTOR: EXPLORING THE BALANCE OF POWER IN RELATIONSHIPS

**Power**, the potential to influence, plays a part in every relationship—although we hope not in abusive or exploitative ways.[2] Whether you are interacting with a close friend and exerting an equal amount of power, with an employer who exerts more power than you, or with a partner who acquiesces to your every request, power is present. Perceptions of power affect our respect for others, our fear of them, our feelings of confidence or dependence, and even our decisions about whose company we seek.[3] The power dynamics of our relationships determine who we are able to influence or control, who is able to influence or control us, and whether we are comfortable with our position on the power seesaw.

We test the balance of power in our relationships routinely. Sometimes we feel in control or powerful in a relationship, while other times we feel out of control or powerless. A sense of powerlessness can feed on itself, contributing to our

Moviestore collection Ltd/Ysanne Slide/Alamy Stock Photo

Superheroes repeatedly demonstrate that with power comes responsibility.

actually becoming more vulnerable to another's power. In contrast, when we exert power and succeed, feelings of powerfulness can contribute to our becoming more influential. The "me too." movement testifies to this. As the movement took shape, we saw what could happen when people who once felt powerless to act against those who repeatedly abused their power by sexually harassing or assaulting them decided that they no longer would cede control to the more powerful, but instead would exert their own power by speaking up, exposing their abusers, and taking control back.[4]

## FEELING POWERFUL VERSUS POWERLESS

If you find yourself feeling powerless a lot of the time, chances are that you're also unhappy and dissatisfied with a number of your important relationships. When we lose the ability to exert power, we also lose the ability to direct our future. Others end up making choices for us—choices that likely are not in our best interest.

### Are You Socially Anxious?

Emotions influence how powerful or powerless we feel. If you feel nervous or overly emotional in social situations, you may suffer from social anxiety, which probably makes it more difficult for you to project a powerful image. Those who are socially anxious find it difficult to enjoy themselves in public settings. They are likely to feel that others are judging them. Because this anxiety is so painful, some who experience it decide to stay away from social situations altogether, which makes it unlikely that they will influence anyone.

The socially anxious are especially fearful of authority figures, such as supervisors at work or anyone whom they perceive to be better or more important than they are. Upon meeting authority figures, people with social anxiety may experience a lump in the throat and their facial muscles may freeze up. Because their focus is on not failing, they are unlikely even to remember what was said in conversation.[5]

### Are You on a Power Trip?

At the extreme, some emotions can send you on a *power trip*—you feel so capable and secure that you imagine you can manipulate others to do whatever you want with little effort. The term *Machiavellian* refers to people who use a variety of ploys to make choices for and control others. If you score high in Machiavellianism, you have the drive to control others. If you score low in Machiavellianism, you are likely more susceptible to the interpersonal persuasion of others.[6]

## TRY THIS

## What's Your Power Orientation?

The amount of Machiavellianism you possess influences how likely you are to try to control others.

For each statement below, select a numerical response on a scale from 1 to 5, where 1 is "disagree a lot" and 5 is "agree a lot" and write it down next to the statement.

*(Continued)*

(Continued)

1. The best way to handle people is to tell them what they want to hear. ____

2. When you ask someone to do something for you, it is best to give the real reason for wanting it rather than giving reasons that might carry more weight. ____

3. Anyone who completely trusts anyone else is asking for trouble. ____

4. It is hard to get ahead without cutting corners here and there. ____

5. It is safest to assume that everyone has a vicious streak, which will come out when given a chance. ____

6. One should take action only when it is morally right. ____

7. Most people are basically good and kind. ____

8. There is no excuse for lying to someone else. ____

9. Most people more easily forget the death of their father than the loss of property. ____

10. Generally speaking, people won't work hard unless they're forced to do so. ____

To determine your score, follow these steps.

Reverse the scores on items 2, 6, 7, and 8 as follows:

| IF YOU RESPONDED WITH | CHANGE IT TO |
| --- | --- |
| 5 | 1 |
| 4 | 2 |
| 3 | 3 |
| 2 | 4 |
| 1 | 5 |

Add together your answers for all questions, being certain to use the reverse numbers for questions 2, 6, 7, and 8.

If your total score is between 35 and 50, you are likely a high Machiavellian. If you score between 10 and 15, you are probably a low Machiavellian. The majority of responses fall between these extremes.

Do you believe that your results on this test accurately describe you? Do your results support or contradict research findings that men generally are more Machiavellian than women, older adults tend to have lower scores than younger adults, and those with higher scores tend to be in professions that require one to exert control over others? To what extent, if any, do you see your score reflected in how you interact with others and your decisions regarding whether or not to exert power over the choices others make?

Source: From R. Christie and F. L. Geis, *Studies in Machiavellianism*. Academic Press 1970. © Elsevier Science & Technology Books.

# WHERE DOES POWER COME FROM?

Power is relational. The person who has power derives it from the social relationship itself. Another person assents, overtly or covertly, to their use of power. The greater our power, the greater our ability to make things happen—or prevent them from happening. When we have power, we simply are better able to control what happens to us when in the company of others. Your judgment of the amount of power you or another have is based on the resources you or the other control; this determines the degree to which either one of you feels dependent in the relationship.

# POWER CATEGORIES

When we have power, we possess a resource others value.[7] Researchers identify six categories of power that we use to control and influence others: reward, coercive, expert, legitimate, referent, and persuasive (see Table 10.1).[8] The extent to which we use each of these currencies of power in our relationships reveals our influence preferences.

## Reward Power

The person in a relationship who controls something valued by the other person in the relationship is said to hold **reward power**. The person with reward power knows what the other person wants, is able to provide it, lets the other know this ability exists, and reveals what the other needs to do for

### TABLE 10.1  TYPES OF POWER

| TYPE | DEFINITION | EXAMPLE |
|---|---|---|
| **Reward power** | One party in the relationship controls something valued by the other party. | Instructors hold reward power over their students in the form of grades. |
| **Coercive power** | One party in the relationship can deliver negative consequences in response to the actions of another. | Individuals who threaten to boycott a business unless certain actions are taken hold coercive power over the business owners. |
| **Expert power** | One party in the relationship possesses special knowledge or skill that another individual believes he or she needs. | Physicians hold expert power in the eyes of patients in the form of specific diagnoses or treatments. |
| **Legitimate power** | Because of his or her position, one party in the relationship is able to control the other party. | Employers hold legitimate power over their employees. |
| **Referent power** | Because of the respect and admiration accorded him or her, one party in the relationship is able to convince others. | An older sibling may have referent power over a younger brother or sister. |
| **Persuasive power** | One party in the relationship is able to persuade another to believe or act as he or she wants. | Through the use of logic, well-conceived and developed arguments, and emotional appeals, lawyers hold persuasive power over jurors. |

the reward to be released. Rewards may be tangible (job, money) or intangible (friendship, security). The extent to which one person values the rewards determines the amount of power the other is able to exercise. If you have the ability either to deliver positive consequences or to remove negative ones, you will be more likely to get another person to comply with your requests. Every relationship implies some degree of reward power. The more fulfilling we find a relationship, the more we perceive it to have such power.

## Coercive Power

Unlike reward power, **coercive power** is typically associated with force. Individuals with coercive power can deliver negative consequences or remove positive ones in response to another's actions. When using coercive power, people need to be prepared both to escalate the threats they make and to have others resent or dislike them for threatening them in the first place. To exercise coercive power, you need to identify the specific consequences another person most fears, have the ability to mete out those consequences at will, let the other person know you have that ability, and convince them that unless they behave as you want, you will act accordingly.

By exercising psychological coercive power, someone can compel us to maintain a relationship we might otherwise choose to end. Because we fear the punishment the other person can inflict—whether that fear is of being demeaned, or something else—the threats made can be a powerful interpersonal motivator.

Comstock/Comstock/Thinkstock

Being able to develop logical arguments can increase your power.

## Expert Power

A person with **expert power** is presumed to possess a special knowledge or skill others believe they need. Expert power holders have the ability to influence us because of their training, background, or accomplishments. Such power is further enhanced when we believe the expert source to be unbiased, with nothing to gain personally from influencing us. For example, a physician may persuade us to follow specific instructions concerning our health if we are convinced that her credentials qualify her to dispense such advice, and we trust that she will not profit unduly if we follow her instructions. If, on the other hand, a salesperson recommends you purchase a product for which he will earn a higher fee, you might doubt his actual expertise.

## Legitimate Power

When a person's position enables him or her to control another, that person has **legitimate power.** Most of us believe that some people have a right to exert power over us merely because of the roles they perform, who they are, or the positions they hold. For example, students perceive their teachers to have legitimate power and employees perceive their employers to have legitimate power. Often used to reduce conflict, legitimate power convinces those with less power to adhere to the requests of the more powerful.

## Referent Power

When someone has **referent power**, we do as they request because we identify with, respect, or like them, and we want them to like us. The relationship is a simple one. As our desire to be like someone increases, so does that individual's referent power in our eyes. The more attractive we find someone and the more respect and admiration we have for them, the greater our tendency to mirror that person's behavior and do as they want rather than contradict their actions and fail to conform with their wishes. Thus, a person who serves as our referent can get us to do many things we might not otherwise do.

## Persuasive Power

Sometimes a person has power because of their ability to persuade by conveying information in well-thought-out arguments. **Persuasive power** is based on the logic or reasonableness of the person's arguments or the demonstrated superiority of their knowledge. Those who possess persuasive power need not be experts; they only need to know how to use speech powerfully and reason intelligently.

## TRY THIS

## Powerful People and Power Plays

In your relationships, the more powerful person is the one in control of the situation. Think of three current relationships.

1. For each, identify the relationship's nature—that is, is it based primarily on friendship, family ties, work, or health needs?

2. Compare and contrast the amount of power you perceive yourself and the other person to wield. In each instance, who is more powerful and why?

3. Compare your perceptions of the amount of power you have in each of the three relationships. In which of your relationships is power balanced? In which is it imbalanced? How do you account for the differences?

Although we can use any of these types of power in our relationships, some are more effective and less damaging than others to the sense of self of the less powerful member. By analyzing the types of power that characterize your meaningful relationships, you gain insight into how balanced or unbalanced, personally costly or beneficial, and effective or ineffective the use of power and personal influence is in your life.[9]

# EXERCISING PERSUASION

How often do you succeed in exercising power and influencing others to see things your way? How often do you give in to others whom you perceive to have more power? Successful persuaders understand the attitudes, beliefs, and values others hold dear and use these to accomplish their persuasive goals. Once we identify how we can best influence others, our interpersonal effectiveness may improve markedly.

When seeking to influence another, usually we try to modify that person's thinking, feelings, or behavior so that it becomes more compatible with ours. Seeking to exert personal influence is normal, but some of us become so preoccupied with the effort that our central aim in our relationships becomes to create similarity of thought, feeling, and behavior.

To this end, let us explore the roles that attitudes, beliefs, and values play in this process, and how attitudes, beliefs, and values are internalized, maintained, or changed through interaction.

## THE ROLE OF ATTITUDES

Although we cannot see, hear, or touch an attitude, we can examine the behavior that results from holding that attitude. We use verbal and nonverbal cues to communicate attitudes, our positive, negative, mixed, or indifferent evaluations of particular individuals, objects, or ideas. Facial expressions, postures, and gestures are attitude revealers, attesting to the intensity of our feelings.[10] Each time we socialize, attend class, or go to a meeting, we put our attitudes on display. They affect who we are and how we relate.

### What Is an Attitude?

Most psychologists define an **attitude** as a mental set or readiness to respond that causes us to react in a particular way to a given stimulus. Each of our attitudes represents a predisposition to react positively or negatively, ambivalently, or apathetically toward certain people, ideas, things, or situations. In other words, our attitudes represent our evaluations. They help us sort our perceptions into categories.

In large measure, our attitudes determine our communication preferences and behavior. They lead us to behave in certain ways and increase the likelihood that specific kinds of reactions will occur.

### Where Do Our Attitudes Come From?

We act according to pictures we carry in our heads—pictures that do not necessarily correspond with reality. To understand why we hold the attitudes we do, we can try to identify the forces that help us create and sustain those pictures.

The roots of our attitudes extend in many directions. Among the forces feeding them and contributing to their growth are family, religion, education, economic and social class, and culture.

- *Family:* Few of us escape the strong influences our family members exert. Our parents communicate their attitudes, and eventually we acquire and hold at least a number of them.

- *Religion:* Religion affects both believers and nonbelievers. In fact, its impact has become even more widespread in recent decades, with churches striving to influence attitudes on such social issues as gun control, immigration, violence in media, and economic disparities.

- *Education:* We attend school for more years now than ever before. Many of us start before we are 5 years old and attend until we are well into our 20s. In addition, adults are returning to school in record numbers. What we are taught, who teaches us, and the articles, books, films, and other media we are assigned all help shape our attitudes.

- *Economic and social class:* Our economic status helps determine the social arena we frequent. The company we keep and the amount of money we have influence our thoughts about the world and its problems.

- *Culture:* The customs and beliefs of a society make up its culture. Culture is passed on to us by our family, friends, and the groups we belong to, and it helps coordinate our actions and the norms and rules we live by. Once we share a culture, we also share similar meanings.

## THE ROLE OF BELIEFS

Although the term *attitude* is sometimes used interchangeably with the term *belief*, the two are distinguishable. While we internalize many attitudes, we form an even greater number of beliefs.

### What Are Beliefs?

Beliefs are to attitudes as bricks are to buildings. In other words, **beliefs** provide the basis or foundation for our attitudes.

Whereas attitudes are measured on a favorable–unfavorable or good–bad continuum, beliefs are measured on a true–false or probable–improbable continuum. Thus, if we say that we think something is true, we really are saying that we believe it.

We believe information for a variety of reasons. Sometimes we believe it because we read it somewhere or saw it on the news, and we have blind faith in the media, never recognizing that authors and reporters may be wrong or biased. Other times, we believe information because an authority or a friend says it is so or because "everyone else believes it." Our beliefs are not necessarily logical. Rather, in large part, we hold them as a result of what we want or need to believe, what we are able to believe, or what others teach us to believe. Consequently, we don't always require proof to believe. Instead, we allow our beliefs to influence our interpretations, using them to manipulate or distort what we see and hear. We act in ways that are consistent with what we think is true. As a result, at least to some degree, what we believe restricts what we perceive.

Our belief system is made up of everything with which we agree.[11] It includes all the information and biases we have accumulated since birth. Formed along with our belief system is our disbelief system. It is composed of all the things with which we disagree. Together, the two systems influence our processing of information.

iStock.com/imtmphoto

Few of us escape the strong influences of family members.

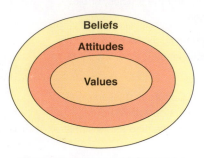

## FIGURE 10.1
Interpersonal Influencers

We exert interpersonal influence by tapping into the attitudes, beliefs, and values of others.

## THE ROLE OF VALUES

Like attitudes and beliefs, our values influence our communication, affecting our relationships (see Figure 10.1). We define **values** as ideas about what is important in our lives. Our values represent our feelings about the worth of something.

Our values provide us with a relatively persistent framework for deciding what we think is right or wrong, which goals to aspire to, whose company to seek, whom to listen to, and how to live. They provide us with criteria for evaluating the people in our lives, including their ideas and actions. They indicate what we find desirable and to what extent, and consequently, they influence what we are willing to strive for.

## GAINING COMPLIANCE IN INTERPERSONAL RELATIONSHIPS

Because we are always forming new relationships and having new experiences, we may find it necessary or perhaps expedient to adjust our attitudes. Sometimes, for example, we interact with another whose actions conflict with our beliefs. When this occurs, we may try to take steps to reduce or eliminate the conflict. We work hard to gain compliance so that we are able to maintain internal balance among our actions, feelings, and beliefs.

### Strategies for Gaining Compliance

We use a variety of persuasive strategies to gain compliance from others. For example, we may try to influence another toward a particular action, attitude, or belief by making a direct request such as "Will you drive me to the library so that I can get a book I need on genetics?" This is the most straightforward way to gain compliance. Studies demonstrate that simply asking someone for something with which he or she can easily comply succeeds 90 percent of the time. In one study, when a person asked those waiting in a line if she could cut ahead of them because she was in a rush, most acquiesced. Sometimes we're on autopilot, complying to a request, even without a good reason. More than 60 percent even let the person cut in when the reason offered was weak: "I have to make some copies."[12]

Adding supportive evidence can strengthen a request: "I really would like to be able to put the latest research into my report, and to do that I need the new genetics book the library is holding for me." Or we might offer a trade, such as "If you drive me to the library, I'll cook you a great dinner." The norm of reciprocity—the fact that we feel obligated to return another's favor, even if the person is someone we are not crazy about—often elicits compliance.[13]

Instead of trying to strike a deal, we might try to coerce the other person into complying by threatening him or her with a punishment for inaction: "I can't believe you. I'm only asking you to drive me to the library, not around the world. If you don't take me, I won't go with you to that dinner that's so important to you."

Similarly, we might describe another benefit—that is, we might offer one or more reasons that help the other person perceive what he or she stands to gain from helping us: "If I get that book, I'm much more likely to get a good grade, so I'll qualify for a research assistantship, which means I won't have to get a second job, and I'll have more time to spend with you."

Although simply asking for what we want is often effective, at times we might find it more desirable to use an indirect approach, reciting emotion-laden statements designed to help us maintain face: "You know I really want to get a good grade on my research assignment, but I won't be able to do it without that book. I just wish I could get to the library." Or we might aim to instill empathy for our situation by appealing to the other's love and concern for our welfare: "Come on," we might say, "We always help each other out because my doing well is important to you and your doing well is equally important to me."[14] Successfully persuading others increases our sense of personal power and helps to facilitate our psychological balance (see Table 10.2).

### TABLE 10.2 COMPLIANCE-GAINING STRATEGIES

| WHICH OF THE INTERPERSONAL PERSUASION STRATEGIES DO YOU CONSIDER ETHICAL? WHICH ARE YOU COMFORTABLE USING? WHICH HAVE YOU FOUND WORK THE BEST? | |
| --- | --- |
| Strategy | Example |
| Make a direct request. | Will you drive me to the airport? |
| Strengthen a request with supporting evidence. | Will you drive me to the airport so that we can talk about what needs to be done while I'm away? |
| Strike a deal/offer a trade. | If you drive me to the airport, I'll treat you to a great dinner at that restaurant you wanted to go to. |
| Exert coercion. | I can't believe that you haven't offered to drive me to the airport. If you don't help out, I'll complete the report while I'm away, and I won't put your name on it. |
| Identify compliance benefits. | If you drive me to the airport, I'll be more likely to have time to hear your ideas on the project you'd like to be involved in, which means I'll be able to recommend you to the president. |
| Use emotion-laden statements. | I really want to be able to recommend to the president that you be a part of the special team that's being formed, but I need to learn more about how you think. I just wish you'd take me to the airport so we'd have time to talk. |
| Instill empathy with an appeal directed at your welfare. | Come on. Take me to the airport. I know that you care about how I do on this trip. If I'm rested, my chances of succeeding are greater. I know that's important to you. |

## STRATEGIES FOR ACHIEVING RELATIONAL BALANCE

Balance is a state of psychological health or comfort in which our actions, feelings, and beliefs are related in a way we like them to be. When in a balanced state, we feel content and satisfied. When our actions, feelings, and beliefs are not balanced, we experience discomfort and tension.

### Balance Theory

We can illustrate our need for consistency by referring to a model of attitude change called **balance theory**, developed by Fritz Heider.[15] In Heider's model we symbolize our relationships with plus and minus signs. A plus sign signifies a positive feeling or attitude; a minus signifies a negative feeling or

Do you feel balanced?

attitude. According to Heider, we expect people we like to like what we like and people we don't like to dislike what we like. Thus, whenever the model contains three pluses or one plus and two minuses, the interpersonal relationship is balanced. For example, you like dining out (+), you like David (+), and David likes dining out (+). Your relationship is balanced. Your relationship is also balanced if you don't like dining out (−), you like David (+), and David doesn't like dining out (−).

When our relationships are balanced, we exist in a state of equilibrium; people we share relationships with think the same way we do. When our relationships are unbalanced, however, we exist in a state of disequilibrium. Things don't fit together as we want them to. Thus, we try to make adjustments to restore balance.

At times, each of us purposefully avoids interacting with another person because we fear we will dislike or disagree with him or her. This is one way we try to maintain a state of consistency or balance. At other times, however, we are unable to avoid interacting with someone who threatens our balance. This is especially true if we really like another person and our relationship with him or her is important to us. When a relationship we value is endangered by inconsistencies that cause us discomfort, we can attempt to restore balance in a number of ways. First, we can change our attitude toward the problem. We can reassess our stand and decide that our original judgment was in error. Second, we can try to change the other person by giving him or her information that supports our point of view. Third, we can simply decide that whether we agree on the issue is not of vital importance to our relationship. Fourth, we can misinterpret the other's position, convincing ourselves that the person does not really mean what he or she is saying—that is, we convince ourselves that the person really agrees with us. Finally, we can choose to view the imbalance as an asset, telling ourselves that it demonstrates the maturity of our relationship. We then can disagree without feeling excessive discomfort.

## TRY THIS

### Tensions and Tactics

According to balance theory, when two people interact in relation to an event or object of mutual concern, the situations they find themselves in are either balanced or not. An unbalanced situation precipitates tension, motivating persuasion—a change in attitude in an effort to restore balance.

Recall a personal experience in which you and another person existed in an imbalanced situation due to your mismatching attitudes relevant to some object of mutual concern. Specify the steps you and/or the other took in an effort to restore balance, describing how the "felt tension" contributed to interpersonal persuasive efforts on either your part or your partner's.

The Interpersonal Communication Playbook

## Cognitive Dissonance Theory

The theory of ==cognitive dissonance== offers another approach to explain how we compensate when we find ourselves doing things that fail to fit with what we know or have opinions that fail to fit with other opinions we hold.[16] According to Leon Festinger, the theory's formulator, dissonance is an aversive drive that propels us toward consistency. In other words, once we have acted, we feel compelled to bring our beliefs into harmony with our actions. For example, imagine that you are a heavy smoker who knows about all the medical reports on the dangers of smoking. Your knowledge conflicts with your behavior. According to Festinger, something has to give: Either you will give up smoking, or you will alter your belief that smoking will harm you, whichever action is easiest.

When knowledge and behavior conflict, dissonance exists.

Festinger identifies three mental means we use to ensure that our actions and attitudes support each other. The first, selective exposure, reduces dissonance by ensuring we avoid information and people likely to contradict our beliefs (as briefly discussed in Chapter 3). This explains why a political rally is likely to attract mostly members of the party holding the rally. The second, the ==need for reassurance==, ensures that we will seek out information and social support confirming that we made the right decision. This explains why, after being persuaded to make a significant purchase such as a car, you might pore over copies of *Consumer Reports* or notice that others have bought cars like yours too. The third, ==minimal justification for action==, suggests that small incentives are more effective than large ones at creating dissonance and inducing attitude change. This is counter to what we might expect, but it reveals that when the incentive to alter behavior is small, we really do have to change our attitude to bring it in line with our behavior. Doing so also allows us to appear reasonable to ourselves.

# ROUTES TO INTERPERSONAL INFLUENCE

Which influence route do you travel—a peripheral or offhand route, or a central, more thoughtful route? Before you answer, realize that we are exposed to so many persuasive messages during interpersonal encounters that we virtually are certain to take the lazy approach unless the subject is one in which we are personally involved.

Those of us who are relatively easily influenced are likely to respond to what psychologist Robert Cialdini calls ==trigger cues==—cues that stimulate programmed responses to persuasive appeals.[17] These cues take six forms: reciprocation ("You owe me one."), consistency ("This has always worked before."), social proof ("The whole administration is in favor of this approach."), liking ("Love me, support my ideas."), authority ("Because I want you to."), and scarcity ("Hurry, before it's no longer possible for you to do so."). Trigger cues lead us to take a cognitive shortcut, or a peripheral route, one that requires little effort or thought.

According to psychologists Richard Petty and John Cacioppo, "A more thoughtful alternative cognitive process, the central route, involves message elaboration, the careful thinking about issue-relevant arguments contained in a persuasive communication."[18] Once we travel this route, a number of other factors, among them our motivation and ability to concentrate and resist distractions, determine our success.

# THE IMPACT OF CULTURE, GENDER, MEDIA, AND TECHNOLOGY ON CONCEPTIONS OF POWER

How do culture, gender, and media and technology influence our thoughts and actions when it comes to exerting our power and influence and responding to the efforts of others to do the same? How does each serve to modify our approach to power and our reactions when the target of another's influence attempts?

## CULTURE, VALUES, AND RELATIONAL POWER

According to theorist Geert Hofstede, culture influences and modifies four value dimensions affecting relational power: individualism and collectivism, uncertainty avoidance, masculinity and femininity, and power distance.

### Individualism and Collectivism

One of the key variables determining human action is whether one's primary orientation is individual or collective in nature. In individualistically oriented countries such as the United States, Great Britain, and Australia, the individual is of central importance; independence is stressed, with personal goals taking priority over allegiance to a group; personal achievement is rewarded; and uniqueness is an asset. In collectivistically oriented countries such as Taiwan, Colombia, and Pakistan, the individual is dependent on the in-group, the views and needs of the in-group are valued over the views and needs of the individual, and the individual sacrifices personal rights and places trust in group decisions.[19] A number of co-cultures in the United States, including Mexican American and African American cultures, are collectivistically oriented.[20]

### Uncertainty Avoidance

Some cultures perceive uncertainty or ambiguous situations as threatening. This orientation, predominant in countries such as Japan, Portugal, and Greece, leads people to develop written rules and regulations and hold rituals and ceremonies that add structure to life. In contrast, countries such as the United States, Denmark, and Ireland, have a low need for uncertainty avoidance and thus a low tolerance for structure. These countries instead value initiative and risk more highly.

### Masculinity and Femininity

By "masculinity and femininity," Hofstede refers to the extent to which a country values male-oriented or female-oriented traits. Among the countries that value such masculine traits as ambition, achievement, and the acquisition of money are Ireland, Japan, and Mexico, where men are taught to be assertive, ambitious, and domineering. In contrast, femininity-valuing cultures such as Sweden and the Netherlands stress caring, nurturing, and sexual equality.[21]

## Power Distance

Different cultures endow the parties to a relationship with different levels of social power or status. In some cultures, for example, wealth gives individuals more power, whereas in others age, education, occupation, and even family background are more important than wealth as sources of power. Whereas some cultures minimize social or class inequalities, others emphasize them, sometimes even asserting that each person has a protected place in the culture's social order and that individuals with high social status have the right to use their power as they see fit. Such variations are a measure of power distance, the extent to which the culture's members believe that institutional and organizational power should not be shared equally and that all decisions by power holders must be accepted.[22] At one end are cultures such as Israel and Denmark, which believe in minimizing social or class imbalances, challenging authority figures, and using power only for legitimate purposes. On the other end of the scale are Saudi Arabia and Syria, which prefer the maintenance of large power distances (see Table 10.3).

### TABLE 10.3  POWER DISTANCE AND BEHAVIOR

| BEHAVIORS CHARACTERISTIC OF LOW-POWER-DISTANCE CULTURES | BEHAVIORS CHARACTERISTIC OF HIGH-POWER-DISTANCE CULTURES |
|---|---|
| Minimizing class and social differences | Treating power as a fact of life |
| Challenging authority figures | Accepting inequalities in society |
| Using power for legitimate purposes only | Bypassing subordinates in decision making |

In some cultures, individuals are free to take power when they feel it is rightfully theirs rather than allowing others to have power over them. In other cultures, such verbal assertions of the right to power on the part of individuals are repressed. Members of cultures that have nonverbal rather than verbal traditions do not tell others that they seek power; rather, these individuals believe that they can intuit where power lies. Thus, for members of these cultures, power does not need to be claimed. If they have power, others will know. Unlike North American cultures, where power can be enhanced through communication, in Eastern cultures, members believe such communication is unnecessary and out of place.[23]

Our interpersonal relationships benefit when we understand how views of power differ across cultures. Developing a clearer vision of the kinds of power people in different cultures value and the extent to which the members of a culture will or will not engage in conflict with people in power enhances our ability to interpret another's responses to power.

## GENDER AND THE BALANCE OF POWER

Society's tendency to view women as less powerful than men influences our everyday relationships. In fact, some women and men maintain the traditional belief that men should be more powerful, earning more money and achieving more status than women.[24] When these expectations go unmet, however, their relationships may suffer. Prevailing economic realities place increased pressure on men as it becomes harder for them to be the sole or prime wage earners in their families.

Although women now contribute significantly to family income, which should increase their decisional power in the family, they still perceive themselves to have primary responsibility for seeing that domestic responsibilities are met. Inequitable workloads can lead to relationship resentment, dissatisfaction, and dissolution. In contrast, more equitable distribution of out-of-home and in-home work leads to more relationship satisfaction and stability.[25]

Women are expected to be work specialists, home specialists, health specialists, and life-cycle specialists, people adept at coping with crises during any life stage. Women are supposed to monitor relationships and make sure things get done when scheduled, yet accede to or comply with the preferences or beliefs of their partners whenever their opinions differ—effectively ceding power to a partner. Thus, while women may be gaining increased access to resources, some hesitate to use those resources independently in order to change the power dynamics.[26]

## TRY THIS

## Who Has the Power?

Interview a person from a culture other than your own. Ask your interviewee to answer the following questions about three relationships: one he or she shares with a parent, one with a coworker, and one with a significant other.

1. Who in each relationship tends to have the power?

2. What kind of power does that person use most?

3. What, if anything, does the less powerful member in the relationship do to balance the power?

To what extent, if any, does the research on how members of this culture handle power lead you to expect what your interviewee has reported?

Generally, men engage in more efforts to exert control and dominate in relationships than do women. Socialized to dominate rather than to reveal their vulnerabilities, some become trapped in their images of male power. For such men, manliness is equated with having power over others.

It could be that women and men conceive of power differently. Powerful women need not be thought of as men wearing dresses. Instead of practicing male patterns of behavior, many women seek alternative means of gaining, maintaining, and exerting their power. Thus, in general, American women do not epitomize attributes such as control and domination—so prominent in the traditional power displays of men—but instead practice power based on a model of personal authority, empowerment, or reciprocal empowerment.[27]

**Sexual harassment**, defined as "unwelcome sexual behavior that takes place in person or electronically," represents an abuse of power affecting men and women.[28] Being subjected to inappropriate sexual comments or jokes, inappropriate touching, sexual intimidation; receiving unwelcome sexualized photos through texts or e-mail; and having sexual rumors or pictures spread are included among examples of sexual harassment. In a national survey of middle and high school students conducted during the 2010–2011 school year, girls reported being harassed more than boys—56 percent compared with 40 percent, with boys more frequently identified as the harassers. Of the students surveyed, 44 percent reported being harassed in person, while 30 percent reported online incidents of harassment.[29]

Sexual harassment also affects men and women at work, with male–female, male–male, and female–female harassment reported. Although more formal processes

Sexual harassment is an abuse of power that occurs too frequently in the workplace.

exist for reporting sexual harassment today than in the past, and many employers have instituted anti-harassment policies and workshops, each year thousands of incidents of sexual harassment are still reported to local, state, and federal agencies. That so much sexualized aggression still occurs is evidence of inequitable power and continued gender discrimination in the workplace.[30]

# REFLECT ON THIS

## *Power Issues by Gender*

Researchers report that working women with children have larger workloads than the respective dads, logging 5 more hours of in-home work each week. About a decade ago, researchers had reported that in families where both partners worked full-time, the women averaged more than 26 hours a week in household labor, while the men averaged 10. Thus, while not yet equal, the workloads of men and women appear to be on a trend toward equalizing. In fact, a recent study conducted for the Families and Work Institute confirmed that men now experience even

*(Continued)*

(Continued)

more work–family conflicts than women. Despite these improvements, however, many women remain dissatisfied, pointing out that whatever leisure time they have is often interrupted, while men appear better at protecting their leisure time.

With this information as background, consider how work is distributed among the members of your family. Next, think about how the work each family member is expected to perform affects the dynamics of power in your family. To do this, first answer the following questions. Then ask a peer in your major field the same questions and compare and contrast the responses you receive with your own.

1. How many hours per week does each family member work?

2. How many hours per week does each family member spend performing household chores?

3. Which members of the household have the power to decide who engages in what activities, how money is spent, how leisure time is spent, and so forth?

4. Which family member's leisure time is subject to more interruptions?

5. To what extent, if any, do you perceive in the family a relationship between the exercise of power and gender?

Sources: See the December 2009 issue of *Social Forces* and results of the 2010 American Time Use Survey from the U.S. Bureau of Labor Statistics, http://www.bls.gov/news.release/archives/atus_06222011.pdf.

See Daphne Spain, *Gendered Spaces.* Chapel Hill: University of North Carolina Press, 1992.

Ruth Davis Konigsberg, "Chore Wars," *Time,* July 21, 2011, pp. 45–49.

Kerstin Aumann, Ellen Galinsky, and Kenneth Matos, *The New Male Mystique,* Families and Work Institute, Corporate Leadership Circle Conference Call, September 8, 2011, http://www.familiesandwork.org/site/support/110908_clc_ppoint.pdf.

Konigsberg, "Chore Wars," p. 45.

## MEDIA, TECHNOLOGY, AND POWER SHIFTS

How complicit are the media and technology in shaping perceptions of relational power? The media present us with numerous models of people on the giving and receiving ends of power. Technology facilitates the spreading of influence. Both affect how we respond to and use power in personal encounters.

The power of female action heroes comes not from their sexualization or beauty but from their skill and expertise.

## Media Power

Because women are consistently underrepresented in the media,[31] we may be left with the impression that men are typically in charge, occupy more high-status positions, and set the cultural standards. Men, not women, are held up by the media as authorities. In newscasts, more men than women hold the position of anchor, reinforcing the impression that men are the voice of authority. This perception is reinforced by commercials, where male voice-overs predominate, supporting the impression that women depend on men for direction.[32] In contrast, when women are portrayed in power positions, they often are depicted as lonely or embittered. Thus, we are led to believe that men are entitled to exert power over others, while women are not.[33]

The power that is left to women appears to be sexual power. Women are generally encouraged to hone their powerlessness, while men are encouraged to develop their aggressiveness and strength. Exceptions may be found in recent years, however. For example, in popular films such as *The Hunger Games* and *Wonder Woman,* the audience is presented with heroic female leads whose power stems not from being sexualized or beautiful but rather from skill and athletic prowess—they are portrayed as capable, cunning, and compassionate.[34] And in *Black Panther*, it is Shuri, the sister of the Black Panther T'Challa, who endows him and their kingdom with the innovations they need to give them control, meet the needs of the underserved, and build the future they seek.[35] Such characters have proved very popular, especially among teens.

In depictions of power and powerlessness in the media, minorities generally fare even worse than women. Minority men still are cast in stereotypical roles, presented as lazy and unable to handle authority, and minority women are still depicted as misusing power in their efforts to dominate others or as sex objects. In addition, the media too often present distorted depictions of older people that reinforce notions that they are sickly and less powerful members of society.

Because of social media, however, traditional media power may be ebbing. By reducing the time that people spend with other media, some see computers decreasing the amount of power the traditional media are able to exert. Do you agree?

Cyberbullying extends the bully's reach, magnifying the harm to a victim.

## Technological Power

Is technology capable of getting us to do things we never imagined we would do? Is it capable of socially manipulating us?[36] And when it comes to power, is the Internet a power equalizer or distorter? What do you think?

**Social Control.** Facebook and other social media want to keep our eyes on their sites. To keep us engaged, they populate our feeds with information they believe we want to see. Since most people prefer to see content that reinforces their current thinking, Facebook walls and Instagram feeds become echo chambers, protecting us from views that differ from our own and distorting our reality without our even being aware of it.[37] Others pay to modify our behavior to their advantage. "Fake news" and paid "likes" feed our illusions. Fake accounts, known as bots, sway us, reshaping the beliefs we hold. Twitter followers and retweets are bought by celebrities, businesses, and anyone else who wants to appear to be more popular than they actually are or who desires to exert outsize online influence.[38] Social media train us to respond—manipulating us with promises of rewards—which also can end up as our punishments. Social media fraud is big business.

**Power Equalizer.** From one vantage point, the Internet is perceived more as a power equalizer than traditional media in that it can be color- and gender-blind. As a result, women, minorities, and older people are apt to find themselves with wider audiences and receiving more respect online than off. In this way, the Internet is seen as empowering, giving its users a sense of their interpersonal power as it enables them to share ideas and concerns and otherwise feel more in control and less isolated and lonely.

**Power Distorter.** Unfortunately, from another vantage point, the Internet is perceived more as distorting power relationships. On Instagram, for example, users are free to feature the most positive aspects of their personalities and lives. This contributes to others viewing them more favorably—thereby increasing their power and influence.[39] By taking time away from face-to-face interaction, however, is technology helping to insulate you from more intimate settings?

Technology has the potential to create magic as well as magnify danger. When it comes to computer and video games, for example, often players must take part in virtual violence to prevail. Sadly, too often, this reinforces cultural views of men as powerful aggressors, females as sexual objects, and violence as a turn-on.[40]

Perhaps one of the most serious dangers of technology's ability to create an imbalance of power is the penchant of some users to engage in cyberbullying. Promoting their own power at others' expense, bullies equate power with force. Among some of the reasons people report being bullied are their looks, sexual orientation, race/ethnicity, religious beliefs, and lack of money.[41] Bullying is by no means new, but the advent of the Internet has extended the bully's reach. Since bullying no longer is confined to the schoolyard or halls, safe havens for the bullied no longer exist. Bullying follows the bullied wherever they go. Intimidating messages such as "Why don't you kill yourself like everyone hopes?" are instantly accessible to millions and thereby magnify the bully's potential to harm his or her victim(s). Cyberbullying is a prime example of the misuse of power. A number of teenagers have committed suicide allegedly because of being subjected to relentless malicious taunting and other actions by cyberbullies.[42] Cyberbullies experience extreme online disinhibition effects, since they are not face-to-face with their targets, leading to their feeling even freer to disparage, slander, or threaten their victims. Online bullies doctor photographs, post embarrassing videos, and use texts, webcams, and cell phone cameras to put technology to malicious use. What actions do you think should be taken to address the dangers of cyberbullying and empower the victims of cyberbullies?

# GAINING COMMUNICATION COMPETENCE: SKILLS FOR BALANCING POWER IN RELATIONSHIPS

You can increase your interpersonal communication competence by following these guidelines concerning power.

## USE POWER WISELY

You have the option to use different kinds of power in your relationships. How you choose to use your power says a lot about you. What kinds of power bind others to you, willingly and unwillingly? What kinds of power enable you to make the most of relational opportunities? What kinds limit or debilitate you? Having a range of effective power and influence strategies can make it easier for you to satisfy your relational needs.

## UNDERSTAND HOW BELIEFS, VALUES, AND ATTITUDES AFFECT RELATIONAL COMFORT

Your interactions with others are facilitated when you understand your own attitudes, beliefs, and values as well as theirs. How do you respond when your significant beliefs are challenged? Some beliefs are more meaningful to you than to others, and the more central a belief is, the harder each of you works to defend it, the less willing you are to change it, and the more resistant you become to compliance-gaining efforts.

## CAPITALIZE ON THE NEED FOR BALANCE

Recognize the extent to which your drive for consistency influences the nature and tone of your interpersonal relationships. When we want to convince another to think and feel as we do, we can create or point out an imbalance in his or her life, and then demonstrate how thinking or feeling as we do will help restore a sense of internal consistency.

## The Case of the Power Moment

Tilda was given the task of assessing the productivity and performance of employees in various divisions of the company where she works. Included among those she would have to report on was her live-in boyfriend, Larry, who was a division head. Tilda's boss told her to deliver copies of a preliminary report to all division heads once the report was complete, prior to its being disseminated to a wider company audience.

After reading Tilda's preliminary report, which was somewhat critical of a number of people in his division, Larry hit the roof. If his people were targets of criticism, the clear implication was that he was not doing his job. When Larry told Tilda his reaction and concerns, she became defensive and insisted that the information in her report was accurate. Larry cautioned Tilda that if she didn't alter her report, he would end their relationship. It was that important to him.

Larry didn't want his anger to become evident to others at work, so he interacted with Tilda at work with the same level of professionalism he had always exhibited. Their private communication was another matter, however. All week, when they were at home together, Larry pressured Tilda to revise the report, pointing out time and again the errors he believed she was making and reminding her of the consequences she would face if she failed to comply.

Tilda was in emotional turmoil. What could she do in the face of Larry's power play?

### Consider the following questions:

1. If you were Tilda, how would you respond to Larry's ultimatum?

2. What kind(s) of power had Larry attempted to use?

3. What steps might Tilda and Larry take to resolve their impasse?

# REVIEW THIS

1. **Define power, comparing and contrasting the following types of power: reward, coercive, expert, legitimate, referent, and persuasive.** ☐

Power is the ability to influence and control others. It is dependent on the resources one is able to control.

When a person has reward power, he or she controls something another person values. With coercive power, one person can deliver negative consequences to another. A person with expert power possesses special knowledge or skill that another thinks he or she needs. With legitimate power, one party's position lets him or her control another. A person has referent power when another person respects and admires him or her. A person with persuasive power is skilled at using logic, well-conceived arguments, and emotional appeals to persuade others to believe or behave as he or she desires.

2. **Define and distinguish among attitudes, beliefs, and values as persuasive forces, discussing strategies to help elicit compliance and restore relational balance.** ☐

An attitude is a mental set or readiness to respond in a predetermined way to a particular stimulus. Beliefs are the building blocks of attitudes. They are one's assessment of what is true or false, probable or improbable. Values represent our ideas of what is important in life.

Together, these affect the nature and tone of relationships. Communicated through behavior, they influence whose company we seek, with whom we are most comfortable, and what we need to do to maintain a state of internal consistency or balance.

Balance theory is a model of attitude change that recognizes our desire to live in a state of equilibrium. Cognitive dissonance is an aversive drive that propels us toward consistency. Interpersonal persuasion occurs first by creating imbalance and then finding a solution that restores balance.

3. **Discuss how culture, gender, and media and technology influence the exercise of and responses to power.** ☐

Culture influences and modifies four value dimensions: individualism and collectivism, uncertainty avoidance, masculinity and femininity, and power distance.

Gender expectations reinforce the belief that men should be powerful. In general, men engage in more efforts to exert control, while women practice reciprocal empowerment. Abuses of power, including sexual harassment, affect men and women in school and in the workplace.

The media present men more often than women in positions of power. The Internet affords power to those with access. For some, technology is interpersonally empowering, and it also decreases the amount of power other media exert. For others, technology exacerbates the creation of imbalances of power, contributing to cyberbullying.

**4. Identify guidelines for balancing relational power.** ☐

By using power wisely, understanding how beliefs, values, and attitudes influence relational comfort, and capitalizing on the need for balance, you can increase your ability to develop more healthful relationships.

## CHECK YOUR UNDERSTANDING

1. Can you provide examples of appropriate and inappropriate uses of different kinds of power? What kind(s) of power do you think you wield? (See pages 266–270.)

2. Can you explain how the attitudes, beliefs, and values of two people could influence the course of their relationship? (See pages 270–275.)

3. Can you explain the relationship between power and compliance? (See pages 275–279.)

4. Can you offer scenarios to illustrate the roles that balance theory and cognitive dissonance play in interpersonal persuasion? (See pages 279–281.)

5. Can you identify ways in which culture, gender, the media, and technology influence perceptions of power in the United States? In what ways are the messages sent positive? In what ways are they negative? (See pages 283–288.)

## KEY TERMS

Attitude  276

Balance theory  279

Beliefs  277

Coercive power  274

Cognitive dissonance  281

Expert power  274

Legitimate power  274

Minimal justification for action  281

Need for reassurance  281

Persuasive power  275

Power  270

Referent power  275

Reward power  273

Sexual harassment  285

Trigger cues  281

Values  278

Get the tools you need to sharpen your study skills. **SAGE edge** offers a robust online environment featuring an impressive array of free tools and resources. Access practice quizzes, eFlashcards, video, and multimedia at **edge.sagepub.com/gambleicp**.

**11**

# Conflict in Relationships

## Learning Objectives

### AFTER COMPLETING THIS CHAPTER, YOU SHOULD BE ABLE TO

1. Define conflict, discuss its nature, and explain the difference between functional and dysfunctional conflict

2. Identify conflict sources and classifications

3. Distinguish between conflict management styles

4. Discuss productive ways to communicate during conflict

5. Distinguish between the following conflict expression styles: assertive, nonassertive, and aggressive

6. Explain culture's influence on conflict

7. Discuss how gender influences the handling of conflict

8. Describe the ways media portrayals and technology affect perceptions of conflict

9. Demonstrate how to resolve conflict effectively

Conflict is drama, and how people deal with conflict shows you the kind of people they are.

—Stephen Moyer

· · · · · · · · · · · · · · · · · · · · · · · · · · · · · · · · · · · · · · · · · · · · · · · · · · · · · · · · · · · · ·

Once upon a time, you were in a conflict with a friend/significant other/family member/ co-worker (select one). As a result of the conflict, your relationship with that person became stronger/weaker/more of the same (select one).

Conflict happens when one person interferes with or frustrates the desires of another person to obtain a goal. Most of our interpersonal conflicts involve people with whom we're close or with whom we work. Many revolve around money, sex, chores or responsibilities, trust issues, and erroneous assumptions about the other.[1] Sometimes conflict ensues simply because we think a partner should realize, without our telling them, why we're upset. Sometimes we expect those who know us to be able to read our minds and respond as we'd like them to. This rarely is the case.[2]

We witness conflicts playing out on the world stage. We also experience conflicts vicariously via media offerings. Conflicts highlighted in reality television programs such as *Big Brother* and *Survivor*, although they may seem contrived, do make for compelling and interesting story lines. Sometimes, participants are seen losing control, unable or unwilling to resolve their conflict. And now and again, we find the parties engaged in creative negotiations in the effort to resolve the conflict. Despite all the dramatic contrivances, we can learn much about the handling of conflict by observing the players in action and thinking through how we would respond to each of the conflict-producing situations were we in their shoes.[3]

While conflict has a dark side that too often surfaces as bullying, interpersonal violence, or outright war, the interpersonal conflicts we experience need not become dysfunctional. An inevitable part of life, interpersonal conflicts touch us all sooner or later. Every one of our relationships of any significance involves conflict from time to time. When a relationship is conflict-free, it probably is not genuine.[4] ■

# WHAT DO YOU KNOW?

Before continuing your reading of this chapter, which of the following five statements do you believe to be true, and which do you believe to be false?

| | | | |
|---|---|---|---|
| 1. | A conflict-free relationship is not healthy. | T | F |
| 2. | Some interpersonal conflicts take on a life of their own, with participants unable to control them. | T | F |
| 3. | Some interpersonal arguments are less destructive than others, but all of them have negative consequences. | T | F |
| 4. | Most people have a stylized way of dealing with conflict that is unique to their own context and culture. | T | F |
| 5. | Movies and video games have a powerful influence on how we learn to deal with conflict. | T | F |

Read the chapter to discover if you're right or if you've made any erroneous assumptions.

ANSWERS: 1. T; 2. F; 3. F; 4. T; 5. T

# THE MEANING OF CONFLICT

Conflict can be a positive or negative experience. Given that conflict is a common occurrence, it makes sense to learn how to handle it constructively, so that its presence improves our relationships. In this chapter, we explore the nature of interpersonal conflict, how it arises, how it affects us, and what we can do to manage it more effectively.

## CONFLICT DEFINED

Interpersonal conflict is a struggle between interdependent parties that occurs whenever one person's thoughts or actions are perceived to limit or interfere with those of the other person.[5] For example, when you and a friend want to play the same position on a team, or apply for the same job, or ask the same person to be your date to a wedding, your attempt to maximize your personal satisfaction or meet your personal needs can interfere with your friend's ability to do the same. When both parties to the conflict are aware of a disagreement and perceive their goals to be incompatible, each will do their best to prevail. It even doesn't matter if their goals are in fact compatible. What matters is that one or both believe the goals to be mutually exclusive and are operating as if there is not enough of something to satisfy both of them.[6]

Conflict develops for a variety of reasons. It's how you handle it that matters.

## CONFLICT IS BASED ON INTERACTION

How much disagreement are you able to put up with before perceiving conflict in your relationship? Your answer represents your tolerance for disagreement.[7] Some of us are able to tolerate less disagreement, and so perceive a conflict's presence sooner than others.

Conflict is created and maintained through behavior, and it tests every relationship. How do you react upon discovering you are in conflict? Do you take it personally, interpreting it as a personal attack? If you do, do you characteristically respond with avoidant or aggressive behavior? Are you likely to strike out at the other person, compete with them, suppress your feelings, negotiate the situation, or deal with the conflict directly? Do your actions demonstrate your inflexibility, functioning to escalate the conflict you're in, or do you use constructive patterns enabling you to manage a conflict more effectively? How conflict is handled determines if your welfare and relationship satisfaction are secure once a conflict is behind you.[8]

## COMPLEMENTARY, SYMMETRICAL, AND PARALLEL APPROACHES

Your approach to conflict is based on how you and another person characteristically interact with each other. If your relationship is long term, you likely have developed a relational conflict style—the pattern of disagreement management you typically enact. In relationships based on a complementary conflict style, partners display opposite behaviors that are mutually reinforcing. For example, one partner complains and the other withdraws. In contrast, in relationships featuring a symmetrical conflict style, both partners believe themselves equals, mirroring each other's behavior, but as the conflict continues, one partner comes to perceive himself or herself as "more equal" or more deserving of winning than the other, and the conflict escalates out of control. In effect, both partners complain, each competing to complain more. Finally, in relationships with a parallel conflict style, partners shift approaches based on the situation.

## FEELINGS ABOUT CONFLICT

Where have your feelings about conflict come from? Dictionaries tell us that conflict is disagreement or war, suggesting that it is a negative force that leads to undesirable consequences. Some of us believe that conflict is one of the prime causes of divorce or relational violence, and that disagreeing or fighting with another either will dissolve whatever relationship exists or prevent one from forming. Others of us have been taught that nice people don't fight or make waves. And still others fear that if we don't smile and act cheerfully, others won't like us. The more awful we think conflict is, the more we typically try to avoid it.

It is not conflict that creates problems, however, but the way we approach it.[9] In and of itself, conflict is neither a positive nor a negative force. How we perceive it and handle it—whether the conflict is functional or dysfunctional—determines the health of our interpersonal relationships and our satisfaction with them.[10]

## Functional Conflict

Conflict can have real benefits. When we handle conflict well, it helps us develop insights into our relationships and more effective means of relating to one another. **Functional conflicts** build in us a clearer understanding of each other's needs, attitudes, or beliefs, strengthening our relationships.

According to conflict experts, when handled well, conflict performs these valuable functions:

- Conflict helps us learn better ways of handling future disagreements and thereby reduces the probability of more serious conflicts.

- Conflict fosters innovation by helping us acquire new ways of thinking and behaving.

- Conflict develops in us a renewed sense of cohesiveness by increasing our understanding of one another as well as our perceptions of closeness and trust.

- Conflict provides opportunities to assess the viability of our relationships.

- Conflict, once resolved, helps to strengthen our relationships.[11]

When approaching conflict with a functional orientation, we are willing to listen to opposing viewpoints, open to changing troublesome behaviors, and accepting of others' differences. Because they are constructive, functional conflicts don't damage relationships.

## Dysfunctional Conflict

When conflicts are poorly handled, they may escalate and become dysfunctional, precipitating destructive outcomes. A **dysfunctional conflict** can create serious problems for a relationship, often resulting in personal pain, emotional strain, and lasting resentments. Individuals engaged in dysfunctional conflict characteristically rely on threats, deception, force, and violence to achieve their goals, which typically include the desire to defeat or hurt the other person. The parties to a dysfunctional conflict tend to demonstrate rigid inflexibility. They attempt to serve their own interests by undercutting the other person and making them look bad. As a result, dysfunctional conflict tends to grow worse, become destructive, harm both mental and physical health, and ultimately damage or destroy their relationships.[12]

**Crazymaking behavior**, a conflict-producing technique that figuratively can drive a partner crazy, is often at the root of dysfunctional conflict. For example, imagine the outcome of the following conversation between a husband and wife after the husband has been waiting at a taxi stand for his wife, who arrives late:

**He:** Why were you late?

**She:** I tried my best.

**He:** Yeah? You and who else? Your mother is never on time either.

**She:** That's got nothing to do with it.

**He:** The hell it doesn't. You're just as sloppy as she is.

**She:** You don't say! Who picks your dirty underwear off the floor every morning?

**He:** I happen to go to work. What do you do all day?

**She:** I'm trying to get along on the money you don't make, that's what I do all day.

**He:** Why should I knock myself out for a lazy ingrate like you?

This exchange illustrates the crazymaking technique of *gunnysacking*, in which the user saves all of their complaints, as though stuffing them in a gunnysack, and then makes a mess of things by emptying the sack during a heated moment, allowing the stockpiled complaints to cascade out. When we drag irrelevant past issues—such as the mother-in-law mentioned in the preceding dialogue—into a conflict, we end up venting pent-up aggressions and exchanging insults.

Crazymakers typically display passive-aggressive behavior, catching a person off guard, confusing him or her, and arousing anger. Instead of addressing a relational complaint constructively, crazymakers resort to insidious approaches. Other kinds of crazymaking behavior are guiltmaking, beltlining, avoiding, and withholding. *Guiltmaking* occurs when one party makes the other responsible for causing pain: "It's okay; don't worry about me. Your feelings are more important," whines the guiltmaker. *Beltlining* involves the voicing of comments that "hit below the belt," such as bringing up a person's unattractive physical attributes or perceived lack of intelligence. *Avoiding* occurs when a party to a conflict refuses to face an issue, leaving the other person frustrated. *Withholding* involves the denial of affection, humor, a material possession, or some other desirable thing or behavior because of the conflict. Any one of these inappropriate responses to conflict can contribute to the buildup of relationship resentments.[13]

Among other dysfunctional conflict producing behaviors apt to precipitate relational conflict are preemptive striking, forcing, and blaming. *Preemptive striking* occurs when one partner attacks the other, verbally or physically, without warning. Because he or she is unprepared to handle the conflict, the conflict is likely either to escalate or to be postponed by the attackee's immediate departure. *Forcing* is in play when one partner imposes his or her position on the other. We do not like to feel compelled to do something, nor do we enjoy feeling that we cannot extricate ourselves from a situation. When this occurs, a relationship may suffer serious damage. *Blaming* presents itself when one party blames the other for some wrong suffered. Blame does nothing to resolve a relationship problem, but it does expose the raw feelings that one party is experiencing. Blame relies on the delivery of messages that attack rather than messages that attempt to resolve disagreements.

In lieu of enacting any of these dysfunctional behaviors, when a conflict arises, follow these five guidelines:

1. Be specific when you introduce a complaint.
2. Ask for change that will make the situation better.

3. Be tolerant of your partner.

4. Attack the issue, not the other person.

5. Think about what you have to say before you say it.[14]

## TRY THIS

# Thinking Through Conflict

Review several situations in which you and another person were in conflict and examine the feelings you had at those times. Then use the following scales to measure those feelings. For example, for the first item, "good" versus "bad," if you feel that the conflict was completely good, circle 1. If you feel that the conflict was completely bad, circle 5. If you feel neutral about the conflict, circle 3.

### Conflict

| Good | 1 | 2 | 3 | 4 | 5 | Bad |
|------|---|---|---|---|---|-----|
| Rewarding | 1 | 2 | 3 | 4 | 5 | Threatening |
| Normal | 1 | 2 | 3 | 4 | 5 | Abnormal |
| Constructive | 1 | 2 | 3 | 4 | 5 | Destructive |
| Necessary | 1 | 2 | 3 | 4 | 5 | Unnecessary |
| Challenging | 1 | 2 | 3 | 4 | 5 | Overwhelming |
| Desirable | 1 | 2 | 3 | 4 | 5 | Undesirable |
| Inevitable | 1 | 2 | 3 | 4 | 5 | Avoidable |
| Healthy | 1 | 2 | 3 | 4 | 5 | Unhealthy |
| Clean | 1 | 2 | 3 | 4 | 5 | Dirty |

Compute your score by adding up the numbers you have circled.

*Total Score* _____

If your score is:

10–14   You think conflict is definitely a positive experience.

15–20   You think conflict can be helpful.

21–30   You have very ambivalent feelings toward conflict.

31–40   You think conflict is something to avoid.

41–50   You think conflict is definitely a negative experience.

If possible, collect the scores of all the students in your class and compute the averages for men and women. How does your score compare to the average score for your gender? What conclusions, if any, can you draw from this?

# SOURCES AND CLASSIFICATIONS OF CONFLICT

Anyone can start a conflict. Conflict also can occur in any setting. Forces within us that oppose each other can build to create a conflict, or we may find ourselves experiencing tension as outside forces combine to create conflict. An **intrapersonal conflict** originates within a single person. For example, a person who is going to school full-time while raising children may feel conflicted about whether to spend time studying or watching his or her child's Little League game.

Interpersonal conflict can result from real or imagined differences.

Interpersonal conflict involves a communication situation in which the people involved are interdependent—that is, the actions or beliefs of one person are likely to have some impact on the other person.[15] Conflict is apt to occur in the following situations:

- When we perceive *individual difference* in beliefs, opinions, perceptions, values, needs, assumptions, interests, or goals. For example, you believe that taking personal risks and relocating to accept a new job is necessary for you to grow and develop in your career, whereas your partner believes that stability and roots are more important. The difference in the way you and your partner think is apt to produce conflict.

- When we observe a *scarcity of certain resources* such as time, money, power, popularity, space, or position. For example, you may feel that sharing a bank account with your partner is keeping you from realizing your personal goals. If you had your own bank account, you tell yourself, you would be better able to fulfill your personal needs. Thus, the shared bank account becomes a source of relational conflict.

- When we *engage in a rivalry* or compete with someone else. For example, if you and a friend are applying for the same job, conflict may arise between you.

- When we *disagree over how to define a relationship*. For instance, you may want to stay just friends, but he or she wants more, which can trigger conflict between you.

- When we *misinterpret another's intent*. When you misunderstand another person's intentions, your assumptions can lead to conflict. For instance, if a friend does not call because she is planning to surprise you, but you conclude that she is avoiding you, your misinterpretation may result in conflict.

A conflict can result from real differences or from misunderstandings, anger, or expecting too much or too little from another person.

# How Verbally Aggressive Are You?

Complete the Inventory of Verbal Aggressiveness using the following scale:

**1** = almost never true

**2** = rarely true

**3** = occasionally true

**4** = often true

**5** = almost always true

_____ **1.** I try not to attack someone's intelligence when I attack his or her ideas.

_____ **2.** In order to counter a person's stubbornness, I use insults.

_____ **3.** I try to preserve another's self-concept as I try to influence him or her.

_____ **4.** When someone has no reason that I can see for refusing to complete a task that I think is important, I tell him or her how unreasonable she or he is.

_____ **5.** When others do things I perceive as stupid, I'm gentle in telling them what I think.

_____ **6.** I attack the characters of others when I think they deserve it.

_____ **7.** When I don't like how someone is behaving, I insult him or her to wake him or her up.

_____ **8.** Even when I think another's ideas are stupid, I'll try to make him or her feel good about himself or herself.

_____ **9.** When people are fixed in their ways of thinking or acting, I lose my temper and say things to them I shouldn't say.

_____ **10.** I take criticism well and do not retaliate by criticizing another.

_____ **11.** I enjoy telling others off after they insult me.

_____ **12.** When I do not like someone, I try not to show it.

_____ **13.** To stimulate their intelligence, I enjoy belittling people who do what I consider to be stupid things.

_____ **14.** I try not to harm another person's self-concept even when I attack his or her ideas.

_____ **15.** I go out of my way not to offend those I try to influence.

_____ 16. When others are cruel or mean, I attack their characters in an effort to correct their behavior.

_____ 17. I won't engage in an argument that involves personal attacks.

_____ 18. Yelling and screaming work to involve others I am trying to influence when all else fails.

_____ 19. When I am unsuccessful refuting another's position, I'll make him or her feel defensive to try to weaken his or her resolve.

_____ 20. When an argument becomes a personal attack, I try to change the subject.

Follow these steps to compute your verbal aggressiveness score:

1. Add the scores on items 2, 4, 6, 7, 9, 11, 13, 16, 18, 19.

2. Add the scores on items 1, 3, 5, 8, 10, 12, 14, 15, 17, 20.

3. Subtract the Step 2 score from 60.

4. Add the score from Step 1 to the score you computed in Step 3.

If you scored between 59 and 100, you are highly verbally aggressive.

If you scored between 39 and 58, you are somewhat verbally aggressive.

If you scored between 20 and 38, you are rarely verbally aggressive.

Does your score surprise you? Do you think it would surprise those you interact with frequently? Ask them. Do their responses confirm or contradict your beliefs? If you scored high in verbal aggressiveness, what might you change about the way you share your ideas with others to avoid becoming verbally combative?

Source: Inventory of Verbal Aggressiveness adapted from Dominic A. Infante and Charles J. Wigley III, "Verbal Aggressiveness: An Interpersonal Model and Measure," *Communication Monographs,* Volume 53, March 1986, p. 64. Reprinted by permission of Taylor & Francis Ltd., http://www.tandf.co.uk/journals/titles/03637751.html, and Professor Dominic A. Infante.

# CLASSIFYING CONFLICTS

Classifying a conflict lets us better understand the conflict's cause. Once we understand the cause, we can address the conflict more effectively. We can classify an interpersonal conflict in several different ways: by the nature of the goal of the parties, by the conflict's level of intensity, and by the general character of the conflict. We explore each in turn below.

## The Nature of the Goal

We can categorize conflict based on whether the parties involved seek a **shareable** or **nonshareable goal**. A goal is shareable if each participant to the conflict possesses some of it. It is nonshareable if it must be fully claimed and possessed by only one party. Two people competing for the highest score on a test are competing for a shareable goal because they conceivable could earn the same grade. Two people competing for the same job are competing for a nonshareable goal.

## The Intensity of the Conflict

The level of intensity we bring to a conflict depends on how strongly we feel about winning. Those engaged in a **low-intensity conflict** usually don't seek to undermine one another. Instead, they devise a strategy to help control their communications that permits the discovery of a mutually beneficial solution. A disagreement about where to eat dinner may constitute a low-intensity conflict. In a **medium-intensity conflict**, although each person wants to win, winning itself is believed sufficient. Those involved don't seek to hurt each other in the process. Competing with a friend to be captain of a sports team may create a medium-intensity conflict. In contrast, in a **high-intensity conflict,** one party to the conflict aims to do serious damage to the other. Winning is no longer enough. Victory must be total. Two people engaged in a highly contested divorce may find themselves in a high-intensity conflict.

## The Character of the Conflict

In addition to the intensity level, it is important to consider the character of the conflict—the basic disagreement at the root of the problem. When we categorize a conflict by its character, we identify it as a pseudoconflict, a content conflict, a value conflict, or an ego conflict.

A **pseudoconflict** has the appearance of a conflict but is not one. It occurs when one person mistakenly believes that the parties to the conflict cannot simultaneously achieve their goals. Typically, pseudoconflicts revolve around erroneous either/or judgments (either you or I win) or around simple misunderstandings in which one or both parties fail to perceive that they actually agree. The parties to a pseudoconflict resolve it when they realize no conflict actually exists. For example, suppose Allie and Buffy are going to spend an evening watching DVDs. Allie wants to watch one DVD, and Buffy wants to watch another. If one of them is willing to delay watching the one she wants until a bit later, they can watch both. In this way, both parties' goals can be met.

A **content conflict** occurs when two parties disagree over matters of fact: the definition of a term, the solution to a problem, or accuracy of information. Once they accept that facts can be verified, inferences tested, definitions checked, and solutions evaluated against established criteria, they then are able to settle their conflict rationally. If you and a partner disagree about how much money is in your joint savings account, a trip to the bank can resolve your disagreement.

A **value conflict** occurs when the parties hold disparate views on an issue important to each. A person who values individual independence is apt to have different opinions of government aid programs than someone who believes that we are all ultimately accountable for the well-being of others. If both can agree that it is all right to disagree, they will be able to discuss the issue, share

How strongly we feel about winning affects the intensity of our conflict.

insights, understand each other's positions, and learn from each other, even though they might continue to disagree.

Of all the conflict categories, an **ego conflict** has the greatest potential to ruin a relationship. People involved in an ego conflict seek to win at all costs because they think that losing will damage their self-worth, their prestige, or others' perception of their competence. Because they believe that their credibility is on the line, it's no longer the issue itself that is important. Rational decision making suffers as both strive to win to protect their egos. For example, when each of two friends believes that he or she is the best person to run for class president, and neither will back down, they will likely engage in an ego conflict.

# CONFLICT MANAGEMENT STYLES

Let's look at a number of different paradigms to help us understand and represent the strategies we rely on as we work to resolve conflicts. Among the most widely used is Blake and Mouton's **conflict resolution grid**. Theorists Robert Blake and Jane Srygley Mouton originated the concept of preferred conflict resolution style.[16] By identifying five distinct types of conflict behavior and placing them on a grid, they were able to represent graphically the different ways people resolve conflicts. The grid depicts the extent to which individuals employ *assertive strategies* to satisfy their own concerns or *cooperative strategies* to satisfy the concerns of another as a means of resolving a conflict. You can use Blake and Mouton's approach to help you select the behavioral strategy most appropriate for resolving a specific conflict.

The grid, as shown in Figure 11.1, has two scales. The vertical scale, assertiveness, measures the extent to which a person acts to attain personal goals, and the horizontal scale, cooperativeness, represents the extent to which that person exhibits behavior intended to satisfy a concern for others. The interface between the two scales represents how strongly the individual feels about each component—that is, how the person's concern is apportioned or how he or she behaves. On the basis of this measure, Blake and Mouton identified five **conflict styles**: avoiding, competitive, compromising, accommodative, and collaborative.

## Avoiding

A person with an **avoiding style** (1,1 on the grid) is unassertive and uncooperative. The avoider's approach to conflict is to withdraw. The person may actually physically leave the scene of the conflict. The avoider aims to maintain the appearance of indifference. Avoiders view conflict as a useless, potentially punishing endeavor. By refusing to deal with the conflict, they relieve themselves of the psychological burdens it imposes. Avoiders also give up their personal goals and sometimes their relationships.

## Competitive

A person with a **competitive style** (1,9) is high in assertiveness and low in cooperation. Competitors strive to force their position on others. They seek to maximize the importance of their needs by minimizing the needs of others.[17] Competitors exhibit an overwhelming need to defeat those with whom they are in conflict. They fight to defend their positions, often confronting others, attacking their self-concepts, and compelling them to concur by physical force or psychological domination.

## FIGURE 11.1

Blake and Mouton's Conflict Resolution Grid

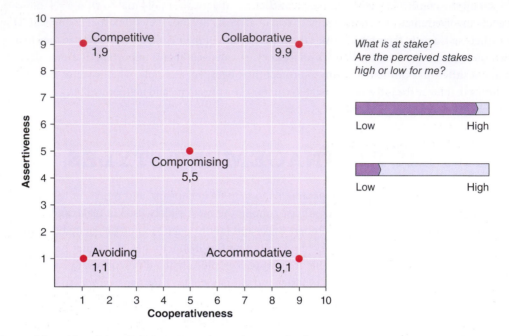

Source: Adapted from Robert R. Blake and Jane Srygley Mouton, "The Fifth Achievement," *Journal of Applied Behavioral Science,* Vol. 6, No. 4, 1970, p. 418. Copyright © 1970 by NTL Institute for Applied Behavioral Science.

They threaten, accuse, name-call, confront, deny responsibility for wrongdoing, and generally do everything they can to prove how right they are. Competitors do this despite the costs incurred, the harm inflicted, or the fact that others may find their means of handling the conflict destructive. Bullies, for example, exhibit such behaviors.

### Compromising

Someone who has a **compromising style** (5,5) is in the middle range in both assertiveness and cooperativeness. Compromisers aim to find the middle ground by working to permit each party to a conflict to gain something. While that may happen, each also gives up something to reach the agreement. This style leaves users only partially satisfied, and because of this it is sometimes referred to as the "lose–lose" approach. Part of a goal or a relationship is sacrificed to reach agreement—for the common good.

Compromisers typically appeal to fairness and negotiate trade-offs to find a reasonable, quick solution to the conflict they face. As such, compromising is only moderately effective, requires both parties to sacrifice, and precludes the search for more creative solutions.

### Accommodative

People with an **accommodative style** (9,1) are unassertive and cooperative. Because they are likely to overvalue the maintenance of relationships and undervalue the attainment of their own goals, accommodators' main concern is to smooth things over and ensure that others accept them, like them, and maintain a relationship with them. Accommodators tend to gloss over differences and downplay disagreements. Their actions can precipitate an uneasy, tense relational state characterized by a weak, self-sacrificing approach and nervous laughter. The style is perceived as generally ineffective, if only because its users usually fail to meet their personal goals, adding to the strains their relationships are under.

When in a conflict, how assertive and cooperative are you?

## Collaborative

A person with a **collaborative style** (9,9) is high in both assertiveness and cooperativeness. Collaborators exhibit a "win-win" orientation. They are problem solvers, actively seeking to satisfy their own goals as well as those of others. Users of this style seek to integrate the needs of both parties to the conflict so that each attains full satisfaction with the solution. Collaborators recognize that conflict is normal and can be helpful, believing that every person involved in a conflict holds an opinion that deserves to be aired and considered. They openly discuss differences without resorting to personal attacks. Collaborators tend to be highly competent communicators who preserve and promote opportunities for sharing and continued interaction.

Each of the five conflict styles has its place and can be useful given different relationships, circumstances, and contexts.[18] How you manage conflicts is affected by the importance of your personal goals versus the importance of your relationships. For example, avoidance may be the best approach when a conflict is minor. Likewise, accommodation may be an appropriate choice when the conflict's outcome is more important to the other person than to you. A competitive strategy may be appropriate when you do not need the continued goodwill and cooperation of the other person. By becoming more mindful of such possibilities, we can vary our responses according to what will work best in particular situations.

## TRY THIS

## Where Are You on the Grid?

Think about how you characteristically deal with conflict. Then respond to each of the statements on a scale of 1 to 7, where 1 indicates that you strongly disagree with the statement and 7 indicates that you strongly agree with it.

1. I discuss the problem to reach a mutual understanding. _____

2. I stick to my argument. _____

*(Continued)*

(Continued)

3. I give in to my partner to keep my relationship satisfying. _____

4. I sometimes sacrifice my own goals so my partner can meet his or hers. _____

5. I try to find a new solution that will satisfy all our needs. _____

6. I usually try to win arguments. _____

7. I do not like to talk about issues of disagreement. _____

8. I am willing to give up some of my goals in exchange for achieving other goals. _____

9. I try to get all my concerns and my partner's concerns out in the open. _____

10. I usually try to forget about issues of disagreement so I don't have to confront my partner. _____

11. I try to think of a compromise that satisfies both our needs. _____

12. I argue until my ideas are accepted. _____

13. It is important to get both our points of view out in the open. _____

14. I try to convince my partner that my position is right. _____

15. I try to meet my partner halfway. _____

16. If the issue is very important to my partner I usually give in. _____

17. I attempt to work with my partner to find a creative solution we both like. _____

18. I usually let my partner take responsibility for bringing up conflict issues. _____

19. I would rather not get into a discussion of unpleasant issues. _____

20. I avoid bringing up certain issues if my arguments might hurt my partner's feelings. _____

21. I might agree with some of my partner's points to make my partner happy. _____

22. I avoid talking with my partner about disagreements. _____

23. I try to find a "middle ground" position that is acceptable to both of us. _____

24. I try to influence my partner so he or she will see things my way. _____

25. I believe that you have to "give a little to get a little" during a disagreement. _____

In order to determine your preferred style of conflict, add your scores for the following items:

3, 4, 16, 20, 21   (accommodating)  _____

7, 10, 18, 19, 22   (avoiding)  _____

1, 5, 9, 13, 17   (collaborating)  _____

2, 6, 12, 14, 24   (competing)  _____

8, 11, 15, 23, 25   (compromising)  _____

Higher scores indicate that you tend toward that particular style.

As you consider the Blake and Mouton conflict grid and its five styles, keep your preferred style(s) in mind in an effort to determine if those you habitually use are effective in resolving relational conflict.

Source: This inventory, based on the work of Blake and Mouton, appears in "Put Yourself to the Test," in Laura K. Guerrero, Peter A. Andersen, and Walid A. Afifi, *Close Encounters: Communication in Relationships*, Thousand Oaks, CA: Sage, 2011, pp. 336–338.

# COMMUNICATING DURING CONFLICT

As we seek to resolve conflict, we need to avoid using relationship-destroying behaviors. By eliminating destructive communication behaviors from our repertoire and substituting constructive communication behaviors in their place, we become better able to manage interpersonal conflict.

## COMPETITIVE COMMUNICATION BEHAVIORS

When a conflict first develops, one of the variables affecting its outcome is whether participants intend to cooperate or compete with each other. If both bring a competitive orientation to the conflict, each will likely be ego involved and view winning the conflict as an affirmation of personal worth. When parties to a conflict are deceitful rather than open, when they fail to respect each other or view each other as equals, when they don't try to understand the conflict from the other's point of view, when they neglect to ask questions, or when they ignore or fail to clarify the assumptions under which they're operating, they also are likely to rely on strategies that suppress rather than encourage the free exchange of ideas. As a result, they will impede, not facilitate, the identification of a mutually satisfactory solution.

Parties to a conflict who lack openness are usually only concerned with their own feelings, believing it unnecessary for the other party to benefit from the outcome. They absolve themselves of any responsibility for creating the conflict and tend to use power techniques that further inhibit freedom of expression while trying to inflict psychological pain on the other person.

## COOPERATIVE COMMUNICATION BEHAVIORS

When parties to a conflict define it as mutually noncompetitive—a "win-win" opportunity—they express themselves openly and honestly, view each other as equals, and respect and work to understand each other's positions. In order for both parties to win, they must use effective listening

Expressing yourself openly and honestly can create a "win-win" opportunity. Is that happening here?

techniques (see Chapter 4) and perception validation techniques (see Chapter 3) to ensure understanding of the other's perspective. They must encourage a free exchange of ideas, engage in open discussion of alternatives, and integrate their needs in their effort to identify a mutually satisfactory solution.

As a result of using constructive conflict resolution behaviors, each party avoids behaving in a way that could escalate the situation by causing the other to become defensive or combative. Instead, each seeks to view the conflict through the other's eyes. Employing **role reversal** is one way to learn conflict resolution strategies. Through this technique, in which each person imagines himself or herself as the other, the parties come to understand each other, discover creative ways to integrate their interests and concerns, and work toward a common goal. Once statements such as "You're wrong" and "That's ridiculous" are replaced with statements such as "What you believe is not what I believe," individuals are on their way to developing a cooperative conflict resolution orientation based on effective communication.

## DESC SCRIPTS

A strategy that can help manage and resolve conflict is the **DESC script**, a means of expressing our feelings and understanding the feelings of another person.[19] DESC is an acronym for *describe*, *express*, *specify*, and *consequences*.

### Describe

You initiate a DESC script by *describing* to the other party, as specifically and objectively as possible, why a situation troubles you. While describing the situation, you also give yourself the opportunity to examine and define your personal needs and goals. Once you identify what you perceive as negative about the situation, you are in a better position to resolve it. It is important that your words describing the situation be simple, concrete, specific, and unbiased. For example, instead of yelling, "You're infatuated with Danielle; when she's around you wish I'd disappear," observe, "The last two times we've been with Danielle, you've ignored me."

How successful are you at expressing your feelings?

### Express

The second step in the DESC approach is to *express* how you feel about the situation. Here it is important to use personal statements that make it clear you are expressing what *you* feel and what *you* think. The key to making a personal statement is to use the pronouns *I*, *me*, or *my*; for example, use phrases such as "I feel," or "It appears to me." You can name a feeling: "I feel disappointed" or "I feel angry." You can use comparisons: "I feel invisible." Or you can indicate the type of action your feelings prompt you to display: "I feel like running away." By disclosing your feelings, you help the other become aware of your position without alienating him or her.

## Specify

Once you have described the problem and expressed your feelings, the next step is to *specify* how you would like to see the situation resolved. In effect, you request that the other person stop behaving one way and start behaving another. For instance, "When you know you will be late, please call to warn me."

## Consequences

All behavioral changes have *consequences* in the form of punishments or rewards. In the last phase of DESC, you spell out the consequences of the status quo, the change, or both. When possible, you should emphasize positive rather than negative outcomes. For example, it is probably more effective to say, "If you stop belittling me in front of Nick and Alisha, I'll feel better and we'll have more fun," than it would be to say, "If you continue to make fun of me, I'll have to start making fun of you."

The following example illustrates how a DESC script could help resolve the relationship difficulties between two friends:

**Describe:**   We hardly see or speak to each other anymore. It's been weeks since we've talked or gone out for a drink.

**Express:**   I feel bad about how our schedules are making it difficult for us to get together, especially since I value your friendship, and I want us to stay in touch.

**Specify:**   Can we get together for a latte and see how we can make more time for each other?

**Consequences:**   If we can find a way to schedule friendship breaks like others schedule coffee breaks, I think we'd feel better and not find ourselves so stressed.

# YOUR EXPRESSIVE STYLE

We have choices when facing conflict-producing situations: We can opt to respond nonassertively, aggressively, or assertively (see Figure 11.2). Our choice ultimately determines the conflict's resolution. Let's explore the characteristics of each approach.

### FIGURE 11.2
Expressive Style Scale

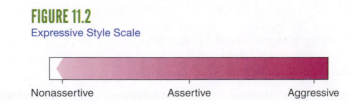

Nonassertive        Assertive        Aggressive

# A Self-Assessment

Respond to the statements below to assess the extent to which you characteristically respond assertively to interpersonal conflict. Use the following scale to evaluate the degree to which each statement typifies your behavior.

For each statement, assign a score of 5 to 1, according to the following criteria:

5  You almost always display the behavior.

4  You display the behavior about 75 percent of the time.

3  You have a 50–50 chance of displaying the behavior.

2  You sometimes, but not frequently, behave this way.

1  You almost never display the behavior.

*You and a friend disagree over who works harder to make your friendship work. You*

_____  try not to make your friend feel guilty.

_____  calmly let your friend know what upsets you about his or her behavior.

_____  avoid blaming your friend for any relationship problems.

_____  look directly at your friend when talking to him or her.

_____  make no assumptions about how your friend feels.

_____  question your friend in an effort to avoid misunderstanding him or her.

_____  avoid using sarcasm as a communication strategy.

_____  refrain from becoming anxious about discussing the problem.

_____  use appropriately forceful voice tone, body language, facial expressions, and gestures to support your feelings.

_____  avoid cursing and using obscenities to make your point.

_____  present your thought in an organized manner.

_____  consider the impact of your actions.

_____  *Total*

*You and a professor disagree about a grade. You*

_____  try not to make your professor feel guilty.

_____  calmly let your professor know what upsets you about his or her behavior.

_____ avoid blaming your professor for any relationship problems.

_____ look directly at your professor when talking to him or her.

_____ make no assumptions about how your professor feels.

_____ question your professor in an effort to avoid misunderstanding him or her.

_____ avoid using sarcasm as a communication strategy.

_____ refrain from becoming anxious about discussing the problem.

_____ use appropriately forceful voice tone, body language, facial expressions, and gestures to support your feelings.

_____ avoid cursing and using obscenities to make your point.

_____ present your thought in an organized manner.

_____ consider the impact of your actions.

_____ *Total*

To determine your total score, add the values in each of the sections above.

If you consistently score near 60 for each situation, you are likely comfortable handling conflict. If you consistently score near 12, you likely are not. Reexamine each set of responses. With which person were you most effective? Most ineffective? Why? Circle the items to which you responded with a 1, 2, or 3. These are the behaviors you may want to work on.

## NONASSERTIVENESS

When we are fearful or hesitate to express our feelings and thoughts, we exhibit a **nonassertive expression style** in which we do not try to satisfy our own concerns. By adopting such an avoidance-based strategy, we allow others to intimidate us and usually ensure that our own feelings will remain bottled up inside us and that our needs will go unmet. Out of fear, we fail to let another know of our displeasure, and we do not take whatever steps are needed to improve an unsatisfying relationship. We offer excuse after excuse, never quite finding the right time or the right words to express how we really feel, and we avoid confronting the individual or situation that is causing us discomfort. Using a nonassertive style can result in performing a favor when you cannot really spare the time or staying in a relationship you find demeaning. Why would you not assert yourself?

### Why We Don't Assert Ourselves

A number of factors account for nonassertiveness. Sometimes it is inertia—we are merely lazy. After all, it's easier to do nothing.

Hemera Technologies/AbleStock.com/Thinkstock

How would you describe the behavior pictured? Can you tell a story about it?

Assertion takes energy. At other times, it's merely that we don't care enough about the conflict to assert ourselves. At still other times, our *fear* compels us to adopt a nonassertive style. We may, for example, fear rejection or making someone unhappy with us. Shyness is also a factor. Shy people devote a lot of time to worrying about what others think of them.

## Nonassertive Language

Suppose someone who is shy (Person A) wants another person (B) to help plan a friend's party. Their conversation might proceed like this:

**A:**    Um, hey, this really isn't important, but you know Angela's birthday is coming up, and I was wondering if you would be willing to take a few minutes and help me plan a party for her.

**B:**    *(Head buried in a book)* Can't do it now. I'm busy.

**A:**    Oh, sure. Sorry.

We associate various nonverbal and verbal behaviors with shyness and nonassertiveness. Nonassertive nonverbal cues include downcast eyes or evasive eye contact, excessive head nodding, body gestures such as hand wringing, slouched posture, and a low, whining, hesitant, or giggly voice. Nonassertive verbal behaviors include fillers like "uh," "um," and "you know"; negators such as "This really isn't important, but"; qualifiers such as "just" and "I guess"; an overuse of apologetic words; and a disconnected speech pattern. Generally, nonassertive behaviors reduce the impact of what is said. That is one reason individuals fearing rejection resort to them—their aim is to appease others.

# AGGRESSIVENESS

In contrast to people who are nonassertive, people who exhibit an ==aggressive expression style== express their needs, wants, and ideas openly, even if doing so hurts another person. In the effort to stand up for themselves, those who are aggressive often ignore or violate the rights of others with whom they conflict. As a result, aggressive people get more of their needs met than do nonassertive people—but at someone else's expense. The aggressor's aim is to dominate and win; merely breaking even is not enough.

## Why We Act Aggressively

People act aggressively for a number of reasons. First, we may lash out simply because we feel vulnerable; we make an effort to protect ourselves from the perceived threat of powerlessness. Second, unresolved, emotionally volatile experiences can trigger an aggressive reaction, causing an overreaction when we face conflict. Third, we may believe that the only way to get our ideas and feelings across is through aggression. For some reason, we may convince ourselves that others will not listen to or react to our words if we are mild-mannered. And finally, we may not understand how to channel or handle aggressive impulses. Our aggressive style may be related to repeated past instances of nonassertive behavior. The hurt, disappointment, bewilderment, and sense of personal violation that accompany nonassertion may have reached a boiling point. No longer able to contain our feelings, we abruptly vent them. As a result, aggression may do damage to or even destroy a relationship.

## Aggressive Language

The message sent by the aggressive person is selfish: "This is what I want; what you want doesn't count and is of no consequence to me." Let's revisit the party-planning scenario above, but this time Person A exhibits an aggressive style. The conversation might go like this:

**A:** I'm fed up with you. I'm sick of listening to you tell me you don't have time to plan this party. You'd better make time for me now!

**B:** *(Head buried in a book)* Can't do it now. I'm busy.

**A:** You can do it now. You're just selfish. You don't have time for anyone but yourself.

**B:** Not so.

**A:** That's a lie. Who always does everything? I do. All you ever do is read or watch videos. You're just lazy! I'm sick and tired of talking to you.

Compared to the nonassertive person, who starts hesitantly, the aggressive person begins by attacking and uses nonverbal and verbal cues in support. Nonverbal cues include "stare-down" messages; a raised, harsh, strident voice; a cold, sarcastic, or demeaning tone; excessive finger pointing and fist pounding; and a willingness to invade another's personal space. Aggressors often interrupt or answer before another is finished speaking and use threats such as "You'd better" or "I'm warning you." They are also prone to making evaluative judgments and accusative statements such as "That's bad" and "Your approach is inferior," and degrading comments such as "You can't be serious" and "Shut up." In some exchanges, the conversation escalates out of control because the aggressor's target feels the need to retaliate. When his happens, they reach a stalemate, and no one wins.

# ASSERTIVENESS

While the nonassertive person wants to avoid conflict, even at the cost of sacrificing needs and wants, and the aggressive person wants to dominate, even if this domination causes another harm, the person exhibiting an **assertive expression style** wants to communicate honestly, clearly, and directly, and to stand up for what he or she believes without harming anyone—including himself or herself. Behaving in this way promotes a healthy interpersonal climate for the handling of conflict.

Acting assertively tends to be rewarding. When we accomplish our goals and act in our own best interest without harming or depreciating someone else, we feel good. The same holds true when we elicit a positive response from another and can openly express our feelings and thoughts.

## Learning Assertive Behavior

Learning assertive skills can help you refrain from sending nonassertive or aggressive messages when doing so would be inappropriate. By attending to feelings and using specific verbal and nonverbal skills, you can resolve interpersonal conflict. Nonassertive people create a power imbalance by giving everyone more rights than they give themselves, and aggressive people create an imbalance by giving themselves more rights than others. Assertive individuals try to balance social power and thereby equalize the nature of their relationships.

## Using Assertive Language

As with nonassertion and aggression, particular nonverbal and verbal cues characterize assertion. An important one is good eye contact. When we avoid eye contact we send the message that we are

When you assert yourself, you make more of your own decisions.

nervous, anxious, uncomfortable, or even incompetent. When we stare at another, our gaze suggests we hold the person in contempt. However, when we look at another with interest and focus on him or her during a conversation, we communicate our concern. Likewise, a strong, well-modulated steady voice signals we are in control and sincere. We saw in Chapter 8 that using "I" language helps others accept responsibility for their feelings. In similar fashion, the verbal characteristics of assertive individuals include an ability and willingness to send "I" messages and "we" messages. Those who are assertive let us know what they think and feel ("I want," "I don't like"). They are willing to cooperate for a relationship's betterment ("Let's," "We can"). When we communicate assertively, we also use empathetic statements of interest ("What do you think?" or "How do you see this?"). Absent from the assertive person's conversations are wishy-washy statements such as "I guess," fillers such as "um," and self-demeanors such as "I know this sounds dumb, but . . ." In addition, when we display an assertive style, we don't offer blame statements or send "you" messages. Instead, we express ourselves in personally fulfilling and interpersonally effective ways.

Let's consider the party-planning scenario one more time, with Person A exhibiting an assertive style:

**A:** It's March, and that means it's time to begin planning Tim's party.

**B:** *(Head buried in a book)* Can't do it now. I'm busy.

**A:** I think the party will have a better chance of succeeding if we give ourselves plenty of time to get organized.

**B:** It's going to be impossible for me to give it much thought.

**A:** I've already jotted down some preliminary ideas. I hope you'll look at them when you finish the chapter you're reading.

**B:** Do I have to do it today?

**A:** Is there another day that would be better for you?

**B:** Oh, I don't know.

**A:** Well, let's talk about it when you complete your reading. Are we agreed?

**B:** All right.

**A:** Good! It shouldn't take more than 30 minutes, and I'll really feel better when we've at least gone over these ideas.

The ability to communicate assertively usually puts you at an advantage when you are involved in a conflict. Your perception of your role in a relationship affects your choice of conflict resolution strategy. Imagine you and Sheila work for the same company. Sheila asks you to pick her up and drop her off at the train every day. You feel this will cause you unnecessary delays. You respond:

1. "Um, well, I guess it's possible . . . Oh, all right." (nonassertive)

2. "You're kidding! You really have nerve! Why should I do that for you?" (aggressive)

3. "I understand you get tired of having to walk to the station every day, but still, I'd rather not commit myself to picking you up and driving you there every day. I'd be glad to help you once or twice a week." (assertive)

Which response would you choose?

We can be assertive, nonassertive, or aggressive in various ways. When we interact with someone, we can communicate our nonassertiveness by demeaning ourselves, by keeping silent, or by hesitating when stating a position. We can communicate our aggressiveness by being openly hostile, sarcastic, or rude. And we can communicate our assertiveness by standing up for our rights, openly expressing our beliefs, and stating our positions directly. Although there is no one way you need to act in every interpersonal conflict, each choice you make regarding how to act influences the eventual outcome of the conflict.

# CULTURE AND CONFLICT RESOLUTION

Because culture is the lens through which we view the world, cultural background influences our response to conflict. For example, people from individualist cultures such as the United States prefer to deal directly with conflict, whereas those from collectivist cultures such as Japan are more comfortable with an indirect approach.[20] People from individualist cultures use controlling and overt confrontational strategies, whereas people from collectivist cultures prefer to use smoothing or avoidance strategies in the effort to help those they are in conflict with save face.[21]

In the United States, an emphasis is placed on the individual's rights, mainly on whether a person's needs are given their proper due. In contrast, most Latin American and Asian countries emphasize the concerns of the group rather than the rights and needs of individuals.[22] In one study, university students from different cultures were asked if they would permit aggressive behavior in their children to help protect what they perceived rightfully to be theirs. The highest percentage of affirmative responses came from U.S. parents (61 percent).[23]

## ANALYZE THIS: EDWARD DE BONO

iStock.com/T Turovska

Edward de Bono is a physician and leading authority on creative thinking. What does the following excerpt from de Bono's *I Am Right—You Are Wrong* suggest about how the Japanese handle conflict?

Every day the leading executives in the Japanese motor industry meet for lunch in their special club. They discuss problems common to the whole motor industry. But a soon as lunch is over and they step over the

*(Continued)*

(Continued)

threshold of the club, out into the street, they are bitter enemies seeking to kill each other's business by marketing, technical changes, pricing policy, etc. For the Japanese, who do not have the tradition of Western logic, there is no contradiction at all between "friend" and "enemy." They find it easy to conceive of someone as a friend–enemy or enemy–friend.

Source: Edward de Bono, *I Am Right—You Are Wrong,* New York: Viking, 1991, p. 196.

We also distinguish cultures by whether they use high- or low-context communication. Cultures using high-context communication are tradition-bound and emphasize politeness and indirectness in relationships. Some might interpret such behavior as nonassertive. In contrast, members of low-context communication cultures exhibit a more direct communication style, which some might interpret as assertive. Thus, people from low-context cultures such as the United States are likely to communicate openly and directly, whereas members of high-context cultures such as Japan and Korea prefer to avoid confrontation and to preserve a sense of harmony in an effort to help others maintain their self-esteem.[24] This orientation may be changing, however, since young adults favor collaborative problem-solving to resolve a conflict, rather than avoidance.[25]

Because of the inevitability of conflict in relationships, people from different cultures need to recognize and acknowledge their differences. By becoming less ethnocentric and more culturally aware, we can learn to handle conflict with people from different cultures as effectively as we handle conflict with people from our own culture. The next time you are involved in a conflict with someone from a different culture, ask yourself:

1. Which of my behaviors is my partner having difficulty understanding or accepting?
2. Which of his or her behaviors am I having difficulty with?
3. To what extent is this person more or less cooperative or competitive than me?
4. To what degree is this person more or less open, direct, and assertive or more or less reticent, indirect, and nonassertive than me?

By making an effort to understand how the experiences of people from other cultures lead them to develop perspectives on conflict that differ from yours, you can appreciate and embrace the flexibility necessary to resolve conflict.[26]

When it comes to age as a cultural variable, developing the ability to empathize can bridge the generation gap that fuels many intergenerational conflicts. Older people complain that members of younger generations stereotype them as "old geezers," making them feel worthless and discarded. Members of the "sandwich generation" complain about the burden they have to shoulder in both caring for their own children and "parenting" their aged parents, who have numerous "aches and pains" and—from their adult children's perspective—rarely seem to be content. If members of the older and younger generations could empathize with one another—that is, identify with and understand each other's feelings and motives—and could share their thoughts, a fuller, more meaningful understanding might develop between them, helping to defuse perceived or imagined intergenerational conflicts.[27]

# GENDER AND CONFLICT RESOLUTION

Can women and men work together effectively to resolve conflict? Do they share the same priorities when it comes to alleviating conflict? Adult men and women tend to respond dissimilarly to conflict. Women, it appears, specialize in communication that builds support, while men tend to focus on task-related issues.[28] However, both kinds of behavior can actually complement each other and work in unison to resolve conflict.

## EARLY LEARNING

When growing up, boys and girls may be socialized to approach conflict differently. Boys often learn to resolve their conflicts more directly with verbal assaults or by physically fighting. Girls are likely encouraged to use more indirect methods, relying primarily on gossip and the threat of social isolation to address conflicts.

## THE GENDERING OF CONFLICT RELATED COMMUNICATION

Neither men nor women may be aware of their contributions to or strategies for conflict resolution. When adults, men tend to use communication to solve problems and to assert their points of view. They see talk as a means of establishing superiority and winning others' respect. They become ego-involved. For women, conversation provides the means to work out conflicts and relationship problems. Whereas men use talk to negotiate for power and influence, women use it to build connections and include others. Men put priority on outcomes, and women put it on the relationship itself. As a result, while men may be better at staying focused on the goal gained from resolving a conflict, women are likely better prepared to interpret the feelings, moods, and needs of those they are in conflict with. They are better at asking questions and avoiding the putdowns that make conflict resolution unnecessarily difficult.[29]

## RESOLUTION PREFERENCES

Men and women differ in how committed they are to conflict resolution. Men are sometimes quicker than women to withdraw from conflict. Women may want to talk it out, but men may simply want to be done with it—something they often achieve by leaving.[30] Women also tend to do more compromising and accommodating than men, who are likely to use somewhat more forceful and direct means to get their way. Men and women need to be aware that they tend to bring different orientations to conflict that influence their responses.

When we compare heterosexual couples and gay and lesbian partners, we discover that gays and lesbians

1. Are less likely to become hostile after a conflict
2. Don't display dominance while engaging in conflict
3. Rarely take conflict personally
4. Diffuse conflict with humor
5. In general, stay calmer in the midst of conflict[31]

# MEDIA, TECHNOLOGY, AND CONFLICT RESOLUTION: MODELS OR MADNESS

How we arrive at a solution when involved in an interpersonal conflict is revealing. For example, we can try one approach after another and then weigh the consequences of potential options, or we can rely on the power of example and then enact what we have observed, effectively learning vicariously. Media and technology facilitate the vicarious approach, providing abundant models of people embroiled in conflict. They also supply the means to communicate about and spread conflict, at times contributing to conflicts going viral. As such, both media and technology play parts in helping and hindering conflict resolution.

## MEDIA PORTRAYALS: MODEL THE WAY

According to **social learning theory**, we learn at least some of what we know by observing others and then modeling the behavior of those we have observed. Thus, through observation and modeling of mediated characters, we acquire a wide range of behaviors and solutions to potential problems that we otherwise might not have had the resources, inclination, or time to figure out. In this way, media offerings (including video games) can lead us to practice certain behaviors while also inhibiting our use of others.

# REFLECT ON THIS

### Lessons Learned

Social learning theory explains that "children and adults acquire attitudes, emotional responses, and new styles of conduct through filmed and televised modeling." This statement, delivered by psychologist and social learning expert Albert Bandura, implies that the prevalence and efficacy of violence on television demonstrate to viewers that violence is a viable solution to life's problems.

In other words, by watching television programs and films and playing video games in which violent behavior gets results, viewers and gamers may come to believe that aggression is a valid means of resolving conflicts. Thus, media offerings may without intention make the once unthinkable more thinkable.

Provide an example of something that you believe was once unthinkable that mediated portrayals have now made acceptable.

Source: Albert Bandura, *Social Learning Theory,* Englewood Cliffs, NJ: Prentice Hall, 1977, p. 27.

Both news and entertainment offerings involve depictions of different kinds of conflicts. News stories, for example, may describe the nature and outcomes of gang violence, union-management disputes, political rivalries, or a war's battles. Entertainment shows abound with conflicts resulting from family disputes, love entanglements, and disagreements over job-related issues such as promotions and/or money. Some of these conflicts have positive outcomes, and others have negative ones. All, however, affect our attitudes toward the means used to resolve them. We learn what works and what doesn't.

Media offerings influence attitudes toward conflict in another way as well. A program may improve on "real life" by tying up into neat packages situations that in reality would leave us feeling confused or would require more effort to resolve. To suit entertainment needs, for example, most television programs fit time slots of 30, 60, or 120 minutes. Few conflicts go unresolved within those time blocks. Rarely are we left hanging or in despair. Instead, we are presented with fabricated versions of conflict resolution. To be sure, most of us realize that drama and real life are different, but media can twist our expectations about the world in ways we don't even realize.

# TECHNOLOGY: REAL AND UNREAL

What do we learn about conflict when online? Do we learn myths or the realities of conflict?

## Gaming

*Call of Duty* and *Battlefield* are popular video game franchises that have morphed into cultural institutions. These games realistically simulate high-tech military combat—vividly re-creating the experiences of fighting in a war. How does taking war and turning it into a game affect us, especially when the line between warrior and civilian is often unclear and the visuals are frighteningly close to YouTube footage of real wars?[32] Real war, however, is not "fun" or "entertaining," as these games are intended to be. While some believe these games trivialize military conflict and have little cultural impact, others believe they are akin to movies, such as *American Sniper, The Hurt Locker* and *Black Hawk Down*, that comment on war.

In your opinion, what does playing computer games teach us about conflict? Whether or not we take these games seriously, to what extent might they be influencing the approaches we use to handle conflict in our personal and professional lives? Could they influence us to use destructive approaches to conflict resolution when less aggressive, more accommodating approaches might be wiser? Could such games be encouraging us to display more aggressive behavior in our personal relationships? What about games that reward players for killing the innocent, members of law enforcement, or prostitutes or for displaying skill using a range of weapons, or in which players assume the role of a criminal?

Research has found that immediately after playing violent games, the possibility that the player will interpret a mild or ambiguous provocation in a hostile fashion increases, as do the player's general arousal level and dominant behavioral proclivities. In effect, through playing such games, players learn aggressive life scripts and come to de-emphasize negative reactions to conflict and violence.[33]

## Factors Influencing Online Interactions

During online interactions, the heated discussion of real-world political, social, religious, or economic issues may result in flaming and cyberbullying, with communication becoming hostile, threatening, and personally insulting. From a conflict perspective, flaming is an outgrowth of one person's perception that the other is being patently unfair. Related to bullying, it typically provokes angry responses that sometimes result in flame wars between the parties, ultimately drawing in more participants who perpetuate the online harassment. Some attribute flaming and bullying to de-individuation and a general lack of awareness of the feelings of others, asserting that in U.S. culture, we spend so much time online that we have individualized our leisure time, reducing our dependence on others and precipitating what has been called the "bowling alone" syndrome characterized by a lack of in-person socializing.[34]

Others contend that it's the **online disinhibition effect** that escalates the conflict further. They assert that people are more willing to speak out or misbehave online than they are in person.[35] According to this argument, striking out at another person online feels less like a confrontation than would telling that person the same thing over the phone or face-to-face. Being very frank, of course, likely provokes the target of that frankness to retaliate with vitriolic remarks, and so on.

What do you think? And to what extent, if any, do you believe that social networking might be used to ameliorate or perpetuate such behavior? For example, one kind of response to relational conflict is *ghosting*, which destroys the relationship. When engaged in ghosting, one person in the relationship calls it quits, completely severing communication with the other but with absolutely no warning or explanation. Suddenly one party simply avoids all contact with the other party, erasing the person from social media, and blocking all of the ghosted person's on and offline communication efforts.[36] Ghosting can be devastating to the person who is ghosted.[37] How did or do you imagine you would feel if someone with whom you shared a relationship resolved their feelings of conflict by erasing you from their lives without first speaking with you about it?

### It's Not All Bad

On the other hand, newer technologies are not without their benefits for conflict resolution. In fact, at times their availability can help users defuse rather than heat up a conflict. For example, individuals who are very angry at one another may find that texting and instant messaging actually foster their communication. These means allow people with a conflict to interact while avoiding the shouting match that would likely take place if they were in the same room. By slowing things down a bit and freeing them to think things through before responding, communicating in cyberspace may help to lower the tension level and reduce the number of potentially hurtful and thoughtless retorts they might otherwise make to one another. Because online interaction tends to be asynchronous, we're not compelled to handle the conflict in real time, but can delay our response.

## TRY THIS

### It's War!

First, view a film (e.g., *Black Panther*) or television offering (e.g., *Game of Thrones*) or play a computer game (e.g., Mortal Kombat) that focuses on the handling of interpersonal conflict.

1. Describe the nature of the conflict presented in the film or game.

2. Discuss how the characters attempt to handle the conflict, identifying both their negative and positive behaviors.

3. Describe the outcome of the conflict and the extent to which its resolution strengthened or weakened the relationship of the characters.

4. Explain your views regarding the ethics and viability of the means used to resolve conflict in film and games.

Next, select a current issue of a major newspaper, an online news site, or a broadcast/cable news show.

1. Identify articles/stories focused on conflict of different kinds. For example, stories may be devoted to gang fights, domestic violence, management-labor disputes, class warfare, or war.

2. Keep a tally of which conflict-focused articles/stories have positive slants and which have negative slants, which have positive resolutions and which have negative resolutions.

3. Discuss what your findings suggest regarding the coverage of conflict.

4. How might the nature of news coverage influence reader/viewer attitudes toward the effect and value of conflict?

# GAINING COMMUNICATION COMPETENCE: GUIDELINES FOR SKILLFULLY RESOLVING CONFLICT

By applying principles of effective communication, we can resolve interpersonal conflict productively. Using effective communication techniques can help us reduce the likelihood that our behavior will escalate a conflict. Learning to handle conflict successfully is an obtainable goal leading to increased self-confidence, improved relationships, and a greater ability to handle stressful situations. The following guidelines summarize how we can use interpersonal skills to resolve conflict.

## RECOGNIZE THAT CONFLICT CAN BE RESOLVED RATIONALLY

Sometimes when we step back from a situation, we find the perspective to realize that we can resolve a conflict. Similarly, withdrawing or postponing a discussion of the conflict until you are in control of your emotions can be the most rational decision, just as smoothing or apologizing when you feel that engaging would be wrong may well be best. At times, deciding who needs a goal most and letting that person have it is the rational choice. Of course, meeting in the middle and facing the conflict head-on are also valid. Recognizing when to use which behavior and sensing when a behavioral choice will be productive or not are first steps in learning to handle conflict more effectively. Being able to switch approaches according to what will work best is a key to conflict resolution.

## AGREE ABOUT HOW TO DEFINE THE CONFLICT

Once we acknowledge that we can handle a conflict rationally, we are ready to identify the reason for the conflict by asking questions: What is the nature of our conflict? Which of us feels more strongly about the issue? What can we do about it?

Communication during this stage will be more effective if, when sharing feelings and reactions, we send "I" messages ("I don't like having to do all the work") rather than "you" messages and avoid sending blame messages ("You ruin everything."). This stage has no place for labeling, accusing, or insulting. Instead, both sides need to be specific regarding the reasons for the conflict and in explaining what is needed to find a beneficial solution—a solution in which neither will lose and both will win. In other words, if we find a way to define the conflict as a mutual problem rather than as a win–lose battle, it will be easier to resolve.

## EXCHANGE PERCEPTIONS: DESCRIBE, EXPRESS, SPECIFY, AND NOTE BEHAVIORAL CONSEQUENCES

When each party proposes a solution that underscores the intention to cooperate, defensiveness and egocentrism levels are reduced. Such a solution requires that each person understands the other's perspective and be able to keep it in mind as the sides resolve the differences between them. To settle a conflict, each party must understand—but not necessarily agree with—the motivation behind the other's actions. Only by considering the perspective of another can we invent an array of possible solutions based on a clear understanding of each side and the emotional force underlying each position.

## ASSESS ALTERNATIVE SOLUTIONS AND CHOOSE THE ONE THAT SEEMS BEST

After conceiving possible solutions, we must assess which solution each of the parties considers best. Will one solution lead to a one-sided "win" at the other's expense, will everyone "lose," or will everyone "win"? Make a note of which solutions are totally unacceptable and those that are mutually acceptable. The conflict is resolved when the parties select a solution that satisfies each of them and to which they agree to abide. Usually, this is the solution with the most advantages and fewest disadvantages for each side—the one that appears to be the fairest when measured against agreed-on criteria.

## IMPLEMENT AND EVALUATE THE SELECTED SOLUTION

During this stage, we test the chosen solution. We identify who is doing what, when, where, and under what conditions. We seek to know whether the adopted solution has alleviated the conflict's causes and whether the outcome has been as rewarding as anticipated. If it has not, then it is time to restart the conflict resolution process. Agreements that do not improve the ability of the parties to relate typically fail because they usually are inconsistent with, rather than supportive of, each person's needs and goals.

# The Case of the Jousting Roommates

Jim and Jack share an apartment. Jim likes to rise early and enrolls in 8:00 A.M. classes. Jack likes to sleep in; he carries a heavy late-afternoon and evening course load. Jim likes a quiet place to study. Jack loves to read with music blasting. Jim is a neat freak. Jack leaves his things wherever he happens to drop them.

As roommates, Jim and Jack shared a relationship that could be described as tenuous at best, until . . .

It was about 2:00 A.M. Jim had been asleep for about 3 hours. Jack arrived home and immediately turned on his music—it was blaring so loud that it virtually knocked Jim out of bed. Jim yelled at Jack to turn the speakers off and put his headset on. Jack yelled back at Jim to get a life. Jim was so angry that he hurled a book across the room; it hit the ceiling and set off the fire alarm. As the engines arrived, Jack and Jim began to wonder if they might consider alternatives to screaming and throwing things at each other.

Now, consider these questions:

1. In your opinion, will Jack and Jim survive a year together?

2. What will need to happen for them to develop a more positive and cooperative relationship?

3. How would you advise these roommates to resolve their conflict?

# REVIEW THIS

1. **Define conflict and discuss its nature, explaining the difference between functional and dysfunctional conflict.** ☐

Conflict is inevitable in any relationship. Anyone can start a conflict, and a conflict can occur in any setting. It can involve a single person (intrapersonal conflict) or two or more people (interpersonal conflict). Conflict occurs whenever the thoughts or actions of one person are perceived by another to limit or interfere with his or her own thoughts or actions. Once aware of their disagreement and the incompatibility of their goals, both parties to the conflict try to prevail. Conflicts that are functional are constructive; they help us better understand one another as well as strengthen our relationships. Conflicts that are dysfunctional damage or even destroy relationships.

2. **Identify conflict sources.** ☐

Conflicts arise from perceived individual differences, scarcity of resources, rivalries, relationship disagreements, and misinterpretations. Every conflict can be described according to the nature of the goal of the parties (shareable or nonshareable), the conflict's level of intensity (low, medium, or high), and the general character of the conflict (pseudoconflict, content conflict, value conflict, or ego conflict).

3. **Distinguish between conflict management styles.** ☐

Among the most popular means to depict preferred conflict resolution styles is Blake and Mouton's conflict resolution grid. The five styles identified in the grid are avoiding, accommodative, competitive, compromising, and collaborative.

4. **Discuss productive ways to communicate during conflict.** ☐

Employing role reversal is one communication technique that helps to resolve conflict. Another is the use of a DESC script. DESC is an acronym for *describe*, *express*, *specify*, and *consequences*.

5. **Compare and contrast the following conflict expression styles: assertive, nonassertive, and aggressive.** ☐

A person who approaches conflict nonassertively attempts to avoid it, even if this means giving up his or her own needs and wants. A person who approaches conflict aggressively aims to dominate in a relationship, even if this means hurting the other party. A person who approaches conflict assertively communicates honestly, clearly, and directly about the conflict, standing up for what he or she believes without harming the other party or himself or herself.

6. **Explain culture's influence on conflict.** ☐

People from individualist, low-context communication cultures prefer to deal directly with conflict, whereas people from collectivist, high-context communication cultures are more comfortable dealing with conflict indirectly.

· · · · · · · · · · · · · · · · · · · · · · · · · · · ·

**7.** **Discuss differences and similarities in how men and women approach and handle conflict.** ☐

Men tend to pursue their own self-interests without orienting themselves to a partner's perspective; women tend to attempt to meet others' needs. Men focus on problem-solving and task-related issues, while women try to build support as they work out relationship problems.

· · · · · · · · · · · · · · · · · · · · · · · · · · · ·

**8.** **Discuss how media portrayals and technology affect perceptions of conflict.** ☐

We acquire attitudes, emotional responses, and styles of conduct by modeling what we observe on television, in films, and in games. Communicating online may also lower the tension level associated with face-to-face conflict. At the same time, television and film may delude us into thinking that conflicts can be resolved quickly.

· · · · · · · · · · · · · · · · · · · · · · · · · · · ·

**9.** **Identify how to resolve conflict effectively.** ☐

To resolve conflict, we must recognize that conflict can be resolved rationally, agree on a definition of the conflict, exchange perceptions, communicate tentative solutions illustrating cooperative intentions, choose the best solution, implement it, and evaluate it.

· · · · · · · · · · · · · · · · · · · · · · · · · · · ·

## CHECK YOUR UNDERSTANDING

**1.** Can you deconstruct a specific conflict situation by identifying the parties to the conflict, the sources of the conflict, the goal(s) sought, the nature of the conflict, and its resolution? (See pages 270–275.)

**2.** Can you differentiate between functional and dysfunctional conflict? Which kind do you experience most frequently in your close relationships? (See pages 294–298.)

**3.** Can you create scenarios illustrating the differences among nonassertive, assertive,

and aggressive approaches to a conflict-laden situation? (See pages 279–283.)

**4.** Can you provide examples of how gender, culture, and media and technology influence both attitudes toward and behaviors exhibited during conflict? (See pages 315–320.)

**5.** Can you assess your own conflict management skills? (See pages 320–321.)

## KEY TERMS

Accommodative style  306

Aggressive expression style  314

Assertive expression style  315

Avoiding style  305

Collaborative style  307

Competitive style  305

Get the tools you need to sharpen your study skills. **SAGE edge** offers a robust online environment featuring an impressive array of free tools and resources. Access practice quizzes, eFlashcards, video, and multimedia at **edge.sagepub.com/gambleicp**.

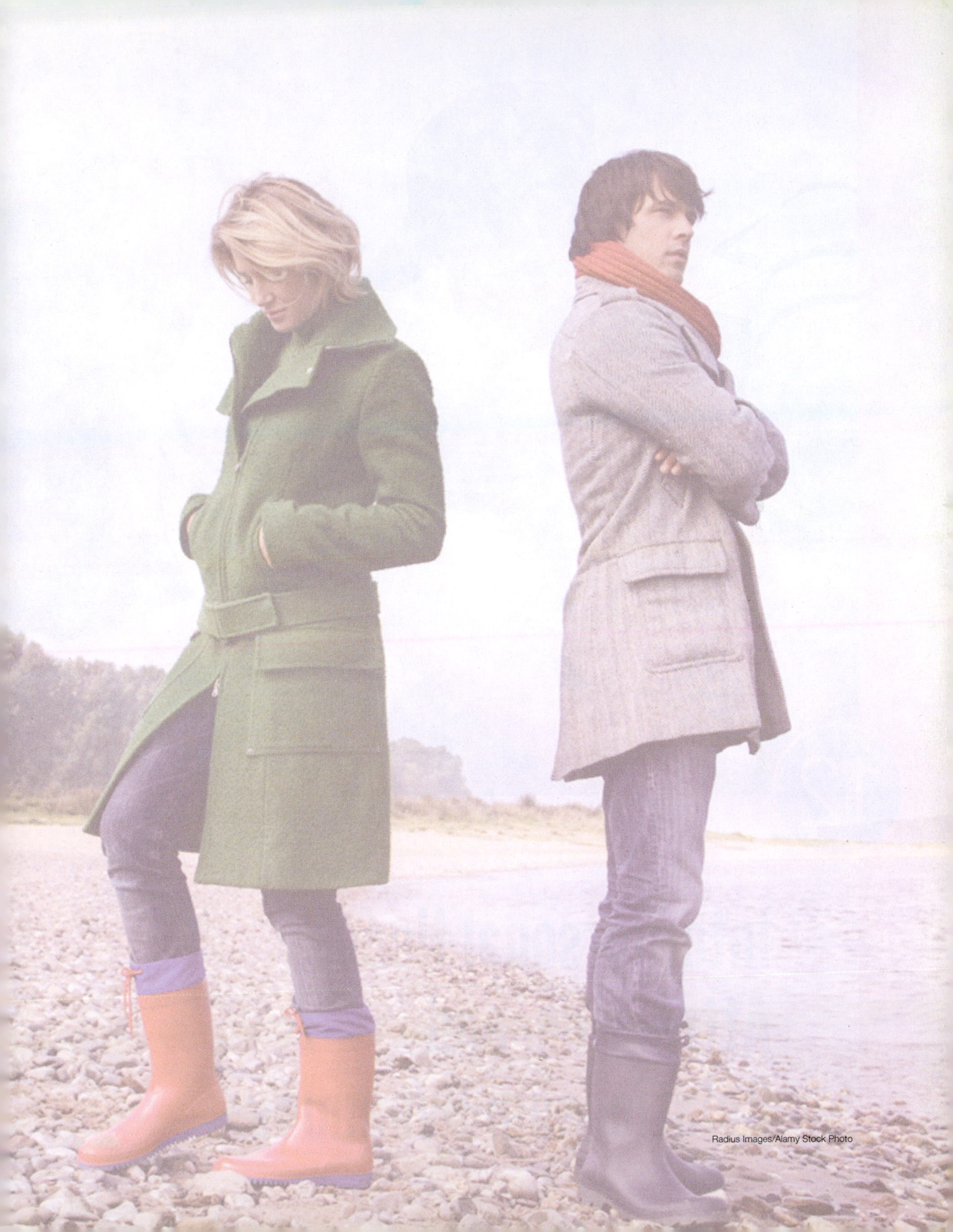

Radius Images/Alamy Stock Photo

**12**

# Interpersonal Needs, Attraction, and Relationship Dynamics

## Learning Objectives

### AFTER COMPLETING THIS CHAPTER, YOU SHOULD BE ABLE TO

1. Discuss the functions and needs relationships serve

2. Identify characteristics distinguishing one relationship from another

3. Describe factors influencing interpersonal attraction

4. Explain the relationship spectrum using Rawlins's friendship model, Sternberg's triangle of love, and Knapp and Vangelisti's relationship model to distinguish among acquaintanceships, friendships, and romantic relationships

5. Identify how culture, gender, and media and technology impact the nature of our relationships

6. Apply specific techniques to facilitate mastery of relationship dynamics

> To suggest that one simply starts a friendship, courtship, romantic partnership or marriage and "off it goes" is simple-minded. It is like believing that one can drive down the street merely by turning the ignition key, sitting back, and letting the car take care of itself.
>
> —Steve Duck

# WHAT DO YOU KNOW?

Before continuing your reading of this chapter, which of the following five statements do you believe to be true, and which do you believe to be false?

| | | | |
|---|---|---|---|
| 1. | Happy people tend to live longer than unhappy people. | T | F |
| 2. | As time passes, passionate love increases. | T | F |
| 3. | "What's up?" is a question that opens a communication channel between two people. | T | F |
| 4. | By talking about *my* friends instead of *our* friends, partners are able to bond more easily. | T | F |
| 5. | Less talk about fewer topics increases a relationship's strength. | T | F |

Read the chapter to discover if you're right or if you've made any erroneous assumptions.

ANSWERS: 1. T; 2. F; 3. T; 4. F; 5. F

Which fascinates you more: your own relationships or those you experience vicariously? We seem to be intrigued with the array of relationships depicted on reality TV. The *Real Housewives* franchise attests to this.[1] Viewers watch avidly as the women on these shows and their spouses or significant others, assorted friends, and family members experience relationship highs and lows. We observe as the characters figure out the ground rules for each relationship and decide whether to take a particular relationship to another level, to work through the relationship's challenges, or to terminate it.

Relationship dramas—both the ups and the downs—are at the heart of all the offerings in the *Real Housewives* franchise. Each episode presents a case study focused on evolving relationship dynamics. We are privy to weddings, breakups, and squabbles among family members and friends. Some featured relationships fall apart quickly, others experience significant alternations, and a number are shown as just beginning. While some of the story lines likely are manufactured, they still afford us the chance to compare the dynamics of the relationships they feature with our own—past and present. And as we revise our feelings toward those with whom we share real relationships, how we feel about the characters on these shows also changes. And sometimes, as executive producer Andy Cohen notes, our greatest satisfaction comes when we think, "I would never do that!"[2]

Relationships are the fabric of our lives. In fact, our happiness depends on how satisfied we are with them.[3] Whether we are friends or family, linked romantically or through our careers, relationships matter. To lay a foundation for a better understanding of why we enter into relationships, consider what a relationship is and the needs and functions it fulfills.

# WHY WE FORM RELATIONSHIPS

The term **relationship** refers to a wide array of social connections that to varying degrees meet our interpersonal needs. When we speak of interpersonal relationships, we are concerned with the relationships we have with our parents, significant other, siblings, friends, employer or employees, physician, and instructors, among others.

Our expectations for a relationship depend on its nature. For example, we likely have different relational expectations for a doctor, a coworker, a friend, a lover, and a family member. As a result, we probably use different rules to guide our behavior in relating to each of them, and we measure each relationship's effectiveness according to somewhat different criteria that we establish based on our goals for the particular relationship.

Goals vary from relationship to relationship. When interacting with a physician, for example, our goals are more than likely different from those we have when interacting with a friend. Despite these differences, however, there are commonalities in the way we approach and communicate with others.

Relationships also help meet our personal needs. Perhaps we are lonely and seek an outlet from our isolation. Maybe we feel a need to release pent-up tensions, discuss our interests, or share concerns and feelings. Perhaps we want to change another's beliefs or attitudes. Or maybe we aspire to learn more about ourselves. Whatever our personal reasons for reaching out to another human being, the desire to interact with and develop meaningful relationships lives in us all, helping to define our humanness. We need interpersonal contact to survive.

## RELATIONSHIPS PRESERVE HAPPINESS AND HEALTH

A correlation exists between happiness and relationship effectiveness. One also exists between happiness and longevity, with those who report feeling happy living up to 35 percent longer.[4] Unhappiness results from a lack of relational attention and poorly handled relationship problems.[5] Family, friends, and associates, however, can function as social support and help us get through the stresses and challenges of life.

We all need person-to-person contact. Without it, we feel lonely and isolated.

Not only do relationships help preserve our mental well-being, but they also affect us physically.[6] People involved in problematic relationships experience more medical problems than do those with better-functioning relationships.[7] The incidence of heart attacks and traffic accident injuries is higher among people whose relationships are failing than it is among those whose relationships are thriving.[8] Mortality rates are higher for those with deficient social support systems, who don't feel part of a group or a family, or don't feel that they "fit in."[9] People with terminal illnesses tend to die sooner if they have only a small group of friends rather than a large array of family members and friends on whom they can rely. Widowed men who do not remarry have higher mortality rates than those who do. The immune systems of widows are weaker than those of their married counterparts. Lonely people die sooner and younger.[10]

## RELATIONSHIPS PREVENT SOCIAL ISOLATION AND LONELINESS

We all need person-to-person contact. If isolated, we suffer. When our social surroundings fail to reflect our needs and wishes, we try to manufacture situations that do, even if only subconsciously. For example, hermits are prone to hallucinating that other people are present and speaking to them, the bereaved are apt to imagine their dead loved ones are there with them, and those who are incarcerated dream about meeting their family members, friends, and other people on the outside.[11] We humans have the need to belong.[12]

## ANALYZE THIS: BY YOURSELF

Upon hearing his name called, James J. Pelosi prepared himself for one last humiliating moment. As he approached the podium to accept his diploma from the U.S. Military Academy at West Point, he expected to hear a chorus of boos. There were no boos, only silence. Upon returning to his seat, however, he was surprised by the handshakes he received from those around him.

Why had James Pelosi expected to be booed by his peers? While a West Point cadet, Pelosi had been

*(Continued)*

accused of cheating. He maintained his innocence, but was convicted by the Honor Committee, before his conviction was ultimately thrown out on appeal. But the academy reserves the right to subject those it believes guilty—despite insufficient evidence for a conviction—of an Honor Code violation to "the silencing." Thus, for his last 2 years at West Point, Pelosi was ostracized—virtually no one spoke a word to him. Most cadets are unable to withstand the pressure of such treatment and resign, but not James Pelosi. Steadfast in asserting his innocence and unwilling to bend under the punishment of having to live alone and eat every meal alone, of being constantly treated as if he didn't matter, and even though he lost 26 pounds, Pelosi persisted as a cadet.

Pelosi was among a handful of cadets who graduated after undergoing the silencing. When interviewed about the experience, he observed: "I've taken a psychology course, and I know what isolation does to animals. No one at the Academy asks how it affects a person. Doesn't that seem strange?"

Answer these questions:

1. Would you have endured the treatment James Pelosi received? Why or why not?

2. How does Pelosi's experience compare with that of an individual bullied and/or taunted on the Internet by people who urge others to ignore and ostracize her or him?

3. What role does resilience play in each of the preceding instances?

4. What steps would you advise others to take to cope with feelings of isolation?

Sources: For more detail, see "The Silencing," *Newsweek,* June 18, 1973, p. 42.

## RELATIONSHIPS MEET INTERPERSONAL NEEDS

A number of researchers have addressed the notion of interpersonal needs, among them William Schutz, who formulated a three-dimensional theory of interpersonal behavior known as **fundamental interpersonal relations orientation**, and Abraham Maslow, the creator of a well-known hierarchy of human needs.

### Fundamental Interpersonal Relations Orientation

According to Schutz, we meet three of our basic interpersonal needs through our relationships: inclusion, control, and affection.[13] Let us see how these needs play out in our lives.

*Inclusion* relates to the extent to which we feel the need to establish and maintain a feeling of mutual interest with others. Most of us want to be included. We want others to acknowledge us and want to learn more about us. Some of us know what it feels like to be excluded—to be the last asked to join a team or work on a project or to have to eat alone in the cafeteria. When our **inclusion needs** go unmet, we feel isolated and lonely. In contrast, when our inclusion needs are satisfied, we develop a sense of enhanced self-worth and feel fulfilled.

*Control* relates to our need to establish and maintain relationships that facilitate our experiencing satisfactory levels of influence and power. To varying degrees, we need to feel capable of having someone else in charge. We differ in how necessary it is for us to be a controlling or supporting player. When our **control needs** go unmet, we may conclude that others fail to value or respect our abilities and that, consequently, we are unable to make sound decisions, direct our future, or influence another's.

*Affection* relates to our need to give and receive love and to experience emotionally close relationships. Should our **affection needs** go unfulfilled, we may feel unlovable and long for meaningful relationships that will keep us from being emotionally detached. In contrast, when our affection needs are met, we are comfortable sharing intimate and friendly relationships. Not every relationship develops into one based on love.

Typically, the need for inclusion impels us to build relationships. Once we do, these relationships also meet our control and affection needs. The extent to which we feel and are able to realize these needs varies. In fact, we can classify people according to their specific "need levels." If, for example, individuals rarely attempt to satisfy a specific need, we say their need level is deficient. On the other hand, if they are consumed with satisfying a specific need, we say their need level is excessive. People with a deficient need for inclusion are referred to as *undersocial*, those with a deficient need for affection are *underpersonal*, and people with little need to control others are known as *abdicrats*. Those in whom these needs are excessive are referred to, respectively, as *oversocial*, *overpersonal*, and *autocrats*.

Individuals who are undersocial, for example, try to avoid interacting with others, preferring their privacy and alone time. Oversocial people, in contrast, continually seek to be with others. However, both experience a fear of isolation, but they compensate for their fear using opposite strategies. The same holds true for individuals with deficient and excessive control needs. *Abdicrats* are afraid to exert control, so they readily cede it; autocrats fear not having control, so they grab the reins of power. Finally, individuals who are underpersonal do their best to keep relationships superficial, while those who are overpersonal try to increase their closeness to others. Both groups, however, are motivated by the need for affection and a fear of being rejected.

Unlike people in the groups just described, many of us are quite satisfied with our relationships. We find our need levels fulfilled and express our needs comfortably and naturally. People in this group are described as *social* (comfortable with people or alone), *democratic* (willing to give or take orders depending on the situation), and *personal* (at ease sharing both close and distant relationships).

### Maslow's Hierarchy of Needs

In contrast to Schutz, Abraham Maslow conceived of human needs as forming a pyramidal hierarchy, now known as **Maslow's needs hierarchy**, with our most basic needs located at or near the base, and our higher-order needs closer to or at the apex (see Figure 12.1).[14] Once our physiological and safety needs are met—the basic necessities of life (shelter, food, water, and safety)—we can move on to meeting our needs for belonging. These needs are usually satisfied through the attainment of a certain level of success in work, friendship, and love relationships and self-esteem. Ultimately, if we are fortunate, we find another who cares enough for us to help us in pursuit of realizing our full potential.

## RELATIONSHIPS SERVE AS BEHAVIORAL ANCHORS

In addition to meeting our inclusion, control, and affection needs, relationships serve as points of reference for appropriate behavioral and emotional responses. They help us express grief, happiness, and a host of other feelings in culturally acceptable ways. By comparing how we react with how friends and family members react, we become more comfortable and gain a greater sense of emotional stability.

FIGURE 12.1
Maslow's Hierarchy of Needs

Self-actualization

Esteem

Belongingness

Security

Physiological

Source: Abraham Maslow, *Toward a Psychology of Being*, New York: John Wiley, 1962.

## RELATIONSHIPS FUNCTION AS COMMUNICATION CONDUITS

Relationships are a kind of communication pipeline. They are the places where communication about anything can occur. They give us the opportunity to talk about the important and the trivial, the meaningful and the insignificant. They provide an audience for our self-disclosures. They provide someone for us to talk to as we attempt to make sense of our life and experiences.

## TRY THIS

## How Do You Feel About Being In/Out, Up/Down, or Close/Far?

We frequently assume that others share the same needs for inclusion, control, and affection, but that may not necessarily be the case. First, answer the following questions by selecting a number on a scale of 1 to 5, where 1 is "not at all" and 5 is "very." Then ask three men and three women from three different cultures to respond to the same questions.

1. How important is it to you to feel included as a part of a group?

2. To what extent is your need to be included currently fulfilled?

3. How important is it to you to be able to exert power and control in a relationship?

4. To what extent is your need to exert influence and power currently fulfilled?

5. How important is it to you to be involved in a close or an intimate relationship—one based on love?

6. To what extent is your need for love fulfilled currently?

Compare and contrast the need assessments of those whom you interviewed with your assessment of your own needs. What conclusions, if any, are you able to draw?

## GOOD RELATIONSHIPS HELP MAINTAIN OUR SENSE OF WORTH

To be sure, there are qualitative differences among our relationships. When healthy and functional, relationships enhance our sense of self. By supporting us, attending to us, and providing us with a sense of community, those with whom we share relationships help us preserve our self-esteem and opinions of our self-worth.

# RELATIONSHIP CHARACTERISTICS

Various characteristics differentiate one relationship from another. We choose to spend more time with some people, perhaps because we have ties to them or they support our goals and are there for us when we need them. We distance ourselves from others, believing they may be threats to our well-being.

## DURATION

How long did your longest relationship to date last? What about your shortest? Why did one thrive while the other withered? Relational duration differs by relationship type. For example, you have probably known your mother from birth or since you were adopted. Meaningful relationships require significant attention if they are to endure. In general, the stronger a relationship, the more time it has to develop and the longer it lasts.

## CONTACT FREQUENCY

Duration and contact often go hand in hand. We are likely to engage in more frequent interaction with people to whom we are personally tied. The more frequent our contact, the greater our opportunity to understand one another and develop the ability to predict one another's behavior. Compare, for example, your ability to predict the behavior of a close friend with your ability to predict the behavior of an acquaintance. Probably because you and the close friend interact more frequently, you know that person better and thus are more accurate in predicting his or her behavior.

## SHARING

The longer a relationship lasts, and the more frequent our contacts, the more information we are likely to share about ourselves. Usually this sharing of our innermost thoughts and feelings does not occur early in a relationship, but gradually, over a significant time.

This couple has been married for 30 years. What is your longest relationship to date?

## SUPPORT

When we think about another person's needs and act to help meet those needs, we provide support. For instance, we may try to decrease the stress felt by another by helping him or her cope with problems or handle anxieties. We may also provide support for someone by alleviating his or her sense of isolation or loneliness and by being available to that person physically or emotionally whenever we are needed.

## INTERACTION VARIABILITY

When the kinds of contacts we have with a single person vary, our relationship with him or her can be described as having greater breadth. For example, your authors work together writing books, socialize together, and live together. Thus, our interactions are characterized by greater variability than they would be if we were merely coauthors.

## EXPECTATIONS AND GOALS

We bring expectations and goals to our relationships. Often, for example, we expect those with whom we share relationships to be interested in us and in our welfare. We expect them to support us rather than to frustrate us, to help alleviate our fears rather than add to them. We want significant others to be attentive and honest and to help us develop and understand ourselves. We want them to feel affection for us, to want to be with us, to enjoy our company, and, as we get closer, to want to share themselves with us.

Tristan Fewings/Stringer/Getty Images Entertainment/Getty Images

# RELATIONSHIP ATTRACTORS

How do you decide when you would like to meet or get to know someone better? Each of us is drawn to some people more than others. Typically, we won't start a relationship with someone who turns us off. What makes us want to keep our distance from some of the people we meet? What causes us to decide *not* to try to get closer? According to a survey of singles in America conducted for the dating website Match.com, the top five relationship turnoffs are having a disheveled or unclean appearance, appearing lazy, being too needy, lacking a sense of humor, and distance—that is, living more than 3 hours apart.[15]

That said, how do we identify those forces that do make us want to get to know some of those "strangers" we meet a lot better? When it comes to choosing the people with whom we *will* develop relationships, interpersonal attraction is key. In fact, interpersonal attraction is the main reason we initiate contacts that we hope will develop into more meaningful relationships.

As you read about interpersonal attraction, remember that attraction is not necessarily mutual. We may find ourselves drawn to someone who does not reciprocate our feelings. Furthermore, attraction is not necessarily long-lived. We may discover that we were wrong about the qualities we thought another person possessed, or we may discover that the qualities that drew us in are insufficient to sustain our relationship.

As our relationship changes, so do our feelings of attraction. As we become closer to someone, we also become more highly attracted to them. The amount of attraction we feel for another depends on our relationship. We feel differently about our casual friends and our best friends, as we do about someone we hardly know and someone with whom we would like to be or have been intimate. Intimacy and attraction correlate positively.

Researchers identify a number of variables that influence how attracted or drawn we feel to another. Included among these are physical attractiveness, social attractiveness, task attractiveness, proximity, reinforcement, similarity, and complementarity (see Table 12.1).

## TABLE 12.1  RELATIONSHIP ATTRACTORS

| | |
|---|---|
| **Physical attractiveness** | Physical appeal can lead to the initiation of a relationship. |
| **Social attractiveness** | Personality and demeanor can be engaging. |
| **Task attractiveness** | When we enjoy working together, we seek more interpersonal contact. |
| **Proximity** | We are apt to enjoy interacting with people who work or live near us. |
| **Reinforcement** | We tend to persist in interacting with people whose company we find personally rewarding. |
| **Similarity** | We are apt to like people whose way of thinking resembles our own. |
| **Complementarity** | We find ourselves attracted to people who are different from us, but whose personalities complement ours in some way. |

## PHYSICAL ATTRACTIVENESS

*Physical attractiveness* serves as one of the main components we use to determine who we might want to share a relationship with.[16] How someone looks—whether it's the person's eyes, clothing, body shape, or some other aspect of appearance—determines whether or not we will find ourselves drawn to that person. For the most part, we prefer to initiate relationships with those we find physically appealing.

## SOCIAL ATTRACTIVENESS

A person with *social attractiveness* has the kind of personality or interpersonal demeanor we admire. We simply feel comfortable interacting with him or her. Perceptions of social attractiveness correlate with favorable personality attributions such as kindness, warmth, and intelligence.[17]

# REFLECT ON THIS

## *The Romantic Attraction Factor*

Even the most charming person may not inspire romantic desire in us. So, what is that causes us to come to think romantically about someone? While it is likely that the characteristics important to each of us in a romantic partner differ, research suggests that if our ideal partner preferences match the traits we perceive a potential partner to have, a positive outcome for the relationship is likely. Below are two different means of gauging romantic attraction:

1. What characteristics are most important to you in a romantic partner? With these traits in mind, how does either your current or a prospective partner measure up? For instance, how important to you are a partner's physical attractiveness, earning prospects, and warm characteristics?

2. Use the 9-point tool below to express your romantic interest in either a current or a desired partner. Using a scale of 1 to 9, where 1 is "agree" and 9 is "disagree," score your response to each statement that follows.

### Passion

1. I feel a great deal of sexual desire for _____.

2. _____ is the only person I want to be romantically involved with.

3. _____ always seems to be on my mind.

### Bondedness

1. It is important to me to see or talk to _____ regularly.

2. _____ is the first person I'd turn to if I had a problem.

3. If I achieved something good, _____ is the person I would tell first.

4. When I am away from _____, I feel down.

## TASK ATTRACTIVENESS

If we enjoy working with someone, we experience *task attractiveness*, and are apt to want to have more contact with him or her. We value the person's presence not just because he or she is adept at doing a job or enhances our productivity, but also because we find him or her engaging and want to sustain the interaction. As a result, what starts off solely as a business relationship may in time develop into a friendship.

## PROXIMITY

If you think about those people with whom you enjoy interacting, you may find that for the most part, they are individuals who work or live near you. *Proximity*, or physical nearness, increases opportunities to interact, share experiences, and form attachments. The more we interact, the more familiar we become, and the greater our chances of discovering other areas of common interest that could further increase a person's attractiveness in our eyes. Thus, the closer two

Interpersonal attraction plays a key role in relationship development.

people are geographically, the more likely it is they will be attracted to each other and develop an intimate relationship.

This is not to say that familiarity cannot also breed contempt. According to researchers Ellen Berscheid and Elaine Hatfield Walster, the more closely some people live, the greater the likelihood that they come to dislike each other. Berscheid and Walster note, "While propinquity (or nearness) may be a necessary condition for attraction, it probably is also a necessary condition for hatred."[18] How proximity functions depends on the people involved and their feelings toward each other. To what extent, if any, have your experiences revealed the truth of this claim?

## REINFORCEMENT

Another factor influencing interpersonal attraction is *reinforcement*. We enjoy sustaining contacts that are rewarding, and we refrain from maintaining those we judge punishing. Consequently, all things being equal, we enjoy being in personally rewarding relationships. We like people who praise and like us more than those who criticize and dislike us. But as is so often the case, too much of a good thing can backfire. Too much reinforcement can make us question another's sincerity or motivation.

## SIMILARITY

In general, we find ourselves attracted to those whose appearance, behavior, values, attitudes, experiences, beliefs, ideas, and interests are compatible with ours, and who like and dislike the same things we do. Typically, we like people whose way of thinking resembles our own more than we like those who disagree with us, especially when the topic under consideration is important to us. In fact, the more salient an issue, the more important being similar becomes. Similarity offers us "social validation": the input we need to confirm the "correctness" of positions taken.

We also expect people with attitudes similar to ours to like us more than would those whose attitudes differ substantially from ours. By associating with and establishing relationships with people we perceive to be most like us, we play it safe. In fact, according to the **matching hypothesis** developed by Elaine Hatfield Walster and her colleagues, although you may be attracted to the most physically attractive people, you will most likely date and enter into a long-term relationship with someone similar to yourself in physical attractiveness.[19]

## COMPLEMENTARITY

Not all research suggests that we develop relationships only with those who are like us. The variable of *complementarity* suggests that opposites also attract (though not as commonly or as easily as people who are more alike). At times, instead of falling for someone who is our replica, we find ourselves attracted to someone very different, perhaps because he or she exhibits characteristics we admire but do not possess. Thus, an introverted person might be attracted to someone who is extroverted. Interacting with our "opposites" can help us learn different ways of thinking. Sometimes it also can lead to relationship control and management issues.[20]

## THE UPSHOT

While each of the characteristics described in the above sections plays its part in our choice of a romantic partner, it is what we find attractive in a potential partner that leads us to desire that person in particular. Which characteristic(s) drew you to your partner?

A few years ago, a number of airlines began allowing passengers to select their seatmates based on the perusal of information uploaded from fellow travelers' Facebook or LinkedIn profiles.[21] That way they can try to sit next to someone who seems interesting to them. The airlines call this "social seating." What would you look for in a potential seatmate? Do you think having such profiles available would improve your chances of meeting someone with whom you would not only like to chat during the flight but also continue to interact after landing? Why or why not?

# THE RELATIONSHIP SPECTRUM

We come into contact with many different people daily. Some of them we will never see again. As a result, our relationships will never progress beyond the superficial. Others we will decide to get to know better. Some of these people will become acquaintances. We will connect briefly when opportunities arise, but our interactions with them usually will be limited in quality and quantity. Usually, with time, we simply drift away from each other. With others, however, we will develop long-lasting, meaningful friendships and/or romantic relationships.

## HOW CLOSE ARE WE?

It is impossible to have close relationships with everyone. We can characterize each of our relationships according to the amount and kind of closeness that we share.

**Intimacy** is a measure of closeness.[22] Intimate closeness may involve physical contact, shared ideas and value principles, disclosure of emotional feelings, and participation in shared activities. While some intimate relationships exhibit all four qualities, others exhibit only one or two. The amount of intimacy shared with acquaintances differs from the amount of intimacy shared with friends, which, in turn, differs from the amount of intimacy shared in romantic relationships.

Communication expectations for each type of relationship also differ. For example, we expect close friends and romantic partners to make more of an emotional investment toward understanding who we are than we would expect colleagues at work to exhibit. We count on friends and partners more and are more influenced by them, and we believe that others cannot easily replace their roles in our lives. (We discuss intimacy in greater detail in Chapter 13.)

## THE NATURE OF ACQUAINTANCESHIP

*Acquaintances* are people we know, usually by name, with whom we converse when given the opportunity, but with whom our interaction is typically limited in scope and quality. Unless we harbor a desire for more than acquaintanceship, rarely do we go out of our way to see an acquaintance, preferring to leave our meetings to chance.

## Measuring Intimacy

Think of five friends. Fill in each blank below with as many of the five names as are applicable:

1. _____ and I reveal our deepest feelings and thoughts to each other.

2. _____ and I understand each other.

3. _____ and I rely on each other for help and support.

4. _____ and I trust each other.

5. _____ and I accept each other as we are.

6. _____ and I expect our relationship to last a long time.

7. _____ and I have a lot in common.

8. _____ and I enjoy doing things together.

9. _____ and I meet each other's needs.

10. _____ and I enjoy each other's company.

Based on your responses, with which person do you believe you share the most and the least intimacy? In most cases, the greater your interdependence with another, the more important and significant this person is in your life.

A. F. Archive/Alamy

*The Big Bang Theory* centers on the friendships and romances of physicists Sheldon Cooper (Jim Parsons, lower center) and Leonard Hofstadter (Johnny Galecki, top center). In one episode, Sheldon tries to overcome his poor social skills by employing a scientific approach to making friends: the "Friendship Algorithm."

## THE NATURE OF FRIENDSHIP

Over time, some acquaintanceships develop into *friendships*. Unlike acquaintances, friends voluntarily seek each other out, enjoy each other's company, and display a strong mutual regard. Friends accept each other, confide in each other, trust one another to keep confidences, understand and provide emotional support to each other, share significant interests, and expect the relationship to endure.[23]

We are closer to some friends than we are to others. Our closest friends are those to whom we confide our innermost feelings and thoughts. We share a greater degree of intimacy with them. We also have the desire to learn more about them and share personal aspects of ourselves with them.

Friendships take time to develop. As we progress from the initial stages of contact into a more planned but still casual friendship, we begin to increase our knowledge of and trust in each other, and both the depth and the breadth of the relationship increase. As our friendship intensifies, we are likely to become more "other-oriented," a quality we demonstrate by going out of our way for the other person, becoming more open and expressive toward and more accepting of one another.

Communication researcher and friendship expert W. K. Rawlins developed a "6-stage model of friendship" that provides a useful explanation of how this kind of relationship develops (see Table 12.2).[24] We discuss each of the 6 stages next.

## TABLE 12.2  MODELS OF FRIENDSHIP AND RELATIONSHIPS

| RAWLINS'S 6-STAGE MODEL OF FRIENDSHIP | KNAPP AND VANGELISTI'S 10-STAGE MODEL OF RELATIONSHIPS |
|---|---|
| Role-limited interaction | Initiating |
| Friendly relations moving toward friendship | Experimenting |
| Nascent friendship | Intensifying |
| Stabilized friendship | Integrating |
| | Bonding |
| Waning friendship | Differentiating |
| | Circumscribing |
| | Stagnating |
| | Avoiding |
| | Terminating |

## Role-Limited Interaction

Friendships usually start with two people making limited initial contact in some context. For example, we might meet another at work, in a restaurant, or on a train. This initial meeting, or role-limited interaction, represents the first stage of friendship. During this stage, because we are unsure of how or if a relationship will develop, we relate somewhat tentatively. We possess little personal knowledge about each other, and we are reluctant to reveal personal information. We rely on polite exchanges, stereotypes of social roles, and standard scripts in our initial conversations.

## Friendly Relations

During the next stage, we progress to friendly relations, in which we continue the effort to determine whether we have enough in common to continue building a relationship. We increase the amount of small talk as we test the waters to see whether interest is reciprocated. We become somewhat less guarded, a bit more openly expressive, and more interested in having the other respond to our overtures.

## Moving Toward Friendship

As our desire for friendship increases, we cautiously step beyond conventional social rules and role playing, making small disclosures to demonstrate that we would like to expand our friendship. We invite the other to spend time voluntarily with us in a context outside the naturally occurring one we have shared to this point. We might, for example, ask a classmate if she would like to study with us, or ask someone we work with if he would like to stop at a coffee shop with us on the way home. Once we have the opportunity to interact more personally, naturally, and in a more relaxed setting, we may also reveal our attitudes, beliefs, and values to each other.

## Nascent Friendship

As our moves toward friendship are reciprocated, we begin to consider ourselves friends. At this point, nascent friendship, significant changes in how we communicate with one another occur. We augment the social stereotypes and standards that once regulated our interactions and begin working out our own rules. We may, for instance, opt to get together to play tennis every Thursday afternoon or have dinner together some Sundays. We select the activities we will do together, and our interactions become more regularized or patterned.

## Stabilized Friendship

Once it is apparent that friendship will continue, and we can count on each other to be there, we enter into a stage of stabilized friendship. We trust each other and respond to each other in ways that confirm our trustworthiness. We interact more frequently and across a greater number of settings. We give each other emotional support, share more intimate information, and reveal fears or vulnerabilities we keep secret from most others.

## Waning Friendship

Friendships don't maintain themselves. We need to work at them. Once we take a friendship for granted, or make less of a personal effort or investment to keep it going, we may find ourselves in the waning friendship stage. Why do once good friends drift apart? Sometimes, life circumstances, including interests, careers, or personal obligations, change. Such changes can alter friendship needs. In other cases, trust is violated or unspoken rules are broken, causing individuals to become less willing to disclose or to be more protective of personal information. Such feelings may also arise because one person habitually misbehaves. Sometimes friendships wane because people simply tire of each other. Once this happens, the friendship is likely to dissolve. Having run its course, it simply ends.[25]

But how do you end a friendship? How do you ultimately tell a once good friend that it's over? Some people just stop calling or are always too busy to get together, hoping their friend will eventually get the hint. Others fail to return texts. Facebook has normalized the practice of defriending, which allows you to remove a friend with the click of a mouse. Some endings leave lasting resentments, but other friendships terminate without ill will, leaving open the possibility that at some point in the future you just might "friend" one another again—if only on Facebook.[26]

# ROMANCE: COMING TOGETHER AND BREAKING APART

The love we feel for the person we have a **romantic relationship** with is different from our love for friends or family. Even though approximately 50 percent of all marriages in the United States end in divorce, when we enter into marriage, typically we expect it to be permanent, and that expectation of permanence, at least in part, distinguishes a romantic relationship from others.

## Love's Dimensions

Love has different dimensions. We can, for example, view it as passionate or as companionate. What's the difference? Passionate love is what we feel when we first fall in love; it signals our attraction to and focus on a single person. While some manage to sustain passionate love over a lifetime, it often decreases in intensity over time.[27] In contrast, companionate love increases over time. As a couple's feelings of trust and caring for one another grow, they engage themselves in one another's lives and mutually respond to one another's needs.

An alternative means of looking at types of love is attributed to sociologist John Alan Lee, who differentiated romantic relationships from nonromantic ones by describing them according to whether they are based primarily on *eros, ludis, storge, mania, pragma,* or *agape.*[28] The type of love experienced reveals the nature of the relationship shared. *Eros* (erotic love) is sexual love that brings couples together. *Ludis* is the game of love; partners seek affection and immediate gratification, but they don't see their relationship as lasting. They simply enjoy the idea of being in love. *Storge,* in contrast, is the kind of love we have for good friends and family members. It does not involve sex at all, though at one time or another, we may find ourselves feeling sexual attraction. *Mania* is more like obsessive love, with a partner experiencing frequent relationship highs and lows because of his or her unyielding need for attention and/or low self-esteem. *Pragma* has the same root as the word *pragmatic*; arranged marriages, for example, are often planned for pragmatic reasons. *Agape* love has a spiritual quality, often being described as a love that is pure. One person devotes himself or herself to another but expects nothing in return. A parent and a child are said to experience such love. Differentiating one type of love from another in this way makes love's many aspects clear.

## The Triangle of Love

What other characteristics differentiate romantic relationships? Researchers have concluded that the ingredients necessary for building a romantic love-based relationship are *commitment,* or an intention to remain in the relationship even if trouble occurs; *passion,* or intensely positive feelings of attraction that motivate each partner to want to be with the other person; and *intimacy,* or sustained feelings of closeness and connection.[29] According to Robert Sternberg's ==triangular theory of love==, varying combinations of intimacy, passion, and commitment create different types of love (see Figure 12.2).[30] Every love relationship, says Sternberg, has these three elements in various amounts. For some couples, intimacy dominates, with commitment and passion playing supporting roles. For others, little commitment to the relationship exists, but there is an abundance of passion and intimacy.

Sternberg asserts that intimacy, often the most central component within a love relationship, is the variable providing the foundation for love's development. It remains relatively stable over a relationship's course—or at least until the relationship partners no longer find the relationship satisfying and no longer feel emotionally close. Think of the warm feelings you get when hugging someone

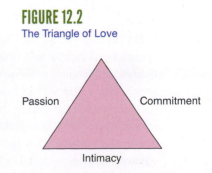

**FIGURE 12.2**
The Triangle of Love

you love. You feel close and connected. This is *manifest intimacy*. But we can also experience feelings of intimacy or connection that are not directly apparent to others; this is *latent intimacy*.

Passion, according to Sternberg, is love's "hot" component. Included in passion are sexual attraction and arousal, as well as motivation. Passion is the variable most important at the beginning of a love relationship, since it functions as an initial attractor. This does not mean that long-term relationships lack passion; rather, in developed relationships, passion tends to occur in "sparks and spurts" rather than at a sustained high level.

The third component in Sternberg's love triangle is the "cooler" variable of commitment. A decision to love someone requires a commitment to maintain and sustain that love. Because commitment is based on decision making, it is the most stable component in the triangle and is the strongest predictor of relational satisfaction. Although any one element can exist without the others, all three are necessary for a romantic relationship to exist.

## Love's Stages

Knapp and Vangelisti's 10-stage model of relationships suggests that we perceive our relationships, including our romantic ones, as escalating/intensifying, stabilizing, or deteriorating/atrophying over time as we grow closer and more intimate. We become comfortable with our relational culture—the rules or routines we have worked out for our relationship—or grow apart from each other. According to Knapp and Vangelisti, our relationships are in a constant state of flux: They either grow stronger or weaker with time. As they strengthen or weaken, they pass through some or all of the 10 relationship stages they identify in their model and that we can use to characterize the nature of a relationship at any particular moment in its evolution (see Figure 12.3).[31] As you read about these stages, consider how, without labeling it good or bad, you would describe a romantic relationship you are in currently.

**FIGURE 12.3**
Relationship Stages

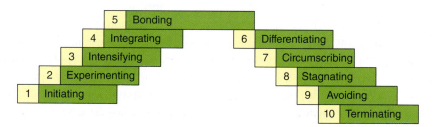

**Stage 1: Initiating.** During the initiating stage of a relationship, we ask ourselves whether someone is appealing enough for us to initiate interaction with him or her. If the answer is yes, we display our interest and attempt to show why this person would, in turn, enjoy interacting with us. In other words, we do what we can to make the person perceive us as likable and friendly.

Communication during this phase is typically brief and formularized or ritualistic. We greet one another with a handshake, engage in phatic communication—superficial, casual interaction designed simply to open the channel between us—and search for an appropriate conversation opener, often opting to talk about an insignificant topic such as the weather, just so that contact

Love relationships evolve. Typical romances today may involve such phases as "going out" when a teenager, "hooking up" or having a "friend with benefits" when a college student, seriously dating but delaying commitment in your 20s, and marrying or deciding not to somewhere around 30. Many people spend significant periods of their adult lives in committed relationships, but not necessarily married. Thus, we now also have different love relationship categories, such as the following:

iStock.com/TriggerPhoto

- Stay-over relationships: committed, monogamous partnerships, common among college students, that the parties find comfortable and convenient but do not entail a loss of independence

- Living apart together relationships: committed relationships in which the parties maintain separate residences, common among those who are divorced and don't want to uproot their children or themselves

Marriage is a public ritual that confirms a relationship's exclusiveness.

- Living together apart relationships: relationships in which the parties have children together and continue to cohabit even though their love connection is over, so that they can share parenting responsibilities and resources.[37]

Whatever the nature or status of a love relationship, romantic attraction probably played a role initially. We had to decide whether to pursue a relationship and came to a preliminary conclusion that there was something about the other person that attracted us.

## ANALYZE THIS: STATUS UPDATES

When Facebook founder Mark Zuckerberg and his longtime girlfriend, Priscilla Chan, married, they both updated their relationship status on Facebook to "married," announcing their union by making it "Facebook official." Many responded with surprise, since the couple had succeeded in keeping their plans a secret.

1. Have you used Facebook to announce similar status changes? If so, how have others responded to your status alterations?

2. What in your mind justifies a status change?

3. Were you ever taken aback by a status change announced by a friend or romantic partner? How did you respond?

# HOW CULTURE, GENDER, AND THE MEDIA AND TECHNOLOGY INFLUENCE OUR RELATIONSHIPS

Culture, gender, and the media and technology have roles to play in how and with whom we form relationships.

## CULTURE'S EFFECTS

Although we all have a need to make contact and connect with others, culture leads us to do these things in different ways. Culture guides us in deciding whether to speak to strangers and in understanding relationship customs and practices globally. For example, how we define who is a "stranger"

Culture guides us in understanding relationship customs and practices.

reveals some of the challenges we face in interacting with people from diverse cultures. In cultures that promote individualistic values, the concept of the stranger is easier to penetrate than it is in cultures that promote collectivistic values. Collectivistic culture members create strong in-group bonds to separate insiders from outsiders. For example, in Greek the word for *stranger* literally means "non-Greek"; in Korea, strangers are seen as "nonpersons."[38]

In most cultures, only loose connections exist between acquaintances. Because acquaintances do not usually confide in one another, they limit their conversations to ritualistic small talk. Even the topics of small talk may be culturally regulated. For example, although it may be perfectly accept-

able in the United States to inquire about another's spouse, in some Arab countries, it may be seen as a breach of etiquette to ask a male acquaintance about his wife.[39] Intercultural conceptions of friendship may also vary. In some countries, such as Thailand, a person is accepted completely as a friend or not at all, so if you disapprove of any aspect of another's behavior, that person cannot be your friend.[40] In contrast, many Americans simply choose not to discuss those aspects of their friends to which they take exception or with which they disagree, such as their political or religious beliefs.

Cultural expectations for friendships differ in other ways too. Whereas cultures with individualistic orientations refer to friends as "friends," cultures with collectivistic orientations refer to friends with labels that individualistic cultures typically reserve for family members: brother, sister, or cousin. These labels suggest that the bonds of friendship are not transient, but lasting.

Cultural customs concerning romance and marriage also vary widely. For example, in countries such as India and Afghanistan, parents arrange the marriages of their children. As a result, dating prior to marriage in these countries is rare. The same is true in many Middle Eastern countries; in some, such as Iran, dating is even against the law. In Central and South America, most young people do not date until they are well into their teens, and in Japan and Korea, significant dating first begins during college. In many European countries, dating is a group activity rather than a couples' activity.[41]

Jupiterimages/Photos.com/Thinkstock

Because culture affects communication, it also affects our responses to those whose cultures differ from ours. By answering the following questions, you can remove barriers and improve your ability to communicate with others from different cultures.

### Does the Culture Place More Stress on Individuals or on Social Relationships?

While some cultures emphasize social relationships, others stress individualism. To determine what your culture has taught you, ask yourself if you give preference to your own private interests or the interests of the group when interacting. According to researchers, individualism lies at the very heart of American culture, while for members of other cultural groups, such as those from East Asian countries, the social relationship is paramount.[42]

### Does the Culture Promote Development of Short- or Long-Term Relationships?

While Americans may find it easy to drop in and out of relationships and organizations, members of East Asian cultures believe that relationships ought to last and that individuals are obligated to show loyalty to others. Because of this perspective, in these cultures business and personal relationships are mixed together, last longer, and are based on mutual expectations of reciprocity and congeniality. Thus, whereas Americans typically want to get right down to business, individuals from East Asian countries feel more comfortable if their business interactions occur on a more personal level, believing that for an effective business relationship to develop, a warm personal relationship must first exist.

### Does the Culture Value Results or the Natural Relationship Process?

Americans are highly results oriented, often wanting instant answers—even from a relationship. Compared with individuals from other cultures, they are more spontaneous in their interactions and more apt to reveal themselves to others. In contrast, in most Asian countries, people tend to be less revealing and more willing to devote significantly longer periods to getting to know each other.

## GENDER AND RELATIONSHIP DEVELOPMENT

Lessons we've internalized about gender influence the roles we play in our relationships and the rules or behavioral norms that guide our interactions.

We learn to perform roles. We are not born knowing how to enact them. Our learning, however, starts early—virtually as soon as we are born. For example, studies reveal that nurses in U.S. hospital nurseries handle boy and girl babies differently, raising the pitch of their voices as much as a third higher when talking to girls and using larger gestures when interacting with boys.[43] In part because of the ways many in U.S. society interact, we develop different expectations for men and women. As a result, we may expect them to behave differently, dress differently, play differently, and perform different jobs. On the other hand, people who grow up in families that treat boys and girls as equals are likely to develop or acquire views of their prospective roles that differ from the long-held traditional expectations.

In general, U.S. culture has taught that men are to perform **instrumental roles** and women are to perform **expressive roles**. The expectation is for men to focus on getting things done and for women to focus on helping, supporting, nurturing, and being responsive to others' needs. Consequently, male communication is primarily task oriented and female communication is primarily relationship oriented.

Over time, it has become increasingly acceptable for men and women to be more **androgynous** in their roles—that is, to share both instrumental and expressive roles. As perceptions of men and women have changed, so have expectations for them. When we view male and female roles as androgynous, we make it feasible for men and women to be behaviorally flexible and to display an array of what were once more limited, sex-typed characteristics. Thus, men can be both nurturing and competitive, and females can be both assertive and submissive.

As Rachel Bertsche, author of *MWF Seeking BFF: My Yearlong Search for a New Best Friend,* observes, friendship is terribly important in our lives.[44] Yet, too often it becomes a luxury, something we try to fit in after career and family. When compared with the friendships of men, women's friendships are often de-emphasized by the media, which often trivialize them while treating men's friendships with dignity and respect. Friends, however, are of vital importance to the members of both sexes, though not for the same reasons. Female friendships tend to be expressive, centering on sharing disclosures and developing loyalty and trust, so women choose friends they can confide in.[45] Women focus on relational matters and are sensitive to what happens to their friends. Men, in contrast, have "chumships."[46] Instead of basing their friendships around talk, men tend to befriend others with whom they share hobbies, play sports, and so forth. Whereas women's friendships emphasize face-to-face interaction, those shared by men emphasize side-to-side interaction. On the other hand, male-female friendships tend to be more active and less intense than female friendships and more emotionally fulfilling and expressive than male friendships.

What about dating? Men are less likely to want to date a woman who's more ambitious or intelligent than themselves. Women, in comparison, penalize neither intelligence nor ambitiousness in men.[47] When women and men date, the women typically want to talk more than the men. Men tend to approach conversation functionally, with the goal of sharing information or solving problems, whereas women are more likely to view conversation as an ingredient essential to the relationship's development. Thus, it is often the woman who keeps the conversation going. Linguistic theorist Deborah Tannen explains that women use "rapport talk" while men use "report talk": Women talk to establish and negotiate relationships; men talk to preserve independence and negotiate status.[48] When selecting a romantic relationship partner, American men tend to look for stereotypically feminine women (women who are attractive, slim, and sexy), and women are likely to look for men with stereotypically masculine qualities (men who are ambitious, energetic, and strong).[49] A quarter century ago, many American women reported that they expected their spouses to be their superiors in intelligence, ability, education, and job success.[50] Currently men and women alike put emphasis on their partner's economic and social status.[51]

## MEDIA, TECHNOLOGY, AND SOCIAL WORLDS

While the media and technology reflect existing societal expectations, we also use the portrayals and communication examples they feature as models of what to do or not do when building, maintaining, and ending relationships of our own.

### Media Portrayals of Friendship and Romance

Media portrayals mimic cultural expectations for gender. As such, they reinforce how we perceive men and women and shape our views of effective communication and relationships.

Until recently, media offerings largely featured dependent women and independent men, suggesting that incompetent women need to rely on men to succeed, that men are the breadwinners and women the caregivers, and that men are the aggressors and women the victims.[52] These depictions reinforced the public's consciousness, causing many of us to limit our perceptions of ourselves and perpetuating unrealistic images of what we should be like and how we should interact when in one another's company. For example, a prominent stereotype is the macho man, who demonstrates his manliness by announcing his toughness or by degrading women.[53]

When it comes to portrayals of friendships, the *Housewives* series have depicted female friendships negatively by highlighting the participants' rude, nasty, and backbiting behavior. Negative images of male friendships also abound, however, as men sharing friendships frequently are depicted in media offerings as slovenly, inebriated, and self-centered. And when the media focus on cross-sex friendships, the male and the female often end up in bed. On the other hand, *I am Jazz*, a reality show that follows the life of a transgender teen, lets us see friends try to protect her from being bullied.

## Technology: Meeting in Cyberspace

Technology affects both communication and relationships. The media scholar Neil Postman believed us to be living in a **technopoly**, a society in which all forms of cultural life (including relationships) are subordinate to technology.[54] Do you agree?

The Internet has brought a plethora of social networks into our lives. Developing friendships and romantic relationships online is now commonplace. For centuries, the elite used paintings of themselves to represent their status and present themselves as they wished to be seen. Now we all have the ability to present digital portraits of ourselves and share them with the world. We use these digital representations to connect with others—to "friend" them—on Facebook and other sites. In effect, we sell ourselves and promote our lifestyles. Some view the number of social network friends attracted (even if a majority of them are weak ties) as a status enhancer.[55] Being well liked becomes itself a preoccupation. Indeed, a large number of us keep careful count of online friends and Twitter followers, correlating our worth with their numbers.[56]

Interestingly, women update their status on Facebook more frequently than men do, making an average of 21 updates per week, while men average six. Women also comment more frequently on others' updates. Even in the online world, women take charge of social relationships.[57]

It's not just about friends, however. While people still use singles bars, parties, cruises, and ads to meet potential romantic partners, the twenty-first century finds us increasingly relying on sites such as Match.com and OkCupid for romantic relationship building. We now shop for a love connection as we shop for everything else. While women are more likely than men to form personal relationships online, both participate in the digital domain to form friendships and romantic

The media often feature individuals in stereotypical relationships.

More and more friendships and romantic relationships are developing online.

relationships, with increasing numbers of these transferring into physical space. A little over a decade ago, some 21 percent of heterosexual couples and 61 percent of same-sex couples in the United States met online.[58] In 2017, some 70 percent of gay relationships started online, and more than one-third of marriages began there.

According to researchers, however, these websites do not actually improve dating outcomes. The partner choices made by members are based on more than personality similarities. Instead, they often are comprised of objectifications or over-interpretations of a potential partner's social clues. Ultimately, this can lead to disappointment should the parties meet. At least in part, this is attributed to the development of a two- versus a three-dimensional impression of a potential partner, and as a result, a rational decision cannot necessarily be made.[59]

Now, even a cell phone can function as a matchmaker for love and friendship connections. Looking for love nearby is a common practice, and growing numbers of people now use cell phone applications to make instant dates based on proximity.[60] Users post their profiles (sometimes only a picture) and scan lists of others who have done the same. They exchange messages, and if a mutual interest surfaces, they can decide to meet. These apps offer opportunities for quick interaction (an advantage for the time-challenged). When using an app like Tinder, in contrast, we expose ourselves to an expanded pool of partner possibilities. Then we simply can swipe right (if a photo of someone appeals to us) or left (if it doesn't) to indicate whether we would like to begin a relationship with a person. We can decide later if we want to turn it into a real-life relationship. Thus, digital media make it easier for us both to flirt and to follow up on our initial flirtations by messaging interest.[61]

Why has online socializing taken off? Unlike our more traditionally established relationships, relationships that are built online promote intimacy through the sharing of more personal mutual disclosures. According to communication researcher Joseph Walther, the online environment encourages interaction to become *hyperpersonal*, meaning in cyberspace we share information we might not when face-to-face. Perhaps this is because we feel less inhibited online and because we have not yet interacted with them in person, we view our partners more positively, a perception that accelerates our feelings of closeness.[62] In addition, online interactions help us maintain connections. "Away messages," posts on Facebook, and numerous texts let our friends and significant others know what we are up to and vice versa. Researchers believe that those who use these means of communication to stay connected with others do so because they do not want to be out of the loop. They also employ them to control others' impressions of them. For example, you can post a "social butterfly"-type message even if you are home watching a Netflix movie. Or you can make a boyfriend or girlfriend think you're out with someone else when you're not. The best result is to return to a screen full of messages sent in response to your posts or texts. The worst is to return to an empty screen. Thus, responses to posts can serve as a litmus test of social capital.[63]

Thus, online social networks both facilitate and complicate relationship building. While they encourage mutual disclosures that help build intimacy, they also give users more control over how others perceive them than they otherwise would be able to exert. By limiting face-to-face interaction, they may be impeding our ability to "think on our feet." We may be skilled at "conversing" with our fingertips, but this may not be a skill that carries over into our face-to-face encounters.

# GAINING COMMUNICATION COMPETENCE: GUIDELINES FOR SKILLFULLY NAVIGATING THE RELATIONSHIP SPECTRUM

Relationships are complex. The more we can learn about how we form them and why they do or don't work, the better able we will be to navigate their complexities. What can we do to improve our relationships?

## ACKNOWLEDGE THAT RELATIONSHIPS DON'T JUST HAPPEN

Working to improve relationships is a lifelong endeavor. We can work to develop meaningful relationships, or we can let them falter or wither away. By focusing on the nature of relationships and why we have them in the first place, we are able to discover what we will miss when one goes awry.

## OWN YOUR NEED FOR OTHERS

What happens to those who feel cut off from others? Feelings of isolation increase the risk of death.[64] Relationships combat loneliness and increase feelings of belonging. When they are lacking, we are often left with a sense of doom.

## UNDERSTAND THE NATURE OF FRIENDSHIP AND ROMANTIC RELATIONSHIPS

People in healthy relationships enjoy the following:

- They look forward to being together because they enjoy each other's company.

- They accept each other as they are, are free to be themselves, and make few, if any, demands on the other person to change.

- They trust each other and are willing to put themselves in the hands of the other, because each assumes that the other will act in his or her best interest.

- They share a high level of commitment and are willing to help and support each other.

- They respect each other.

- They are willing to share personal information and engage in high levels of self-disclosure. As a result, they are better able to predict each other's actions.

## MEET THE CHALLENGES MEDIA AND TECHNOLOGY POSE

Our relational repertoire grows larger as the media and technological innovations make new ways of interacting possible. How we develop and grow future relationships may be different from how we grew and nurtured them in the past. We may become attracted to people in different ways and for different reasons. Originating, pacing, or repairing a relationship begun on the Internet may require different skills than beginning, maintaining, or reinvigorating one established face-to-face. We need to remain open to using both traditional and new approaches to building and sustaining meaningful relationships.

## CONNECT THE CASE

# The Case of the Job Promotion

Susan and Bob are married and have two children. To ensure the lifestyle they want for their family, both Susan and Bob work more than 40 hours per week. Though Bob tries to do his share of household chores, Susan somehow ends up more exhausted at week's end.

Susan figures out how to get the kids to and from soccer and softball practice, where they go after school, and how they spend their time on weekends. That seems fair to Bob, since he makes more money than Susan, or, as he puts it, "brings home the lion's share of the bacon," so they can afford to take great family vacations, buy designer clothes, and eat in fine restaurants.

Given Bob's position, Susan wonders how he will handle the latest news about her career.

Susan had nearly floated out of the CEO's office. Not only had she been promoted, but she had also been given a substantial salary increase—she would now be making more money than her husband. Yet the excitement and pride she felt was tinged with concern and uncertainty because she wasn't sure how Bob would react to the news. She sat down at her desk, took a deep breath, took out her cell, and called Bob at his office. She told herself he should be pleased, since now they would have even more money to spend on those extras that help make their lives easier. Bob answered her call: "Hi, Susan. What's up?"

### Consider these questions:

1. If you were Susan, how would you reveal the good news to Bob? What would you say?

2. How do you imagine Bob will respond to Susan's news?

3. In what ways, or to what extent, do you think Susan's promotion and new salary will change Susan and Bob's relationship?

# REVIEW THIS

## CHAPTER SUMMARY

1. **Discuss the functions relationships serve.** ☐

Relationships help preserve our happiness and health; prevent our isolation; meet our needs for inclusion, control, and affection; offer a point of reference for checking if our behavior and emotional responses are culturally acceptable; serve as a communication pipeline; and maintain our sense of worth.

. . . . . . . . . . . . . . . . . . . . . . . . . . . . . . . .

2. **Identify characteristics distinguishing one relationship from another.** ☐

We can compare and contrast relationships based on their duration, the frequency of interpersonal contacts, how much people reveal to each other, the kind of support they offer one another, the variability of their interactions, and their goals.

. . . . . . . . . . . . . . . . . . . . . . . . . . . . . . . .

3. **Describe factors influencing interpersonal attraction.** ☐

The primary motive for initiating a relationship is attraction. Among the variables influencing the amount of attraction are physical attractiveness, social attractiveness, task attractiveness, proximity, reinforcement, similarity, and complementarity.

. . . . . . . . . . . . . . . . . . . . . . . . . . . . . . . .

4. **Explain the relationship spectrum using Rawlins's friendship model, Sternberg's triangle of love, and Knapp and Vangelisti's relationship model to distinguish among acquaintanceships, friendships, and romantic relationships.** ☐

The stages of Rawlins's 6-stage model of friendship are role-limited interaction, friendly relations, moving toward friendship, nascent friendship, stabilized friendship, and waning friendship. Sternberg's triangle of love identifies commitment, passion, and intimacy as necessary components in a romantic relationship. Knapp and Vangelisti identify the following relationship stages: initiating, experimenting, intensifying, integrating, bonding, differentiating, circumscribing, stagnating, avoiding, and terminating. Not every relationship goes through all 10 stages. Relationships may progress, retreat, advance again, and/or deteriorate. Relationship stabilization occurs at the level both parties agree is satisfying and meets their needs.

. . . . . . . . . . . . . . . . . . . . . . . . . . . . . . . .

5. **Identify how culture, gender, the media, and technology impact the nature of our relationships.** ☐

Culture guides us in understanding relationship customs and practices globally. Whether a culture promotes individualism or collectivism, developing short- or long-term relations, and results or the natural relational process, affects attitudes toward friendship, romance, and marriage.

Gender influences relationship roles and rules as well as the expectations developed for males and females. Societal norms can lead men to perform more instrumental roles and women to perform roles that are more expressive. As perceptions of men and women change, androgyny has become more accepted.

The media and technology tend to reinforce cultural and gender expectations, with stereotypical portrayals abounding. While shaping our image of an effective relationship, they also help broaden our concept of acceptable means of interacting.

6. **Identify specific techniques that can facilitate our mastery of relationship dynamics.** ☐

Once we acknowledge that relationships don't just happen, recognize our need for others, understand the nature of friendship, and display the ability to meet the challenges the media and emerging technologies pose, we become better able to demonstrate mastery of relationship dynamics.

## CHECK YOUR UNDERSTANDING

1. Can you list the functions that relationships fulfill in your life? (See pages 328–333.)

2. Can you use Rawlins's friendship model and Sternberg's triangle of love to summarize the similarities and differences between a relationship based on friendship and one based on love? If you were creating a list of rules to follow for friendship and romance, what rules would be on your list and why? (See pages 336–340.)

3. Can you create a 10-stage scenario to illustrate Knapp and Vangelisti's relationship model in action? (See pages 340–345.)

4. Can you explain which attraction factors are important to you and why? (See pages 345–349.)

5. Can you give examples of how your gender and/or culture or the media and technology you prefer have influenced the course of a relationship? (See pages 350–356.)

## KEY TERMS

Affection need  335

Androgynous  354

Control need  334

Expressive roles  353

Fundamental interpersonal relations orientation  334

Inclusion need  334

Instrumental roles  353

Intimacy  343

Knapp and Vangelisti's 10-stage model of relationships  348

Maslow's needs hierarchy  335

Matching hypothesis  342

Relational culture  348

Relationships  332

Romantic relationship  346

Technopoly  355

Triangular theory of love  347

Get the tools you need to sharpen your study skills. **SAGE edge** offers a robust online environment featuring an impressive array of free tools and resources. Access practice quizzes, eFlashcards, video, and multimedia at **edge.sagepub.com/gambleicp**.

13

# Intimacy and Distance in Relationships

## Learning Objectives

### AFTER COMPLETING THIS CHAPTER, YOU SHOULD BE ABLE TO

1. Define self-disclosure and intimacy, using social penetration theory to describe a relationship's breadth and depth and the Johari window to explore how self-awareness and self-disclosure affect relationships

2. Define and explain the effects of relational dialectics

3. Discuss factors influencing relationship maintenance

4. Discuss whether and how to repair a relationship

5. Define and explain toxic communication, describing the four stages in an abusive relationship

6. Explain the grief cycle, describing what occurs when a relationship ends with a loved one's death

7. Identify how culture, gender, and media and technology influence notions of intimacy and disclosure

8. Discuss strategies for handling closeness and distance in relationships more effectively

> I believe we're all secretly happy we can't figure our relationships out. It keeps our minds working.
>
> —Jerry Seinfeld

Through the ups and downs of our relationships, how and what we communicate about ourselves and our relational goals either can help bring us closer together, enable us to maintain a relational steady state, or create relationship obstacles—some of which may be insurmountable. Some of us are happy and satisfied with our relationships, and some of us are not. Some of us are in healthy and fulfilling relationships, while others of us are in poor relationships beset with problems and dangers. What happens should we want to deepen a friendship, develop a romance, extricate ourselves from a relationship we no longer find satisfying, or terminate a relationship we believe to be dysfunctional? What happens, for example, should one partner begin to obsess over the other, turning what once appeared to be a healthy relationship into an unhealthy one? ■

# WHAT DO YOU KNOW?

Before continuing your reading of this chapter, which of the following five statements do you believe to be true, and which do you believe to be false?

1.  Self-disclosure involves willingly revealing private information about ourselves to another person.      T     F

2.  Self-disclosure carries no risks.      T     F

3.  Intimacy and self-disclosure are positively related.      T     F

4.  When disclosures occur too early in a relationship, the person being confided in is likely to feel uncomfortable.      T     F

5.  While technologically equipped to handle a long-distance relationship, we may not be able to meet the emotional challenges such a relationship presents.      T     F

Read the chapter to discover if you're right or if you've made any erroneous assumptions.

ANSWERS: 1. T; 2. F; 3. T; 4. T; 5. T

In Chapter 12, we looked at different kinds of interpersonal relationships. In this chapter, we delve into those qualities that distinguish close and satisfying interpersonal relationships from those that are dysfunctional. When they are very good, close relationships help make us healthier and extend our lives, but when they are very bad, they may threaten both our health and our happiness.

# SELF-DISCLOSURE AND INTIMACY

In the age of social networking, managing how much other people know about you isn't easy. When and with whom are you most comfortable talking about yourself? Under what conditions and to whom do you reveal information about you that you normally keep to yourself?

When we self-disclose, we willingly reveal otherwise private information about ourselves to another person. By definition, messages of **self-disclosure** generally include personal facts about us that someone would be unlikely to discover on his or her own. Among Westerners, self-disclosure is a sign of closeness.[1] As we disclose more about ourselves, our communication becomes more intimate; similarly, when we refrain from self-disclosing or backtrack in revealing personal information, our communication becomes less intimate and more impersonal.

Sometimes we use self-disclosure as a tool to get to know others.[2] People skilled in establishing connections offer self-disclosures that make it easier for a partner to reciprocate. They know that there are different depths of information and that the depth of disclosures should correlate with the appropriate relationship stage.[3]

## THE NORM OF RECIPROCITY

Self-disclosure carries risk. By revealing our likes, dislikes, feelings, fears, strengths, and weaknesses, we increase our vulnerability, risking rejection and criticism. For that reason, we typically first reveal small amounts of low-risk information. For example, "I love the color blue because it reminds me of my grandmother." We save more risky disclosures, such as "I am an atheist" or "I don't ever want to get married or have kids," until we confirm that the other person is willing to match both the level and the nature of our disclosing. In other words, we act in accordance with the **norm of reciprocity**, the expectation that others will return our self-disclosures in kind.[4] When another person reveals the same kind of information as we have revealed, we feel safer, display a greater willingness to move self-disclosing to a deeper level, and, over time, become even more willing to relate increasingly intimate information.[5] In contrast, lack of such reciprocation indicates that the other person is not yet ready to openly disclose, that things need to go more slowly, or that our relationship may be one-sided and not likely to develop fully.

Highly intimate relationships have significant amounts of breadth and depth.

If we are careless and inadequately or inappropriately engage in self-disclosure, others may view us negatively. The satisfactory development of our relationships hinges on our appropriate use of self-disclosures, which typically occur incrementally during the course of a positive relationship.

Thus, self-disclosure and intimacy correlate positively in our relationships. Discovering another person's inner nature involves peeling back the series of layers that protect the individual's inner self. The more layers we peel back, the more is revealed about the person, and the closer we become.

## SOCIAL PENETRATION THEORY

We may judge a relationship's strength and health by assessing the breadth and depth of the information shared. **Relationship breadth** is related to the number of different topics we discuss with another. **Relationship depth**, in contrast, is reflected in how central the topics we discuss are to our self-concept, how much we reveal about ourselves, and how we feel about doing so. The more we reveal, the deeper others are able to penetrate into our core.

Social psychologists and communication practitioners use the model depicted in Figure 13.1 to describe how breadth and depth of communication relate. In the model, the circle represents

When disclosures occur too early in a relationship, the person being confided in is likely to feel uncomfortable.

the complete individual, composed of many different wedge-shaped aspects (e.g., religion, work, school, social life). The aspects are, of course, different for each of us. The concentric rings indicate the information a person reveals during conversation, with the outer circles representing casual conversations and the inner circles representing very intimate conversations. By noting which segments of the circle are active in a relationship, we can use this model to illustrate the relationship's intimacy level.

To understand how the model works, it is necessary to understand **social penetration theory**, first proposed in 1973 by psychologists Irwin Altman and Dalmas Taylor.[6] According to this theory, relationships typically begin with relatively narrow breadth, in which we discuss few topics with each other, and shallow depth, in which our conversations about these topics remain relatively superficial. We may, for example, talk about where we grew up, what we are majoring in, and the kind of job we would like to hold. We depict this type of relationship as shown on the left-hand side of Figure 13.2; it is a casual relationship.

However, over time, the amount of intimacy we share increases and the level of intensity we feel deepens. As a result, highly intimate relationships have significant amounts of breadth and depth; the range of topics increases along with the amount of information revealed about the self and feelings. We may share our political and religious beliefs, our fears, talents, and secret ambitions. Such changes are shown on the right-hand side of Figure 13.2.

The social penetration model is useful for a number of reasons. First, it provides us with a two-dimensional depiction of our relationships, showing both the range of topics we talk about and the extent to which we reveal ourselves through our conversations. Second, it enables us to understand why some of our relationships seem stronger than others. As a relationship increases in strength, we become more willing to discuss particular subjects and more comfortable revealing more about ourselves. We give that person greater access, allowing her or him to venture inward, toward our circle's center—or our core. This increases our relational bonds. We also share more about our thoughts and feelings on an array of topics, broadening our relationship. Thus, when your communication with someone lacks breadth or depth, although your relationship may be satisfying, it will likely remain quite casual. To change things, you would need to take steps to enhance the scope and nature of your interactions, perhaps by disclosing your personal values and sharing private feelings about yourself.

## FIGURE 13.1
Altman and Taylor's Social Penetration Model: Breadth and Depth in Relationships

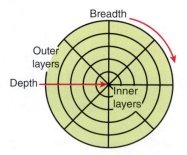

## FIGURE 13.2
Social Penetration in a Casual and an Intimate Relationship

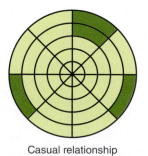

Casual relationship

Intimate relationship

At times, our wanting to get to know someone better causes us to discuss topics at a depth we would normally reserve for those with whom we share a core intimate relationship. When such disclosures or revelations occur prematurely—before both partners are ready—they may contribute to feelings of discomfort in one or both of us. We are likely to judge those who reveal too much to us too soon as indiscreet, untrustworthy, or just plain odd. We may even perceive those who try to get us to do more disclosing than we are ready for as pushy and overbearing.[7] On the other hand, when we are ready to deepen the relationship, increases in breadth and depth occur naturally and cause little, if any, relational discomfort.

Responses to the self-disclosure of positive and negative information are also time related. We tend to dislike those who disclose positive information about themselves in the very early stages of our relationship, especially if they are bragging. In contrast, the disclosure of negative information early in a relationship may be a positive, because, for some reason, we tend to be attracted to people who are willing to be honest and take responsibility for their actions.[8] Thus, if a person tells you that he failed a course but then recommitted to studying and passed the course with an A the second time he took it, your respect for this person might actually grow.

Of course, it is neither possible nor desirable to have close relationships with everyone; every relationship has an optimal level. Current relationships that are more distant, if given the right opportunities, may become deeper and more significant. We need time to absorb information about each other. The satisfactory development of a relationship—whether a friendship or a romance—depends on our being able to pace our self-disclosures properly.

Opening the relational self to others is a process, not a single action, with some of our disclosures revealing more than others. There is a difference between saying "I love my job" and "I'm in love with my boss." The latter is a more significant revelation than the former, especially if it was never shared with anyone before.

## TRY THIS

## Social Penetration—In Casual and Intimate Relationships

Think about the nature of your conversations in four different relationships:

**a.** A new friendship

**b.** A long-lasting, meaningful friendship

**c.** A current relationship with a parent or caregiver

**d.** A romantic relationship

For each relationship, label the pie-shaped wedges of the corresponding diagram below with the various aspects of your life. Then color in the segments that correspond to the level of self-disclosures you share with the person. The resulting

*(Continued)*

(Continued)

diagrams will illustrate graphically the amount of social penetration you have with each individual. How do the similarities and differences in your diagrams explain the different types of relationships? Explain.

FIGURE 13.3

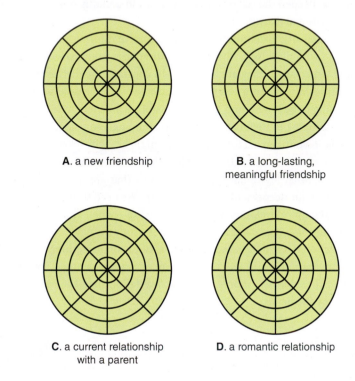

**A**. a new friendship

**B**. a long-lasting, meaningful friendship

**C**. a current relationship with a parent

**D**. a romantic relationship

FIGURE 13.4

ME

## THE JOHARI WINDOW AND SELF-DISCLOSURE

The **Johari window** is another model we can use to explore the roles that self-awareness and self-disclosure play in relationship building. "Johari" is a combination of the first names of the model's two creators: Joseph Luft and Harrington Ingham. The model uses a depiction of a window with four panes to help us explore how self-awareness and self-disclosure are relationship dependent.[9]

The entire window represents yourself (see Figure 13.4). It is divided by two axes, creating four panes.

By dividing the window in half with an axis, we create sections representing what we do and do not know about ourselves (see Figure 13.5). Then by dividing the window again with a horizontal axis, we are able to represent what another person does and does not know about us (see Figure 13.6). Finally, by putting the two axes together, we create four panes descriptive of a relationship (see Figure 13.7).

Pane 1, the *open* area, represents information about you that is known both to you and to another person. For example, you may have divulged your religious background, tastes in food, or career aspirations. As you and the other person grow closer, the size of the open area grows larger.

Pane 2, the *blind* area, signifies information about you that the other person is aware of but that you are not. For example, you may consider yourself to be very confident, while another sees that you are extremely insecure. We learn of information in our blind area primarily through feedback.

Pane 3, the *hidden* area, signifies information that you know about yourself but are unwilling to reveal. Items in the hidden area usually become known only as a result of self-disclosure. During this process information is moved from Pane 3 into Pane 1, the open area. Thus, as you share more about yourself with another, the size of Pane 3 shrinks, while the size of Pane 1 grows.

Pane 4, the *unknown* area, signifies information unknown to both you and the other person. Pane 4 exists because we constantly learn new things about ourselves. Over time, education or life experience brings some of this pane's mysteries into the open. For example, we may discover that we have a previously unrecognized fear, prejudice, or talent. The more introspective we are, the smaller the size of our unknown area.

Because our development of self-awareness depends on our being able to gain information about the self, we need to be open to learning more about our blind and unknown areas. By understanding how others see us, we can also develop greater self-insight. Perspective taking is key to establishing meaningful relationships.

Similar to the way we use the social penetration model to represent our relationships, we can use the Johari window to represent how we feel about another person and how comfortable we are revealing personal information to him or her. Consider the four relationships diagrammed in Figure 13.8. Window A shows a fairly impersonal relationship. The relatively large size of the unknown area and the relatively small size of the open area tell us that the people involved in this relationship are not particularly introspective, are apt to withdraw from contact with one another, and refrain from self-disclosing. Thus, in such a relationship, all you may know about the other person is his taste in music because he plays the songs he has downloaded loudly enough for you to hear.

**FIGURE 13.5**

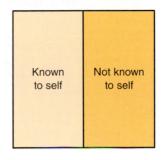

**FIGURE 13.6**

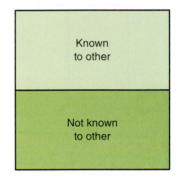

**FIGURE 13.7**
The Johari Window

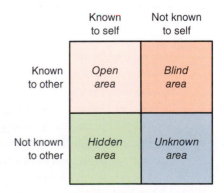

Source: Joseph Luft, *Group Processes: An Introduction to Group Dynamics,* 3rd ed., Palo Alto, CA: Mayfield, 1984, p. 60.

**FIGURE 13.8**
Relationship Windows

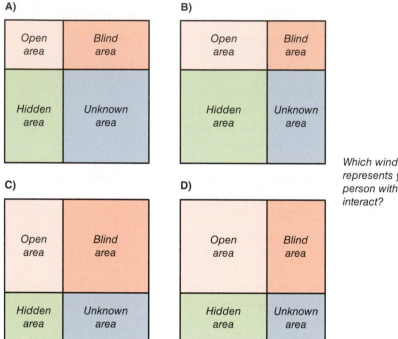

**A)**

| Open area | Blind area |
| Hidden area | Unknown area |

**B)**

| Open area | Blind area |
| Hidden area | Unknown area |

**C)**

| Open area | Blind area |
| Hidden area | Unknown area |

**D)**

| Open area | Blind area |
| Hidden area | Unknown area |

*Which window best represents you and another person with whom you interact?*

Window B shows a relationship with a dominant hidden area. This tells us that an individual sharing such a relationship fears exposure of some weakness and lacks trust in the other, believing that he or she might exploit any information revealed. The person is likely to feel it necessary to create and maintain a facade in an effort to pretend to be something he or she is not. Perhaps the person is contemplating suicide but communicates no clues.

Window C shows a relationship with a dominant blind area. When involved in such a relationship, we usually are unaware of how we are affecting or being perceived by the other because we are overly concerned with our own self-presentation. Maybe we don't think of ourselves as popular because we do not recognize how many friends we have or how many people care about us.

Window D depicts a relationship with a particularly large open area. Such a relationship usually involves significant self-disclosing and is characterized by candor and sensitivity to the needs and insights of the other. The individuals help each other to see into their blind areas, and they come to trust each other enough to share their most fundamental beliefs.

Thus, when we choose not to disclose information about ourselves to others, our windows have smaller open areas and larger hidden, blind, or unknown areas. In contrast, when we feel comfortable with another person and want to maintain or increase our feelings of closeness, our windows have larger open areas and smaller hidden, blind, and unknown areas.

# Window Gazing

Consider once again the four relationships you analyzed in the previous "Try This" box: a new friendship; a long-lasting, meaningful friendship; a current relationship with a parent or caregiver; and a romantic relationship. Then draw a Johari window to represent each of the four relationships.

Explain what the relative sizes of the panes in your windows tell you about yourself in relation to the four people you selected. Also consider the extent to which you think each person's own window would mirror the one you drew. Then ask each person to draw one. Compare and contrast each of their windows with yours. How do the similarities and differences help explain your relationship with each individual?

## SELF-DISCLOSURE: RATIONALES AND RISKS

As noted earlier in this chapter, self-disclosure and relationship success share a positive correlation. The higher the quality of our self-disclosures, the more satisfying we find the relationship. Feeling comfortable being honest and self-revealing are key to relationship health, whether we are talking about the health of a marriage or grandchild–grandparent interaction.[10] This does not mean, however, that we should self-disclose without considering the risks—remember our discussion of trust in Chapter 9.

To evaluate the level of self-disclosure appropriate for you in a given relationship, ask yourself these questions:

1. Do I want to take the relationship to a deeper level?
2. Do I feel comfortable and safe doing so?
3. Is the disclosing I intend to do appropriate and relevant?
4. Will my partner reciprocate?
5. Will the disclosure have a positive impact on our relationship?

If you cannot answer all five of these questions with a yes, then it may not be the right time for you to self-disclose, or your relationship partner might not be the right person with whom you should share more information about yourself.

Disclosing personal information always carries some risk—both for you and for the other person. The other person may reject you or form a negative impression of you because of what you reveal. In addition, your disclosure may communicate a previously unknown weakness, which may leave you with less control over the relationship. While what you disclose may help you feel more honest and forthcoming, the truth you reveal may hurt your partner or be more than he or she wishes to know.

On the other hand, self-disclosing can bring benefits and strengthen a relationship. Of course, developing a mutually satisfying relationship depends on more than reciprocal self-disclosing. Relationships worth having are going to evolve, and, as they do we need to respond to the changes.

# USING RELATIONAL DIALECTICS THEORY TO UNDERSTAND RELATIONSHIPS

As some relational forces pull us toward intimacy, opposing forces may pull us in the opposite direction. The road to a happy relationship is not always smooth. Partners do not necessarily want the same things from their relationship at the same time. Developed by communication theorist Leslie Baxter, **relational dialectics theory** explains the ups and downs and pushes and pulls that dynamic, healthy relationships experience.

While some models portray relationships developing in stages—recall both Knapp and Vangelisti's 10-stage model of relationships and Rawlins's 6-stage model of friendship discussed in Chapter 12—others suggest that rather than proceeding through set stages, a relationship evolves and changes over time as the parties sharing it repeatedly reevaluate and redefine their goals and needs while trying to manage the relationship's course. Since a relationship's context is ever changing, relational partners need to resolve a series of dialectical tensions—the conflicts created when the goals and expectations of one partner clash with the goals and expectations of the other.

Dialectical tensions may occur in any interpersonal relationship in any context. According to Baxter, relationships experience both internal and external tensions. Internal tensions include how the partners communicate with each other, while external tensions occur between the partners and the rest of society. Among the dialectical forces making relationship maintenance challenging are the push and pull partners feel toward integration versus separation, stability versus change, and expression versus privacy.[11]

## INTEGRATION–SEPARATION

The dialectic of integration–separation focuses on the tension between the desire to be socially integrated and the desire to be self-sufficient. From an internal perspective, a person's desire for connection clashes with the need for autonomy. For example, we want to be connected to our partner but independent of him or her too. If you have ever felt smothered by a partner in a relationship, you were likely experiencing a need for more autonomy. On the other hand, if you have ever felt as if your partner was ignoring you, you were probably expressing your desire for greater connection.

Externally, we express this pull–push dialectic by wanting to introduce our partner to others and at the same time wanting to keep him or her to ourselves—an inclusion-seclusion tension.

## STABILITY–CHANGE

Do you like to get comfortable in a relationship, or do you enjoy change? The internal manifestation of the stability–change dialectic is a tension between desiring consistency in a relationship and desiring novelty. For any relationship to last, each partner needs to be able to count on the other to perform certain relational roles. In other words, our lives need to have some routines, or we experience chaos. When our lives become nothing but routine, and we feel we know everything about the other person, however, life becomes stale, and we find ourselves longing for excitement and something different. But when relationships are characterized by too much novelty or surprise, we may feel overwhelmed by our lack of control.

Externally, the stability–change dialectic manifests itself as tension between a desire to have a conventional relationship that conforms to social norms and a desire to demonstrate the uniqueness in our relationship.[12]

## EXPRESSION–PRIVACY

Do you disclose or keep things to yourself? The internal tension between openness and privacy determines how much partners reveal to one another.[13] The push-pull here is between wanting to get closer by revealing thoughts and feelings and wanting to protect ourselves from criticism by withholding personal information that could increase vulnerability.

Externally, this dialectic manifests itself in how much we choose to reveal about our relationship versus how much we conceal. What do you

How much newness and novelty do you desire in your relationship?

tell your best friend about a dysfunctional romantic relationship? While we may want to reveal a relationship, we may think it best to conceal it from public scrutiny, fearing what could happen if others intervene. Unfortunately, such fears can allow an abusive relationship to continue.[14]

## WORKING THROUGH DIALECTICAL TENSIONS

Which of the preceding relational dialectics cause you the most problems? If you are like many partners, the dialectic producing the most tension in your close relationships is that of autonomy–connection, followed in descending order by predictability–novelty, inclusion–seclusion, openness–closeness, conventionality–uniqueness, and revelation–concealment.[15] Some researchers support the preeminence of autonomy–connection but believe that the openness–closeness dialectic also significantly influences relational progress or deterioration.[16]

The real challenge lies in managing the problems created by the contradictory pushes and pulls. Researchers have identified a number of ways of handling these dialectical tensions practically.[17] Among them are denial, disorientation, spiraling alternation, segmentation, balance, integration, recalibration, and reaffirmation.

When you practice *denial*, you respond to one pole of a dialectical challenge, while ignoring the other. For example, when caught between conflicting desires for autonomy and connection, you might opt for connection only, choosing to spend all your time with your partner. You satisfy one need, while denying the other.

When you practice *disorientation*, you feel overwhelmed and opt to give in to feelings of helplessness. This response is nonfunctional, because all dialogue between you and your partner stops as you retreat into yourself.

The response of *spiraling alternation* finds you caught in a repetitive cycle of alternating tensions, causing you to move repeatedly from one side of the dialectic to the other. You might choose to draw close emotionally, but then argue that you need more space, only to draw close once more.

When you engage in *segmentation*, you and your partner isolate different relationship aspects and deal with them in separate situations of relational life. For example, you may choose to share some activities but have independent interests in other life spheres. You might emphasize different sides of the dialectic depending on the topic being discussed or the context in which you find yourselves. For example, you might be open to discussing everything except politics or religion.

## TRY THIS

### Try to See It My Way

The prevalence of popular expressions reflecting relational dialectics in daily life is testimony to their importance. Identify some adages—such as "I need my space" or "Out of sight, out of mind"—that reflect or allude to the pull–push nature of relational dialectics.

*Balance* is another compromise approach in which both partners see dialectical tension poles as legitimate and attempt to deal with their opposing needs by moderating their response. By engaging both sides of the dialectic—choosing to be moderately open or moderately connected, you strive to reach a midpoint that tips in neither direction.

*Integration* finds you responding to opposing forces without denying or diluting them. You might, for example, relish certainty but embrace its opposite by doing something that you have never done before on weekends.

When you *recalibrate* a relational tension, you reframe it. Though this tactic does not ensure a solution to the tensions, it does allow partners to redefine the nature of the challenge they face so that it is not perceived as a permanent oppositional pull or contradiction.

Finally, *reaffirmation* involves the realization by both partners that dialectical tensions will persist in relationships if only because relationships are rich and complex. Working through tensions becomes a promise of what the relationship can accomplish rather than a threat to its survival. We discuss relationship maintenance in greater depth in the next section.

# FOCUSING ON RELATIONSHIP MAINTENANCE

Though we may find the relationships we share satisfying and mutually rewarding, we still have to commit to working to maintain each one—that is, we need to engage in **relationship maintenance**. Should we grow lazy or careless, expecting a relationship to take care of itself, the relationship could end up suffering from a lack of nourishment and waste away.[18]

According to researchers Kathryn Dindia and Leslie Baxter, we need to use the following strategies to maintain a relationship's health:

- We need to take time to talk to one another and share our feelings and concerns in an open and honest manner.

- We need to talk about *how* we talk to each other—that is, engage in *metacommunication* (as discussed in Chapter 6).

- We need to rely on prosocial approaches, including showing that we affirm, support, and value our partner, being cheerful in each other's presence, and refraining from criticizing each other.

- We need to celebrate the relationship itself by engaging in activities that mark the relationship's very existence and confirm its importance.

- We need to have fun simply spending time together.[19]

To want to invest in and work at maintaining their relationship, partners need to feel treated fairly. According to equity theory, each partner needs to feel that both are equally committed to preserving the relationship, that neither is taking advantage of the other, and that the resources are being shared equitably. If one party in a relationship is effectively in charge of relationship maintenance, that does not bode well for the relationship's future. When one party demonstrates concern about the relationship and seeks to adapt, but the other fails to do so, the relationship could be in danger.

Relationships take work to maintain.

As a relationship's strength grows, the partners become more secure and feel less pressure to reciprocate every relationship contribution equally or quickly. Instead of focusing on the short-term relationship balance sheet, they focus on the long-term future, and thus they feel confident enough to postpone the personal rewards they expect their connection to each other to deliver. This, however, does not mean that the fairness quotient of the relationship can stay unbalanced too long without causing the partners to suggest changing the state of equity. By periodically assessing our relationship's equity and quality, we demonstrate our interest in its general state or climate, not merely in what we are currently gaining or losing by maintaining it.[20]

## TRY THIS

### What's Fair?

To evaluate a relationship, we may try to assess whether it is based on fairness or is one-sided.

Consider a relationship you are currently in and one that has terminated. Compare and contrast them based on the extent to which you and your current and former partner do or did each of the following:

*(Continued)*

1. Experience(d) feelings of being let down

2. Feel/felt rewarded

3. Share(d) resources

4. Feel/felt pressured to reciprocate the other's good deeds

5. Believe(d) the relationship survived only because of one person's efforts

6. Handle(d) and resolve(d) relational problems and conflicts fairly

Based on your responses, how important would you say fairness is to you in maintaining a satisfying relationship?

In the relationships that have the healthiest climates and make us feel the happiest, most rewarded, and most secure, we tend to perceive ourselves as investing equally in the relationship's well-being and its future. In contrast, when we believe we are the one investing more in the relationship, we tend to become resentful and might even conclude we are being "used." At the same time, when our partner makes more of a psychological or physical investment than we do, we could experience guilt. Perceived imbalance in either direction reduces relationship satisfaction, possibly eroding the relationship's effectiveness and curtailing its future.[21] Once we believe a relationship has no future, we no longer perceive the need to weather bad times, and suddenly problems and conflicts we once would have attempted to work out responsibly now appear not worth the time or effort. When a relationship reaches this point, we also are less likely to trust one another. Thus, we tell each other less, and as a result, we continue growing apart.

# RELATIONSHIPS IN NEED OF REPAIR: FIX IT OR END IT

When a relationship fails to satisfy, we need to decide whether we want to work to repair it and, if so, how to go about it. Of course, before we can take steps toward relationship repair or dissolution, we should identify what caused our relationship's communication climate to become negative in the first place.

## IDENTIFY THE PROBLEM

The first task is to identify, as clearly as possible, why the relationship is not working. What is the problem? What exactly is it that you find dissatisfying?

As you learned in Chapter 2, the primary factor that leads to relationship problems is a partner or friend's sending disconfirming rather than confirming messages. Whereas **confirming messages** demonstrate that we value the relationship, disconfirming messages show our disregard.

When we send **disconfirming messages**, we exhibit a lack of recognition of the other and his or her needs. We fail to acknowledge the other person's ideas or feelings. We refrain from supporting him or her, and we limit the amount of information we share. Through our behavior, we let the other know we are ignoring him or her, that the person is unworthy of our serious attention, that because we now believe him or her to be insignificant, we are able to display a basic lack of concern for his or her needs. We may verbally abuse our partner, continually complain about his or her shortcomings, pretend he or she is not present, and make a concerted effort to prove our own importance by demonstrating that whatever we do matters, while the other's words and actions do not count. Over time, the absence of confirmation curtails effective communication and reshapes the relationship into one that is very uncomfortable.

What kinds of changes are you willing to make should a relationship you share experience problems?

## IDENTIFY STRATEGIES TO REPAIR THE PROBLEM

Next, friends or partners need to agree on what to do to restore the relationship to a state each will find rewarding and reinforcing, one that affirms each party. This is the point at which we ask what kinds of changes, if any, we each would be willing to make in our behavior that could improve our satisfaction with the relationship, including its emotional tone or communication climate. For example, we take a giant step toward confirming the importance of our relationship with another if we (1) demonstrate our willingness to acknowledge the person's significance; (2) work to sustain both a verbal and a nonverbal dialogue that demonstrates our respect for him or her; (3) reflect back to that person that we care about, understand, and respect his or her feelings; and (4) encourage him or her to share thoughts and feelings with us.

## DECIDE TO DISSOLVE OR SAVE THE RELATIONSHIP

**Relationship repair** depends on our being able to talk about what we feel and want from each other. It is not always successful. When a relationship is stressed, the parties tend to exchange and perceive a lot more negativity than previously. Comments to each other become tinged with sarcasm. They argue more, and problems tend to escalate rather being resolved to their mutual satisfaction.[22] When the parties to a relationship fail to receive the rewards they expect, see no purpose in maintaining the relationship, or are unable to handle the strain that trying to maintain the relationship presents, they are liable to part ways.

Breaking up a relationship is rarely easy. However, you can employ two key strategies to avoid an ugly scene. First, do not overpersonalize the relationship's end by feeling a need to blame yourself or the other person for the relationship's dissolution. Asking questions such as "What's wrong with him?" or "How could I have been so stupid?" usually solves nothing. The fact is that sometimes circumstances rather than people cause a relationship to end.[23] Second, keep a sense of perspective and recognize that a relationship that does not survive probably was not meant to survive. When you are no longer able to meet each other's needs, or when you feel that the relationship is stifling your personal growth, it may be better to end it.

On the other hand, when one or both partners are motivated to repair the relationship, by questioning themselves and each other about the relationship and by making a commitment to change how each relates to the other, they can renegotiate the relationship, transform it, and facilitate its continued growth.

# THE DARK SIDE OF RELATIONSHIPS: DYSFUNCTIONS AND TOXIC COMMUNICATION

In the United States, a woman is battered by an intimate partner approximately every 15 seconds. Every day, four women die from violence committed by people close to them. Some 50 percent of women have been physically or emotionally abused. It is estimated that 85 percent of relationship abuse is perpetrated by men against women, but women can be highly verbally abusive toward their male partners, and homosexual couples also experience partner abuse.[24] When a sexual relationship goes awry, why does it too often culminate in emotional or physical violence?[25]

While we may think of romantic relationships as based in love, some have a dark side that makes them dysfunctional.[26] They are unhealthy, destructive, and characterized by episodes of toxic communication. Both physical and psychological forms of relational abuse are toxic and leave psychological scars from which victims find it difficult to recover. The fact that men commit most of the violence that is perpetrated against women underscores the unequal balance of power in many relationships. In general, men have been socialized to assert themselves, compete, and focus on outcomes, whereas society has conditioned women to defer, compromise, and focus more on nurturing others.

Why do some men abuse their partners? Why do too many women remain in these relationships? Perhaps it is because of learned myths such as "love can jump hurdles." As the media fill our minds with romantic notions of dangerous yet attractive male figures and charming but helpless women such as those featured in the *Twilight* and *Fifty Shades of Grey* novels and films, some women are apt to become overly dependent, leading to the toleration of abuse and contributing to increased physical and emotional risk.[27]

Romanticized notions encourage the abused to downplay relational violence by blaming it on uncontrollable passion or too much alcohol rather than on the abuser. As a result, both victim and aggressor ignore or reframe abusive incidents. Abusive people have strong masculine gender orientations, relish controlling others, and aggressively seek to dominate. Victims who remain in such unhealthy relationships likely have been socialized into combining the emotionally supportive feminine role with one of feelings of helplessness and fear. Additionally, they probably have been socialized to be deferential and to value interpersonal harmony. When in an abusive courtship relationship, the predominant theme the man enacts is control, while the predominant theme the woman enacts is dependence.[28] The perpetrators of violence against relational partners also take pains to isolate their partners from financial resources, leaving them without access to cash, bank accounts, or credit cards. They also may threaten to harm any children or to isolate their partner from their children.[29]

Like friendships and romantic relationships, dysfunctional relationships pass through a predictable set of stages as illustrated in the model of the cycle of abuse (see Figure 13.9). During the first stage, relational tensions build in the abuser, who blames the partner for problems or for not being supportive and looks for an excuse to vent anger. In the second stage, the tensions erupt into violence, and one or more battering incidents occur. In the third stage, the abuser experiences remorse and resolves to make it up to the victim, typically promising that it will never happen again. In the fourth stage, there is a lull in violence, and the victim again feels loved until relational tensions build and the cycle of abuse repeats.[30] For abuse to persist, the victim must be isolated from family and friends who could otherwise offer solace, support, and a means of escape.[31]

**FIGURE 13.9**
The Cycle of Abuse

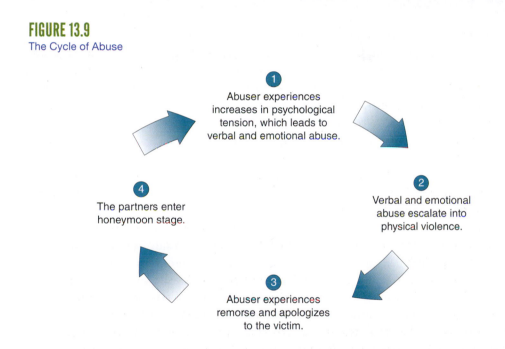

Why do some stay in unhappy relationships? Usually people stay because they want to. Why do some stay in abusive relationships? Most stay because they think they have to.[32] Relationships involving psychological or physical violence are ineffective, unhealthy, and often personally devastating. Violence has no place in any relationship. If you find yourself in an abusive relationship, do not think you can make it better by loving your partner more. That simply doesn't work. Call the National Domestic Violence Hotline (at 1-800-799-SAFE, or 1-800-799-7233) for advice and then seek protection in a safe place such as a battered women's shelter. While all relationships encounter challenges, violence devalues the very meaning of love and is never an acceptable option.

# RELATIONSHIPS AND DEATH: PROCESSING GRIEF

Not all relationship terminations are the result of a decision made by one or both parties to the relationship. Unfortunately, some of our strongest relationships terminate due to a loved one's death. Many report death to be the most painful of all relationship endings, and it is one that all of us will experience at some point in our lives. When a loved one dies, survivors can be left with feelings of loneliness and despair that may damage psychological and physical health. In fact, bereaved individuals are at greater risk than others for psychological and health problems.[33] At the same time, however, some people may not be devastated by the death of a relational partner. Whether devastated or not, a person grieving should be allowed to recover in her or his own way.[34]

What steps can we take to rescue ourselves from grief? First, it is useful to understand the **grief process**, which has been characterized as consisting of five stages (see Figure 13.10). The first stage, denial, finds the griever refusing to accept what has happened. Reality, however, prompts him or her to acknowledge the magnitude of the loss and the feelings of loneliness accompanying it. The second stage, anger, leaves the person in grief feeling powerless as he or she rages against the loss. During the third stage, guilt, the griever turns anger inward, regretting anything he or she

Hemera Technologies/AbleStock.com/Thinkstock

Some of our strongest relationships end with a loved one's death.

might ever have done or said to hurt the person who has died. This leads into the fourth stage, depression, during which the grieving person feels as if his or her former life is over, and nothing will ever be right again. He or she may find it virtually impossible to envision a future. Finally, in the acceptance stage, the person realizes that, while things will never again be the same, he or she will make it through and continue living.[35]

During the mourning period, those closest to the person who has suffered the loss typically try to offer protection by shielding him or her from feeling sad. Denying sadness, however, rarely makes it go away. Rather than attempting to suppress or ignore feelings of sadness, mourners need to be permitted to experience and express it. Submerged grief usually does more harm than its expression. By allowing grieving people to process their feelings, we help free them to continue with their lives.[36] Here, a social support network can play a critical role.

Writing an obituary for the deceased loved one may also help a bereaved person to work through his or her grief, providing an opportunity to recollect, honor, and commemorate what was appreciated most about the person who passed away while simultaneously facilitating the forming of memories. After the terrorist attacks of September 11, 2001, reporters for the *New York Times* interviewed the families of victims to help them create obituaries as tributes to those who had been killed.[37] An obituary performs the valuable act of remembering.[38]

Interestingly, an erroneous stereotype regarding romantic relationships in which one partner has died is that women grieve, while men replace. Actually, significant numbers of both men and women form new intimate relationships over time after recovering from the deaths of romantic partners.

A separate issue related to death is that of "virtual immortality." What happens to a person's online existence after death? Does the cyberself pass away or remain vital on Facebook's memorial pages? Who has the power (and the passwords) to sort through a former digital life?[39]

**FIGURE 13.10**
Working Through Grief

1  Denial
2  Anger
3  Guilt
4  Depression
5  Acceptance

# THE EFFECTS OF CULTURE, GENDER, AND MEDIA AND TECHNOLOGY ON RELATIONAL INTIMACY

Culture, gender, and media and technology mediate notions of intimacy, including ideas about self-disclosure, relationship maintenance and termination, and expression of grief.

## CULTURE'S IMPACT

Around the world, and even within U.S. culture, not all people necessarily approach intimacy in the same way. For example, the Japanese use friendship as a pathway to greater intimacy, while Americans rely more on romantic relationships to attain intimacy. Thus, the Japanese perceive best-friend relationships as more intimate than boyfriend or girlfriend relationships.

On the other hand, both Japanese and Americans perceive strangers to be the least intimate relationship, see acquaintance relationships as less intimate than relationships with friends, and view best-friend relationships as more intimate than "just friends" relationships. These similarities in perception suggest that the stages of relationships discussed previously may cut across cultures.[40]

Within the United States, African Americans and Caucasians hold the most permissive sexual attitudes, while individuals of Asian, Latino, and Middle Eastern heritage typically display more conservative attitudes.[41] Similarly, both Caucasians and African Americans believe that talking about sexual intimacy with a partner is a sign of a strong relationship, whereas Asian and Hispanic Americans are much less likely to discuss their more intimate relationship moments.[42]

Notions of how much self-disclosing is appropriate also vary among cultures. Those born in the United States tend to be high disclosers, even demonstrating a willingness to disclose information about themselves to strangers.[43] This may explain why Americans seem particularly easy to meet, are proficient at cocktail-party conversation, and are perceived as exhibitionists by those from more non-disclosing cultures. Conversely, Japanese tend to do little disclosing about themselves to others except to the few people with whom they are very close. In general, Asians do not reach out to strangers. They do, however, demonstrate great care for each other, since they view harmony as essential to relationship nurturance. They work hard to prevent those they perceive as outsiders from obtaining information they believe reflects poorly on them.[44]

Members of cultures with a strong group orientation do not value privacy as much as do members of cultures with an individualistic orientation. Thus, members of Arabic, Greek, and Spanish cultures have a lesser need for privacy in relationships than do members of Western or North American cultures.[45] Similarly, members of Western cultures depend on actions rather than words to cement trust. Westerners tend to perceive commitment as a bond connecting two people. Asians, Hispanics, and African Americans perceive commitment as a bond linking the members of groups.[46]

Members of diverse cultures also express and cope with grief differently. Relationship scholar Steve Duck notes that in some cultures, it is acceptable to fall to the ground, cover oneself with dust, and wail loudly in a public display of grief; other cultures emphasize public composure and view the showing of such emotion as unacceptable.[47]

## GENDER, INTIMACY, AND DISTANCE

Understanding alternative ways of developing and maintaining intimacy is an important part of our ability to sustain relationships. While both women and men value friendships and romantic relationships, they are apt to express closeness dissimilarly. For example, most men define intimacy in terms of what two people *do* together, whereas most women define it in terms of what they *talk about* together. Thus, men engage in shared activities as a means to achieve closeness, while women participate in shared emotional talk.[48] Men assume the value of a relationship; they don't feel a deep need to talk about it. Women, in contrast, feel that discussion of a relationship's dynamics is important. This can create relationship problems, because as men attempt to develop intimacy with women, they will plan activities, whereas women might prefer to be in a situation in which they would have an increased opportunity for talking and self-disclosing, not just doing.[49]

Men and women define intimacy differently.

Men and women also assign different weights to autonomy and connection. Because men are more likely to be socialized toward independence, they tend to prefer autonomy to interrelatedness; in contrast, women tend to need autonomy less and connection more. This preference disparity may lead a woman to think that her partner does not value their relationship and lead a man to think that his partner wants to consume his time with intrusive talk. What creates comfort for many women is what creates discomfort for many men. Women likewise tend to disclose more intimate information to partners than do men. Perhaps this is because women have been encouraged to be more personal and open about their thoughts, feelings, and fears than men. Thus, men tend to ask women more questions about themselves than women ask of men. At the same time, women hope that their male partners will voluntarily reciprocate with self-disclosures of their own.[50]

In general, women watch the progress of relationships more carefully. As a result, women tend to detect relationship troubles sooner and are apt to surpass men in both expressing feelings of vulnerability and providing emotional support. Whereas women are more comfortable revealing their feelings and providing overt expressions of **caring**, men tend to be at ease using covert caring signals such as teasing, joking, and providing companionship.

Contrary to the image presented in romance novels and films, men are more likely to initiate a declaration of love than are women.[51] They are also more likely to fall in love first.[52] More often than not, a woman will wait until she hears her male partner say "I love you" before she reciprocates. Men have been socialized to take the lead in love.

# ANALYZE THIS: FEELINGS

In the poem "To Women, as Far as I'm Concerned," D. H. Lawrence expresses his opinion of feelings.

The feelings I don't have, I don't have.

The feelings I don't have, I won't say I have.

The feelings you say you have, you don't have.

The feelings you would like us both to have, we neither of us have.

The feelings people ought to have, they never have.

If people say they've got feelings, you may be pretty sure they haven't got them.

So if you want either of us to feel anything at all

you'd better abandon all idea of feelings altogether.

**Consider these questions:**

1. With which, if any, of the poet's observations do you agree?

2. In what ways, if any, do you think the poet's perceptions express a male point of view? Explain.

## MEDIA AND TECHNOLOGY: THE DECLINE OF PRIVACY AND DISTANCE

Social networks enable us to keep in touch with those who live near and at a distance, some of whom we see regularly and others whom we may never see face-to-face, making the Internet the ultimate noncontact, person-to-person network.[53] This is particularly important because of changing attitudes toward privacy and the reality that **long-distance relationships** are increasingly common.

The current economic environment has made us more transient; in growing numbers, we are compelled to move to wherever jobs exist, to travel extensively for work, and to venture to distant training locations requiring us to spend more time away from home. Yet we and our friends, family members, and significant others can commit to staying close and "staying together" psychologically. Certainly, long-distance relationships are not new. When separated by distance, your grandparents and parents may have exchanged love letters. The Internet, however, has changed things in that some relationships that now exist may not have begun were it not for the **virtual communities** that brought the partners together.[54]

How good do you think you would be at maintaining a romantic relationship if you and your significant other lived far apart from one another? This is a relationship challenge many students like yourself face as they leave their hometowns to attend college and their romantic partners remain behind or select other colleges hundreds of miles away. College students have company. Dual-career couples who work in widely separated locations, whether by choice or because of limited job availability, face similar problems. While increasingly common, long-distance relationships can be fraught with complications—exposing the limits of technology, especially if trust becomes an issue.[55] However, if one partner in the long-distance relationship idealizes the other, the relationship tends to have more stability than even a geographically close one—that is, until the partners stage a reunion and reality intrudes.[56]

Have you considered the kinds of problems that can beset long-distance relationships? When separated by distance, partners may spend significant time texting, Skyping, and calling one another in the effort to continue the relationship they began when both lived in the same town. Just working out a time when one of them can fly to see the other is a challenge. In time, some partners find themselves arguing about such things as whether or not to have "phone sex."

Like any other relationship, a long-distance relationship has a greater chance of success if both partners are willing to solve problems jointly and to be open to one another by engaging in self-disclosure.[57]

## TRY THIS

### At a Distance

Work demands compel more and more of us to experience long-distance relationships. Interview three people of your generation (identifying their approximate ages and types of work) and three people from an older or younger generation (similarly identifying their approximate ages and types of work) regarding whether they expect to experience or have experienced a long-distance relationship (whether regional or international) because of job demands. Also ask them to describe what they consider to be the biggest hurdles of such relationships and how they have or would overcome them.

More than ever before, we are technologically equipped to handle the challenges of long-distance relationships—whether friendships or romantic relationships. Previously, when individuals carried on such relationships, they were aware that the geographic distance created a special fragility in the relationships, which they were apt to characterize as tenuous and uncertain. The parties to long distance relationships then lacked something we tend to take for granted: routine interactions about nothing—that is, talk about routine, seemingly unimportant daily events or activities.[58] Now we have the technological means to maintain frequent low-cost contact with those who are geographically distant from us, facilitating the small talk that increases relationship health, durability, and longevity. We have become more accessible—even immediately accessible—although miles apart. This sense of immediacy helps to nurture long-distance relationships by allowing the parties to sustain a sense of personal commitment and continuity. Because long-distance relationships no longer engender decreased contact, rather than concluding that a relationship should end because of geographic distance, we may now feel more equipped to cope. Technology serves up instant connectivity, allowing us to continue weaving our daily lives together. Though far apart, we have the ability to feel the closeness required for relational depth.

Technology facilitates the development and maintenance of relationships in other ways as well. When communicating online, some of us actually become more talkative. There are fewer awkward silences and embarrassing moments. Some even feel less vulnerable talking about feelings online than they do face-to-face.[59]

How else does online interaction affect our relationships? In Chapter 12, we noted that interacting online facilitates hyperpersonal communication, likely precipitating greater intimacy and social attraction than would a comparable amount of face-to-face interaction. Communicating online leads partners to construct idealized impressions of one another, heightening their expectations for the relationship and contributing to their continuing contact.[60] In general, women disclose more than men, though there is a smaller difference relative to self-disclosure between them than once thought.[61]

Facebook's users are more connected than ever.[62] While the adage says there are "6 degrees of separation" between any two people on the planet, the average Facebook user is a mere 4.74 degrees away from any other user. While some of our ties may be weak, they shrink the world, bringing us closer together nonetheless.[63]

When Facebook started, the amount of private information that members shared was minimal. Now users share virtually everything. In addition, Facebook's Timeline keeps a record of each user's past posts, back to the account's creation, allowing others to gain a more comprehensive understanding of a person's online identity by providing a kind of life story.[64] Unless a user is vigilant about who can see old posts, however, his or her life can become literally an open book. The tug between privacy and transparency continues. Interestingly, active Facebook users demonstrated less concern with privacy than did infrequent users.[65] Privacy concerns reasserted themselves, however, as a result of Facebook coming under fire for sharing the personal information of approximately 50 million users.[66]

Additionally, online journals—blogs—facilitate emotional purging and self-other insight. Bloggers write about issues of importance to them, even reporting on painful traumas; the soliciting of reader feedback and the reading of each other's entries brings users closer together.[67]

# GAINING COMMUNICATION COMPETENCE: HANDLING RELATIONAL CLOSENESS AND DISTANCE SKILLFULLY

By now it should be apparent that negotiating closeness and distance in relationships is complex. By considering the following questions, you will be better able to select the level of closeness appropriate for you.

## HOW IMPORTANT TO YOU IS THIS PERSON?

We typically want to get closer to and share more about ourselves with those whose friendship or romantic involvement is important to us. One measure of how important a person is in your life is the extent to which you are willing to invest time, effort, and energy to build and maintain a relationship with him or her.

## ARE YOU WILLING TO INITIATE INTERACTION?

No matter how interested you and another person might be in one another, you stand little chance of developing a meaningful relationship unless you begin to communicate. If either of you hesitates or for some reason is unable to initiate contact, you are less likely to build the foundation needed for an effective relationship. Thus, it is necessary to use appropriate conversation openers.

Being willing to initiate interaction is necessary to begin a relationship.

## HOW MUCH AND WHAT KIND OF INTIMACY DO YOU DESIRE?

Many of us hope to realize emotional closeness with friends and lovers. We expect to reveal our inner selves and hope they will reciprocate. The ways we express intimacy, however, depend on our background. Some of us will build intimacy through expressive disclosure talk, while others will build it instrumentally by participating in activities together and by being there and doing things for one another.

## HOW ACCEPTING ARE YOU OF THE OTHER PERSON?

To what degree are you able to accept the other person for who that person is and what he or she represents? Do you feel that in order for you to accept him or her fully, the other person must change? With our friends and lovers, we should feel that we can be ourselves and that we can reveal our feelings without having them or ourselves rejected.

## HOW ARE YOU WILLING TO SUPPORT THE OTHER PERSON?

Support is a basic expectation of most relationships based on friendship or love.[68] We show support in different ways: by listening, talking through problems, empathizing, or being there in times of need or even when we disagree.

## DO YOU RECOGNIZE THAT YOUR RELATIONSHIP WILL CHANGE?

Changes in relationships are a natural and a continuous part of the life cycle. Relationships evolve. They are dynamic. Relationship changes may challenge or upset us, excite or thrill us. We may welcome some changes, curse others, be delighted or disoriented by them. But they will continue. The people whose lives we touch, and vice versa, will influence us and change us in ways we are unable to predict. Our relationship choices, and whether we manage or mismanage them (expecting instant gratification or having the patience necessary for a meaningful relationship to grow) will affect and transform us.

## CAN YOUR RELATIONSHIP SURVIVE THE DISTANCE TEST?

While we are likely to remain close to those we see regularly, what do you imagine would happen to your friendships and romantic relationships if you had to relocate to a different part of the country or the world? Which of your relationships do you think would survive the test of distance? What specific steps would you take to ensure intimacy and the relationship's maintenance? How would you keep your lives interwoven?

## DO YOU KNOW WHEN TO CONTINUE AND WHEN TO END A RELATIONSHIP?

Not every relationship should be sustained or maintained. When a relationship turns dark, is destructive, deteriorates into verbal or physical violence, or drains our energy and self-confidence, we need to end it before it does irreparable harm. However, there are some relationships we do not want to end, such as family relationships. In these cases, we may need to seek professional help.

## CONNECT THE CASE

### The Case of the Plane Trip

Samantha sat down in her first-class seat. Her company had paid for her to travel coach, but she had used some of her frequent-flier miles to treat herself to a first-class return flight. After all, she told herself, she had sold more than anyone in her division, and she really deserved the upgrade.

The first-class seats were so-o-o comfortable. After texting her friend that she was on the plane and had just ordered a drink, Samantha settled in to read a magazine. She briefly gazed out the window, watching the last-minute preparations of the ground crew. Then Tom arrived and sat in the seat next to hers. From his opening greeting, Samantha knew that the flight might not be the dream she had envisioned; it would likely be awkward and uncomfortable instead.

"What are your plans for tonight?" Tom nonchalantly asked her. At first, Samantha thought he must be joking, and she smiled faintly. But he wasn't joking. He continued saying, "I have tickets to the hockey game. Want to go?"

Samantha answered that she had other plans, but added, "Thank you, anyway." Tom, however, pressed on: "I've just broken up with my girlfriend. Are you seeing anyone? Even if you are, what about tomorrow night, sweetheart?"

It wasn't just his sexist language that bothered her—it was the tone and content. Tom acted as if they were vacationing together, as if he knew her well and could confide in her, when they didn't know each other at all. Not only had he skipped any rapport-building stages, he was attempting to move too quickly for friendship between them to even have a chance of developing.

Samantha was uncertain how to handle the situation. She could ask to change her seat. She could tell Tom that he was bothering her and that she found his manner offensive. She could take out her phone and text a friend. She turned away from him and looked out the window.

Suddenly, the decision was no longer hers. Tom stood up and asked to change his seat. As the plane slowly pulled away from the gate, Samantha heard him asking someone else, "Would you like to go to a hockey game?"

### Consider these questions:

1. If you had been in Samantha's position, how would you have responded to Tom?

2. What relationship-building mistakes, if any, do you think are exhibited in this case study?

3. What might Tom do differently if given the opportunity to replay his part?

# REVIEW THIS

1. **Define self-disclosure and intimacy, using social penetration theory to describe a relationship's breadth and depth and the Johari window to explore how self-awareness and self-disclosure affect our relationships.** ☐

Self-disclosure occurs when we willingly tell others things about ourselves that they otherwise would not know. How much you reveal about yourself to another is a measure of intimacy.

We can describe every relationship in terms of its breadth, or the number of topics we talk about, and its depth, or how central the discussed topics are to our self-concept and how much we reveal about ourselves during our conversations. According to social penetration theory, most of our relationships begin with relatively narrow breadth and shallow depth. As the relationships grow and increase in strength, however, both breadth and depth increase also.

The Johari window is a four-paned model used to explore the nature of relationships. The sizes of the panes signify what you do and do not know about yourself and what another person does and does not know about you. The four panes are termed the open, blind, hidden, and unknown areas. As information is moved from the hidden, blind, and unknown areas into the open area, we engage in self/other disclosure and gain self-awareness and self-insight.

2. **Define and explain the effects of relational dialectics.** ☐

While some relational forces pull us toward intimacy, others pull us in the opposite direction. Relational dialectics reflect the dynamic nature of relational ties and tugs such as integration–separation, stability–change, and expression–privacy, tensions that we need to resolve.

3. **Discuss factors influencing relationship maintenance.** ☐

We use relationship maintenance techniques to nourish relationships we find satisfying and mutually rewarding. This involves being mindful, taking time to talk with each other, and demonstrating commitment.

4. **Discuss whether and how to repair a relationship.** ☐

When a relationship fails to satisfy, we need to decide whether we want to work to repair it. If we can't repair it, the relation usually ends. To repair a relationship, partners need to be able to talk about what they feel and want from each other. Efforts do not always succeed.

5. **Define and explain toxic communication and identify the four stages in an abusive relationship.** ☐

Unfortunately, not all of our relationships are characterized by the presence of healthy patterns of communication. Some are dysfunctional, and in these, the use of toxic communication is common. Dysfunctional relationships are also noted for the presence of verbal or physical abuse. Abusive relationships are characterized by four repeating stages: (1) the experiencing of psychological tension, to which the abuser responds by engaging in verbal and/or emotional abuse; (2) escalation into physical violence; (3) abuser remorse and apologies; and (4) a honeymoon stage until tensions increase again.

**6. Explain the grief cycle, describing what occurs when a relationship ends with a loved one's death.** ☐

The grief process consists of five stages: denial, anger, guilt, depression, and acceptance. Mourners need to be permitted to experience and express their feelings.

**7. Identify how culture, gender, the media, and technology influence notions of intimacy and disclosure.** ☐

Attitudes toward intimacy and disclosure differ from one culture to another. Members of different cultures may view strangers differently, hold more or less restrictive sexual attitudes, and engage in more or less self-disclosure. Like culture, gender influences preferences for developing and maintaining intimacy. Most men define

intimacy in terms of what two people do together, whereas most women define it in terms of what they talk about together. Men and women also assign different weights to autonomy and connection. The media and technology also play roles in maintaining relationships, especially long-distance ones. We are a more transient society. Technology facilitates our committing ourselves psychologically to each other, though separated by great distance.

**8. Discuss strategies for handling closeness and distance in relationships more effectively.** ☐

Deciding how important another is to you, creating a climate fostering information seeking and giving, distinguishing the amount of intimacy desired, being accepting and supportive, acknowledging that changes occur in relationships, figuring out if a relationship can survive the distance test, and knowing when to end a relationship are necessary for gaining competence in handling closeness and distance in relationships.

## CHECK YOUR UNDERSTANDING

1. Can you explain the relationship between self-disclosure and intimacy, using yourself or a close friend or relative to make your points? (See pages 364–365.)

2. Can you compare a relationship that has little breadth and depth with one that has great breadth and little depth, and then with one that has both great breadth and great depth? (See pages 365–366.)

3. Can you use a Johari window to analyze one of your important relationships? (See pages 367–371.)

4. Can you summarize the dialectical tensions that can arise in a relationship? Which have arisen in your relationship with a family member? With a friend? With a romantic partner? In what ways are the tensions experienced similar and different? (See pages 371–374.)

5. Can you provide examples of how gender, culture, the media, and technology influence attitudes toward intimacy and distance in relationships? (See pages 381–384.)

## KEY TERMS

Caring 383

Confirming messages 376

Disconfirming messages 377

Grief process 380

Johari window 368

Long-distance relationship 384

Norm of reciprocity 365

Relational dialectics theory 372

Relationship breadth 365

Relationship depth 365

Relationship maintenance 374

Relationship repair 377

Self-disclosure 364

Social penetration theory 366

Toxic communication 378

Virtual community 384

Get the tools you need to sharpen your study skills. **SAGE edge** offers a robust online environment featuring an impressive array of free tools and resources. Access practice quizzes, eFlashcards, video, and multimedia at **edge.sagepub.com/gambleicp**.

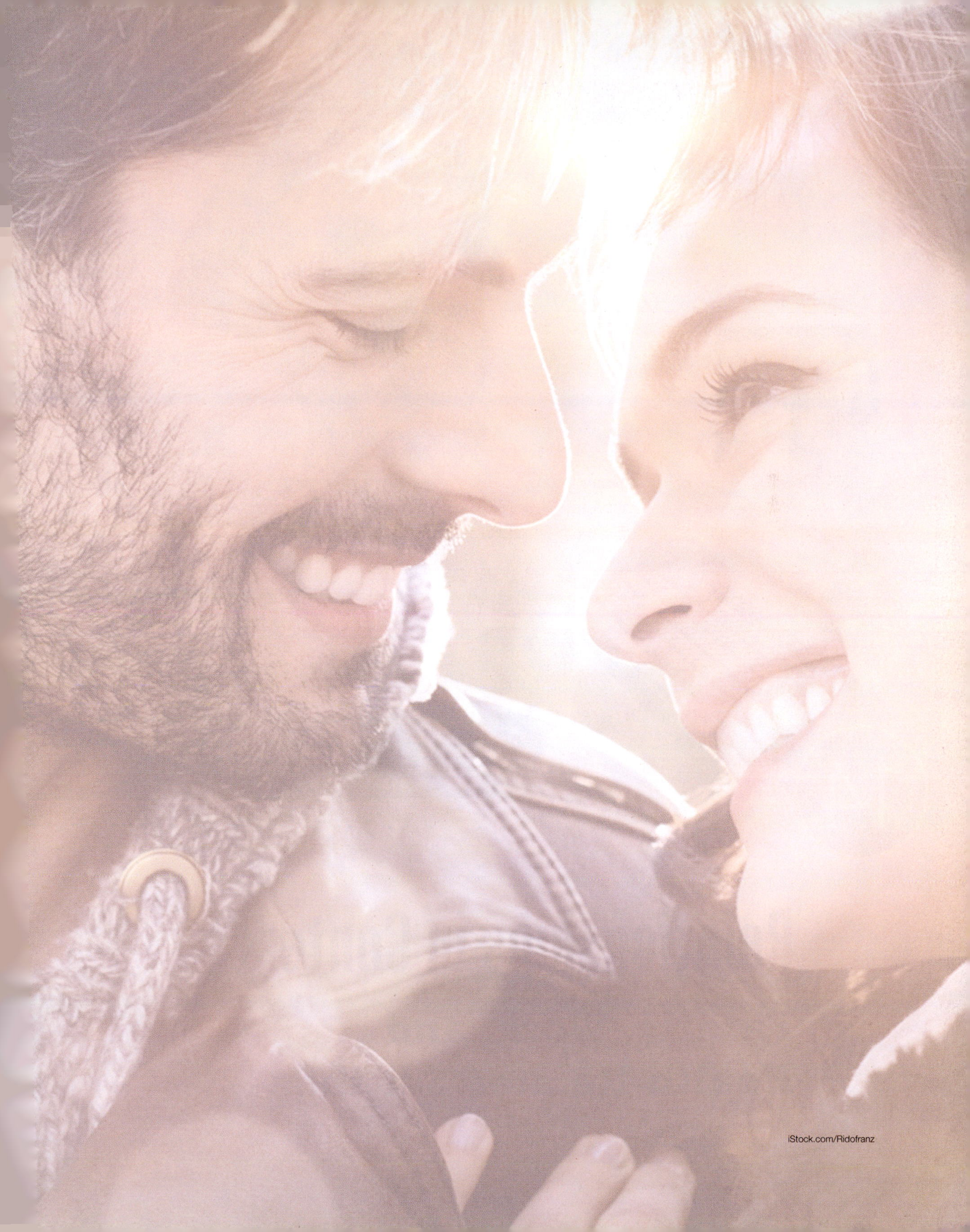

iStock.com/Ridofranz

iStock.com/bowdenimages

# Relationships in Context

## Family, Work, and Health-Related Settings

## Learning Objectives

### AFTER COMPLETING THIS CHAPTER, YOU SHOULD BE ABLE TO

1. Discuss the nature of interpersonal communication in families

2. Discuss the nature of interpersonal communication in the workplace

3. Explain the relationship between interpersonal communication and health

4. Identify how you can gain communication competence and apply skills across contexts

> They always say that time changes things, but you actually have to change them yourself.
>
> —Andy Warhol

How satisfied are you as a family member? An employee? A patient? When navigating family, work, and health, does the following ring true? A Better Me + A Better You = A Better Us.[1] The preceding equation should work no matter the communication context. We all have multiple versions of ourselves and different mixes of family, work, and health. How is it going for you in each life arena? Where do your worlds complement each other, and where do they clash? ■

# WHAT DO YOU KNOW?

Before continuing your reading of this chapter, which of the following five statements do you believe to be true, and which do you believe to be false?

| | | | |
|---|---|---|---|
| **1.** | Fewer than half of all American families include a married couple. | T | F |
| **2.** | If a family has more than two people, then its members live in triangles. | T | F |
| **3.** | Mindguards facilitate groupthink. | T | F |
| **4.** | An iron maiden is a woman who wears men's clothing. | T | F |
| **5.** | Cyberslacking occurs when you grow tired of playing online games. | T | F |

Read the chapter to discover if you're right or if you've made any erroneous assumptions.

ANSWERS: 1. T; 2. T; 3. T; 4. F; 5. F

Family, work, and health settings are contexts in which many of our most important interactions occur. How we interact and the kinds of relationships we share in each of these communication arenas influence our personal, economic, mental, and physical well-being. What happens in our family, professionally, and with our health impacts our sense of self and whether we feel physically and emotionally able to meet life's daily challenges.

We begin by exploring the nature of family communication. After all, much of what we know about communication stems from our upbringing.

# THE NATURE OF FAMILIAL COMMUNICATION

It is in our family that we first learn how to create, maintain, and end relationships; how to express ourselves; how to argue; how to display affection; how to choose acceptable topics for conversation in mixed company; how work affects home life; how to cope with stress and illness, and more. What it means to be a family member and how the lessons we learned in childhood affect our health and relationship expectations are key issues.

What is a family? Do you consider yours to be typical? Family communication researchers use a number of definitions, including describing a family as a network of people who live together and support each other,[2] as a group of intimates with strong ties of loyalty and emotion,[3] and as a group of two or more individuals who are interdependent because of their blood connection, legal bonds, and/or explicit verbal promise.[4] Some define family narrowly, others more broadly. Definitions of family have become more flexible and reflective of diverse forms of contemporary families. We think family should be defined in terms of what it means to you. In other words, when you list the members of your family, you are revealing what family means to you.[5]

For some of us the concept of family brings to mind a picture of the traditional ==nuclear family==, one with a mother, a father, and one or more children. The nuclear family no longer constitutes the "average" American family. Others picture a ==blended family==, one including two adults and children (biological or adopted) from one or both of the adults' previous relationships, and potentially additional children from the current relationship. Others picture a ==single-parent family==, also known as a primary-parent family, one in which the mother or father is solely responsible for the biological or adopted child(ren), responsible for carrying out all parental obligations. Families can be composed of parents of any gender or orientation but also include committed partners who opt not to have children. As long as we are legally or emotionally connected to one or more people, we may consider ourselves part of a family.

Currently, more than half of all births in the United States are to single women, most of whom are not college educated.[6] In 1950, only 4 million Americans lived alone, approximately 9 percent of households. Today, according to U.S. Census data, about 33 million Americans live alone, making up 28 percent of all households, nearly tied with childless couples as the most prominent residential type.[7] Also, the Census Bureau reports that less than 50 percent of families in the United States include a married couple. That means that single adults or cohabiting couples now head more than half of all U.S. households.[8]

## FIGURE 14.1

Percentage of One-Person Households in the United States, by Decade

Source: Based on information from the U.S. Census Bureau.

Recent years have seen an increase in the number of extended or intergenerational families living together—that is, in households shared by parents and their children along with the children's grandparents, and perhaps also aunts, uncles, and cousins (see Figure 14.2).[9] Economic conditions have led people of all age groups to move back to their family home, creating a **boomerang family** or an accordion family.[10] While some cultures always have lived in multigenerational households, this form of family living has not previously been the norm in the United States. Also increasing in number are **commuter families**, in which—again often for economic reasons—one or more members commute from a primary residence to a work location in a distant city, where they remain for periods of time.

In any discussion of family interaction, it is important to distinguish between family of origin and current family status. Your family of origin is the family in which you grew up. According to family therapist Virginia Satir, the family of origin provides the pattern for "peoplemaking."[11]

## THE FAMILY AS COMMUNICATION SYSTEM

It is virtually impossible to assign a beginning or an end to communicative exchanges between family members. Familial exchanges are in process, continually evolving, providing a unique context for studying communication in which each member interprets experience based on his or her personal perspective.

There is a dynamic interplay among family members. According to **systems theory**, family members are interdependent, with the actions of an individual family member understood only in relation to all family members and to the functioning of the family as a whole.[12] How one family member behaves affects how every other family member behaves, both in and out of the family

## FIGURE 14.2

Multigenerational Households in the United States, 2000 and 2010

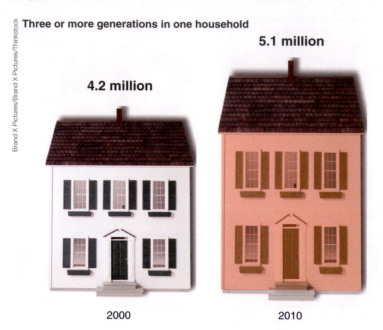

**Three or more generations in one household**

5.1 million

4.2 million

2000          2010

Source: Based on information from the U.S. Census Bureau.

setting. For example, choosing to end contact with one family member affects the entire family.[13] Consequently, the verbal and nonverbal actions of any one family member cannot be understood in isolation from those of other family members (remember our discussion of Watzlawick, Beavin, and Jackson's axioms of communication in Chapter 1).

## Family Members Are Interdependent

To fully grasp the concept of family member interdependence, picture family members connected by pieces of rope. As one member moves, his or her movement tugs on or affects all the others. Sometimes as family members move they tie each other up in knots, at other times they try to pull away from one another, and at still other times they give each other enough rope to experience the freedom necessary for personal growth.

## The Family Is Greater Than the Sum of Its Parts

Recall from Chapter 1 that the principle of nonsummativity tells us that the whole is greater than the sum of its parts. Summing up the characteristics of individual family members does not allow us to understand the family. Instead, we need to attend to how together the members of a family function as a whole, the ways in which they are connected, and the interaction patterns they use. By becoming more aware of the family system and discovering their part in it, including who they are and the connections between them and others, family members open the way to talking about their respective perceptions and any desire they may have to reshape either the roles members assume or the interaction patterns in use.

## Families Change

Families are complex and in flux. They need to be adaptive. Because they are made up of people, and people change as they age, families are continually dealing with change, processing new information, negotiating meaning, meeting member needs, and adapting to transitions. At the same time, members try to maintain a sense of stability and a balanced state in order to facilitate the family's maintenance.

None of this is simple. Change can lead to unresolved feelings, stress, and conflict. Families' attempts to meet such challenges and realize their goals reveal much about how they communicate.

David Sacks/Lifesize/Thinkstock

Every family has a unique communication dynamic.

## Family Members Engage in Mutual Influence

Family members are engaged in the complex process of mutual influence. As members decode, create, and share meaning, they interact and work out their relationships. Every family member, whether living or deceased, is connected to and has the ability to influence others in the family.

---

## TRY THIS

## Virginia Satir on "Peoplemaking"

Virginia Satir was a pioneering family therapist and author. Read her comments below about the nature of families and answer her questions:

When I was five, I decided that when I grew up I'd be a "children's detective on parents." I didn't quite know what I would look for, but I realized a lot went on in families that didn't meet the eye. . . .

It is now clear to me that the family is a microcosm of the world. To understand the world, we can study the family: issues such as power, intimacy, autonomy, trust, and communication skills are vital parts underlying how we live in the world. To change the world is to change the family. . . .

Does it feel good to you to live with your family right now? . . .

Do you feel you are living with friends, people you like and trust, and who like and trust you? . . .

Is it fun and exciting to be a member of your family?

*(Continued)*

(Continued)

Now complete the following exercise:

1.  Identify the members of your immediate family.

2.  Use a series of words and then images to describe each person on your list. For example, you might describe your brother as *wired*, *tight*, and *frenetic* and choose a jack-in-the-box as the image that represents him.

3.  Provide an example for each family member illustrating how that person affects your relationship with each other member of your family.

4.  Identify which member(s) in your family fulfill(s) the following roles:

    a.  *the blamer* (the person who holds others responsible for what goes wrong)
    b.  *the soother* (the person who tries to make peace)
    c.  *the robot* (the person who tries to reason logically)
    d.  *the distracter* (the person who tries to defuse a conflict by providing a distraction)

5.  Which of these roles make things better? Which make them worse? Which role is yours?

Source: Virginia Satir, *The New Peoplemaking,* Mountain View, CA: Science and Behavior Books, 1988.

## FAMILY COMMUNICATION: ROLES AND RULES

Family members are expected to play certain roles and follow specific rules in relation to each other and to the family as a whole.

### Roles

A **role** is a set of prescribed behaviors. Wage earner, homemaker, financial manager, child-care provider, and social planner are among the roles family members perform. In some families, roles are shared. In others, each role is the primary responsibility of one family member. Whereas some families exhibit significant role versatility and turn-taking, others adhere strictly to stereotypical role definitions. Contemporary family members play an expanding number of roles, a demand that may increase stress.

In families that practice healthy communication, role relationships constantly evolve. As a family progresses through various developmental stages, different family members may perform different roles. Family members who were advice givers may become advice takers, and vice versa. One of the challenges facing modern families concerns the support that many aging parents need from their adult children. As Americans live longer, the parent–child relationship lasts longer. Thus, members of the so-called sandwich generation face dual responsibilities as they raise children of their own and take care of aging parents.

# ANALYZE THIS: TRANSITIONS

Begin by considering these questions: In what ways, if any, has your family and the roles you and others play as family members evolved over time? To what extent are you satisfied/dissatisfied with how your family has adapted to family member transitions?

In the following poem by Linda Pastan, the speaker offers us a mother's perception of her developing daughter:

## To a Daughter Leaving Home

When I taught you
at eight to ride
a bicycle, loping along
beside you
as you wobbled away
on two round wheels,
my own mouth rounding
in surprise when you pulled
ahead down the curved path of the park,
I kept waiting

for the thud
of your crash as I
sprinted to catch up,
while you grew
smaller, more breakable
with distance,
pumping, pumping
for your life, screaming
with laughter,
the hair flapping
behind you like a
handkerchief waving
goodbye.

### Now consider these questions:

1. What does the poem tell us about the parent–child relationship?

2. What does it tell us about the author's view of family?

Source: "To a Daughter Leaving Home". Copyright © 1988 by Linda Pastan, from CARNIVAL EVENING: NEW AND SELECTED POEMS 1968–1998 by Linda Pastan. Used by permission of W. W. Norton & Company, Inc.

---

Families share a history and the prospect of a future. Past interactions, rituals, and celebrations pave the way for present exchanges and indicate the potential for mutually influential relationships to continue. What changes have you perceived in your family?

## Rules

Implied or spoken understandings—**rules**—guide family communication. Through repeated exposure, we come to recognize and internalize these rules.[14] Some rules are passed down through generations; others are new and negotiated directly. Family rules regulate family interaction and, among other things, let members know how to divide tasks, who is in charge of what, and who talks and listens to whom. For example, which, if any, of the following rules do members of your family accept?

- Children should be seen and not heard.
- Children should speak only when spoken to.
- Don't talk about family matters outside the family.
- No arguing at the dinner table.
- Never go into Mom and Dad's room.
- Don't lie.
- Don't answer back when scolded.
- Never raise your voice.
- Don't show when you have been hurt.
- Don't express fear.
- Don't ask for the car when Mom or Dad is in a bad mood.
- Don't interrupt an adult when he or she is speaking.

## Expectations

Family members develop expectations for each other that, if realized, increase their satisfaction. For example, many expect family members to offer each other emotional support no matter what.

Family members share expectations for one another. Are yours realized?

To this end, we make time for each other and recognize our obligation to help others in our family by providing social support and doing whatever we can to help them cope with everyday realities. What relational contributions do you make to your family? What relational benefits do you derive from it?

Through sustained interaction, we clarify our expectations regarding how family members should behave in relation to each other and toward us. Understanding these rules and their effects leads us to understand whether we communicate as effectively as we could and what rules, if any, we would like to renegotiate to improve family interaction.

## TRY THIS

## The Rules We Live By

One by one, interview each member of your immediate family, asking the following questions:

1. What are the rules that guide our life as a family?

2. Where did the rules come from?

3. What are your feelings about these rules?

4. What new rules would improve the balance in or operation of our family?

Identify those rules that all your family members agree on and those roles that at least one family member thinks are unfair or in need of revision. To what extent do you agree with family members' assessments?

# COMMUNICATION PATTERNS IN FAMILIES

Families evolve habitual patterns of communication. Some patterns facilitate effective interaction, while others impede it.

## Problematic Communication Patterns

In some families, the rules are too restrictive to be healthy. The term often used to describe a family with problematic communication is *dysfunctional*. When a family's rules prohibit a member from adequately expressing his or her feelings or needs, they also deter the sharing of important personal information and aspects of the self. Inhibiting a family member can be emotionally devastating and can harm the person in ways that may not be known for years. For example, if every time you bring a problem to your father he explodes with rage, you soon learn not to approach him with your problems. You may also learn to express anger inappropriately.

Some families suffer from frequent episodes of *communication dysfunction*. Instead of supporting one another, family members crash into each other. Instead of exhibiting family cohesion and pulling together emotionally, they come unglued. The communication characteristics of dysfunctional families enable at least one family member to inflict pain on or denigrate one or more other members systematically.

Among the harmful messages that may be communicated in dysfunctional families are physical, sexual, or emotional abuse; messages of worthlessness, intimidation, and manipulation; and the idea that one person has a right to use any and all compliance-gaining or power strategies to control fully another's actions. The targets of dysfunctional communication often blame themselves for causing this. They label themselves inadequate and come to believe that they are powerless to control their lives. Consequently, they may lack the self-confidence to counter the abuse they receive.

## Productive Communication Patterns

More healthy or productive family communication patterns occur in families whose members have the freedom to express their feelings. The members of such families have the following qualities:

- They are able to offer emotional and physical support to each other.
- They are comfortable revealing their feelings and thoughts to one another.

Abuse is never justified.

- They are confident about the family's ability to meet each member's needs.

- They are flexible and open enough to adapt and respond to situations that produce conflict or unexpected change.

Communication is the greatest single factor that determines the health of families' members and how their members interact.[15] Families whose members communicate effectively are more adaptable to changes in the family's power structure, role relationships, and rules.[16] They also are more willing to negotiate seemingly incompatible goals.

## Your Family Network

We can learn a lot about how our family communicates by drawing a family network map.[17] A family can create such a map by taking the following steps:

1. Have one family member tack a large sheet of paper to the wall where all members can see it clearly.

2. Draw a circle for each person who is a part of the family, including extended family members who are part of the household. If someone was a part of the family but now is gone, represent that person with a filled-in circle.

3. To show how family members are connected, draw lines between them. For example, a family may have marital pairs, parent–child pairs, and sibling pairs (see Figure 14.3).

4. Identify what each role means to each family member. For example, what does performing the role of parent, significant other, child, or sibling mean?

5. Compare and contrast family role definitions. After sharing ideas, family members may develop new understandings about the members of their family and their relationships to one another.

6. Each person should think about the particular relationship he or she has with every other family member and describe how he or she feels about each connection.

## FIGURE 14.3

The Family Network: How Families Are Connected

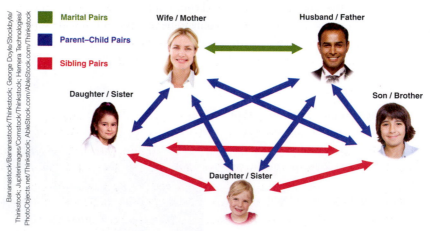

Source: Based on figure in *New Peoplemaking*, Virginia Satir. Science and Behavior Books, Inc.

The lines of the family network reveal that in families of more than two people, we do not live in pairs but in triangles. As Virginia Satir explains, a triangle is a pair plus one. Because only two people can relate at one time, any other person is left out. This person faces a dilemma: work to break up the relationship between the other two, support it, or withdraw. The third person's decision is critical in affecting how the family network operates.[18]

In more nurturing families, these relationships and the perceptions of family members are open to discussion. In less nurturing families, family members are unaware of these networks and their effects and are either unwilling or unable to talk about them. By discussing connections, however, family members can develop the insights they need for the family to function more effectively as a unit.

## CULTURE AND THE FAMILY

Although the concept of family is universal, the nature of the family is not. Because culture shapes families, the word means different things to members of different cultures. Families do not develop rules, beliefs, and rituals in isolation. How members think, act, and speak is drawn from the wider cultural context—both the culture the family members live in and the culture to which they trace their ancestry.[19]

### Varying Family Composition

One culture's definition of family is no more correct or acceptable than another's—except, of course, to members of that culture. In many cultures, the extended family household is the norm. For example, in Mexico, it is standard for grandparents to live with their adult children and their grandchildren, not in retirement communities. In the United States, the nuclear family was considered the ideal household group for quite some time, though that seems to be changing as a result of the economy and immigration.[20]

### Varying Communication Styles

Members of diverse cultures often differ in the extent to which they adhere to traditional sex roles, tolerate uncertainty and change, share or disclose their feelings and affections, retain individual identities, and assert individual rights. Mexicans, for example, provide a very supportive environment to family members. As a result, Mexican children are raised to rely upon and provide support to the family unit. Mexicans judge their level of success based on the family's achievements. In contrast, children in the United States are taught to place a high value on individual ability and initiative.[21]

### Varying Family Roles

Some families are more position oriented than person oriented, and vice versa. In position-oriented families, roles are more rigidly related to sex and age, whereas in person-oriented families, individual comfort levels and needs demarcate roles. Person-oriented families tend to practice democratic decision making, with roles negotiated, individualism fostered, and interaction between family members emphasized. In position-oriented families, status and roles are ascribed, and members follow rules without questioning the authority figure.[22] Thus, in some cultures, but not others, the sex of the parent determines who possesses the power to influence other family members.

The family also influences perception and communication. Chinese children, for example, are taught to respect and feel a lifelong obligation to their parents. The Chinese proverb "To forget one's ancestors is to be a brook without a source, a tree without a root" reflects this belief. In other cultures, such as India, it is common for males to be perceived as superior and for men and women to eat separately, or for the women to eat only once the men have finished. In Indian culture, boys usually have more freedom of expression than do girls.[23]

However, it is important to remember that variation within cultures exists. The family experience of one person will differ from that of another. As a result, when two people from different families decide to create a new family of their own, they may enter their partnership with different value systems and role and rule definitions. Unless we talk about our differences and reveal our expectations, we may fail to clarify assumptions, clash regarding our roles and responsibilities, and be unable to negotiate our differences. This makes it more likely that we will fail to meet many of the challenges of family communication.

## GENDER AND THE FAMILY

The family is an important source of our attitudes regarding gender and what it means to be male, female, or transgender. Different families deal with such issues as gender identity and male and female authority and power in different ways. Through both overt and unconscious communication, families contribute to male and female role assignments. Consider your own family. To what extent do the notions it espouses regarding household roles, occupational choices, areas of responsibility, sources of emotional support, and how men and women should interact with sons and daughters and with each other reveal its feelings about gender issues?

### Who Has the Responsibility?

In the United States, men were long given primary responsibility for meeting their families' financial needs. Now, women share or perform this role. Similarly, while women were more likely than men to provide comfort, care, and warmth for family members, now these responsibilities also tend to be shared. Still, women continue to devote more time to housework and child care than do men.[24] As you grew up, the role expectations held by your family members—the kinds of activities in which they encouraged you to engage, the kinds of emotional behavior they expected you to exhibit—likely influenced your personal perceptions of what is appropriate.

### What Are the Gender Expectations?

In addition to role assignments, parental communication affects gender expectations, traditionally by reinforcing cooperation, helpfulness, and nurturance in girls and competition, independence, industriousness, and assertiveness in boys.[25] Parents communicate gender expectations to children in the ways they relate to their children, the clothes and toys they buy for them, the chores they assign to them, and how they speak to them. Girls, for example are often asked to help take care of and be responsible for other children, while boys are assigned to take care of things.[26] In addition, parents are likely to address boys in a more active, content-focused manner, whereas they address girls in softer tones, with content often focused on thoughts and feelings.

Although children of both sexes are socialized regarding the importance of being masculine or feminine, positive changes are occurring in societal views of what constitute masculinity and femininity. The increased sharing of tasks by men and women correlates positively with increased disclosure and relationship maintenance. Children encouraged to grow up outside conventional gender roles are likely to exhibit broader sex-role views and broader communication repertoires than those from families in which traditional gender roles are strictly followed.

Does life in your family ever resemble life in a sitcom?

## MEDIA, TECHNOLOGY, AND THE FAMILY

What do we learn from the media, particularly "reality" shows and sitcoms, concerning family member communication? Many programs continue to offer distorted, stereotypical views of contemporary family members, though they are changing. Men still tend to be presented as aggressive, confident, and powerful, while women too often are depicted as obsessed with shopping, overly emotional, and highly sexualized.[27] Yet, there is hope. Newer media offerings present more complex depictions, portraying men and women with combinations of qualities and responsibilities. The sitcom *Modern Family*, for example, depicts both traditional and nontraditional masculinity and femininity, with kind and gentle men, gay couples, and independent women. *Dirty Little Liars*, in contrast capitalized on presenting strong, smart, but cunning women who pursued their goals with a "no matter what" approach.

## TRY THIS

### The TV Family

1. While viewing a contemporary sitcom or drama that depicts a family, identify the following:

    a. The members of the family, their roles, and their relationships to one another
    b. The factors that seem to hold family members together
    c. The subjects about which family members communicate
    d. The nature of a conflict they experience
    e. How they resolve the conflict

2. Compare and contrast the television family with your own family. Based on your analysis, imagine a sitcom or drama involving your family. What conclusions can you draw about the nature of communication in your own family?

When it comes to technology, social media tools keep family members who may be widely dispersed across a state, a country, or the world closer by facilitating their continued interaction. They facilitate long distance familial relationships just as they do romantic ones. Soldiers deployed abroad are able to video-chat with their families virtually daily.[28]

# INTERPERSONAL COMMUNICATION AT WORK

Whether we are in an entry-level position or the CEO, our work depends on our ability to negotiate the roles and rules of the workplace. How effectively we communicate at work can make the difference between career success and failure. In fact, it is hard to imagine any work-related activity that does not depend on some form of interpersonal communication. Whether we are concerned with management–employee relations, conflict resolution, decision making, problem solving, or leadership, good interpersonal skills are necessary. Determining why some organizations function well and others do not may be as simple as identifying the kinds of interpersonal relationships that the people who work in them have.[29]

## RELATIONSHIPS ARE THE ORGANIZATION

Like family members, organizational personnel share interdependent relationships. In fact, were it not for their interaction, there would be no organization. Being savvy and knowledgeable about how to build person-to-person relationships is key to nurturing both individual and organizational growth. Chapters 2 and 13 we discussed some of the effects of loneliness. Loneliness, it turns out, is not merely a personal issue. It also can be an organizational issue, limiting productivity and increasing employee anxiety. Like anger and happiness, loneliness may be contagious. Having close relationships with colleagues—even just one—can make a difference.[30] Rugged individualism no longer dominates the thinking of successful organizations. Team players are seen as increasingly important. Thus, we need to take time to explore how a workplace organizes and energizes those who work in it.[31]

## THE DYAD AND THE ORGANIZATION

As we noted in Chapter 1, the dyad, or two-person relationship, is the most basic level of interpersonal interaction. Numerous instances of dyadic interaction occur daily in organizational settings as co-workers interact with each other and the organization's leaders. The relationship level is where most of the organization's work gets done. It is also where we encounter frequent difficulties.

Communication in the workplace can flow either horizontally or vertically. Among the dyads formed in organizations are co-worker relationships, in which communication flows horizontally; leader–follower relationships, in which communication flows upward and downward; worker–customer/client relationships, in which communication flows horizontally; and mentoring relationships, in which communication flows upward and downward. An increasing number of younger workers are mentoring top managers on how to use social media and other technology

Interpersonal communication sustains work relationships.

trends, a practice known as *reverse mentoring*.[32] Whatever the dyads' composition, the effectiveness of the workplace depends on the effectiveness of dyads.

## A Question of Power and Independence

Some people in organizations are its leaders, while others work with and under them. Although the organization's leaders and team members depend on each other, those in leadership positions exert varying degrees of control over others. Still by networking, building their innovation skills, and cultivating charisma, younger employees are able to gain informal power unconnected to the organization chart.[33]

When leaders' interactions are perceived as supportive, open, and honest, employees tend to find their jobs more satisfying. Another contributor to employee satisfaction is the degree of *argumentativeness* present. In this context, argumentativeness is not a negative. Rather, it is the tendency to recognize controversial issues in communication situations, to present and defend positions taken on the issues, and to question the positions others have taken.[34] When workers perceive their bosses to be high in argumentativeness and low in verbal aggressiveness—that is, their managerial style neither blames workers nor denies them the right to disagree—workers are likely to have higher levels of job satisfaction. The nurturance of independent-mindedness, or allowing workers to express their opinions and interests without denying those of others, plays an important role in the relational satisfaction the organization's members.[35]

This doesn't mean that working with those who see things as we do doesn't matter to us, because it does. It is comfortable to work with those who share our goals and values. Yet, to sustain relational satisfaction, we also need to be comfortable expressing differences. That said, we appreciate working with and for others whose tolerance for disagreement is high.[36]

## A Question of Trust

When workers perceive an organization's climate to be trusting and supportive, their relational satisfaction is generally high. A culture of openness makes genuine expressions of ideas and feelings possible. If employees fear being punished for revealing true feelings, they will suppress them. We are more likely to trust those whose behavior is consistent and who increase our own feelings of security.

Trust is built through risk and confirmation and destroyed through risk and disconfirmation (see Chapter 9). When you disclose your thoughts and feelings to a co-worker, and that person responds with acceptance, support, and cooperation, as well as reciprocating by disclosing their feelings, you are more apt to trust that person. We demonstrate trustworthiness by not exploiting another's vulnerabilities.

## A Question of Perception

Workers who understand each other's job responsibilities and problems tend to exhibit higher morale and openness than those whose perceptions clash.[37] If, when communicating, employees are overly ambitious, then they are more likely to distort information as it is passed up to the organization's leadership in the effort to please. Thus, such employees answer questions with what they think the boss wants to hear, not with what they actually think. Leaders, in contrast, may discount positive information about employees, but pay more attention to critical information.[38] What impact might such a perceptual practice have on your career trajectory?

Jupiterimages/liquidlibrary/Thinkstock

Brainstorming encourages a free exchange of ideas.

## NETWORKS, INTERACTION, AND RELATIONSHIP SATISFACTION

Workplace networks are communication paths affecting the amount and type of communication employees send and receive, and how freely ideas and feelings flow through the organization. **Organizational networks** may be formal, describing structured, established, official lines of communication, or they may be informal, describing the unofficial channels of communication—who actually talks to whom and about what.[39]

Workers network both offline and online, connecting with others to share resources, deepen knowledge, complete assignments, and reach goals.[40] Just as in a family, an organization's network reveals the extent to which every member functions as an active member in relationships with others. People who occupy central positions in a network are more satisfied, have higher morale, and have greater ability to exert influence than those occupying peripheral positions. Organizations that allow workers to circulate and make new connections are more likely to prosper.[41]

## WORKING IN TEAMS

Although interaction at the dyadic level serves as the most basic unit for exploring organizational interaction, communication within and between teams is central.

### Creating a Healthy Work Climate

In his classic book *Communication Within the Organization,* Charles Redding identifies components of an effective work climate: supportiveness, participative decision making, trust among group members, openness and candor, and high-performance goals.[42] The healthier a work group's climate, the more effectively the team's members are able to work. Likewise, Douglas McGregor, an expert in organizational communication, attributes the effectiveness of work groups to these characteristics:

- The working atmosphere tends to be informal, comfortable, and relaxed.

- There is ample discussion pertinent to the task at hand, in which virtually all participate.

- Members understand, accept, and commit themselves to the group's task or objective.

- Members listen to each other. Every idea put forth is given a fair hearing.

- Disagreements are not suppressed. Rather, the reasons for disagreement are examined carefully as the group seeks to resolve them rationally rather than to dominate or silence dissenters.

- Most important decisions are reached by consensus in which it is clear that everyone generally agrees and is willing to support the decision.

- Criticism is frequent, frank, and relatively comfortable. There is little evidence of personal attack, either overt or hidden.

- Members freely express their feelings.

- When action needs to be taken, clear assignments are made and accepted.

- The chairperson does not dominate, nor do members defer to the chair. In fact, the group's leadership shifts, depending on circumstances. The issue is not who controls the group, but how the job is done.

- The group is cognizant of its own operation.[43]

## Practice Effective Decision Making

How well groups work depends at least in part on their decision making. To work effectively, groups are likely to rely on a number of methods designed to increase problem-solving effectiveness, among which are reflective thinking, brainstorming, and the conscious avoidance of groupthink.

**Use reflective thinking.** The **reflective thinking framework**, first proposed by John Dewey in 1910, remains a favored problem-solving approach. It consists of 6 steps:

1. What is the problem?
2. What are the facts of the situation?
3. What criteria must an acceptable solution meet?
4. What are the possible solutions?
5. Which is the best solution?
6. How can the solution be implemented?

For the reflective thinking framework to work as intended, the team's members need to suspend judgment and open themselves to all available ideas, facts, and opinions. To ensure this occurs, as they make their way through the sequence's steps, team members ask themselves questions such as the following:

- Are we using all of the group's resources?

- Are we using our time well?

- Are we open, engaging in fact-finding and inquiry?

- Are we listening to and demonstrating respect for each other?

- Are we resisting pressuring those who disagree?

- Is the atmosphere in which we are working supportive, trusting, and collaborative?

**Use brainstorming.** A technique for promoting the free flow of ideas during problem solving, **brainstorming** was devised in 1957 by advertising executive Alex Osborn.[44] To ensure that brainstorming sessions are successful, team members need to

- Temporarily suspend judgment. Do not evaluate or criticize ideas as they are suggested.

- Encourage freewheeling. It is easier to tame a wild idea than to give life to one that is inert.

- Stress quantity of ideas. The greater the number of ideas, the better the chance of finding a good one.

- Build on the ideas of other members. Modify, combine, and mix together ideas to generate different combinations or patterns.

- Record all ideas.

- Only after brainstorming is completed do members evaluate ideas for their usefulness and applicability.

By following the brainstorming guidelines, groups can avoid shooting down ideas before having the chance to consider them fully. Defeatist phrases such as "That won't work" and "You've got to be kidding" have no place.

While criticism is discouraged during the brainstorming process, after the brainstorming session ends, it is important for team members to debate and assess the contributions and viewpoints it has produced. Doing this enhances productivity. Dissent wakes up participants, encouraging them to dig beneath the surface of their ideas.[45]

**Avoid groupthink.** The third strategy, the avoidance of **groupthink**, finds the group making a conscious effort not to pressure individual members to conform to the majority opinion in order to reach consensus.[46] Instead, the group works to realistically appraise alternative courses of actions, while ensuring that minority or unpopular views are expressed and listened to. When working in a group, members should be alert to the following symptoms of groupthink:

- There is an *illusion of invulnerability*. Members feel so secure about a group decision that they ignore warning signs that the decision may be flawed.

- Members use *rationalizations* to discount warnings.

- There is an unquestioned belief in the *inherent morality* of the group and its actions.

- Those who disagree with the group are *stereotyped* as evil, weak, or stupid. An "us" versus "them" attitude is fostered.

- The group applies direct *pressure* to any members who question the stereotypes. The guiding ethic is that if you are a loyal member, you will not question the group's direction.

- *Self-censorship* occurs as members strive not to have others perceive them as deviating from the group's consensus.

- The *illusion of unanimity* causes group members to interpret silence as agreement.

- Members serve as self-appointed *mindguards* in an effort to protect the group and its leader from adverse information.

Groups engaging in groupthink let a desire for consensus interfere with the need to think critically. The mental efficiency of the group deteriorates when members exhibit defensive avoidance and when healthy disagreements and conflicts are suppressed. Work groups that consciously seek to avoid becoming trapped by the dynamics of groupthink produce better decisions.

# CULTURE AND THE WORKPLACE

Our shrinking world requires enhanced understanding of diverse cultures. Although English serves as the international language of business, there remain significant differences in how people around the world relate to each other at work.

For example, the **participative leadership** style common in many American companies may be less effective and less used in countries where **authoritarian leadership** is practiced.[47] Authoritarian leaders use a dominating and directive communication style as they determine policies and make decisions that team members are expected to support. Participative leaders, in contrast, act as guides to team members who are free to identify goals, establish procedures, and reach their own conclusions. In organizations with participative leaders, virtually any member may fulfill any leadership function.

Similarly, the common American practice of organizations rewarding their best workers with bonuses would not be well received by Japanese workers, who are unaccustomed to being singled out and do not like receiving individual attention. The Japanese also are unaccustomed to the bluntness and independence often displayed by U.S. business representatives.

We can all benefit from increasing our understanding of how cultural differences affect on-the-job relationships. As we explore some of these differences, however, keep in mind that characterizing a national work culture does not mean that every person in that country ascribes to that culture. Individual variations and differences will always exist.

## Are Workers Dominant or Submissive?

Some cultures instill in their members a desire to dominate their environment, while others promote a desire to live in harmony with it. Workers in the United States, for example, interact directly with each other, typically seeking to dominate their environment by directly influencing or even controlling those with whom they work. Workers in Asian cultures, in contrast, work instead to preserve the peace, interacting with one another much more indirectly and often less offensively. American businesspeople generally prefer that others get to the point and put all their cards on the table.[48] In contrast, Asian businesspeople try not to reveal their emotions, may practice avoidance, use third-party intermediaries, and go out of their way to help others save face.

## Are Workers Individualistic or Collectivistic?

Whereas workplaces in the United States, Great Britain, and Canada historically have promoted individualism, in other countries, such as Japan, China, and Israel, the emphasis has been placed on group harmony and loyalty instead. As discussed in Chapter 7, in individualistic cultures people tend to think more of themselves, their personal goals and potential for success, and the needs of their immediate families. In collectivistic cultures, people are likely to show considerable allegiance to their organizations. Members of individualistic cultures base decisions on what is good for the individual. Those in collectivistic cultures, in contrast, weigh the benefits to the individual and the benefits to the group and opt for what is best for the group. Members of individualistic cultures are known to use confrontational strategies when handling interpersonal issues. Members of collectivistic cultures characteristically do not, believing that "the nail that sticks up gets pounded down."

## How Do Workers Perceive the Need for Space?

Members of different cultures perceive space differently. In the United States, for example, employees prefer private space and have a greater need for personal space than do members of other cultures. The harder it is to gain access to someone who works in an organization, the more important that person is perceived to be. In Japan and the Middle East, in contrast, leaders and followers often share the same space.[49] In organizations, furniture may be used to communicate space needs. For example, when workers from the United States meet to talk they generally prefer a face-to-face arrangement or one in which their chairs are placed at right angles. Workers belonging to Asian cultures, however, generally prefer a side-by-side arrangement; the desire to avoid direct eye contact may account for this preference (see Figure 14.4).[50] What advantages and disadvantages do you see for each type of arrangement?

### FIGURE 14.4
Preferred Furniture Arrangements: U.S. and Asian Cultures

Preferred by people in the United States

Preferred by Asian cultures

Face-to-face          Right angles          Side-by-side

## How Do Workers Perceive Time?

Culture influences our perception of time. While people in some societies are oriented toward the past, others, including those in the United States and Canada, place more emphasis on the present or the future. The business strategies used by organizations in these countries are not as concerned with where the organizations have been as they are with where they are now and where they are going. People from Asian countries tend to be even more future oriented and consider long timeframes in planning.

Cultural preferences regarding time similarly affect whether someone thinks it rude for another to do two things at once, such as texting or reading e-mail during a meeting. In cultures with a monochromic time orientation, such as the United States, Germany, and Switzerland, time is perceived to be linear and segmented. In these cultures, most believe that only one thing should be done at a time. In cultures with a polychromic time orientation, such as Latin American and Middle Eastern cultures, time is perceived more loosely, and people rather than tasks are central. In these cultures, it is more acceptable to devote attention to several activities simultaneously. Thus, people in monochromic cultures schedule appointments, don't run late, and believe in following a plan. In polychromic cultures, maintaining harmonious relations is seen as more important than the agenda.[51]

# Culture Can Shock

What happens when the communication customs of businesspeople from different cultures clash? What can be done to resolve the resulting problems? Consider the following observation of a business meeting made by practitioner Richard G. Linowes more than two decades ago.

Around a conference table in a large U.S. office tower, three American executives sat with their new boss, Mr. Akiro Kusumoto, the newly appointed head of a Japanese firm's subsidiary, and two of his Japanese lieutenants. The meeting was called to discuss ideas for reducing operating costs. Mr. Kusumoto began by outlining his company's aspirations for its long-term U.S. presence. He then turned to the current budgetary matter. One Japanese manager politely offered one suggestion, and an American then proposed another. After gingerly discussing the alternatives for quite some time, the then exasperated American blurted out: "Look, that idea is just not going to have much impact. Look at the numbers! We should cut this program, and I think we should do it as soon as possible!" In the face of such bluntness, uncommon and unacceptable in Japan, Mr. Kusumoto fell silent. He leaned back, drew air between his teeth, and felt a deep longing to "return East." He realized his life in this country would be filled with many such jarring encounters, and lamented his posting to a land of such rudeness.

1. Why do you think Mr. Kusumoto was shocked by the American executive's outburst?

2. What, in your opinion, caused the American executive to become exasperated in the first place?

3. Were you in the shoes of Mr. Kusumoto or the American executive, how would you have responded?

Source: Richard G. Linowes, "The Japanese Manager's Traumatic Entry into the United States: Understanding the American-Japanese Cultural Divide," *Academy of Management Executive*, November 1993.

What it means to be "on time" also differs among cultures. Being punctual for business meetings is very important in the United States, Germany, and Switzerland. In Latin American and Middle Eastern countries, however, businesspeople typically display a much more casual approach to punctuality. Arabs, for example, believe that God alone decides when things get accomplished.[52]

## How Diverse Are the Interpersonal Needs and Skills of Workers?

Members of Asian cultures are likely to stress the meeting of collective needs, while among Americans, meeting individual needs usually is the priority. Thus, while helping workers attain self-actualization may be a goal of U.S. organizations, in Asian cultures, the goal is belonging.

The practice of interpersonal skills also differs. In some countries, such as Spain and Portugal, managers are likely to be more aware of employees' feelings and more concerned with their welfare, whereas German and French managers are less so. Whereas the Dutch appear quite willing to cooperate, the French are often the least willing. The Japanese tend to rely on objectivity in decision making, but in Latin America, intuition often rules. While managers in the United States and Latin America are often praised for having interpersonal competence, this does not mean they are perfect.[53]

## Are Members of Different Generations Prepared to Work Together?

In recent years, some American workplaces have included employees from five generations. In ascending chronological order, they are the Greatest Generation (1901–1924), the Silent Generation (1925–1946), the Baby Boomers (1946–1964), Generation X (1965 through the very early 1980s), the Millennials, also known as Generation Y (early1980s through 1994). As the youngest members of the Greatest Generation have left the workforce, the oldest members of the Gen Z or the iGeneration (since 1994) have begun to enter. Since the generation we were born into influences our communication, members of different generations need to understand one another in order to determine how best to work together.[54]

For example, nearly all the members of the Greatest Generation, known for their hard work and respect for authority, are now likely retired. Though half of all Boomers are expected to have retired by 2018, many still seek personal fulfilment through work, having expected to be employed long term and loyal toward employers. Boomers tend to be optimistic, involved, and not afraid to question authority. Members of Gen X are both individualistic and team players but seek more work–life balance than the Boomers and tend to be more skeptical, challenging others. Millennials, though reputed to feel special and entitled, are also team oriented, technologically savvy, capable of multitasking, and achievement motivated.[55] Finally, though the characteristics of members of the iGen are still being revealed, there is little doubt that they are being influenced by ubiquitous technology and their need to multi-task. For members of this generation, their phone is a computer.[56] They also are more entrepreneurial and more global in their thinking.[57] Of course, not every person in a generation displays all of the characteristics generally associated with that generation.

When it comes to offices, workers from earlier generations tended to work in cubicles. Millennials and iGen members, in contrast, prefer open spaces—with large kitchens and communal areas where employees mingle and share ideas. The goal? To make the workplace homey and less formal.[58] What's your preference?

iStock.com/Dean Mitchell

How prepared are you to work with people from different cultures and generations?

Earlier in this chapter we noted the increase in reverse mentoring. Many older workers, however, don't enjoy being mentored by someone younger. How would you navigate such a situation?

# GENDER AND THE WORKPLACE

Cultural views of gender influence communication in organizational settings. Only a short time ago, the sexual division of labor was a fundamental feature of the workplace. Although the divisions are no longer so extreme, gender inequality and discrimination still exist.[59] Bro culture and sexual harassment continue in some workplaces. However, bad behavior has no place in any organization.[60]

Let us explore some of the prescriptive roles once accorded to men and women, the ways in which these stereotypes devalued women's work, and efforts made to diminish such stereotypical assumptions.

## Stereotypes of Women in Organizations

About a half century ago, organizational theorist and Harvard educator Rosabeth Moss Kanter observed that some organizations exhibited a tendency to classify women into one of four roles: sex object, mother, child, or iron maiden.[61] While some believe these stereotypes are outdated, they continue to be debated. Let us explore each in turn.

When a woman is seen in the role of sex object, conversations are likely to focus on a woman's appearance or on sex, rather than on her performance, and may constitute sexual harassment.

The stereotype of women as mothers also influences their treatment in organizations. When male co-workers or supervisors are in need of support or sympathy, they characteristically seek to interact with a woman rather than with another man. Also, working women who have children are believed to be less committed to their work than are men with children, causing women to be passed over more frequently for training and advancement opportunities.

The stereotype of women as children reinforces men's need to protect them. By asserting that women are not mature enough to make difficult decisions, men also restrict women's opportunities to lead.

The stereotype of women as iron maidens reflects the belief that women who succeed in achieving positions of power get there because of their unwomanliness—that is, because they possess characteristics such as independence, ambition, toughness, and forcefulness, all of which are usually associated with men.[62]

Any of these stereotypes can keep women from advancing in their careers and from having successful marriages. Because of perceived incompetence or lack of femininity, women may be held back from realizing their full potential. Despite ample evidence to the contrary, a feeling persists among some that because women tend to be more affiliative and nurturing than men, they are less able to make tough decisions, are not assertive enough, and are too worried about disappointing others to be effective leaders.

## Stereotypes of Men in Organizations

Men are also stereotyped in organizations, but, as communication expert Julia Wood observes, the stereotypes attributed to men tend to be more positive. Men are seen as sturdy oaks, fighters, and breadwinners.[63] The stereotype suggests that men who are tough, self-sufficient, and in control of their feelings are "real men" and are thus of more value to the organization than are men who lean on others, complain, or give in to their fears. As a result, men sometimes choose to hide mistakes and suffer stress-related ailments in silence.

The stereotype of men as breadwinners reflects society's expectation that men be their families' primary wage earners. Frequently, a man's ability to earn a good income is a measure of his success. This takes a toll on men. In fact, CDC data reveal that men are 3.5 times as likely to commit suicide as women, with male suicide rates peaking in middle age.[64] In 1992, Willard Gaylin hypothesized that the higher suicide rates of men was attributed to the social humiliations they experienced when perceived as workplace failures.[65] While these stereotypes of men have little if any validity, they also limit women's chances for comparable workplace growth.

## Gender and Work–Life Mix

Sheryl Sandberg's book *Lean In*, and the movement of the same name, push women to be more ambitious.[66] Interestingly, some men react negatively to women's career success, with divorce rates increasing in the marriages of successful women but not in the marriages of successful men. Women also continue to spend more time on household chores than men, even when both are employed full time.[67]

Women's struggle to balance work and personal life has been discussed for some time, but in recent years, it has become increasingly common to hear about men's pursuit of such balance. More and more men desire to spend time with their families and have their work reflect their interests. Companies that have made allowances for the personal lives of women are similarly making allowances for the personal lives of men.

## Leadership and Management Style

According to the International Women's Forum, the management styles of men and women tend to differ. Male managers describe their style in terms of a series of exchanges involving rewards or punishments for the actions of others. In contrast, female managers are more concerned with exhibiting interactive leadership—in encouraging and sharing both power and decision making with others.[68] Of note, qualities such as assertiveness, competitiveness, and instrumentality—usually associated with men—are valued in leaders. On the other hand, so are characteristics such as supportiveness, receptiveness, participation, and collaboration—skills more typically attributed to women. In addition, bringing women into positions of power boosts the bottom line.[69]

Work life and home life are colliding. What will you do to maintain a healthy work–life mix?

When men and women are able to work together well, they complement and enhance each other's performance.[70]

## Workplace Pathologies

Bullying and sexual harassment are dysfunctional workplace behaviors. All too prevalent, verbal or nonverbal hostility toward workers and unwelcome sexual overtures or demands render the workplace an offensive and intimidating environment.

**Bullying.** Workplace bullying is too common.[71] Anyone in an organization can be a bully's target.

Workplace bullying generally involves verbal abuse and typically includes gossiping about a target, online and/or offline; insulting and threatening the target; acting unkindly toward, humiliating, and being harshly critical of the target; assaulting the target's dignity; denigrating the target publicly; and excluding the target from social functions. (Unlike school bullying, workplace bullying does not typically involve physical abuse.)

While most workplace bullies are male, bullies may operate in groups, attacking male and female targets in approximately equal numbers.[72] While peer-to-peer bullying occurs, most bullies are in higher-ranking positions than their targets. To combat bullying, workplaces need to communicate their opposition to it by establishing a policy of zero tolerance and taking action when it is observed or reported.

**Sexual harassment.** The U.S. Equal Employment Opportunity Commission defines sexual harassment as unsolicited and unwelcome behavior of a sexual nature that makes the target uncomfortable. Members of either sex can be sexually harassed—usually for not living up to another's expectations for their gender—but a 2018 survey revealed that 81 percent of women reported having been sexually harassed.[73] There are two categories of sexual harassment:

- *Quid pro quo harassment* ("something for something") makes employment opportunities dependent on the granting of sexual favors. Negative consequences are the cost of a refusal, and promotions and expensive gifts are common rewards.
- *Hostile work environment harassment* includes sexual conduct such as posting sexually explicit photos, telling sexually charged jokes, making lewd remarks and gestures, and engaging in sexual banter that makes a worker uncomfortable and intimidates him or her.

In the United States, companies are not permitted to suspend or reassign employees who complain about being sexually harassed.[74] To educate their employees and to protect themselves, many workplaces now require that all employees attend programs aimed at the prevention of sexual harassment.

Because neither bullying nor sexual harassment has been eradicated from the workplace, both problems need continuing attention. We can help to reduce their incidence by challenging these behaviors when they occur.

# MEDIA, TECHNOLOGY, AND THE WORKPLACE

How have the pervasiveness of the media and technology influenced both perceptions and realities of the workplace? In what ways have they contributed to global thinking and personalization?

## Media Portrayals

Workplace situations depicted in TV programs and feature films frequently highlight casual sexism and worker harassment. The portrayals of leaders and supervisors have ranged from comic, to misguided, to corrupt. Similarly, workers have been portrayed as overly ambitious, technologically gifted or inept, cunning, lazy, and stressed. All the foibles of the modern workplace have been put under a spotlight—including depictions of men and women.

When depicted in the media as members of a workforce, women are sometimes shown having trouble juggling work and personal relationships. More frequently than men, women are shown discussing love interests, problems with their children, their clothing, or other non-work issues, making them appear less professional. Women also are depicted spending significant amounts of time watching the men work.[75] Men are usually presented as job focused and helpers of less competent women. They also are depicted as "in-charge" more often. In contrast, women are more frequently portrayed as career driven and ambitious, conniving and promiscuous, or isolated and lonely. Such portrayals do little to allay the persistence of the "glass ceiling."[76]

## Technological Realities

Workplace communication is no longer limited to face-to-face interactions, phone conversations, or paper or e-mail memos. Newer technologies continue to redefine our work lives, making it more difficult for us to separate our work and personal lives. While technology affords us the freedom to work in multiple environments, including at home, it also means we are reachable 24/7.[77]

Many of us now spend significant segments of the day with our smartphones, laptops, and tablets, texting and/or tweeting. Virtual teams—made up of members who do not have to assemble physically to work together—are commonplace. Such teams, composed of people who may live in different countries, locations, and time zones, can tackle and accomplish assignments quickly and efficiently—that is, if the technology is used appropriately and not to engage in non-work-related online activities, such as playing games, shopping, and updating Facebook, during work hours.[78]

How technology is used in an organization often indicates whether its leaders care for and respect those who work in them. For example, do the organization's leaders rely on technology to deliver bad news, or do they do it personally? Firing an employee via tweet or text message is simply inappropriate.

By using social networking, we can facilitate communication and collaboration with co-workers as well as peers in our field. Cross-functional teams (teams that run across different areas of a company) create new social connections that facilitate the exchange and building of knowledge, while fostering team members' embeddedness in one another's lives.[79] Multi-teaming—that is, being a member of several teams—and publicly relating to co-workers through internal and personal social networking, including tweeting and retweeting, can also help enhance professional visibility. As we share information and experiences online, we also extend our reach, widen our perspective, and advance our professional reputation by growing our social capital and driving others to our online presence.[80]

Increasing numbers of employers now turn to Facebook, Instagram, Twitter, and LinkedIn to derive information about both job applicants' and employees' character, personality, and potential for job success. Our online and professional lives are crashing into each other, with some people losing their jobs over their online activity.[81] Others may miss out on job opportunities because of what they have posted.[82]

# INTERPERSONAL COMMUNICATION IN HEALTH CARE SETTINGS

The field of **health communication** is concerned with the study of human interaction in the health care process.[83] Whether we succeed at maintaining our health or are able to help others maintain theirs depend in part on the following three factors:

1. How effective we are at interacting interpersonally in diverse health care settings

2. How capable we are at developing and maintaining effective health care relationships

3. How adept we are at resolving health-related conflicts and communication problems

Many of our communicative interactions about health occur not in formal health care settings but in more informal settings such as in our homes, over the Internet, or in our workplaces, when, for example, we converse with a co-worker about a health matter and offer our social support. It is probable that you offer others more social support than you realize. When you listen to a grieving parent or help someone search the Internet for information, you are offering social support. Social support enhances healing, reduces stress, and builds feelings of self-worth. Thus, receiving and offering social support can be health enhancing.[84]

# THE CONSUMER–HEALTH CARE PROVIDER DYAD

Communication serves four key functions in the relationship between a health care consumer and a health care provider, each dependent on interpersonal communication:

1. *Diagnosis:* requires data gathering, data interpretation, and problem-solving skills

2. *Cooperation:* requires skill in developing quality interactions that foster effective provider–patient interactions; involves eliciting patient consent, including an agreement to follow prescribed measures

3. *Counseling:* relates to the provider's effectiveness in delivering therapeutic communication

4. *Educating:* involves the provider in disseminating information to others in the effort to reduce health risks and increase health care effectiveness

How can we improve our abilities to interact with each other to fulfill these functions? What can we do to ensure the sharing of sufficient information to facilitate correct diagnosis, needed cooperation, and proper treatment? The answers to these questions lie less in what we need to do alone and more in what we need to do together.

While medical advances have been significant, consumers continue to accuse some health care providers of insensitivity, inability to empathize, lack of trust, and deficient listening skills. Recognizing that effective interpersonal communication and trust are essential for the creation of satisfactory provider–consumer relationships, medical schools are increasingly integrating communication training into their curricula.

## Sensitivity Matters

Provider insensitivity and consumer dissatisfaction are correlated. Consider your own situation with your medical provider. You likely become upset and apprehensive when your provider does not pay sufficient attention to your medical concerns. On the other hand, your compliance with your provider's recommendations probably increases when you feel you have been listened to.

## Clear Communication Matters

To develop open and trusting provider–consumer relationships, we need to be skilled at exchanging health-based messages.[85] Finding the right words to use when communicating about health—particularly sexual health—can be difficult, but it is extremely important. Not talking about safer sex or the dangers of opioids, for example, increases the chances that individuals will engage in risky behavior.[86]

We need to be aware of the messages sent and received. Some messages frighten or confuse us. If we have difficulty describing or explaining our symptoms, others may misinterpret our words. Contributing to the clarity problem is the tendency for health care providers to use jargon, a practice that makes it more likely for us to misunderstand a diagnosis or treatment regimen and, thus, fail to comply with the provider's instructions.

## Compliance Matters

There are two key message-sending strategies for providers that influence the consumer's willingness to comply: *emphasizing of expertise* ("If you comply with my recommendations, your symptoms should diminish.") and, if the consumer resists, *threats* ("If you fail to follow my recommendations, you're a prime candidate for a stroke.").

Along with verbal messages, health care providers use a wide range of nonverbal communication cues—some that enhance and some that unintentionally undermine consumer compliance. By moving physically closer to clients, smiling, or exhibiting pleasant facial expressions, head nods, or vocal reinforcers such as "uh-huh," providers communicate high sensory involvement and caring, both enhancers of compliance.

## Perceptions Matter

In addition to misunderstanding each other, providers and consumers may misperceive or stereotype one another, further complicating their relationship. We sometimes have unreasonable performance expectations for health care providers, expecting miracle cures. Such perceptions make it highly unlikely that providers will be able to measure up in our eyes. At the same time, providers often stereotype health care consumers. They may underestimate clients' intelligence or, based on assumptions related to age, sex, or level of attractiveness, fail to foster honest exchanges of information and feelings.

## Decision Making Matters

How decisions are made and who makes them also influence patient satisfaction, compliance with prescribed treatment, and recuperation. The continuum of health care decision making shown in Figure 14.5 identifies the factors at work.[87]

At the *physician control* end of the continuum, the provider is responsible for all decision making. Because the physician has superior knowledge and abilities, the patient ought to trust him or

### FIGURE 14.5
Health Care Decision Making Continuum

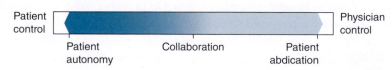

Source: Deborah Ballard-Reisch, "Health Care Providers and Consumers: Making Decisions Together," in Barbara C. Thornton and Gary L. Kreps, eds., *Perspectives on Health Communication*, Long Grove, IL: Waveland Press, 1993, p. 70.

The Interpersonal Communication Playbook

her. In the past, this was the most common model. In such a relationship, the physician does most of the talking, asks the majority of questions, frequently interrupts the patient, abruptly changes topics, or even ignores the patient. The interaction is dominated and controlled by the physician.

At the opposite end of the continuum is *patient control*. In such a relationship, the patient exercises his or her right to self-determination and assumes complete responsibility for decision making. The proliferation of health care information resources on the Internet has facilitated this option.

At the scale's midpoint is *collaboration*. In this kind of relationship, provider and patient share information, negotiate perspectives, and reach a mutually satisfactory decision. Typically more time consuming than the alternatives, this approach preserves the patient's right to participate fully in decisions affecting his or her health and allows for more balanced interaction and consensus building.

How would you describe your physician's communication effectiveness?

## CULTURE AND HEALTH COMMUNICATION

The cultural backgrounds of health care providers and the clients they treat often differ. While this does not necessarily cause problems, they can surface if either fails to recognize how culture and prevailing stereotypes influence communication about health.

When it comes to health and perceptions of illness, it is important to consider an individual's beliefs, values, and attitudes as they influence those symptoms we are prone to consult a provider about, what we expect the provider to do, and how we are likely to react when confronting a health issue.

Misunderstandings occur when people from different cultures have conflicting ideas about the nature of disease and the meaning of illness. For instance, providers who fail to understand that people from Asian cultures may perceive mental illness as dishonoring their family and community may be confused when an Asian consumer strongly denies being depressed even when all the symptoms suggest it.[88]

Providers may benefit from understanding how members of different cultures cope with the uncertainty that illness presents. Here William B. Gudykunst's uncertainty reduction theory (see Chapter 3), which addresses the desire to gather enough information to make a social encounter predictable, plays a role. In high-context cultures such as Japan, uncertainty reduction predicts if individual patients will follow group norms, while in low-context cultures such as the United States, the focus is on predicting the actions of individual patients, not group behavior. A provider's having contact with the relatives and friends of clients from high-context cultures could help to reduce the provider's uncertainty regarding patient responses.[89]

When interacting with members of different cultures, health care providers can benefit from asking the following questions: What are the person's space needs? Does he or she respond to touch? What kind of eye contact will foster trust? Are there any special rules of protocol to follow? Are there any role models that might increase treatment compliance?

## GENDER AND HEALTH CARE

Research indicates that female and male health care providers may relate to their patients differently. Male physicians tend to have stronger systematizing skills, while female physicians have stronger empathizing and social support skills.[90]

On average, compared with their male counterparts, female health care providers spend more time with patients, interrupt less frequently, elicit more medical information, and are more responsive to issues related to reproduction and sexuality. Patient visits to female providers typically last longer than visits with male providers.[91] The female physician–female patient dyad tends to be the most interactive.

## MEDIA, TECHNOLOGY, AND HEALTH CARE

Media and technology influence our interactions with health care providers; they also influence what we eat and drink, and how long we live.

### Media Messages

Although current prime-time health-related television programs do include more interesting professional women than were featured years ago, they also often contain high levels of sexual and occupational stereotyping. For examples, the female medical professionals depicted tend to be younger than the men, and they are less often identified as the people in charge.

In addition, media depictions of men as sexual aggressors and women as sex objects contribute to the pathologizing of women's bodies and the legitimating of unhealthy and destructive behaviors such as anorexia and battering. Similarly, the emphasis on eroticism and sex in entertainment helps to create a societal atmosphere that is conducive to risky sexual practices. Television also provides many models of eating and drinking practices that are not conducive to maintaining good health. Yet, despite their poor diets, with few exceptions, characters are rarely overweight. Such depictions may contribute to weight gain and dental problems in individuals who watch a lot of television.

Media portrayals of medical practitioners also help to develop a distorted picture of illness and available medical treatments. Rarely do television dramas deal with the long-term consequences of chronic illness. Instead, week after week, they present examples of acute illness, crisis situations, and injuries. What is more, the health care providers portrayed in these shows make few diagnostic errors and frequently cure dire ailments. In addition, rarely is the patient depicted as taking an active role in his or her care.

Finally, the influence on health care consumers of talk shows such as *Dr. Oz* and *The Doctors* should not be discounted. Although they enable consumers to learn about health away from the tensions of a doctor's examining room, such programs cannot substitute for the one-to-one nature of the consumer–health care provider relationship, in part because of the questionable reliability of the advice they offer consumers.

### Technology Messages

The Internet and computers have become thriving parts of the health care arena, enabling us, if we want to, to take more control over our medical futures than was previously possible. There are numerous websites devoted to disseminating health-related information, and we can even video-chat with health care providers. Burgeoning electronic communities also facilitate consumer research and consumer-to-consumer interactions. Consumers are able to explore the medical literature and compare notes with others who experience the same symptoms and afflictions. Internet support groups may also facilitate recovery and health maintenance.

Technology has improved not only our ability to process health-related information but also our ability to develop effective interpersonal relationships with health care practitioners, so that we are able to talk openly and candidly about our health and health-related issues. Apps like OurNotes makes it easier for patients to share thoughts with physicians as well as access their records.[92] This improvement in communication can itself be health enhancing.

# GAINING COMMUNICATION COMPETENCE ACROSS CONTEXTS

In our highly mobile, stress-filled technological society, life is never static. Family relationships transition or dissolve; new ones are created. Deaths, departures, and arrivals may elicit a range of emotions, from grief, resentment, fear, and jealousy to happiness. Similar comings, goings, and health-related challenges occur in organizational life. In every context, from family, to work, to health, we find ourselves needing to adapt by renegotiating the nature of our relationships.

## PREPARE TO HANDLE CONFLICT ACROSS CONTEXTS

You have a disagreement with a friend and choose to simply walk away. You disagree with a mechanic about the cost of repairing your car, but you pay up, telling yourself that you will never take your car to be fixed at that shop again. It is not so easy, however, to walk away from family or work conflicts or disagreements with health care providers. To avoid creating high-pressure situations that can result in out-of-control interactions, we need to rely on effective problem-solving and conflict resolution techniques (see also Chapter 11). We can use the following rules to foster the sharing of perceptions:

- Respond to what is going on rather than what you *think* is going on; clarify messages by paraphrasing.

- Ask for help and emotional support when you need it.

- Express your dreams and vision for the future.

- Refrain from blaming and judging others.

- Express your feelings directly without concealing them or becoming physically or verbally aggressive.

- Observe your own behavior, noticing what you say, how you sound, and what you feel during an interaction.

## RECOGNIZE THAT YOU CANNOT ALWAYS BE HAPPY AND IN GOOD HEALTH

Whether it is in a family, work, or health-related context, it is important to be able to communicate honestly, admit when you have a problem, and seek help when you are unable to resolve it on your own. Follow these guidelines to address issues as they emerge:

- Share responsibilities.

- Maintain a high level of self-disclosure and trust.

- Deal directly with unmet or unrealized expectations.

- Deal directly with changing rules and role conflicts.

- Ask questions.

- Listen more, paying attention to verbal and nonverbal cues.

- Remain open to change and be willing to relate to the person or condition that is, rather than the one that was.

## LEARN ABOUT EACH OTHER

When you share effective interpersonal family, work, and health care relationships, you focus on and talk about issues that may help you adapt to change and face new situations and circumstances. Exhibiting an "other-orientation"— focusing not just on yourself but on the other person's perceptions—facilitates this. Offer support when it is needed, take a sincere interest in another's welfare, and use online resources to help maintain social and work networks and acquire knowledge relevant to your and others' well-being. Additionally, become aware of how cultural customs and gender practices affect relationships in different contexts.

## CONNECT THE CASE

### The Case of the Problematic Reunion

"It seemed like such a good idea!" Jade moaned to Dominic, her husband. "I thought that for too long we've only been communicating on Facebook and that hosting a family reunion would be a fun way of finally getting all of us together. Now I just want to call the whole thing off! Facebook is easier."

Both Jade and Dominic work full-time jobs. Taking their two kids, ages 6 and 10, to school and then to an array of after-school and weekend activities, making child-care arrangements, and serving as caregivers for an ailing grandparent (taking him to and from doctor visits), plus a host of other responsibilities, make their lives a constant juggling act. They see their siblings, parents, aunts and uncles, and cousins far less frequently than they did when they married 15 years earlier. A family reunion seemed like the perfect way to see everybody again. So, Jade had e-mailed a bunch of invitations.

It seemed that as soon as Jade pressed *send* she was flooded with a bunch of replies asking for more information. There were questions about the date and the food she would serve, requests for transportation, queries regarding who else was invited, and complaints about who should not have been invited—it seemed that everyone had advice to offer and a hidden agenda.

No one had told Dominic's parents in advance about the reunion, and they had already planned a vacation cruise. Uncle Fred was not speaking with cousin Jennifer. Cousins Olivia and Jason were going to be away on a business trip. Nieces Jane and Keri and nephews Elijah and Conner were committed to playing in assorted Little League and soccer games. Jade's mom did not want to stay overnight at Jade's home. Aunt Tessie would love to come, but she needed someone to fly down to where she lived and help her travel to the reunion.

Jade and Dominic were ready to cancel the reunion when their children started whining that they wanted to have a party.

### Consider these questions:

1. What advice would you give Jade and Dominic about family, work, and health issues?

2. Have you or someone you know faced a similar situation? How was it resolved?

3. What kinds of attitudes or behavioral orientations would help turn this experience into a more positive one for Jade and Dominic?

# REVIEW THIS

**1. Discuss the nature of interpersonal communication in families.** ☐

The family is the core of early communicative and socialization experiences. According to systems theory, the behavior of one family member may be understood only in relation to the behavior of every other family member. Families are defined in many different ways, and many different family forms are common. In any family, however, members perform roles and have responsibilities. They create rules that guide family communication and regulate family member interaction. A family's cultural background influences its preferred communication style and whether it is position or person oriented. The family is also a source of member attitudes regarding what it means to be male or female, directly influencing the roles and responsibilities of family members. Mediated images of family affect family member satisfaction; technological innovations enable family members to maintain contact with one another.

**2. Discuss the nature of interpersonal communication in the workplace.** ☐

Those who work in organizations share interdependent relationships. The kinds of communication and the networks at play affect the organization's ability to fulfill its functions and facilitate employee morale and job satisfaction. Culture influences whether participative or authoritarian leadership is practiced. Whether employees are dominant or submissive, individualistic or collectivistic, and how they perceive space, time, and their needs are also affected by culture. In addition, cultural views of gender influence workplace roles, interactions, and expectations, and workplace relationships are influenced by both media portrayals and technological innovations.

**3. Explain the relationship between interpersonal communication and health.** ☐

People in health-related settings rely on interpersonal communication as they present, process, and react to health-related messages. No matter the setting, it is important that both parties to an interaction be sensitive to each other's needs, have an awareness of mutual expectations, understand how their manner of encoding and decoding messages and interacting with others influences relations, and recognize how to overcome perceptual barriers. When not acknowledged, cultural influences and stereotypes can interfere with communication about health, leading to misunderstandings and affecting the delivery of health care. Media representations too frequently reinforce gender stereotypes and promote unhealthy practices. Technology is facilitating a more active role for health care consumers, fostering both consumer–provider interaction and ease of finding information and support online.

**4. Identify how you can gain communication competence across contexts.** ☐

In any context, constructive observation, verbalization and discussion, problem solving, and joint decision making enhance communication.

## CHECK YOUR UNDERSTANDING

1. Can you evaluate the relational consequences of not attaining work–life balance? (See pages 391–392.)

2. Can you provide scenarios to explain how the family context influences the nature of interpersonal communication? How important to you is the performance of particular familial roles? (See pages 392–401.)

3. Can you offer examples of how gender, culture, the media, and technology influence both family and workplace relationships? (See pages 410–418.)

4. Can you explain the interface between healthy relationships and personal health? (See pages 418–423.)

5. Can you summarize steps you can take to enhance your interpersonal competence across contexts? (See pages 423–424.)

## KEY TERMS

Authoritarian leadership 413

Blended family 396

Boomerang family 397

Brainstorming 411

Commuter family 397

Groupthink 412

Health communication 420

Nuclear family 396

Organizational networks 410

Participative leadership 413

Reflective thinking framework 411

Roles 400

Rules 401

Single-parent family 396

Systems theory 397

Get the tools you need to sharpen your study skills. **SAGE edge** offers a robust online environment featuring an impressive array of free tools and resources. Access practice quizzes, eFlashcards, video, and multimedia at **edge.sagepub.com/gambleicp**.

iStock.com/bowdenimages

# Glossary

**Accommodative style:** A style of resolving conflict that is unassertive and cooperative.

**Adaptors:** Unintentional movements of the body that reveal information about psychological state or inner needs, such as nervousness.

**Affect displays:** Unintentional movements of the body that reflect the intensity of an emotional state of being.

**Affection need:** The need to give and receive love and to experience emotionally close relationships.

**Aggressive expression style:** A style of communication involving the open expression of one's needs, wants, and ideas, even at the expense of another person.

**Allness:** A perceptual fallacy that allows a person to believe that he or she knows everything about something.

**Allocentric orientation:** A perspective displayed by people who are primarily collectivistic in their thinking and behaving.

**Androgynous:** Having both masculine and feminine traits.

**Appreciative listening:** Listening engaged in for pleasure.

**Argot:** The language used by members of a co-culture.

**Assertive expression style:** A style of communication that is honest, clear, and direct.

**Attending:** Paying attention; the willingness to organize and focus on particular stimuli.

**Attitude:** A mental set or readiness that causes one to respond in a particular way to a given stimulus.

**Attribution theory:** A theory that posits that we assign meaning to behavior by ascribing motives and causes.

**Authoritarian leadership:** A style of leadership characterized by the use of dominating and directive communication.

**Avoiding style:** A style of resolving conflict that is unassertive and uncooperative.

**Balance theory:** A mode of attitude change that demonstrates the desire to live in a state of equilibrium.

**Beliefs:** The building blocks of attitudes; one's assessment of what is true or false, probable or improbable.

**Blended family:** A family with two adults and children from one or both of the adults' previous relationships, as well as possibly children from the current relationship.

**Blindering:** The unconscious adding of restrictions that do not actually exist.

**Boomerang family:** Family households containing adult children who the family thought had left permanently but have unexpectedly returned.

**Brainstorming:** A technique designed to encourage idea generation.

**Bypassing:** A communication problem that occurs when individuals think they understand each other but actually miss each other's meaning.

**Caring:** The level of emotional involvement we convey to one another.

**Category-based processing:** The processing of information about a person that is influenced by attitudes toward the group into which the person is placed.

**Channel:** A medium or passageway through which a message travels.

**Chronemics:** The study of how humans use time to communicate.

**Closed-ended question:** A question that forces the respondent to choose a specific response.

**Closure:** The process by which one fills in a missing perceptual piece.

**Co-culture:** A group of people who share a culture within a society but outside its dominant culture.

**Coercive power:** The ability to deliver negative consequences in response to the action of another; power derived from force or the threat of force.

**Cognitive dissonance:** An aversive drive propelling one toward consistency.

**Collaborative style:** A style of resolving conflict that is high in both assertiveness and cooperativeness.

**Collectivistic cultures:** Cultures in which group goals are given a higher priority than individual goals.

**Communication:** A process involving both deliberate and accidental transfer of meaning.

**Communication accommodation theory:** A theory that asserts that we adjust our language patterns to reflect how we feel about another person.

**Communication convergence:** The matching of vocabulary, speaking rate, and use of pauses with another as part of building a relationship.

**Communication divergence:** The purposeful adoption of a style of speaking that contrasts with the style of speaking of a person from whom one desires to distance oneself.

**Communication presence:** The unique composite of characteristics we present in both the physical and online worlds.

**Commuter family:** A family that includes one or more members who commute from the household's primary residence to distant work location(s) and remain there for long periods.

**Comparison level for alternatives:** A comparison of profits and costs derived from one relationship with those that might be derived from another relationship.

**Competitive relationship:** A relationship characterized by the presence of defensive and threatening behavior; a relationship in which one party aims to win, or to beat or outsmart the other party.

**Competitive style:** A style of resolving conflict that is high in assertiveness and low in cooperation.

**Complementary relationship:** A relationship based on difference in which the parties engage in opposite behaviors.

**Comprehensive listening:** Listening engaged in to gain knowledge.

**Compromising style:** A style of resolving conflict that is in the middle range in both assertiveness and cooperativeness.

**Confirmation:** A communication that tells another person that his or her self-image is affirmed.

**Confirming messages:** Messages that convey value for another person.

**Conflict resolution grid:** A model that measures an individual's preferred style of handling conflict.

**Conflict styles:** Individuals' characteristic approaches to conflict with respect to measures of assertiveness and cooperativeness.

**Connotative meaning:** Subjective meaning; personal meaning.

**Content conflict:** A conflict that revolves around a matter of fact.

**Context:** The setting in which communication takes place.

**Control need:** The need to establish and maintain relationships that allow one to experience satisfactory levels of influence and power.

**Conversation:** A relatively informal social interaction in which the roles of speaker and listener are exchanged in a nonautomatic fashion under the collaborative management of all parties.

**Conversation deprivation:** A lack of aural communication.

**Conversational rules:** Behaviors that are established, preferred, or prohibited during social exchanges.

**Conversational structure:** The typical format for conversation, comprising the greeting, topic priming, the heart of the conversation, preliminary processing, and the closing.

**Cooperative relationship:** A relationship based on supportiveness, sharing, interdependent efforts, and trust.

**Coping:** The managing of emotions.

**Cost-benefit theory:** A theory that states that we work to sustain relationships that give us the greatest total benefit and that a relationship will be sustained only as long as perceived benefits outweigh emotional expenditures; also known as social exchange theory.

**Counterfeit relationship:** A relationship based on a lie.

**Crazymaking behavior:** Behavior believed to be at the root of dysfunctional conflict.

**Critical or deliberative listening:** Listening that involves working to understand, analyze, and assess content.

**Cultural awareness:** The ability to understand the role cultural prescriptions play in shaping communication.

**Debilitative emotion:** An emotion that impedes a person's ability to function effectively.

**Defensive climate:** The climate that results when a party to a relationship perceives or anticipates a threat.

**Denotative meaning:** Dictionary meaning; emotion-free meaning.

**DESC script:** A strategy for expressing one's own feelings and understanding the feelings of others; DESC is an acronym for describe, express, specify, and consequences.

**Describing feelings:** Revealing how another's behavior affects one without expressing any judgment of that behavior.

**Descriptive statements:** Statements that recount observable behavior without judgment.

**Dialogic listening:** Listening that involves give-and-take between persons interacting as they cocreate a relationship.

**Disconfirmation:** Communication that denies another person's significance.

**Disconfirming messages:** Messages that convey disregard for another person.

**Displacement:** A defense mechanism through which one releases anger or frustration by communicating feelings to people or objects perceived to be more accessible and less dangerous than the person who precipitated the feelings.

**Displaying feelings:** Overtly enacting one's feelings.

**Dominant culture:** The culture that has the most power.

**Dyad:** Two individuals interacting; a two-person relationship.

**Dysfunctional conflict:** Conflict that creates one or more serious relationship problems.

**Effect:** The result of a communication episode.

**Ego conflict:** A conflict that revolves around an individual's self-worth.

**Emblems:** Deliberate movements of the body that are consciously sent and easily translated into speech.

**Emotion contagion:** The passing of a mood from person to person, influenced by individuals' ability to respond to emotion in kind or to exhibit a parallel response.

**Emotion state:** An emotion of limited endurance.

**Emotion trait:** An emotion that persists during person-to-person interactions regardless of with whom one is interacting.

**Emotional ineptitude:** The inability to handle and control one's emotional responses.

**Emotional intelligence:** The ability to motivate oneself or to persist in the face of frustration; to control impulse and delay gratification; to regulate one's mood and keep distress from swamping the abilities to think, empathize, and hope.

**Emotionally tone-deaf:** Unable to listen empathetically.

**Emotions:** The feelings one experiences in reaction to one's surroundings.

**Emotive language:** Language that announces the user's attitude toward a subject.

**Empathetic listening:** Listening that involves understanding and internalizing the emotional content of a message.

**Empathetic responsiveness:** A listener's experiencing of an emotional response that corresponds with the emotions a speaker is experiencing.

**Empathy:** The ability to understand another's thoughts and feelings and to communicate that understanding to the person; the ability to comprehend another's point of view.

**Equivocal language:** Words that may be interpreted in more than one way.

**Ethnocentrism:** The tendency to perceive what is right or wrong, good or bad, according to the categories and values of one's own culture.

**Euphemism:** Less direct or inoffensive language substituted for blunt language.

**Evaluative feedback:** Feedback that reveals one's feelings or reactions to what one heard, providing a positive or a negative assessment.

**Evaluative statements:** Judgmental pronouncements.

**Expectancy violation theory:** A theory that addresses our reactions to nonverbal behavior and notes that violations of nonverbal communication norms can be positive or negative.

**Expected self:** The self that others assume one will exhibit.

**Expert power:** Power derived from having special knowledge or skills that another thinks he or she needs.

**Expressive roles:** Roles focused on helping, supporting, nurturing, and being responsive to the needs of others; relationship-oriented roles.

**Extensional orientation:** The type of orientation one displays when not blinded by labels.

**External feedback:** Responses received from others.

**Face-saving:** The preservation of a person's dignity; may involve giving indirect answers to avoid hurting or embarrassing another person.

**Facial Action Coding System:** A virtual taxonomy of more than three thousand facial expressions used to interpret emotions and detect deception.

**Facilitative emotion:** An emotion that promotes effective functioning.

**Fact-inference confusion:** The tendency to treat observations and assumptions similarly.

**Feedback:** Information received in exchange for a message sent.

**Feedforward:** A variant of feedback sent prior to a message's delivery as a means of revealing something about to follow.

**Figure-ground principle:** A strategy that facilitates the organization of stimuli by enabling one to focus on different stimuli alternately.

**Fixed-feature space:** Space as defined by the permanent characteristics of an environment.

**Flame war:** An exchange of out-of-control online messages.

**Flaming:** The losing of emotional self-control while sending a message online.

**Frozen evaluation:** A perceptual fallacy that discourages flexibility and encourages rigidity; an evaluation of a person that ignores changes.

**Functional conflict:** A conflict that develops a clearer understanding of needs, attitudes, or beliefs.

**Fundamental attribution error:** The overemphasis of internal or personal factors.

**Fundamental interpersonal relations orientation:** A three-dimensional theory of interpersonal behavior highlighting the needs for inclusion, control, and affection.

**Gender:** The socially constructed roles and behaviors that the members of a given society believe to be appropriate for men and women.

**Gender identity:** An inner sense of being male or female.

**Gender prescriptions:** The roles and behaviors that a culture assigns to males and females.

**Genderlect:** Deborah Tannen's term for language differences attributed to gender.

**Grief process:** A five-stage process during which the feelings a grieving individual experiences begin with denial and then pass through anger, guilt, and depression before resolving with acceptance.

**Grit:** A combination of passion and perseverance for a singularly important goal, together with resilience and a tolerance for feeling frustrated.

**Groupthink:** A communication dysfunction in which some group members attempt to protect the group's harmony by exerting irrational pressures on one or more members so that genuine opinions are suppressed.

**Halo effect:** The perception of positive qualities in a person one likes.

**Haptics:** The study of how touch communicates.

**Health communication:** A field of study concerned with human interaction in the health care process.

**Hearing:** An involuntary physiological response in which sound waves are transformed into electrical impulses and processed by the brain.

**High-context cultures:** Cultures in which people tend to be very polite and indirect when interacting with others.

**High-intensity conflict:** Extreme conflict in which one party aims to destroy or debilitate the other.

**High-monitored feedback:** Feedback offered to serve a specific purpose; feedback that is sent intentionally.

**Horn effect:** The perception of negative qualities in a person one dislikes.

**HURIER model:** A model of listening that focuses on the following stages: hearing, understanding, remembering, interpreting, evaluating, and responding.

**"I" messages:** Nonevaluative forms of feedback that reveal a speaker's feelings about the situation faced by another person.

**Ideal self:** The self one would like to be.

**Idiocentric orientation:** An orientation displayed by people who are primarily individualistic in their ways of thinking and behaving.

**Illustrators:** Bodily cues designed to enhance receiver comprehension of speech by supporting or reinforcing it.

**Impression management:** The exercising of control over one's behaviors in an effort to make the desired impression.

**Inclusion need:** The social need to feel a sense of belonging or mutual interest in relationship to others.

**Indiscrimination:** A perceptual barrier that causes one to emphasize similarities and neglect differences.

**Individualistic culture:** A culture in which individual identity is paramount.

**Informal space or non-fixed-feature space:** The invisible space each person carries around.

**Instrumental roles:** Roles that are focused on getting things done; task-oriented roles.

**Intensional orientation:** The type of orientation displayed when one responds to a label rather than to what the label actually represents.

**Interaction model:** A representation of communication as a back-and-forth process.

**Internal feedback:** A person's response to his or her own performance.

**Interpersonal communication:** The ongoing, ever-changing process that occurs when one person interacts with another person, forming a dyad; communication occurring within a relationship.

**Interpersonal competence:** The ability to use appropriate communication to build and maintain an effective relationship.

**Interpersonal conflict:** A struggle between interdependent parties that occurs whenever one individual's thoughts or actions are perceived to limit or interfere with those of another; conflict that originates between two or more interdependent people.

**Intimacy:** A measure of closeness; sustained feelings of closeness and connection.

**Intimate distance:** From skin contact to 18 inches from another person; the distance usually used by people who trust each other or who share an emotional bond or closeness.

**Intrapersonal communication:** Communication requiring only a single communicator; communication with oneself.

**Intrapersonal conflict:** Conflict that originates within a single person.

**Johari window:** A model containing four panes—the open area, the blind area, the hidden area, and the unknown area—that is used to explain the roles that self-awareness and self-disclosure play in relationship building.

**Kinesics:** The study of human body motion.

**Knapp and Vangelisti's 10-stage model of relationships:** A model of relational development and deterioration created by Mark L. Knapp and Anita L. Vangelisti.

**Language:** A code or system of arbitrary symbols shared by a group and used by its members to communicate with each other.

**Legitimate power:** The type of power in which one party in a relationship controls the other.

**Lie:** The deliberate distortion or concealment of information; the intentional deception of another person to convince him or her of something one knows to be untrue.

**Linguistic determinism:** The view that language shapes thinking.

**Linguistic relativity:** The view that languages contain unique embedded elements.

**Listening:** A voluntary psychological process consisting of the following stages: sensing, attending, understanding/interpreting, evaluating, responding, and remembering.

**Long-distance relationship:** A relationship between individuals who are geographically separated.

**Low-context culture:** A culture in which people typically exhibit a direct communication style.

**Low-intensity conflict:** Conflict in which the parties involved devise strategies to create a solution beneficial to both.

**Low-monitored feedback:** Feedback that is sincere and spontaneous; feedback delivered without careful planning.

**Make-believe media:** Media offerings that make us believe things that are not necessarily true.

**Manner maxim:** The premise that when conversing, one should use diction that is appropriate to the receiver and the interaction's context.

**Maslow's needs hierarchy:** A 5-level pyramidal hierarchy of human needs developed by Abraham Maslow.

**Matching hypothesis:** The theory that we enter into a long-term relationship with someone similar to ourselves in physical attractiveness.

**Media models:** The images depicted in the mass media.

**Medium-intensity conflict:** Conflict in which each of the persons involved wants to win.

**Messages:** The content of communication.

**Metacommunicative functions:** Communication about communication.

**Meta-conversation:** Conversation about conversation.

**Minimal justification for action:** The principle that small rather than large incentives are more effective at creating dissonance and inducing attitude change.

**Need for reassurance:** The need to seek out information to confirm a decision.

**Negative feedback:** Responses that stop behavior in progress.

**Negative Pygmalion:** An individual who negatively influences one's perceptions of one's own abilities.

**Noise:** Anything that interferes with or impedes the ability to send or receive a message.

**Nonassertive expression style:** A style of communication characterized by hesitation in expressing one's feelings and thoughts.

**Non-evaluative feedback:** Feedback that is nonjudgmental.

**Non-listening:** A kind of deficient listening behavior in which the receiver tunes out.

**Nonshareable goal:** A goal that can be fully claimed and possessed by a single individual only.

**Nonverbal communication:** Communication that does not include words; messages expressed by nonlinguistic means; people's actions or attributes, including their use of objects, sounds, time, and space, that have socially shared significance and stimulate meaning in others.

**Norm of reciprocity:** The expectation of self-disclosure equity in a relationship.

**Nuclear family:** A household family unit that includes a mother, a father, and one or more children.

**Olfactics:** The study of the sense of smell.

**Online disinhibition effect:** The willingness to say what one really thinks or to misbehave when online.

**Open-ended question:** A question that allows the respondent free rein in answering.

**Organizational networks:** Patterns of communication in organizations.

**Paralanguage:** Messages sent using only vocal cues.

**Participative leadership:** Leadership in which leaders act as guides to others who remain free to identify their own goals, establish their own procedures, and reach their own conclusions.

**Perceived self:** A reflection of one's self-concept; the person one believes oneself to be when one is being honest with oneself.

**Perception:** The process used to make sense of experience.

**Perceptual constancy:** The tendency to maintain the way one sees the world.

**Perceptual sets:** Organizational constructions that condition a readiness to perceive, or a tendency to interpret stimuli in ways to which one has been conditioned.

**Personal distance:** From 18 inches to 4 feet from a person; the distance at which we are most apt to converse informally.

**Person-based processing:** The processing of information about a person based on perceptions of the individual, not on his or her membership in a particular group.

**Perspective taking:** Adopting the viewpoint of another person.

**Persuasive power:** The ability of one party in a relationship to persuade the other party to act in a desired way.

**Polarizing language:** Language that describes experience in either-or terms.

**Positive feedback:** Responses that enhance behavior in progress.

**Positive Pygmalion:** An individual who positively influences one's perceptions of one's own abilities.

**Possible self:** The self that one might become someday.

**Power:** The potential to influence others.

**Power distance:** The extent to which individuals are willing to accept power differentials.

**Pragmatic code:** The agreement to consider the context of an interaction, the interdependent nature of the relationship, and the goal of the exchange in deciphering meaning.

**Prejudiced talk:** Talk that includes racist, sexist, or ageist comments or comments denigrating any other kind of group.

**Presentational facial expressions:** Facial expressions that are consciously controlled.

**Probing:** A nonevaluative technique in which one solicits additional information from another.

**Proxemics:** The study of how space and distance are used to communicate.

**Pseudoconflict:** A situation that, while not an actual conflict, gives the appearance of one.

**Public distance:** A distance of 12 feet and beyond; the distance we use to remove ourselves physically from interaction, to communicate with strangers, or to address large groups.

**Purr words:** Words that register social approval.

**Quality maxim:** The premise that persons engaged in conversation do not offer comments known to be false.

**Quantity maxim:** The premise that persons conversing provide as much information as is needed to communicate a message's meaning and continue the conversation.

**Racial profiling:** A form of stereotyping attributed to racism.

**Rationalization:** The provision of a logical or reasonable explanation for an unrealistic thought or feeling.

**Reasoned sense making:** The ability to predict and account for the behavior of a particular person.

**Red-flag word:** A word that triggers emotional deafness in the receiver, dropping listening efficiency to zero.

**Referent power:** Power that is based in other persons' respect for or identification with the power holder.

**Reflected appraisal theory:** A theory that states that the self a person presents is in large part based on the way others categorize the individual, the roles they expect him or her to play, and the behaviors or traits they expect him or her to exhibit.

**Reflective thinking framework:** A problem-solving system designed to encourage critical inquiry.

**Regulators:** Communication cues intentionally used to influence turn taking and to control the flow of conversation.

**Rejection:** The negation of or disagreement with a self-appraisal.

**Relational culture:** The ways in which the parties to a relationship work out the rules or routines of the relationship.

**Relational dialectics theory:** A theory that explores the pushes and pulls partners feel toward integration versus separation, stability versus change, and expression versus privacy.

**Relationship breadth:** An aspect of a relationship measured by how many topics the parties discuss.

**Relationship depth:** An aspect of a relationship measured by how central the topics discussed are to the self-concepts of the individuals involved and how much the parties are willing to reveal about themselves and their feelings.

**Relationship maintenance:** The work that is needed to keep a relationship healthy.

**Relationship repair:** The work that is needed when a relationship fails to satisfy.

**Relationships:** A wide array of social connections that to varying degrees meet our interpersonal needs.

**Relevancy maxim:** The premise that persons engaged in conversation do not purposefully go off on tangents or digress.

**Representational facial expressions:** Exhibited facial expressions that communicate genuine inner feelings.

**Repression:** The forgetting or denial of disturbing stimuli.

**Resilience:** The ability to cope with and recover quickly from disappointments.

**Retrospective sense making:** The ability to make sense of one's own behavior once it has occurred.

**Reward power:** Power based in the fact that one party in a relationship controls something valued by the other party.

**Role duality:** The simultaneous performance of the roles of sender and receiver by the members of a dyad.

**Role reversal:** Imagining or acting by one party in a relationship or an exchange that he or she is the other party.

**Roles:** The parts that people play when interacting.

**Romantic relationship:** A love-based relationship built on commitment, passion, and intimacy.

**Rules:** Behavioral norms; implied or spoken understandings.

**Sapir–Whorf hypothesis:** A theory that proposes that language influences perception by revealing and reflecting one's worldview; language is determined by the perceived reality of a culture.

**Schemata:** The mental templates or knowledge structures that individuals carry with them.

**Scripts:** The general ideas that individuals have about persons and situations and how things should play out.

**Selective attention:** The means by which one focuses on certain cues while ignoring others.

**Selective exposure:** The practice of exposing oneself to people and messages that confirm one's existing beliefs, values, or attitudes.

**Selective perception:** The aspect of perception comprising selective exposure, selective attention, and selective retention, which enables individuals to see, hear, and believe only what they want to.

**Selective retention:** The recalling of things that reinforce one's thinking and the forgetting of things one finds objectionable.

**Self-awareness:** Personal reflection on and monitoring of one's own behavior.

**Self-concept:** The relatively stable set of perceptions one attributes to oneself.

**Self-disclosure:** The willing sharing of information about the self with others.

**Self-efficacy:** A positive belief in one's own abilities, competence, and potential.

**Self-esteem:** Your self-evaluation and estimation of your self-worth.

**Self-fulfilling prophecy:** A prediction or expectation that comes true simply because one acts as if it were true.

**Self-image:** The mental picture one has of oneself.

**Self-serving bias:** The overemphasizing of external factors as influences on one's behavior.

**Semantic code:** The agreement to use the same symbols to communicate.

**Semi-fixed-feature space:** Space in which movable objects are used to identify boundaries and promote or inhibit interaction.

**Serial construction of meaning model:** A model positing that shared meaning results from commonality, mutuality, and the equivalence of our evaluation.

**Sexual harassment:** Unwelcome sexual behavior that takes place in person or electronically.

**Shareable goal:** A goal that both parties to a conflict can possess.

**Silence:** The absence of vocal communication.

**Single-parent family:** A family in which one parent is solely responsible for the care of a biological or adopted child or children.

**Small talk:** Spontaneous conversation that lays the foundation for an interpersonal relationship.

**Snarl words:** Words that register social disapproval.

**Social comparison theory:** A theory affirming that individuals compare themselves to others to develop a feel for how their talents, abilities, and qualities measure up.

**Social distance:** From 4 feet to 12 feet from another person; the interpersonal distance we usually use to conduct business or discuss nonpersonal issues.

**Social identity model of de-individuation effects:** A theory that states that each individual has different identities that make themselves visible in different situations.

**Social intelligence:** The ability to understand and relate to people.

**Social learning theory:** A theory that asserts that individuals learn at least some of what they know by observing others and then modeling the behaviors that they have observed.

**Social penetration theory:** A theory that states that relationships typically begin with relatively narrow breadth and shallow depth and develop both over time.

**Social presence theory:** A perception among social media users that others are listening to them when they post, perceiving themselves as being face-to-face, rather than in a digital environment.

**Speech–thought differential:** The difference between the rate of speech and the rate at which speech can be comprehended.

**Spotlighting:** The highlighting of a person's sex for emphasis.

**Standpoint theory:** A theory that one's place in the power hierarchy influences the accuracy of one's perception of social life.

**Stereotypes:** Rigid perceptions that are applied to all members of a group or to an individual over time, regardless of individual variations.

**Supportive climate:** A climate in which the level of threat that individuals experience is reduced.

**Supportive environment:** An environment that builds trust and maintains each person's sense of worth.

**Supportive feedback:** Nonevaluative feedback that indicates that another's problem is viewed as important.

**Sympathetic responsiveness:** Feeling for, rather than with, another.

**Syntactic code:** Conventions that guide word use; the agreement to use the same rules regarding word use.

**Systems theory:** An approach to communication that stresses the interaction of all elements in a communication network.

**Technopoly:** A culture whose thought world is monopolized by technology.

**Telepresence:** The sense of physically being in a different place or time through virtual reality.

**Territoriality:** The claiming or identifying of space as one's own.

**Toxic communication:** Communication that is verbally or physically abusive.

**Transactional model:** A representation of communication that depicts transmission and reception occurring simultaneously, demonstrating that source and receiver continually influence one another.

**Triangle of meaning:** A model that demonstrates the relationships that exist among words, things, and thoughts.

**Triangular theory of love:** A theory developed by Robert Sternberg that states that varying combinations of intimacy, passion, and commitment create different types of love.

**Trigger cues:** Cues that stimulate "click, whirr" programmed responses to persuasive appeals.

**Trust:** The belief that one can rely on another; made up of two components: trusting behavior and trustworthy behavior.

**Trusting behavior:** Behavior that accords with the belief that another will not take advantage of one's vulnerabilities.

**Trustworthy behavior:** Behavior that does not take advantage of another's vulnerabilities.

**Uncertainty reduction theory:** A theory that states that individuals learn more about each other by monitoring their social environment.

**Unconscious bias:** A bias we are unaware that we harbor.

**Value conflict:** Conflict that revolves around the importance of an issue.

**Values:** One's ideas about what is important in life.

**Virtual community:** A community that exists only in cyberspace.

**Word mask:** Ambiguous language meant to confuse.

**Word wall:** Language that impedes understanding.

# Notes

## CHAPTER 1

1. Hilary Sheinbaum, "The Wi-Fi Version of Vanity Plates," *The New York Times,* September 14, 2017, p. D6.

2. Aaron Smith, "Americans and Text Messaging," Pew Internet & American Life Project, September 19, 2011, http//www.pewinternet .org/2011/09/19/how-americans-use-text-messaging.aspx.

3. See Julia T. Wood, *Communication Theories in Action: An Introduction,* 9th ed., Boston: Wadsworth, 2011; and W. W. Wilmot, *Relational Communication,* New York, NY: McGraw-Hill, 1999.

4. See Julia T. Wood, *Relational Communication,* 2nd ed., Belmont, CA: Wadsworth, 1997.

5. For a review of the research on interpersonal communication competence, see J. M. Wiemann and M. O. Wiemann, *Interpersonal Competence,* Newbury Park, CA: Sage, 1991.

6. I. Lau, C. Chiu, and Y. Hong, "I Know What You Know: Assumptions about Others' Knowledge and Their Effects on Message Construction," *Social Cognition,* 19, 2001, pp. 587–600.

7. See, for example, Kevin B. Wright, Lisa Sparks, and Dan O'Hair, *Health Communication in the 21st Century,* Malden, MA: Blackwell, 2007; and Dhruv Khullar, "How Social Isolation is Killing Us," December 22, 2016, nytimes.com. http://www .nytimes.com/2016/12/22/upshot/ how-social-isolation-is-killing-us .html?smid=nytcore-iphone-share&smprod=nytcore-iphone

8. Erica Goode, "Rethinking Solitary Confinement," *NYTimes.com,* March 11, 2012, pp. 1, 19.

9. See Thomas Hora in Paul H. Watzlawick, Janet H. Beavin, and Don D. Jackson, *Pragmatics of Human Communication: A Study of Interactional Patterns, Pathologies, and Paradoxes,* New York, NY: Norton, 1967.

10. William Schutz, *The Interpersonal Underworld,* Palo Alto, CA: Science and Behavior Books, 1966.

11. C. R. Berger, *Planning Strategic Interaction: Attaining Goals through Communication Action,* Mahwah, NJ: Lawrence Erlbaum, 1997.

12. See also Richard West and Lynn H. Turner, *Understanding Interpersonal Communication,* 2nd ed., Boston: Wadsworth, 2011.

13. See Mark L. Knapp and John A. Daly, eds., *The SAGE Handbook of Interpersonal Communication,* 4th ed., Thousand Oaks, CA: Sage, 2011.

14. Paul H. Watzlawick, Janet H. Beavin, and Don D. Jackson, *Pragmatics of Human Communication: A Study of Interactional Patterns, Pathologies, and Paradoxes,* New York: Norton, 1967.

15. Edward T. Hall, *The Silent Language,* New York: Fawcett, 1959.

16. William B. Gudykunst, *Bridging Differences: Effective Intergroup Communication,* 4th ed., Thousand Oaks, CA: Sage, 2004.

17. See Geert Hofstede, *Culture's Consequences: Comparing Values, Behaviors, Institutions, and Organizations across Nations,* 2nd ed., Thousand Oaks, CA: Sage, 2001.

18. See Edward T. Hall, *Beyond Culture,* New York: Doubleday, 1959.

19. See Julia T. Wood, *Gendered Lives: Communication, Gender, and Culture,* 9th ed., Boston: Wadsworth, 2011.

20. Elizabeth Fox-Genovese, *Feminism without Illusions,* Chapel Hill: University of North Carolina Press, 1991, p. 20.

21. Marshall McLuhan, *Understanding Media: The Extension of Man,* New York: McGraw-Hill, 1964.

22. Quoted in D. Kirkpatrick, "Here Comes the Payoff from PCs," *Fortune,* March 23, 1992, pp. 93–102.

23. "Exactly How Much Are the Times A-Changin'?" *Newsweek,* July 26, 2010, p. 56.

24. Evan Asano, "How Much Time Do People Spend on Social Media?" *Social Media Today,* January 4, 2017. https://www.socialmediatoday .com/marketing/how-much-time-do-people-spend-social-media-infographic

25. "U.S. Adults Now Spend 12 Hours, 7 Minutes a Day Consuming Media," *Media Buying,* May 1, 2017. https://www.emarketer.com/ Article/US-Adults-Now-Spend-12-Hours-7-Minutes-Day-Consuming-Media/1015775

26. A. Ramirez and S. Zhang, "When Online Meets Offline: The Effect of Modality-Switching on Relational Communication," *Communication Monographs,* 74, 2007, pp. 287–310.

27. See "The Information: How the Internet Gets Inside Us," *The New Yorker,* February 14 and 21, 2011, pp. 124–130.

28. For a discussion of contemporary breakups, see Benoi Denizet-Lewis, "It's Not U, It's Me: (," *New York Times Magazine,* August 7, 2011, p. 14.

# CHAPTER 2

1. See, for example, Arthur C. Brooks, "Are You Narcissistic? Who, Moi?" *The New York Times,* February 14, 2016, p. 10; and Joseph Burgo, *The Narcissist You Know: Defending Yourself Against Extreme Narcissists in an All-About-Me Age.* New York: Touchstone, 2015.

2. Lionel Tiger, "Zuckerberg: The World's Richest Primatologist," *Wall Street Journal,* February 6, 2012, p. A11.

3. Shannon Greenwood, Andrew Perrin, and Maeve Duggan, "Social Media Update, 2016," November 11, 2016. http://www.pewinternet .org/2016/11/11/social-media-update-2016/

4. See, for example, Amy Gonzales and Jeffrey T. Hancock, "Mirror, Mirror on My Facebook Wall: Effects of Exposure to Facebook on Self-Esteem," *Cyberpsychology, Behavior, and Social Networking,* 14, 2011, pp. 41–49; and N. B. Ellison, C. Steinfield, and C. Lampe, "The Benefits of Facebook 'Friends': Social Capital and College Students' Use of Online Social Network Sites," *Journal of Computer-Mediated Communication,* 12:4, 2007, http:// jcmc.indiana.edu/vol12/issue4/ ellison.html.

5. As quoted in *Life* magazine, April 21, 1961.

6. S. I. Hayakawa and Alan R. Hayakawa, *Language in Thought and Action,* 5th ed., New York: Harcourt Brace Jovanovich, 1990. For a recent discussion of the self in relationship to others, see David Brooks, *The Social Animal: The Hidden Sources of Love, Character, and Achievement,* New York: Random House, 2011.

7. See Christopher J. Mruk, *Self-Esteem Research, Theory, and Practice: Toward a Positive Psychology of Self-Esteem,* 3rd ed., New York: Springer, 2006; and Don Hamacheck, *Encounters with the Self,* 3rd ed., Fort Worth, TX: Holt, Rinehart & Winston, 1992, pp. 3–5.

8. See, for example, Neff and Geers, "Optimistic Expectations in Early Marriage," *Journal of Personality and Social Psychology,* July 2013, pp. 38–60.

9. See Lauren Slater, "The Trouble with Self-Esteem," *New York Times Magazine,* February 3, 2002, pp. 44–47.

10. R. F. Baumeister, L. Smart, and J. M. Boden, "Relation of Threatened Egotism to Violence and Aggression: The Dark Side of High Self-Esteem," *Psychological Review,* 103, 1996, pp. 5–33.

11. R. Brooks and S. Goldstein, *Raising Resilient Children,* New York: Contemporary Books, 2001.

12. William James, *The Principles of Psychology,* New York: Dover, 1890.

13. Charles Horton Cooley, *Human Nature and the Social Order,* New York: Scribner's, 1912.

14. See, for example, C. Jaret, D. Teitzes, and N. Shapkina, "Reflected Appraisals and Self-Esteem," *Sociological Perspectives,* 48, 2005, pp. 403–419.

15. Leon Festinger, "A Theory of Social Comparison Processes," *Human Relations,* 2, 1954, pp. 117–140.

16. L. B. Whitbeck and D. R. Hoyt, "Social Prestige and Assortive Mating: A Comparison of Students from 1950 and 1988," *Journal of Social and Personal Relationships,* 11, 1994, pp. 137–145.

17. Roy F. Baumeister, Jennifer D. Campbell, Joachim I. Krueger, and Kathleen D. Vohs, "Does High Self-Esteem Cause Better Performance, Interpersonal Success, Happiness, or Healthier Lifestyles?" *Psychological Science in the Public Interest,* 4:1 (May 2003), pp. 1–44.

18. J. Saunders, "The Role of Self-Esteem in the Misinformation Effect," *Memory,* 20(2), 2012, pp. 90–99.

19. Marlene Zuk, "A Case of Unwarranted Self-Regard," *The Record,* May 30, 2005, p. L7.

20. Angela Duckworth, "The Grit Factor," *The New York Times,* April 10, 2016, p. EL7.

21. See Rosabeth Moss Kanter, *Confidence: How Winning Streaks and Losing Streaks Begin and End.* New York: Crown, 2004.

22. Laura Landro, "Why Learning to Be Resilient Is Good for Your Health," *The Wall Street Journal,* February 16, 2016, p. D2.

23. Sharon Begley, "Real Self-Esteem Builds on Achievement, Not Praise for Slackers," *Wall Street Journal,* April 16, 2003, p. B1.

24. Ashley Parker, "My Bitmoji, My (Better) Self," *The New York Times,* October 4, 2015, ST 12.

25. D. M. Tice and J. Faber, "Cognitive and Motivational Process in Self-Presentation," in J. P. Forgas, K. D. Williams, and L. Wheeler, eds., *The Social Mind: Cognitive and Motivational Aspects of Interpersonal Behavior,* New York: Cambridge University Press, 2001, pp. 139–156.

26. See Erving Goffman, *The Presentation of Self in Everyday Life.* Garden City, NY: Doubleday, 1959.

27. Paul H. Watzlawick, Janet H. Beavin, and Don D. Jackson, *Pragmatics of Human Interaction: A Study of Interactional Patterns, Pathologies, and Paradoxes,* New York: Norton, 1967.

28. See Kim Giffin and Bobby R. Patton, "The Search for Self Identity," in *Fundamentals of Interpersonal Communication,* New York: Harper & Row, 1971; and George H. Mead, *Mind, Self and Society,* Chicago, IL: University of Chicago Press, 1934, pp. 144–164.

29. See Albert Bandura, *Self-Efficacy: The Exercise of Control,* New York: Freeman, 1997; and Meg Jay, "The Secrets of Resilience," *The Wall Street Journal,* Saturday/Sunday, November 11–12, 2017. pp. C1, C2.

30. See, for example, Robert Rosenthal and Lenore Jacobson, *Pygmalion in the Classroom,* New York: Holt, Rinehart & Winston, 1968; Len Sandler, "Self-Fulfilling Prophecy: Better Management by Magic," *Training Magazine,* February 1986; and Adreu Termes Lopez, "Galatea and Pygmalion Glances: Perception and Strategies of the 'Other' in Front of (Pre)judices," *Race, Ethnicity and Education,* 20:1, January 2017, pp. 132–145.

31. Rosenthal and Jacobson, *Pygmalion in the Classroom.*

32. See, for example, Michael L. Hecht, Ronald L. Jackson II, and Sidney A. Ribeau, *African American Communication: Exploring Identity and Culture,* Mahwah, NJ: Lawrence Erlbaum, 2003.

33. Larry A. Samovar and Richard E. Porter, *Communication between Cultures,* Belmont, CA: Wadsworth, 1991; Richard Brislin, *Understanding Culture's Influence on Behavior,* Orlando, FL: Harcourt Brace Jovanovich, 1993, p. 47.

34. See Judith Martin and Thomas Nakayama, *Experiencing Intercultural Communication: An Introduction,* 3rd ed., New York: McGraw-Hill, 2008; and William B. Gudykunst and Stella Ting-Toomy, *Culture and Interpersonal Communication,* Newbury Park, CA: Sage, 1988.

35. S. Kitayama and H. R. Markus, "Culture and Self: Implications for Internationalizing Psychology," in N. R. Goldberger and J. B. Veroff, eds., *The Culture and Psychology Reader,* New York: New York University Press, 1995, p. 44.

36. Harry C. Triandis, Kwok Leung, Marcelo J. Villareal, and Felicia I. Clack, "Allocentric versus Idiocentric Tendencies: Convergent and Discriminant Validation," *Journal of Research in Personality,* 19, 1985, pp. 395–415.

37. J. A. Vandello and D. Cohen, "Patterns of Individualism and Collectivism across the United States," *Journal of Personality and Social Psychology,* 77, 1999, pp. 279–292.

38. See, for example, W. B. Gudykunst, Y. Matsumoto, S. Ting-Toomey, T. Nishida, K. Kim, and S. Heyman, "The Influence of Cultural Individualism-Collectivism, Self-Construals, and Individual Values on Communication Styles across Cultures," *Human Communication Research,* 22, 1996, pp. 510–543.

39. For a discussion of cultural variations in power distance, see Judith N. Martin and Thomas K. Nakayama, *Intercultural Communication in Contexts,* 5th ed., New York: McGraw-Hill, 2010.

40. Robert Atkinson, "The Universal Teenager," *Psychology Today,* October 1988. See also Amy Novotney, "R U Friends 4 Real?," *Monitor on Psychology,* 43, February 2012, p. 62.

41. Ibid.

42. Ceylan Yeginsu, "Britain Tackles Loneliness," *The New York Times,* January 18, 2018, p. A7; see also Eric Klineberg, "Is Loneliness a Health Epidemic?" *The New York Times,* February 11, 2018; p. SR8.

43. Elizabeth Bernstein, "New Research on Overcoming the Loneliness Spiral," *The Wall Street Journal,* September 22, 2015, p. D3.

44. Darlene Powell Hopson and Derek Hopson, *Different and Wonderful: Raising Black Children in a Race-Conscious Society,* Upper Saddle River, NJ: Prentice Hall, 1991.

45. See Philip Jordan and Maria Hernandez Reif, "Reexamination of Young Children's Racial Attitudes and Skin Tone Preferences," *Journal of Black Psychology,* 35, 2009, pp. 388–403.

46. Jamil Smith, "Super-Powered: *Black Panther* Marks a Major Milestone for Culture," *Time,* February 19, 2018, pp. 38–45.

47. Quoted in Joel Wells, *Who Do You Think You Are?* Chicago: Thomas More Press, 1989, pp. 92–93.

48. Ibid, p. 93.

49. M. Kremar, S. Giles, and D. Helme, "Understanding the Process: How Mediated and Peer Norms Affect Young Women's Body Esteem," *Communication Quarterly,* 56, 2008, pp. 111–130.

50. See, for example, C. M. Strong, "The Role of Exposure to Media Idealized Male Physiques on Men's Body Image," *Dissertation Abstracts International,* 65, 2005, p. 4306.

51. Julia T. Wood, *Gendered Lives: Communication, Gender, and Culture,* 9th ed., Boston: Wadsworth, 2011, p. 176.

52. Ibid.

53. Renee Engeln, "The Problem with 'Fat Talk,'" *The New York Times,* March 15, 2015, p. 12.

54. Michael Parenti, "The Make Believe Media," *The Humanist,* November–December, 1990.

55. Lee Margulies, "Females Under-represented in Top U.S. Films, Study Says," *The Record* (Bergen County, NJ), May 17, 2012, p. BL4.

56. Stuart Ewen, *All Consuming Images: The Politics of Style in Contemporary Culture,* New York: Basic Books, 1988, p. 89.

57. Amanda Lenhart, Lee Rainie, and Oliver Lewis, *Teenage Life Online: The Rise of the Instant-Message*

*Generation and the Internet's Impact on Friendships and Family Relationships,* Washington, DC: Pew Internet & American Life Project, 2001, http://www.pewinternet .org/2001/06/20/the-rise-of-the-instant-message-generation/

58. For example, see B. Marcus, F. Machilek, and A. Schutz, "Personality in Cyberspace: Personal Web Sites as Media for Personality Expressions and Impressions," *Journal of Personality and Social Psychology,* 90, 2007, pp. 1014–1031; and M. K. Matsuba, "Searching for Self and Relationships Online," *Cyberpsychology and Behavior,* 9, 2006, pp. 275–284.

59. Sherry Turkle, *Alone Together: Why We Expect More from Technology and Less from Each Other,* New York: Basic Books, 2011, pp. 12, 14, 178.

60. See Gonzales and Hancock, "Mirror, Mirror on My Facebook Wall."

61. Christopher Carpenter, "Narcissism on Facebook: Self-Promotion and Anti-social Behavior," *Personality and Individual Differences,* 52, 2012, pp. 482–486; and Kate Murphy, "What Selfie Sticks Really Tell Us About Ourselves," *The New York Times,* August 9, 2015, p. 5SR.

62. Tara Parker-Pope, "All about You," *New York Times Magazine,* May 20, 2012, p. 16.

63. Roni Caryn Rabin, "Internet Use Tied to Depression in Youths," *New York Times,* August 10, 2010, p. D6.

64. Shirley Kramer and Becky Inkster, "#Status of Mind: Social Media and Young People's Mental Health and Wellbeing," RSPH, May 2017. http://www.infocoponline.es/pdf/SOCIAL MEDIA-MENTALHEALTH.pdf

65. Ibid.

66. Lynda Edwards, "What Might Have Been," *New York Times,* January 2, 1994, sec. 9, p. 1.

67. Claudette Mackay-Lassonde, "Butterflies, Not Pigeonholes," *Vital Speeches of the Day,* January 1, 1994, p. 183.

## CHAPTER 3

1. See, for example, Marian L. Houser, Sean M. Horan, and Lisa A. Furler, "Predicting Relational Outcomes: An Investigation of Thin Slice Judgments in Speed Dating," *Human Communication,* 10:2, 2007, pp. 69–81; and Christopher A. Pepping, "Attachment, Culture and Initial Romantic Attraction: A Speed-Dating Study," *Personality and Individual Differences,* vol. 108, April 2017, pp. 79–85.].

2. Malcolm Gladwell, *Blink: The Power of Thinking without Thinking,* New York: Little, Brown, 2005.

3. See also Marian L. Houser, Sean M. Horan, and Lisa A. Furler, "Dating in the Fast Lane: How Communication Predicts Speed Dating Success," *Journal of Social and Personal Relationships,* 24, 2008, pp. 749–768.

4. Houser et al., "Predicting Relational Outcomes."

5. See, for example, Paul W. Eastwick, Eli J. Finkel, and Alice H. Eagly, "When and Why Do Ideal Partner Preferences Affect the Process of Initiating and Maintaining Romantic Relationships?" *Journal of Personality and Social Psychology,* 101, 2011, pp. 1012–1032.

6. Houser et al., "Dating in the Fast Lane."

7. Robert Lee Hotz, "Project to Explore Human Perception," *Wall Street Journal,* March 22, 2012, p. A2.

8. Nicholas St. Fleur, "Perception Is in the Eye (and Nose) of the Beholder," *The New York Times,* November 24, 2017, p. C18.

9. Jessica K. Witt and Dennis R. Proffitt, "See the Ball, Hit the Ball," *Psychological Science,* 16, 2005, pp. 937–938.

10. Joe Palca, "Can You Think Your Way to That Hole-in-One?," NPR Science, April 18, 2012, http://m.npr.org/ news/science/150813843.

11. Ibid.

12. William Wan, "Many People Can't Tell When Photos Are Fake. Can You?" *The Washington Post,* July 17, 2017.

13. Adam Liptak, "Often Wrong but Rarely in Doubt: Eyewitness IDs Will Get a Fresh Look," *New York Times,* August 23, 2011; and Erica Goode and John Schwartz, "Police Lineups Start to Face Fact: Eyes Can Lie," *New York Times,* August 29, 2011, pp. A1, A3.

14. Eric Schwitzgebel, *Perplexities of Consciousness,* Cambridge: MIT Press, 2011.

15. Stephen R. Covey, *The Seven Habits of Highly Effective People,* New York: Simon & Schuster, 1990, p. 28.

16. See, for example, Donna J. Haraway, "Situated Knowledges: The Science Question in Feminism and the Privilege of Partial Perspectives," in *Simians, Cyborgs, and Women: The Reinvention of Nature,* New York: Routledge, 1991; and Sandra Harding, ed., *The Feminist Standpoint Theory Reader: Intellectual and Political Controversies,* New York: Routledge, 2003.

17. Claire Cain Miller, "Sexes Differ on Persistence of Sexism," *The New York Times,* January 19, 2017, p. A3.

18. See, for example, P. H. Collins, "Learning from the Outsider Within," *Social Programs,* 33, 1986, pp. 514–532.

19. Sandra Harding, *Whose Science? Whose Knowledge? Thinking from Women's Lives,* Ithaca, NY: Cornell University Press, 1991.

20. See, for example, Charles R. Berger, "Uncertain Outcome Values in Predicted Relationships: Uncertainty Reduction Theory Then and Now," *Human Communication Research,* 13, 1986, pp. 34–38.

21. See "Information Theory," *Encyclopedia Britannica Online,* http://www.britannica.com/ EBchecked/topic/287907/ Information-theory.

22. See, for example, Mark Changizi, "Masters of Distraction," *Wall Street Journal,* August 20–21, 2011, p. C9.

23. Quoted in Jonah Lehrer, "Learning How to Focus on Focus," *Wall Street Journal,* September 3–4, 2011, p. C12.

24. See Benedict Carey, "The Then and Now of Memory," *New York Times,* July 5, 2011, p. D4.

25. See, for example, Christopher Chabris and Daniel Simons, *The Invisible Gorilla and Other Ways Our Intuitions Deceive Us,* New York: Crown, 2010.

26. V. Nanusov, "It Depends on Your Perspective: Effects of Stance and Beliefs about Intent on Person Perception," *Western Journal of Communication,* 57, 1993, pp. 27–41.

27. Sharon Begley, "The Memory of Sept. 11 Is Seared in Your Mind, But Is It Really True?" *Wall Street Journal,* September 13, 2002, p. B1.

28. Jill Harness, "Tricks Our Minds Play on Us," Neatorama, September 29, 2010, http://www.neatorama.com/2010/09/29/tricks-our-minds-play-on-us.

29. Michael D. Lemonick, "When Our Memories Are Both Vivid and Wrong," *The Wall Street Journal,* January 28/29, 2017, p. C3.

30. C. Routledge, J. Juhl, A. Abeyta, and C. Roylance, C. "Using the Past to Promote a Peaceful Future: Nostalgia Mitigates Existential Threat Induced Nationalistic and Religious Self-sacrifice. *Social Psychology,* 45: 2014, pp. 339–346.

31. Evan J. Fishman, and Jenifer Husman, "Extending Attribution Theory: Considering Students Perceived Control of the Attribution Process," *Journal of Educational Psychology,* 109:4, May 2017, pp. 559–573.

32. Saul Kassin, *Psychology,* 2nd ed., Upper Saddle River, NJ: Prentice Hall, 1998.

33. See, for example, Narciso Cellan, "We Are, Therefore I Am: Social Media and Ethnocentrism," *International Journal of Technology, Knowledge and Society: Annual Review,* 13:1, March 2017, pp. 11–25.

34. See, for example, Larry A. Samovar, Richard E. Porter, and Edwin R. McDaniel, *Communication between Cultures,* 7th ed., Boston: Wadsworth, 2010.

35. Ibid.

36. Donald R. Arkinson, George Morten, and Derald Wing Sue, "Minority Group Counseling: An Overview," in Larry A. Samovar and Richard E. Porter, eds., *Intercultural Communication: A Reader,* 4th ed., Belmont, CA: Wadsworth, 1982, p. 172.

37. Irene V. Blair, Charles M. Judd, Melody S. Sadler, and Christopher Jenkins, "The Role of Afrocentric Features in Person Perception: Judging by Features and Categories," *Journal of Personality and Social Psychology,* 83, 2002, pp. 5–25.

38. See, for example, M. E. Hill, "Color Difference in the Socioeconomic Status of African American Men: Results of a Longitudinal Study," *Social Forces,* 78, pp. 1437–1460.

39. See Alison L. Chasteen, "The Role of Age and Age-Related Attitudes in Perceptions of Elderly Individuals," *Basic and Applied Social Psychology,* 22, 2000, 147–156.

40. S. T. Fiske and S. L. Neuberg, "A Continuum of Impression Formation, from Category-Based to Individuating Processes: Influences of Information and Motivation on Attention and Interpretation," in M. P. Zanna, ed., *Advances in Experimental Social Psychology,* vol. 23, New York: Academic Press, 1990, pp. 1–74.

41. M. Snyder and P. K. Miene, "Stereotyping of the Elderly: A Functional Approach," *British Journal of Social Psychology,* 33, 1994, pp. 63–82.

42. Ibid.

43. Tim Hartford, "The Problem with Facts," *The Financial Times,* March 11/12, 2017, pp. 15, 19.

44. Irving J. Lee, *How to Talk with People,* San Francisco: International Society for General Semantics, 1982.

45. Mary Morain, ed., *Classroom Exercises in General Semantics,* San Francisco: International Society for General Semantics, 1980, pp. 17–18.

46. J. W. Bagby, "A Cross-Cultural Study of Perceptual Predominance in Binocular Rivalry," *Journal of Abnormal and Social Psychology,* 54, 1957, pp. 331–334.

47. "In Depth: Race Relations," Gallup: http://news.gallup.com/poll/1687/race-relations.aspx

48. See Julia T. Wood, *Gendered Lives: Communication, Gender, and Culture,* 9th ed., Boston: Wadsworth, 2011.

49. Kevin Quealy, "Media Bias of Different Sort: Readers Skip Some Stories," *The New York Times,* February 27, 2017, p. A3.

50. See George Gerbner, Larry P. Gross, Michael Morgan, and Nancy Signorielli, "Growing Up with Television: The Cultivation Perspective," in Jennings Bryant and Dolf Zillmann, eds., *Media Effects: Advances in Theory and Research,* Hillsdale, NJ: Lawrence Erlbaum, 1994, pp. 17–41.

51. See George Gerbner, Larry P. Gross, Michael Morgan, and Nancy Signorielli, "The 'Mainstreaming' of America: Violence Profile No. 11," *Journal of Communication,* 30, 1980, pp. 10–29; and George Gerbner, "The Politics of Media Violence: Some Reflections," in Cees J. Hamelink and Olga Linné, eds., *Mass Communication Research: On Problems and Policies,* Norwood, NJ; Ablex, 1994.

52. See, for example, Robin L. Nabi, "Cosmetic Surgery Makeover Programs and Intentions to Undergo Cosmetic Enhancements:

A Consideration of Three Models of Media Effects," *Human Communication Research,* 35, 2009, pp. 1–27; and L. J. Shrum and Valerie Darmanin Bischak, "Mainstreaming, Resonance, and Impersonal Impact: Testing Moderators of the Cultivation Effect for Estimates of Crime Risk," *Human Communication Research,* 27, 2001, 187–215.

53. See, for example, Laura Burkhart, Andrea Hoopes, and Megan Moreno, "'Why is this Person Writing this Stuff on Facebook?' Female College Students Perceptions of Sexual Reference Displays on Facebook," *College Student Journal,* 51:3, Fall 2017, pp. 337–346.

54. See Tom Postmes, Russell Spears, and Martin Lea, "Breaching or Building Social Boundaries? SIDE-Effects of Computer Mediated Communication," *Communication Research,* 25, 1998, pp. 689–715.

55. See, for example, Russell Spears, Tom Postmes, Martin Lea, and Susan E. Watt, "A SIDE View of Social Influence," in Joseph P. Forgas and Kipling D. Williams, eds., *Social Influence: Direct and Indirect Processes,* Philadelphia: Psychology Press, 2001, pp. 331–350.

56. Iowa State University, "Violent Video Games and Hostile Personalities Go Together," *Science Daily,* April 4, 2007, http://www.sciencedaily.com/releases/2007/04/070404162247.htm.

57. Sharon Begley, "The Kid Flunked, But He Sure Pays Attention," *Wall Street Journal,* May 29, 2003, pp. B1, B8.

58. Sandra Blakeslee, "Video-Game Killing Builds Visual Skills, Researchers Report," *New York Times,* May 29, 2003, pp. A1, A25.

59. Jeremy Bailenson, *Experience on Demand: What Virtual Reality Is, How It Works, and What It Can Do.* New York: W. W. Norton & Company, 2018. See also Jason Lanier, *Dawn of the New Everything: Encounters with Reality and Virtual Reality.* New York: Henry Holt & Company, 2017.

60. Randall Stross, "The Second Screen, Trying to Complement the First," *New York Times,* March 4, 2012, p. BU5.

61. Cathy N. Davidson, *Now You See It: How the Brain Science of Attention Will Transform the Way We Live, Work, and Learn,* New York: Viking, 2011.

62. Jessica Guynn, "Snapchat Snapping Up Young Users Fleeing Facebook, *USA Today,* January 13, 2018, p. 3B.

63. Patricia Cohen, "Internet Use Affects How We Remember," *New York Times,* July 15, 2011, p. A14; and Katherine Hobson, "Relying on Internet Affects the Way We Remember," *Wall Street Journal,* July 19, 2011, p. D2.

64. R. A. Geist, "How the Empathic Process Heals: A Microprocess Perspective: *International Journal of Psychoanalytic Self Psychology,* 8, 2013, pp. 265–281.

65. Peggy Orenstein, "I Tweet, Therefore I Am," *New York Times Magazine,* August 1, 2010, pp. 11–12.

## CHAPTER 4

1. See, for example, David Glenn, "Divided Attention: In an Age of Classroom Multitasking, Scholars Probe the Nature of Learning and Memory," *Chronicle of Higher Education,* February 28, 2010, http://chronicle.com/article/Scholars-Turn-Their-Attention/63746.

2. Ibid.

3. Faith Brynie, "The Madness of Multitasking," *Psychology Today,* Brain Sense blog, August 24, 2009, http://www.psychologytoday.com/blog/brain-sense/200908/the-madness-multitasking

4. Joanna Nikas, "No More Small Talk," *The New York Times,* September 17, 2017, p. D6.

5. Celeste Headlee, "The Right Way to Have Difficult Conversations," *The Wall Street Journal,* September 9–10, 2017, p. C3.

6. Ibid.; see also, Eli Amdur, "The Most Important Communication Skill of All," *The Record,* November 29, 2015, p. J1.

7. See, for example, R. Emanuel, J. Adams, K. Baker, E. K. Daufin, C. Ellington, E. Fitts, J. Himsel, L. Holladay, and D. Okeowo, "How College Students Spend Their Time Communicating," *International Journal of Listening,* 22, 2008, pp. 13–28; L. Barker, R. Edwards, C. Gaines, K. Gladney, and F. Holley, "An Investigation of Proportional Time Spent in Various Communication Activities by College Students," *Journal of Applied Communication Research,* 8, 1981, pp. 101–109; and Andrew Wolvin and Carolyn Coakley, "A Survey of the Status of Listening Training in Some *Fortune* 500 Corporations," *Communication Education,* 40, 1991, pp. 152–164.

8. M. L. Beall, J. Gill-Rosier, J. Tate, and A. Matten, "State of the Context: Listening in Education," *International Journal of Listening,* 22, 2008, pp. 123–132.

9. A. Dubber, *Radio in the Digital Age.* Cambridge, MA: Polity Press, 2013.

10. See Denisa R. Superville, "Digitally Distracted: Hours Spent Wired Changing How Kids Think and Interact," *The Record* (Bergen County, NJ), May 15, 2010, pp. A1, A8; and Virginia Rideout, Ulla G. Foehr, and Donald F. Roberts, *Generation M2: Media in the Lives of 8–18-Year-Olds,* A Kaiser Family Foundation Study, January, 2010, https://files.eric.ed.gov/fulltext/ED527859.pdf

11. See R. N. Bostrom, "The Process of Listening," in O. Hargie, ed., *Handbook of Communication Skills,* 3rd ed., New York: Routledge, pp. 267–291; and Andrew Wolvin

and Carolyn Gwynn Coakley, *Listening,* 5th ed., Dubuque, IA: Brown & Benchmark, 1996.

12. See Judi Brownell, *Listening: Attitudes, Principles, and Skills,* 3rd ed., Boston: Allyn & Bacon, 2006.

13. Teddy Wayne, "Engulfed in the Artificial Audioscape," *The New York Times,* February 11, 2018, p. ST2.

14. Cited in Arthur K. Robertson, *The Language of Effective Listening,* Carmel, IN: Scott Foresman Professional Books, 1991, pp. 44–45.

15. Cathy N. Davidson, *Now You See It: How the Brain Science of Attention Will Transform the Way We Live, Work, and Learn,* New York: Viking, 2011.

16. See M. Imhof, "Who Are We as We Listen? Individual Listening Profiles in Varying Contexts," *International Journal of Listening,* 18, 2004, pp. 36–45; and K. W. Watson, L. L. Barker, and J. B. Weaver, "The Listening Styles Profiles: Development and Validation of an Instrument to Assess Four Listening Styles," *International Journal of Listening,* 9, 1995, pp. 1–13.

17. See, for example, M. Snyder, "A Gender-Informed Model of Couple and Family Therapy: Relationship Enhancement Therapy," *Contemporary Family Therapy,* 14, 1992, pp. 15–31; and B. I. Omdahl, *Cognitive Appraisal, Emotion, and Empathy,* Mahwah, NJ: Lawrence Erlbaum, 1995.

18. J. B. Weaver III and M. B. Kirley, "Listening Styles and Empathy," *Southern Communication Journal,* 60, 1995, pp. 131–140.

19. Frank I. Luntz, *Win: The Key Principles to Take Your Business from Ordinary to Extraordinary,* New York: Hyperion, 2011.

20. See, for example, Wolvin and Coakley, *Listening.*

21. R. Preiss and L. Wheeless, "Affective Responses in Listening," *Journal of the International Listening Association,* 3, 1989, pp. 72–102.

22. See, for example, J. B. Bavelas and T. Johnson, "Listeners as Co-narrators," *Journal of Personality and Social Psychology,* 79, 2002, pp. 941–952.

23. Quoted in Adam Bryant, "Want to Inspire? Don't Sugarcoat Your Feedback," *New York Times,* September 11, 2011, p. BU2.

24. John Stewart and M. Thomas, "Dialogic Listening: Sculpting Mutual Meanings," in John Stewart, ed., *Bridges Not Walls: A Book about Interpersonal Communication,* 6th ed., New York: McGraw-Hill, 1995, pp. 184–201.

25. See, for example, H. S. Park and X. Guan, "Cultural Differences in Self versus Others' Self-Construals: Data from China and the United States," *Communication Research Reports,* 24, 2007, pp. 21–28.

26. C. Y. Cheng, "Chinese Philosophy and Contemporary Communication Theory," in D. I. Kincaid, ed., *Communication Theory: Eastern and Western Perspectives,* New York: Academic Press, 1987.

27. See Stella Ting-Toomey, "Toward a Theory of Conflict and Culture," in William B. Gudykunst, Lea P. Stewart, and Stella Ting-Toomey, eds., *Communication, Culture, and Organizational Processes,* Beverly Hills, CA: Sage, 1985, pp. 71–86.

28. Larry A. Samovar and Richard E. Porter, *Communication between Cultures,* 5th ed., Belmont, CA: Wadsworth, 2004, pp. 211–212.

29. See T. S. Lebra, "The Cultural Significance of Silence in Japanese Communication," *Multilingua,* 6, 1987, pp. 343–357.

30. William B. Gudykunst, *Bridging Differences: Effective Intergroup Communication,* 4th ed., Thousand Oaks, CA: Sage, 2004, pp. 196–197.

31. Deborah Tannen, *You Just Don't Understand: Women and Men in Conversation.* New York: Morrow, 1990.

32. M. Booth-Butterfield, "She Hears . . . He Hears: What They Hear and Why," *Personnel Journal,* 44:3, 1984, pp. 36–42.

33. M. Messner, "Boyhood, Organized Sports, and the Construction of Masculinities," in E. Disch, ed., *Reconstructing Gender,* Mountain View, CA: Mayfield, 1997, pp. 57–73.

34. See Julia T. Wood, *Gendered Lives: Communication, Gender, and Culture,* 10th ed., Boston: Wadsworth, 2013, p. 127.

35. Diana K. Ivy and Phil Backlund, *Exploring GenderSpeak: Personal Effectiveness in Gender Communication,* New York: McGraw-Hill, 1994, p. 225.

36. N. Newcombe and D. B. Arnkoff, "Effects of Speech Style and Sex of Speaker on Person Perception," *Journal of Personality and Social Psychology,* 37, 1999, pp. 1293–1303.

37. A. Mulac, C. R. Incontro, and M. R. James, "Comparison of the Gender-Linked Language Effect and Sex Role Stereotypes," *Journal of Personality and Social Psychology,* 49, 1985, pp. 1098–1109.

38. Davidson, *Now You See It,* pp. 23–31.

39. Ibid.

40. See Leonard Miakotko, "The Impact of Smart Phones and Mobile Devices on Human Health and Life," www.nyu.edu/classes/keefer/waoe/miakotkol.pdf; and Emma Seppala, "What is Your Phone Doing to Your Relationships?" *Mindful,* November 14, 2017, https://www.mindful.org/what-is-your-phone-doing-to-your-relationships/

41. See, for example, C. Bracken and P. Skalski, "Telepresence and Video Games: The Impact of Image Quality." *PsychNology Journal,* 7:1, 2009, pp. 101–112.

42. K. Crawford, "Following You: Disciplines of Listening in Social Media," *Continuum: Journal of Media & Cultural Studies,* 23:4, 2009, pp. 525–535.

43. Danny Hakim, "Alexa, Stop Listening! Hey Google, You Too,"

The New York Times, December 10, 2017, p. BU7.

## CHAPTER 5

1. Mark Santora, "Holocaust Law in Poland Chips at Shared Pain," *The New York Times*, February 7, 2018, pp. A1, A9.

2. Dan Bilefsky, "Quebec Tries to Say Au Revoir to 'Hi,' and Hello to 'Bonjour,'" *The New York Times*, December 6, 2017, p. A7.

3. C. K. Ogden and I. A. Richards, *The Meaning of Meaning,* New York: Harcourt Brace Jovanovich, 1930.

4. Anemona Hartocollis, "At Harvard, 'House Master' is Discontinued as Job Title," *The New York Times*, December 3, 2015, p. A22.

5. See, for example, Ralph Keyes, *Euphemania: Our Love Affair with Euphemisms,* New York: Little, Brown, 2011.

6. For a discussion of politeness in non-Western cultures, see M. S. Kim, *Non-Western Perspectives in Human Communication,* Thousand Oaks, CA: Sage, 2002.

7. William Lutz, *Doublespeak Defined,* New York: Harper Resource, 1999; and National Council of Teachers of English, "The 1999 Doublespeak Awards," *ETC.: A Review of General Semantics,* 56, 1999–2000, p. 484.

8. A. Brown, *Hate Speech Law: A Philosophical Examination.* New York: Routledge, 2015.

9. Mark Vilensky, "School Rethinks Mr., Ms. Labels," *The Wall Street Journal,* January 27, 2015, pp. A13, A14.

10. William Haney, *Communication and Organizational Behavior,* 3rd ed., Homewood, IL: Richard D. Irwin, 1973, pp. 247–248.

11. See "Mokusatsu: One Word, Two Lessons," www.nsa.gov/public_info/_files/tech_journals/mokusatsu.pdf.

12. William B. Gudykunst, "Uncertainty and Anxiety," in Young Yun Kim and William B. Gudykunst, eds., *Theories in Intercultural Communication,* Newbury Park, CA: Sage, 1988, p. 129.

13. Dean C. Barnlund, *Public and Private Self in Japan and the United States: Communicative Styles in Two Cultures,* Yarmouth, ME: Intercultural Press, 1989, p. 57; and Tomohiro Hasegawa and William B. Gudykunst, "Silence in Japan and the United States," *Journal of Cross-Cultural Psychology,* 29, 1998, pp. 668–684.

14. See Richard E. Nisbett, "Living Together versus Going It Alone," in Larry A. Samovar, Richard E. Porter, and Edwin R. McDaniel, *Intercultural Communication: A Reader,* 12th ed., Boston: Wadsworth, 2009, pp. 134–144.

15. Steve Duck, "Talking Relationships into Being," *Journal of Social and Personal Relationships,* 12, 1995, pp. 535–540.

16. Howard Giles, Nikolas Coupland, and Justine Coupland, "Accommodation Theory: Communication, Context, and Consequence," in Howard Giles, Nikolas Coupland, and Justine Coupland, eds., *Contexts of Accommodation: Developments in Applied Sociolinguistics,* New York: Cambridge University Press, 1991, pp. 1–68.

17. Y. Baruch and S. Jenkins, "Swearing at Work and Permissive Leadership Culture: When Anti-social Becomes Social and Incivility Is Acceptable," *Leadership and Organization Development Journal,* 28, 2006, pp. 492–507.

18. Edward Sapir, *Selected Writings of Edward Sapir,* David W. Mandelbaum, ed., Berkeley: University of California Press, 1949, p. 162.

19. Robert Sapolsky, "Language Shapes Thoughts and Storm Preparations,"

*The Wall Street Journal,* April 25–26, 2015, p, C2.

20. E. M. Rogers and T. M. Steinfatt, *Intercultural Communication,* Prospect Heights, IL: Waveland Press, 1998, p. 135.

21. B. L. Whorf, *Language, Thought, and Reality: Selected Writings of Benjamin Lee Whorf,* J. B. Carroll, ed., Cambridge: MIT Press, 1940/1956, p. 239.

22. Sapir, *Selected Writings,* p. 162.

23. See Fiona Cowie, *What's Within? Nativism Reconsidered,* New York: Oxford University Press, 1999; also see J. H. McWhorter, *The Language Hoax: Why the World Looks the Same in Any Language.* Oxford, England: Oxford University Press, 2014.

24. See Farzad Sharifian, "Cultural Linguistics and Linguistic Relativity," *Language Sciences,* vol. 59, January 2017, pp. 83–92.

25. Larry A. Samovar and Richard E. Porter, *Communication between Cultures,* Belmont, CA: Wadsworth, 1991, p. 152.

26. See, for example, Margaret K. Nydel, *Understanding Arabs: A Guide for Modern Times,* 4th ed., New York: Nicholas Brealey, 2005.

27. See, for example, Edwin R. McDaniel, Larry A. Samovar, and Richard E. Porter, "Understanding Intercultural Communication: The Working Principles," in Larry A. Samovar, Richard E. Porter, and Edwin R. McDaniel, eds., *Intercultural Communication: A Reader,* 12th ed., Boston: Wadsworth, 2009, pp. 6–17.

28. Sharon Begley, "West Brain, East Brain: What a Difference Culture Makes," *Newsweek,* March 1, 2010, p. A6.

29. Lera Boroditsky, "Lost in Translation," *Wall Street Journal,* July 24–25, 2010, p. W3.

30. Nancy M. Henley, "Molehill or Mountain? What We Know and Don't Know about Sex Bias in

Language," in Mary Crawford & Margaret Gentry, eds., *Gender and Thought: Psychological Perspectives,* New York: Springer-Verlag, 1989, pp. 59–78.

31. See, for example, J. Gastil, "Generic Pronouns and Sexist Language: The Oxymoronic Character of Masculine Generics," *Sex Roles,* 23, 1990, pp. 629–643; and J. Y. Switzer, "The Impact of Generic Word Choices: An Empirical Investigation of Age- and Sex-Related Differences," *Sex Roles,* 22, 1990, pp. 69–82.

32. Christina Passariello and Ray A. Smith, "Grab Your 'Murse,' Pack a 'Mankini' and Don't Forget the 'Mewelry,'" *Wall Street Journal,* September 8, 2011, pp. A1, A12.

33. Deborah Tannen, "Gender Differences in Conversational Coherence: Physical Alignment and Topical Cohesion," in Bruce Dorval, ed., *Conversational Organization and Its Development,* Norwood, NJ: Ablex, 1990, pp. 167–206.

34. Julia T. Wood, *Gendered Lives: Communication, Gender, and Culture,* 9th ed., Boston: Wadsworth, 2011.

35. Jennifer Coates, *Women, Men, and Language: A Sociolinguistic Account of Gender Differences in Language,* 2nd ed., New York: Longman, 1993.

36. See, for example, Karina Schumann and Michael Ross, "Why Women Apologize More than Men: Gender Differences in Thresholds for Perceiving Offensive Behavior," *Psychological Science,* 21, 2010, pp. 1649–1655.

37. Campell Leaper and Rachel D. Robnett, "Women Are More Likely than Men to Use Tentative Language, Aren't They? A Meta-analysis Testing for Gender Differences and Moderators," *Psychology of Women Quarterly,* 35, 2011, pp. 129–142.

38. Robin Lakoff, *Language and Woman's Place,* New York: Harper & Row, 1975.

39. See, for example, S. Mills, "Discourse Competence: Or How to Theorize Strong Women," in C. Hendricks and K. Oliver, eds., *Language and Liberation,* Albany: State University of New York Press, 1999, pp. 81–97.

40. Deborah Tannen, *You Just Don't Understand: Women and Men in Conversation,* New York: Morrow, 1990.

41. Ibid., p. 42. See also, Deborah Tannen, *You're the Only One I Can Tell: Inside the Lanugage of Women's Friendships.* New York: Ballantine Books, 2017.

42. L. Tamir, *Men in Their Forties: The Transition to Middle Age,* New York: Springer, 1982.

43. J. Harwood, H. Giles, S. Fox, E. B. Ryan, and A. Williams, "Patronizing Young and Elderly Adults: Response Strategies in a Community Setting," *Journal of Applied Communication Research,* 21, 1993, pp. 211–226.

44. Naomi Wolf, *The Beauty Myth,* New York: Morrow, 1991.

45. Susan F. Rasky, "Study Reports Sex Bias in News Organizations," *New York Times,* April 11, 1989, p. C22.

46. Kevin Maney, "There are No Words . . ." *Newsweek,* April 8, 2016, pp. 46–47.

47. Howard Rheingold, "A Slice of Life in My Virtual Community," in Linda M. Harasim, ed., *Global Networks: Computers and International Communication,* Cambridge, MA: MIT Press, 1993, p. 61.

48. Pamela Paul, "Cracking Teenagers' Online Codes," *New York Times,* January 22, 2012, pp. ST1, ST9.

49. See Susannah Griffee, "First Grade Teacher Calls Students 'Future Criminals,'" April 2, 2011, https://www.nbcnewyork.com/news/local/First-Grade-Teacher-Calls-Students-Future-Criminals-119071054.html

50. T. Wofford, "The FBI Has a File on Gamergate," *Newsweek.* December 19, 2014.

51. Stephanie Raposo, "Quick! Tell Us What KUTGW Means," *Wall Street Journal,* August 5, 2009, pp. D1, D3.

52. See Carolyn Tagg, "A Corpus Linguistics Study of SMS Text Messaging," doctoral dissertation, University of Birmingham, March 2009.

53. John McWhorter, "Is Texting Killing the English Language?" *Time,* April 25, 2013, http://ideas.time.com/2013/04/25/is-texting-killing-the-english-language/

54. C. Wood, N. Kemp, and S. Waldron, "Exploring the Longitudinal Relationships Between the Use of Grammar in Text Messaging and Performance on Grammatical Tasks," *British Journal of Developmental Psychology,* 3s, 2014, pp. 415–429.

55. Lauren Collister, "There's a Reason Using a Period in a Text Message Makes You Sound Angry," *Quartz,* January 3, 2018. https://qz.com/1169792/theres-a-reason-using-a-period-in-a-text-message-makes-you-sound-angry/

56. Katie Roiphe, "The Language of Fakebook," *New York Times,* August 15, 2010, p. 2; and Aimee Lee Ball, "Talking (Exclamation) Points," *New York Times,* July 3, 2011, p. 2.

57. Holly Corbett Bristol, "Women Set Casual Tone on Social Media (v. eexxcciiittting!)," *USA Today,* December 8, 2011, p. 3D.

58. See "Say What??? Campaigns That Failed to Translate," https://glantz.net/blog/campaigns-that-failed-to-translate

## CHAPTER 6

1. Farhad Manjoo, "The Post-Text Future is Here (You Read That Right)," *The New York Times,* February 12, 2018, p. F2.

2. In "The Art of Original Filmmaking: Interview with Bérénice Bejo," The Writing Studio, http://www.writingstudio.co.za/page3974.html,

as cited in "Business Communication Lessons from 'The Artist,'" Presence and Impact: The Art and Practice of Communication Mastery, March 8, 2012, http://presenceandimpact.com/2012/03/08/business-communication-lessons-from-the-artist-3. For more background, see also Sheila Roberts, Jean Dujardin and Bérénice Bejo, The Artist Interview, November 23, 2011, http://collider.com/jean-dujardin-and-berenice-bejo-the-artist-interview/

3. Teri Kwal Gamble and Michael Gamble, Nonverbal Messages Tell More: A Practical Guide to Nonverbal Communication. New York: Routledge Taylor & Francis Group, 2017.

4. See Paul Ekman, Telling Lies: Clues to Deceit in the Marketplace, Politics, and Marriage. New York: Norton, 1992.

5. Ibid, p. 43.

6. See David B. Buller and Judee K. Burgoon, "Interpersonal Deception Theory," Communication Theory, 6, 1996, pp. 203–242.

7. See Paul Ekman, "Mistakes When Deceiving," in Thomas A. Sebeok and Robert Rosenthal, eds., The Clever Hans Phenomenon: Communication with Horses, Whales, Apes, and People, New York: New York Academy of Sciences, 1981, pp. 269–278; Paul Ekman, Emotions Revealed: Recognizing Faces and Feelings to Improve Communication and Emotional Life, New York: Henry Holt, 2003; and Malcolm Gladwell, "The Naked Face," The New Yorker, August 3, 2002, pp. 38–49.

8. Ekman, Emotions Revealed.

9. See Wilhelm Oliver and Werner Sommer, "Emotion Recognition in Nonverbal Face-to-Face Communication," Journal of Nonverbal Behavior, 41:3, September 2017, pp. 221–238.

10. Quoted in Daniel Goleman, "Sensing Silent Cues Emerges as Key Skill," New York Times, October 10, 1989. See also Joe Navarro with Marvin Karlins, What Every BODY Is Saying: An Ex-FBI Agent's Guide to Speed-Reading People, New York: HarperCollins, 2008.

11. See H. D. Ellis and A. W. Young, "Are Faces Special?" in A. W. Young and H. D. Ellis, eds., Handbook of Research in Face Processing, Amsterdam: North Holland, 1989, pp. 1–26.

12. Steve Lohr, "Facial Recognition Works Best If You're a White Guy" The New York Times, January 12, 2018, pp. B1, B5.

13. See M. D. Alicke, R. H. Smith, and M. L. Klotz, "Judgments of Physical Attractiveness: The Role of Faces and Bodies," Personality and Social Psychology Bulletin, 12, 1986, pp. 381–389.

14. D. S. Berry, "What Can a Moving Face Tell Us?" Journal of Personality and Social Psychology, 58, 1990, pp. 1004–1014.

15. E. H. Hess and J. M. Polt, "Pupil Size as Related to Interest Value of Visual Stimuli," Science, 132, August 5, 1960, pp. 349–350.

16. See C. L. Kleinke, "Gaze and Eye Contact: A Research Review," Psychological Bulletin, 100, 1986, pp. 78–100.

17. M. Argyle and J. Dean, "Eye Contact, Distance, and Affiliation," Sociometry, 28, 1965, pp. 289–394.

18. See M. LaFrance and C. Mayo, Moving Bodies: Nonverbal Communication in Human Interaction, 2nd ed., New York, NY: Holt, 1978.

19. Paul Ekman and Wallace V. Friesen, Unmasking the Face: A Guide to Recognizing Emotions from Facial Expressions, Englewood Cliffs, NJ: Prentice Hall, 1984.

20. Paul Ekman and Wallace V. Friesen, "The Repertoire of Nonverbal Behavior: Categories, Origins, Usage and Coding," Semiotica, 69, 1969, pp. 49–97.

21. See P. D. Krivonos and M. L. Knapp, "Initiating Communication: What Do You Say When You Say Hello?" Central States Journal, 26, 1975, pp. 115–125; and M. L. Knapp, R. P. Hart, and G. W. Friedrich, "Nonverbal Correlates of Human Leave Taking," Communication Monographs, 40, 1973, pp. 182–198.

22. M. L. Knapp, "Nonverbal Communication: Basic Perspectives," in John Stewart, ed., Bridges Not Walls: A Book about Interpersonal Communication, 5th ed., New York: McGraw-Hill, 1990.

23. See M. Hodgins and K. Miyake, "The Vocal Attractiveness Stereotype: Replication and Elaboration," Journal of Nonverbal Behavior, 14, 1990, pp. 97–112.

24. R. N. Bond, S. Feldsteen, and S. Simpson, "Relative and Absolute Judgments of Speech Rate from Masked and Content-Standard Stimuli: The Influence of Vocal Frequency and Intensity," Human Communication Research, 14, 1988, pp. 548–568.

25. Edward T. Hall, The Hidden Dimension, New York: Doubleday, 1969.

26. A. G. Halberstadt, "Race, Socioeconomic Status, and Nonverbal Behavior," in A. W. Wiegman and S. Feldstein, eds., Multichannel Integrations of Nonverbal Behavior, Mahwah, NJ: Lawrence Erlbaum, 1985, pp. 195–225.

27. See J. K. Burgoon, "Privacy and Communication," in M. Burgoon, ed., Communication Yearbook 6, Beverly Hills, CA: Sage, 1982, pp. 206–249; J. K. Burgoon and L. Aho, "Three Field Experiments on the Effects of Violations of Conversational Distance," Communication Monographs, 49, 1982, pp. 71–88; and J. K. Burgoon and J. B. Walther, "Nonverbal

Expectations and the Evaluative Consequence of Violations," *Human Communication Research,* 17, 1990, pp. 232–265.

28. Hall, *Hidden Dimension*; and A. Rapoport, *The Meaning of the Built Environment,* Beverly Hills, CA: Sage, 1982.

29. See U. J. Derliga, R. J. Lewis, S. Harrison, B. A. Winstead, and R. Costanza, "Gender Differences in the Initiation and Attribution of Tactile Intimacy," *Journal of Nonverbal Behavior,* 13, 1989, pp. 83–96.

30. See D. K. Fromme, W. E. Jaynes, D. K. Taylor, E. G. Harold, J. Daniell, J. R. Rountree, and M. L. Fromme, "Nonverbal Behavior and Attitudes toward Touch," *Journal of Nonverbal Behavior,* 13, 1989, pp. 3–14.

31. S. E. Jones and A. E. Yarbrough, "A Naturalistic Study of the Message of Touch," *Communication Monographs,* 52, 1985, pp. 19–56; and Argyle, *Bodily Communication.*

32. Nancy Henley, *Body Politics: Power, Sex, and Nonverbal Communication,* New York: Simon & Schuster, 1986.

33. S. Kaiser, *The Social Psychology of Clothing: Symbolic Appearances in Context,* 2nd ed., New York: Macmillan, 1990.

34. See, for example, M. S. Singer and A. E. Singer, "The Effect of Police Uniforms on Interpersonal Perception," *Journal of Psychology,* 119, 1985, pp. 157–161.

35. Robin Givhan, "The Casual-Friday Campaign," *Newsweek,* August 15, 2011, p. 61.

36. See Brooks Barnes, "Hollywood Still Likes Its Women Skinny," *The New York Times,* August 20, 2017, pp. AR2, AR10; and Kathleen Kennedy Townsend, "What Should a Powerful Woman Look Like," *The New York Times,* July 3, 2016, p. SR2.

37. Dahlia Lithwick, "Our Beauty Bias Is Unfair," *Newsweek,* June 14, 2010, p. 20; Jessica Bennett, "The Beauty Advantage," *Newsweek,* July 26,

2010, pp. 46–48; Maureen Dowd, "Dressed to Distract," *New York Times,* June 6, 2010, p. WK11; and Harriet Brown, "For Obese People, Prejudice in Plain Sight," *New York Times,* March 16, 2010, p. D6.

38. See, for example, Hajo Adam and Adam D. Galinsky, "Enclothed Cognition," *Journal of Experimental Social Psychology,* 2012, doi:10,1016/j.jesp.2012.02.008.

39. N. Wade, "Scent of a Man Is Linked to a Woman's Selection," *New York Times,* January 22, 2002, p. F2.

40. N. Wade, "For Gay Men, Different Scent of Attraction," *New York Times,* May 10, 2005, pp. A1, A14.

41. Lauran Neergaard, "Researchers Find Bad Times Really Do Stink," *The Record* (Bergen County, NJ), March 28, 2008, p. A6.

42. Max Luscher, *The Luscher Color Test,* New York: Simon & Schuster, 1980; and Max Luscher, *The Four Color Person,* New York: Simon & Schuster, 1980.

43. Ibid.

44. Simon Garfield, *Timekeepers: How the World Become Obsessed with Time.* New York: Cannongate Books, 2016.

45. Robert Levine, "Waiting Is a Power Game," *Psychology Today,* April 1987, p. 30.

46. A. Moon and S. Chen, "The Power to Control Time: Power Influences How Much Time (You Think) You Have," *Journal of Experimental and Social Psychology,* 54, 2014, pp. 97–101; and Daniel H. Pink, *When: The Scientific Secrets of Perfect Timing.* New York: Riverhead Books, 2018.

47. Peter Anderson, "Exploring Intercultural Differences in Nonverbal Communication," in L. A. Samovar and R. E. Porter, eds., *Interpersonal Communication: A Reader,* 5th ed., Belmont, CA: Wadsworth, 1998, pp. 272–282.

48. See, for example, P. A. Andersen and H. Wang, "Unraveling Culture

Cues: Dimensions of Nonverbal Communication across Cultures," in L. A. Samovar, R. E. Porter, and E. R. McDaniel, eds., *Intercultural Communication: A Reader,* 11th ed., Belmont, CA: Wadsworth, 2006, pp. 250–266.

49. Larry A. Samovar, Richard E. Porter, and Edwin R. McDaniel, *Communication between Cultures,* 7th ed., Boston: Wadsworth, 2010, pp. 260–265.

50. Larry A. Samovar, Richard E. Porter, and Lisa A. Stefani, *Communication between Cultures,* 3rd ed., Belmont, CA: Wadsworth, 1998, p. 159.

51. Michael L. Hecht, Ronald L. Jackson II, and Sidney A. Ribeau, *African American Communication,* 2nd ed., Mahwah, NJ: Lawrence Erlbaum, 2003. See also K. R. Johnson, "Black Kinesics: Some Nonverbal Communication Patterns in the Black Culture," in R. L. Jackson, ed., *African American Communication and Identities,* Thousand Oaks, CA: Sage, 2004, pp. 39–46.

52. M. P. Orbe and T. M. Harris, *Interracial Communication Theory into Practice,* New York: Thompson Learning, 2001.

53. "If You're Minding Manners, One Gesture Isn't OK in Brazil," *The Record* (Bergen County, NJ), July 6, 2008, p. T1.

54. Austin Considine, "A Little Imperfection for That Smile," *New York Times,* October 23, 2011, p. ST6.

55. Judith A. Hall, *Nonverbal Sex Differences: Communication Accuracy and Expressive Style,* Baltimore: Johns Hopkins University Press, 1984, p. 3.

56. B. Ueland, "Tell Me More: On the Fine Art of Listening," *Utne Reader,* November/December 1992, pp. 104–109; A. Mulac, "Men's and Women's Talk in Some Gender and Mixed Gender Dyads: Power or Polemic?" *Journal of Language and Social Psychology,* 8, 1989, pp. 249–270.

57. J. F. Dovidio, S. L. Ellyson, C. F. Keating, K. Heltman, and C. E. Brown, "The Relationship of Social Power to Visual Displays of Dominance between Men and Women," *Journal of Personality and Social Psychology,* 54, 1988, pp. 233–242.

58. K. Floyd, "Affectionate Same-Sex Touch: The Influence of Homophobia on Observers' Perceptions," *Journal of Social Psychology,* 140, 2000, pp. 774–788.

59. See, for example, Nancy Briton and Judith Hall, "Gender-Based Expectancies and Observer Judgments of Smiling," *Journal of Nonverbal Behavior,* 19, 1995, p. 49; and Diane Hales, *Just Like a Woman,* New York: Bantam Books, 1999, p. 270.

60. Julia T. Wood, *Gendered Lives: Communication, Gender, and Culture,* 9th ed., Boston: Wadsworth, 2011, p. 130.

61. See, for example, Lucy Rycroft-Smith, "Switching to Men's Clothing Taught Me That the World Doesn't Want Women to Get Too Comfortable," *Quartz,* February 27, 2017, https://qz.com/916148/ switching-to-mens-clothing-taught-me-that-the-world-doesnt-want-women-to-get-too-comfortable/

62. Tricia Romano, "A Tall Tale, but True: Men in Heels," *New York Times,* October 16, 2011, p. ST12; Alexis Tarrazi, "What's in Store: Brogues/Oxfords," *The Record* (Bergen County, NJ), October 16, 2011, F3.

63. Stephanie Clifford, "Men Step Out of the Recession, Bag on Hip, Bracelet on Wrist," *New York Times,* February 20, 2012, pp. A1, B3.

64. See, for example, Bill Puka, "The Liberation of Caring: A Different Voice for Gilligan's Different Voice," *Hypatia,* 5, 1990, pp. 59–82; and J. A. Hall, "Gender, Gender-Roles, and Nonverbal Communication Skills," in R. Rosenthal, ed., *Skill in Nonverbal Communication: Individual Differences,* Cambridge, MA: Oelgeschlager, Gunn & Hain, 1979.

65. Carol Gilligan, *In a Different Voice: Psychological Theory and Women's Development,* Cambridge, MA: Harvard University Press, 1982; and Carol Gilligan, Nona P. Lyons, and Trudy J. Hanmer, eds., *Making Connections: The Relational Worlds of Adolescent Girls at Emma Willard School,* Cambridge, MA: Harvard University Press, 1990.

66. See, for example, "Why We Flirt," *Time,* February 4, 2008; and Deborah A. Lott and Frank Veronsky, "The New Flirting Game," *Psychology Today,* January 1, 1999, http://www.psychologytoday .com/articles/199901/ the-new-flirting-game.

67. See, for example, Jean Kilbourne, "The More You Subtract, the More You Add: Cutting Girls Down to Size," in Joan Z. Spade and Catherine G. Valentine, eds., *The Kaleidoscope of Gender: Prisms, Patterns, and Possibilities,* Belmont, CA: Wadsworth, 2004, pp. 234–244.

68. Wood, *Gendered Lives,* pp. 257–283.

69. Brandon Griggs, "Why Computer Voices Are Mostly Female," CNN, October 21, 2011, http://www.cnn .com/2011/10/21/tech/innovation/ female-computer-voices/index .html?hpt.

70. Barbara Ortutay, "Picking New Emojis is a Process," *The Record,* January 15, 2018, p. 2BL.

71. K. Skovholt, A. Gronning, and A. Kankaanranta, "The Communicative Functions of Emoticons in Workplace E-mails," *Journal of Computer-Mediated Communication,* 19, 2014, pp. 780–797.

72. I. Vandergriff, "Emotive Communication Online: A Contextual Analysis of Computer-Mediated Communication Cues," *Journal of Pragmatics,* 51, 2013, pp. 1–12.

73. See D. N. Gunraj, A. M. Drumm-Hewitt, E. M. Dashow, S. S. N. Upadhyay, and C. M. Kline, "Texting Insincerely: The Role of the Period in Text Messages," *Computers in Human Behavior,* 55, 2016, pp. 1067–1075.

74. Adrienne LaFrance, "Why Do So Many Digital Assistants Have Female Names?" March 30, 2016, https://www.theatlantic.com/ technology/archive/2016/03/why-do-so-many-digital-assistants-have-feminine-names/475884/

75. H. S. Hodgkins and C. Belch, "Interparental Violence and Nonverbal Abilities," *Journal of Nonverbal Behavior,* 24, 2000, pp. 3–24.

76. See, for example, N. Miczo, C. Segrin, and L. E. Allspach, "Relationship between Nonverbal Sensitivity, Encoding, and Relational Satisfaction," *Communication Reports,* 14, 2001, pp. 39–48.

## CHAPTER 7

1. Rachel Dodes, "The New Water Cooler Is a TV Show," *Wall Street Journal,* February 10, 2012, p. D4.

2. Jefferson Graham, "TV Networks Count on 'Social' TV Viewers," *USA Today,* May 3, 2012, p. 3B; and Alan Reisberg, "The Relationship Between Social Media and TV Viewing," *Capital Media,* http:// www.capmediagroup.com/the-relationship-between-social-media-and-tv-viewing/.

3. O. Weisman, I. M. Aderka, H. Hermesh, and E. Gilboa-Schectman, "Social Rank and Affiliation in Social Anxiety Disorder," *Behavior Research and Therapy,* 49, 2011, pp. 399–405.

4. Sue Shellenbarger, "The Best Ways to Network at a Party," *The Wall Street Journal,* September 15, 2015, pp. D1, D4.

5. Elizabeth Bernstein, "Speaking Up Is Hard to Do: Researchers Explain

Why," *Wall Street Journal,* February 7, 2012, pp. D1, D4.

6. Andrea Bartz, "How to Talk to Anyone: Awkward Much? Don't Sweat It. Everyone Is. Get Ready to Master the Almost-Lost (But Life-Changing!) Art of Face-to-Face Conversation," *Scholastic Choices,* 33:3, November/December 2017, pp. 6–9.

7. Stephanie Hayes, "Nice Day, Eh?" *The Atlantic,* October 2016, p. 22.

8. See Margaret L. McLaughlin, *Conversation: How Talk Is Organized,* Beverly Hills, CA: Sage, 1984; and N. J. Enfield, *How We Talk: The Inner Workings of Conversation.* New York: Basic Books, 2017.

9. Steve Duck, *Understanding Relationships,* New York: Guilford Press, 1991, p. 16. See also Steve Duck, *Human Relationships,* 4th ed., Thousand Oaks, CA: Sage, 2007.

10. Gerald Coffee, *Beyond Survival,* New York: Putnam, 1990.

11. See, for example, Susan Cain, *Quiet: The Power of Introverts in a World That Can't Stop Talking,* New York: Crown, 2012.

12. See, for example, Ed Keller and Brad Faye, *The Face-to-Face Book: Why Relationships Rule in a Digital Marketplace,* New York: Free Press, 2012.

13. See Steven W. Duck, *Human Relationships,* 4th ed., London: Sage, 2007; and Steven W. Duck, *Meaningful Relationships: Talking Sense, and Relating,* Thousand Oaks, CA: Sage, 1994.

14. Matt Huston, "Finding Your Crowd," *Psychology Today,* July/August 2017, p. 9.

15. Susan Shimanoff, *Conversational Rules,* Beverly Hills, CA: Sage, 1980, p. 57.

16. Steve Duck, *Human Relationships,* 3rd ed., Thousand Oaks, CA: Sage, 1998, p. 7. See also Duck, *Human Relationships,* 4th ed.

17. See, for example, Scott Jacobs and Sally Jackson, "Speech Act Structure in Conversation: Rational Aspects of Pragmatic Coherence," in Robert T. Craig and Karen Tracy, eds., *Conversational Coherence: Form, Structure, and Strategy,* Beverly Hills, CA: Sage, 1983, pp. 47–66.

18. See Robert E. Nofsinger, *Everyday Conversation,* Newbury Park, CA: Sage, 1991, p. 6. For a discussion of criteria used to assess conversational effectiveness, see Daniel J. Canary, Michael J. Cody, and Valerie L. Manusov, *Interpersonal Communication: A Goals-Based Approach,* 3rd ed., Boston: Bedford/St. Martin's Press, 2003, pp. 520–523.

19. Thomas E. Murray, "The Language of Singles Bars," *American Speech,* 60, 1985, pp. 17–30.

20. Chris Kleinke, *Meeting and Understanding People,* New York: W. H. Freeman, 1986.

21. Gregory Stock, *The Book of Questions,* New York: Workman, 1987.

22. Mark L. Knapp, Roderick P. Hart, Gustav W. Friedrich, and Gary M. Shulman, "The Rhetoric of Goodbye: Verbal and Nonverbal Correlates of Human Leave-Taking," *Speech Monographs,* 40, August 1973, pp. 182–198.

23. Agnes Alsious and K. G. Munhall, "Seeing the Way: The Role of Vision in Conversation Turn Exchange Perception," *Multisensory Research,* 30:7/8, 2017, pp. 653–679.

24. N. J. Enfield, "Speech Relies on Some Little Words," *The Wall Street Journal,* October 28–29, 2017, p. C4.

25. H. P. Grice, "Logic and Conversation," in P. Cole and J. L. Morgan, eds., *Syntax and Semantics,* vol. 3, *Speech Acts,* New York: Seminar Press, 1975, pp. 41–58; and K. Lindblom, "Cooperating with Grice: A Cross-Disciplinary Metaperspective on Uses of Grice's Cooperative Principle," *Journal of Pragmatics,* 33, 2001, pp. 1601–1623.

26. McLaughlin, *Conversation,* pp. 88–89.

27. See, for example, K. Midooka, "Characteristics of Japanese Style Communication," *Media, Culture, and Society,* 12, 1990, pp. 477–489; and Y. Gu, "Polite Phenomena in Modern Chinese," *Journal of Pragmatics,* 14, 1990, pp. 237–257.

28. P. Brown and S. Levinson, *Politeness: Some Universals in Language Usage,* New York: Cambridge University Press, 1987.

29. Robert Lee Hotz, "Science Reveals Why We Brag So Much," *Wall Street Journal,* May 8, 2012, p. D1.

30. Diana I. Tamir and Jason P. Mitchell, "Disclosing Information about the Self Is Intrinsically Rewarding," *Proceedings of the National Academy of Sciences,* May 7, 2012, published online before print, doi:10.1073/pnas.1202129109, http://wjh.harvard.edu/~dtamir/Tamir-PNAS-2012.pdf.

31. Ibid.

32. Elizabeth Bernstein, "How to Navigate Difficult Conversations," *The Wall Street Journal,* July 17, 2017, https://www.wsj.com/articles/how-to-navigate-difficult-conversations-1500310034

33. Anthony M. Grant, "Conversational Mapping: Coaching Others (and Ourselves) to Better Have Difficult Conversations," *Coaching Psychologist,* 13:1, June 2017, pp. 34–40.

34. William B. Gudykunst, *Bridging Differences: Effective Intergroup Communication,* 2nd ed., Thousand Oaks, CA: Sage, 1994, p. 83. See also William B. Gudykunst, *Bridging Differences: Effective Intergroup Communication,* 3rd ed., Thousand Oaks, CA: Sage, 1998.

35. Gudykunst, *Bridging Differences,* 2nd ed., p. 139.

36. See, for example, Stella Ting-Toomey and Leeva C. Chung, *Understanding Intercultural Communication,* 2nd ed., New York:

Oxford University Press, 2012, pp. 118–120; and Edward C. Stewart and Milton J. Bennett, *American Cultural Patterns: A Cross-Cultural Perspective,* 2nd ed., London: Nicholas Brealey, 2005.

37. Ibid.

38. T. S. Lebra, "The Cultural Significance of Silence in Japanese Communication," *Multilingua,* 6, 6, 1987, pp. 343–357.

39. Halim Barakat, *The Arab World: Society, Culture, and State,* Berkeley: University of California Press, 1993.

40. Ibid.

41. M. S. Morris, *Saying and Meaning in Puerto Rico,* Elmsford, NY: Pergamon, 1981, pp. 135–136.

42. H. Yamada, "Topic Management and Turn Distributions in Business Meetings: American versus Japanese Strategies," *Text,* 10, 1990, 272–295.

43. See, for example, L. K. Acitelli, "Gender Differences in Relationship Awareness and Marital Satisfaction among Young Married Couples," *Personality and Social Psychology Bulletin,* 18, 1992, pp. 102–110; and Julia T. Wood and Christopher C. Inman, "In a Different Mode: Masculine Styles of Communicating Closeness," *Journal of Applied Communication Research,* 21, 1993, pp. 279–295.

44. Deborah Tannen, *You Just Don't Understand: Women and Men in Conversation,* New York: Morrow, 1990, p. 24–25.

45. Alice Greenwood, "Discourse Variation and Social Comfort: A Study of Topic Initiation and Interruption Patterns in the Dinner Conversations of Preadolescent Children," doctoral dissertation, City University of New York, 1989.

46. Deborah Tannen, *Gender and Discourse,* New York: Oxford University Press, 1994, pp. 61–67.

47. Alison Gendar, "Let'salltalkovereachother," *Daily News,* October 18, 2011, p. 11.

48. See Sherry Turkle, *Alone Together: Why We Expect More from Technology and Less from Each Other,* New York: Basic Books, 2011; and Sherry Turkle, "The Flight from Conversation," *New York Times Sunday Review,* April 22, 2012, p. SR1, SR6–7.

49. Turkle, "Flight from Conversation," p. SR6.

50. Ibid.

51. Sherry Turkle, "Stop Googling. Let's Talk," *The New York Times,* September 25, 2015.

52. Jennifer Breheny Wallace, "The Big Benefits of a Little Small Talk," *The Wall Street Journal,* October 1–2, 2016, p. C3.

53. See Amanda Lenhart, "Teens, Smartphones and Texting," Pew Internet & American Life Project, March 19, 2012, http://pewinternet .org/Reports/2012/Teens-and-smartphones.aspx; Amanda Lenhart, "Teens, Cell Phones and Texting: Text Messaging Becomes Centerpiece Communication," Pew Internet & American Life Project, April 20, 2010, http:// pewresearch.org/pubs/1572/teens-cell-phones-text-messages, and Kenneth Burke; "Seventy-Three Texting Statistics That Answer All Your Questions," May 24, 2016, https://www.textrequest.com/blog/ texting-statistics-answer-questions/.

54. Turkle, "Stop Googling. Let's Talk."

55. Robert Lee Hotz, "Decoding Our Chatter," *Wall Street Journal,* October 1–2, 2011, pp. C1–C2.

56. See Roy Pea, Clifford Nass, Lyn Meheula, Marcus Rance, Aman Kumar, Holden Bamford, et al., "Media Use, Face-to-Face Communication, Media Multitasking, and Social Well-Being Among 8- to 12-Year-Old Girls," *Developmental Psychology,* 48, 2012, pp. 327–336; Rachel Emma Silverman, "Study: Face Time Benefits Preteens," *Wall Street Journal,* January 31, 2012, p. D2.

57. Ibid.

58. Pamela Paul, "A Blog as Therapy for Teenagers," *New York Times,* January 20, 2012, p. ST6.

59. Geert Lovink, *Zero Comments: Blogging and Critical Internet Culture,* New York: Routledge, 2008, p. 10.

## CHAPTER 8

1. Danielle Ofri, "Doctors Have Feelings, Too," *New York Times,* March 27, 2012, p. A27.

2. Ellen Peters, Daniel Västfjäll, Tommy Gärling, and Paul Slovic, "Affect and Decision Making: A 'Hot' Topic," *Journal of Behavioral Decision Making,* 19, 2006, pp. 79–85.

3. See, for example, Robin L. Nabi, "Exploring the Framing Effects of Emotion: Do Discrete Emotions Differentially Influence Information Accessibility, Information Seeking, and Policy Preference?" *Communication Research,* 30, 2003, pp. 224–247.

4. Daniel Goleman, *Emotional Intelligence,* New York: Bantam Books, 1995, p. x.

5. See Nico H. Frijda, *The Laws of Emotion,* New York: Lawrence Erlbaum, 2007; and Richard S. Lazarus, *Emotion and Adaptation,* New York: Oxford University Press, 1991.

6. See Richard J. Davidson and Sharon Begley, *The Emotional Life of Your Brain,* New York: Hudson Street Press, 2012.

7. Carroll E. Izard, *Human Emotions,* New York: Plenum, 1977, p. 10.

8. Howard Gardner, *Multiple Intelligences: The Theory in Practice,* New York: Basic Books, 1993, p. 9.

9. See Davidson and Begley, *Emotional Life of Your Brain.*

10. Ibid., p. 34. See also Daniel Goleman, *Social Intelligence,* New York: Bantam, 2006.

11. I. Ruisel, "Social Intelligence: Conception and Methodological Problems," *Studia Psychologica,* 34, 1992, pp. 281–296.

12. J. D. Mayer and P. Salovey, "The Intelligence of Emotional Intelligence," *Intelligence,* 17, 1993, pp. 433–442.

13. See Goleman, *Emotional Intelligence,* p. 43.

14. Sharon Jayson, "Botox May Deaden Perception, Study Says," *USA Today,* April 22, 2011, p. 3A.

15. L. Nummenmaa, E. Glerean, R. Hari, and J. K. Hietanen, "Bodily Maps of Emotions," *PNAS,* 111, pp. 646–651.

16. Paul Ekman, *Darwin and Facial Expression,* New York: Academic Press, 1973.

17. Victoria Brescoli and Eric Luis Uhlmann, "Can an Angry Woman Get Ahead? Status Conferral, Gender, and Expression of Emotion in the Workplace," *Psychological Science,* 19:3, March 2008, pp. 268–275.

18. Rebecca Traister, "Hillary, Heated," *New York Magazine,* 18, October 1, 2017, pp. 23–24.

19. Goleman, *Emotional Intelligence,* p. 6.

20. E. Nagourney, "Blow a Gasket for Your Heart," *New York Times,* February 11, 2003, p. F6.

21. American Psychological Association, "Strategies for Controlling Your Anger," October 2011, http://www.apa.org/helpcenter/controlling-anger.aspx.

22. "Psychologist Produces the First-Ever 'World Map of Happiness,'" *Science Daily,* November 13, 2006, https://www.google.com/search?q=%E2%80%9CPsychologist+Produces+the+First-Ever+%E2%80%98World+Map+of+Happiness%2C%E2%80%99%E2%80%9D+Science+Daily%2C+November+13%2C+2006&oq=%E2%80%9CPsychologist+Produces+the+First-Ever+%E2%80%98World+Map+of+Happiness%2C%E2%80%99%E2%80%9D+Science+Daily%2C+November+13%2C+2006&aqs=chrome..69i57.1576j0j7&sourceid=chrome&ie=UTF-8; and Dan Buettner, "The World's Happiest Places," *National Geographic,* November 2017, pp. 30–59.

23. Gorman, "Laughter Feels So Good," p. A14.

24. See, for example, Nick Powdthavee, *The Happiness Equation: The Surprising Economics of Our Most Valuable Asset,* New York: Icon Books, 2011.

25. Buettner, p. 36.

26. Daniel Gilbert, "The Science Behind the Smile," interview by Gardiner Morse, *Harvard Business Review,* January–February, 2012, pp. 85–90. See also Daniel Gilbert, *Stumbling on Happiness,* New York: Knopf, 2006.

27. Virginia Konchan, "Synthetic Happiness," *Michigan Quarterly Review* blog, February 17, 2012, http://www.michiganquarterlyreview.com/2012/02/synthetic-happiness.

28. "A Quick and Easy Guide to Happiness," *Time,* October 2, 2017, p. 33.

29. James Gorman, "Survival's Ick Factor," *New York Times,* January 24, 2012, pp. D1, D4.

30. Daniel Goleman, "A Feel-Good Theory: A Smile Affects Mood," *New York Times,* July 19, 1989, p. C1.

31. Robert Plutchik, "Emotions: A General Psychoevolutionary Theory," in Klaus R. Scherer and Paul Ekman, eds., *Approaches to Emotion,* Hillsdale, NJ: Lawrence Erlbaum, 1984, pp. 197–219.

32. See, for example, Daniel Goleman, "Happy or Sad, a Mood Can Prove Contagious," *New York Times,* October 15, 1991, p. C1; and Ellen O'Brien, "Moods Are as Contagious as the Office Cold," *The Record* (Bergen County, NJ), November 15, 1993, p. B3.

33. B. Aubrey Fisher and Katherine L. Adams, *Interpersonal Communication: Pragmatics of Human Relationships,* New York: McGraw-Hill, 1994, p. 290.

34. Ibid.

35. Izard, *Human Emotions,* p. 5.

36. Goleman, "Happy or Sad."

37. Ibid.

38. Lazarus, *Emotion and Adaptation.*

39. Albert Ellis and R. Harper, *A New Guide to Rational Living,* North Hollywood, CA: Wilshire Books, 1977.

40. Joseph P. Forgas, "Affect and Person Perception," in Joseph P. Forgas, ed., *Emotion and Social Judgments,* New York: Pergamon, 1991, p. 288.

41. Sandra Metts and John Waite Bowers, "Emotion in Interpersonal Communication," in Mark L. Knapp and Gerald R. Miller, eds., *Handbook of Interpersonal Communication,* 2nd ed., Thousand Oaks, CA: Sage, 1994.

42. Cited in Elizabeth Bernstein, "Show Me the Love . . . or Not," *Wall Street Journal,* February 21, 2012, pp. D1, D2.

43. See also Amir Levine and Rachel Heller, *Attached: The New Science of Adult Attachment and How It Can Help You Find—and Keep—Love,* New York: Tarcher, 2011.

44. See, for example, K. Nishiyama, *Doing Business with Japan,* Honolulu: University of Hawaii Press, 2000.

45. Larry A. Samovar, Richard E. Porter, and Edwin R. McDaniel, *Communication between Cultures,* 7th ed., Boston: Wadsworth, 2010, p. 316.

46. J. A. Soto, R. W. Levenson, and R. Ebling, "Cultures of Moderation and Expression: Emotional Experience, Behavior, and Physiology in Chinese Americans and Mexican Americans," *Emotion,* 5, 2005, pp. 154–165.

47. J. W. Pennebaker, B. Rime, and V. E. Blankenship, "Stereotypes

of Emotional Expressiveness of Northerners and Southerners: A Cross-Cultural Test of Montesquieu's Hypotheses," *Journal of Personality and Social Psychology,* 70, 1996, pp. 372–380.

48. Stella Ting-Toomey, "The Matrix of Face: An Updated Face-Negotiation Theory," in William B. Gudykunst, ed., *Theorizing about Intercultural Communication,* Thousand Oaks, CA: Sage, 2005, p. 73.

49. Julia T. Wood and Christopher C. Inman, "In a Different Mode: Masculine Styles of Communicating Closeness," *Journal of Applied Communication Research,* 21, 1993, pp. 279–295.

50. Scott Swain, "Covert Intimacy: Closeness in Men's Friendships," in Barbara J. Risman and Pepper Schwartz, eds., *Gender in Intimate Relationships: A Microstructural Approach,* Belmont, CA: Wadsworth, 1989, pp. 71–86; and Drury Sherrod, "The Influence of Gender on Same-Sex Friendships," in Clyde Hendrick, ed., *Close Relationships,* Newbury Park, CA: Sage, 1989, pp. 164–186.

51. Christopher Shea, "What's a 'Good Cry'?" *Wall Street Journal,* July 16–17, 2011, p. C4; A. M. Kring and A. H. Gordon, "Sex Differences in Emotion: Expression, Experience, and Physiology," *Journal of Personality and Social Psychology,* 74, 1998, pp. 686–703.

52. See, for example, E. J. Coats and R. S. Feldman, "Gender Differences in Nonverbal Correlates of Social Status," *Personality and Social Psychology Bulletin,* 22, 1996, pp. 1014–1022.

53. D. J. Goldsmith and P. A. Fulfs, "'You Just Don't Have the Evidence': An Analysis of Claims and Evidence in Deborah Tannen's *You Just Don't Understand,*" in M. E. Roloff, ed., *Communication Yearbook 22,* Thousand Oaks, CA: Sage, 1999, pp. 1–49; and J. Swenson and F. L.

Casmir, "The Impact of Culture-Sameness, Gender, Foreign Travel, and Academic Background on the Ability to Interpret Facial Expression of Emotion in Others," *Communication Quarterly,* 46, 1998, pp. 214–230.

54. Judith A. Hall, *Nonverbal Sex Differences: Accuracy of Communication and Expressive Style,* Baltimore: Johns Hopkins University Press, 1984, pp. 182–184.

55. Leslie Jamison, "I Don't Get Angry, I Get Sad," *The New York Times Magazine,* January 21, 2018, pp. 30–35.

56. See, for example, Carolyn Zahn-Waxler, "The Development of Empathy, Guilt, and Internalization of Distress: Implications for Gender Differences in Internalizing and Externalizing Problems," in Richard J. Davidson, ed., *Anxiety, Depression, and Emotion,* New York: Oxford University Press, 2000, pp. 222–265.

57. R. A. Buhrke and D. R. Fuqua, "Sex Differences in Same and Cross-Sex Supportive Relationships," *Sex Roles,* 17, 1987, pp. 339–352.

58. Diane F. Witmer and Sandra Lee Katzman, "On-Line Smiles: Does Gender Make a Difference in the Use of Graphic Accents?," *Journal of Computer-Mediated Communication,* 2:4, 1997, http://jcmc.indiana.edu/vol2/issue4/witmer1.html.

59. Anthony Pratkanis and Elliot Aronson, *Age of Propaganda: The Everyday Use and Abuse of Persuasion,* New York: W. H. Freeman, 1992, p. 52.

60. Ibid., p. 54.

61. Funda Kivran-Swaine and Mor Naaman, "Network Properties and Social Sharing of Emotions in Social Awareness Streams," paper presented at the Association for Computing Machinery Conference on Computer Supported Cooperative Work, March 19–23, 2011, https://dl.acm.org/citation

.cfm?id=2141562 ; and Nasir Naveed, Thomas Gottron, Jérôme Kunegis, and Arifah Che Alhadi, "Bad News Travel Fast: A Content-Based Analysis of Interestingness on Twitter," paper presented at the Web Science Conference, June 14–17, 2011, https://www.websci11.org/www.websci11.org/fileadmin/websci/Papers/50_paper.pdf.

62. Scott A. Golden and Michael W. Macy, "Diurnal and Seasonal Moods Vary with Work, Sleep, and Daylength Across Diverse Cultures," *Science,* 333, September 30, 2011, pp. 1878–1881.

63. Benedict Carey, "Study of Twitter Messages Tracks When We Are :)," *New York Times,* September 30, 2011, p. A16.

64. Jenna Wortham, "Whimsical Text Icons Get a Shot at Success," *New York Times,* December 7, 2011, pp. B1, B10.

65. R. C. Martin, K. R. Coyier, I. M. VanSistine, and K. I. Schroeder, "Anger on the Internet: The Perceived Value of Rant-Sites," *Cyberpsychology, Behavior, and Social Networking,* 16, 2013, pp. 119–122.

66. Martin Lindstrom, "You Love Your iPhone. Literally," *New York Times,* October 1, 2011, p. A21.

67. A. Muise, E. Christofides, and S. Desmarais, "More Information Than You Ever Wanted: Does Facebook Bring Out the Green-Eyed Monster of Jealousy?" *CyberPsychology and Behavior,* 132, 2009, pp. 441–444; and "'Creeping' or Just Information Seeking: Gender Differences in Partner Monitoring in Response to Jealousy on Facebook," *Personal Relationships,* 21, 2014, pp. 35–50.

68. Albert Ellis, "Why Rational-Emotive Therapy to Rational Emotive Behavior Therapy?" *Psychotherapy,* 36, 1999, pp. 154–159.

69. See, for example, A. M. Bippus and S. L. Young, "Owning Your Emotions: Reactions to Expressions

of Self- versus Other-Attributed Positive and Negative Emotions," *Journal of Applied Communication Research,* 33, 2005, pp. 26–45.

70. Albert Ellis, *A New Guide to Rational Living,* North Hollywood, CA: Wilshire Books, 1977.

## CHAPTER 9

1. Tim Cole, "Lying to the One You Love: The Use of Deception in Romantic Relationships," *Journal of Social and Personal Relationships,* 18, 2001, pp. 107–129.

2. Alice Park, "White Coats, White Lies: How Honest Is Your Doctor?," *Time,* February 9, 2012, p. 15.

3. See, for example, Rachel Botsman, *Who Can You Trust? How Technology Brought Us Together and Why It Might Drive Us Apart.* New York: Public Affairs, 2017.

4. Antoine de Saint-Exupéry, *The Little Prince,* K. Woods, trans., New York: Reynal & Hitchcock, 1943, p. 45.

5. See, for example, James Jaska and Michael W. Pritchard, *Communication Ethics: Methods of Analysis,* Belmont, CA: Wadsworth, 1988.

6. Abraham Maslow, *Motivation and Personality,* New York: Harper & Row, 1970.

7. Fred Luskin, *Forgive for Good,* San Francisco: HarperCollins, 2002.

8. Fred Luskin, "Four Steps toward Forgiveness," *Healing Currents Magazine,* September/October, 1996, https://www.newconversations .net/fred-luskin-two-articles-on-forgiveness/.

9. Linda Berlin, "Forgive: Stanford Program Teaches How to Let Go of Grudges," *SFGate,* September 24, 1999, http://www.sfgate.com/ default/article/FORGIVE-Stanford-program-teaches-how-to-let-go-2906556.php.

10. F. M. Luskin, K. Ginzburg, and C. E. Thoresen, "The Effect of Forgiveness Training on Psychosocial Factors in College-Age Adults," *Humboldt Journal of Social Relations,* 29, 2005, pp. 163–184. See a summary of this study on the Forgive for Good website, https://learningtoforgive .com/.

11. Luskin, "Four Steps toward Forgiveness."

12. A. H. Harris, F. M. Luskin, S. V. Benisovich, S. Standard, J. Bruning, S. Evans, and C. Thoresen, "Effects of a Group Forgiveness Intervention on Forgiveness, Perceived Stress, and Trait Anger: A Randomized Trial," *Journal of Clinical Psychology,* 62, 2006, pp. 715–733. See a summary of this study on the Forgive for Good website, https://learningtoforgive .com/research/effects-of-group-forgiveness-intervention-on-perceived-stress-state-and-trait-anger-symptoms-of-stress-self-reported-health-and-forgiveness-stanford-forgiveness-project/.

13. Cited in Jennifer Kavanaugh, "Getting Down to the Heart of Forgiveness," *Palo Alto Weekly,* February 10, 1999.

14. See John W. Thibaut and Harold H. Kelley, *The Social Psychology of Groups,* New York: John Wiley, 1959; Kenneth J. Gergen, Martin S. Greenberg, and Richard H. Willis, eds., *Social Exchange: Advances in Theory and Research,* New York: Plenum, 1980; and Dalmas Taylor and Irwin Altman, "Self-Disclosure as a Function of Reward-Cost Outcomes," *Sociometry,* 38, 1975, pp. 18–31.

15. Ellen Berscheid, "Interpersonal Attraction," in Gardner Lindzey and Elliot Aronson, eds., *Handbook of Social Psychology,* 3rd ed., New York: Random House, 1985, pp. 413–484.

16. Stephen R. Covey, *The Seven Habits of Highly Effective People,* New York: Simon & Schuster, 1989, p. 188.

17. Jack R. Gibb, "Defensive Communication," *Journal of Communication,* 2, 1961, pp. 141–148.

18. Patrik Jonsson, "We're Becoming Truth-Challenged, and That's No Lie," *The Record* (Bergen County, NJ), July 24, 2011, pp. O1, O4.

19. See, for example, James B. Stewart, *Tangled Webs: How False Statements Are Undermining America—From Martha Stewart to Bernie Madoff,* New York: Penguin Press, 2011.

20. See Sissela Bok, *Lying,* New York: Random House, 1989; and Steven A. McCornack and Timothy R. Levine, "When Lies Are Uncovered: Emotional and Relational Outcomes of Discovered Deception," *Communication Monographs,* 57, 1990, pp. 119–138.

21. See, for example, Frank Bruni, "True Believers, All of Us," *New York Times,* August 7, 2011, p. SR3.

22. Walter Isaacson, *Steve Jobs,* New York: Simon & Schuster, 2011.

23. Carolyn Saarni and Michael Lewis, "Deceit and Illusion in Human Affairs," in Michael Lewis and Carolyn Saarni, eds., *Lying and Deception in Everyday Life,* New York: Guilford Press, 1993, p. 7.

24. Ibid., p. 8.

25. C. Camden, M. T. Motley, and A. Wilson, "White Lies in Interpersonal Communication: A Taxonomy and Preliminary Investigation of Social Motivations," *Western Journal of Speech Communication,* 48, 1984, pp. 309–325.

26. See, for example, Matthew Feinberg, Robb Willer, Jennifer Stellar, and Dacher Keltner, "The Virtues of Gossip: Reputational Information Sharing as Prosocial Behavior," *Journal of Personality and Social Psychology,* 102, 2012, pp. 1015–1030; Jennifer Coates, "Gossip Revisited: Language in All-Female Groups," and Jane Pilkington, "Don't Try to Make Out That I'm Nice! The Different Strategies Women and Men Use When Gossiping," in Jennifer Coates, ed., *Language and Gender: A Reader,* Malden, MA: Blackwell, 1998, pp. 226–253 and

pp. 254–269; and Lubna Abdel Aziz, "Why We Gossip," *Al-Abram Weekly* online, November 28–December 4, 2002, http://weekly.ahram.org.eg/2002/614/pe2.htm.

27. Suzanne Eggins and Diana Slade, *Analysing Casual Conversation,* London: Cassell, 1997.

28. Jack Levin and Arnold Arluke, *Gossip: The Inside Scoop,* New York: Plenum, 1987.

29. Robin Dunbar, *Grooming, Gossip, and the Evolution of Language,* Cambridge, MA: Harvard University Press, 1998.

30. Sameer Hinduja and Justin W. Patchin, *Bullying beyond the Schoolyard: Preventing and Responding to Cyberbullying.* Thousand Oaks, CA: Corwin Press, 2009. See also Sameer Hinduja and Justin W. Patchin, *Cyberbullying and Suicide* (Cyberbullying Research Summary), http://www.cyberbullying.us/cyberbullying_and_suicide_research_fact_sheet.pdf.

31. William B. Gudykunst, *Bridging Differences: Effective Intergroup Communication,* 2nd ed., Thousand Oaks, CA: Sage, 1994, pp. 74–75.

32. See, for example, M. Hecht, S. Ribeau, and M. Sedane, "A Mexican-American Perspective on Interethnic Communication," *International Journal of Intercultural Relations,* 14, 1990, pp. 31–55.

33. John G. Holmes and John K. Rempel, "Trust in Close Relationships," in Clyde Hendrick, ed., *Close Relationships,* Newbury Park, CA: Sage, 1989, p. 204.

34. Drury Sherrod, "The Influence of Gender on Same-Sex Friendships," in Clyde Hendrick, ed., *Close Relationships,* Newbury Park, CA: Sage, 1989, pp. 164–186.

35. See, for example, Harry T. Reis, "Gender Differences in Intimacy and Related Behaviors: Context and Process," in Daniel J. Canary and Kathryn Dindia, eds., *Sex Differences and Similarities in Communication: Critical Essays and Empirical Investigations of Sex and Gender in Interaction,* Mahwah, NJ: Lawrence Erlbaum, 1998, pp. 203–231.

36. Bella M. DePaulo, Jennifer A. Epstein, and Melissa M. Wyer, "Sex Differences in Lying: How Women and Men Deal with the Dilemma of Deceit," in Michael Lewis and Carolyn Saarni, eds., *Lying and Deception in Everyday Life,* New York: Guilford Press, 1993, pp. 126–147.

37. Ibid.

38. Louis A. Day, *Ethics in Media Communications: Cases and Controversies,* Belmont, CA: Wadsworth, 1991, p. 279.

39. Susan Faludi, *Backlash: The Undeclared War against American Women,* New York: Crown, 1991; and Julia T. Wood, *Gendered Lives: Communication, Gender, and Culture,* 10th ed., Boston: Wadsworth, 2013.

40. Amitai Etzioni, "E-Communities Build New Ties, but Ties That Bind," *New York Times,* February 10, 2000, p. G7.

41. Ray A. Smith, "Some Ads Get Less Racy and More Realistic," *The Wall Street Journal,* March 6, 2018, p. A11.

42. See, for example, Bruce E. Johansen, "Race, Ethnicity, and the Media," in Alan Wells, ed., *Mass Media and Society,* Lexington, MA: D. C. Heath, 1987, p. 441.

43. James E. Murphy and Sharon M. Murphy, "American Indians and the Media: Neglect and Stereotype," in Ray Heibert and Carol Reuss, eds., *Impact of Mass Media,* 2nd ed., New York: Longman, 1988, pp. 312–322; and Beverly R. Singer, *Wiping the War Paint off the Lens: Native American Film and Video,* Minneapolis: University of Minnesota Press, 2001.

44. Friend and Nicola. See also A. M. Boyle, L. F. O'Sullivan, "Staying Connected: Computer Mediated and Face-to-Face Communication in College Students' Dating Relationships," *Cyberpsychology, Behavior and Social Networking,* 19, 2016, pp. 299–307.

45. Cited in Cristen Conger, "Do People Lie More On the Internet?," ABC News online, March 5, 2011, http://abcnews.go.com/Technology/people-lie-internet/story?id=13060797.

46. Kevin Roose, "It Was Only a Matter of Time: Here Comes an App for Fake Videos," *The New York Times,* March 5, 2018, pp. A1, A18.

47. See, for example, Catalina L. Toma, Jeffrey T. Hancock, and Nicole B. Ellison, "Separating Fact from Fiction: An Examination of Deceptive Self-Presentation in Online Dating Profiles," *Personality and Social Psychology Bulletin,* 34, 2008, pp. 1023–1036.

48. Catalina L. Toma and Jeffrey T. Hancock, "What Lies Beneath: The Linguistic Traces of Deception in Online Dating Profiles," *Journal of Communication,* 62, 2012, pp. 78–97.

49. Matt Richtel, "Young, in Love and Sharing Everything, Including a Password," *New York Times,* January 18, 2012, pp. A1, A11.

50. Sheri Madigan, Anh Ly, Christina L. Rash, et al., "Prevalence of Multiple Forms of Sexting Behavior Among Youth: A Systemic Review and Meta-Analysis," *JAMA Pediatrics*, Published online February 26, 2018. doi:10.1001/jamapediatrics.2017.5314

## CHAPTER 10

1. Stanley Milgram, *Obedience to Authority.* New York: Harper Perennial, 1974.

2. See J. P. Dillard and L. J. Marshall, "Persuasion as a Social Skill," in J. O. Greene and B. R. Burleson, eds., *Handbook of Communication and Social Interaction Skills,* Mahwah, NJ: Lawrence Erlbaum, 2003, pp. 479–513.

3. Lin Farley, "Reclaiming 'Sexual Harassment,'" *The New York Times,* October 19, 2017, p. A27.

4. Rebecca Traister, "This Moment Isn't (Just) About Sex: It's About Sexism," *New York,* December 11–24, 2017, pp. 17–18.

5. See "Social Anxiety Fact Sheet," Social Phobia/Social Anxiety Association, http://www.socialphobia.org/fact.html.

6. See Dan O'Hair, and Michael J. Cody, "Machiavellian Beliefs and Social Influence," *Western Journal of Speech Communication,* 51, 1987, pp. 286–287.

7. See William W. Wilmot and Joyce L. Hocker, *Interpersonal Conflict,* 6th ed., New York: McGraw-Hill, 2001.

8. John R. French and Bertram Raven, "The Bases of Social Power," in Dorwin Cartwright, ed., *Studies in Social Power,* Ann Arbor: University of Michigan Press, 1959, pp. 150–167; and Bertram H. Raven, Richard Centers, and Aroldo Rodrigues, "The Bases of Conjugal Power," in Ronald E. Cromwell and David H. Olson, eds., *Power in Families,* Beverly Hills, CA: Sage, 1975, pp. 217–232.

9. Malcolm R. Parks, *Personal Relationships and Personal Networks,* Mahwah, NJ: Lawrence Erlbaum, 2007.

10. R. G. Maio and G. Haddock, *The Psychology of Attitudes and Attitude Change,* 2nd ed., Thousand Oaks, CA: Sage, 2015.

11. See Milton Rokeach, *The Open and Closed Mind,* New York: Basic Books, 1960; and Milton Rokeach, *Beliefs, Attitudes, and Values,* San Francisco, CA: Jossey-Bass, 1970.

12. E. J. Langer, "Rethinking the Role of Thought in Social Interaction," in J. H. Harvey, W. J. Ickes, and R. F. Kidd, eds., *New Directions in Attribution Research,* vol. 2, Hillsdale, NJ: Lawrence Erlbaum, 1978, pp. 35–58.

13. Robert B. Cialdini, *Influence: Science and Practice,* 5th ed., Boston: Allyn & Bacon, 2009.

14. See, for example, G. R. Miller, F. Boster, M. E. Roloff, and D. Seibold, "MBRS Rekindled: Some Thoughts on Compliance Gaining in Interpersonal Settings," in M. E. Roloff and G. R. Miller, eds., *Interpersonal Processes: New Directions in Communication Research,* Newbury Park, CA: Sage, 1987, pp. 89–116.

15. Fritz Heider, *The Psychology of Interpersonal Relations,* New York: John Wiley, 1958.

16. Leon Festinger, "Social Communication and Cognitions: A Very Preliminary and Highly Tentative Draft," in Eddie Haron-Jones and Judson Mills, eds., *Cognitive Dissonance: Progress on a Pivotal Theory in Social Psychology,* Washington, DC: American Psychological Association, 1999, p. 361.

17. Cialdini, *Influence.*

18. Richard E. Petty and John T. Cacioppo, *Communication and Persuasion: Central and Peripheral Routes to Attitude Change,* New York: Springer-Verlag, 1986, p. 7.

19. Geert Hofstede, *Culture's Consequences: Comparing Values, Behaviors, Institutions, and Organizations across Nations,* 2nd ed., Thousand Oaks, CA: Sage, 2001.

20. See Michael L. Hecht, Mary Jane Collier, and Sidney A. Ribeau, *African American Communication: Ethnic Identity and Cultural Interpretation,* Newbury Park, CA: Sage, 1993, p. 97; and H. Riemer, S. Shavitt, M. Koo, and H. Markus, "Preferences Don't Have to be Personal: Expanding Attitude Theorizing With a Cross-Cultural Perspective," *Psychological Review,* 221, 2014, pp. 619–648.

21. Hofstede, *Culture's Consequences.*

22. See Geert Hofstede, *Cultures and Organizations: Software of the Mind,* London: McGraw-Hill, 1991.

23. Jan Servaes, "Cultural Identity in East and West," *Howard Journal of Communication,* 1:2, 1988, p. 64.

24. See, for example, J. M. Steil and K. Weltman, "Marital Inequality: The Importance of Resources, Personal Attributes, and Social Norms on Career Valuing and the Allocation of Domestic Responsibilities," *Sex Roles,* 24, 1991, pp. 161–179; and W. Farrell, "Men as Success Objects," *Utne Reader,* May/June 1991, pp. 81–84.

25. See, for example, Kenneth C. Dempsy, "Men and Women's Power Relationships and the Persisting Inequitable Division of Housework," *Journal of Family Studies,* 6, 2000, pp. 7–24.

26. Graham Allen, *Family Life,* New York: Blackwell, 1993.

27. See, for example, Patricia S. E. Darlington and Becky Michele Mulvaney, *Women, Power, and Ethnicity: Working toward Reciprocal Empowerment,* New York: Haworth Press, 2003.

28. Jenny Anderson, "National Study Finds Widespread Sexual Harassment of Students in Grades 7 to 12," *New York Times,* November 7, 2011, p. A14.

29. See Associated Press, "National Study Finds Sexual Harassment Pervasive," November 14, 2011, available at http://www.in.gov/icrc/2557.htm.

30. Hilary Stout, "Less 'He Said, She Said' in Sex Harassment Cases," *New York Times,* November 5, 2011, p. BU10.

31. Julia T. Wood, *Gendered Lives: Communication, Gender, and Culture,* 9th ed., Boston: Wadsworth, 2011.

32. See Susan A. Basow, *Gender: Stereotypes and Roles,* 3rd ed., Pacific Grove, CA: Brooks/Cole, 1992.

33. Dwight E. Brooks and Lisa P. Hébert, "Gender, Race, and Media Representation," in Bonnie J. Dow and Julia T. Wood, eds., *The SAGE Handbook of Gender and Communication,* Thousand Oaks, CA: Sage, 2006, pp. 297–317.

34. See, for example, Angela Watercutter, "*The Hunger Games*' Katniss Everdeen: The Heroine the World Needs Right Now," Wired.com, March 22, 2012, http://www.wired.com/underwire/2012/03/katniss-everdeen-hollywood-heroines/all/1.

35. "'Black Panther' to Fund Youth STEM Programs," *The New York Times,* February 28, 2018, p. C3.

36. Maureen Dowd, "Soothsayer Sees Tech's Dark Side," *The New York Times,* November 9, 2017, pp. D1, D8.

37. Benedict Carey, "How Fiction Becomes Fact on Social Media," *The New York Times,* October 24, 2017, pp. D1, D4.

38. Nicholas Confesore, Gabriel J. X. Dance, Richard Harris, and Mark Hansen, "Buying Online Influence From a Shadowy Market," *The New York Times,* January 28, 2018, pp. 1, 18–20.

39. Erin A. Vogel and Jason P. Rose, "Perceptions of Perfection: The Influence of Social Media on Interpersonal Evaluations," *Basic and Applied Social Psychology,* 39:6, 2017, pp. 317–325.

40. James D. Ivory, "The Games, They Are a-Changin': Technological Advancements in Video Games and Implications for Effects on Youth," in Patrick E. Jamieson and Daniel Romer, eds., *The Changing Portrayal of Adolescents in the Media since 1950,* New York: Oxford University Press, 2008, pp. 347–376.

41. Charles M. Blow, "The Bleakness of the Bullied," *New York Times,* October 15, 2011, p. A19.

42. See, for example, Susan Donaldson James, "Immigrant Teen Taunted by Cyberbullies Hangs Herself," ABC News, January 26, 2010, http://abcnews.go.com/Health/cyber-bullying-factor-suicide-massachusetts-teen-irish-immigrant/story?id=9660938; and Alfred P. Doblin "Through Tyler Clementi's Looking Glass," *The Record* (Bergen County, NJ), September 12, 2011, p. A13.

# CHAPTER 11

1. J. A. Lavner, B. R. Karney, and T. N. Bradbury, "Relationship Problems Over the Early Years of Marriage: Stability or Change?" *Journal of Family Psychology,* 28, 2014, pp. 979–985.

2. C. N. Wright, and M. E. Roloff, "You Should Just Know Why I'm Upset: Expectancy Violation Theory and the Influence of Mind Reading Expectations (MRE) on Responses to Relational Problems," *Communication Research Reports,* 32, 2015, pp. 10–19.

3. W. Wagner, D. T. Ostick, and S. R. Komives, *Leadership for a Better World: Understanding the Social Change Model of Leadership Development—Instructor's Manual,* San Francisco: Jossey-Bass, 2007.

4. See, for example, D. H. Cloven and M. E. Roloff, "Sense-Making Activities and Interpersonal Conflict: Communicative Cures for the Mulling Blues," *Western Journal of Speech Communication,* 55, 1991, pp. 134–158; and A. S. Rancer and T. A. Avtgis, *Argumentative and Aggressive Communication: Theory, Research, and Application,* Thousand Oaks, CA: Sage, 2006.

5. See, for example, Joyce L. Hocker and William W. Wilmot, *Interpersonal Conflict,* 3rd ed., Dubuque, IA: William C. Brown, 1991, p. 12; William W. Wilmot and Joyce L. Hocker, *Interpersonal Conflict,* 8th ed., New York: McGraw-Hill, 2011; Dudley D. Cahn, "Intimates in Conflict: A Research Review," in Dudley D. Cahn, ed., *Intimates in Conflict: A Communication Perspective,* Hillsdale, NJ: Lawrence Erlbaum, 1990; and Joseph P. Folger, Marshall Scott Poole, and Randall K. Stutman, *Working through Conflict,* 2nd ed., New York: HarperCollins, 1993.

6. See G. L. Welton, "Parties in Conflict: Their Characteristics and Perceptions," in K. G. Duffy, J. W. Grosch, and P. V. Olczak, eds., *Community Mediation: A Handbook for Practitioners and Researchers,* New York: Guilford Press, 1991, pp. 105–118; and Laura K. Guerrero, Peter A. Andersen, and Walid A. Afifi, *Close Encounters: Communication in Relationships,* 2nd ed., Thousand Oaks, CA: Sage, 2007.

7. See V. P. Richmond, J. C. McCroskey, and L. Powell, *Organizational Communication for Survival,* Boston: Pearson, 2013.

8. See A. J. Johnson and I. A. Cionea, "Serial Arguments in Interpersonal Relationships: Relational Dynamics and Interdependence," in J. A. Samp, ed., *Communicating Interpersonal Conflict in Close Relationships: Contexts, Challenges and Opportunities.* New York: Routledge, 2017, pp. 111–127; and C. Miller Waite, and M. E. Roloff, "When Hurt Continues: Taking Conflict Personally Leads to Rumination, Residual Hurt, and Negative Emotions Toward Someone Who Hurt Us," *Communication Quarterly,* 62, 2014, pp. 193–213.

9. See, for example, Lavinia Hall, ed., *Negotiation: Strategies for Mutual Gain,* Newbury Park, CA: Sage, 1993; and F. F. Jordan-Jackson, Y. Lin, A. S. Rancer, and D. A. Infante, "Perceptions of Males and Females' Use of Aggressive Affirming and Nonaffirming Messages in an Interpersonal Dispute: You've Come a Long Way Baby?" *Western Journal of Communication,* 72, 2008, pp. 239–258.

10. See R. Fisher and S. Brown, *Getting Together: Building Relationships as We Negotiate,* Boston: Houghton Mifflin, 1988.

11. Alan C. Filley, *Interpersonal Conflict Resolution*, Glenview, IL: Scott Foresman, 1975; Mark L. Knapp and Anita L. Vangelisti, *Interpersonal Communication and Human Relationships*, 2nd ed., Boston: Allyn & Bacon, 1994; and J. Gottman, "Why Marriages Fail," in K. M. Galvin and P. J. Cooper, eds., *Making Connections: Readings in Relational Communication*, 4th ed., 2006, pp. 228–236.

12. Folger et al., *Working through Conflict*, pp. 8–10. See also C. Segrin and J. Flora, "Family Conflict is Detrimental to Physical and Mental Health," in J. A. Samp, ed., *Communicating Interpersonal Conflict in Close Relationships: Contexts, Challenges, and Opportunities*. New York: Routledge, 2017, pp. 207–224.

13. G. R. Bach and P. Wyden, *The Intimate Enemy: How to Fight Fair in Love and Marriage*, New York: William Morrow, 1969, p. 3; A. M. Hicks and L. M. Diamond, "How Was Your Day? Couples' Affect When Telling and Hearing Daily Events," *Personal Relationships*, 15, 2008, pp. 205–228; and L. N. Olson and D. O. Braithwaite, "'If You Hit Me Again, I'll Hit You Back': Conflict Management Strategies of Individuals Experiencing Aggression during Conflicts," *Communication Studies*, 55, 2004, pp. 271–285.

14. G. R. Back and R. Deutsch, *Pairing*, New York: Peter Wyden, 1970; G. Back, *Stop! You're Driving Me Crazy*, New York: Putnam, 1985.

15. John Stewart, ed., *Bridges Not Walls: A Book about Interpersonal Communication*, New York: McGraw-Hill, 1995, p. 401.

16. Robert R. Blake and Jane Srygley Mouton, *The Managerial Grid*, Houston: Gulf, 1964.

17. M. J. Papa and D. J. Canary, "Communication in Organizations: A Competence-Based Approach," in A. M. Nicotera, ed., *Conflict and Organizations: Communicative Processes*, Albany: State University of New York Press, 1995, pp. 153–179; and Joyce L. Hocker and William W. Wilmot, *Interpersonal Conflict*, 5th ed., Dubuque, IA: Brown & Benchmark, 1998.

18. See W. W. Wilmot and J. L. Hocker, *Interpersonal Conflict*, 9th ed., New York: McGraw-Hill, 2014.

19. Sharon Anthony Bower and Gordon H. Bower, *Asserting Yourself: A Practical Guide for Positive Change*, updated ed., Reading, MA: Perseus Books, 1991, pp. 111–113.

20. See, for example, Stella Ting-Toomey, and John G. Oetzel, *Managing Intercultural Conflict Effectively*, Thousand Oaks, CA: Sage, 2001.

21. Stella Ting-Toomey, "Intercultural Conflict Styles: A Face-Negotiation Theory," in Young Yun Kim and William B. Gudykunst, eds., *Theories in Intercultural Communication*, Newbury Park, CA: Sage, 1988.

22. See, for example, Stella Ting-Toomey, "Managing Conflict in Intimate Intercultural Relationships," in Dudley D. Cahn, ed., *Conflict in Personal Relationships*, Hillsdale, NJ: Lawrence Erlbaum, 1994.

23. Deborah Tannen, *The Argument Culture: Moving from Debate to Dialogue*, New York: Random House, 1998, p. 206.

24. See Stella Ting-Toomey and Jiro Takai, "Explaining Intercultural Conflict: Promising Approaches and Future Directions," in John G. Oetzel and Stella Ting-Toomey, eds., *The Sage Handbook of Conflict Communication*, Thousand Oaks, CA: Sage, 2006, pp. 691–723.

25. See Y. Xie, D. Hample, and X. Wan, "A Cross-Cultural Analysis of Argument Predispositions in China: Argumentativeness, Verbal Aggressiveness, Argument Frames and Personalization of Conflict," *Argumentation*, 29, 2015, pp. 265–284.

26. William B. Gudykunst, *Bridging Differences: Effective Intergroup Communication*, 2nd ed., Thousand Oaks, CA: Sage, 1994.

27. Malcolm Boyd, "Empathy Can Span the Abyss," Modern Maturity, 1992. See also Leora Lawton, Merril Silverstein, and Vern Bengtson, "Affection, Social Contact, and Geographic Distance between Adult Children and Their Parents," *Journal of Marriage and the Family*, 56, 1994, pp. 57–68.

28. Julia T. Wood, *Gendered Lives: Communication, Gender, and Culture*, 5th ed., Belmont, CA: Wadsworth, 2003, p. 202.

29. M. Fox, M. Gibbs, and D. Auerback, "Age and Gender Dimensions of Friendship," *Psychology of Women Quarterly*, 9, 1985, pp. 489–502.

30. J. M. Gottman, "The Roles of Conflict Engagement, Escalation, or Avoidance in Marital Interaction: A Longitudinal View of Five Types of Couples," *Journal of Consulting and Clinical Psychology*, 61, 1993, pp. 6–15.

31. See J. M. Gottman, R. W. Levenson, C. Swanson, K. Swanson, R. Tyson, and D. Yoshimoto, "Observing Gay, Lesbian, and Heterosexual Couples' Relationships: Mathematical Modeling of Conflict Interaction," *Journal of Homosexuality*, 45, 2003, pp. 65–91.

32. Lev Grossman and Evan Narcisse, "Conflict of Interest: Video Games Based on America's Real Wars Are Big Business," *Time*, October 21, 2011, pp. 70–75.

33. See Craig A. Anderson, "Violent Video Games: Myths, Facts, and Unanswered Questions," in Alison Alexander and Janice Hanson, eds., *Taking Sides: Clashing Views in Mass Media and Society*, 11th ed., New York: McGraw-Hill, 2011, pp. 94–98.

34. See, for example, Robert Putnam, *Bowling Alone: The Collapse and Revival of American Community*, New York: Simon & Schuster, 2000.

35. Matt Ridley, "Internet On, Inhibitions Off: Why We Tell All," *Wall Street Journal,* February 18–19, 2012, p. C4.

36. V. Safronova, "Exes Explain Ghosting, the Ultimate Silent Treatment," *The New York Times,* June 26, 2015.

37. J. Vilhauer, "Why Ghosting Hurts So Much," *Psychology Today,* November 27, 2015.

## CHAPTER 12

1. Lawrence Yee, "Andy Cohen on the Future of 'Real Housewives': Why He Didn't Want to be Paid for Hosting Reunions," *Variety,* December 2, 2016, http://variety.com/2016/tv/news/andy-cohen-real-housewives-spinoffs-next-city-1201932262/

2. Andy Cohen, "*Housewives* and the Hill," *Huffington Post,* June 14, 2010, http://www.huffingtonpost.com/andy-cohen/housewives-and-the-hill_b_612040.html.

3. See Emily Impett, Amy Strackman, Eli J. Finkel, and Shelly L. Gable, "The Best of Times, the Worst of Times: The Place of Close Relationships in Psychology and Our Daily Lives," *Journal of Personality and Social Psychology,* 94, 2008, pp. 808–823.

4. Sharon Jayson, "People Who Say They Feel Happy May Live 35% Longer," *USA Today,* November 1, 2011, p. 2A.

5. Steve Duck, *Understanding Relationships,* New York: Guilford Press, 1991, pp. 1–2.

6. See H. K. Kim and P. McKenry, "The Relationship between Marriage and Psychological Well-Being," *Journal of Family Issues,* 23, 2002, pp. 885–911.

7. See R. M. Kaplan and R. G. Kronick, "Marital Status and Longevity in the United States Population," *Journal of Epidemiology and Community Health,* 60, 2006, pp. 760–765.

8. James J. Lynch, *The Broken Heart: The Medical Consequences of Loneliness,* New York: Basic Books, 1977.

9. Jean Seligmann with Nina Archer Biddle, "The Death of a Spouse," *Newsweek,* May 9, 1994, p. 57.

10. "Lonely People 'More Likely to Die Young,'" *Daily Mail* online, September 14, 2007, http://www.dailymail.co.uk/health/article-481791/Lonely-people-likely-die-young.html.

11. Duck, *Understanding Relationships,* p. 9.

12. Phyllis Korkki, "Building a Bridge to a Lonely Colleague," *New York Times,* January 29, 2012, p. BU8; S. Cacioppo, A. J. Grippo, S. London, L. Goossens, and J. T. Cacioppo, "Loneliness: Clinical Import and Interventions," *Perspectives on Psychological Science,* 10, 2015, pp. 238–249.

13. Ibid., p. 24.

14. Abraham Maslow, *Motivation and Personality,* 3rd ed., New York: HarperCollins, 1954; and Abraham Maslow, *Toward a Psychology of Being,* New York: John Wiley, 1962.

15. Sharon Jayson, "Many Singles Looking for Love, but Not Marriage," *USA Today,* February 2, 2012, p. 4D.

16. E. J. Finkel and R. F. Baumeister, "Attraction and Rejection," in R. F. Baumeister and E. J. Finkel, eds., *Advanced Social Psychology: The State of the Science.* New York: Oxford University Press, 2010, pp. 419–459.

17. Ray Bull and Nichola Rumsey, *The Social Psychology of Facial Appearance,* New York: Springer-Verlag, 1988.

18. Ellen Berscheid and Elaine Hatfield Walster, *Interpersonal Attraction,* 2nd ed., Reading, MA: Addison-Wesley, 1978.

19. See Elaine Walster, G. William Walster, and Ellen Berscheid, *Equity: Theory and Research,* Boston: Allyn & Bacon, 1978; and Elaine Hatfield and Susan Sprecher, "Matching Hypothesis," in Harry T. Reis and Susan Sprecher, eds., *Encyclopedia of Human Relationships,* vol. 2, New York: Sage, 2009, pp. 1065–1067.

20. S. I. Rick, D. A. Small, and E. J. Finkel, "Fatal (Fiscal) Attraction: Spendthrifts and Tightwads in Marriage," *Journal of Marketing Research,* 48, 2011, pp. 228–237.

21. Nicola Clark, "Making the Skies Friendlier," *New York Times,* February 24, 2012, p. B1, B2.

22. Robert J. Sternberg, *The Triangle of Love: Intimacy, Passion, Commitment,* New York: Basic Books, 1988.

23. See David M. Buss and David P. Schmitt, "Sexual Strategies Theory: An Evolutionary Perspective on Human Mating," *Psychological Review,* 100, 1993, pp. 204–232.

24. William K. Rawlins, "Friendship as a Communicative Achievement: A Theory and an Interpretive Analysis of Verbal Reports," doctoral dissertation, Temple University, Philadelphia, 1981.

25. See William K. Rawlins, *Friendship Matters: Communication, Dialectics, and the Life Course,* New York: Aldine de Gruyter, 1992; and William K. Rawlins, *The Compass of Friendship: Narratives, Identities, and Dialogues,* Thousand Oaks, CA: Sage, 2009.

26. Alex Williams, "It's Not Me, It's You," *New York Times,* January 28, 2012, pp. ST1, ST8.

27. H. T. Reis and A. Aron, "Love: What Is It, Why Does It Matter, and How Does It Operate?" *Perspectives on Psychological Science,* 3, 2009, pp. 80–86.

28. John Alan Lee, "A Typology of Styles of Loving," *Personality and Social Psychology Bulletin,* 3, 1977, pp. 173–182.

29. Robert J. Sternberg, "A Triangular Theory of Love," *Psychological Review,* 93, 1986, pp. 119–135; and Sternberg, *The Triangle of Love.*

30. Ibid.; and Robert J. Sternberg, "Triangulating Love," in Robert J. Sternberg and Michael L. Barnes, eds., *The Psychology of Love,* New Haven, CT: Yale University Press, 1988, pp. 119–138.

31. See Mark L. Knapp and Anita L. Vangelisti, *Interpersonal Communication and Human Relationships,* 3rd ed., Boston: Allyn & Bacon, 1996.

32. See Charles R. Berger and James J. Bradac, *Language and Social Knowledge: Uncertainty in Interpersonal Relations,* London: Arnold, 1982.

33. Ibid.

34. See Laura K. Guerrero and Paul A. Mongeau, "On Becoming 'More than Friends': The Transition from Friendship to Romantic Relationship," in Susan Sprecher, Amy Wenzel, and John Harvey, eds., *Handbook of Relationship Initiation,* New York: Psychology Press, 2008, pp. 175–194; S. Planalp and A. Benson, "Friends' and Acquaintances' Conversations I," *Journal of Social and Personal Relationships,* 9, 1992, pp. 483–506; and S. Planalp, "Friends' and Acquaintances' Conversations II," *Journal of Social and Personal Relationships,* 10, 1993, pp. 339–354.

35. Mark L. Knapp and Anita L. Vangelisti, *Interpersonal Communication and Human Relationships,* 2nd ed., Boston: Allyn & Bacon, 1992, p. 41.

36. See Lawrence B. Rosenfield and Daniella Bordaray-Sciolino, "Self Disclosure as a Communication Strategy during Relationship Termination," paper presented at the national meeting of the Speech Communication Association, Denver, November 1985.

37. Rose Pastore, "The New Lexicon of Love," *Psychology Today,* December 2011.

38. Myron W. Lustig and Jolene Koester, *Intercultural Competence: Interpersonal Communication across Cultures,* 2nd ed., New York: HarperCollins, 1996, p. 243.

39. See Geert Hofstede, "Cross-Cultural Management II: Empirical Studies," *International Studies of Management and Organization,* 13, 1983, pp. 46–74.

40. John Paul Feig, *A Common Core: Thais and Americans,* Yarmouth, ME: Intercultural Press, 1989, p. 50.

41. See, "Dating Customs around the World," FactMonster.com, https://www.factmonster.com/cool-stuff/dating-and-marriage/dating-customs-around-world.

42. Hervé Varenne, *Americans Together: Structured Diversity in a Midwestern Town,* New York: Teacher's College Press, 1977.

43. Paul Bohannan, *We, the Alien: An Introduction to Cultural Anthropology,* Prospect Heights, IL: Waveland Press, 1992, p. 57.

44. Rachel Bertsche, *MWF Seeking BFF: My Yearlong Search for a New Best Friend,* New York: Ballantine, 2011.

45. Pharme M. Camarena, Pamela A. Sarigiani, and Anne C. Peterson, "Gender-Specific Pathways to Intimacy in Early Adolescence," *Journal of Youth and Adolescence,* 19:1, 1990, pp. 19–32.

46. William Pollack, *Real Boys: Rescuing Our Sons from the Myths of Boyhood,* New York: Random House, 1998, p. 181.

47. See, for example, Jena E. Pincott, "Why Some Men Are Intimated by Smarter Women," *Psychology Today,* May 7, 2016, https://www.psychologytoday.com/us/articles/201605/why-some-men-are-intimidated-smarter-women; D. Fisman, S. Iyengar, E. Kamenica, and I. Simonson, "Gender Differences in Mate Selection: Evidence from a Speed Dating Experiment," http://faculty.chicagobooth.edu/emir.kamenica/documents/genderdifferences.

pdf; and P. Regan, L. Levin, S. Sprecher, F. Christopher, and R. Cate, "Partner Preferences: What Characteristics Do Men and Women Desire in Their Short-Term Sexual and Long-Term Romantic Partners?" *Journal of Psychology and Human Sexuality,* XII, 2000, pp. 1–21.

48. Deborah Tannen, *You Just Don't Understand: Women and Men in Conversation,* New York: Morrow, 1990, p. 77.

49. S. Davis, "Men as Success Objectives and Women as Sex Objects: A Study of Personal Advertisements," *Sex Roles,* 23, 1990, pp. 43–50; and J. E. Smith, V. A. Waldorf, and D. L. Trembath, "Single White Male Looking for Thin, Very Attractive . . . ," *Sex Roles*, 23, 1990, pp. 675–685.

50. L. H. Ganong and M. Coleman, "Gender Differences in Expectations of Self and Future Partner," *Journal of Family Issues,* 13, 1992, pp. 55–64.

51. N. Shpancer, "Laws of Attraction: How Do We Select a Life Partner?" *Psychology Today,* December 2, 2014, https://www.psychologytoday.com/us/blog/insight-therapy/201412/laws-attraction-how-do-we-select-life-partner.

52. Tannen, *You Just Don't Understand,* pp. 238–244.

53. Frank Bruni, "Trump, Manly He-Man, *The New York Times,* February 28, 2018, p. A23.

54. Steve Lohr, "Reluctant Conscripts in the March of Technology," *New York Times,* September 17, 1995, p. 16.

55. Christine Rosen, "Virtual Friendship and the New Narcissism," in Mark Bauerlein, ed., *The Digital Divide,* New York: Penguin, 2011, pp. 172–188.

56. See, for example, Charles Isherwood, "'Salesman' Comes Calling, Right on Time," *New York Times,* February 26, 2012, pp. AR6, AR27.

57. Keith N. Hampton, Lauren Sessions Goulet, Cameron Marlow, and Lee Rainie, *Why Most Facebook*

*Users Get More than They Give,* Pew Internet & American Life Project, February 3, 2012, http://pewinternet.org/Reports/2012/Facebook-users.aspx.

58. Stephanie Rosenbloom, "Love, Lies, and What They Learned," *New York Times,* November 13, 2011, p. ST1, ST8–ST9; See also "Online Dating Statistics & Facts," *Dating Sites Reviews.com,* https://www.datingsitesreviews.com/staticpages/index.php?page=Online-Dating-Industry-Facts-Statistics.

59. Eli J. Finkel, Paul W. Eastwick, Benjamin R. Karney, Harry T. Reis, and Susan Sprecher, "Online Dating: A Critical Analysis from the Perspective of Psychological Science," *Psychological Science in the Public Interest,* 13:1, 2012, pp. 3–66.

60. Jenna Wortham, "With an App, Your Next Date Could Be Just around the Corner," *New York Times,* November 3, 2011, pp. A1, B4.

61. Teddy Wayne, "Swiping Them Off Their Feet," *The New York Times,* November 9, 2014, p. ST14; Eli J. Finkel, "In Defense of Tinder," *The New York Times,* February 8, 2015; p. SR9.

62. See, for example, Joseph B. Walther, "Computer-Mediated Communication: Impersonal, Interpersonal, and Hyperpersonal Interaction," *Communication Research,* 23, 1996, pp. 3–43; and J. R. Suler, "The Online Disinhibition Effect," *Cyberpsychology and Behavior,* 7, 2004, pp. 321–326.

63. See, for example, Joyce Conen, "Making a Statement in Absentia," *New York Times,* March 20, 2003, pp. G1, G4.

64. Lynch, *The Broken Heart.*

# CHAPTER 13

1. Valerian J. Derlega and John H. Berg, eds., *Self-Disclosure: Theory, Research, and Therapy,* New York: Plenum, 1987.

2. D. E. Miell, "Cognitive and Communicative Strategies in Developing Relationships," doctoral thesis, University of Lancaster, 1984.

3. See, for example, Patricia Parr, Rebecca A. Boyle, and Laura Tejada, "I Said, You Said: A Communication Exercise for Couples," *Contemporary Family Therapy,* 30, 2008, pp. 167–173.

4. See, for example, B. Aubrey Fisher and Katherine L. Adams, *Interpersonal Communication: Pragmatics of Human Relationships,* New York: McGraw-Hill, 1994, p. 309.

5. S. Sprecher, S. Treger, J. D. Wondra, N. Hilaire, and K. Wallpe, "Taking Turns: Reciprocal Self-Disclosure Promotes Liking in Initial Interactions," *Journal of Experimental Social Psychology,* 49, 2013, pp. 860–866.

6. Irwin Altman and Dalmas Taylor, *Social Penetration: The Development of Interpersonal Relationships,* New York: Holt, Rinehart & Winston, 1973.

7. Steve Duck, *Understanding Relationships,* New York: Guilford Press, 1991, p. 80.

8. Ibid.

9. Joseph Luft, *Group Processes: An Introduction to Group Dynamics,* 2nd ed., Palo Alto, CA: Mayfield, 1970.

10. See, for example, F. D. Fincham and T. N. Bradbury, "The Impact of Attributions in Marriage: An Individual Difference Analysis," *Journal of Social and Personal Relationships,* 6, 1989, pp. 69–85; and V. G. Downs, "Grandparents and Grandchildren: The Relationship between Self-Disclosure and Solidarity in an Intergenerational Relationship," *Communication Research Reports,* 5, 1988, pp. 173–179.

11. Leslie A. Baxter, "The Social Side of Personal Relationships: A Dialectical Perspective," in Steve Duck, ed., *Social Context and Relationships,* Newbury Park, CA: Sage, 1993, pp. 139–165.

12. Ibid.

13. Sandra Petronio, "The Boundaries of Privacy: Praxis of Everyday Life," in Sandra Petronio, ed., *Balancing the Secrets of Private Disclosure,* Mahwah, NJ: Lawrence Erlbaum, 2000, pp. 37–49.

14. Renate Klein and Robert M. Milardo, "Third-Party Influences on the Management of Personal Relationships," in Steve Duck, ed., *Social Context and Relationships,* Newbury Park, CA: Sage, 1993, pp. 55–77.

15. D. R. Pawlowski, "Dialectical Tensions in Marital Couples' Accounts of Their Relationships," *Communication Quarterly,* 46, 1998, pp. 396–416.

16. L. A. Baxter and L. A. Erbert, "Perceptions of Dialectical Contradictions in Turning Points of Development in Heterosexual Romantic Relationships," *Journal of Social and Personal Relationships,* 16, 1999, pp. 547–569.

17. See, for example, L. A. Baxter, "Dialectical Contradictions in Relationship Development," *Journal of Social and Personal Relationships,* 7, 1990, pp. 69–88; and E. M. Griffin, *A First Look at Communication Theory,* 5th ed., New York: McGraw-Hill, 2003, pp. 157–170.

18. Duck, *Understanding Relationships,* p. 122.

19. Kathryn Dindia and Leslie A. Baxter, "Strategies for Maintaining and Repairing Marital Relationships," *Journal of Social and Personal Relationships,* 4, 1987, pp. 143–158; and Kathryn Dindia, "A Multiphasic View of Relationship Maintenance Strategies," in D. J. Canary and L. Stafford, eds., *Communication and Relational Maintenance,* San Diego, CA: Academic Press, 1994, pp. 91–112.

20. Duck, *Understanding Relationships,* pp. 125–126.

21. Sharon S. Brehm, *Intimate Relationships,* 2nd ed., New York: McGraw-Hill, 1992.

22. Katherine A. McGonagle, Ronald C. Kessler, and Ian H. Gotlib, "The Effects of Marital Disagreement Style, Frequency, and Outcome on Marital Disruption," *Journal of Social and Personal Relationships,* 10, 1993, pp. 385–404.

23. Duck, *Understanding Relationships,* pp. 168–169.

24. Julie Mehta, "Tainted Love," *Current Health,* 32, January 2006, pp. 18–21.

25. See Michael P. Johnson, "Violence and Abuse in Personal Relationships: Conflict, Terror, and Resistance in Intimate Partnerships," in Anita L. Vangelisti and Daniel Perlman, eds., *The Cambridge Handbook of Personal Relationships,* New York: Cambridge University Press, 2006, pp. 557–576; and Susan Murphy-Milano, *Defending Our Lives: Getting Away from Domestic Violence and Staying Safe,* New York: Anchor/Doubleday, 1996.

26. See, for example, Brian H. Spitzberg and William R. Cupach, eds., *The Dark Side of Interpersonal Communication,* Mahwah, NJ: Lawrence Erlbaum, 2007.

27. Sally A. Lloyd and Beth C. Emery, *The Dark Side of Courtship: Physical and Sexual Aggression,* Thousand Oaks, CA: Sage, 2000, p. 27.

28. Sally A. Lloyd, "The Dark Side of Courtship," *Family Relations,* 40, 1991, pp. 14–20.

29. M. F. Davis and S. J. Kraham, "Protecting Women's Welfare in the Face of Violence," *Fordham Urban Law Journal,* 22, 1995, pp. 1141–1157.

30. Julia T. Wood, *Gendered Lives: Communication, Gender, and Culture,* Belmont, CA: Wadsworth, 1994, p. 202.

31. J. E. McConnell, "Beyond Metaphor: Battered Women, Involuntary Servitude, and the Thirteenth Amendment," *Yale Journal of Law and Feminism,* 4, 1992, pp. 207–253.

32. M. P. Johnson, "Social and Cognitive Features of the Dissolution of Commitment to Relationships," in Steve Duck, ed., *Dissolving Personal Relationships,* New York: Academic Press, 1982, pp. 51–73.

33. See George A. Bonanno, *The Other Side of Sadness: What the New Science of Bereavement Tells Us about Life and Loss,* New York: Basic Books, 2009; and James J. Lynch, *The Broken Heart: The Medical Consequences of Loneliness,* New York: Basic Books, 1977.

34. Hal Arkowitz and Scott O. Lilienfeld, "Grief without Tears," *Scientific American Mind,* November/December 2011, pp. 68–69.

35. This process is described in Harold S. Kushner, *When Bad Things Happen to Good People,* New York: Schocken Books, 1981. See also K. Doka, "Living With Heartbreak: The Grief Process," *Caring and the Human Spirit,* Spring/Summer, 2016.

36. See, for example, Erica Goode, "Experts Offer Fresh Insights into the Mind of the Grieving Child," *New York Times,* March 28, 2000, pp. F7, F12.

37. Janice Hume, "'Portraits of Grief,' Reflectors of Values: *The New York Times* Remembers Victims of September 11," *Journalism and Mass Communication Quarterly,* 80, 2003, pp. 166–182.

38. S. K. Bonsu, "The Presentation of Dead Selves in Everyday Life: Obituaries and Impression Management," *Symbolic Interaction,* 30, 2007, pp. 199–219.

39. See "Virtual Immortality," *The Record* (Bergen County, NJ), February 25, 2012, p. A 13.

40. William B. Gudykunst, "The Influence of Cultural Variability on Perceptions of Communication Behavior Associated with Relationship Terms," *Human Communication Research,* 13, 1986, pp. 147–166; and Kyoko Seki, David Matsumoto, and T. Todd Imahori, "The Conceptualization and Expression of Intimacy in Japan and the United States," *Journal of Cross-Cultural Psychology,* 33, 2002, pp. 303–319.

41. Susan Sprecher and Kathleen McKinney, *Sexuality,* Newbury Park, CA: Sage, 1993.

42. Robert Crooks and Karla Baur, *Our Sexuality,* 7th ed. Pacific Grove, CA: Brooks/Cole, 1999.

43. Gudykunst, "Influence of Cultural Variability."

44. See, for example, M. Kito, "Self-Disclosure in Romantic Relationships and Friendships among American and Japanese College Students," *Journal of Social Psychology,* 145, 2005, pp. 127–140.

45. Carol Zinner Dolphin, "Beyond Hall: Variables in the Use of Personal Space in Intercultural Transactions," *Howard Journal of Communications,* 1, 1988, pp. 28–29.

46. Stanley O. Gaines, Jr., "Relationships among Members of Cultural Minorities," in Julia T. Wood and Steve Duck, eds., *Under-studied Relationships: Off the Beaten Track,* Thousand Oaks, CA: Sage, 1995, pp. 51–88.

47. Duck, *Understanding Relationships,* p. 12.

48. Scott Swain, "Covert Intimacy: Closeness in Men's Friendships," in Barbara J. Risman and Pepper Schwartz, eds., *Gender in Intimate Relationships: A Microstructural Approach,* Belmont, CA: Wadsworth, 1989, pp. 71–86; and E. Paul and K. White, "The Development of Intimate Relationships in Late Adolescence," *Adolescence,* 25, 1990, pp. 375–400.

49. Julia T. Wood and Christopher C. Inman, "In a Different Mode:

Masculine Styles of Communicating Closeness," *Journal of Applied Communication Research,* 21, 1993, pp. 279–295.

50. See, for example, Judy Cornelia Pearson, Lynn H. Turner, and William Todd-Mancillas, *Gender and Communication,* 2nd ed., Dubuque, IA: William C. Brown, 1991, pp. 170–171.

51. W. F. Owen, "The Verbal Expression of Love by Women and Men as a Critical Communication Event in Personal Relationships," *Women's Studies in Communication,* 10, 1987, pp. 15–24.

52. Brehm, *Intimate Relationships.*

53. Michelle M. Kazmer and Caroline Haythornthwaite, "Juggling Multiple Social Worlds: Distance Students Online and Offline," *American Behavioral Scientist,* 45, 2001, pp. 510–529.

54. See Henry Jenkins, "Love Online," in Mark Bauerlein, ed., *The Digital Divide,* New York: Penguin, 2011, pp. 160–165.

55. Sue Shellenbarger, "The Long Distance Relationship That's Built to Last," *The Wall Street Journal,* August, 18, 2018, https://www.wsj.com/articles/the-long-distance-marriage-thats-built-to-last-1534252845; Halhi Patell, "Social Media Helps Couples Plug into Their Relationships," February 13, 2012, http://www.sbstatesman.com/social-media-helps-couples-plug-into-their-relationships; See also, Amanda Roosa, "How to Stay Sane in a Long Distance Relationship," *Huffington Post,* December 6, 2017, https://www.huffingtonpost.com/amanda-roosa/how-to-stay-sane-in-a-lon_b_8023796.html.

56. Laura Stafford and Andy J. Merolla, "Idealization, Reunions, and Stability in Long-Distance Dating Relationships," *Journal of Social and Personal Relationships,* 24, 2007, pp. 37–54.

57. Katheryn C. Maguire and Terry A. Kinney, "When Distance Is Problematic: Communication, Coping, and Relational Satisfaction in Female College Students' Long-Distance Dating Relationships," *Journal of Applied Communication Research,* 38, 2010, pp. 27–46.

58. Duck, *Understanding Relationships,* p. 163.

59. Ruth Padawer, "Teens Get Closer from Afar with Instant Messages," *The Record* (Bergen County, NJ), June 17, 2003, pp. A1, A8.

60. Artemio Ramirez, Jr., and Shuangyur Zhang, "When Online Meets Offline: The Effect of Modality Switching on Relational Communication," *Communication Monographs,* 74, 2007, pp. 287–310.

61. J. Wu and H. Lu, "Cultural and Gender Differences in Self-Disclosure on Social Networking Sites," in J. Petley, ed., *Media and Public Sharing: Drawing the Boundaries of Disclosure.* London: I. B. Tauris and Co., 2013.

62. See, for example, N. B. Elison, J. Vitak, R. Gray, and C. Lampe, "Cultivating Social Resources on Social Network Sites: Facebook Relationship Maintenance Behaviors and Their Role in Social Capital Processes," *Journal of Computer-Mediated Communication,* 19, 2014, pp. 855–870.

63. John D. Sutter, "On Facebook, It's Now 4.74 Degrees of Separation," CNN.com, http://www.cnn.com/2011/11/22/tech/social-media/facebook-six-degrees/index.html?hpt.

64. Michaelle Bond, "Your Facebook Past on Display?," *USA Today,* November 3, 2011, p. 3B.

65. Ibid.

66. Carol Cadwalladr and Emma Graham-Harrison, "How Cambridge Analytica Turned Facebook 'Likes' into a Lucrative Political Tool," *The Guardian,*

March 17, 2018, https://www.theguardian.com/technology/2018/mar/17/facebook-cambridge-analytica-kogan-data-algorithm.

67. Marilyn Elias, "You've Got Trauma, but Writing Can Help," *USA Today,* July 1, 2002, p. G6.

68. See B. R. Burleson and W. Samter, "A Social Skills Approach to Relationship Maintenance: How Individual Differences in Communication Skills Affect the Achievement of Relationship Functions," in D. J. Canary and L. Stafford, eds., *Communication and Relational Maintenance,* Orlando, FL: Academic Press, 1994.

# CHAPTER 14

1. B. Burnett and D. Evans, *Designing Your Life: How to Build a Well-Lived, Joyful Life,* New York: Knopf, 2016.

2. Kathleen M. Galvin, Carma L. Bylund, and Bernard J. Brommel, *Family Communication: Cohesion and Change,* 8th ed., Boston: Allyn & Bacon, 2012, p. 4.

3. Patricia Noller and Mary Anne Fitzpatrick, *Communication in Family Relationships,* Englewood Cliffs, NJ: Prentice Hall, 1993; and Lynn Turner and Richard West, *Perspectives on Family Communication,* New York: McGraw-Hill, 2005.

4. Laurie P. Arliss, *Contemporary Family Communication: Messages and Meanings,* New York: St. Martin's Press, 1993, p. 7.

5. See Jane Jorgenson, "Where Is the 'Family' in Family Communication? Exploring Families' Self-Definitions," *Journal of Applied Communication Research,* 17, 1989, pp. 27–41.

6. Jason DeParle and Sabrina Tavernise, "Unwed Mothers Now a Majority Before Age of 30," *New York Times,* February 19, 2012, pp. A1, A16.

7. Eric Klinenberg, "Living Alone Is the New Norm," *Time,* March 11, 2012, pp. 60–62.

8. U.S. Census Bureau, 2009, American Community Survey, http://www.census.gov/acs/www.

9. Sharon Jayson, "All Together Now: Extended Families," *USA Today,* November 23–24, 2011, pp. 1A, 2A.

10. See Katherine S. Newman, *The Accordion Family: Boomerang Kids, Anxious Parents, and the Private Toll of Global Competition,* New York: Beacon Press, 2012; and Rachel Louise Ensign, "When the Budget Calls for a Move Back Home," *Wall Street Journal,* November 27, 2011, p. B3.

11. Virginia Satir, *The New Peoplemaking.* Mountain View, CA: Science and Behavior Books, 1988.

12. Arliss, *Contemporary Family Communication,* p. 57.

13. Catherine Saint Louis, "When Families Fall Out," *The New York Times,* December 26, 2017, pp. D1, D4.

14. Galvin et al., *Family Communication.*

15. Satir, *New Peoplemaking,* p. 79.

16. David H. Olson and Associates, *Families: What Makes Them Work,* Beverly Hills, CA: Sage, 1983.

17. Satir, *New Peoplemaking,* pp. 182–193.

18. Ibid.

19. See Monica McGoldrick, "Ethnicity, Cultural Diversity, and Normality," in Froma Walsh, ed., *Normal Family Processes,* 2nd ed., New York: Guilford Press, 1993.

20. Jayson, "All Together Now."

21. John W. Santrock, *Life Span Development,* 4th ed., Dubuque, IA: William C. Brown, 1992, p. 261.

22. Stella Ting-Toomey and Leeva C. Chung, *Understanding Intercultural Communication,* 2nd ed., New York: Oxford University Press, 2012, p. 68.

23. Julia T. Wood, *Gendered Lives: Communication, Gender, and Culture,* 9th ed., Boston: Wadsworth, 2011, p. 190.

24. Judy C. Pearson, *Communication in the Family: Seeking Satisfaction in Changing Times,* 2nd ed., New York: HarperCollins, 1993, p. 80.

25. Wood, *Gendered Lives,* pp. 169–181.

26. Ibid.

27. See, for example, Dwight E. Brooks and Lisa P. Hébert, "Gender, Race and Media Representation," in Bonnie J. Dow and Julia T. Wood, eds., *The SAGE Handbook of Gender and Communication,* Thousand Oaks, CA: Sage, 2006, pp. 297–317; and Jennifer L. Walsh and L. Monique Ward, "Adolescent Gender Role Portrayals in the Media: 1950 to the Present," in Patrick E. Jamieson and Daniel Romer, eds., *The Changing Portrayal of Adolescents in the Media since 1950,* New York: Oxford University Press, 2008, pp. 132–164.

28. Mike Chalmers, "Deployed? Facebook Puts Family in Your Face," *USA Today,* November 25, 2011, p. 3A.

29. See P. M. Sias, K. J. Krone, and F. M. Jablin, "An Ecological Systems Perspective on Workplace Relationships," in M. L. Knapp and J. A. Daly, eds., *Handbook of Interpersonal Communication,* 3rd ed., Thousand Oaks, CA: Sage, 2002, pp. 615–642; and Margaret J. Wheatley, *Leadership and the New Science,* San Francisco: Berrett-Koehler, 1994, p. 23.

30. Phyllis Korkki, "Building a Bridge to a Lonely Colleague," *New York Times,* January 29, 2012, p. BU8.

31. Marvin R. Weisbord, *Discovering Common Ground: How Future Search Conferences Bring People Together to Achieve Breakthrough Innovation, Empowerment, Shared Vision, and Collaborative Action,* San Francisco: Berrett-Koehler, 1992.

32. Leslie Kwoh, "Reverse Mentoring Cracks Workplace," *Wall Street Journal,* November 28, 2011, p. B7.

33. Sue Shellenbarger, "Gaining Power at Work When You Have None," *The Wall Street Journal,* March 7, 2018, p. A15.

34. D. A. Infante and A. S. Rancer, "A Conceptualization and Measure of Argumentativeness," *Journal of Personality Assessment,* 45, 1982, pp. 72–80.

35. D. A. Infante and W. I. Gorden, "Superiors' Argumentativeness and Verbal Aggressiveness as Predictors of Subordinates' Satisfaction," *Human Communication Research,* 12, 1985, pp. 117–125; and D. A. Infante and W. I. Gorden, "Superior and Subordinate Communicator Profiles: Implications for Independent-Mindedness and Upward Effectiveness," *Central States Speech Journal,* 38, 1987, pp. 73–80.

36. Virginia P. Richmond and James C. McCroskey, *Organizational Communication for Survival,* 4th ed., Boston: Pearson, 2009, pp. 174–178.

37. Gerald M. Goldhaber, *Organizational Communication,* 5th ed., Dubuque, IA: William C. Brown, 1990, p. 214.

38. Fred Dansereau and Steven E. Markham, "Superior-Subordinate Communication: Multiple Levels of Analysis," in Fredric M. Jablin et al., eds., *Handbook of Organizational Communication: An Interdisciplinary Perspective,* Newbury Park, CA: Sage, 1987, pp. 343–353.

39. Richmond and McCroskey, *Organizational Communication for Survival,* pp. 27–28.

40. Dawn R. Gilpin, "Working the Twittersphere," in Zizi Papacharissi, ed., *A Networked Self: Identity, Community, and Culture on Social Network Sites,* New York: Routledge, 2011, pp. 232–250.

41. Wheatley, *Leadership and the New Science,* p. 107.

42. Charles Redding, *Communication within the Organization,* New York: Industrial Communication Council, 1972.

43. Douglas McGregor, *The Human Side of Enterprise,* New York: McGraw-Hill, 1960.

44. Alex F. Osborn, *Applied Imagination,* New York: Scribner's, 1957.

45. Jonah Lehrer, "Groupthink," *The New Yorker,* January 30, 2012, pp. 22–27.

46. Irving Janis, *Groupthink,* Boston: Houghton Mifflin, 1982.

47. See, for instance, Lisa A Mainiero, "Participation? Nyet. Rewards and Praise? Da!" *Academy of Management Executive,* August 1993, p. 87; and Diane H. B. Welsh, Fred Luthans, and Steven M. Sommer, "Managing Russian Factory Workers: The Impact of U.S. Based Behavioral and Participative Techniques," *Academy of Management Journal,* February 1993, pp. 57–59.

48. Lillian H. Chaney and Jeanette S. Martin, *Intercultural Business Communication,* Englewood Cliffs, NJ: Prentice Hall, 1995, p. 41.

49. See, for example, *Diversity Leadership Guide,* Diversity Management Office, NASA, January/February 2007, https://missionstem.nasa.gov/diversity-inclusion-leadrshp.html.

50. Chaney and Martin, *Intercultural Business Communication.* See also C. Chiu, L. Mallorie, H. T. Keh, and W. Law, "Perceptions of Culture in Multicultural Space: Joint Presentation of Images from Two Cultures Increases In-Group Attribution of Culture-Typical Characteristics," *Journal of Cross-Cultural Psychology,* 40, 2009, pp. 282–300.

51. Larry A. Samovar, Richard E. Porter, and Edwin R. McDaniel, *Communication between Cultures,* 7th ed., Boston: Wadsworth, 2010, p. 278.

52. Christopher Engholm, *When Business East Meets Business West,* New York: John Wiley, 1991.

53. See, for example, Geert Hofstede, *Culture's Consequences: Comparing Values, Behaviors, Institutions, and Organizations across Nations,* 2nd ed., Thousand Oaks, CA: Sage, 2001; and Anne-Marie Soderberg and Nigel Holden, "Rethinking Cross-Cultural Management in a Globalizing Business World," *International Journal of Cross-Cultural Management,* 2, 2002, pp. 103–121.

54. See, for example, Owen Proctor, "Reshaping Roche Campus with Millennials in Mind," *The Record,* March 8, 2018, pp. 1L, 7L.

55. Greg Hammill, "Mixing and Managing Four Generations of Employees," *FDR Magazine Online,* Winter/Spring 2005, https://www.fdu.edu/newspubs/magazine/05ws/generations.htm; and Lindsay Gellman, "Bosses Try to Decode Millennials," *The Wall Street Journal,* May 18, 2016, pp. B1, B7.

56. Larry D. Rosen, "Welcome to the iGeneration," *Psychology Today,* May 27, 2010, https://www.psychologytoday.com/blog/rewired-the-psychology-technology/201003/welcome-the-igeneration.

57. George Beall, "8 Key Differences Between Gen Z and Millennials," *Huffington Post,* November 6, 2017, https://www.huffingtonpost.com/george-beall/8-key-differences-between_b_12814200.html.

58. Pilita Clark, "The Sound of Taylor Swift at My Desk? No Thanks," *The Financial Times*, March 5, 2018, p. 12.

59. See, for example, J. T. Wood, *Gendered Lives: Communication, Gender, & Culture,* Stamford, CT: Cengage Learning, 2015.

60. David Gelles and Claire Cain Miller, "Schools Teach M.B.A.s Perils of 'Bro' Ethos," *The New York Times,* December 26, 2017, pp. A1, A15.

61. Rosabeth Moss Kanter, *Men and Women of the Corporation,* New York: Basic Books, 1977.

62. Barbara Garlick, Suzanne Dixon, and Pauline Allen, eds., *Stereotypes of Women in Power: Historical Perspectives and Revisionist Views,* Westport, CT: Greenwood Press, 1992.

63. Wood, *Gendered Lives,* pp. 234–235.

64. See American Society for Suicide Prevention, https://afsp.org/about-suicide/suicide-statistics/.

65. Willard Gaylin, *The Male Ego,* New York: Viking, 1992.

66. Sheryl Sandberg, *Lean In: Women, Work, and The Will to Lead,* New York: Knopf, 2013.

67. Sendhil Mullainathan, "The Hidden Taxes That Challenge Women," *The New York Times,* March 4, 2018, p. BU4.

68. Richmond and McCroskey, *Organizational Communication for Survival,* pp. 114–117.

69. Sarah Gordon, "Female Leaders Boost the Bottom Line," *The Financial Times,* September 27, 2017, p. 9.

70. Wood, *Gendered Lives,* pp. 250–251.

71. S. Magnuson and K. Norem, "Bullies Grow Up and Go to Work," *Journal of Professional Counseling, Practice, Theory, and Research,* 37:2, 2009, pp. 34–51.

72. See Gary Namie and Pamela E. Lutgen-Sandvik, "Active and Passive Accomplices: The Communal Character of Workplace Bullying," *International Journal of Communication,* 4, 2010, pp. 343–373.

73. Rhitu Chatterjee, "A New Survey Finds 81 Percent of Women Have Experienced Sexual Harassment," National Public Radio, February 21, 2018, https://www.npr.org/sections/thetwo-way/2018/02/21/587671849/a-new-survey-finds-eighty-percent-of-women-have-experienced-sexual-harassment.

74. J. F. Andronici and D. S. Katz, "The Right to Complain," *Ms.,* Spring 2007, p. 59.

75. See, for example, R. E. Thompson, "The Changing Face of Gender Issues in the 21st Century

Workplace," *Physician Executive,* 31:1, 2005, pp. 64–65; and J. N. Cleveland, M. Stockdale, and K. R. Murphy, *Women and Men in Organizations: Sex and Gender Issues at Work,* Mahwah, NJ: Lawrence Erlbaum, 2000.

76. Souha R. Ezzedeen, "Portrayals of Career Women in Hollywood Films: Implications for the Glass Ceiling's Persistence," *Gender in Management: An International Journal,* 30:3, 2015, pp. 239–264.

77. S. Ladner, "Laptops in the Living Room: Mobile Technologies and the Divide between Work and Private Time among Interactive Agency Workers," *Canadian Journal of Communication,* 33, 2008, pp. 465–489.

78. R. K. Garrett and J. N. Danziger, "Disaffection or Expected Outcomes: Understanding Personal Internet Use During Work," *Journal of Computer-Mediated Communication,* 13, 2008, pp. 937–958; and R. K. Garrett, and J. N. Danziger, "On Cyberslacking: Workplace Status and Personal Internet Use at Work," *Cyberpsychology and Behavior,* 11, 2008, pp. 287–292.

79. Mary Beth Watson-Manheim, "Exploring the Use of Social Network Sites in the Workplace," in Zizi Papacharissi, ed., *A Networked Self: Identity, Community, and Culture on Social Network Sites,* New York: Routledge, 2011, pp. 169–182.

80. Gilpin, "Working the Twittersphere."

81. Jon Johnson, "How One Stupid Tweet Blew Up Justine Sacco's Life," *The New York Times Magazine,* February 12, 2015, https://www.nytimes.com/2015/02/15/magazine/how-one-stupid-tweet-ruined-justine-saccos-life.html.

82. Rex W. Huppke, "Facebook Profile Can Predict Job Success," *Sun Sentinel,* March 12, 2012, p. 2D.

83. See Kevin B. Wright, Lisa Sparks, and H. Dan O'Hair, *Health Communication in the 21st Century,* Malden, MA: Blackwell, 2008, p. 5; and Gary L. Kreps and Barbara C. Thornton, *Health Communication: Theory and Practice,* 2nd ed., Prospect Heights, IL: Waveland Press, 1992, p. 2.

84. See J. B. Bowen, M. A. Stewart, and B. L. Ryan, "Outcomes of Patient-Provider Interaction," in T. L. Thompson, A. M. Dorsey, K. I. Miller, and R. Parrot, eds., *Handbook of Health Communication,* Mahwah, NJ: Lawrence Erlbaum, 2003, pp. 141–161; S. Cohen and T. A. Wills, "Stress, Social Support, and Buffering Hypothesis," *Psychological Bulletin,* 98, 1985, pp. 310–157; and T. Ferguson, "Health Care in Cyberspace: Patients Lead a Revolution," *The Futurist,* 31, November–December 1997, pp. 29–34.

85. For an early discussion of the value of interpersonal communication in health care settings, see T. L. Thompson, "Patient Health Care: Issues in Interpersonal Communication," in E. Berlin Ray and L. Donohew, eds., *Communication and Health,* Hillsdale, NJ: Lawrence Erlbaum, 1990, pp. 27–50. See also V. Batenburg and J. A. Small, "Does a Communication Skills Course Influence Medical Students' Attitudes?" *Medical Teacher,* 19, 1997, pp. 263–269.

86. Peggy Clarke, "Finding the Words to Communicate about Sexual Health," paper presented at the "Communication and Health" conference of the Speech Communication Association, Washington, DC, July 19–23, 1995, p. 2.

87. See also D. Ballard-Reisch, "A Model of Participative Decision Making for Physician-Patient Interaction," *Health Communication,* 2, 1990, pp. 91–104.

88. Athena du Pre, *Communicating about Health: Current Issues and Perspectives,* Mountain View, CA: Mayfield, 2000, p. 157.

89. See Gary L. Kreps and Elizabeth N. Kunimoto, *Effective Communication in Multicultural Health Care Settings,* Thousand Oaks, CA: Sage, 1994; and D. E. Brashers, "Communication and Uncertainty Management," *Journal of Communication,* 51, 2001, pp. 477–497.

90. Theodore A. Avtgis and E. Phillips Polack, *Medical Communication: Defining the Discipline,* 2nd ed., Dubuque, IA: Kendall Hunt, 2017.

91. Peter Franks and Klea D. Bertakis, "Physician Gender, Patient Gender, and Primary Care," *Journal of Women's Health,* 12, 2003, pp. 73–80.

92. Barbara Sadick, "Physicians, It's Time to Listen More," *The Wall Street Journal,* February 26, 2018, p. R2.

# Index